Memoir, [illegible]

Miscellanies, From the Papers of

Thomas Jefferson

(Volume 2)

Thomas Jefferson

Thomas Jefferson Randolph

Alpha Editions

This edition published in 2022

ISBN : 9789356894686

Design and Setting By
Alpha Editions
www.alphaedis.com
Email - info@alphaedis.com

LETTER I.—TO RICHARD HENRY LEE, April 22, 1786

TO RICHARD HENRY LEE.

London, April 22, 1786.

Dear Sir,

In your letter of October the 29th, you desired me to send you one of the new lamps. I tried at every probable place in Paris, and could not get a tolerable one. I have been glad of it since I came here, as I find them much better made here. I now deliver one, with this letter, into the hands of Mr. Fulwar Skipwith, a merchant from Virginia, settled here, who promises to send it to you, with one for Mr. C. Thomson. Of this be pleased to accept, from me. It is now found, that they may be used with almost any oil.

I expect to leave this place in about three days. Our public letters, joint and separate, will inform you what has been done, and what could not be done here. With respect to a commercial treaty with this country, be assured, that this government not only has it not in contemplation at present to make any, but that they do not conceive that any circumstances will arise, which shall render it expedient for them to have any political connection with us. They think we shall be glad of their commerce on their own terms. There is no party in our favor here, either in power or out of power. Even the opposition concur with the ministry and the nation in this. I can scarcely consider as a party, the Marquis of Lansdowne, and a half dozen characters about him, such as Dr. Price, &c. who are impressed with the utility of a friendly connection with us. The former does not venture this sentiment in parliament, and the latter are not in situations to be heard. The Marquis of Lansdowne spoke to me affectionately of your brother, Doctor Lee, and desired his respects to him, which I beg leave to communicate through you. Were he to come into the ministry (of which there is not the most distant prospect), he must adopt the King's system, or go out again, as he did before, for daring to depart from it. When we see, that through all the changes of ministry, which have taken place during the present reign, there has never been a change of system with respect to America, we cannot reasonably doubt, that this is the system of the King himself. His obstinacy of character we know; his hostility we have known, and it is embittered by ill success. If ever this nation, during his life, enter into arrangements with us, it must be in consequence of events, of which they do not at present see a possibility. The object of the present ministry is to buoy up the nation with flattering calculations of their present prosperity, and to make them believe they are better without us than with us. This they seriously believe; for what is it men cannot be made to believe? I dined the other day in a company of the ministerial party. A General Clark, a Scotchman and ministerialist, sat next to me. He introduced the subject of American affairs, and in the course of the conversation told me, that were America to petition parliament to be again received on their former footing, the petition would be very generally rejected. He was serious in this, and I think it was the sentiment of the company, and is the sentiment perhaps of the nation. In this they are wise, but for a foolish reason. They think they lost more by suffering us to participate of their commercial privileges, at home and abroad, than they lose by our political severance. The true reason, however, why such an application should be rejected, is, that in a very short time we should oblige them to add another hundred millions to their debt, in unsuccessful attempts to retain the subjection offered to them. They are at present in a frenzy, and will not be recovered from it, till they shall have leaped the precipice they are now so boldly advancing to. Writing from England, I write you nothing but English news. The continent, at present, furnishes nothing interesting. I shall hope the favor of your letters, at times. The proceedings and views of Congress and of the Assemblies, the opinions and dispositions of our people in general, which, in governments like ours, must be the foundation of measures, will always be interesting to me, as will whatever respects your own health and happiness; being with great esteem,

Dear Sir, your most obedient

and most humble servant,

Th: Jefferson

LETTER II.—TO CHARLES THOMSON, April 22, 1786

TO CHARLES THOMSON.

London, April 22, 1786.

Dear Sir,

In one of your former letters, you expressed a wish to have one of the newly invented lamps. I find them made here much better than at Paris, and take the liberty of asking your acceptance of one, which will accompany this letter. It is now found, that any tolerable oil may be used in them. The spermaceti oil is best, of the cheap kinds.

I could write you volumes on the improvements which I find made, and making here, in the arts. One deserves particular notice, because it is simple, great, and likely to have extensive consequences. It is the application of steam, as an agent for working grist-mills. I have visited the one lately made here. It was at that time turning eight pair of stones. It consumes one hundred bushels of coal a day. It is proposed to put up thirty pair of stones. I do not know whether the quantity of fuel is to be increased. I hear you are applying the same agent in America to navigate boats, and I have little doubt, but that it will be applied generally to machines, so as to supersede the use of water ponds, and of course to lay open all the streams for navigation. We know, that steam is one of the most powerful engines we can employ; and in America fuel is abundant. I find no new publication here worth sending to you. I shall set out for Paris within three or four days. Our public letters will inform you of our public proceedings here.

I am, with sincere esteem, Dear Sir,

your friend and servant,

Th: Jefferson.

LETTER III.—TO JOHN JAY, April 23, 1786

TO JOHN JAY.

London, April 23, 1786.

Sir,

In my letter of March the 12th, I had the honor of explaining to you the motives which had brought me to this place. A joint letter from Mr. Adams and myself, sent by the last packet, informed you of the result of our conferences with the Tripoline minister. The conferences with the minister of Portugal have, been drawn to a greater length than I expected. However, every thing is now agreed, and the treaty will be ready for signature the day after to-morrow. I shall set out for Paris the same day. With this country nothing is done: and that nothing is intended to be done, on their part, admits not the smallest doubt. The nation is against any change of measures: the ministers are against it; some from principle, others from subserviency: and the King, more than all men, is against it. If we take a retrospect to the beginning of the present reign, we observe, that amidst all the changes of ministry, no change of measures with respect to America ever took place; excepting only at the moment of the peace; and the minister of that moment was immediately removed. Judging of the future by the past, I do not expect a change of disposition during the present reign, which bids fair to be a long one, as the King is healthy and temperate. That he is persevering, we know. If he ever changes his plan, it will be in consequence of events, which, at present, neither himself nor his ministers place among those which are probable. Even the opposition dare not open their lips in favor of a connection with us, so unpopular would be the topic. It is not, that they think our commerce unimportant to them. I find that the merchants here set sufficient value on it. But they are sure of keeping it on their own terms. No better proof can be shown of the security in which the ministers think themselves on this head, than that they have not thought it worth while to give us a conference on the subject, though, on my arrival, we exhibited to them our commission, observed to them that it would expire on the 12th of the next month, and that I had come over on purpose to see if any arrangements could be made before that time. Of two months which then remained, six weeks have elapsed without one scrip of a pen, or one word from a minister, except a vague proposition at an accidental meeting. We availed ourselves even of that, to make another essay to extort some sort of declaration from the court. But their silence is invincible. But of all this, as well as of the proceedings in the negotiation with Portugal, information will be given you by a joint letter from Mr. Adams and myself. The moment is certainly arrived, when, the plan of this court being out of all doubt, Congress and the States may decide what their own measures should be.

The Marquis of Lansdowne spoke of you in very friendly terms, and desired me to present his respects to you, in the first letter I should write. He is thoroughly sensible of the folly of the present measures of this country, as are a few other characters about him. Dr. Price is among these, and is particularly disturbed at the present prospect. He acknowledges, however, that all change is desperate: which weighs the more, as he is intimate with Mr. Pitt. This small band of friends, favorable as it is, does not pretend to say one word in public on our subject.

I have the honor to be, with sentiments of the highest esteem and respect,

Sir, your most obedient

and most humble servant,

Th: Jefferson.

LETTER IV.—TO JOHN JAY, April 23, 1786

TO JOHN JAY.

London, April 23, 1786.

Sir,

In another letter of this day, I stated to you what had passed with public characters since my arrival here. Conversations with private individuals, I thought it best not to mingle with the contents of that letter. Yet, as some have taken place, which relate to matters within our instructions, and with persons whose opinions deserve to have some weight, I will take the liberty of stating them. In a conversation with an ancient and respectable merchant of this place, such a view of the true state of the commercial connections of America and Great Britain was presented to him, as induced him to acknowledge they had been mistaken in their opinions, and to ask, that Mr. Adams and myself would permit the chairman of the committee of American merchants to call on us. He observed, that the same person happened to be also chairman of the committee of the whole body of British merchants; and that such was the respect paid to his person and office, that we might consider what came from him, as coming from the committees themselves. He called on us at an appointed hour. He was a Mr. Duncan Campbell, formerly much concerned in the American trade. We entered on the subject of the non-execution of the late treaty of peace, alleged on both sides. We observed, that the refusal to deliver the western posts, and the withdrawing American property, contrary to express stipulation, having preceded what they considered as breaches on our part, were to be considered as the causes of our proceedings. The obstructions thrown by our legislatures in the way of the recovery of their debts, were insisted on by him. We observed to him, that the great amount of the debt from America to Great Britain, and the little circulating coin in the formeer country, rendered an immediate payment impossible; that time was necessary; that we had been authorized to enter into explanatory arrangements on this subject; that we had made overtures for the purpose, which had not been attended to, and that the States had, therefore, been obliged to modify the article for themselves. He acknowledged the impossibility of immediate payment, the propriety of an explanatory convention, and said, that they were disposed to allow a reasonable time. We mentioned the term of five years, including the present; but that judgments might be allowed immediately, only dividing the execution into equal and annual parts, so that the last should be levied by the close of the year 1790. This seemed to be quite agreeable to him, and to be as short a term as would be insisted on by them. Proceeding to the sum to be demanded, we agreed that the principal, with the interest incurring before and after the war, should be paid; but as to that incurring during the war, we differed from him. He urged its justice with respect to themselves, who had laid out of the use of their money during that period. This was his only topic. We opposed to it all those which circumstances, both public and private, gave rise to. He appeared to feel their weight, but said the renunciation of this interest was a bitter pill, and such a one as the merchants here could not swallow. He wished, that no declaration should be made as to this article: but we observed, that if we entered into explanatory declarations of the points unfavorable to us, we should expect, as a consideration for this, corresponding declarations on the parts in our favor. In fact, we supposed his view was to leave this part of the interest to stand on the general expressions of the treaty, that they might avail themselves, in individual cases, of the favorable dispositions of debtors or of juries. We proceeded to the necessity of arrangements of our future commerce, were it only as a means of enabling our country to pay its debts. We suggested, that they had been contracted while certain modes of remittance had existed here, which had been an inducement to us to contract these debts. He said he was not authorized to speak on the subject of the future commerce. He appeared really and feelingly anxious, that arrangements should be stipulated as to the payment of the old debts, said he would proceed in that moment to Lord Caermarthen's, and discuss the subject with him, and that we might expect to hear from him. He took leave, and we have never since heard from him or any other person on the subject. Congress will judge how far these conversations should influence their future proceedings, or those of the States.

I have the honor to be, with the highest respect and esteem, Sir, your most obedient, humble servant,

Th: Jefferson.

LETTER V.—TO JAMES MADISON, April 25, 1786

TO JAMES MADISON.

London, April 25, 1786.

Dear Sir,

Some of the objects of the joint commission, with which we were honored by Congress, called me to this place about six weeks ago. To-morrow I set out on my return to Paris. With this nation nothing is done; and it is now decided, that they intend to do nothing with us.

I wrote you, in a former letter, on the subject of a Mr. Paradise, who owns an estate in Virginia in right of his wife, and who has a considerable sum due to him in our loan office. Since I came here, I have had opportunities of knowing his extreme personal worth, and his losses by the late war. He is, from principle, a pure republican, while his father was as warm a tory. His attachment to the American cause, and his candid warmth, brought him sometimes into altercations on the subject with his father, and some persons interested in their variance, artfully brought up this subject of conversation whenever they met. It produced a neglect in the father. He had already settled on him a sum of money in the funds: but would do no more, and probably would have undone that, if he could. When remittances from Virginia were forbidden, the profits of the Virginia estate were carried into our loan office. Paradise was then obliged to begin to eat his capital in England: from that, to part with conveniences, and to run in debt. His situation is now distressing; and would be completely relieved, could he receive what is due to him from our State. He is coming over to settle there. His wife and family will follow him. I never ask unjust preferences for any body. But if, by any just means, he can be helped to his money, I own I should be much gratified. The goodness of his heart, his kindness to Americans before, during, and since the war, the purity of his political and moral character, interest me in the events impending over him, and which will infallibly be ruinous, if he fails to receive his money. I ask of you, on his behalf, that in pursuing the path of right, you will become active for him, instead of being merely quiescent, as you might be, were his merit and his misfortunes unknown to you.

I have put into the hands of Mr. Fulwar Skipwith for you, a packet containing some catalogues, which he will forward. I am, with very sincere esteem, Dear Sir,

your friend and servant,

Th: Jefferson.

LETTER VI.—TO THE COUNT DE VERGENNES, May 3, 1786

TO THE COUNT DE VERGENNES.
Paris, May 3, 1786.
Sir,
After begging leave to present my respects to your Excellency, on my return to this place, I take the liberty of offering to your attention some papers, which I found on my arrival here, written by sundry merchants of L'Orient and others, some of whom are citizens of the United States, and all of them concerned in the trade between the two countries. This has been carried on by an exchange of the manufactures and produce of this country, for the produce of that, and principally for tobacco, which, though, on its arrival here, confined to a single purchaser, has been received equally from all sellers. In confidence of a continuance of this practice, the merchants of both countries were carrying on their commerce of exchange. A late contract by the Farm has, in a great measure, fixed in a single mercantile house the supplies of tobacco wanted for this country. This arrangement found the established merchants with some tobacco on hand, some on the seas coming to them, and more still due. By the papers now enclosed, it seems, that there are six thousand four hundred and eight hogsheads in the single port of L'Orient. Whether government may interfere, as to articles furnished by the merchants after they had notice of the contract before mentioned, must depend on principles of policy. But those of justice seem to urge, that, for commodities furnished before such notice, they should be so far protected, as that they may wind up, without loss, the transactions in which the new arrangement found them actually engaged. Your Excellency is the best judge, how far it may be consistent with the rules of government, to interfere for their relief, and with you, therefore, I beg leave entirely to rest their interests. Information lately received, relative to the Barbary States, has suggested, that it might be expedient, and perhaps necessary for us, to pave the way to arrangements with them, by a previous application to the Ottoman Porte. Your Excellency's intimate acquaintance with this subject would render your advice to us equally valuable and desirable. If you would be pleased to permit me to wait on you, any day or hour which shall be most convenient to yourself, I should be much gratified by a little conversation with you on this subject.
I have the honor to be, with great respect, your Excellency's most obedient and most humble servant,
Th: Jefferson.

LETTER VII.—TO JOHN PAGE, May 4, 1786

TO JOHN PAGE.

Paris, May 4, 1786.

Dear Sir,

Your two favors of March the 15th and August the 23, 1785, by Monsieur de la Croix, came to hand on the 15th of November. His return gives me an opportunity of sending you a copy of the Nautical Almanacs for 1786, 7, 8, 9. There is no late and interesting publication here, or I would send it by the same conveyance. With these almanacs, I pack a copy of some Notes I wrote for Monsieur de Marbois, in the year 1781, of which I had a few printed here. They were written in haste, and for his private inspection. A few friends having asked copies, I found it cheaper to print than to write them. They will offer nothing new to you, not even as an oblation of my friendship for you, which is as old almost as we are ourselves. Mazzei brought me your favor of April the 27th. I thank you much for your communications. Nothing can be more grateful at such a distance. It is unfortunate, that most people think the occurrences passing daily under their eyes, are either known to all the world, or not worth being known. They therefore do not give them place in their letters. I hope you will be so good as to continue your friendly information. The proceedings of our public bodies, the progress of the public mind on interesting questions, the casualties which happen among our private friends, and whatever is interesting to yourself and family, will always be anxiously received by me. There is one circumstance in the work you were concerned in, which has not yet come to my knowledge; to wit, How far westward from Fort Pitt, does the western boundary of Pennsylvania pass, and where does it strike the Ohio? The proposition you mention from Mr. Anderson, on the purchase of tobacco, I would have made use of, but that I have engaged the abuses of the tobacco trade on a more general scale. I confess their redress is by no means certain; but till I see all hope of removing the evil by the roots desperate, I cannot propose to prune its branches.

I returned but three or four days ago, from a two months' trip to England. I traversed that country much, and own, both town and country fell short of my expectations. Comparing it with this, I found a much greater proportion of barrens, a soil, in other parts, not naturally so good as this, not better cultivated, but better manured, and therefore more productive. This proceeds from the practice of long leases there, and short ones here. The laboring people here, are poorer than in England. They pay about one half their produce in rent; the English, in general, about a third. The gardening, in that country, is the article in which it surpasses all the earth. I mean their pleasure gardening. This, indeed, went far beyond my ideas. The city of

London, though handsomer than Paris, is not so handsome as Philadelphia. Their architecture is in the most wretched style I ever saw, not meaning to except America, where it is bad, nor even Virginia, where it is worse than in any other part of America which I have seen. The mechanical arts in London are carried to a wonderful perfection. But of these I need not speak, because, of them my countrymen have unfortunately too many samples before their eyes. I consider the extravagance which has seized them, as a more baneful evil than toryism was during the war. It is the more so, as the example is set by the best and most amiable characters among us. Would a missionary appear, who would make frugality the basis of his religious system, and go through the land, preaching it up as the only road to salvation, I would join his school, though not generally disposed to seek my religion out of the dictates of my own reason, and feelings of my own heart. These things have been more deeply impressed on my mind, by what I have heard and seen in England. That nation hate us, their ministers hate us, and their King, more than all other men. They have the impudence to avow this, though they acknowledge our trade important to them. But they think, we cannot prevent our countrymen from bringing that into their laps. A conviction of this determines them to make no terms of commerce with us. They say, they will pocket our carrying trade as well as their own. Our overtures of commercial arrangements have been treated with a derision, which shows their firm persuasion, that we shall never unite to suppress their commerce, or even to impede it. I think their hostility towards us is much more deeply rooted at present, than during the war. In the arts, the most striking thing I saw there, new, was the application of the principle of the steam-engine to grist-mills. I saw eight pair of stones which are worked by steam, and there are to be set up thirty pair in the same house. A hundred bushels of coal, a day, are consumed at present. I do not know in what proportion the consumption will be increased by the additional gear.

Be so good as to present my respects to Mrs. Page and your family, to W. Lewis, F. Willis, and their families, and to accept yourself assurances of the sincere regard, with which I am, Dear Sir, your affectionate friend and servant,

Th: Jefferson.

LETTER VIII.—TO WILLIAM CARMICHAEL

TO WILLIAM CARMICHAEL.

Paris, May 5, 1786.

Dear Sir,

A visit of two months to England has been the cause of your not hearing from me during that period. Your letters of February the 3rd, to Mr. Adams and myself, and of February the 4th, to me, had come to hand before my departure. While I was in London, Mr. Adams received the letters giving information of Mr. Lambe's arrival at Algiers. In London, we had conferences with a Tripoline ambassador, now at that court, named Abdrahaman. He asked us thirty thousand guineas for a peace with his court, and as much for Tunis, for which he said he could answer. What we were authorized to offer, being to this, but as a drop to a bucket, our conferences were repeated, only for the purpose of obtaining information. If the demands of Algiers and Morocco should be proportioned to this, according to their superior power, it is easy to foresee that the United States will not buy a peace with money. What principally led me to England was, the information that the Chevalier del Pinto, Portuguese minister at that court, had received full powers to treat with us. I accordingly went there, and, in the course of six weeks, we arranged a commercial treaty between our two countries. His powers were only to negotiate, not to sign. And as I could not wait, Mr. Adams and myself signed, and the Chevalier del Pinto expected daily the arrival of powers to do the same. The footing on which each has placed the other, is that of the most favored nation. We wished much to have had some privileges in their American possessions: but this was not to be effected. The right to import flour into Portugal, though not conceded by the treaty, we are not without hopes of obtaining.

My journey furnished us occasion to renew our overtures to the court of London; which it was the more important to do, as our powers to that court were to expire on the 12th of this month. These overtures were not attended to, and our commission expiring, we made our final report to Congress; and I suppose this the last offer of friendship, which will ever be made on our part. The treaty of peace being unexecuted on either part, in important points, each will now take their own measures for obtaining execution. I think the King, ministers, and nation are more bitterly hostile to us at present, than at any period of the late war. A like disposition on our part, has been rising for some time. In what events these things will end, we cannot foresee. Our countrymen are eager in their passions and enterprise, and not disposed to calculate their interests against these. Our enemies (for such they are, in fact) have for twelve years past, followed but one uniform rule, that of doing exactly the contrary of what reason points out. Having early, during our contest, observed this in the British conduct, I governed myself by it, in all prognostications of their measures; and I can say, with truth, it never failed me but in the circumstance of their making peace with us. I have no letters from America of later date than the new year. Mr. Adams had, to the beginning of February. I am in hopes our letters will give a new spur to the proposition, for investing Congress with the regulation of our commerce.

This will be handed you by a Baron Waltersdorf, a Danish gentleman, whom, if you did not already know, I should take the liberty of recommending to you. You were so kind as to write me, that you would forward me a particular map, which has not come to hand.

I beg you to be assured of the respect and esteem, with which I have the honor to be, Dear Sir,

your most obedient

and most humble servant,

Th: Jefferson.

LETTER IX.—TO MR. DUMAS, May 6, 1789

TO MR. DUMAS.

Paris, May 6, 1789.

Sir,

Having been absent in England, for some time past, your favors of February the 27th, March the 28th, and April the 11th, have not been acknowledged so soon as they should have been. I am obliged to you, for assisting to make me known to the Rhingrave de Salm and the Marquis de la Coste, whose reputations render an acquaintance with them desirable. I have not yet seen either: but expect that honor from the Rhingrave very soon. Your letters to Mr. Jay and Mr. Van Berkel, received in my absence, will be forwarded by a gentleman who leaves this place for New York, within a few days. I sent the treaty with Prussia by a gentleman who sailed from Havre, the 11th of November. The arrival of that vessel in America is not yet known here. Though the time is not long enough to produce despair, it is sufficiently so to give inquietude lest it should be lost. This would be a cause of much concern to me: I beg the favor of you to mention this circumstance to the Baron de Thulemeyer, as an apology for his not hearing from us. The last advices from America bring us nothing interesting. A principal object of my journey to London was, to enter into commercial arrangements with Portugal. This has been done almost in the precise terms of those of Prussia. The English are still our enemies. The spirit existing there, and rising in America, has a very lowering aspect. To what events it may give birth, I cannot foresee. We are young, and can survive them; but their rotten machine must crush under the trial. The animosities of sovereigns are temporary, and may be allayed: but those which seize the whole body of a people, and of a people, too, who dictate their own measures, produce calamities of long duration. I shall not wonder to see the scenes of ancient Rome and Carthage renewed in our day; and if not pursued to the same issue, it may be, because the republic of modern powers will not permit the extinction of any one of its members. Peace and friendship with all mankind is our wisest policy: and I wish we may be permitted to pursue it. But the temper and folly of our enemies may not leave this in our choice. I am happy in our prospect of friendship with the most estimable powers of Europe, and particularly with those of the confederacy, of which yours is. That your present crisis may have a happy issue, is the prayer and wish of him, who has the honor to be, with great respect and esteem, Sir, your most obedient humble servant,

Th: Jefferson.

LETTER X.—TO WILLIAM DRAYTON, May 6, 1786

TO WILLIAM DRAYTON.

Paris, May 6, 1786.

Sir,

Your favor of November the 23rd came duly to hand. A call to England, soon after its receipt, has prevented my acknowledging it so soon as I should have done. I am very sensible of the honor done me by the South Carolina society for promoting and improving agriculture and other rural concerns, when they were pleased to elect me to be of their body: and I beg leave, through you, Sir, to convey to them my grateful thanks for this favor. They will find in me, indeed, but a very unprofitable servant. At present, particularly, my situation is unfavorable to the desire I feel, of promoting their views. However, I shall certainly avail myself of every occasion, which shall occur of doing so. Perhaps I may render some service, by forwarding to the society such new objects of culture, as may be likely to succeed in the soil and climate of South Carolina. In an infant country, as ours is, these experiments are important. We are probably far from possessing, as yet, all the articles of culture for which nature has fitted our country. To find out these, will require abundance of unsuccessful experiments. But if in a multitude of these, we make one useful acquisition, it repays our trouble. Perhaps it is the peculiar duty of associated bodies, to undertake these experiments. Under this sense of the views of the society, and with so little opportunity of being otherwise useful to them, I shall be attentive to procure for them the seeds of such plants, as they will be so good as to point out to me, or as shall occur to myself as worthy their notice. I send at present, by Mr. McQueen, some seeds of a grass, found very useful in the southern parts of Europe, and particularly, and almost solely, cultivated in Malta. It is called by the names of Sulla, and Spanish St. Foin, and is the *Hedysarum coronarium* of Linnaeus. It is usually sown early in autumn. I shall receive a supply of fresher seed this fall, which I will also do myself the honor of forwarding to you. I expect, in the same season, from the south of France, some acorns of the cork oak, which I propose for your society, as I am persuaded they will succeed with you. I observed it to grow in England, without shelter; not well indeed; but so as to give hopes that it would do well with you. I shall consider myself as always honored by the commands of the society, whenever they shall find it convenient to make use of me, and beg you to be assured, personally, of the sentiments of respect and esteem, with which I have the honor to be, Sir, your most obedient and most humble servant,

Th: Jefferson.

LETTER XI.—TO W. T. FRANKLIN, May 7, 1786

TO W. T. FRANKLIN.

Paris, May 7, 1786.

Dear Sir,

On my return from a two months' visit to England, I found here your favor of January the 18th. This contains the latest intelligence I have from America. Your effects not being then arrived, gives me anxiety for them, as I think they went in a vessel, which sailed from Havre the 11th of November. In this vessel, went also the two Mr. Fitzhughs of Virginia, with the Prussian treaty, our papers relative to the Barbary States, with the despatches for Congress, and letters which I had been writing to other persons in America for six weeks preceding their departure. I am obliged to you for the information as to Dr. Franklin's health, in which I feel a great interest. I concur in opinion with you, that in the present factious division of your State, an angel from heaven could do no good. I have been sorry, therefore, from the beginning, to see such time as Dr. Franklin's wasted on so hopeless a business. You have formed a just opinion of Monroe. He is a man whose soul might be turned wrong side outwards, without discovering a blemish to the world. I wish with all my heart, Congress may call you into the diplomatic line, as that seems to have attracted your own desires. It is not one in which you can do any thing more, than pass the present hour agreeably, without any prospect to future provision. Perhaps the arrangements with Portugal, by adding to the number of those appointments, may give Congress an opportunity of doing justice to your own, and to Dr. Franklin's services. If my wishes could aid you, you have them sincerely. My late return to this place scarcely enables me to give you any of its news. I have not yet called on M. La Veillard, or seen any of your acquaintances. The marriage of the ambassador of Sweden with Miss Necker, you have heard of. Houdon is about taking a wife also. His bust of the General has arrived, and meets the approbation of those who know the original. Europe enjoys a perfect calm, at present. Perhaps it may be disturbed by the death of the King of Prussia, which is constantly expected. As yet, we have no information from the Barbary States, which may enable us to prognosticate the success of our endeavors to effect a peace in that quarter. Present me respectfully and affectionately to Dr. Franklin, and accept assurances of the esteem, with which I am, Dear Sir, your friend and servant,

Th: Jefferson.

LETTER XII.—TO ELBRIDGE GERRY, May 7, 1786

TO ELBRIDGE GERRY.

Paris, May 7, 1786.

Dear Sir,

My last to you was of the 11th of October. Soon after that, your favor of the 12th of September came to hand. My acknowledgment of this is made later than it should have been, by my trip to England. Your long silence I ascribe to a more pleasing cause, that of devoting your spare time to one more capable of filling it with happiness, and to whom, as well as to yourself, I wish all those precious blessings which this change of condition is calculated to give you.

My public letters to Mr. Jay will have apprized you of my journey to England, and of its motives; and the joint letters of Mr. Adams and myself, of its effects. With respect to Portugal, it produced arrangements; with respect to England and Barbary, only information. I am quite at a loss what you will do with England. To leave her in possession of our posts, seems inadmissible; and yet to take them, brings on a state of things, for which we seem not to be in readiness. Perhaps a total suppression of her trade, or an exclusion of her vessels from the carriage of our produce, may have some effect; but I believe not very great. Their passions are too deeply and too universally engaged in opposition to us. The ministry have found means to persuade the nation, that they are richer than they were while we participated of their commercial privileges. We should try to turn our trade into other channels. I am in hopes this country will endeavor to give it more encouragement. But what will you do with the piratical States? Buy a peace at their enormous price; force one; or abandon the carriage into the Mediterranean to other powers? All these measures are disagreeable. The decision rests with you. The Emperor is now pressing a treaty with us. In a commercial view, I doubt whether it is desirable: but in a political one, I believe it is. He is now undoubtedly the second power in Europe, and on the death of the King of Prussia, he becomes the first character. An alliance with him will give us respectability in Europe, which we have occasion for. Besides, he will be at the head of the second grand confederacy of Europe, and may at any time serve us with the powers constituting that. I am pressed on so many hands to recommend Dumas to the patronage of Congress, that I cannot avoid it. Every body speaks well of him, and his zeal in our cause. Any thing done for him will gratify this court, and the patriotic party in Holland, as well as some distinguished individuals. I am induced, from my own feelings, to recommend Colonel Humphreys to your care. He is sensible, prudent, and honest, and may be very firmly relied on, in any office which requires these talents. I pray you to accept assurance of the sincere esteem and respect, with which I am,

Dear Sir, your most obedient

and most humble servant,

Th: Jefferson.

LETTER XIII.—TO JAMES ROSS, May 8, 1786

TO JAMES ROSS.

Paris, May 8, 1786.

Dear Sir,

I have duly received your favor of October the 22nd, and am much gratified by the communications therein made. It has given me details, which do not enter into the views of my ordinary correspondents, and which are very entertaining. I experience great satisfaction at seeing my country proceed to facilitate the intercommunications of its several parts, by opening rivers, canals, and roads. How much more rational is this disposal of public money, than that of waging war.

Before the receipt of your letter, Morris's contract for sixty thousand hogsheads of tobacco was concluded with the Farmers General. I have been for some time occupied in endeavoring to destroy the root of the evils, which the tobacco trade encounters in this country, by making the ministers sensible, that merchants will not bring a commodity to a market, where but one person is allowed to buy it; and that so long as that single purchaser is obliged to go to foreign markets for it, he must pay for it in coin, and not in commodities. These truths have made their way to the minds of the ministry, insomuch, as to have delayed the execution of the new lease of the Farms, six months. It is renewed, however, for three years, but so as not to render impossible a reformation of this great evil. They are sensible of the evil, but it is so interwoven with their fiscal system, that they find it hazardous to disentangle. The temporary distress, too, of the revenue, they are not prepared to meet. My hopes, therefore, are weak, though not quite desperate. When they become so, it will remain to look about for the best palliative this monopoly can bear. My present idea is, that it will be found in a prohibition to the Farmers General, to purchase tobacco any where but in France. You will perceive by this, that my object is to strengthen the connection between this country and my own in all useful points. I am of opinion, that twenty-three thousand hogsheads of tobacco, the annual consumption of this country, do not exceed the amount of those commodities, which it is more advantageous to us to buy here than in England, or elsewhere; and such a commerce would powerfully reinforce the motives for a friendship from this country towards ours. This friendship we ought to cultivate closely, considering the present dispositions of England towards us.

I am lately returned from a visit to that country. The spirit of hostility to us has always existed in the mind of the King, but it has now extended itself through the whole mass of the people, and the majority in the public councils.

In a country, where the voice of the people influences so much the measures of administration, and where it coincides with the private temper of the King, there is no pronouncing on future events. It is true, they have nothing to gain, and much to lose, by a war with us. But interest is not the strongest passion in the human breast. There are difficult points, too, still unsettled between us. They have not withdrawn their armies out of our country, nor given satisfaction for the property they brought off. On our part, we have not paid our debts, and it will take time to pay them. In conferences with some distinguished mercantile characters, I found them sensible of the impossibility of our paying these debts at once, and that an endeavor to force universal and immediate payment, would render debts desperate, which are good in themselves. I think we should not have differed in the term necessary. We differed essentially in the article of interest. For while the principal, and interest preceding and subsequent to the war, seem justly due from us, that which accrued during the war does not. Interest is a compensation for the use of money. Their money, in our hands, was in the form of lands and negroes. Tobacco, the produce of these lands and negroes (or, as I may call it, the interest for them), being almost impossible of conveyance to the markets of consumption, because taken by themselves in its way there, sold during the war at five or six shillings the hundred. This did not pay taxes, and for tools, and other plantation charges. A man who should have attempted to remit to his creditor tobacco, for either principal or interest, must have remitted it three times before one cargo would have arrived safe: and this from the depredations of their own nation, and often of the creditor himself; for some of the merchants entered deeply into the privateering business. The individuals who did not, say they have lost this interest: the debtor replies, that he has not gained it, and that it is a case where, a loss having been incurred, every one tries to shift it from himself. The known bias of the human mind from motives of interest should lessen the confidence of each party in the justice of their reasoning: but it is difficult to say, which of them should make the sacrifice, both of reason and interest. Our conferences were intended as preparatory to some arrangement. It is uncertain how far we should have been able to accommodate our opinions. But the absolute aversion of the government to enter into any arrangement prevented the object from being pursued. Each country is left to do justice to itself and to the other, according to its own ideas as to what is past; and to scramble for the future as well as they can: to regulate their commerce by duties and prohibitions, and perhaps by cannons and mortars; in which event, we must abandon the ocean, where we are weak, leaving to neutral nations the carriage of our commodities; and measure with them on land, where they alone can lose. Farewell, then, all our useful improvements of canals and roads, reformations of laws, and other rational employments. I really doubt, whether there is temper enough, on either side, to prevent this issue of our present hatred. Europe is, at this moment, without the appearance of a cloud. The death of the King of Prussia, daily expected, may raise one. My paper admonishes me, that, after asking a continuance of your favors, it is time for me to conclude with assurances of the esteem with which I am,

Dear Sir, your friend and servant,

Th: Jefferson.

LETTER XIV.—TO T. PLEASANTS, May 8,1786

TO T. PLEASANTS.

Paris, May 8,1786.

Dear Sir,

At the time of the receipt of your favor of October the 24th, the contract between the Farmers General and Mr. Morris, for tobacco, was concluded, and in a course of execution. There was no room, therefore, to offer the proposals which accompanied your letter. I was, moreover, engaged in endeavors to have the monopoly, in the purchase of this article, in this country, suppressed. My hopes on that subject are not desperate, but neither are they flattering. I consider it as the most effectual means of procuring the full value of our produce, of diverting our demands for manufactures from Great Britain to this country, to a certain amount, and of thus producing some equilibrium in our commerce, which at present lies all in the British scale. It would cement an union with our friends, and lessen the torrent of wealth which we are pouring into the laps of our enemies. For my part, I think that the trade with Great Britain is a ruinous one to ourselves; and that nothing would be an inducement to tolerate it, but a free commerce with their West Indies: and that this being denied to us, we should put a stop to the losing branch. The question is, whether they are right in their prognostications, that we have neither resolution nor union enough for this. Every thing I hear from my own country, fills me with despair as to their recovery from their vassalage to Great Britain. Fashion and folly are plunging them deeper and deeper into distress: and the legislators of the country becoming debtors also, there seems no hope of applying the only possible remedy, that of an immediate judgment and execution. We should try, whether the prodigal might not be restrained from taking on credit the gewgaw held out to him in one hand, by seeing the keys of a prison in the other. Be pleased to present my respects to Mrs. Pleasants, and to be assured of the esteem with which I am,

Dear Sir, your friend and servant,

Th: Jefferson.

LETTER XV.—TO COLONEL MONROE, May 10,1786

TO COLONEL MONROE.

Paris, May 10,1786.

Dear Sir,

My last to you was of January the 27th. Since that, I have received yours of January the 19th. Information from other quarters gives me reason to suspect you have in negotiation a very important change in your situation. You will carry into its execution all my wishes for your happiness. I hope it will not detach you from a settlement in your own country. I had even entertained hopes of your settling in my neighborhood: but these were determined by your desiring a plan of a house for Richmond. However reluctantly I relinquish this prospect, I shall not the less readily obey your commands, by sending you a plan. Having been much engaged since my return from England, in answering the letters and despatching other business which had accumulated during my absence, and being still much engaged, perhaps I may not be able to send the plan by this conveyance. If I do not send it now, I will surely by the next conveyance after this. Your *Encyclopédie*, containing eighteen *livraisons*, went off last night for Havre, from whence it will go in a vessel bound to New York. It will be under the care of M. la Croix, a passenger, who, if he does not find you in New York, will carry it to Virginia, and send it to Richmond. Another copy, in a separate box, goes for Currie. I pay here all charges to New York. What may occur afterwards, I desire him to ask either of you or Currie, as either will pay for the other; or to draw on me for them.

My letters to Mr. Jay will have informed you of the objects which carried me to England: and that the principal one, the treaty with Portugal, has been accomplished. Though we were unable to procure any special advantages in that, yet we thought it of consequence to insure our trade against those particular checks and discouragements, which it has heretofore met with there. The information as to the Barbary States, which we obtained from Abdrahaman the Tripoline ambassador, was also given to Mr. Jay. If it be right, and the scale of proportion between those nations, which we had settled, be also right, eight times the sum required by Tripoli will be necessary to accomplish a peace with the whole; that is to say, about two hundred and forty thousand guineas. The continuance of this peace will depend on their idea of our power to enforce it, and on the life of the particular Dey, or other head of the government, with whom it is contracted. Congress will, no doubt, weigh these circumstances against the expense and probable success of compelling a peace by arms. Count d'Estaing having communicated to me verbally some information as to an experiment formerly made by this country, I shall get him to put it into writing, and I will forward it to Congress, as it may aid them in their choice of measures. However, which plan is most eligible can only be known to yourselves, who are on the spot, and have under your view all the difficulties of both. There is a third measure, that of abandoning the Mediterranean carriage to other nations.

With respect to England, no arrangements can be taken. The merchants were certainly disposed to have consented to accommodation, as to the article of debts. I was not certain, when I left England, that they would relinquish the interest during the war. A letter received since, from the first character among the American merchants in Scotland, satisfies me they would have relinquished it, to insure the capital and residue of interest. Would to heaven, all the States, therefore, would settle a uniform plan. To open the courts to them, so that they might obtain judgments; to divide the executions into so many equal annual instalments, as that the last might be paid in the year 1790; to have the payments in actual money; and to include the capital, and interest preceding and subsequent to the war, would give satisfaction to the world, and to the merchants in general. Since it is left for each nation to pursue their own measures, in the execution of the late treaty, may not Congress, with propriety, recommend a mode of executing that article respecting the debts, and send it to each State to be passed into law? Whether England gives up the posts or not, these debts must be paid, or our character stained with infamy among all nations, and through all time. As to the satisfaction for slaves carried off, it is a bagatelle, which, if not made good before the last instalment becomes due, may be secured out of that.

I formerly communicated the overtures for a treaty, which had been made by the imperial ambassador. The instructions from Congress being in their favor, and Mr. Adams's opinion also, I encouraged them. He expected his full powers when I went to England. Yet I did not think, nor did Mr. Adams, that this was of importance enough to weigh against the objects of that journey. He received them soon after my departure, and communicated it to me on my return, asking a copy of our propositions. I gave him one, but observed, our commission had then but a few days to run. He desired I should propose to Congress the giving new powers to go on with this, and said, that, in the mean time, he would arrange with us the plan. In a commercial view, no great good is to be gained by this. But in a political one, it may be expedient. As the treaty would, of course, be in the terms of those of Prussia and Portugal, it will give us but little additional embarrassment, in any commercial regulations we may wish to establish. The exceptions from these, which the other treaties will require, may take in the treaty with the Emperor. I should be glad to communicate some answer, as soon as Congress shall have made up their minds on it. My information to Congress, on the subject of our commercial articles with this country, has only come down to January the 27th. Whether I shall say any thing on it, in my letter to Mr. Jay by this conveyance, depends on its not being too early for an appointment I expect hourly from the Count de Vergennes, to meet him on this and other subjects. My last information was, that the lease was too far advanced to withdraw from it the article of tobacco, but that a clause is inserted in it, empowering the King to discontinue it at any time. A discontinuance is, therefore, the only remaining object, and as even this cannot be effected till the expiration of the old lease, which is about the end of the present year, I have wished only to stir the subject, from time to time, so as to keep it alive. This idea led me into a measure proposed by the Marquis de la Fayette, whose return from Berlin found the matter at that point, to which my former report to Congress had conducted it. I communicated to him what I had been engaged on, what were my prospects, and my purpose of keeping the subject just open. He offered his services with that zeal which commands them on every occasion respecting America. He suggested to me the meeting two or three gentlemen, well acquainted with this business. We met. They urged me to propose to the Count de Vergennes, the appointing a committee to take the matter into consideration. I told them, that decency would not permit me to point out to the Count de Vergennes the mode by which he should conduct a negotiation, but that I would press again the necessity of an arrangement, if, whilst that should be operating on his mind, they would suggest the appointment of a committee. The Marquis offered his services for this purpose. The consequence was the appointment of a committee, and the Marquis as a member of it. I communicated to him my papers. He collected other lights wherever he could, and particularly from the gentlemen with whom we had before concerted, and who had a good acquaintance with the subject. The Marquis became our champion in the committee, and two of its members, who were of the corps of Farmers General, entered the lists on the other side. Each gave in memorials. The lease, indeed, was signed while I was gone to England, but the discussions were, and still are continued in the committee: from which we derive two advantages; 1. that of showing, that the object is not to be relinquished; and 2. that of enlightening government, as to its true interest. The Count de Vergennes is absolutely for it; but it is not in his department. Calonne is his friend, and in this instance his principle seems to be, *Amica veritas, sed magis amicus Plato*. An additional hope is founded in the expectation of a change of the minister of finance. The present one is under the absolute control of the Farmers General. The committee's views have been somewhat different from mine. They despair of a suppression of the Farm, and therefore wish to obtain palliatives, which would coincide with the particular good of this country. I think, that so long as the monopoly in the sale is kept up, it is of no consequence to us, how they modify the pill for their own internal relief: but, on the contrary, the worse it remains, the more necessary it will render a reformation. Any palliative would take from us all those arguments and friends, that would be satisfied with accommodation. The Marquis, though differing in opinion from me on this point, has, however, adhered to my principle of absolute liberty or nothing. In this condition is the matter at this moment. Whether I say any thing on the subject to Mr. Jay, will depend on my interview with the Count de Vergennes. I doubt whether that will furnish any thing worth communicating, and whether it will be in time. I therefore state thus much to you, that you may see the matter is not laid aside.

I must beg leave to recommend Colonel Humphreys to your acquaintance and good offices. He is an excellent man, an able one, and in need of some provision. Besides former applications to me in favor of Dumas, the Rhingrave of Salm (the effective minister of the government of Holland, while their two ambassadors here are ostensible), who is conducting secret arrangements for them with this court, presses his interests on us. It is evident the two governments make a point of it. You ask, why they do not provide for him themselves. I am not able to answer the question, but by a conjecture, that Dumas's particular ambition prefers an appointment from us. I know all the difficulty of this application, which Congress has to encounter. I see the reasons against giving him the primary appointment at that court, and the difficulty of his accommodating himself to a subordinate one. Yet I think something must be done in it, to gratify this court, of which we must be always asking favors. In these countries, personal favors weigh more than public interest. The minister who has asked a gratification for Dumas, has embarked his own feelings and reputation in that demand. I do not think it was discreet, by any means. But this reflection might perhaps aggravate a disappointment. I know not really what you can do: but yet hope something will be done. Adieu, my Dear Sir, and believe me to be

yours affectionately,

Th: Jefferson.

LETTER XVI.—TO JOHN ADAMS, May 11, 1786

TO JOHN ADAMS.

Paris, May 11, 1786.

Dear Sir,

I do myself the honor of enclosing to you, letters which came to hand last night, from Mr. Lambe, Mr. Carmichael, and Mr. Barclay. By these you will perceive, that our peace is not to be purchased at Algiers but at a price far beyond our powers. What that would be, indeed, Mr. Lambe does not say, nor probably does he know. But as he knew our ultimatum, we are to suppose from his letter, that it would be a price infinitely beyond that. A reference to Congress hereon seems to be necessary. Till that can be obtained, Mr. Lambe must be idle at Algiers, Carthagena, or elsewhere. Would he not be better employed in going to Congress? They would be able to draw from him and Mr. Randall, the information necessary to determine what they will do. And if they determine to negotiate, they can re-appoint the same, or appoint a new negotiator, according to the opinion they shall form on their examination. I suggest this to you as my first thoughts; an ultimate opinion should not be formed till we see Mr. Randall, who may be shortly expected. In the mean time, should an opportunity occur, favor me with your ideas hereon that we may be maturing our opinions. I shall send copies of these three letters to Mr. Jay, by the packet which sails from L'Orient the first of the next month.

I have the honor to be, with great esteem, Dear Sir, your most obedient and most humble servant,

Th: Jefferson

LETTER XVII.—TO LISTER ASQUITH, May 22, 1786

TO LISTER ASQUITH.

Paris, May 22, 1786.

Sir,

When I left this place for England, I had no suspicion that any thing more would be necessary on my part for your liberation. Being but lately returned, I could not sooner acknowledge the receipt of your letters of April the 21st and May the 1st. I this day write to M. Desbordes, to pay the charges necessary for your enlargement, to furnish you with a guinea apiece, and to take your draft on Mr. Grand for those sums, and the others which he has furnished you at my request. This being a new case, I am unable to say whether you will be held to repay this money. Congress will decide on that, to whom I shall send a report of the case, and to whom you should apply on your return to America, to know whether you are to repay it or not. During the whole of this long transaction, I have never ceased soliciting your discharge. The evidence furnished by the Farmers to the ministers, impressed them with a belief that you were guilty. However, they obtained a remission of all which the King could remit, which was your condemnation to the galleys, and imprisonment, and the sum in which you were fined. The confiscation belonged to the Farmers, and the expenses of subsistence and of prosecution were theirs also, and so could not be remitted by the King. I wish you to be assured of my sensibility for your sufferings, and of my wishes to have obtained an earlier relief, had it been possible. I shall be glad if you can have an immediate and safe return to your own country, and there find your families well, and make those who may be authorized to decide on your case sensible, that these misfortunes have not been brought on you by any desire of yours, to infringe the laws of the country in which you have suffered. I enclose herewith your log-book and the other papers desired by you, and am, Sir,

your most obedient, humble servant,

Th: Jefferson.

LETTER XVIII.—TO JOHN JAY, May 23, 1786

TO JOHN JAY.

Sir,

Paris, May 23, 1786.

Letters received both from Madrid and Algiers, while I was in London, having suggested that treaties with the States of Barbary would be much facilitated by a previous one with the Ottoman Porte, it was agreed between Mr. Adams and myself, that on my return, I should consult on this subject the Count de Vergennes, whose long residence at Constantinople rendered him the best judge of its expediency. Various circumstances have put it out of my power to consult him, till to-day. I stated to him the difficulties we were likely to meet with at Algiers; and asked his opinion, what would be the probable expense of a diplomatic mission to Constantinople, and what its effect at Algiers. He said that the expense would be very great, for that presents must be made at that court, and every one would be gaping after them: and that it would not procure us a peace at Algiers one penny the cheaper. He observed, that the Barbary States acknowledged a sort of vassalage to the Porte, and availed themselves of that relation, when any thing was to be gained by it; but that whenever it subjected them to a demand from the Porte, they totally disregarded it: that money was the sole agent at Algiers, except so far as fear could be induced also. He cited the present example of Spain, which, though having a treaty with the Porte would probably be obliged to buy a peace at Algiers, at the expense of upwards of six millions of livres. I told him, we had calculated from the demands and information of the Tripoline ambassador, at London, that to make peace with the four Barbary States would cost us between two and three hundred thousand guineas, if bought with money. The sum did not seem to exceed his expectations. I mentioned to him, that considering the uncertainty of a peace, when bought, perhaps Congress might think it more eligible to establish a cruise of frigates in the Mediterranean, and even to blockade Algiers. He supposed it would require ten vessels, great and small. I observed to him that Monsieur de Massiac had formerly done it with five: he said it was true, but that vessels of relief would be necessary. I hinted to him that I thought the English capable of administering aid to the Algerines. He seemed to think it impossible, on account of the scandal it would bring on. I asked him what had occasioned the blockade by Monsieur de Massiac: he said, an infraction of their treaty by the Algerines.

I had a good deal of conversation with him, also, on the situation of affairs between England and the United States: and particularly, on their refusal to deliver up our posts. I observed to him, that the obstructions thrown in the way of the recovery of their debts, were the effect, and not the cause, as they pretended, of their refusal to deliver up the posts; that the merchants interested in these debts, showed a great disposition to make arrangements with us; that the article of time we could certainly have settled, and probably that of the interest during the war: but that, the minister showing no disposition to have these matters arranged, I thought it a sufficient proof that this was not the true cause of their retaining the posts. He concurred as to the justice of our requiring time for the payment of our debts; said nothing which showed a difference of opinion as to the article of interest, and seemed to believe fully, that their object was to divert the channel of the fur-trade, before they delivered up the posts, and expressed a strong sense of the importance of that commerce to us. I told him I really could not foresee what would be the event of this detention; that the situation of the British funds, and the desire of their minister to begin to reduce the national debt, seemed to indicate that they could not wish a war. He thought so, but that neither were we in a condition to go to war. I told him, I was yet uninformed what Congress proposed to do on this subject, but that we should certainly always count on the good offices of France, and I was sure that the offer of them would suffice to induce Great Britain to do us justice. He said that surely we might always count on the friendship of France. I added, that by the treaty of alliance, she was bound to guaranty our limits to us, as they should be established at the moment of peace. He said they were so, '*mais qu'il nous etoit nécessaire de les constater.*' I told him there was no question what our boundaries were; that the English themselves admitted they were clear beyond all question. I feared, however, to press this any further, lest a reciprocal question should be put to me, and therefore diverted the conversation to another object. This is a sketch only of a conference which was long. I have endeavored to give the substance, and sometimes the expressions, where they were material. I supposed it would be agreeable to Congress to have it communicated to them, in the present undecided state in which these subjects are. I should add, that an explanation of the transaction of Monsieur de Massiac with the Algerines, before hinted at, will be found in the enclosed letter from the Count d'Estaing to me, wherein he gives also his own opinion. The whole is submitted to Congress, as I conceive it my duty to furnish them with whatever information I can gather, which may throw any light on the subjects depending before them. I have the honor to be, with the most perfect esteem and respect, Sir, your most obedient and most humble servant,

Th: Jefferson.

LETTER XIX.—TO MR. CARMICHAEL, June 20, 1786

TO MR. CARMICHAEL.

Paris, June 20, 1786.

Dear Sir,

My last to you was of the 5th of May, by Baron Waltersdorff. Since that I have been honored with yours of April the 13th, and May the 16th and 18th. The present covers letters to Mr. Lambe and Mr. Randall, informing them that the demands of Algiers for the ransom of our prisoners and also for peace, are so infinitely beyond our instructions, that we must refer the matter back to Congress, and therefore praying them to come on immediately. I will beg the favor of you to forward these letters. The whole of this business, therefore, is suspended till we receive further orders, except as to Mr. Barclay's mission. Your bills have been received and honored. The first naming expressly a letter of advice, and none coming, it was refused till the receipt of your letter to me, in which you mentioned that you had drawn two bills. I immediately informed Mr. Grand, who thereupon honored the bill.

I have received no public letters of late date. Through other channels, I have collected some articles of information, which may be acceptable to you.

In a letter of March the 20th, from Dr. Franklin to me, is this passage. 'As to public affairs, the Congress has not been able to assemble more than seven or eight States during the whole winter, so the treaty with Prussia remains still unratified, though there is no doubt of its being done soon, as a full Congress is expected next month. The disposition to furnish Congress with ample powers augments daily, as people become more enlightened. And I do not remember ever to have seen, during my long life, more signs of public felicity than appear at present, throughout these States; the cultivators of the earth, who make the bulk of our nation, have made good crops, which are paid for at high prices, with ready money; the artisans, too, receive high wages; and the value of all real estates is augmented greatly. Merchants and shopkeepers, indeed, complain that there is not business enough. But this is evidently not owing to the fewness of buyers, but to the too great number of sellers; for the consumption of goods was never greater, as appears by the dress, furniture, and manner of living, of all ranks of the people.' His health is good, except as to the stone, which does not grow worse. I thank you for your attention to my request about the books, which Mr. Barclay writes me he has forwarded from Cadiz.

I have the honor to be with great respect, Dear Sir, your most obedient, humble servant,

Th: Jefferson.

LETTER XX.—TO MR. LAMBE, June 20,1786

TO MR. LAMBE.

Sir,

Paris, June 20,1786.

Having communicated to Mr. Adams the information received, at different times, from yourself, from Mr. Randall, and Mr. Carmichael, we find that the sum likely to be demanded by Algiers for the ransom of our prisoners, as well as for peace, is so infinitely beyond our powers, and the expectations of Congress, that it has become our duty to refer the whole matter back to them. Whether they will choose to buy a peace, to force one, or to do nothing, will rest in their pleasure. But that they may have all the information possible to guide them in their deliberations, we think it important that you should return to them. No time will be lost by this, and perhaps time maybe gained. It is, therefore, our joint desire, that you repair immediately to New York, for the purpose of giving to Congress all the information on this subject, which your journey has enabled you to acquire. You will consider this request as coming from Mr. Adams as well as myself, as it is by express authority from him, that I join him in it. I am of opinion, it will be better for you to come to Marseilles and by Paris: because there is a possibility that fresh orders to us, from Congress, might render it useful that we, also, should have received from you all possible information on this subject. And perhaps no time may be lost by this, as it might be long before you would set a passage from Alicant to America.

I am, Sir, your most obedient and most humble servant,

Th: Jefferson.

LETTER XXI..—TO MONSIEUR DE REYNEVAL, June 25, 1786

TO MONSIEUR DE REYNEVAL.

Paris, June 25, 1786.

Sir,

I have received letters from two citizens of the United States, of the names of Geary and Arnold, informing me, that having for some time past exercised commerce in London, and having failed, they were obliged to leave that country; that they came over to Dunkirk, and from thence to Brest, where, one of them having changed his name, the more effectually to elude the search of his creditors, they were both imprisoned by order of the commandant; whether at the suit of their creditors, or because one of them changed his name, they are uninformed. But they are told, that the commandant has sent information of his proceedings to your office. I have some reason to suppose, their creditors are endeavoring to obtain leave to remove them to England, where their imprisonment would be perpetual. Unable to procure information elsewhere, I take the liberty of asking you, whether you know the cause of their imprisonment, and of soliciting your attention to them, so far as that nothing may take place against them by surprise, and out of the ordinary course of the law.

I have the honor to be, with sentiments of the most perfect esteem and respect, Sir, your most obedient and most humble; servant,

Th: Jefferson.

LETTER XXII.—TO THE PREVOT DES MARCHANDS, September 27, 1786

TO THE PREVOT DES MARCHANDS ET ECHEVINS DE PARIS.
Paris, September 27, 1786.
Gentlemen,

The commonwealth of Virginia, in gratitude for the services of Major General the Marquis de la Fayette, have determined to erect his bust in their Capital. Desirous to place a like monument of his worth, and of their sense of it, in the country to which they are indebted for his birth, they have hoped that the city of Paris will consent to become the depository of this second testimony of their gratitude. Being charged by them with the execution of their wishes, I have the honor to solicit of Messieurs le Prevot des Marchands et Echevins, on behalf of the city, their acceptance of a bust of this gallant officer, and that they will be pleased to place it where, doing most honor to him, it will most gratify the feelings of an allied nation.

It is with true pleasure that I obey the call of that commonwealth, to render just homage to a character so great in its first developements, that they would honor the close of any other. Their country covered by a small army against a great one, their exhausted means supplied by his talents, their enemies finally forced to that spot whither their allies and confederates were collecting to receive them, and a war which had spread its miseries into the four quarters of the earth thus reduced to a single point, where one blow should terminate it, and through the whole, an implicit respect paid to the laws of the land; these are facts which would illustrate any character, and which fully justify the warmth of those feelings, of which I have the honor, on this occasion, to be the organ.

It would have been more pleasing to me to have executed this office in person, to have mingled the tribute of private gratitude with that of my country, and, at the same time, to have had an opportunity of presenting to your honorable body, the homage of that profound respect which I have the honor to bear them. But I am withheld from these grateful duties, by the consequences of a fall, which confine me to my room. Mr. Short, therefore, a citizen of the State of Virginia, and heretofore a member of its Council of State, will have the honor of delivering you this letter, together with the resolution of the General Assembly of Virginia. He will have that, also, of presenting the bust at such time and place, as you will be so good as to signify your pleasure to receive it. Through him, I beg to be allowed the honor of presenting those sentiments of profound respect and veneration, with which I am, Gentlemen, your most obedient and most humble servant,
Th: Jefferson.

LETTER XXIII.—TO COLONEL MONROE, July 9, 1786

TO COLONEL MONROE.

Paris, July 9, 1786.

Dear Sir,

I wrote you last on the 10th of May; since which your favor of May the 11th has come to hand. The political world enjoys great quiet here. The King of Prussia is still living, but like the snuff of a candle, which sometimes seems out, and then blazes up again. Some think that his death will not produce any immediate effect in Europe. His kingdom like a machine, will go on for some time with the winding up he has given it. The King's visit to Cherbourg has made a great sensation in England and here. It proves to the world, that it is a serious object to this country, and that the King commits himself for the accomplishment of it. Indeed, so many cones have been sunk, that no doubt remains of the practicability of it. It will contain, as is said, eighty ships of the line, be one of the best harbors in the world, and by means of two entrances, on different sides, will admit vessels to come in and go out with every wind. The effect of this, in another war with England, defies calculation. Having no news to communicate, I will recur to the subjects of your letter of May the 11th.

With respect to the new States, were the question to stand simply in this form, How may the ultramontane territory be disposed of, so as to produce the greatest and most immediate benefit to the inhabitants of the maritime States of the Union? the plan would be more plausible, of laying it off into two or three States only. Even on this view, however, there would still be something to be said against it, which might render it at least doubtful. But that is a question, which good faith forbids us to receive into discussion. This requires us to state the question in its just form, How may the territories of the Union be disposed of, so as to produce the greatest degree of happiness to their inhabitants? With respect to the maritime States, little or nothing remains to be done. With respect, then, to the ultramontane States, will their inhabitants be happiest, divided into States of thirty thousand square miles, not quite as large as Pennsylvania, or into States of one hundred and sixty thousand square miles each, that is to say, three times as large as Virginia within the Allegany? They will not only be happier in States of moderate size, but it is the only way in which they can exist as a regular society. Considering the American character in general, that of those people particularly, and the energetic nature of our governments, a State of such extent as one hundred and sixty thousand square miles, would soon crumble into little ones. These are the circumstances, which reduce the Indians to such small societies. They would produce an effect on our people, similar to this. They would not be broken into such small pieces, because they are more habituated to subordination, and value more a government of regular law. But you would surely reverse the nature of things, in making small States on the ocean, and large ones beyond the mountains. If we could, in our consciences, say, that great States beyond the mountains will make the people happiest, we must still ask, whether they will be contented to be laid off into large States. They certainly will not: and if they decide to divide themselves, we are not able to restrain them. They will end by separating from our confederacy, and becoming its enemies. We had better then look forward, and see what will be the probable course of things. This will surely be a division of that country into States, of a small, or, at most, of a moderate size. If we lay them off into such, they will acquiesce; and we shall have the advantage of arranging them, so as to produce the best combinations of interest. What Congress have already done in this matter, is an argument the more, in favor of the revolt of those States against a different arrangement, and of their acquiescence under a continuance of that. Upon this plan, we treat them as fellow-citizens; they will have a just share in their own government; they will love us, and pride themselves in an union with us. Upon the other, we treat them as subjects; we govern them, and not they themselves; they will abhor us as masters, and break off from us in defiance. I confess to you, that I can see no other turn that these two plans would take. But I respect your opinion, and your knowledge of the country, too much, to be over-confident in my own.

I thank you sincerely for your communication, that my not having sooner given notice of the *Arrêts* relative to fish, gave discontent to some persons. These are the most friendly offices you can do me, because they enable me to justify myself, if I am right, or correct myself, if wrong. If those who thought I might have been remiss, would have written to me on the subject, I should have admired them for their candor, and thanked them for it: for I have no jealousies nor resentments at things of this kind, where I have no reason to believe they have been excited by a hostile spirit; and I suspect no such spirit in a single member of Congress. You know there were two *Arrêts*; the first of August the 30th, 1784, the second of the 18th and 25th of September, 1785. As to the first, it would be a sufficient justification of myself, to say, that it was in the time of my predecessor, nine months before I came into office, and that there was no more reason for my giving information of it, when I did come into office, than of all the other transactions, which preceded that period. But this would seem to lay a blame on Dr. Franklin for not communicating it, which I am confident he did not deserve. This government affects a secrecy in all its transactions whatsoever, though they be of a nature not to admit a perfect secrecy. Their *Arrêts* respecting the islands go to those islands, and are unpublished and unknown in France, except in the bureau where they are formed. That of August, 1784, would probably be communicated to the merchants of the seaport towns also. But Paris having no commercial connections with them, if any thing makes its way from a seaport town to Paris, it must be by accident. We have, indeed, agents in these seaports; but they value their offices so little, that they do not trouble themselves to inform us of what is passing there. As a proof that these things do not transpire here, nor are easily got at, recollect that Mr. Adams, Dr. Franklin, and myself were all here on the spot together, from August, 1784, to June, 1785, that is to say, ten months, and yet not one of us knew of the *Arrêt* of August, 1784. September the 18th and 25th, 1785, the second was passed. And here alone I became responsible. I think it was about six weeks before I got notice of it, that is, in November. On the 20th of that month, writing to Count de Vergennes on another subject, I took occasion to remonstrate to him on that. But from early in November, when the Fitzhughs went to America. I had never a confidential opportunity of writing to Mr. Jay from hence, directly, for several months. In a letter of December the 14th, to Mr. Jay, I mentioned to him the want of an opportunity to write to him confidentially, which obliged me at that moment to write by post via London, and on such things only, as both post-offices were welcome to see. On the 2nd of January, Mr. Bingham setting out for London, I wrote to Mr. Jay, sending him a copy of my letter to Count de Vergennes, and stating something, which had passed in conversation on the same subject. I prayed Mr. Bingham to take charge of the letter, and either to send it by a safe hand, or carry it himself, as circumstances should render most advisable. I believe he kept it, to carry himself. He did not sail from London till about the 12th of March, nor arrive in America till the middle of May. Thus you see, that causes had prevented a letter, which I had written on the 20th of November, from getting to America till the month of May. No wonder, then, if notice of this *Arrêt* came first to you by the way of the West Indies: and, in general, I am confident, that you will receive notice of the regulations of this country, respecting their islands, by the way of those islands, before you will from hence. Nor can this be remedied, but by a system of bribery, which would end in the corruption of your own ministers, and produce no good adequate to the expense. Be so good as to communicate these circumstances to the persons who you think may have supposed me guilty of remissness on this occasion.

I will turn to a subject more pleasing to both, and give you my sincere congratulations on your marriage. Your own dispositions, and the inherent comforts of that state, will insure you a great addition of happiness. Long may you live to enjoy it, and enjoy it in full measure. The interest I feel in every one connected with you, will justify my presenting my earliest respects to the lady, and of tendering her the homage of my friendship. I shall be happy at all times to be useful to either of you, and to receive your commands. I enclose you the bill of lading of your *Encyclopédie.* With respect to the remittance for it, of which you make mention, I beg you not to think of it. I know, by experience, that on proceeding to make a settlement in life, a man has need of all his resources; and I should be unhappy, were you to lessen them by an attention to this trifle. Let it lie till you have nothing else to do with your money. Adieu, my Dear Sir, and be assured of the esteem with which I am your friend and servant,

Th: Jefferson.

LETTER XXIV.—TO JOHN ADAMS, July 11, 1786

TO JOHN ADAMS.

Paris, July 11, 1786.

Dear Sir,

Our instructions relative to the Barbary States having required us to proceed by way of negotiation to obtain their peace, it became our duty to do this to the best of our power. Whatever might be our private opinions, they were to be suppressed, and the line marked out to us was to be followed. It has been so, honestly and zealously. It was, therefore, never material for us to consult together on the best plan of conduct towards these States. I acknowledge I very, early thought it would be best to effect a peace through the medium of war. Though it is a question with which we have nothing to do, yet as you propose some discussion of it, I shall trouble you with my reasons. Of the four positions laid down in your letter of the 3rd instant, I agree to the three first, which are, in substance, that the good offices of our friends cannot procure us a peace, without paying its price, that they cannot materially lessen that price; and that paying it, we can have the peace in spite of the intrigues of our enemies. As to the fourth, that the longer the negotiation is delayed, the larger will be the demand; this will depend on the intermediate captures: if they are many and rich, the price may be raised; if few and poor, it will be lessened. However, if it is decided, that we shall buy a peace, I know no reason for delaying the operation, but should rather think it ought to be hastened: but I should prefer the obtaining it by war.

1. Justice is in favor of this opinion. 2. Honor favors it. 3. It will procure us respect in Europe; and respect is a safeguard to interest. 4. It will arm the federal head with the safest of all the instruments of coercion over its delinquent members, and prevent it from using what would be less safe. I think, that so far you go with me. But in the next steps we shall differ. 5. I think it least expensive. 6. Equally effectual. I ask a fleet of one hundred and fifty guns, the one half of which shall be in constant cruise. This fleet, built, manned, and victualled for six months, will cost four hundred and fifty thousand pounds sterling. Its annual expense will be three hundred pounds sterling a gun, including every thing: this will be forty-five thousand pounds sterling a year. I take British experience for the basis of my calculation: though we know, from our own experience, that we can do in this way for pounds lawful, what costs them pounds sterling. Were we to charge all this to the Algerine war, it would amount to little more than we must pay if we buy peace. But as it is proper and necessary, that we should establish a small marine force (even were we to buy a peace from the Algerines), and as that force, laid up in our dock-yard, would cost us half as much annually as if kept

in order for service, we have a right to say, that only twenty-two thousand and five hundred pounds sterling, per annum, should be charged to the Algerine war. 6. It will be as effectual. To all the mismanagements of Spain and Portugal, urged to show that war against those people is ineffectual, I urge a single fact to prove the contrary, where there is any management. About forty years ago, the Algerines having broke their treaty with France, this court sent Monsieur de Massiac, with one large and two small frigates: he blockaded the harbor of Algiers three months, and they subscribed to the terms he proposed. If it be admitted, however, that war, on the fairest prospects, is still exposed to uncertainties, I weigh against this the greater uncertainty of the duration of a peace bought with money, from such a people, from a Dey eighty years old, and by a nation who, on the hypothesis of buying peace, is to have no power on the sea to enforce an observance of it.

So far I have gone on the supposition, that the whole weight of this war would rest on us. But, 1. Naples will join us. The character of their naval minister (Acton), his known sentiments with respect to the peace Spain is officiously trying to make for them, and his dispositions against the Algerines, give the best grounds to believe it. 2. Every principle of reason assures,us, that Portugal will join us. I state this as taking for granted, what all seem to believe, that they will not be at peace with Algiers. I suppose, then, that a convention might be formed between Portugal, Naples, and the United States, by which the burthen of the war might be quotaed on them, according to their respective wealth; and the term of it should be, when Algiers should subscribe to a peace with all three on equal terms. This might be left open for other nations to accede to, and many, if not most of the powers of Europe (except France, England, Holland, and Spain, if her peace be made), would sooner or later enter into the confederacy, for the sake of having their peace with the piratical States guarantied by the whole. I suppose, that, in this case, our proportion of force would not be the half of what I first calculated on.

These are the reasons, which have influenced my judgment on this question. I give them to you, to show you that I am imposed on by a semblance of reason at least; and not with an expectation of their changing your opinion. You have viewed the subject, I am sure, in all its bearings. You have weighed both questions, with all their circumstances. You make the result different from what I do. The same facts impress us differently. This is enough to make me suspect an error in my process of reasoning, though I am not able to detect it. It is of no consequence; as I have nothing to say in the decision, and am ready to proceed heartily on any other plan, which may be adopted, if my agency should be thought useful. With respect to the dispositions of the States, I am utterly uninformed. I cannot help thinking, however, that on a view of all the circumstances, they might be united in either of the plans.

Having written this on the receipt of your letter, without knowing of any opportunity of sending it, I know not when it will go: I add nothing, therefore, on any other subject, but assurances of the sincere esteem and respect, with which I am,

Dear Sir, your friend and servant,

Th: Jefferson.

LETTER XXV.—TO JOHN JAY, August 11, 1786

TO JOHN JAY.

Paris, August 11, 1786.

Sir,

Since the date of my last, which was of July the 8th, I have been honored with the receipt of yours of June the 16th. I am to thank you, on the part of the minister of Geneva, for the intelligence it contained on the subject of Gallatin, whose relations will be relieved by the receipt of it.

The enclosed intelligence, relative to the instructions of the court of London to Sir Guy Carleton, came to me through the Count de la Touche and Marquis de la Fayette. De la Touche is a director under the Marechal de Castries, minister for the marine department, and possibly receives his intelligence from him, and he from their ambassador at London. Possibly, too, it might be fabricated here. Yet weighing the characters of the ministry of St. James's and Versailles, I think the former more capable of giving such instructions, than the latter of fabricating them for the small purposes the fabrication could answer.

The Gazette of France, of July the 28th, announces the arrival of Peyrouse at Brazil, that he was to touch at Otaheite, and proceed to California, and still further northwardly. This paper, as you well know, gives out such facts as the court are willing the world should be possessed of. The presumption is, therefore, that they will make an establishment of some sort on the northwest coast of America.

I trouble you with the copy of a letter from Schweighauser and Dobree, on a subject with which I am quite unacquainted. Their letter to Congress of November the 30th, 1780, gives their state of the matter. How far it be true and just, can probably be ascertained from Dr. Franklin, Dr. Lee, and other gentlemen now in America. I shall be glad to be honored with the commands of Congress on this subject. I have inquired into the state of the arms, mentioned in their letter to me. The principal articles were about thirty thousand bayonets, fifty thousand gunlocks, thirty cases of arms, twenty-two cases of sabres, and some other things of little consequence. The quay at Nantes having been overflowed by the river Loire, the greatest part of these arms was under water, and they are now, as I am informed, a solid mass of rust, not worth the expense of throwing them out of the warehouse, much less that of storage. Were not their want of value a sufficient reason against reclaiming the property of these arms, it rests with Congress to decide, whether other reasons are not opposed to this reclamation. They were the property of a sovereign body, they were seized by an individual, taken cognizance of by a court of justice, and refused, or at least not restored by the sovereign, within whose State they had been arrested. These are circumstances which have been mentioned to me. Doctor Franklin, however, will be able to inform Congress, with precision, as to what passed on this subject. If the information I have received be any thing like the truth, the discussion of this matter can only be with the court of Versailles. It would be very delicate, and could have but one of two objects; either to recover the arms, which are not worth receiving, or to satisfy us on the point of honor. Congress will judge how far the latter may be worth pursuing against a particular ally, and under actual circumstances. An instance, too, of acquiescence on our part under a wrong, rather than disturb our friendship by altercations, may have its value in some future case. However, I shall be ready to do in this what Congress shall be pleased to direct.

I enclose the despatches relative to the Barbary negotiation, received since my last. It is painful to me to overwhelm Congress and yourself continually with these voluminous papers. But I have no right to suppress any part of them, and it is one of those cases, where, from a want of well digested information, we must be contented to examine a great deal of rubbish, in order to find a little good matter.

The gazettes of Leyden and France, to the present date, accompany this, which, for want of direct and safe opportunities, I am obliged to send by an American gentleman, by the way of London. The irregularity of the French packets has diverted elsewhere the tide of passengers who used to furnish me occasions of writing to you, without permitting my letters to go through the post-office. So that when the packets go now, I can seldom write by them.

I have the honor to be, with sentiments of the highest esteem and respect, Sir, your most obedient and most humble servant,

Th: Jefferson.

[The annexed is a translation of the paper referred to in

the preceding letter, on the subject of the instructions

given to Sir Guy Carleton.]

An extract of English political news, concerning North America, July 14th, 1786.

General Carleton departs in a few days with M. de la Naudiere, a Canadian gentleman. He has made me acquainted with the Indian Colonel Joseph Brandt. It is certain that he departs with the most positive instructions to distress the Americans as much as possible, and to create them enemies on all sides.

Colonel Brandt goes loaded with presents for himself, and for several chiefs of the tribes bordering on Canada. It would be well for the Americans to know in time, that enemies are raised against them, in order to derange their system of government, and to add to the confusion which already exists in it. The new possessions of England will not only gain what America shall lose, but will acquire strength in proportion to the weakening of the United States.

Sooner or later, the new States which are forming will place themselves under the protection of England, which can always communicate with them through Canada; and which, in case of future necessity, can harass the United States on one side, by her shipping, and on the other, by her intrigues. This system has not yet come to maturity, but it is unfolded, and we may rely upon the instructions given to Colonel Brandt.

LETTER XXVI.—TO COLONEL MONROE, August 11, 1786

TO COLONEL MONROE.

Paris, August 11, 1786.

Dear Sir,

I wrote you last on the 9th of July; and since that, have received yours of the 16th of June, with the interesting intelligence it contained. I was entirely in the dark as to the progress of that negotiation, and concur entirely in the views you have taken of it The difficulty on which it hangs, is a *sine qua non* with us. It would be to deceive them and ourselves, to suppose that an amity can be preserved, while this right is withheld. Such a supposition would argue, not only an ignorance of the people to whom this is most interesting, but an ignorance of the nature of man, or an inattention to it. Those who see but halfway into our true interest, will think that that concurs with the views of the other party. But those who see it in all its extent, will be sensible that our true interest will be best promoted, by making all the just claims of our fellow-citizens, wherever situated, our own, by urging and enforcing them with the weight of our whole influence, and by exercising in this, as in every other instance, a just government in their concerns, and making common cause, even where our separate interest would seem opposed to theirs. No other conduct can attach us together; and on this attachment depends our happiness.

The King of Prussia still lives, and is even said to be better. Europe is very quiet at present. The only germ of dissension which shows itself at present, is in the quarter of Turkey. The Emperor, the Empress, and the Venetians seem all to be picking at the Turks. It is not probable, however, that either of the two first will do any thing to bring on an open rupture, while the King of Prussia lives.

You will perceive by the letters I enclose to Mr. Jay, that Lambe, under the pretext of ill health, declines returning either to Congress, Mr. Adams, or myself. This circumstance makes me fear some malversation. The money appropriated to this object being in Holland, and having been always under the care of Mr. Adams, it was concerted between us that all the drafts should be on him. I know not, therefore, what sums may have been advanced to Lambe; I hope, however, nothing great. I am persuaded that an angel sent on this business, and so much limited in his terms, could have done nothing. But should Congress propose to try the line of negotiation again, I think they will perceive that Lambe is not a proper agent. I have written to Mr. Adams on the subject of a settlement with Lambe. There is little prospect of accommodation between the Algerines, and the Portuguese and Neapolitans. A very valuable capture too, lately made by them on the Empress of Russia, bids fair to draw her on them. The probability is therefore, that these three nations will be at war with them, and the possibility is that could we furnish a couple of frigates, a convention might be formed with those powers, establishing a perpetual cruise on the coast of Algiers, which would bring them to reason. Such a convention being left open to all powers willing to come into it, should have for its object a general peace, to be guarantied to each, by the whole. Were only two or three to begin a confederacy of this kind, I think every power in Europe would soon fall into it, except France, England, and perhaps Spain and Holland. Of these there is only England who would give any real aid to the Algerines. Morocco, you perceive, will be at peace with us. Were the honor and advantage of establishing such a confederacy out of the question, yet the necessity that the United States should have some marine force, and the happiness of this, as the ostensible cause for beginning it, would decide on its propriety. It will be said, there is no money in the treasury. There never will be money in the treasury till the confederacy shows its teeth. The States must see the rod; perhaps it must be felt by some one of them. I am persuaded, all of them would rejoice to see every one obliged to furnish its contributions. It is not the difficulty of furnishing them, which beggars the treasury, but the fear that others will not furnish as much. Every rational citizen must wish to see an effective instrument of coercion, and should fear to see it on any other element than the water. A naval force can never endanger our liberties, nor occasion bloodshed: a land force would do both. It is not in the choice of the States, whether they will pay money to cover their trade against the Algerines. If they obtain a peace by negotiation, they must pay a great sum of money for it; if they do nothing, they must pay a great sum of money, in the form of insurance; and in either way, as great a one as in the way of force, and probably less effectual.

I look forward with anxiety to the approaching moment of your departure from Congress. Besides the interest of the confederacy and of the State, I have a personal interest in it. I know not to whom I may venture confidential communications, after you are gone. I take the liberty of placing here my respects to Mrs. Monroe, and assurances of the sincere esteem with which I am, Dear Sir, your friend and servant,

Th: Jefferson.

LETTER XXVII.—TO MR. WYTHE, August 13,1786

TO MR. WYTHE.

Paris, August 13,1786.

Dear Sir

Your favors of January the 10th and February the 10th, came to hand on the 20th and 23rd of May. I availed myself of the first opportunity which occurred, by a gentleman going to England, of sending to Mr. Joddrel a copy of the Notes on our country! with a line informing him, that it was you who had emboldened me to take that liberty. Madison, no doubt, informed you of the reason why I had sent only a single copy to Virginia. Being assured by him, that they will not do the harm I had apprehended, but on the contrary may do some good, I propose to send thither the copies remaining on hand, which are fewer than I had intended. But of the numerous corrections they need, there are one or two so essential, that I must have them made, by printing a few new leaves, and substituting them for the old. This will be done while they are engraving a map which I have constructed, of the country from Albemarle sound to Lake Erie, and which will be inserted in the book. A bad French translation which is getting out here, will probably oblige me to publish the original more freely; which it did not deserve, nor did I intend. Your wishes, which are laws to me, will justify my destining a copy for you, otherwise, I should as soon have thought of sending you a horn-book; for there is no truth in it which is not familiar to you, and its errors I should hardly have proposed to treat you with.

Immediately on the receipt of your letter, I wrote to a correspondent at Florence to inquire after the family of Tagliaferro, as you desired. I received his answer two days ago, a copy of which I now enclose. The original shall be sent by some other occasion. I will have the copper-plate immediately engraved. This may be ready within a few days, but the probability is, that I shall be long getting an opportunity of sending it to you, as these rarely occur. You do not mention the size of the plate, but presuming it is intended for labels for the inside of books, I shall have it made of a proper size for that. I shall omit the word *agisos*, according to the license you allow me, because I think the beauty of a motto is to condense much matter in as few words as possible. The word omitted will be supplied by every reader.

The European papers have announced, that the Assembly of Virginia were occupied on the revisal of their code of laws. This, with some other similar intelligence, has contributed much to convince the people of Europe, that what the English papers are constantly publishing of our anarchy, is false; as they are sensible that such a work is that of a people only, who are in perfect tranquillity. Our act for freedom of religion is extremely applauded. The ambassadors and ministers of the several nations of Europe, resident at this court, have asked of me copies of it, to send to their sovereigns, and it is inserted at full length in several books now in the press; among others, in the new *Encyclopédie*. I think it will produce considerable good even in these countries, where ignorance, superstition, poverty, and oppression of body and mind, in every form, are so firmly settled on the mass of the people, that their redemption from them can never be hoped. If all the sovereigns of Europe were to set themselves to work, to emancipate the minds of their subjects from their present ignorance and prejudices, and that, as zealously as they now endeavor the contrary, a thousand years would not place them on that high ground, on which our common people are now setting out. Ours could not have been so fairly placed under the control of the common sense of the people, had they not been separated from their parent stock, and kept from contamination, either from them, or the other people of the old world, by the intervention of so wide an ocean. To know the worth of this, one must see the want of it here. I think by far the most important bill in our whole code, is that for the diffusion of knowledge among the people. No other sure foundation can be devised for the preservation of freedom and happiness. If any body thinks, that kings, nobles, or priests are good conservators of the public happiness, send him here. It is the best school in the universe to cure him of that folly. He will see here, with his own eyes, that these descriptions of men are an abandoned confederacy against the happiness of the mass of the people. The omnipotence of their effect cannot be better proved, than in this country particularly, where, notwithstanding the finest soil upon earth, the finest climate under heaven, and a people of the most benevolent, the most gay and amiable character of which the human form is susceptible; where such a people, I say, surrounded by so many blessings from nature, are loaded with misery by kings, nobles, and priests, and by them alone. Preach, my dear Sir, a crusade against ignorance; establish and improve the law for educating the common people. Let our countrymen know, that the people alone can protect us against these evils, and that the tax which will be paid for this purpose, is not more than the thousandth part of what will be paid to kings, priests, and nobles, who will rise up among us if we leave the people in ignorance. The people of England, I think, are less oppressed than here. But it needs but half an eye to see, when among them, that the foundation is laid in their dispositions for the establishment of a despotism. Nobility, wealth, and pomp are the objects of their admiration. They are by no means the free-minded people, we suppose them in America. Their learned men, too, are few in number, and are less learned, and infinitely less emancipated from prejudice, than those of this country. An event, too, seems to be preparing, in the order of things, which will probably decide the fate of that country. It is no longer doubtful, that the harbor of Cherbourg will be complete, that it will be a most excellent one, and capacious enough to hold the whole navy of France. Nothing has ever been wanting to enable this country to invade that, but a naval force conveniently stationed to protect the transports. This change of situation must oblige the English to keep up a great standing army, and there is no King, who, with sufficient force, is not always ready to make himself absolute. My paper warns me, it is time to recommend myself to the friendly recollection of Mrs. Wythe, of Colonel Taliaferro and his family, and particularly of Mr. R. T. and to assure you of the affectionate esteem, with which I am,

Dear Sir, your friend and servant,

Th: Jefferson.

LETTER XXVIII.—TO MRS. COSWAY, October 12, 1786

TO MRS. COSWAY.

Paris, October 12, 1786.

My Dear Madam,

Having performed the last sad office of handing you into your carriage, at the pavillion de St. Denis, and seen the wheels get actually into motion, I turned on my heel and walked, more dead than alive, to the opposite door, where my own was awaiting me. Mr. Danquerville was missing. He was sought for, found, and dragged down stairs. We were crammed into the carriage, like recruits for the Bastille, and not having soul enough to give orders to the coachman, he presumed Paris our destination, and drove off. After a considerable interval, silence was broke, with a '*Je suis vraiment affligé du depart de ces bons gens.*' This was a signal for mutual confession of distress. We began immediately to talk of Mr. and Mrs. Cosway, of their goodness, their talents, their amiability; and though we spoke of nothing else, we seemed hardly to have entered into the matter, when the coachman announced the rue St. Denis, and that we were opposite Mr. Danquerville's. He insisted on descending there, and traversing a short passage to his lodgings. I was carried home. Seated by my fire-side, solitary and sad, the following dialogue took place between my Head and my Heart.

Head. Well, friend, you seem to be in a pretty trim.

Heart. I am indeed the most wretched of all earthly beings. Overwhelmed with grief, every fibre of my frame distended beyond its natural powers to bear, I would willingly meet whatever catastrophe should leave me no more to feel, or to fear.

Head. These are the eternal consequences of your warmth and precipitation. This is one of the scrapes into which you are ever leading us. You confess your follies, indeed; but still you hug and cherish them; and no reformation can be hoped, where there is no repentance.

Heart. Oh, my friend! this is no moment to upbraid my foibles. I am rent into fragments by the force of my grief! If you have any balm, pour it into my wounds; if none, do not harrow them by new torments. Spare me in this awful moment! At any other, I will attend with patience to your admonitions.

Head. On the contrary, I never found that the moment of triumph, with you, was the moment of attention to my admonitions. While suffering under your follies, you may perhaps be made sensible of them; but, the paroxysm over, you fancy it can never return. Harsh, therefore, as the medicine may be, it is my office to administer it. You will be pleased to remember, that when our friend Trumbull used to be telling us of the merits and talents of these good people, I never ceased whispering to you that we had no occasion for new acquaintances; that the greater their merit and talents, the more dangerous their friendship to our tranquillity, because the regret at parting would be greater.

Heart. Accordingly, Sir, this acquaintance was not the consequence of my doings. It was one of your projects, which threw us in the way of it. It was you, remember, and not I, who desired the meeting at Legrand and Motinos. I never trouble myself with domes nor arches. The *Halle aux bleds* might have rotted down, before I should have gone to see it. But you, forsooth, who are eternally getting us to sleep with your diagrams and crotchets, must go and examine this wonderful piece of architecture; and when you had seen it, oh! it was the most superb thing on earth! What you had seen there was worth all you had yet seen in Paris! I thought so too. But I meant it of the lady and gentleman to whom we had been presented; and not of a parcel of sticks and chips put together in pens. You then, Sir, and not I, have been the cause of the present distress.

Head. It would have been happy for you, if my diagrams and crotchets had gotten you to sleep on that day, as you are pleased to say they eternally do. My visit to Legrand and Motinos, had public utility for its object. A market is to be built in Richmond. What a commodious plan is that of Legrand and Motinos; especially, if we put on it the noble dome of the *Halle aux bleds*. If such a bridge as they showed us, can be thrown across the Schuylkill, at Philadelphia, the floating bridges taken up, and the navigation of that river opened, what a copious resource will be added of wood and provisions, to warm and feed the poor of that city? While I was occupied with these objects, you were dilating with your new acquaintances, and contriving how to prevent a separation from them. Every soul of you had an engagement for the day. Yet all these were to be sacrificed, that you might dine together. Lying messengers were to be despatched into every quarter of the city, with apologies for your breach of engagement. You, particularly, had the effrontery to send word to the Duchess Danville, that on the moment we were setting out to dine with her, despatches came to hand, which required immediate attention. You wanted me to invent a more ingenious excuse; but I knew you were getting into a scrape, and I would have nothing to do with it. Well; after dinner to St. Cloud, from St. Cloud to Ruggieri's, from Ruggieri's to Krumfoltz; and if the day had been as long as a Lapland summer day, you would still have contrived means among you to have filled it.

Heart. Oh! my dear friend, how you have revived me, by recalling to mind the transactions of that day! How well I remember them all, and that when I came home at night, and looked back to the morning, it seemed to have been a month agone. Go on, then, like a kind comforter, and paint to me the day we went to St. Germains. How beautiful was every object! the *Port de Reuilly*, the hills along the Seine, the rainbows of the machine of Marly, the terras of St. Germains, the chateaux, the gardens, the statues of Marly, the pavillion of Lucienne. Recollect, too, Madrid, Bagatelle, the King's garden, the Desert. How grand the idea excited by the remains of such a column. The spiral staircase, too, was beautiful. Every moment was filled with something agreeable. The wheels of time moved on with a rapidity, of which those of our carriage gave but a faint idea. And yet, in the evening, when one took a retrospect of the day, what a mass of happiness had we travelled over! Retrace all those scenes to me, my good companion, and I will forgive the unkindness with which you were chiding me. The day we went to St. Germains was a little too warm, I think; was it not?

Head. Thou art the most incorrigible of all the beings that ever sinned! I reminded you of the follies of the first day, intending to deduce from thence some useful lessons for you, but instead of listening to them, you kindle at the recollection, you retrace the whole series with a fondness, which shows you want nothing but the opportunity, to act it over again. I often told you, during its course, that you were imprudently engaging your affections, under circumstances that must cost you a great deal of pain; that the persons, indeed, were of the greatest merit, possessing good sense, good humor, honest hearts, honest manners, and eminence in a lovely art; that the lady had, moreover, qualities and accomplishments belonging to her sex, which might form a chapter apart for her; such as music, modesty, beauty, and that softness of disposition, which is the ornament of her sex, and charm of ours: but that all these considerations would increase the pang of separation, that their stay here was to be short; that you rack our whole system when you are parted from those you love, complaining that such a separation is worse than death, inasmuch as this ends our sufferings, whereas that only begins them; and that the separation would, in this instance, be the more severe, as you, would probably never see them again.

Heart. But they told me, they would come back again the next year.

Head. But in the mean time, see what you surfer: and their return, too, depends on so many circumstances, that, if you had a grain of prudence, you would not count upon it. Upon the whole, it is improbable, and therefore you should abandon the idea of ever seeing them again.

Heart. May Heaven abandon me, if I do!

Head. Very well. Suppose, then, they come back. They are to stay two months, and when these are expired, what is to follow? Perhaps you flatter yourself they may come to America?

Heart. God only knows what is to happen. I see nothing impossible in that supposition: and I see things wonderfully contrived sometimes to make us happy. Where could they find such objects as in America, for the exercise of their enchanting art; especially the lady, who paints landscapes so inimitably? She wants only subjects worthy of immortality, to render her pencil immortal. The Falling Spring, the Cascade of Niagara, the Passage of the Potomac through the Blue Mountains, the Natural Bridge; it is worth a voyage across the Atlantic to see these objects; much more to paint, and make them, and thereby ourselves, known to all ages. And our own dear Monticello; where has nature spread so rich a mantle under the eye?—mountains, forests rocks, rivers. With what majesty do we there ride above the storms! How sublime to look down into the workhouse of nature to see her clouds, hail, snow, rain, thunder, all fabricated at our feet! and the glorious sun when rising as if out of a distant water, lust gilding the tops of the mountains, and giving life to all nature! 1 hope in God, no circumstance may ever make either seek an asylum from grief! With what sincere sympathy I would open every cell of my composition, to receive the effusion of their woes!

I would pour my tears into their wounds; and if a drop of balm could be found on the top of the Cordilleras, or at the remotest sources of the Missouri, I would go thither myself to seek and to bring it. Deeply practised in the school of affliction, the human heart knows no joy which I have not lost, no sorrow of which I have not drank! Fortune can present no grief of unknown form to me! Who, then, can so softly bind up the wound of another, as he who has felt the same wound himself? But Heaven forbid, they should ever know a sorrow! Let us turn over another leaf, for this has distracted me.

Head. Well. Let us put this possibility to trial, then, on another point. When you consider the character which is given of our country by the lying newspapers of London, and their credulous copyers in other countries; when you reflect, that all Europe is made to believe we are a lawless banditti, in a state of absolute anarchy, cutting one another's throats, and plundering without distinction, how could you expect, that any reasonable creature would venture among us?

Heart. But you and I know, that all this is false: that there is not a country on earth, where there is greater tranquillity; where the laws are milder, or better obeyed; where every one is more attentive to his own business, or meddles less with that of others; where strangers are better received, more hospitably treated, and with a more sacred respect.

Head. True, you and I know this, but your friends do not know it.

Heart. But they are sensible people, who think for themselves. They will ask of impartial foreigners, who have been among us, whether they saw or heard on the spot any instance of anarchy. They will judge, too, that a people occupied, as we are, in opening rivers, digging navigable canals, making roads, building public schools, establishing academies, erecting busts and statues to our great men, protecting religious freedom, abolishing sanguinary punishments, reforming and improving our laws in general; they will judge, I say, for themselves, whether these are not the occupations of a people at their ease; whether this is not better evidence of our true state, than a London newspaper, hired to lie, and from which no truth can ever be extracted, but by reversing every thing it says.

Head. I did not begin this lecture, my friend, with a view to learn from you what America is doing. Let us return, then, to our point. I wish to make you sensible how imprudent it is to place your affections without reserve on objects you must so soon lose, and whose loss, when it comes, must cost you such severe pangs. Remember the last night. You knew your friends were to leave Paris to-day. This was enough to throw you into agonies. All night you tossed us from one side of the bed to the other; no sleep, no rest. The poor Crippled wrist, too, never left one moment in the same position; now up, now down, now here, now there; was it to be wondered at, if its pains returned? The surgeon then was to be called, and to be rated as an ignoramus, because he could not divine the cause of this extraordinary change. In fine, my friend, you must mend your manners. This is not a world to live at random in, as you do. To avoid those eternal distresses, to which you are for ever exposing us, you must learn to look forward before you take a step, which may interest our peace. Every thing in this world is matter of calculation. Advance, then, with caution, the balance in your hand. Put into one scale the pleasures which any object may offer; but put fairly into the other the pains which are to follow, and see which preponderates. The making an acquaintance is not a matter of indifference. When a new one is proposed to you, view it all round. Consider what advantages it presents, and to what inconveniences it may expose you. Do not bite at the bait of pleasure, till you know there is no hook beneath it. The art of life is the art of avoiding pain; and he is the best pilot, who steers clearest of the rocks and shoals with which it is beset. Pleasure is always before us; but misfortune is at our side: while running after that, this arrests us. The most effectual means of being secure against pain, is to retire within ourselves, and to suffice for our own happiness. Those which depend on ourselves, are the only pleasures a wise man will count on; for nothing is ours, which another may deprive us of. Hence the inestimable value of intellectual pleasures. Ever in our power, always leading us to something new, never cloying, we ride serene and sublime above the concerns of this mortal world, contemplating truth and nature, matter and motion, the laws which bind up their existence, and that Eternal Being, who made and bound them up by those laws. Let this be our employ. Leave the bustle and tumult of society to those who have not talents to occupy themselves without them. Friendship is but another name for an alliance with the follies and the misfortunes of others. Our own share of miseries is sufficient: why enter then as volunteers into those of another? Is there so little gall poured into our cup, that we must heed help to drink that of our neighbor? A friend dies, or leaves us: we feel as if a limb was cut off. He is sick: we must watch over him, and participate of his pains. His fortune is shipwrecked: ours must be laid under contribution. He loses a child, a parent, or a partner: we must mourn the loss as if it were our own.

Heart. And what more sublime delight, than to mingle tears with one whom the hand of Heaven hath smitten! to watch over the bed of sickness, and to beguile its tedious and its painful moments! to share our bread with one to whom misfortune has left none! This world abounds indeed with misery: to lighten its burthen, we must divide it with one another. But let us now try the virtue of your mathematical balance, and as you have put into one scale the burthens of friendship, let me put its comforts into the other. When languishing then under disease, how grateful is the solace of our friends! how are we penetrated with their assiduities and attentions! how much are we supported by their encouragements and kind offices! When Heaven has taken from us some object of our love, how sweet is it to have a bosom whereon to recline our heads, and into which we may pour the torrent of our tears! Grief, with such a comfort, is almost a luxury! In a life where we are perpetually exposed to want and accident, yours is a wonderful proposition, to insulate ourselves, to retire from all aid, and to wrap ourselves in the mantle of self-sufficiency! For assuredly nobody will care for him, who cares for nobody. But friendship is precious, not only in the shade, but in the sunshine of life: and thanks to a benevolent arrangement of things, the greater part of life is sunshine. I will recur for proof to the days we have lately passed. On these, indeed, the sun shone brightly! How gay did the face of nature appear! Hills, valleys, chateaux, gardens, rivers, every object wore its liveliest hue! Whence did they borrow it? From the presence of our charming companion. They were pleasing, because she seemed pleased. Alone, the scene would have been dull and insipid: the participation of it with her gave it relish. Let the gloomy monk, sequestered from the world, seek unsocial pleasures in the bottom of his cell! Let the sublimated philosopher grasp visionary happiness, while pursuing phantoms dressed in the garb of truth! Their supreme wisdom is supreme folly: and they mistake for happiness the mere absence of pain. Had they ever felt the solid pleasure of one generous spasm of the heart, they would exchange for it all the frigid speculations of their lives, which you have been vaunting in such elevated terms. Believe me, then, my friend, that that is a miserable arithmetic, which could estimate friendship at nothing, or at less than nothing. Respect for you has induced me to enter into this discussion, and to hear principles uttered, which I detest and abjure. Respect for myself now obliges me to recall you into the proper limits of your office. When nature assigned us the same habitation, she gave us over it a divided empire. To you she allotted the field of science; to me that of morals.

When the circle is to be squared, or the orbit of a comet to be traced; when the arch of greatest strength, or the solid of least resistance is to be investigated, take up the problem; it is yours; nature has given me no cognizance of it. In like manner, in denying to you the feelings of sympathy, of benevolence, of gratitude, of justice, of love, of friendship, she has excluded you from their control. To these she has adapted the mechanism of the heart. Morals were too essential to the happiness of man, to be risked on the uncertain combinations of the head. She laid their foundation, therefore, in sentiment, not in science. That she gave to all, as necessary to all: this to a few only, as sufficing with a few. I know indeed, that you pretend authority to the sovereign control of our conduct, in all its parts: and a respect for your grave saws and maxims, a desire to do what is right, has sometimes induced me to conform to your counsels. A few facts, however, which I can readily recall to your memory, will suffice to prove to you, that nature has not organized you for our moral direction. When the poor wearied soldier, whom we overtook at Chickahominy, with his pack on his back, begged us to let him get up behind our chariot, you began to calculate that the road was full of soldiers, and that if all should be taken up, our horses would fail in their journey. We drove on therefore. But soon becoming sensible you had made me do wrong, that though we cannot relieve all the distressed, we should relieve as many as we can, I turned about to take up the soldier; but he had entered a by-path, and was no more to be found: and from that moment to this, I could never find him out to ask his forgiveness. Again, when the poor woman came to ask a charity in Philadelphia, you whispered, that she looked like a drunkard, and that half a dollar was enough to give her for the ale-house. Those who want the dispositions to give, easily find reasons why they ought not to give. When I sought her out afterwards, and did what I should have done at first, you know, that she employed the money immediately towards placing her child at school. If our country, when pressed with wrongs at the point of the bayonet, had been governed by its heads instead of its' hearts, where should we have been now? Hanging on a gallows as high as Hainan's. You began to calculate, and to compare wealth and numbers: we threw up a few pulsations of our blood; we supplied enthusiasm against wealth and numbers; we put our existence to the hazard, when the hazard seemed against us, and we saved our country: justifying, at the same time, the ways of Providence, whose precept is, to do always what is right, and leave the issue to him. In short, my friend, as far as my recollection serves me, I do not know that I ever did a good thing on your suggestion, or a dirty one without it. I do for ever, then, disclaim your interference in my province. Fill paper as you please with triangles and squares: try how many ways you can hang and combine them together. I shall never envy nor control your sublime delights. But leave me to decide when and where friendships are to be contracted. You say I contract them at random. So you said the woman at Philadelphia was a drunkard. I receive none into my esteem, till I know they are worthy of it. Wealth, title, office, are no recommendations to my friendship. On the contrary, great good qualities are requisite to make amends for their having wealth, title, and office. You confess, that, in the present case, I could not have made a worthier choice. You only object, that I was so soon to lose them. We are not immortal ourselves, my friend; how can we expect our enjoyments to be so? We have no rose without its thorn; no pleasure without alloy. It is the law of our existence; and we must acquiesce. It is the condition annexed to all our pleasures, not by us who receive, but by him who gives them. True, this condition is pressing cruelly on me at this moment. I feel more fit for death than life. But when I look back on the pleasures of which it is the consequence, I am conscious they were worth the price I am paying. Notwithstanding your endeavors, too, to damp my hopes, I comfort myself with expectations of their promised return. Hope is sweeter than despair; and they were too good to mean to deceive me. 'In the summer,' said the gentleman; but 'In the spring,' said the lady; and I should love her for ever, were it only for that! Know, then, my friend, that I have taken these good people into my bosom; that I have lodged them in the warmest cell I could find; that I love them, and will continue to love them through life; that if fortune should dispose them on one side the globe, and me on the other, my affections shall pervade its whole mass to reach them. Knowing then my determination, attempt not to disturb it. If you can at any time furnish matter for their amusement, it will be the office of a good neighbor to do it. I will, in like manner, seize any occasion which may offer, to do the like good turn for you with Condorcet, Rittenhouse, Madison, La Cretelle, or any other of those worthy sons of science, whom you so justly prize.

I thought this a favorable proposition whereon to rest the issue of the dialogue. So I put an end to it by calling for my nightcap. Methinks, I hear you wish to Heaven I had called a little sooner, and so spared you the *ennui* of such a sermon. I did not interrupt them sooner, because I was in a mood for hearing sermons. You, too, were the subject; and on such a thesis, I never think the theme long; not even if I am to write it, and that slowly and awkwardly, as now, with the left hand. But that you may not be discouraged from a correspondence, which begins so formidably, I will promise you, on my honor, that my future letters shall be of a reasonable length. I will even agree to express but half my esteem for you, for fear of cloying you with too full a dose. But on your part, no curtailing. If your letters are as long as the Bible, they will appear short to me. Only let them be brim full of affection. I shall read them with the dispositions with which Arlequin, in *Les Deux Billets*, spelt the words *'Je t'aime,'* and wished that the whole alphabet had entered into their composition.

We have had incessant rains since your departure. These make me fear for your health, as well as that you had an uncomfortable journey. The same cause has prevented me from being able to give you any account of your friends here. This voyage to Fontainebleau will probably send the Count de Moutier and the Marquis de Brehan to America. Danquerville promised to visit me, but has not done it as yet. De la Tude comes sometimes to take family soup with me, and entertains me with anecdotes of his five and thirty years' imprisonment. How fertile is the mind of man, which can make the Bastille and dungeon of Vincennes yield interesting anecdotes! You know this was for making four verses on Madame de Pompadour. But I think you told me you did not know the verses. They were these.

'Sans esprit, sans sentiment,

Sans etre belle, ni neuve,

En France on peut avoir le premier amant:

Pompadour en est Tepreuve.'

I have read the memoir of his three escapes. As to myself, my health is good, except my wrist, which mends slowly, and my mind, which mends not at all, but broods constantly over your departure. The lateness of the season obliges me to decline my journey into the south of France. Present me in the most friendly terms to Mr. Cosway, and receive me into your own recollection with a partiality and warmth, proportioned not to my own poor merit, but to the sentiments of sincere affection and esteem, with which I have the honor to be, my Dear Madam,

Your most obedient, humble servant,

Th: Jefferson.

LETTER XXIX.—TO MRS. COSWAY, October 13, 1786

TO MRS. COSWAY.

Paris, October 13, 1786.

My Dear Madam,

Just as I had sealed the enclosed, I received a letter of a good length, dated Antwerp, with your name at the bottom. I prepared myself for a feast. I read two or three sentences: looked again at the signature, to see if I had not mistaken it. It was visibly yours. Read a sentence or two more. Diable! Spelt your name distinctly. There was not a letter of it omitted. Began to read again. In fine, after reading a little, and examining the signature alternately, half a dozen times, I found that your name was to four lines only, instead of four pages. I thank you for the four lines, however, because they prove you think of me; little, indeed, but better little than none. To show how much I think of you, I send you the enclosed letter of three sheets of paper, being a history of the evening I parted with you. But how expect you should read a letter of three mortal sheets of paper? I will tell you. Divide it into six doses of half a sheet each, and every day, when the toilette begins, take a dose, that is to say, read half a sheet. By this means, it will have the only merit its length and dulness can aspire to, that of assisting your coiffeuse to procure you six good naps of sleep. I will even allow you twelve days to get through it, holding you rigorously to one condition only, that is, that at whatever hour you receive this, you do not break the seal of the enclosed till the next toilette. Of this injunction I require a sacred execution. I rest it on your friendship, and that in your first letter, you tell me honestly, whether you have honestly performed it. I send you the song I promised. Bring me in return the subject, *Jours heureux!* Were I a songster, I should sing it all to these words; '*Dans ces lieux qu'elle tarde à se rendre!*' Learn it, I pray you, and sing it with feeling. My right hand presents its devoirs to you, and sees with great indignation the left supplanting it in a correspondence so much valued. You will know the first moment it can resume its rights. The first exercise of them shall be addressed to you, as you had the first essay of its rival. It will yet, however, be many a day. Present my esteem to Mr. Cosway, and believe me to be yours very affectionately,

Th: Jefferson.

LETTER XXX.—M. LE ROY DE L'ACADEMIE DES SCIENCES, November 13, 1786

M. LE ROY DE L'ACADEMIE DES SCIENCES.

Paris, November 13, 1786.

Sir,

I received the honor of yours of September the 18th, a day or two after the accident of a dislocated wrist had disabled me from writing. I have waited thus long in constant hope of recovering its use. But finding that this hope walks before me like my shadow, I can no longer oppose the desire and duty of answering your polite and learned letter. I therefore employ my left hand in the office of scribe, which it performs indeed slowly, awkwardly, and badly.

The information given by me to the Marquis de Chastellux, and alluded to in his book and in your letter, was, that the sea breezes which prevail in the lower parts of Virginia, during the summer months, and in the warm parts of-the day, had made a sensible progress into the interior country: that formerly, within the memory of persons living, they extended but little above Williamsburg; that afterwards they became sensible as high as Richmond; and that, at present, they penetrate sometimes as far as the first mountains, which are above an hundred miles further from the sea coast, than Williamsburg is. It is very rare, indeed, that they reach those mountains, and not till the afternoon is considerably advanced. A light northwesterly breeze is, for the most part, felt there, while an easterly or northeasterly wind is blowing strongly in the lower country. How far northward and southward of Virginia, this easterly breeze Takes place, I am not informed. I must, therefore, be understood as speaking of that State only, which extends on the sea coast from 36 1/2 to 38° of latitude.

This is the fact. We know too little of the operations of nature in the physical world, to assign causes with any degree of confidence. Willing always, however, to guess at what we do not know, I have sometimes indulged myself with conjectures on the causes of the phenomena above stated. I will hazard them on paper, for your amusement, premising for their foundation some principles believed to be true.

Air resting on a heated and reflecting surface, becomes warmer, rarer, and lighter: it ascends therefore, and the circumjacent air, which is colder and heavier, flows into its place, becomes warmed and lightened in its turn, ascends, and is succeeded as that which went before. If the heated surface be circular, the air flows to it from every quarter, like the rays of a circle to its centre. If it be a zone of determinate breadth and indefinite length, the air will flow from each side perpendicularly on it. If the currents of air flowing from opposite sides, be of equal force, they will meet in equilibrio, at a line drawn longitudinally through the middle of the zone. If one current be stronger than the other, the stronger one will force back the line of equilibrium, towards the further edge of the zone, or even beyond it: the motion it has acquired causing it to overshoot the zone, as the motion acquired by a pendulum in its descent, causes it to vibrate beyond the point of its lowest descent.

Earth, exposed naked to the sun's rays, absorbs a good portion of them; but, being an opaque body, those rays penetrate to a small depth only. Its surface, by this accumulation of absorbed rays, becomes considerably heated. The residue of the rays are reflected into the air resting on that surface. This air, then, is warmed, 1. by the direct rays of the sun; 2. by its reflected rays; 3. by contact with the heated surface. A forest receiving the sun's rays, a part of them enters the intervals between the trees, and their reflection upwards is intercepted by the leaves and boughs. The rest fall on the trees, the leaves of which being generally inclined towards the horizon, reflect the rays downwards. The atmosphere here, then, receives little or no heat by reflection. Again, these leaves having a power of keeping themselves cool by their own transpiration, they impart no heat to the air by contact. Reflection and contact, then, two of the three modes before-mentioned, of communicating heat, are wanting here; and, of course, the air over a country covered by forest must be colder than that over cultivated grounds.

The sea being pellucid, the sun's rays penetrate it to a considerable depth. Being also fluid, and in perpetual agitation, its parts are constantly mixed together; so that instead of its heat being all accumulated in its surface, as in the case of a solid, opaque body, it is diffused through its whole mass. Its surface, therefore, is comparatively cool, for these reasons; to which may be added that of evaporation. The small degree of reflection which might otherwise take place, is generally prevented by the rippled state of its surface. The air resting on the sea, then, like that resting on a forest, receives little or no heat by reflection or contact; and is therefore colder than that which lies over a cultivated country.

To apply these observations to the phenomena under consideration. The first settlements of Virginia were made along the sea coast, bearing from the south, towards the north, a little eastwardly. These settlements formed a zone, in which, though every point was not cleared of its forest, yet a good proportion was cleared and cultivated. The cultivated earth, as the sun advances above the horizon in the morning, acquires from it an intense heat, which is retained and increased through the warm parts of the day. The air resting on it becomes warm in proportion, and rises. On one side is a country still covered with forest: on the other is the ocean. The colder air from both of these, then rushes towards the heated zone, to supply the place left vacant there by the ascent of its warm air. The breeze from the west is light and feeble; because it traverses a country covered with mountains and forests, which retard its current. That from the east is strong; as passing over the ocean, wherein there is no obstacle to its motion. It is probable, therefore, that this easterly breeze forces itself far into, or perhaps beyond, the zone which produces it. This zone is, by the increase of population, continually widening into the interior country. The line of equilibrium between the easterly and westerly breezes is, therefore, progressive.

Did no foreign causes intervene, the sea breezes would be a little southwardly of the east, that direction being perpendicular to our coast. But within the tropics, there are winds which blow continually and strongly from the east. This current affects the course of the air, even without the tropics. The same cause, too, which produces a strong motion of the air, from east to west, between the tropics, to wit, the sun, exercises its influence without those limits, but more feebly, in proportion as the surface of the globe is there more obliquely presented to its rays. This effect, though not great, is not to be neglected when the sun is in or near our summer solstice, which is the season of these easterly breezes. The northern air, too, flowing towards the equatorial parts, to supply the vacuum made there by the ascent of their heated air, has only the small rotary motion of the polar latitudes from which it comes. Nor does it suddenly acquire the swifter rotation of the parts into which it enters. This gives it the effect of a motion opposed to that of the earth, that is to say, of an easterly one. And all these causes together are known to produce currents of air in the Atlantic, varying from east to northeast, as far as the fortieth degree of latitude. It is this current which presses our sea breeze out of its natural southeasterly direction, to an easterly, and sometimes almost a northeasterly one.

We are led naturally to ask, where the progress of our sea breezes will ultimately be stopped? No confidence can be placed in any answer to this question. If they should ever pass the mountainous country which separates the waters of the ocean from those of the Mississippi, there may be circumstances which might aid their further progress, as far as the Mississippi. That mountainous country commences about two hundred miles from the sea coast, and consists of successive ranges passing from northeast to southwest, and rising the one above the other to the Allegany Ridge, which is the highest of all. From that, lower and lower ridges succeed one another again, till having covered, in the whole, a breadth of two hundred miles from southeast to northwest, they subside into a plain, fertile country, extending four hundred miles to the Mississippi, and probably much further on the other side, towards the heads of the western waters. When this country shall become cultivated, it will, for the reasons before explained, draw to it winds from the east and west. In this case, should the sea breezes pass the intermediate mountains, they will rather be aided than opposed in their further progress to the Mississippi. There are circumstances, however, which render it possible that they may not be able to pass those intermediate mountains. 1. These mountains constitute the highest lands within the United States. The air on them must consequently be very cold and heavy, and have a tendency to flow both to the east and west. 2. Ranging across the current of the sea breezes, they are in themselves, so many successive barriers opposed to their progress. 3. The country they occupy is covered with trees, which assist to weaken and spend the force of the breezes. 4. It will remain so covered; a very small proportion of it being capable of culture. 5. The temperature of its air, then, will never be softened by culture.

Whether in the plain country between the Mississippi and Allegany mountains, easterly or westerly winds prevail at present, I am not informed. I conjecture, however, that they must be westerly: and I think with you, Sir, that if those mountains were to subside into plain country, as their opposition to the westerly winds would then be removed, they would repress more powerfully those from the east, and of course would remove the line of equilibrium nearer to the sea coast for the present.

Having had occasion to mention the course of the tropical winds from east to west, I will add some observations connected with them. They are known to occasion a strong current in the ocean, in the same direction. This current breaks on that wedge of land of which Saint Roque is the point; the southern column of it probably turning off and washing the coast of Brazil. I say probably, because I have never heard the fact, and conjecture it from reason only. The northern column, having its western motion diverted towards the north, and reinforced by the currents of the great rivers Orinoko, Amazons, and Tocantin, has probably been the agent which formed the Gulf of Mexico, cutting the American continent nearly in two, in that part. It re-issues into the ocean at the northern end of the Gulf, and passes by the name of the Gulf Stream, all along the coast of the United States, to its northern extremity. There it turns off eastwardly, having formed by its eddy, at this turn, the Banks of Newfoundland. Through the whole of its course, from the Gulf to the Banks, it retains a very sensible warmth. The Spaniards are, at this time, desirous of trading to their Philippine Islands, by the way of the Cape of Good Hope: but opposed in it by the Dutch, under authority of the treaty of Munster, they are examining the practicability of a common passage through the Straits of Magellan, or round Cape Horn. Were they to make an opening through the Isthmus of Panama, a work much less difficult than some even of the inferior canals of France, however small this opening should be in the beginning, the tropical current entering it with all its force, would soon widen it sufficiently for its own passage, and thus complete in a short time, that work which otherwise will still employ it for ages. Less country, too, would be destroyed by it in this way. These consequences would follow. 1. Vessels from Europe or the western coast of Africa, by entering the tropics, would have a steady wind and tide to carry them through the Atlantic, through America and the Pacific ocean, to every part of the Asiatic coast, and of the eastern coast of Africa: thus performing with speed and safety the tour of the whole globe, to within about twenty-four degrees of longitude, or one fifteenth part of its circumference; the African continent, under the line, occupying about that space. 2. The Gulf of Mexico, now the most dangerous navigation in the world on account of its currents and moveable sands, would become stagnant and safe. 3. The Gulf Stream on the coast of the United States would cease, and with that, those derangements of course and reckoning, which now impede and endanger the intercourse with those States. 4. The fogs on the Banks of Newfoundland,* supposed to be the vapors of the Gulf Stream rendered turbid by cold air, would disappear. 5. Those Banks ceasing to receive supplies of sand, weeds, and warm water, by the Gulf Stream, it might become problematical what effect changes of pasture and temperatures would have on the fisheries. However it is time to relieve you from this long lecture. I wish its subject may have been sufficiently interesting to make amends for its details. These are submitted with entire deference to your better judgment. I will only add to them, by assuring you of the sentiments of perfect esteem and respect, with which I have the honor to be, Sir, your most obedient and most humble servant,

Th: Jefferson.

[This ingenious and probable conjecture, I found in a letter from Dr. Franklin to yourself, published in the late volume of the American Philosophical Transactions.]*

LETTER XXXI.—TO GENERAL WASHINGTON, November 14, 1786

TO GENERAL WASHINGTON.

Paris, November 14, 1786.

Sir,

The house of Le Coulteux, which for some centuries has been the wealthiest of this place, has it in contemplation to establish a great company for the fur trade. They propose that partners interested one half in the establishment, should be American citizens, born and residing in the United States. Yet if I understood them rightly, they expect that the half of the company which resides here, should make the greatest part, or perhaps the whole of the advances, while those on our side the water should superintend the details. They had, at first, thought of Baltimore as the centre of their American transactions. I have pointed out to them the advantages of Alexandria for this purpose. They have concluded to take information as to Baltimore, Philadelphia, and New York, for a principal deposit, and having no correspondent at Alexandria, have asked me to procure a state of the advantages of that place, as also to get a recommendation of the best merchant there, to be adopted as partner and head of the business there. Skill, punctuality, and integrity are the requisites in such a character. They will decide on their whole information, as to the place for their principal factory. Being unwilling that Alexandria should lose its pretensions, I have undertaken to procure them information as to that place. If they undertake this trade at all, it will be on so great a scale as to decide the current of the Indian-trade to the place they adopt. I have no acquaintance at Alexandria or in its neighborhood; but believing you would feel an interest in the matter, from the same motives which I do, I venture to ask the favor of you to recommend to me a proper merchant for their purpose, and to engage some well informed person to send me a representation of the advantages of Alexandria, as the principal deposit of the fur trade.

The author of the political part of the *Encyclopédie Méthodique* desired me to examine his article, *Etats Unis.* I did so. I found it a tissue of errors; for in truth they know nothing about us here. Particularly, however, the article Cincinnati was a mere philippic against that institution: in which it appeared that there was an utter ignorance of facts and motives. I gave him notes on it. He reformed it, as he supposed, and sent it again to me to revise. In this reformed state, Colonel Humphreys saw it.

I found it necessary to write that article for him. Before I gave it to him, I showed it to the Marquis de la Fayette, who made a correction or two. I then sent it to the author. He used the materials, mixing a great deal of his own with them. In a work which is sure of going down to the latest posterity, I thought it material to set facts to rights, as much as possible. The author was well disposed; but could not entirely get the better of his original bias. I send you the article as ultimately published. If you find any material errors in it, and will be so good as to inform me of them, I shall probably have opportunities of setting this author to rights. What has heretofore passed between us on this institution, makes it my duty to mention to you, that I have never heard a person in Europe, learned or unlearned, express his thoughts on this institution, who did not consider it as dishonorable and destructive to our governments; and that every writing which has come out since my arrival here, in which it is mentioned, considers it, even as now reformed, as the germ whose developement is one day to destroy the fabric we have reared. I did not apprehend this, while I had American ideas only. But I confess that what I have seen in Europe, has brought me over to that opinion; and that though the day may be at some distance, beyond the reach of our lives perhaps, yet it will certainly come, when a single fibre left of this institution will produce an hereditary aristocracy, which will change the form of our governments from the best to the worst in the world. To know the mass of evil which flows from this fatal source, a person must be in France; he must see the finest soil, the finest climate, the most compact state, the most benevolent character of people, and every earthly advantage combined, insufficient to prevent this scourge from rendering existence a curse to twenty-four out of twenty-five parts of the inhabitants of this country. With us, the branches of this institution cover all the states. The southern ones, at this time, are aristocratical in their dispositions: and that that spirit should grow and extend itself, is within the natural order of things. I do not flatter myself with the immortality of our governments: but I shall think little also of their longevity, unless this germ of destruction be taken out. When the society themselves shall weigh the possibility of evil, against the impossibility of any good to proceed from this institution, I cannot help hoping they will eradicate it. I know they wish the permanence of our governments, as much as any individuals composing them.

An interruption here, and the departure of the gentleman by whom I send this, oblige me to conclude it with assurances of the sincere respect and esteem, with which I have the honor to be, Dear Sir, your most obedient and most humble servant,

Th: Jefferson.

LETTER XXXII.—TO JAMES MADISON, December 16, 1786

TO JAMES MADISON.

Paris, December 16, 1786.

Dear Sir,

After a very long silence, I am at length able to write to you. An unlucky dislocation of my right wrist has disabled me from using that hand, three months. I now begin to use it a little, but with great pain; so that this letter must be taken up at such intervals as the state of my hand will permit, and will probably be the work of some days. Though the joint seems to be well set, the swelling does not abate, nor the use of it return. I am now, therefore, on the point of setting out, to the south of France, to try the use of some mineral waters there, by immersion. This journey will be of two or three months.

I enclose you herein a copy of the letter from the minister of finance to me, making several advantageous regulations for our commerce. The obtaining this has occupied us a twelvemonth. I say us, because I find the Marquis de la Fayette so useful an auxiliary, that acknowledgements for his co-operation are always due. There remains still something to do for the articles of rice, turpentine, and ship duties. What can be done for tobacco when the late regulation expires, is very uncertain. The commerce between the United States and this country being put on a good footing, we may afterwards proceed to try if any thing can be done to favor our intercourse with her colonies. Admission into them for our fish and flour, is very desirable: but, unfortunately, both those articles would raise a competition against their own.

I find by the public papers, that your commercial convention failed in point of representation. If it should produce a full meeting in May, and a broader reformation, it will still be well. To make us one nation as to foreign concerns, and keep us distinct in domestic ones, gives the outline of the proper division of powers between the general and particular governments. But to enable the federal head to exercise the powers given it, to best advantage, it should be organized, as the particular ones are, into legislative, executive, and judiciary. The first and last are already separated. The second should be. When last with Congress, I often proposed to members to do this, by making of the committee of the States an executive committee during the recess of Congress, and during its sessions to appoint a committee to receive and despatch all executive business, so that Congress itself should meddle only with what should be legislative. But I question if any Congress (much less all successively) can have self-denial enough to go, through with this distribution. The distribution, then, should be imposed on them. I find Congress have reversed their division of the western States, and proposed to make them fewer and larger. This is reversing the natural order of things. A tractable people may be governed in large bodies: but in proportion as they depart from this character, the extent of their government must be less. We see into what small divisions the Indians are obliged to reduce their societies. This measure, with the disposition to shut up the Mississippi, gives me serious apprehensions of the severance of the eastern and western parts of our confederacy. It might have been made the interest of the western States to remain united with us, by managing their interests honestly, and for their own good. But the moment we sacrifice their interests to our own, they will see it better to govern themselves. The moment they resolve to do this, the point is settled. A forced connection is neither our interest, nor within our power. The Virginia act for religious freedom has been received with infinite approbation in Europe, and propagated with enthusiasm. I do not mean by the governments, but by the individuals who compose them. It has been translated into French and Italian, has been sent to most of the courts of Europe, and has been the best evidence of the falsehood of those reports, which stated us to be in anarchy. It is inserted in the new *Encyclopédie*, and is appearing in most of the publications respecting America. In fact, it is comfortable to see the standard of reason at length erected, after so many ages, during which the human mind has been held in vassalage by kings, priests, and nobles: and it is honorable for us to have produced the first legislature who had the courage to declare, that the reason of man may be trusted with the formation of his own opinions.

I thank you for your communications in Natural History. The several instances of trees, &c. found far below the surface of the earth, as in the case of Mr. Hay's well, seem to set the reason of man at defiance.

I am, Dear Sir, with sincere esteem, your friend and servant,

Th: Jefferson.

LETTER XXXIII.—TO CHARLES THOMSON, December 17,1780

TO CHARLES THOMSON.

Paris, December 17,1780.

Dear Sir,

A dislocation of my right wrist has for three months past disabled me from writing, except with my left hand, which was too slow and awkward to be employed often. I begin to have so much use of my wrist as to be able to write, but it is slowly, and in pain. I take the first moment I can, however, to acknowledge the receipt of your letters of April the 6th, July the 8th and 30th. In one of these, you say you have not been able to learn, whether, in the new mills in London, steam is the immediate mover of the machinery, or raises water to move it. It is the immediate mover. The power of this agent, though long known, is but now beginning to be applied to the various purposes of which it is susceptible. You observe, that Whitehurst supposes it to have been the agent, which bursting the earth, threw it up into mountains and vallies. You ask me what I think of this book. I find in it many interesting facts brought together, and many ingenious commentaries on them. But there are great chasms in his facts, and consequently in his reasoning, These he fills up by suppositions, which may be as reasonably denied as granted. A sceptical reader, therefore, like myself, is left in the lurch. I acknowledge, however, he makes more use of fact, than any other writer on a theory of the earth. But I give one answer to all these theorists. That is as follows. They all suppose the earth a created existence. They must suppose a creator then; and that he possessed power and wisdom to a great degree. As he intended the earth for the habitation of animals and vegetables, is it reasonable to suppose, he made two jobs of his creation, that he first made a chaotic lump, and set it into rotatory motion, and then waited the millions of ages necessary to form itself? That when it had done this, he stepped in a second time, to create the animals and plants which were to inhabit it? As the hand of a creator is to be called in, it may as well be called in at one stage of the process as another. We may as well suppose he created the earth at once, nearly in the state in which we see it, fit for the preservation of the beings he placed on it. But it is said, we have a proof that he did not create it in its present solid form, but in a state of fluidity: because its present shape of an oblate spheroid is precisely that, which a fluid mass revolving on its axis would assume.

I suppose, that the same equilibrium between gravity and centrifugal force, which would determine a fluid mass into the form of an oblate spheroid, would determine the wise creator of that mass, if he made it in a solid state, to give it the same spheroidical form. A revolving fluid will continue to change its shape, till it attains that in which its principles of contrary motion are balanced. For if you suppose them not balanced, it will change its form. Now the same balanced form is necessary for the preservation of a revolving solid. The creator, therefore, of a revolving solid, would make it an oblate spheroid, that figure alone admitting a perfect equilibrium. He would make it in that form, for another reason; that is, to prevent a shifting of the axis of rotation. Had he created the earth perfectly spherical, its axis might have been perpetually shifting, by the influence of the other bodies of the system; and by placing the inhabitants of the earth successively under its poles, it might have been depopulated; whereas, being spheroidical, it has but one axis on which it can revolve in equilibrio. Suppose the axis of the earth to shift forty-five degrees; then cut it into one hundred and eighty slices, making every section in the plane of a circle of latitude, perpendicular to the axis: every one of these slices, except the equatorial one, would be unbalanced, as there would be more matter on one side of its axis than on the other. There could be but one diameter drawn through such a slice, which would divide it into two equal parts. On every other possible diameter, the parts would hang unequal. This would produce an irregularity in the diurnal rotation. We may, therefore, conclude it impossible for the poles of the earth to shift, if it was made spheroidical; and that it would be made spheroidical, though solid, to obtain this end. I use this reasoning only on the supposition, that the earth has had a beginning. I am sure I shall read your conjectures on this subject with great pleasure, though I bespeak beforehand, a right to indulge my natural incredulity and scepticism. The pain in which I write, awakens me here from my reverie, and obliges me to conclude with compliments to Mrs. Thomson, and assurances to yourself of the esteem and affection with which I am sincerely, Dear Sir, your friend and servant,

Th: Jefferson.

P. S. Since writing the preceding, I have had a conversation on the subject of the steam-mills, with the famous Boulton, to whom those of London belong, and who is here at this time. He compares the effect of steam with that of horses, in the following manner. Six horses, aided with the most advantageous combination of the mechanical powers hitherto tried, will grind six bushels of flour in an hour; at the end of which time they are all in a foam, and must rest. They can work thus six hours in the twenty-four, grinding thirty-six bushels of flour, which is six to each horse, for the twenty-four hours. His steam-mill in London consumes one hundred and twenty bushels of coal in twenty-four hours, turns ten pair of stones, which grind eight bushels of flour an hour each, which is nineteen hundred and twenty bushels in the twenty-four hours. This makes a peck and a half of coal perform exactly as much as a horse in one day can perform.

LETTER XXXIV.—TO COLONEL MONROE, December 18, 1786

TO COLONEL MONROE.

Paris, December 18, 1786.

Dear Sir,

Your letters of August the 19th and October the 12th have come duly to hand. My last to you was of the 11th of August. Soon after that date I got my right wrist dislocated, which has till now deprived me of the use of that hand; and even now I can use it but slowly, and with pain. The revisal of the Congressional intelligence contained in your letters, makes me regret the loss of it on your departure. I feel, too, the want of a person there to whose discretion I can trust confidential communications, and on whose friendship I can rely against the unjust designs of malevolence. I have no reason to suppose I have enemies in Congress; yet it is too possible, to be without that fear. Some symptoms make me suspect, that my proceedings to redress the abusive administration of tobacco by the Farmers General have indisposed towards me a powerful person in Philadelphia, who was profiting from that abuse. An expression in the enclosed letter of M. de Calonne, would seem to imply, that I had asked the abolition of Mr. Morris's contract. I never did. On the contrary, I always observed to them, that it would be unjust to annul that contract. I was led to this, by principles both of justice and interest. Of interest, because that contract would keep up the price of tobacco here to thirty-four, thirty-six, and thirty-eight livres, from which it will fall when it shall no longer have that support. However, I have done what was right, and I will not so far wound my privilege of doing that, without regard to any man's interest, as to enter into any explanations of this paragraph with him. Yet I esteem him highly, and suppose that hitherto he had esteemed me. You will see by Calonne's letter, that we are doing what we can to get the trade of the United States put on a good footing. I am now about setting out on a journey to the south of France, one object of which is to try the mineral waters there for the restoration of my hand; but another is, to visit all the seaports where we have trade, and to hunt up all the inconveniences under which it labors, in order to get them rectified. I shall visit, and carefully examine too, the canal of Languedoc. On my return, which will be early in the spring, I shall send you several *livraisons* of the *Encyclopédie*, and the plan of your house. I wish to Heaven, you may continue in the disposition to fix it in Albemarle. Short will establish himself there, and perhaps Madison may be tempted to do so. This will be society enough, and it will be the great sweetener of our lives. Without society, and a society to our taste, men are never contented. The one here supposed, we can regulate to our minds, and we may extend our regulations to the sumptuary department, so as to set a good example to a country which needs it, and to preserve our own happiness clear of embarrassment. You wish not to engage in the drudgery of the bar. You have two asylums from that. Either to accept a seat in the Council, or in the judiciary department. The latter, however, would require a little previous drudgery at the bar, to qualify you to discharge your duty with satisfaction to yourself. Neither of these would be inconsistent with a continued residence in Albemarle. It is but twelve hours drive in a sulky from Charlottesville to Richmond, keeping a fresh horse always at the half-way, which would be a small annual expense. I am in hopes, that Mrs. M. will have in her domestic cares occupation and pleasure sufficient to fill her time, and insure her against the *tedium vitæ*: that she will find, that the distractions of a town, and the waste of life under these, can bear no comparison with the tranquil happiness of domestic life. If her own experience has not yet taught her this truth, she has in its favor the testimony of one, who has gone through the various scenes of business, of bustle, of office, of rambling, and of quiet retirement, and who can assure her, that the latter is the only point upon which the mind can settle at rest. Though not clear of inquietudes, because no earthly situation is so, they are fewer in number, and mixed with more objects of contentment, than in any other mode of life. But I must not philosophize too much with her, lest I give her too serious apprehensions of a friendship I shall impose on her. I am with very great esteem, Dear Sir, your sincere friend and servant,

Th: Jefferson.

LETTER XXXV.—TO MR. CARMICHAEL, December 26,1786

TO MR. CARMICHAEL.

Paris, December 26,1786.

Dear Sir,

A note from me of the 22nd of September apprized you it would be some time before I should be able to answer your letters. I did not then expect it would have been so long.

I enclose herein a resolution of Congress recalling Mr. Lambe, which I will beg the favor of you to have delivered him. I have written to Mr. Adams on the subject of directing him to settle with Mr. Barclay, and attend his answer. In the mean time, I am not without hopes Mr. Barclay has done the business. I send also a note desiring Mr. Lambe to deliver you his cipher: and a copy of a letter from the minister of finance here to me, announcing several regulations in favor of our commerce.

My Notes on Virginia, having been hastily written, need abundance of corrections. Two or three of these are so material, that I am reprinting a few leaves to substitute for the old. As soon as these shall be ready, I will beg your acceptance of a copy. I shall be proud to be permitted to send a copy also to the Count de Campomanes, as a tribute to his science and his virtues. You will find in them, that the Natural Bridge has found an admirer in me also. I should be happy to make with you the tour of the curiosities you will find therein mentioned. That kind of pleasure surpasses much, in my estimation, whatever I find on this side the Atlantic. I sometimes think of building a little hermitage at the Natural Bridge (for it is my property), and of passing there a part of the year at least.

I have received American papers to the 1st of November. Some tumultuous meetings of the people have taken place in the eastern States; i.e. one in Massachusetts, one in Connecticut, and one in New Hampshire. Their principal demand was a respite in the judiciary proceedings. No injury was done, however, in a single instance, to the person or property of any one, nor did the tumult continue twenty-four hours in any one instance. In Massachusetts this was owing to the discretion which the malcontents still preserved; in Connecticut and New Hampshire the body of the people rose in support of government, and obliged the malcontents to go to their homes. In the last mentioned State they seized about forty, who were in jail for trial. It is believed this incident will strengthen our government. Those people are not entirely without excuse. Before the war these States depended on their whale-oil and fish. The former was consumed in England, and much of the latter in the Mediterranean. The heavy duties on American whale-oil, now required in England, exclude it from that market: and the Algerines exclude them from bringing their fish into the Mediterranean. France is opening her ports for their oil, but in the mean while their ancient debts are pressing them, and they have nothing to pay with. The Massachusetts Assembly, too, in their zeal for paying their public debt, had laid a tax too heavy to be paid, in the circumstances of their State. The Indians seem disposed, too, to make war on us. These complicated causes determined Congress to increase their forces to two thousand men. The latter was the sole object avowed, yet the former entered for something into the measure. However, I am satisfied the good sense of the people is the strongest army our governments can ever have, and that it will not fail them. The commercial convention at Annapolis was not full enough to do business. They found, too, their appointments too narrow, being confined to the article of commerce. They have proposed a meeting at Philadelphia in May, and that it may be authorized to propose amendments of whatever is defective in the federal constitution.

When I was in England, I formed a portable copying press, on the principles of the large one they make there, for copying letters. I had a model made there, and it has answered perfectly. A workman here has made several from that model. The itinerant temper of your court will, I think, render one of these useful to you. You must, therefore, do me the favor to accept of one. I have it now in readiness, and shall send it by the way of Bayonne, to the care of Mr. Alexander there, unless Don Miguel de Lardi-zabal can carry it with him.

My hand admonishes me it is time to stop, and that I must defer writing to Mr. Barclay till to-morrow.

I have the honor to be, with sentiments of the highest esteem and respect,

Dear Sir, your most obedient

and most humble servant,

Th: Jefferson.

LETTER XXXVI.—TO MR. VAUGHAN, December 29, 1786

TO MR. VAUGHAN.

Paris, December 29, 1786.

Sir,

When I had the honor of seeing you in London, you were so kind as to permit me to trouble you, sometimes with my letters, and particularly on the subject of mathematical or philosophical instruments. Such a correspondence will be too agreeable to me, and at the same time too useful, not to avail myself of your permission. It has been an opinion pretty generally received among philosophers, that the atmosphere of America is more humid than that of Europe. Monsieur de Buffon makes this hypothesis one of the two pillars whereon he builds his system of the degeneracy of animals in America. Having had occasion to controvert this opinion of his, as to the degeneracy of animals there, I expressed a doubt of the fact assumed, that our climates are more moist. I did not know of any experiments, which might authorize a denial of it. Speaking afterwards on the subject with Dr. Franklin, he mentioned to me the observations he had made on a case of magnets, made for him by Mr. Nairne in London. Of these you will see a detail in the second volume of the American Philosophical Transactions, in a letter from Dr. Franklin to Mr. Nairne, wherein he recommends to him to take up the principle therein explained, and endeavor to make an hygrometer, which, taking slowly the temperature of the atmosphere, shall give its mean degree of moisture, and enable us thus to make with more certainty a comparison between the humidities of different climates. May I presume to trouble you with an inquiry of Mr. Nairne, whether he has executed the Doctor's idea; and if he has, to get him to make for me a couple of the instruments he may have contrived. They should be made of the same piece, and under like circumstances, that sending one to America, I may rely on its indications there, compared with those of the one I shall retain here. Being in want of a set of magnets also, I would be glad if he would at the same time send me a set, the case of which should be made as Dr. Franklin describes his to have been, so that I may repeat his experiment. Colonel Smith will do me the favor to receive these things from Mr. Nairne, and to pay him for them.

I think Mr. Rittenhouse never published an invention of his in this way, which was a very good one. It was of an hygrometer, which, like the common ones, was to give the actual moisture of the air. He has two slips of mahogany about five inches long, three fourths of an inch broad, and one tenth of an inch thick, the one having the grain running lengthwise, and the other crosswise. These are glued together by their faces, so as to form a piece five inches long, three fourths of an inch broad, and one third of an inch thick, which is stuck by its lower end into a little plinth of wood, presenting their edge to the view. The fibres of the wood you know are dilated, but not lengthened by moisture. The slip, therefore, whose grain is lengthwise, becomes a standard, retaining always the same precise length. That which has its grain crosswise, dilates with moisture, and contracts for the want of it. If the right hand piece be the cross-grained one, when the air is very moist, it lengthens, and forces its companion to form a kind of interior annulus of a circle on the left. When the air is dry, it contracts, draws its companion to the right, and becomes itself the interior annulus. In order to show this dilation and contraction, an index is fixed on the upper end of the two slips; a plate of metal or wood is fastened to the front of the plinth, so as to cover the two slips from the eye. A slit, being nearly the portion of a circle, is cut in this plate, so that the shank of the index may play freely through its whole range. On the edge of the slit is a graduation. The objection to this instrument is, that it is not fit for comparative observations, because no two pieces of wood being of the same texture exactly, no two will yield exactly alike to the same agent. However, it is less objectionable on this account, than most of the substances used. Mr. Rittenhouse had a thought of trying ivory: but I do not know whether he executed it. All these substances not only vary from one another at the same time, but from themselves at different times. All of them, however, have some peculiar advantages, and I think this, on the whole, appeared preferable to any other I had ever seen. Not knowing whether you had heard of this instrument, and supposing it would amuse you, I have taken the liberty of detailing it to you.

I beg you to be assured of the sentiments of perfect esteem and respect with which I have the honor to be, Sir, your most obedient

and most humble servant,

Th: Jefferson.

LETTER XXXVII.—TO JOHN JAY, December 31, 1786

TO JOHN JAY.

Paris, December 31, 1786

Sir,

I had the honor of addressing you on the 12th of the last month; since which your favor of October the 12th has been received, enclosing a copy of the resolution of Congress for recalling Mr. Lambe. My letter by Mr. Randall informed you, that we had put an end to his powers, and required him to repair to Congress. I lately received a letter from him, dated Alicant, October the 10th, of which I have the honor to enclose you a copy: by which you will perceive, that the circumstance of ill health, either true or false, is urged for his not obeying our call. I shall immediately forward the order of Congress. I am not without fear, that some misapplication of the public money may enter into the causes of his declining to return. The moment that I saw a symptom of this in his conduct, as it was a circumstance which did not admit the delay of consulting Mr. Adams, I wrote to Mr. Carmichael, to stop any monies which he might have in the hands of his banker. I am still unable to judge whether he is guilty of this or not, as by the arrangements with Mr. Adams, who alone had done business with the bankers of the United States, in Holland, Mr. Lambe's drafts were to be made on him, and I know not what their amount has been. His drafts could not have been negotiated, if made on us both, at places so distant. Perhaps it may be thought, that the appointment of Mr. Lambe was censurable in the moment in which it was made. It is a piece of justice, therefore, which I owe to Mr. Adams, to declare that the proposition went first from me to him. I take the liberty of enclosing you a copy of my letter to Mr. Adams, of September the 24th, 1785, in which that proposition was made. It expresses the motives operating on my mind in that moment, as well as the cautions I thought it necessary to take. To these must be added the difficulty of finding an American in Europe fit for the business, and willing to undertake it. I knew afterwards, that Dr. Bancroft (who is named in the letter) could not, on account of his own affairs, have accepted even a primary appointment. I think it evident, that no appointment could have succeeded without a much greater sum of money.

I am happy to find that Mr. Barclay's mission has been attended with complete success. For this we are indebted, unquestionably, to the influence and good offices of the court of Madrid. Colonel Franks, the bearer of this, will have the honor to put into your hands the original of the treaty, with other papers accompanying it. It will appear by these, that Mr. Barclay has conducted himself with a degree of intelligence and of good faith which reflects the highest honor on him.

A copy of a letter from Captain O'Bryan to Mr. Carmichael is also herewith enclosed. The information it contains will throw farther light on the affairs of Algiers. His observations on the difficulties which arise from the distance of Mr. Adams and myself from that place, and from one another, and the delays occasioned by this circumstance, are certainly just. If Congress should propose to revive the negotiations, they will judge whether it will not be more expedient to send a person to Algiers, who can be trusted with full powers: and also whether a mission to Constantinople may not be previously necessary. Before I quit this subject, I must correct an error in the letter of Captain O'Bryan. Mr. Lambe was not limited, as he says, to one hundred, but to two hundred dollars apiece for our prisoners. This was the price which had been just paid for a large number of French prisoners, and this was our guide.

I have the honor to be, with the most perfect esteem and respect, Sir, your most obedient and most humble servant,

Th: Jefferson.

LETTER XXXVIII.—TO SAMUEL OSGOOD, January 5, 1787

TO SAMUEL OSGOOD.

Paris, January 5, 1787.

Dear Sir,

I am desired to forward to you the enclosed queries, and to ask the favor of you to give such an answer to them, as may not give you too much trouble. Those which stand foremost on the paper, can be addressed only to your complaisance; but the last may possibly be interesting to your department, and to the United States. I mean those which suggest the possibility of borrowing money in Europe, the principal of which shall be ultimately payable in land, and in the mean time, a good interest. You know best whether the suggestion can be turned to any profit, and whether it will be worth while to introduce any proposition to Congress thereon. Among the possible shapes into which a matter of this kind may be formed, the following is one. Let us suppose the public lands to be worth a dollar, hard money, the acre. If we should ask of a monied man a loan of one hundred dollars, payable with one hundred acres of land at the end of ten years, and in the mean time, carrying an interest of five per cent., this would be more disadvantageous to the lender than a common loan, payable ultimately in cash. But if we should say, we will deliver you the one hundred acres of land immediately, which is in fact an immediate payment of the principal, and will nevertheless pay your interest of five per cent., for ten years, this offers a superior advantage, and might tempt money-holders. But what should we in fact receive, in this way, for our lands? Thirty-seven dollars and one fourth, being left in Europe, on an interest of five per cent., would pay annually the interest of the one hundred dollars for ten years. There would remain then only sixty-two dollars and three quarters, for the one hundred acres of land; that is to say, about two thirds of its price. Congress can best determine, whether any circumstances in our situation, should induce us to get rid of any of our debts in that way. I beg you to understand, that I have named rates of interest, term of payment and price of land, merely to state the case, and without the least knowledge that a loan could be obtained on these terms. It remains to inform you, from whom this suggestion comes. The person from whom I receive it, is a Monsieur Claviere, connected with the monied men of Amsterdam. He is, on behalf of a company there, actually treating with the Comptroller General here, for the purchase of our debt to this country, at a considerable discount. Whether he has an idea of offering a loan to us, on terms such as I have above spoken of, I know not; nor do I know that he is authorized to make the suggestion he has made. If the thing should be deemed worthy the attention of Congress, they can only consider it as a possibility, and take measures to avail themselves of it, if the possibility turns out in their favor, and not to be disappointed if it does not. Claviere's proposition not being formal enough for me to make an official communication of it, you will make what use of it you see best.

I am, with very sincere esteem and attachment, Dear Sir, your most obedient and most humble servant,

Th: Jefferson.

LETTER XXXIX.—TO JOHN JAY, January 9, 1787

TO JOHN JAY.

Paris, January 9, 1787.

Sir,

My last, of December the 31st, acknowledged the receipt of yours of October the 12th, as the present does those of October the 3rd, 9th, and 27th, together with the resolution of Congress of October the 16th, on the claim of Schweighaeuser. I will proceed in this business on the return of Mr. Barclay, who being fully acquainted with all the circumstances, will be enabled to give me that information, the want of which might lead me to do wrong on the one side or the other.

Information of the signature of the treaty with Morocco has been long on its passage to you. I will beg leave to recur to dates, that you may see that no part of it has been derived from me. The first notice I had of it, was in a letter from Mr. Barclay, dated, Daralbeyda, August the 11th. I received this on the 13th of September. No secure conveyance offered till the 26th of the same month, being thirteen days after my receipt of it. In my letter of that date, which went by the way of London, I had the honor to enclose you a copy of Mr. Barclay's letter. The conveyance of the treaty itself is suffering a delay here at present, which all my anxiety cannot prevent. Colonel Franks' baggage, which came by water from Cadiz to Rouen, has been long and hourly expected. The moment it arrives, he will set out to London, to have duplicates of the treaty signed by Mr. Adams, and from thence he will proceed to New York.

The Chevalier del Pinto, who treated with us on behalf of Portugal, being resident at London, I have presumed that causes of the delay of that treaty had been made known to Mr. Adams, and by him communicated to you. I will write to him by Colonel Franks, in order that you may be answered on that subject.

The publication of the enclosed extract from my letter of May the 27th, 1786, will, I fear, have very mischievous effects. It will tend to draw on the Count de Vergennes the formidable phalanx of the Farms; to prevent his committing himself to me in any conversation which he does not mean for the public papers; to inspire the same diffidence into all other ministers, with whom I might have to transact business; to defeat the little hope, if any hope existed, of getting rid of the Farm on the article of tobacco; and to damp that freedom of, communication which the resolution of Congress of May the 3rd, 1784, was intended to re-establish. Observing by the proceedings of Congress, that they are about to establish a coinage, I think it my duty to inform them, that a Swiss, of the name of Drost, established here, has invented a method of striking the two faces and the edge of a coin, at one stroke. By this, and other simplifications of the process of coinage, he is enabled to coin from twenty-five thousand to thirty thousand pieces a day, with the assistance of only two persons, the pieces of metal being first prepared. I send you by Colonel Franks three coins of gold, silver, and copper, which you will perceive to be perfect medals: and I can assure you, from having seen him coin many, that every piece is as perfect as these. There has certainly never yet been seen any coin, in any country, comparable to this. The best workmen in this way acknowledge that his is like a new art. Coin should always be made in the highest perfection possible, because it is a great guard against the danger of false coinage. This man would be willing to furnish his implements to Congress, and if they please, he will go over and instruct a person to carry on the work: nor do I believe he would ask any thing unreasonable. It would be very desirable, that in the institution of a new coinage, we could set out on so perfect a plan as this, and the more so, as while the work is so exquisitely done, it is done cheaper.

I will certainly do the best I can for the reformation of the consular convention, being persuaded that our States would be very unwilling to conform their laws either to the convention, or to the scheme. But it is too difficult and too delicate, to form sanguine hopes. However, that there may be room to reduce the convention, as much as circumstances will admit, will it not be expedient for Congress to give me powers, in which there shall be no reference to the scheme? The powers sent me, oblige me to produce that scheme, and certainly, the moment it is produced, they will not abate a tittle from it. If they recollect the scheme, and insist on it, we can but conclude it; but if they have forgotten it (which may be), and are willing to reconsider the whole subject, perhaps we may get rid of something the more of it. As the delay is not injurious to us, because the convention, whenever and however made, is to put us in a worse state than we are in now, I shall venture to defer saying a word on the subject, till I can hear from you in answer to this. The full powers may be sufficiently guarded, by private instructions to me, not to go beyond the former scheme. This delay may be well enough ascribed (whenever I shall have received new powers) to a journey, I had before apprized the minister that I should be obliged to take, to some mineral waters in the south of France, to see if by their aid I may recover the use of my right hand, of which a dislocation about four months ago, threatens to deprive me in a great measure. The surgeons have long insisted on this measure. I shall return by Bordeaux, Nantes, and L'Orient, to get the necessary information for finishing our commercial regulations here. Permit me, however, to ask, as immediately as possible, an answer, either affirmative or negative, as Congress shall think best, and to ascribe the delay on which I venture, to my desire to do what is for the best.

I send you a copy of the late marine regulations of this country. There are things in it, which may become interesting to us. Particularly, what relates to the establishment of a marine militia, and their classification.

You will have seen in the public papers, that the King has called an Assembly of the Notables of this country. This has not been done for one hundred and sixty years past. Of course, it calls up all the attention of the people. The objects of this Assembly are not named: several are conjectured. The tolerating the Protestant religion; removing all the internal Custom-houses to the frontier; equalizing the *gabelles* on salt through the kingdom; the sale of the King's domains, to raise money; or, finally, the effecting this necessary end by some other means, are talked of. But, in truth, nothing is known about it. This government practises secrecy so systematically, that it never publishes its purposes or its proceedings, sooner or more extensively than necessary. I send you a pamphlet, which, giving an account of the last *Assemblée des Notable*, may give an idea of what the present will be.

A great desire prevails here of encouraging manufactures. The famous Boulton and Watt, who are at the head of the plated manufactures of Birmingham, the steam mills of London, copying presses and other mechanical works, have been here. It is said, also, that Wedgewood has been here, who is famous for his steel manufactories, and an earthen ware in the antique style; but as to this last person, I am not certain. It cannot, I believe be doubted, but that they came at the request of government, and that they will be induced to establish similar manufactures here.

The transferring hither those manufactures, which contribute so much to draw our commerce to England, will have a great tendency to strengthen our connections with this country, and loosen them with that.

The enfranchising the port of Honfleur at the mouth of the Seine, for multiplying the connections with us, is at present an object. It meets with opposition in the ministry; but I am in hopes it will prevail. If natural causes operate, uninfluenced by accidental circumstances, Bordeaux and Honfleur, or Havre, must ultimately take the greatest part of our commerce. The former, by the Garonne and canal of Languedoc, opens the southern provinces to us; the latter, the northern ones and Paris. Honfleur will be peculiarly advantageous for our rice and whale oil, of which the principal consumption is at Paris. Being free, they can be re-exported when the market here shall happen to be overstocked.

The labors of the ensuing summer will close the eastern half of the harbor of Cherbourg, which will contain and protect forty sail of the line. It has from fifty to thirty-five feet of water next to the cones, shallowing gradually to the shore. Between this and Dunkirk, the navigation of the channel will be rendered much safer in the event of a war with England, and invasions on that country become more practicable.

The gazettes of France and Leyden, to the present date, accompany this.

I have the honor to be, with sentiments of the most perfect respect, Sir, your most obedient and most humble servant,

Th: Jefferson.

LETTER XL.—TO JOHN ADAMS, January 11, 1787

TO JOHN ADAMS.

Paris, January 11, 1787.

Dear Sir,

Mr. Jay, in his last letter to me, observes they hear nothing further of the treaty with Portugal. I have taken the liberty of telling him that I will write to you on the subject, and that he may expect to hear from you on it, by the present conveyance. The Chevalier del Pinto being at London, I presume he has, or can inform you why it is delayed on their part. I will thank you also for the information he shall give you.

There is here an order of priests called the Mathurins, the object of whose institution is, the begging of alms for the redemption of captives. About eighteen months ago, they redeemed three hundred, which cost them about fifteen hundred livres a piece. They have agents residing in the Barbary States, who are constantly employed in searching and contracting for the captives of their nation, and they redeem at a lower price than any other people can. It occurred to me, that their agency might be engaged for our prisoners at Algiers. I have had interviews with them, and the last night a long one with the General of the order. They offer their services with all the benignity and cordiality possible. The General told me, he could not expect to redeem our prisoners as cheap as their own, but that he would use all the means in his power to do it on the best terms possible, which will be the better, as there shall be the less suspicion that he acts for our public. I told him I would write to you on the subject, and speak to him again. What do you think of employing them, limiting them to a certain price, as three hundred dollars, for instance, or any other sum you think proper? He will write immediately to his instruments there, and in two or three months we can know the event. He will deliver them at Marseilles, Cadiz, or where we please, at our expense. The money remaining of the fund destined to the Barbary business, may, I suppose, be drawn on for this object. Write me your opinion, if you please, on this subject, finally, fully, and immediately, that, if you approve the proposition, I may enter into arrangements with the General before my departure to the waters of Aix, which will be about the beginning of February,

I have the honor to be, with very sincere esteem and respect, Dear Sir, your most obedient and most humble servant,

Th: Jefferson.

LETTER XLI.—TO MONSIEUR LE DUC D'HARCOURT, January 14, 1787

TO MONSIEUR LE DUC D'HARCOURT, GOUVERNEUR DU DAUPHIN.

Paris, January 14, 1787.

Sir,

In the conversation with which you were pleased to honor me a few days ago, on the enfranchisement of the port of Honfleur, I took the liberty of observing, that I was not instructed by my constituents to make any proposition on that subject. That it would be agreeable to them, however, I must suppose, because it will offer the following advantages.

1. It is a convenient *entrepôt* for furnishing us with the manufactures of the northern parts of France, and particularly of Paris, and for receiving and distributing the productions of our country in exchange.

2. Cowes, on the opposite side of the channel, has heretofore been the deposite for a considerable part of our productions, landed in Great Britain in the first instance, but intended for re-exportation. From thence our rice, particularly, has been distributed to France and other parts of Europe. I am not certain, whether our tobaccos were deposited there, or carried to London to be sorted for the different markets. To draw this business from Cowes, no place is so favorably situated as Honfleur.

3. It would be a convenient deposite for our whale-oil, of which, after the supply of Paris, there will be a surplus for re-exportation.

4. Should our fur-trade be recovered out of the hands of the English, it will naturally come to Honfleur, as the out-port of Paris.

5. Salt is an important article in all our return cargoes; because, being carried as ballast, its freight costs nothing. But on account of some regulations, with which I am not well acquainted, it cannot at present be shipped to advantage from any port on the Seine.

6. Our vessels being built sharp, for swift sailing, suffer extremely in most of the western ports of France, in which they are left on dry ground at every ebb of the tide. But at Honfleur, I am told, they can ride in bold water, on a good bottom, and near the shore, at all times.

These facts may, perhaps, throw some light on the question in which, for the good of both countries, you are pleased to interest yourself. I take the liberty, therefore, of barely mentioning them, and with the more pleasure, as it furnishes me an occasion of assuring you of those sentiments of respect and esteem, with which I have the honor to be your most obedient, humble servant,

Th: Jefferson.

LETTER XLII.—TO MONSIEUR DE CREVE-COEUR, January 15,1787

TO MONSIEUR DE CREVE-COEUR.

Paris, January 15,1787.

Dear Sir,

I see by the Journal of this morning, that they are robbing us of another of our inventions, to give it to the English. The writer, indeed, only admits them to have revived what he thinks was known to the Greeks, that is, the making the circumference of a wheel of one single piece. The farmers in New Jersey were the first who practised it, and they practised it commonly. Dr. Franklin, in one of his trips to London, mentioned this practice to the man now in London, who has the patent for making those wheels. The idea struck him. The Doctor promised to go to his shop, and assist him in trying to make the wheel of one piece. The Jersey farmers do it by cutting a young sapling, and bending it, while green and juicy, into a circle; and leaving it so until it becomes perfectly seasoned. But in London there are no saplings. The difficulty was, then, to give to old wood the pliancy of young. The Doctor and the workman labored together some weeks, and succeeded; and the man obtained a patent for it, which has made his fortune. I was in his shop in London; he told me the whole story himself, and acknowledged not only the origin of the idea, but how much the assistance of Dr. Franklin had contributed to perform the operation on dry wood. He spoke of him with love and gratitude. I think I have had a similar account from Dr. Franklin, but cannot be quite certain. I know, that being in Philadelphia when the first set of patent wheels arrived from London, and were spoken of, by the gentleman (an Englishman) who brought them, as a wonderful discovery, the idea of its being a new discovery was laughed at by the Philadelphians, who, in their Sunday parties across the Delaware, had seen every farmer's cart mounted on such wheels. The writer in the paper supposes the English workman got his idea from Homer. But it is more likely the Jersey farmer got his idea from thence, because ours are the only farmers who can read Homer; because, too, the Jersey practice is precisely that stated by Homer: the English practice very different. Homer's words are (comparing a young hero killed by Ajax to a poplar felled by a workman) literally thus: 'He fell on the ground, like a poplar, which has grown smooth, in the west part of a great meadow; with its branches shooting from its summit. But the chariot-maker, with his sharp axe, has felled it, that he may bend a wheel for a beautiful chariot. It lies drying on the banks of the river.' Observe the circumstances, which coincide with the Jersey practice. 1. It is a tree growing in a moist place, full of juices, and easily bent. 2. It is cut while green. 3. It is bent into the circumference of a wheel. 4. It is left to dry in that form. You, who write French well and readily, should write a line for the Journal, to reclaim the honor of our farmers. Adieu. Yours affectionately,

Th: Jefferson.

LETTER XLIII.—TO COLONEL EDWARD CARRINGTON, January 16, 1787

TO COLONEL EDWARD CARRINGTON.

Paris, January 16, 1787.

Dear Sir,

Uncertain whether you might be at New York at the moment of Colonel Franks' arrival, I have enclosed my private letters for Virginia, under cover to our delegation in general, which, otherwise, I would have taken the liberty to enclose particularly to you, as best acquainted with the situation of the persons to whom they are addressed. Should this find you at New York, I will still ask your attention to them.

In my letter to Mr. Jay, I have mentioned the meeting of the Notables, appointed for the 29th instant. It is now put off to the 7th or 8th of next month. This event, which will hardly excite any attention in America, is deemed here the most important one, which has taken place in their civil line during the present century. Some promise their country great things from it, some nothing. Our friend De la Fayette was placed on the list originally. Afterwards his name disappeared; but finally was reinstated. This shows, that his character here is not considered as an indifferent one; and that it excites agitation. His education in our school has drawn on him a very jealous eye, from a court whose principles are the most absolute despotism. But I hope he has nearly passed his crisis. The King, who is a good man, is favorably disposed towards him; and he is supported by powerful family connections, and by the public good will. He is the youngest man of the Notables, except one, whose office placed him on the list.

The Count de Vergennes has, within these ten days, had a very severe attack of what is deemed an unfixed gout. He has been well enough, however, to do business to-day. But anxieties for him are not yet quieted. He is a great and good minister, and an accident to him might endanger the peace of Europe.

The tumults in America I expected would have produced in Europe an unfavorable opinion of our political state. But it has not. On the contrary, the small effect of these tumults seems to have given more confidence in the firmness of our governments. The interposition of the people themselves on the side of government, has had a great effect on the opinion here. I am persuaded myself, that the good sense of the people will always be found to be the best army. They may be led astray for a moment, but will soon correct themselves. The people are the only censors of their governors; and even their errors will tend to keep these to the true principles of their institution.

To punish these errors too severely, would be to suppress the only safeguard of the public liberty. The way to prevent these irregular interpositions of the people, is to give them full information of their affairs through the channel of the public papers, and to contrive that those papers should penetrate the whole mass of the people. The basis of our governments being the opinion of the people, the very first object should be to keep that right; and were it left to me to decide, whether we should have a government without newspapers, or newspapers without a government, I should not hesitate a moment to prefer the latter. But I should mean, that every man should receive those papers, and be capable of reading them. I am convinced that those societies (as the Indians), which live without government, enjoy in their general mass an infinitely greater degree of happiness, than those who live under the European governments. Among the former, public opinion is in the place of law, and restrains morals as powerfully as laws ever did any where. Among the latter, under pretence of governing, they have divided their nations into two classes, wolves and sheep. I do not exaggerate. This is a true picture of Europe. Cherish, therefore, the spirit of our people, and keep alive their attention. Do not be too severe upon their errors, but reclaim them by enlightening them. If once they become inattentive to the public affairs, you, and I, and Congress, and Assemblies, Judges and Governors, shall all become wolves. It seems to be the law of our general nature, in spite of individual exceptions: and experience declares, that man is the only animal which devours his own kind; for I can apply no milder term to the governments of Europe, and to the general prey of the rich on the poor. The want of news has led me into disquisition instead of narration, forgetting you have every day enough of that. I shall be happy to hear from you sometimes, only observing, that whatever passes through the post is read, and that when you write what should be read by myself only, you must be so good as to confide your letter to some passenger, or officer of the packet. I will ask your permission to write to you sometimes, and to assure you of the esteem and respect with which I have the honor to be,

Dear Sir, your most obedient

and most humble servant,

Th: Jefferson.

LETTER XLIV—TO JAMES MADISON, January 30, 1787 *

TO JAMES MADISON.

Paris, January 30, 1787.

[The latter part of this letter is in cipher; but appended to the copy preserved, are explanatory notes, which have enabled us to publish it entire, except a few words, to which they afford no key. These are either marked thus * * *, or the words, which the context seemed to require, inserted in italics.]*

Dear Sir,

My last to you was of the 16th of December; since which I have received yours of November the 25th and December the 4th, which afforded me, as your letters always do, a treat on matters public, individual and economical. I am impatient to learn your sentiments on the late troubles in the Eastern States. So far as I have yet seen, they do not appear to threaten serious consequences. Those States have suffered by the stoppage of the channels of their commerce, which have not yet found other issues. This must render money scarce, and make the people uneasy. This uneasiness has produced acts absolutely unjustifiable: but I hope they will provoke no severities from their governments. A consciousness of those in power, that their administration of the public affairs has been honest, may, perhaps, produce too great a degree of indignation: and those characters wherein fear predominates over hope, may apprehend too much from these instances of irregularity. They may conclude too hastily, that nature has formed man insusceptible of any other government than that of force, a conclusion not founded in truth nor experience. Societies exist under three forms, sufficiently distinguishable. 1. Without government, as among our Indians. 2. Under governments, wherein the will of every one has a just influence; as is the case in England, in a slight degree, and in our States, in a great one. 3. Under governments of force; as is the case in all other monarchies, and in most of the other republics. To have an idea of the curse of existence under these last, they must be seen. It is a government of wolves over sheep. It is a problem, not clear in my mind, that the first condition is not the best. But I believe it to be inconsistent with any great degree of population. The second state has a great deal of good in it. The mass of mankind under that enjoys a precious degree of liberty and happiness. It has its evils too: the principal of which is the turbulence to which it is subject. But weigh this against the oppressions of monarchy, and it becomes nothing. *Malo periculosam libertatem quam quietam servitutem.* Even this evil is productive of good. It prevents the degeneracy of government, and nourishes a general attention to the public affairs. I hold it, that a little rebellion now and then is a good thing, and as necessary in the political world, as storms in the physical. Unsuccessful rebellions, indeed, generally establish the encroachments on the rights of the people, which have produced them. An observation of this truth should render honest republican governors so mild in their punishment of rebellions, as not to discourage them too much. It is a medicine necessary for the sound health of government.

If these transactions give me no uneasiness, I feel very differently at another piece of intelligence, to wit, the possibility that the navigation of the Mississippi may be abandoned to Spain. I never had any interest westward of the Allegany; and I never will have any. But I have had great opportunities of knowing the character of the people who inhabit that country; and I will venture to say, that the act which abandons the navigation of the Mississippi, is an act of separation between the eastern and western country. It is a relinquishment of five parts out of eight of the territory of the United States; an abandonment of the fairest subject for the payment of our public debts, and the chaining those debts on our own necks, *in perpetuum.* I have the utmost confidence in the honest intentions of those who concur in this measure; but I lament their want of acquaintance with the character and physical advantages of the people, who, right or wrong, will suppose their interests sacrificed on this occasion to the contrary interests of that part of the confederacy in possession of present power. If they declare themselves a separate people, we are incapable of a single effort to retain them. Our citizens can never be induced, either as militia or as soldiers, to go there to cut the throats of their own brothers and sons, or rather, to be themselves the subjects, instead of the perpetrators, of the parricide. Nor would that country quit the cost of being retained against the will of its inhabitants, could it be done. But it cannot be done. They are able already to rescue the navigation of the Mississippi out of the hands of Spain, and to add New Orleans to their own, territory. They will be joined by the inhabitants of Louisiana. This will bring on a war between them and Spain; and that will produce the question with us, whether it will not be worth our while to become parties with them in the war, in order to re-unite them with us, and thus correct our error. And were I to permit my forebodings to go one step further, I should predict, that the inhabitants of the United States would force their rulers to take the affirmative of that question. I wish I may be mistaken in all these opinions.

We have for some time expected, that the Chevalier de la Luzerne would obtain a promotion in the diplomatic line, by being appointed to some of the courts where this country keeps an ambassador. But none of the vacancies taking place, which had been counted on, I think the present disposition is to require his return to his station in America. He told me himself, lately, that he should return in the spring. I have never pressed this matter on the court, though I knew it to be desirable and desired on our part; because if the compulsion on him to return had been the work of Congress, he would have returned in such ill temper with them, as to disappoint them in the good they expected from it. He would for ever have laid at their door his failure of promotion. I did not press it for another reason, which is, that I have great reason to believe, that the character of the Count de Moutier, who would go, were the Chevalier to be otherwise provided for, would give the most perfect satisfaction in America.

As you have now returned into Congress, it will become of importance, that you should form a just estimate of certain public characters; on which, therefore, I will give you such notes as my knowledge of them has furnished me with. You will compare them with the materials you are otherwise possessed of, and decide on a view of the whole.

You know the opinion I formerly entertained of my friend, Mr. Adams. * * * and the Governor were the first who shook that opinion. I afterwards saw proofs, which convicted him of a degree of vanity, and of a blindness to it, of which no germ appeared in Congress. A seven months' intimacy with him here and as many weeks in London, have given me opportunities of studying him closely. He is vain, irritable, and a bad calculator of the force and probable effect of the motives which govern men. This is all the ill which can possibly be said of him. He is as disinterested as the Being who made him: he is profound in his views; and accurate in his judgment, except where knowledge of the world is necessary to form a judgment. He is so amiable, that I pronounce you will love him, if ever you become acquainted with him. He would be, as he was, a great man in Congress.

Mr. Carmichael is, I think, very little known in America. I never saw him, and while I was in Congress I formed rather a disadvantageous idea of him. His letters received then showed him vain, and more attentive to ceremony and etiquette, than we suppose men of sense should be. I have now a constant correspondence with him, and find him a little hypochondriac and discontented. He possesses a very good understanding, though not of the first order. I have had great opportunities of searching into his character, and have availed myself of them. Many persons of different nations, coming from Madrid to Paris, all speak of him as in high esteem, and I think it certain that he has more of the Count de Florida Blanca's friendship, than any diplomatic character at that court. As long as this minister is in office, Carmichael can do more than any other person who could be sent there.

You will see Franks, and doubtless he will be asking some appointment. I wish there may be any one for which he is fit. He is light, indiscreet, active, honest, affectionate. Though Bingham is not in diplomatic office, yet as he wishes to be so, I will mention such circumstances of him, as you might otherwise be deceived in. He will make you believe he was on the most intimate footing with the first characters in Europe, and versed in the secrets of every cabinet. Not a word of this is true. He had a rage for being presented to great men, and had no * * * in the methods by which he could effect it. * * * * *

The Marquis de la Fayette is a most valuable auxiliary to me. His zeal is unbounded, and his weight with those in power, great. His education having been merely military, commerce was an unknown field to him. But his good sense enabling him to comprehend perfectly whatever is explained to him, his agency has been very efficacious. He has a great deal of sound genius, is well remarked by the King, and rising in popularity. He has nothing against him, but the suspicion of republican principles. I think he will one day be of the ministry. His foible is a canine appetite for popularity and fame; but he will get above this. *The Count de Vergennes is ill.* The possibility of his *recovery* renders it dangerous for us to express a doubt of it; but he is in danger. He is a great minister in European affairs, but has very imperfect ideas of our institutions, and no confidence in them. His devotion to the principles of pure despotism, renders him unaffectionate to our governments. But his fear of England makes him value us as a make-weight. He is cool, reserved in political conversations, but free and familiar on other subjects, and a very attentive, agreeable person to do business with. It is impossible to have a, clearer, better organized head; but age has chilled his heart,

Nothing should be spared on our part, to attach this country to us. It is the only one on which we can rely for support, under every event. Its inhabitants love us more, I think, than they do any other nation on earth. This is very much the effect of the good dispositions with which the French officers returned. In a former letter, I mentioned to you the dislocation of my wrist. I can make not the least use of it, except for the single article of writing, though it is going on five months since the accident happened. I have great anxieties, lest I should never recover any considerable use of it. I shall, by the advice of my surgeons, set out in a fortnight for the waters of Aix, in Provence. I chose these out of several they proposed to me, because if they fail to be effectual, my journey will not be useless altogether. It will give me an opportunity of examining the canal of Languedoc, and of acquiring knowledge of that species of navigation, which may be useful hereafter: but, more immediately, it will enable me to make the tour of the ports concerned in commerce with us, to examine, on the spot, the defects of the late regulations, respecting our commerce, to learn the further improvements which may be made in it, and, on my return, to get this business finished. I shall be absent between two and three months, unless anything happens to recall me here sooner, which may always be effected in ten days, in whatever part of my route I may be.

In speaking of characters, I omitted those of Reyneval and Hennin, the two eyes of Count de Vergennes. The former is the most important character, because possessing the most of the confidence of the Count. He is rather cunning than wise, his views of things being neither great nor liberal. He governs himself by principles which he has learned by rote, and is fit only for the details of execution. His heart is susceptible of little passions, but not of good ones. He is brother-in-law to M. Gerard, from whom he received disadvantageous impressions of us, which cannot be effaced. He has much duplicity. Hennin is a philosopher, sincere, friendly, liberal, learned, beloved by every body: the other by nobody. I think it a great misfortune that the United States are in the department of the former. As particulars of this kind may be useful to you, in your present situation, I may hereafter continue the chapter. I know it will be safely lodged in your discretion. Feb. 5. Since writing thus far, Franks has returned from England. I learn that Mr. Adams desires to be recalled, and that Smith should be appointed *Chargé des Affaires* there. It is not for me to decide whether any diplomatic character should be kept at a court, which keeps none with us. You can judge of Smith's abilities by his letters. They are not of the first order, but they are good. For his honesty, he is like our friend Monroe; turn his soul wrong side outwards, and there is not a speck on it. He has one foible, an excessive inflammability of temper, but he feels it when it comes on, and has resolution enough to suppress it, and to remain silent till it passes over.

I send you, by Colonel Franks, your pocket telescope, walking stick, and chemical box. The two former could not be combined together. The latter could not be had in the form you referred to. Having a great desire to have a portable copying machine, and being satisfied from some experiment, that the principle of the large machine might be applied in a small one, I planned one when in England, and had it made. It answers perfectly. I have since set a workman to making them here, and they are in such demand that he has his hands full. Being assured that you will be pleased to have one, when you shall have tried its convenience, I send you one by Colonel Franks. The machine costs ninety-six livres, the appendages twenty-four livres, and I send you paper and ink for twelve livres; in all, one hundred and thirty-two livres. There is a printed paper of directions: but you must expect to make many essays before you succeed perfectly. A soft brush, like a shaving-brush, is more convenient than the sponge. You can get as much ink and paper as you please, from London. The paper costs a guinea a ream. I am, Dear Sir, with sincere esteem and affection, your most obedient, humble servant,

Th: Jefferson.

LETTER XLV.—TO JOHN JAY, February 1, 1787

TO JOHN JAY.

Sir,

Paris, February 1, 1787.

My last letters were of the 31st of December and 9th of January; since which last date, I have been honored with yours of December the 13th and 14th. I shall pay immediate attention to your instructions relative to the South Carolina frigate. I had the honor of informing you of an improvement in the art of coining, made here by one Drost, and of sending you, by Colonel Franks, a specimen of his execution in gold and silver. I expected to have sent also a coin of copper. The enclosed note from Drost will explain the reason why this was not sent. It will let you see also, that he may be employed; as I suppose he is not so certain as he was of being engaged here. Mr. Grand, who knows him, gives me reason to believe he may be engaged reasonably. Congress will decide whether it be worth their attention.

In some of my former letters, I suggested an opportunity of obliging the court, by borrowing as much money in Holland as would pay the debt due here, if such a loan could be obtained; as to which, I was altogether ignorant. To save time, I wrote to Mr. Dumas, to know whether he thought it probable a loan could be obtained, enjoining on him the strictest secrecy, and informing him I was making the inquiry merely of my own motion, and without instruction. I enclose you his answer. He thinks purchasers of the debt could be found, with a sacrifice of a small part of the capital, and a postponement be obtained of some of the first reimbursements. The proposition by him, for an immediate adoption of this measure by me, was probably urged, on his mind by a desire to serve our country, more than a strict attention to my duty, and the magnitude of the object. I hope, on the contrary, that if it should be thought worth a trial, it may be put into the hands of Mr. Adams, who knows the ground, and is known there, and whose former successful negotiations in this line would give better founded hopes of success on this occasion.

I formerly mentioned to you the hopes of preferment, entertained by the Chevalier de la Luzerne. They have been baffled by events; none of the vacancies taking place which had been expected. Had I pressed his being ordered back, I have reason to believe the order would have been given. But he would have gone back in ill humor with Congress, he would have laid for ever at their door the failure of a promotion then viewed as certain; and this might have excited dispositions that would have disappointed us of the good we hoped from his return. The line I have observed with him has been, to make him sensible that nothing was more desired by Congress than his return, but that they would not willingly press it, so as to defeat him of a personal advantage. He sees his prospects fail, and will return in the approaching spring unless something unexpected should turn up in his favor. In this case, the Count de Moutier has the promise of succeeding to him, and if I do not mistake his character, he would give great satisfaction. So that I think you may calculate on seeing one or the other, by midsummer.

It had been suspected that France and England might adopt those concerted regulations of commerce for their West Indies, of which your letter expresses some apprehensions. But the expressions in the 4th, 5th, 7th, 11th, 18th, and other articles of their treaty, which communicate to the English the privileges of the most favored European nation only, has lessened, if not removed those fears. They have clearly reserved a right of favoring, specially, any nation not European; and there is no nation out of Europe, who could so probably have been in their eye at that time, as ours. They are wise. They must see it probable, at least, that any concert with England will be but of short duration; and they could hardly propose to sacrifice for that, a connection with us, which may be perpetual.

We have been for some days, in much inquietude for the Count de Vergennes. He is very seriously ill. Nature seems struggling to decide his disease into a gout. A swelled foot, at present gives us a hope-of this issue. His loss would at all times have been great; but it would be immense during the critical poise of European affairs, existing at this moment. I enclose you a letter from one of the foreign officers, complaining of the non-payment of their interest. It is only one out of many I have received. This is accompanied by a second copy of the Moorish declaration sent me by Mr. Barclay. He went to Alicant to settle with Mr. Lambe; but on his arrival there, found he was gone to Minorca. A copy of his letter will inform you of this circumstance, and of some others relative to Algiers, with his opinion on them. Whatever the States may enable Congress to do for obtaining the peace of that country, it is a separate question whether they will redeem our captives, how, and at what price. If they decide to redeem them, I will beg leave to observe, that it is of great importance that the first redemption be made at as low a price as possible, because it will form the future tariff. If these pirates find that they can have a very great price for Americans, they will abandon proportionably their pursuits against other nations, to direct them towards ours. That the choice of Congress may be enlarged, as to the instruments they may use for effecting the redemption, I think it my duty to inform them, that there is here an order of priests called the Mathurins, the object of whose institution is to beg alms for the redemption of captives. They keep members always in Barbary, searching out the captives of their country, and redeem, I believe, on better terms than any other body, public or private. It occurred to me, that their agency might be obtained for the redemption of our prisoners at Algiers. I obtained conferences with the General, and with some members of the order. The General, with all the benevolence and cordiality possible, undertook to act for us if we should, desire it. He told me that their last considerable redemption was of about three hundred prisoners, who cost them somewhat upwards of fifteen hundred livres apiece. But that they should not be able to redeem ours, as cheap as they do their own; and that it must be absolutely unknown that the public concern themselves in the operation, or the price would be greatly enhanced. The difference of religion was not once mentioned, nor did it appear to me to be thought of. It was a silent reclamation and acknowledgment of fraternity, between two religions of the same family, which historical events of ancient date had rendered more hostile to one another, than to their common adversaries. I informed the General, that I should communicate the good dispositions of his order, to those who alone had the authority to decide whatever related to our captives. Mr. Carmichael informs me, that monies have been advanced for the support of our prisoners at Algiers, which ought to be replaced. I infer from the context of his letter, that these advances have been made by the court of Madrid. I submit the information to Congress.

A treaty of commerce is certainly concluded between France and Russia. The particulars of it are yet secret.

I enclose the gazettes of France and Leyden to this date, and have the honor of assuring you of those sentiments of perfect esteem and respect, with which I am, Sir, your most obedient and most humble servant,

Th: Jefferson.

LETTER XLVI.—TO MRS. BINGHAM, February 7, 1787

TO MRS. BINGHAM.

Paris, February 7, 1787.

I know, Madam, that the twelve-month is not yet expired; but it will be, nearly, before this will have the honor of being put into your hands. You are then engaged to tell me, truly and honestly, whether you do not find the tranquil pleasures of America, preferable to the empty bustle of Paris. For to what does that bustle tend? At eleven o'clock, it is day, *chez madame*, the curtains are drawn. Propped on bolsters and pillows, and her head scratched into a little order, the bulletins of the sick are read, and the billets of the well. She writes to some of her acquaintance, and receives the visits of others. If the morning is not very thronged, she is able to get out and hobble round the cage of the Palais Royal; but she must hobble quickly, for the coiffeurs turn is come; and a tremendous turn it is! Happy, if he does not make her arrive when dinner is half over! The torpitude of digestion a little passed, she flutters half an hour through the streets, by way of paying visits, and then to the spectacles. These finished; another half hour is devoted to dodging in and out of the doors of her very sincere friends, and away to supper. After supper, cards and after cards, bed; to rise at noon the next day, and to tread, like a mill-horse, the same trodden circle over again. Thus the days of life are consumed, one by one, without an object beyond the present moment; ever flying from the ennui of that, yet carrying it with us; eternally in pursuit of happiness, which keeps eternally before us. If death or bankruptcy happen to trip us out of the circle, it is matter for the buzz of the evening, and is completely forgotten by the next morning. In America, on the other hand, the society of your husband, the fond cares for the children, the arrangements of the house, the improvements of the grounds, fill every moment with a healthy and an useful activity. Every exertion is encouraging, because to present amusement it joins the promise of some future good. The intervals of leisure are filled by the society of real friends, whose affections are not thinned to cobweb, by being spread over a thousand objects. This is the picture, in the light it is presented to my mind; now let me have it in yours. If we do not concur this year, we shall the next; or if not then, in a year or two more. You see I am determined not to suppose myself mistaken.

To let you see that Paris is not changed in its pursuits, since it was honored with your presence, I send you its monthly history. But this relating only to the embellishments of their persons, I must add, that those of the city go on well also. A new bridge, for example, is begun at the *Place Louis Quinze*; the old ones are clearing of the rubbish which encumbered them in the form of houses 5 new hospitals erecting; magnificent walls of inclosure, and Custom-houses at their entrances, &c. &c. &c. I know of no interesting change among those whom you honored with your acquaintance, unless Monsieur de Saint James was of that number. His bankruptcy, and taking asylum in the Bastille, have furnished matter of astonishment. His garden, at the Pont de Neuilly, where, on seventeen acres of ground he had laid out fifty thousand louis, will probably sell for somewhat less money. The workmen of Paris are making rapid strides towards English perfection. Would you believe, that in the course of the last two years, they have learned even to surpass their London rivals in some articles? Commission me to have you a phaeton made, and if it is not as much handsomer than a London one, as that is than a fiacre, send it back to me. Shall I fill the box with caps, bonnets, &c.? Not of my own choosing, but I was going to say, of Mademoiselle Bertin's, forgetting for the moment, that she too is bankrupt. They shall be chosen then by whom you please; or, if you are altogether nonplused by her eclipse, we will call an *Assemblées des Notables*, to help you out of the difficulty, as is now the fashion. In short, honor me with your, commands of any kind, and they shall be faithfully executed. The packets now established from Havre to New York furnish good opportunities of sending whatever you wish.

I shall end where I began, like a Paris day, reminding you of your engagement to write me a letter of respectable length, an engagement the more precious to me, as it has furnished me the occasion, after presenting my respects to Mr. Bingham, of assuring you of the sincerity of those sentiments of esteem and respect, with which I have the honor to be, Dear Madam, your most obedient and most humble servant,

Th: Jefferson,

LETTER XLVII.—TO GOVERNOR RANDOLPH, February 7, 1787

TO GOVERNOR RANDOLPH.

Paris, February 7, 1787.

I have the honor of enclosing to your Excellency a report of the proceedings on the inauguration of the bust of the Marquis de la Fayette, in this city. This has been attended with a considerable, but a necessary delay. The principle that the King is the sole fountain of honor in this country, opposed a barrier to our desires, which threatened to be insurmountable. No instance of a similar proposition from a foreign power, had occurred in their history. The admitting it in this case, is a singular proof of the King's friendly dispositions towards the States of America, and of his personal esteem for the character of the Marquis de la Fayette.

I take this, the earliest occasion, of congratulating my country on your excellency's appointment to the chair of government, and of assuring you, with great sincerity, of those sentiments of perfect esteem and respect, with which I have the honor to be your. Excellency's most obedient and most humble servant,

Th: Jefferson.

LETTER XLVIII.—TO JOHN JAY, February 8, 1787

TO JOHN JAY.

Paris, February 8, 1787.

Sir,

The packet being to sail the day after to-morrow, I have awaited the last possible moment of writing by her, in hopes I might be able to announce some favorable change in the situation of the Count de Vergennes. But none has occurred, and in the mean time he has become weaker by the continuance of his illness. Though not desperately ill, he is dangerously so. The Comptroller General, M. de Calonne, has been very ill also, but he is getting well. These circumstances have occasioned the postponement of the Assemblée des Notables to the 14th instant, and will probably occasion a further postponement. As I shall set out this day se'nnight for the waters of Aix, you will probably hear the issue of the Count de Vergennes illness through some other channel, before I shall have the honor of addressing you again. I may observe the same as to the final decision for the enfranchisement of Honfleur, which is in a fair way of being speedily concluded. The exertions of Monsieur de Creve-coeur, and particularly his influence with the Duke d'Harcourt, the principal instrument in effecting it, have been of chief consequence in this matter.

I have the honor to be, with the most perfect esteem and respect, Sir, your most obedient and most humble servant,

Th: Jefferson.

LETTER XLIX.—TO MR. DUMAS, February 9, 1787

TO MR. DUMAS.

Paris, February 9, 1787.

Sir,

My last to you was dated December the 25th; since which I have been honored with your several favors of December the 29th, January the 5th, 9th, and 23rd. I thought that your affairs could not be more interesting than they have been for a considerable time. Yet in the present moment they are become more so, by the apparent withdrawing of so considerable a personage in the drama, as the King of Prussia. To increase this interest, another person, whose importance scarcely admits calculation, is in a situation which fills us with alarm. Nature is struggling to relieve him by a decided gout; she has my sincere prayers to aid her, as I am persuaded she has yours. I have letters and papers from America as late as the 15th of December. The government of Massachusetts had imprisoned three of the leaders of their insurgents. The insurgents, being collected to the number of three or four hundred, had sent in their petition to the government, praying another act of pardon for their leaders and themselves, and on this condition offering to go every man home, and conduct himself dutifully afterwards. This is the latest intelligence.

I thank you for your attention to the question I had taken the liberty of proposing to you. I think with you, that it would be advisable to have our debt transferred to individuals of your country. There could and would be no objection to the guarantee remaining as you propose; and a postponement of the first payments of capital would surely be a convenience to us. For though the resources of the United States are great and growing, and their dispositions good, yet their machine is new, and they have not got it to go well. It is the object of their general wish at present, and they are all in movement, to set it in a good train; but their movements are necessarily slow. They will surely effect it in the end, because all have the same end in view; the difficulty being only to get all the thirteen States to agree on the same means. Divesting myself of every partiality, and speaking from that thorough knowledge which I have of the country, their resources, and their principles, I had rather trust money in their hands, than in that of any government on earth; because, though for a while the payments of the interest might be less regular, yet the final reimbursement of the capital would be more sure.

I set out next week for the south of France, to try whether some mineral waters in that quarter, much recommended, will restore the use of my hand. I shall be absent from Paris two or three months; but I take arrangements for the regular receipt of your favors, as if I were here. It will be better, however, for you to put your letters to Mr. Jay under cover to Mr. Short, who remains here, and will forward them.

I have thought it my duty to submit to Congress the proposition about the French debt, and may expect their answer in four months.

I have the honor to be, with sincere esteem and respect, Sir, your most obedient and most humble servant,

Th: Jefferson.

LETTER L.—TO JOHN JAY, February 14, 1787

TO JOHN JAY.

Paris, February 14, 1787.

Sir,

In the letter of the 8th instant, which I had the honor of writing you, I informed you that the Count de Vergennes was dangerously ill. He died yesterday morning, and the Count de Montmorin is appointed his successor. Your personal knowledge of this gentleman renders it unnecessary for me to say any thing of him.

Mr. Morris, during his office, being authorized to have the medals and swords executed, which had been ordered by Congress, he authorized Colonel Humphreys to take measures here for the execution. Colonel Humphreys did so; and the swords were finished in time for him to carry them. The medals not being finished, he desired me to attend to them. The workman who was to make that of General Greene, brought me yesterday the medal in gold, twenty-three in copper, and the die. Mr. Short, during my absence, will avail himself of the first occasion which shall offer, of forwarding the medals to you. I must beg leave, through you, to ask the pleasure of Congress as to the number they would choose to have struck. Perhaps they might be willing to deposite one of each person in every college of the United States. Perhaps they might choose to give a series of them to each of the crowned heads of Europe, which would be an acceptable present to them. They will be pleased to decide. In the mean time I have sealed up the die, and shall retain it till I am honored with their orders as to this medal, and the others also when they shall be finished.

I have the honor to be, with sentiments of the most perfect esteem and respect,

Sir, your most obedient

and most humble servant,

Th: Jefferson.

LETTER LI.—TO JOHN JAY, February 23, 1787

TO JOHN JAY.

Paris, February 23, 1787.

Sir,

The *Assemblée des Notables* being an event in the history of this country which excites notice, I have supposed it would not be disagreeable to you to learn its immediate objects, though no way connected with our interests. The Assembly met yesterday: the King, in a short but affectionate speech, informed them of his wish to consult with them on the plans he had digested, and on the general good of his people, and his desire to imitate the head of his family, Henry IV., whose memory is so dear to the nation. The *Garde des Sceaux* then spoke about twenty minutes, chiefly in compliment to the orders present. The Comptroller General, in a speech of about an hour, opened the budget, and enlarged on the several subjects which will be under their deliberation. He explained the situation of the finances at his accession to office, the expenses which their arrangement had rendered necessary, their present state with the improvements made in them, the several plans which had been proposed for their further improvement, a change in the form of some of their taxes, the removal of the interior Custom-houses to the frontiers, and the institution of Provincial Assemblies. The Assembly was then divided into committees, with a prince of the blood at the head of each. In this form they are to discuss separately the subjects which will be submitted to them. Their decision will be reported by two members to the minister, who, on view of the separate decisions of all the committees, will make such changes in his plans, as will best accommodate them to their views, without too much departing from his own, and will then submit them to the vote (but I believe not to the debate) of the General Assembly, which will be convened for this purpose one day in every week, and will vote individually.

The event ©f the Count de Vergennes'death, of which I had the honor to inform you in a letter of the 14th instant, the appointment of the Count Montmorin, and the propriety of my attending at his first audience, which will be on the 27th, have retarded the journey I had proposed a few days.

I shall hope, on my return, to meet here new powers for the consular convention, as, under those I have, it will be impossible to make the changes in the convention, which may be wished for.

I have the honor to be, with sentiments of the most perfect esteem and respect, Sir, your most obedient and most humble servant,

Th: Jefferson.

LETTER LII.—TO THE MARQUIS DE LA FAYETTE, February 28, 1787

TO THE MARQUIS DE LA FAYETTE.

Paris, February 28, 1787.

Dear Sir,

I am just now in the moment of my departure. Monsieur de Montmorin having given us audience at Paris yesterday, I missed the opportunity of seeing you once more. I am extremely pleased with his modesty, the simplicity of his manners, and his dispositions towards us. I promise myself a great deal of satisfaction in doing business with him. I hope he will not give ear to any unfriendly suggestions. I flatter myself I shall hear from you sometimes. Send your letters to my hotel as usual, and they will be forwarded to me. I wish you success in your meeting. I should form better hopes of it, if it were divided into two Houses instead of seven. Keeping the good model of your neighboring country before your eyes, you may get on, step by step, towards a good constitution. Though that model is not perfect, yet, as it would unite more suffrages than any new one which could be proposed, it is better to make that the object. If every advance is to be purchased by filling the royal coffers with gold, it will be gold well employed. The King, who means so well, should be encouraged to repeat these Assemblies. You see how we republicans are apt to preach, when we get on politics. Adieu, my dear friend.

Yours affectionately,

Th: Jefferson.

LETTER LIII.—TO MADAME LA COMTESSE DE TESSE, March 20, 1787

TO MADAME LA COMTESSE DE TESSE.

Nismes, March 20, 1787.

Here I am, Madam, gazing whole hours at the *Maison Quarrée*, like a lover at his mistress. The stocking-weavers and silk-spinners around it, consider me as a hypochondriac Englishman, about to write with a pistol the last chapter of his history. This is the second time I have been in love since I left Paris. The first was with a Diana at the Chateau de Lay-Epinaye in Beaujolois, a delicious morsel of sculpture, by M. A. Slodtz. This, you will say, was in rule, to fall in love with a female beauty: but with a house! It is out of all precedent. No, Madam, it is not without a precedent, in my own history. While in Paris, I was violently smitten with the Hotel de Salm, and used to go to the Tuileries almost daily to look at it. The *loueuse des chaises*, inattentive to my passion, never had the complaisance to place a chair there, so that, sitting on the parapet, and twisting my neck round to see the object of my admiration, I generally left it with a torticollis.

From Lyons to Nismes I have been nourished with the remains of Roman grandeur. They have always brought you to my mind, because I know your affection for whatever is Roman and noble. At Vienne I thought of you. But I am glad you were not there; for you would have seen me more angry than I hope you will ever see me. The Praetorian palace, as it is called, comparable, for its fine proportions, to the *Maison Quarrée*, defaced by the barbarians who have converted it to its present purpose, its beautiful fluted Corinthian columns cut out in part to make space for Gothic windows, and hewed down in the residue to the plane of the building, was enough, you must admit, to disturb my composure. At Orange, too, I thought of you. I was sure you had seen with pleasure the sublime triumphal arch of Marius at the entrance of the city. I went then to the Arena. Would you believe, Madam, that in this eighteenth century, in France, under the reign of Louis XVI., they are at this moment pulling down the circular wall of this superb remain to pave a road? And that too from a hill which is itself an entire mass of stone, just as fit, and more accessible? A former intendant, a M. de Basville, has rendered his memory dear to the traveller and amateur, by the pains he took to preserve and restore these monuments of antiquity. The present one (I do not know who he is) is demolishing the object to make a good road to it. I thought of you again, and I was then in great good humor, at the *Pont du Gard*, a sublime antiquity, and well preserved. But most of all here, where Roman taste, genius, and magnificence excite ideas analogous to yours at every step. I could no longer oppose the inclination to avail myself of your permission to write to you, a permission given with too much complaisance by you, and used by me with too much indiscretion. Madame de Tott did me the same honor.

But she being only the descendant of some of those puny heroes who boiled their own kettles before the walls of Troy, I shall write to her from a Grecian, rather than a Roman canton: when I shall find myself, for example, among her Phocæan relations at Marseilles.

Loving, as you do, Madam, the precious remains of antiquity, loving architecture, gardening, a warm sun, and a clear sky, I wonder you have never thought of moving Chaville to Nismes. This, as you know, has not always been deemed impracticable; and, therefore, the next time a *Surintendant des bailments du roi*, after the example of M. Colbert, sends persons to Nismes to move the *Maison Quarrée* to Paris, that they may not come empty-handed, desire them to bring Chaville with them to replace it. *A propos* of Paris. I have now been three weeks from there, without knowing any thing of what has passed. I suppose I shall meet it all at Aix, where I have directed my letters to be lodged, *poste restante*. My journey has given me leisure to reflect on this *Assemblée des Notables*. Under a good and a young King, as the present, I think good may be made of it. I would have the deputies, then, by all means, so conduct themselves as to encourage him to repeat the calls of this Assembly. Their first step should be to get themselves divided into two chambers instead of seven; the Noblesse and the Commons separately. The second, to persuade the King, instead of choosing the deputies of the Commons himself, to summon those chosen by the people for the Provincial administrations. The third, as the Noblesse is too numerous to be all of the Assemblée, to obtain permission for that body to choose its own deputies. Two Houses, so elected, would contain a mass of wisdom, which would make the people happy, and the King great; would place him in history where no other act can possibly place him. They would thus put themselves in the track of the best guide they can follow, they would soon overtake it, become its guide in turn, and lead to the wholesome modifications wanting in that model, and necessary to constitute a rational government. Should they attempt more than the established habits of the people are ripe for, they must lose all, and retard indefinitely the ultimate object of their aim. These, Madam, are my opinions; but I wish to know yours, which I am sure will be better.

From a correspondent at Nismes you will not expect news. Were I to attempt to give you news, I should tell you stories one thousand years old. I should detail to you the intrigues of the courts of the Cæsars, how they affect us here, the oppressions of their praetors, prefects, &c. I am immersed in antiquities from morning to night. For me the city of Rome is actually existing in all the splendor of its empire. I am filled with alarms for the event of the irruptions daily making on us by the Goths, the Visigoths, Ostrogoths, and Vandals, lest they should re-conquer us to our original barbarism. If I am sometimes induced to look forward to the eighteenth century, it is only when recalled to it by the recollection of your goodness and friendship, and by those sentiments of sincere esteem and respect, with which I have the honor to be,

Madam, your most obedient

and most humble servant,

Th: Jefferson.

LETTER LIV.—TO THE MARQUIS DE LA FAYETTE, April 11, 1787

TO THE MARQUIS DE LA FAYETTE.

Nice, April 11, 1787.

Your head, my dear friend, is full of *Notable* things; and being better employed, therefore, I do not expect letters from you. I am constantly roving about to see what I have never seen before, and shall never see again. In the great cities, I go to see what travellers think alone worthy of being seen; but I make a job of it, and generally gulp it all down in a day. On the other hand, I am never satiated with rambling through the fields and farms, examining the culture and cultivators with a degree of curiosity, which makes some take me to be a fool, and others to be much wiser than I am. I have been pleased to find among the people a less degree of physical misery than I had expected. They are generally well clothed, and have a plenty of food, not animal indeed, but vegetable, which is as wholesome. Perhaps they are over-worked, the excess of the rent required by the landlord obliging them to too many hours of labor in order to produce that, and wherewith to feed and clothe themselves. The soil of Champagne and Burgundy I have found more universally good than I had expected, and as I could not help making a comparison with England, I found that comparison more unfavorable to the latter than is generally admitted. The soil, the climate, and the productions are superior to those of England, and the husbandry as good, except in one point; that of manure. In England, long leases for twenty-one years, or three lives, to wit, that of the farmer, his wife, and son, renewed by the son as soon as he comes to the possession, for his own life, his wife's, and eldest child's, and so on, render the farms there almost hereditary, make it worth the farmer's while to manure the lands highly, and give the landlord an opportunity of occasionally making his rent keep pace with the improved state of the lands. Here the leases are either during pleasure, or for three, six, or nine years, which does not give the farmer time to repay himself for the expensive operation of well manuring, and therefore, he manures ill, or not at all. I suppose, that could the practice of leasing for three lives be introduced in the whole kingdom, it would, within the term of your life, increase agricultural productions fifty per cent.; or were any one proprietor to do it with his own lands, it would increase his rents fifty per cent, in the course of twenty-five years. But I am told the laws do not permit it. The laws then, in this particular, are unwise and unjust, and ought to give that permission. In the southern provinces, where the soil is poor, the climate hot and dry, and there are few animals, they would learn the art, found so precious in England, of making vegetable manure, and thus improving the provinces in the article in which nature has been least kind to them. Indeed, these provinces afford a singular spectacle. Calculating on the poverty of their soil, and their climate by its latitude only, they should have been the poorest in France. On the contrary, they are the richest, from one fortuitous circumstance. Spurs or ramifications of high mountains, making down from the Alps, and, as it were, reticulating these provinces, give to the vallies the protection of a particular inclosure to each, and the benefit of a general stagnation of the northern winds produced by the whole of them, and thus countervail the advantage of several degrees of latitude. From the first olive fields of Pierrelatte, to the orangeries of Hieres, has been continued rapture to me. I have often wished for you. I think you have not made this journey. It is a pleasure you have to come, and an improvement to be added to the many you have already made. It will be a great comfort to you, to know, from your own inspection, the condition of all the provinces of your own country, and it will be interesting to them at some future day, to be known to you. This is, perhaps, the only moment of your life in which you can acquire that knowledge. And to do it most effectually, you must be absolutely incognito, you must ferret the people out of their hovels as I have done, look into their kettles, eat their bread, loll on their beds under pretence of resting yourself, but in fact to find if they are soft. You will feel a sublime pleasure in the course of this investigation, and a sublimer one hereafter, when you shall be able to apply your knowledge to the softening of their beds, or the throwing a morsel of meat into their kettle of vegetables.

You will not wonder at the subjects of my letter: they are the only ones which have been presented to my mind for some time past; and the waters must always be what are the fountains from which they flow. According to this, indeed, I should have intermixed, from beginning to end, warm expressions of friendship to you. But, according to the ideas of our country, we do not permit ourselves to speak even truths, when they may have the air of flattery. I content myself, therefore, with saying once for all, that I love you, your wife, and children. Tell them so, and adieu.

Yours affectionately,

Th: Jefferson.

LETTER LV.—TO WILLIAM SHORT, April 12, 1787

TO WILLIAM SHORT.

Nice, April 12, 1787,

Dear Sir,

At Marseilles, they told me I should encounter the rice fields of Piedmont soon after crossing the Alps. Here they tell me there are none nearer than Vercelli and Novara, which is carrying me almost to Milan. I fear that this circumstance will occasion me a greater delay than I had calculated on. However, I am embarked in the project, and shall go through with it. To-morrow, I set out on my passage over the Alps, being to pursue it ninety-three miles to Coni, on mules, as the snows are not yet enough melted to admit carriages to pass. I leave mine here, therefore, proposing to return by water from Genoa. I think it will be three weeks before I get back to Nice. I find this climate quite as delightful as it has been represented. Hieres is the only place in France, which may be compared with it. The climates are equal. In favor of this place, are the circumstances of gay and dissipated society, a handsome city, good accommodations, and some commerce. In favor of Hieres, are environs of delicious and extensive plains, a society more contracted, and therefore more capable of esteem, and the neighborhood of Toulon, Marseilles, and other places, to which excursions may be made. Placing Marseilles in comparison with Hieres, it has extensive society, a good theatre, freedom from military control, and the most animated commerce. But its winter climate is far inferior. I am now in the act of putting my baggage into portable form for my bat-mule; after praying you, therefore, to let my daughter know I am well, and that I shall not be heard of again in three weeks, I take my leave of you for that time, with assurances of the sincere esteem with which I am, Dear Sir, your friend and servant,

Th: Jefferson.

LETTER LVI.—TO JOHN JAY, May 4, 1787

TO JOHN JAY.

Marseilles, May 4, 1787.

Sir,

I had the honor of receiving at Aix, your letter of February the 9th, and immediately wrote to the Count de Montmorin, explaining the delay of the answer of Congress to the King's letter, and desired Mr. Short to deliver that answer, with my letter, to Monsieur de Montmorin, which he informs me he has accordingly done.

My absence prevented my noting to you, in the first moment, the revolution which has taken place at Paris, in the department of finance, by the substitution of Monsieur de Fourqueux in the place of Monsieur de Calonne; so that you will have heard of it through other channels, before this will have the honor of reaching you.

Having staid at Aix long enough to prove the inefficacy of the waters, I came on to this place, for the purpose of informing myself here, as I mean to do at the other seaport towns, of whatever may be interesting to our commerce. So far as carried on in our own bottoms, I find it almost nothing; and so it must probably remain, till something can be done with the Algerines. Though severely afflicted with the plague, they have come out within these few days, and showed themselves in force along the coast of Genoa, cannonading a little town and taking several vessels.

Among other objects of inquiry, this was the place to learn something more certain on the subject of rice, as it is a great emporium for that of the Levant, and of Italy. I wished particularly to know, whether it was the use of a different machine for cleaning, which brought European rice to market less broken than ours, as had been represented to me, by those who deal in that article in Paris. I found several persons who had passed through the rice country of Italy, but not one who could explain to me the nature of the machine. But I was given to believe, that I might see it myself immediately on entering Piedmont. As this would require but about three weeks, I determined to go, and ascertain this point; as the chance only of placing our rice above all rivalship in quality, as it is in color, by the introduction of a better machine, if a better existed, seemed to justify the application of that much time to it. I found the rice country to be in truth Lombardy, one hundred miles further than had been represented, and that though called Piedmont rice, not a grain is made in the country of Piedmont. I passed through the rice-fields of the Vercellese and Milanese, about sixty miles, and returned from thence last night, having found that the machine is absolutely the same as ours, and of course, that we need not listen more to that suggestion. It is a difference in the species of grain; of which the government of Turin is so sensible, that, as I was informed, they prohibit the exportation of rough rice, on pain of death. I have taken measures, however, which I think will not fail, for obtaining a quantity of it, and I bought on the spot a small parcel, which I have with me. As further details on this subject to Congress would be misplaced, I propose, on my return to Paris, to communicate them, and send the rice to the society at Charleston for promoting agriculture, supposing that they will be best able to try the experiment of cultivating the rice of this quality, and to communicate the species to the two States of South Carolina and Georgia, if they find it answers. I thought the staple of these two States was entitled to this attention, and that it must be desirable to them, to be able to furnish rice of the two qualities demanded in Europe, especially, as the greater consumption is in the forms for which the Lombardy quality is preferred. The mass of our countrymen being interested in agriculture, I hope I do not err in supposing, that in a time of profound peace, as the present, to enable them to adapt their productions to the market, to point out markets for them, and endeavor to obtain favorable terms of reception, is within the line of my duty.

My journey into this part of the country has procured me information, which I will take the liberty of communicating to Congress. In October last, I received a letter, dated Montpelier, October the 2nd, 1786, announcing to me that the writer was a foreigner, who had a matter of very great consequence to communicate to me, and desired I would indicate the channel through which it might pass safely. I did so.

I received soon after, a letter in the following words, omitting only the formal parts. [*A translation of it is here given.*]

'I am a native of Brazil. You are not ignorant of the frightful slavery under which my country groans. This continually becomes more insupportable, since the epoch of your glorious independence; for the cruel Portuguese omit nothing which can render our condition more wretched, from an apprehension that we may follow your example. The conviction, that these usurpers against the laws of nature and humanity only meditate new oppressions, has decided us to follow the guiding light which you have held out to us, to break our chains, to revive our almost expiring liberty, which is nearly overwhelmed by that force, which is the sole foundation of the authority that Europeans exercise over America. But it is necessary that some power should extend assistance to the Brazilians, since Spain would certainly unite herself with Portugal; and in spite of our advantages for defence, we could not make it effectual, or, at least, it would be imprudent to hazard the attempt, without some assurance of success. In this state of affairs, Sir, we can, with propriety, look only to the United States, not only because we are following her example, but, moreover, because nature, in making us inhabitants of the same continent, has in some sort united us in the bonds of a common patriotism. On our part, we are prepared to furnish the necessary supplies of money, and at all times to acknowledge the debt of gratitude due to our benefactors. I have thus, Sir, laid before you a summary of my views. It is in discharge of this commission that I have come to France, since I could not effect it in America without exciting suspicion. It now remains for you to decide whether those views can be accomplished. Should you desire to consult your nation on them, it is in my power to give you all the information you may require.'

As by this time, I had been advised to try the waters of Aix, I wrote to the gentleman my design, and that I would go off my road as far as Nismes, under the pretext of seeing the antiquities of that place, if he would meet me there. He met me, and the following is the sum of the information I received from him. 'Brazil contains as many inhabitants as Portugal. They are, 1. Portuguese. 2. Native whites. 3. Black and mulatto slaves. 4. Indians, civilized and savage. 1. The Portuguese are few in number, mostly married there, have lost sight of their native country, as well as the prospect of returning to it, and are disposed to become independent. 2. The native whites form the body of their nation. 3. The slaves are as numerous as the free. 4. The civilized Indians have no energy, and the savage would not meddle. There are twenty thousand regular troops. Originally these were Portuguese. But as they died off, they were replaced by natives, so that these compose at present the mass of the troops, and may be counted on by their native country. The officers are partly Portuguese, partly Brazilians: their bravery is not doubted, and they understand the parade, but not the science of their profession. They have no bias for Portugal, but no energy either for any thing. The priests are partly Portuguese, partly Brazilians, and will not interest themselves much. The Noblesse are scarcely known as such. They will, in no manner, be distinguished from the people. The men of letters are those most desirous of a revolution. The people are not much under the influence of their priests, most of them read and write, possess arms, and are in the habit of using them for hunting. The slaves will take the side of their masters. In short, as to the question of revolution, there is but one mind in that Country. But there appears no person capable of conducting a revolution, or willing to venture himself at its head, without the aid of some powerful nation, as the people of their own might fail them. There is no printing press in Brazil. They consider the North American revolution as a precedent for theirs. They look to the United States as most likely to give them honest support, and, from a variety of considerations, have the strongest prejudices in our favor. This informant is a native and inhabitant of Rio Janeiro, the present metropolis, which contains fifty thousand inhabitants, knows well St. Salvador, the former one, and the *mines d'or*, which are in the centre of the country. These are all for a revolution; and, constituting the body of the nation, the other parts will follow them, The King's fifth of the mines, yields annually thirteen millions of crusadoes or half dollars. He has the sole right of searching for diamonds and other precious stones, which yield him about half as much. His income from those two resources alone, then, is about ten millions of dollars annually; but the remaining part of the produce of the mines, being twenty-six millions, might be counted on for effecting a revolution. Besides the arms in the hands of the people, there are public magazines. They have abundance of horses, but only a part of their country would admit the service of horses. They would want cannon, ammunition, ships, sailors, soldiers, and officers, for which they are disposed to look to the United States, it being always understood, that every service and furniture will be well paid. Corn costs about twenty livres the one hundred pounds. They have flesh in the greatest abundance, insomuch, that in some parts, they kill beeves for the skin only. The whale fishery is carried on by Brazilians altogether, and not by Portuguese; but in very small vessels, so that the fishermen know nothing of managing a large ship. They would want of us; at all times, shipping, corn, and salt fish. The latter is a great article, and they are at present supplied with it from Portugal. Portugal being without either army or navy, could not attempt an invasion under a twelvemonth. Considering of what it would be composed, it would not be much to be feared, and if it failed, they would probably never attempt a second. Indeed, this source of their wealth being intercepted, they are scarcely capable of a first effort. The thinking part of the nation are so sensible of this, that they consider an early separation inevitable. There is an implacable hatred between the Brazilians and Portuguese; to reconcile which, a former minister adopted the policy of letting the Brazilians into a participation of public offices; but subsequent administrations have reverted to the ancient policy of keeping the administrations in the hands of native Portuguese. There is a mixture of natives, of the old appointments, still remaining in office. If Spain should invade them on their southern extremities, these are so distant from the body of their settlements, that they could not penetrate thence; and Spanish enterprise is not formidable. The *mines d'or* are among mountains, inaccessible to any army; and Rio Janeiro is considered the strongest port in the world after Gibraltar. In case of a successful revolution, a republican government in a single body would probably be established.'

I took care to impress on him, through the whole of our conversation, that I had neither instructions nor authority to say a word to any body on this subject, and that I could only give him my own ideas, as a single individual: which were, that we were not in a condition at present to meddle nationally in any war; that we wished particularly to cultivate the friendship of Portugal, with whom we have an advantageous commerce. That yet, a successful revolution in Brazil could not be uninteresting to us. That prospects of lucre might possibly draw numbers of individuals to their aid, and purer motives our officers, among whom are many excellent. That our citizens being free to leave their own country individually, without the consent of their governments, are equally free to go to any other.

A little before I received the first letter of the Brazilian, a gentleman informed me there was a Mexican in Paris, who wished to have some conversation with me. He accordingly called on me. The substance of the information I drew from him, was as follows. He is himself a native of Mexico, where his relations are, principally. He left it about seventeen years of age, and seems now to be about thirty-three or thirty-four. He classes and characterizes the inhabitants of that country, as follows. 1. The natives of Old Spain, possessed of most of the offices of government, and firmly attached to it. 2. The clergy, equally attached to the government. 3. The natives of Mexico, generally disposed to revolt, but without instruction, without energy, and much under the dominion of their priests. 4. The slaves, mulatto and black; the former enterprising and intelligent, the latter brave, and of very important weight, into whatever scale they throw themselves; but he thinks they will side with their masters. 5. The conquered Indians, cowardly, not likely to take any side, nor important which they take. 6. The free Indians, brave and formidable, should they interfere, but not likely to do so, as being at a great distance. I asked him the numbers of these several classes, but he could not give them. The first, he thought very inconsiderable; that the second formed the body of the freemen; the third equal to the two first; the fourth, to all the preceding: and as to the fifth, he could form no idea of their proportion. Indeed, it appeared to me, that his conjectures as to the others were on loose grounds. He said he knew from good information, there were three hundred thousand inhabitants in the city of Mexico. I was still more cautious with him than with the Brazilian, mentioning it as my private opinion (unauthorized to say a word on the subject, otherwise), that a successful revolution was still at a distance with them; that I feared they must begin by enlightening and emancipating the minds of their people; that as to us, if Spain should give us advantageous terms of commerce, and remove other difficulties, it was not probable that we should relinquish certain and present advantages, though smaller, for uncertain and future ones, however great. I was led into this caution by observing, that this gentleman was intimate at the Spanish ambassador's, and that he was then at Paris, employed by Spain to settle her boundaries with France, on the Pyrenees. He had much the air of candor, but that can be borrowed; so that I was not able to decide about him in my own mind.

Led by a unity of subject, and a desire to give Congress as general a view of the disposition of our southern countrymen, as my information enables me, I will add an article which, old and insulated, I did not think important enough to mention at the time I received it. You will remember, Sir, that during the late war, the British papers often gave details of a rebellion in Peru. The character of those papers discredited the information. But the truth was, that the insurrections were so general, that the event was long on the poise. Had Commodore Johnson, then expected on that coast, touched and landed there two thousand men, the dominion of Spain in that country would have been at an end. They only wanted a point of union, which this body would have constituted. Not having this, they acted without concert, and were are length subdued separately. This conflagration was quenched in blood; two hundred thousand souls, on both sides, having perished; but the remaining matter is very capable of combustion. I have this information from a person who was on the spot at the time, and whose good faith, understanding, and means of information leave no doubt of the facts. He observed, however, that the numbers above supposed to have perished were on such conjectures only as he could collect.

I trouble Congress with these details, because, however distant we may be, both in condition and dispositions, from taking an active part in any commotions in that country, nature has placed it too near us to make its movements altogether indifferent to our interests, or to our curiosity.

I hear of another *Arrêt* of this court, increasing the duties on foreign stock-fish, and the premium on their own imported into their islands; but not having yet seen it, I can say nothing certain on it. I hope the effect of this policy will be defeated by the practice which, I am told, takes place on the Banks of Newfoundland, of putting our fish into the French fishing-boats, and the parties sharing the premium, instead of ours paying the duty.

I am in hopes Mr. Short will be able to send you the medals of General Gates by this packet. I await a general instruction as to these medals. The academies of Europe will be much pleased to receive each a set.

I propose to set out the day after to-morrow for Bordeaux (by the canal of Languedoc), Mantes, L'Orient, and Paris.

I have the honor to be, with sentiments of the most perfect esteem and respect, Sir, your most obedient and most humble servant,

Th: Jefferson.

LETTER LVII.—TO M. GUIDE, May 6, 1787

TO M. GUIDE.

Marseilles, May 6, 1787.

Sir,

A desire of seeing a commerce commenced between the dominions of his Majesty, the King of Sardinia, and the United States of America, and a direct exchange of their respective productions, without passing through a third nation, led me into the conversation which I had the honor of having with you on that subject, and afterwards with Monsieur Tallon at Turin, to whom I promised that I would explain to you, in writing, the substance of what passed between us. The articles of your produce wanted with us are brandies, wines, oil, fruits, and manufactured silks: those with which we can furnish you are indigo, potash, tobacco, flour, salt-fish, furs and peltries, ships and materials for building them. The supply of tobacco, particularly, being in the hands of government solely, appeared to me to offer an article for beginning immediately the experiment of direct commerce. That of the first quality can be had at first hand only from James river in Virginia; those of the second and third from the same place, and from Baltimore in Maryland. The first quality is delivered in the ports of France at thirty-eight livres the quintal, the second at thirty-six livres, the third at thirty-four livres, weight and money of France, by individuals generally. I send you the copy of a large contract, wherein the three qualities are averaged at thirty-six livres. They may be delivered at Nice for those prices. Indeed, it is my opinion, that by making shipments of your own produce to those places, and buying the tobaccos on the spot, they may be had more advantageously. In this case, it would be expedient that merchants of Nice, Turin, and America, should form a joint concern for conducting the business in the two countries. Monsieur Tallon desired me to point out proper persons in America who might be addressed for this purpose. The house of the most extensive reputation, concerned in the tobacco trade, and on the firmest funds, is that of Messrs. Ross and Pleasants at Richmond, in Virginia. If it should be concluded on your part to make any attempt of this kind, and to address yourselves to these gentlemen, or any others, it would be best to write them your ideas, and receive theirs, before you make either purchases or shipments. A more hasty conduct might occasion loss, and retard, instead of encouraging, the establishment of this commerce. I would undertake to write, at the same time, to these or any other merchants whom you should prefer, in order to dispose them favorably, and as disinterestedly as possible, for the encouragement of this essay. I must observe to you, that our vessels are fearful of coming into the Mediterranean on account of the Algerines: and that if you should freight vessels, those of the French will be most advantageous for you, because received into our ports without paying any duties on some of those articles, and lighter than others on all of them. English vessels, on the other hand, are distinguished by paying heavier duties than those of any other nation. Should you desire any further information, or to pass letters with certainty to any mercantile house in America, do me the favor to address yourselves to me at Paris, and I shall do whatever depends on me for this object.

I have the honor to be, with sentiments of high esteem and respect, Sir, your most obedient, humble servant,

Th: Jefferson.

MEMORANDA TAKEN ON A JOURNEY FROM PARIS IN 1787

Memoranda taken on a Journey from Paris into the Southern Parts of France, and Northern of Italy, in the year 1787.

CHAMPAGNE. March 3. *Sens* to *Vermanton.* The face of the country is in large hills, not too steep for the plough, somewhat resembling the Elk hill and Beaver-dam hills of Virginia. The soil is generally a rich mulatto loam, with a mixture of coarse sand, and some loose stone. The plains of the Yonne are of the same color. The plains are in corn, the hills in vineyard, but the wine not good. There are a few apple-trees, but none of any other kind, and no enclosures. No cattle, sheep, or swine; fine mules.

Few *chateaux*; no farm-houses, all the people being gathered in villages. Are they thus collected by that dogma of their religion, which makes them believe, that to keep the Creator in good humor with his own works, they must mumble a mass every day? Certain it is, that they are less happy and less virtuous in villages, than they would be insulated with their families on the grounds they cultivate. The people are illy clothed. Perhaps they have put on their worst clothes at this moment, as it is raining. But I observe women and children carrying heavy burthens, and laboring with the hoe. This is an unequivocal indication of extreme poverty. Men, in a civilized country, never expose their wives and children to labor above their force and sex, as long as their own labor can protect them from it. I see few beggars. Probably this is the effect of a police.

BURGUNDY. March 4. *Lucy-le-Bois. Cussy-les-Forges. Rouvray. Maison-neuve. Vitieaux. La Chaleure. Pont de Panis. Dijon.* The hills are higher, and more abrupt. The soil a good red loam and sand, mixed with more or less grit, small stone, and sometimes rock. All in corn. Some forest wood here and there, broom, whins, and holly, and a few enclosures of quick-hedge. Now and then a flock of sheep.

The people are well clothed, but it is Sunday. They have the appearance of being well fed. The Chateau de Sevigny, near Cussy-les-Forges, is a charming situation. Between Maison-neuve and Vitteaux the road leads through an avenue of trees, eight American miles long, in a right line. It is impossible to paint the ennui of this avenue. On the summits of the hills, which border the valley in which Vitteaux is, there is a parapet of rock, twenty, thirty, or forty feet perpendicular, which crowns the hills. The tops are nearly level, and appear to be covered with earth. Very singular. Great masses of rock in the hills between La Chaleure and Pont de Panis, and a conical hill in the approach to the last place.

Dijon. The tavern price of a bottle of the best wine (e. g. of Vaune) is four livres. The best round potatoes here, I ever saw. They have begun a canal thirty feet wide, which is to lead into the Saone at ————-. It is fed by springs. They are not allowed to take any water out of the riviere d'Ouche, which runs through this place, on account of the mills on that river. They talk of making a canal to the Seine, the nearest navigable part of which, at present, is fifteen leagues from hence. They have very light wagons here for the transportation of their wine. They are long and narrow; the fore-wheels as high as the hind. Two pieces of wine are drawn by one horse in one of these wagons. The road in this part of the country is divided into portions of forty or fifty feet by stones, numbered, which mark the task of the laborers.

March 7 and 8. From *La Baraque* to *Chagny*. On the left are plains, which extend to the Saone; on the right the ridge of mountains, called the Cote. The plains are of a reddish-brown, rich loam, mixed with much small stone. The Cote has for its basis a solid rock, on which is about a foot of soil and small stone, in equal quantities, the soil red, and of middling quality. The plains are in corn; the Cote in vines. The former have no enclosures, the latter is in small ones, of dry stone wall. There is a good deal of forest. Some small herds of small cattle and sheep. Fine mules, which come from Provence, and cost twenty louis. They break them at two years old, and they last to thirty.

The corn-lands here rent for about fifteen livres the arpent. They are now planting, pruning, and sticking their vines. When a new vineyard is made, they plant the vines in gutters about four feet apart. As the vines advance, they lay them down. They put out new shoots, and fill all the intermediate space, till all trace of order is lost. They have ultimately about one foot square to each vine. They begin to yield good profit at five or six years old, and last one hundred, or one hundred and fifty years. A vigneron at Volnay carried me into his vineyard, which was of about ten arpents. He told me, that some years it produced him sixty pieces of wine, and some not more than three pieces. The latter is the most advantageous produce, because the wine is better in quality, and higher in price, in proportion as less is made; and the expenses, at the same time, diminish in the same proportion. Whereas, when much is made, the expenses are increased, while the quality and price become less. In very plentiful years, they often give one half the wine for casks to contain the other half. The cask for two hundred and fifty bottles costs six livres in scarce years, and ten in plentiful. The feuillette is of one hundred and twenty-five bottles, the piece of two hundred and fifty, and the queue or botte of five hundred. An arpent rents at from twenty to sixty livres. A farmer of ten arpents has about three laborers engaged by the year. He pays four louis to a man, and half as much to a woman, and feeds them. He kills one hog, and salts it, which is all the meat used in the family during the year. Their ordinary food is bread and vegetables. At Pomard and Volnay, I observed them eating good wheat bread; at Meursault, rye. I asked the reason of the difference. They told me, that the white wines fail in quality much oftener than the red, and remain on hand. The farmer, therefore, cannot afford to feed his laborers so well. At Meursault only white wines are made, because there is too much stone for the red. On such slight circumstances depends the condition of man! The wines which have given such celebrity to Burgundy grow only on the Cote, an extent of about five leagues long, and half a league wide. They begin at Chambertin, and go through Vougeau, Romanie, Veaune, Nuits, Beaune, Pomard, Volnay, Meursault, and end at Monrachet. Those of the two last are white; the others red. Chambertin, Vougeau, and Beaune are the strongest, and will bear transportation and keeping. They sell, therefore, on the spot for twelve hundred livres the queue, which is forty-eight sous the bottle. Volnay is the best of the other reds, equal in flavor to Chambertin, &c., but being lighter, will not keep, and therefore sells for not more than three hundred livres the queue, which is twelve sous the bottle. It ripens sooner than they do, and consequently is better for those who wish to broach at a year old. In like manner of the white wines, and for the same reason, Monrachet sells for twelve hundred livres the queue (forty-eight sous the bottle), and Meursault of the best quality, viz. the *Goutte d'or*, at only one hundred and fifty livres (six sous the bottle). It is remarkable, that the best of each kind, that is, of the red and white, is made at the extremities of the line, to wit, at Chambertin and Monrachet. It is pretended, that the adjoining vineyards produce the same qualities, but that, belonging to obscure individuals, they have not obtained a name, and therefore sell as other wines. The aspect of the Cote is a little south of east. The western side is also covered with vines, and is apparently of the same soil; yet the wines are only of the coarsest kinds. Such, too, are those which are produced in the plains; but there the soil is richer, and less strong. Vougeau is the property of the monks of Citeaux, and produces about two hundred pieces. Monrachet contains about fifty arpents, and produces, one year with another, about one hundred and twenty pieces. It belongs to two proprietors only, Monsieur de Clarmont, who leases to some wine-merchants, and the Marquis de Sarsnet, of Dijon, whose part is farmed to a Monsieur de la Tour, whose family, for many generations, have had the farm. The best wines are carried to Paris by land. The transportation costs thirty-six livres the piece. The more indifferent go by water. Bottles cost four and a half sous each.

March 9. *Chalons. Sennecey. Tournus. St. Albin. Macon.* On the left are the fine plains of the Saone; on the right high lands, rather waving than hilly, sometimes sloping gently to the plains, sometimes dropping down in precipices, and occasionally broken into beautiful vallies[sp.] by the streams which run into the Saone. The plains are a dark rich loam, in pasture and corn; the heights more or less red or reddish, always gritty, of middling quality only, their sides in vines, and their summits in corn. The vineyards are enclosed with dry stone-walls, and there are some quick-hedges in the corn-grounds. The cattle are few and indifferent. There are some good oxen, however. They draw by the head. Few sheep, and small. A good deal of wood-lands.

I passed three times the canal called Le Charollois, which they are opening from Chalons on the Saone to Dijon on the Loire. It passes near Chagny, and will be twenty-three leagues long. They have worked on it three years, and will finish it in four more. It will reanimate the languishing commerce of Champagne and Burgundy, by furnishing a water transportation for their wines to Nantes, which also will receive new consequence by becoming the emporium of that commerce. At some distance on the right are high mountains, which probably form the separation between the waters of the Saone and Loire. Met a malefactor in the hands of one of the Marichausee; perhaps a dove in the talons of the hawk. The people begin now to be in separate establishments, and not in villages. Houses are mostly covered with tile.

BEAUJOLOIS.[Sp.] *Maison Blanche. St. George. Chateau de Laye-Epinaye.* The face of the country is like that from Chalons to Macon. The plains are a dark rich loam, the hills a red loam of middling quality, mixed generally with more or less coarse sand and grit, and a great deal of small stone. Very little forest. The vineyards are mostly enclosed with dry stone-wall. A few small cattle and sheep. Here, as in Burgundy, the cattle are all white. This is the richest country I ever beheld. It is about ten or twelve leagues in length, and three, four, or five in breadth; at least that part of it, which is under the eye of a traveller. It extends from the top of a ridge of mountains, running parallel with the Saone, and sloping down to the plains of that river, scarce any where too steep for the plough. The whole is thick set with farm-houses, chateaux, and the bastides of the inhabitants of Lyons. The people live separately, and not in villages. The hill-sides are in vine and corn: the plains in corn and pasture. The lands are farmed either for money, or on half-stocks. The rents of the corn-lands, farmed for money, are about ten or twelve livres the arpent. A farmer takes perhaps about one hundred and fifty arpents, for three, six, or nine years. The first year they are in corn; the second in other small grain, with which he sows red clover. The third is for the clover. The spontaneous pasturage is of greensward, which they call fromenteau. When lands are rented on half-stocks, the cattle, sheep, &c. are furnished by the landlord. They are valued, and must be left of equal value. The increase of these, as well as the produce of the farm is divided equally. These leases are only from year to year. They have a method of mixing beautifully the culture of vines, trees, and corn. Rows of fruit-trees are planted about twenty feet apart. Between the trees, in the row, they plant vines four feet apart, and espalier them. The intervals are sowed alternately in corn, so as to be one year in corn, the next in pasture, the third in corn, the fourth in pasture, &c. One hundred toises of vines in length, yield generally about four pieces of wine. In Dauphine, I am told, they plant vines only at the roots of the trees, and let them cover the whole trees. But this spoils both the wine and the fruit. Their wine, when distilled, yields but one-third its quantity in brandy. The wages of a laboring man here are five louis; of a woman, one half. The women do not work with the hoe: they only weed the vines, the corn, &c, and spin. They speak a patois very difficult to understand. I passed some time at the Chateau de Laye-Epinaye. Monsieur de Laye has a seignory of about fifteen thousand arpents, in pasture, corn, vines, and wood. He has over this, as is usual, a certain jurisdiction, both criminal and civil. But this extends only to the first crude examination, which is before his judges. The subject is referred, for final examination and decision, to the regular judicatures of the country. The Seigneur is keeper of the peace on his domains. He is therefore subject to the expenses of maintaining it. A criminal prosecuted to sentence and execution costs M. de Laye about five thousand livres. This is so burthensome to the Seigneurs, that they are slack in criminal prosecutions. A good effect from a bad cause. Through all Champagne, Burgundy, and the Beaujolois, the husbandry seems good, except that they manure too little. This proceeds from the shortness of their leases. The people of Burgundy and Beaujolois are well clothed, and have the appearance of being well fed. But they experience all the oppressions which result from the nature of the general government, and from that of their particular tenures, and of the seignorial government to which they are subject. What a cruel reflection, that a rich country cannot long be a free one. M. de Laye has a Diana and Endymion, a very superior morsel of sculpture by Michael Angelo Slodtz, done in 1740. The wild gooseberry is in leaf; the wild pear and sweet-briar in bud.

Lyons. There are some feeble remains here of an amphitheatre of two hundred feet diameter, and of an aqueduct in brick. The Pont d'Ainay has nine arches of forty feet from centre to centre. The piers are of six feet. The almond is in bloom.

DAUPHINE. From *St. Fond* to *Mornant.* March 15, 16, 17, 18. The Rhone makes extensive plains, which lie chiefly on the eastern side, and are often in two stages. Those of Montelimart are three,or four miles wide, and rather good. Sometimes, as in the neighborhood of Vienne, the hills come in precipices to the river, resembling then very much our Susquehanna and its hill, except that the Susquehanna is ten times as wide as the Rhone. The highlands are often very level. The soil both of hill and plain, where there is soil, is generally tinged, more or less, with red. The hills are sometimes mere masses of rock, sometimes a mixture of loose stone and earth. The plains are always stony, and as often as otherwise covered perfectly with a coat of round stones, of the size of the fist, so as to resemble the remains of inundations, from which all the soil has been carried away. Sometimes they are middling good, sometimes barren. In the neighborhood of Lyons there is more corn than wine. Towards Tains more wine than corn. From thence the plains, where best, are in corn, clover, almonds, mulberries, walnuts: where there is still some earth, they are in corn, almonds, and oaks. The hills are in vines. There is a good deal of forest-wood near Lyons, but not much afterwards. Scarcely any enclosures. There are a few small sheep before we reach Tains; there the'number increases.

Nature never formed a country of more savage aspect, than that on both sides the Rhone. A huge torrent rushes like an arrow between high precipices, often of massive rock, at other times of loose stone, with but little earth. Yet has the hand of man subdued this savage scene, by planting corn where there is a little fertility, trees where there is still less, and vines where there is none. On the whole, it assumes a romantic, picturesque, and pleasing air. The hills on the opposite side of the river, being high, steep, and laid up in terraces, are of a singular appearance. Where the hills are quite in waste, they are covered with broom, whins, box, and some clusters of small pines. The high mountains of Dauphine and Languedoc are now covered with snow. The almond is in general bloom, and the willow putting out its leaf. There were formerly olives at Tain; but a great cold, some years ago, killed them, and they have not been replanted. I am told at Montelimart, that an almond tree yields about three livres profit a year. Supposing them three toises apart, there will be one hundred to the arpent, which gives three hundred livres a year, besides the corn growing on the same ground. A league below Vienne, on the opposite side of the river, is Cote Rotie. It is a string of broken hills, extending a league on the river, from the village of Ampuis to the town of Condrieu. The soil is white, tinged a little, sometimes, with yellow, sometimes with red, stony, poor, and laid up in terraces. Those parts of the hills only, which look to the sun at mid-day, or the earlier hours of the afternoon, produce wines of the first quality. Seven hundred vines, three feet apart, yield a *feuillette*, which is about two and a half *pièces*, to the arpent. The best red wine is produced at the upper end, in the neighborhood of Ampuis; the best white, next to Condrieu. They sell of the first quality and last vintage, at one hundred and fifty livres the *pièce*, equal to twelve sous the bottle. Transportation to Paris is sixty livres, and the bottle four sous; so it may be delivered at Paris in bottles, at twenty sous. When old, it costs ten or eleven louis the *pièce*. There is a quality which keeps well, bears transportation, and cannot be drunk under four years. Another must be drunk at a year old. They are equal in flavor and price.

The wine called Hermitage, is made on the hills impending over the village of Tain; on one of which is the hermitage which gives name to the hills for about two miles, and to the wine made on them. There are but three of those hills which produce wine of the first quality, and of these, the middle regions only. They are about three hundred feet perpendicular height, three quarters of a mile in length, and have a southern aspect. The soil is scarcely tinged red, consists of small rotten stone, and is, where the best wine is made, without any perceptible mixture of earth. It is in sloping terraces. They use a little dung. An *homme de vignes*, which consists of seven hundred plants, three feet apart, yields generally about three quarters of a *pièce*, which is nearly four *pièces* to the arpent. When new, the pièce is sold at about two hundred and twenty-five livres; when old, at three hundred. It cannot be drunk under four years, and improves fastest in a hot situation. There is so little white made in proportion to the red, that it is difficult to buy it separate. They make the white sell the red. If bought separately, it is from fifteen to sixteen louis the pièce, new, and three livres the bottle, old. To give quality to the red, they mix one eighth of white grapes. Portage to Paris is seventy-two livres the pièce, weighing six hundred pounds. There are but about one thousand *pièces* of both red and white, of the first quality, made annually. Vineyards are never rented here, nor are laborers in the vineyard hired by the year. They leave buds proportioned to the strength of the vine, sometimes as much as fifteen inches. The last hermit died in 1751.

In the neighborhood of Montelimart, and below that, they plant vines in rows, six, eight, or ten feet apart, and two feet asunder in the row, filling the intervals with corn. Sometimes the vines are in double rows, two feet apart. I saw single asses in ploughs proportioned to their strength. There are few chateaux in this province. The people, too, are mostly gathered into villages. There are, however, some scattering farm-houses. These are made either of mud, or of round stone and mud. They make enclosures also, in both those ways. Day-laborers receive, sixteen or eighteen sous the day, and feed themselves. Those by the year receive, men three louis, women half that, and are fed. They rarely eat meat; a single hog, salted, being the year's stock for a family. But they have plenty of cheese, eggs, potatoes, and other vegetables, and walnut oil with their salad. It is a trade here, to gather dung along the road for their vines. This proves they have few cattle. I have seen neither hares nor partridges since I left Paris, nor wild fowl on any of the rivers. The roads from Lyons to St. Rambert are neither paved nor gravelled. After that, they are coated with broken flint. The ferry-boats on the Rhone and the Isere, are moved by the stream, and very rapidly. On each side of the river is a moveable stage, one end of which is on an axle and two wheels, which, according to the tide, can be advanced or withdrawn, so as to apply to the gunwale of the boat. The Praetorian Palace at Vienne, is forty-four feet wide, of the Corinthian order, four columns in front, and four in flank. It was begun in the year 400, and finished by Charlemagne.

The sepulchral Pyramid, a little way out of the town, has an order for its basement, the pedestal of which, from point to point of its cap, is twenty-four feet, one inch. At each angle, is a column, engaged one fourth in the wall. The circumference of the three fourths disengaged, is four feet four inches; consequently, the diameter is twenty-three inches. The base of the column indicates it to be Ionic, but the capitals are not formed. The cornice, too, is a bastard Ionic, without modillions or dentils. Between the columns, on each side, is an arch of eight feet, four inches, opening with a pilaster on each side of it. On the top of the basement is a zocle, in the plane of the frieze below. On that is the pyramid, its base in the plane of the collarins of the pilaster below. The pyramid is a little truncated on its top. This monument is inedited.

March 18. *Principality of Orange.* The plains on the Rhone here, are two or three leagues wide, reddish, good, in corn, clover, almonds, olives. No forests. Here begins the country of olives, there being very few till we enter this principality. They are the only tree which I see planted among vines. Thyme grows wild here on the hills. Asses, very small, sell here for two or three louis. The high hills in Dauphine are covered with snow. The remains of the Roman aqueduct are of brick: a fine pièce of Mosaic, still on its bed, forming the floor of a cellar. Twenty feet of it still visible. They are taking down the circular wall of the Amphitheatre to pave a road.

March 19 to 23. LANGUEDOC. *Pont-St.-Esprit. Bagnols. Connaux. Valignitres. Remoulins. St. Gervasy. Vismes. Pont d'Aries.* To Remoulins, there is a mixture of hill and dale. Thence to Nismes, hills on the right, on the left, plains extending to the Rhone and the sea. The hills are rocky. Where there is soil, it is reddish and poor. The -plains generally reddish and good, but stony. When you approach the Rhone, going to Arles, the soil becomes a dark gray loam with some sand, and very good. The culture is corn, clover, saintfoin, olives, vines, mulberries, willow, and some almonds. There is no forest. The hills are enclosed in dry stone-wall. Many sheep.

From the summit of the first hill, after leaving Pont-St.-Esprit, there is a beautiful view of the bridge at about two miles' distance, and a fine landscape of the country both ways. From thence, an excellent road, judiciously conducted, through very romantic scenes. In one part, descending the face of a hill, it is laid out in serpentine, and not zigzag, to ease the descent. In others, it passes through a winding meadow, from fifty to one hundred yards wide, walled, as it were, on both sides, by hills of rock; and at length issues into plain country. The waste hills are covered with thyme, box, and chene-vert. Where the body of the mountains has a surface of soil, the summit has sometimes a crown of rock, as observed in Champagne. At Nismes, the earth is full of lime-stone. The horses are shorn. They are now pruning the olive. A very good tree produces sixty pounds of olives, which yield fifteen pounds of oil: the best quality selling at twelve sous the pound, retail, and ten sous, wholesale. The high hills of Languedoc still covered with snow. The horse-chestnut and mulberry are leafing; apple trees and peas blossoming. The first butterfly I have seen. After the vernal equinox, they are often six or eight months without rain. Many separate farm-houses, numbers of people in rags, and abundance of beggars. The *mine* of wheat, weighing thirty pounds, costs four livres and ten sous. Wheat bread, three sous the pound. *Vin ordinaire*, good, and of a strong body, two or three sous the bottle. Oranges, one sous apiece. They are nearly finishing at Nismes a great mill, worked by a steam-engine, which pumps water from a lower into an upper cistern, from whence two overshot wheels are supplied, each of which turns two pair of stones. The upper cistern being once filled with water, it passes through the wheels into the lower one, from whence it is returned to the upper by the pumps. A stream of water of one quarter or one half inch diameter, supplies the waste of evaporation, absorption, fee. This is furnished from a well by a horse. The arches of the Pont-St.-Esprit are of eighty-eight feet. Wild figs, very flourishing, grow out of the joints of the Pont-du-Gard. The fountain of Nismes is so deep, that a stone was thirteen seconds descending from the surface to the bottom.

March 24. From Nismes to Arles. The plains extending from Nismes to the Rhone, in the direction of Aries, are broken in one place by a skirt of low hills. They are red and stony at first, but as you approach the Rhone, they are of a dark gray mould, with a little sand, and very good. They are in corn and clover, vines, olives, almonds, mulberries, and willow. There are some sheep, no wood, no enclosures.

The high hills of Languedoc are covered with snow. At an ancient church, in the suburbs of Aries, are some hundreds of ancient stone coffins, along the road-side. The ground is thence called *Les Champs Elysees*. In a vault in a church, are some curiously wrought, and in a back yard are many ancient statues, inscriptions, &c. Within the town are a part of two Corinthian columns, and of the pediment with which they were crowned, very rich, having belonged to the ancient capitol of the place.

But the principal monument here, is an amphitheatre, the external portico of which is tolerably complete. How many porticoes there were, cannot be seen; but at one of the principal gates there are still five, measuring, from out to in, seventy-eight feet, ten inches, the vault diminishing inwards. There are sixty-four arches, each of which is, from centre to centre, twenty feet, six inches. Of course, the diameter is of four hundred and thirty-eight feet; or of four hundred and fifty feet, if we suppose the four principal arches a little larger than the rest. The ground floor is supported on innumerable vaults. The first story, externally, has a tall pedestal, like a pilaster, between every two arches; the upper story, a column, the base of which would indicate it Corinthian.

Every column is truncated as low as the impost of the arch, but the arches are all entire. The whole of the upper entablature is gone, and of the Attic, if there was one. Not a single seat of the internal is visible. The whole of the inside, and nearly the whole of the outside, is masked by buildings. It is supposed there are one thousand inhabitants within the amphitheatre. The walls are more entire and firm than those of the *ampitheatre* at Nismes. I suspect its plan and distribution to have been very different from that.

Terrasson. The plains of the Rhone from Arles to this place, are a league or two wide; the mould is of a dark gray, good, in corn and lucerne. Neither wood, nor enclosures. Many sheep.

St. Remy. From Terrasson to St. Remy, is a plain of a league or two wide, bordered by broken hills of massive rock. It is gray and stony, mostly in olives. Some almonds, mulberries, willows, vines, corn, and lucerne. Many sheep. No forest, nor enclosures.

A laboring man's wages here, are one hundred and fifty livres, a woman's half, and fed. Two hundred and eighty pounds of wheat sell for forty-two livres. They make no butter here. It costs, when brought, fifteen sous the pound. Oil is ten sous the pound. Tolerably good olive trees yield, one with another, about twenty pounds of oil. An olive tree must be twenty years old before it has paid its own expenses. It lasts for ever. In 1765, it was so cold, that the Rhone was frozen over at Aries for two months. In 1767, there was a cold spell of a week, which killed all the olive trees. From being fine weather, in one hour there was ice hard enough to bear a horse. It killed people on the road. The old roots of the olive trees put out again. Olive grounds sell for twenty-four livres a tree, and lease at twenty-four sous the tree. The trees are fifteen pieds apart. But lucerne is a more profitable culture. An arpent yields one hundred quintals of hay a year, worth three livres the quintal. It is cut four or five times a year. It is sowed in the broadcast, and lasts five or six years. An arpent of ground for corn rents at from thirty to thirty-six livres. Their leases are for six or nine years. They plant willow for fire-wood, and for hoops to their casks. It seldom rains here in summer. There are some chateaux, many separate farm-houses, good, and ornamented in the small way, so as to show that the tenant's whole time is not occupied in procuring physical necessaries.

March 25. *Orgon. Pontroyal. St. Cannat.* From Orgon to Pontroyal, after quitting the plains of the Rhone, the country seems still to be a plain, cut into compartments by chains of mountains of massive rock, running through it in various directions. From Pontroyal to St. Cannat, the land lies rather in basins. The soil is very various, gray and clay, gray and stony, red and stony; sometimes good, sometimes middling, often barren. We find some golden willows. Towards Pontroyal, the hills begin to be in vines and afterwards in some pasture of greensward and clover. About Orgon are some enclosures of quick-set, others of conical yews planted close. Towards St. Cannat, they begin to be of stone.

The high mountains are covered with snow. Some separate farm-houses of mud. Near Pontroyal is a canal for watering the country; one branch goes to Terrasson, the other to Arles.

March 25, 26, 27, 28. *Aix.* The country is waving, in vines, pasture of greensward and clover, much enclosed with stone, and abounding with sheep.

On approaching Aix, the valley which opens from thence towards the mouth of the Rhone and the sea, is rich and beautiful; a perfect grove of olive trees, mixed among which are corn, lucerne, and vines. The waste grounds throw out thyme and lavender. Wheat bread is three sous the pound. Cow's milk sixteen sous the quart, sheep's milk six sous, butter of sheep's milk twenty sous the pound. Oil, of the best quality, is twelve sous the pound, and sixteen sous if it be virgin oil. This is what runs from the olive when put into the press, spontaneously; afterwards they are forced by the press and by hot water. Dung costs ten sous the one hundred pounds. Their fire-wood is chene-vert and willow. The latter is lopped every three years. An ass sells for from one to three louis; the best mules for thirty louis. The best asses will carry two hundred pounds; the best horses three hundred pounds; the best mules six hundred pounds. The temperature of the mineral waters of Aix is 90° of Fahrenheit's thermometer, at the spout. A mule eats half as much as a horse. The allowance to an ass for the day, is a handful of bran mixed with straw. The price of mutton and beef, about six and a half sous the pound. The beef comes from Auvergne, and is poor and bad. The mutton is small, but of excellent flavor. The wages of a laboring man are one hundred and fifty livres the year, a woman's sixty to sixty-six livres, and fed. Their bread is half wheat, half rye, made once in three or four weeks, to prevent too great a consumption. In the morning they eat bread with an anchovy, or an onion. Their dinner in the middle of the day is bread, soup, and vegetables. Their supper the same. With their vegetables, they have always oil and vinegar. The oil costs about eight sous the pound. They drink what is called *piquette.* This is made after the grapes are pressed, by pouring hot water on the pumice. On Sunday they have meat and wine. Their wood for building comes mostly from the Alps, down the Durance and Rhone. A stick of pine, fifty feet long, girting six feet and three inches at one end, and three feet three inches at the other, costs, delivered here, from fifty-four to sixty livres. Sixty pounds of wheat cost seven livres. One of their little asses will travel with his burthen about five or six leagues a day, and day by day; a mule from six to eight leagues.*

** It is twenty American miles from Aix to Marseilles, and they call it five leagues. Their league, then, is of four American miles.*

March 29. Marseilles. The country is hilly, intersected by chains of hills and mountains of massive rock. The soil is reddish, stony, and indifferent where best. Wherever there is any soil, it is covered with olives. Among these are corn, vines, some lucerne, mulberry, some almonds, and willow. Neither enclosures, nor forest. A very few sheep.

On the road I saw one of those little whirlwinds which we have in Virginia, also some gullied hill-sides. The people are in separate establishments. Ten morning observations of the thermometer, from the 20th to the 31st of March inclusive, made at Nismes, St. Remy, Aix, and Marseilles, give me an average of 52 1/2°, and 46° and 61°, for the greatest and least morning heats. Nine afternoon observations, yield an average of 62 2/3°, and 57° and 66°, the greatest and least. The longest day here, from sunrise to sunset, is fifteen hours and fourteen minutes; the shortest is eight hours and forty-six minutes; the latitude being ————.

There are no tides in the Mediterranean. It is observed to me, that the olive tree grows nowhere more than thirty leagues distant from that sea. I suppose, however, that both Spain and Portugal furnish proofs to the contrary, and doubt its truth as to Asia, Africa, and America. They are six or eight months at a time, here, without rain. The most delicate figs known in Europe, are those growing about this place, called *figues Marseilloises*, or *les veritables Marseilloises*, to distinguish them from others of inferior quality growing here. These keep any length of time. All others exude a sugar in the spring of the year, and become sour. The only process for preserving them, is drying them in the sun, without putting any thing to them whatever. They sell at fifteen sous the pound, while there are others as cheap as five sous the pound. I meet here a small dried grape from Smyrna, without a seed. There are few of the plants growing in this neighborhood. The best grape for drying, known here, is called *des Panses*. They are very large, with a thick skin and much juice. They are best against a wall of southern aspect, as their abundance of juice requires a great deal of sun to dry it. Pretty good fig trees are about the size of the apricot tree, and yield about twenty pounds of figs when dry, each. But the largest will yield the value of a louis. They are sometimes fifteen inches in diameter. It is said that the Marseilles fig degenerates when transported into any other part of the country. The leaves of the mulberry tree will sell for about three livres, the purchaser gathering them. The caper is a creeping plant. It is killed to the roots every winter. In the spring it puts out branches, which creep to the distance of three feet from the centre. The fruit forms on the stem, as that extends itself, and must be gathered every day, as it forms.

This is the work of women. The pistache grows in this neighborhood also, but not very good. They eat them in their milky state. Monsieur de Bergasse has a wine-cellar two hundred and forty *pieds* long, in which are one hundred and twenty tons, of from fifty to one hundred *pièces* each. These tons are twelve *pieds* diameter, the staves four inches thick, the heading two and a half *pouces* thick. The temperature of his cellar is of 9 1/2° of Reaumur. The best method of packing wine, when bottled, is to lay the bottles on their side, and cover them with sand. The 2d of April, the young figs are formed; the 4th we have Windsor beans. They have had asparagus ever since the middle of March. The 5th, I see strawberries and the Guelder rose in blossom. To preserve the raisin, it is first dipped into ley, and then dried in the sun. The aloe grows in the open ground. I measure a mule, not the largest, five feet and two inches high. Marseilles is in an amphitheatre, at the mouth of the Veaune, surrounded by high mountains of naked rock, distant two or three leagues. The country within that amphitheatre is a mixture of small hills, vallies, and plains. The latter are naturally rich. The hills and vallies are forced into production. Looking from the *Chateau de Notre Dame de la Garde*, it would seem as if there was a *bastide* for every arpent. The plain-lands sell for one hundred louis the *carterelle*, which is less than an acre. The ground of the arsenal in Marseilles sold for from fifteen to forty louis the square verge, being nearly the square yard English. In the fields open to the sea, they are obliged to plant rows of canes, every here and there, to break the force of the wind. Saw at the Chateau Borelli pumps worked by the wind.

April 6. From *Marseilles* to *Aubagne*. A valley on the Veaune, bordered on each side by high mountains of massive rock, on which are only some small pines. The interjacent valley is of small hills, vallies, and plains, reddish, gravelly, and originally poor, but fertilized by art, and covered with corn, vines, olives, figs, almonds, mulberries, lucerne, and clover. The river is twelve or fifteen feet wide, one or two feet deep, and rapid.

From *Aubagne* to *Cuges, Beausset, Toulon*. The road, quitting the Veaune and its wealthy valley, a little after Aubagne, enters those mountains of rock, and is engaged with them about a dozen miles. Then it passes six or eight miles through a country still very hilly and stony, but laid up in terraces, covered with olives, vines, and corn. It then follows for two or three miles a hollow between two of those high mountains, which has been, found or made by a small stream. The mountains then reclining a little from their perpendicular, and presenting a coat of soil, reddish, and tolerably good, have given place to the little village of Olioules, in the gardens of which are oranges in the open ground. It continues hilly till we enter the plain of Toulon. On different parts of this road there are figs in the open fields. At Cuges is a plain of about three fourths of a mile diameter, surrounded by high mountains of rock. In this the caper is principally cultivated. The soil is mulatto, gravelly, and of middling quality, or rather indifferent. The plants are set in *quincunx*, about eight feet apart. They have been covered during winter by a hill of earth a foot high. They are now enclosing, pruning, and ploughing them.

Toulon. From Olioules to Toulon the figs are in the open fields. Some of them have stems of fifteen inches diameter. They generally fork near the ground, but sometimes have a single stem of five feet long. They are as large as apricot trees. The olive trees of this day's journey are about the size of large apple trees. The people are in separate establishments. Toulon is in a valley at the mouth of the Goutier, a little river of the size of the Veaune; surrounded by high mountains of naked rock, leaving some space between them and the sea. This space is hilly, reddish, gravelly, and of middling quality, in olives, vines, corn, almonds, figs, and capers. The capers are planted eight feet apart. A bush yields, one year with another, two pounds, worth twelve sous the pound. Every plant, then, yields twenty-four sous, equal to one shilling sterling. An acre, containing six hundred and seventy-six plants, would yield thirty-three pounds sixteen shillings sterling. The fruit is gathered by women, who can gather about twelve pounds a day. They begin to gather about the last of June, and end about the middle of October. Each plant must be picked every day. These plants grow equally well in the best or worst soil, or even in the walls, where there is no soil. They will last the life of a man, or longer. The heat is so great at Toulon in summer, as to occasion very great cracks in the earth. Where the caper is in a soil that will admit it, they plough it. They have pease here through the winter, sheltering them occasionally; and they have had them ever since the 25th of March, without shelter.

April 6. *Hieres.* This is a plain of two or three miles diameter, bounded by the sea on one side, and mountains of rock on the other. The soil is reddish, gravelly, tolerably good, and well watered. It is in olives, mulberries, vines, figs, corn, and some flax. There are also some cherry trees. From Hieres to the sea, which is two or three miles, is a grove of orange trees, olives, and mulberries. The largest orange tree is of two feet diameter one way, and one foot the other (for the section of all the larger ones would be an oval, not a round), and about twenty feet high. Such a tree will yield about six thousand oranges a year. The garden of M. Fille has fifteen thousand six hundred orange, trees. Some years they yield forty thousand livres, some only ten thousand; but generally about twenty-five thousand. The trees are from eight to ten feet apart. They are blossoming and bearing, all the year, flowers and fruit in every stage at the same time. But the best fruit is that which is gathered in April and May. Hieres is a village of about five thousand inhabitants, at the foot of a mountain, which covers it from the north, and from which extends a plain of two or three miles to the sea-shore. It has no port. Here are palm trees twenty or thirty feet high, but they bear no fruit. There is also a botanical garden kept by the King. Considerable salt-ponds here. Hieres is six miles from the public road. It is built on a narrow spur of the mountain. The streets in every direction are steep, in steps of stairs, and about eight feet wide. No carriage of any kind can enter it. The wealthier inhabitants use *chaises à porteurs*. But there are few wealthy, the bulk of the inhabitants being laborers of the earth. At a league's distance in the sea is an island, on which is the Chateau de Géans, belonging to the Marquis de Pontoives: there is a causeway leading to it. The cold of the last November killed the leaves of a great number of the orange-trees, and some of the trees themselves.

From Hieres to *Cuers, Pignans, Luc*, is mostly a plain, with mountains on each hand at a mile or two distance. The soil is generally reddish, and the latter part very red and good. The growth is olives, figs, vines, mulberries, corn, clover, and lucerne. The olive trees are from three to four feet in diameter. There are hedges of pomegranates, sweet-briar, and broom. A great deal of thyme growing wild. There are some enclosures of stone; some sheep and goats.

April 9. From Luc to *Vidavban, Muy, Frejus*, the road leads through vallies, and crosses occasionally the mountains which separate them. The vallies are tolerably good, always red and stony, gravelly or gritty. Their produce as before. The mountains are barren.

Lesterelle, Napoule. Eighteen miles of ascent and descent of a very high mountain. Its growth, where capable of any, two-leaved pine, very small, and some chêne vert.

Antibes, Nice. From Napoule the road is generally near the sea, passing over little hills or strings of vallies, the soil stony, and much below mediocrity in its quality. Here and there is a good plain.

There is snow on the high mountains. The first frogs I have heard are of this day (the 9th). At Antibes are oranges in the open ground, but in small enclosures; palm trees also. From thence to the Var are the largest fig trees and olive trees I have seen. The fig trees are eighteen inches in diameter, and six feet stem; the olives sometimes six feet in diameter, and as large heads as the largest low-ground apple trees. This tree was but a shrub where I first fell in with it, and has become larger and larger to this place. The people are mostly in villages. The several provinces, and even cantons, are distinguished by the form of the women's hats, so that one may know of what canton a woman is by her hat.

Nice. The pine-bur is used here for kindling fires. The people are in separate establishments. With respect to the orange, there seems to be no climate on this side of the Alps sufficiently mild in itself to preserve it without shelter. At Olioules they are between two high mountains; at Hieres covered on the north by a very high mountain; at Antibes and Nice covered by mountains, and also within small, high enclosures. *Quære.* To trace the true line from east to west, which forms the northern and natural limit of that fruit? Saw an elder tree (sambucus) near Nice, fifteen inches in diameter, and eight feet stem. The wine made in this neighborhood is good, though not of the first quality. There are one thousand mules, loaded with merchandise, which pass every week between Nice and Turin, counting those coming as well as going.

April 13. *Scarena. Sospello.* There are no orange trees after we leave the environs of Nice. We lose the olive after rising a little above the village of Scarena, on Mount Braus, and find it again on the other side, a little before we get down to Sospello. But wherever there is soil enough it is terraced, and in corn. The waste parts are either in two-leaved pine and thyme, or of absolutely naked rock. Sospello is on a little torrent, called Bevera, which runs into the river Roia, at the mouth of which is Ventimiglia. The olive trees on the mountain are now loaded with fruit; while some at Sospello are in blossom. Fire-wood here and at Scarena costs fifteen sous the quintal.

April 14. *Ciandola. Tende.* In crossing Mount Brois we lose the olive tree after getting to a certain height, and find it again on the other side at the village of Breglio. Here we come to the river Roia, which, after receiving the branch on which is Sospello, leads to the sea at Ventimiglia. The Roia is about twelve yards wide, and abounds with speckled trout. Were a road made from Breglio, along the side of the Roia to Ventimiglia, it might turn the commerce of Turin to this last place instead of Nice; because it would avoid the mountains of Braus and Brois, leaving only that of Tende; that is to say, it would avoid more than half the difficulties of the passage. Further on, we come to the Chateau di Saorgio, where a scene is presented the most singular and picturesque I ever saw. The castle and village seem hanging to a cloud in front. On the right is a mountain cloven through, to let pass a gurgling stream; on the left, a river, over which is thrown a magnificent bridge. The whole forms a basin, the sides of which are shagged with rocks, olive trees, vines, herds, &c. Near here I saw a tub-wheel without a ream; the trunk descended from the top of the water-fall to the wheel in a direct line, but with the usual inclination. The produce along this passage is most generally olives, except on the heights as before observed; also corn, vines, mulberries, figs, cherries, and walnuts. They have cows, goats, and sheep. In passing on towards Tende, olives fail us ultimately at the village of Fontan, and there the chestnut trees begin in good quantity. Ciandola consists of only two houses, both taverns. Tende is a very inconsiderable village, in which they have not yet the luxury of glass windows: nor in any of the villages on this passage have they yet the fashion of powdering the hair. Common stone and limestone are so abundant, that the apartments of every story are vaulted with stone to save wood.

April 15. *Limone. Coni.* I see abundance of lime-stone as far as the earth is uncovered with snow; i.e. within half or three quarters of an hour's walk of the top. The snows descend much lower on the eastern than western side. Wherever there is soil, there is corn quite to the commencement of the snows, and I suppose under them also. The waste parts are in two-leaved pine, lavender, and thyme. From the foot of the mountain to Coni the road follows a branch of the Po, the plains of which begin narrow, and widen at length into a general plain country, bounded on one side by the Alps. They are good, dark-colored, sometimes tinged with red, and in pasture, corn, mulberries, and some almonds. The hill-sides bordering these plains are reddish, and where they admit of it are in corn; but this is seldom. They are mostly in chestnut, and often absolutely barren. The whole of the plains are plentifully watered from the river, as is much of the hill-side. A great deal of golden willow all along the rivers on the whole of this passage through the Alps. The southern parts of France, but still more the passage through the Alps, enable one to form a scale of the tenderer plants, arranging them according to their several powers of resisting cold. Ascending three different mountains, Braus, Brois, and Tende, they disappear one after another: and descending on the other side, they show themselves again one after another. This is their order, from the tenderest to the hardiest. Caper, orange, palm, aloe, olive, pomegranate, walnut, fig, almond. But this must be understood of the plant; for as to the fruit, the order is somewhat different. The caper, for example, is the tenderest plant, yet being so easily protected, it is the most certain in its fruit. The almond, the hardiest plant, loses its fruit the oftenest on account of its forwardness. The palm, hardier than the caper and the orange, never produces perfect fruit in these parts. Coni is a considerable town, and pretty well built. It is walled.

April 16. *Centale. Savigliano. Racconigi. Poirino. Turin.* The Alps, as far as they are in view from north to south, show the gradation of climate by the line which terminates the snows lying on them. This line begins at their foot northwardly, and rises as they pass on to the south, so as to be half way up their sides on the most southern undulations of the mountain now in view. From the mountains to Turin we see no tree tenderer than the walnut. Of these, as well as of almonds and mulberries, there are a few: somewhat more of vines, but most generally willows and poplars. Corn is sowed with all these. They mix with them also clover and small grass. The country is a general plain; the soil dark, and sometimes, though rarely, reddish. It is rich, and much infested with wild onions. At Racconigi I see the tops and shocks of maize, which prove it is cultivated here: but it can be in small quantities only, because I observe very little ground but what has already something else in it. Here and there are small patches prepared, I suppose, for maize. They have a method of planting the vine, which I have not seen before. At intervals of about eight feet they plant from two to six plants of vine in a cluster At each cluster they fix a forked staff, the plane of the prongs of the fork at a right angle with the row of vines. Athwart these prongs they lash another staff, like a handspike, about eight feet long, horizontally, seven or eight feet from the ground. Of course, it crosses the rows at right angles. The vines are brought from the foot of the fork up to this cross-piece, turned over it, and conducted along over the next, the next, and so on, as far as they will extend, the whole forming an arbor eight feet wide and high and of the whole length of the row, little interrupted by the stems of the vines, which being close around the fork, pass up through hoops, so as to occupy a space only of small diameter. All the buildings in this country are of brick, sometimes covered with plaister, sometimes not. There is a very large and handsome bridge, of seven arches, over the torrent of Sangone. We cross the Po in swinging batteaux. Two are placed side by side, and kept together by a plank-floor, common to both, and lying on the gunwales. The carriage drives on this, without taking out any of the horses. About one hundred and fifty yards up the river is a fixed stake, and a rope tied to it, the other end of which is made fast to one side of the batteaux, so as to throw them oblique to the current. The stream then acting on them, as on an inclined plane, forces them across the current in the portion of a circle, of which the rope is the radius. To support the rope in its whole length, there are two intermediate canoes, about fifty yards apart, in the heads of which are short masts. To the top of these the rope is lashed, the canoes being free otherwise to concur with the general vibration in their smaller arcs of circles. The Po is there about fifty yards wide, and about one hundred in the neighborhood of Turin.

April 17, 18. *Turin.* The first nightingale I have heard this year is to-day (18th). There is a red wine of Nebiule made in this neighborhood, which is very singular. It is about as sweet as the silky Madeira, as astringent on the palate as Bordeaux, and as brisk as Champagne. It is a pleasing wine. At Moncaglieri, about six miles from Turin, on the right side of the Po, begins a ridge of mountains, which, following the Po by Turin, after some distance, spreads wide, and forms the duchy of Montferrat. The soil is mostly red, and in vines, affording a wine called Montferrat, which is thick and strong.

April 19. *Settimo. Chivasso. Ciliano. S. Germano. Vercelli.* The country continues plain and rich, the soil black. The culture, corn, pasture, maize, vines, mulberries, walnuts, some willow, and poplar. The maize bears a very small proportion to the small grain. The earth is formed into ridges from three to four feet wide, and the maize sowed in the broad-cast, on the higher parts of the ridge, so as to cover a third or half of the whole surface. It is sowed late in May. This country is plentifully and beautifully watered at present. Much of it is by torrents, which are dry in summer. These torrents make a great deal of waste ground, covering it with sand and stones. These wastes are sometimes planted in trees, sometimes quite unemployed. They make hedges of willows, by setting the plants from one to three feet apart. When they are grown to the height of eight or ten feet, they bend them down, and interlace them one with another. I do not see any of these, however, which are become old. Probably, therefore, they soon die. The women here smite on the anvil, and work with the maul and spade. The people of this country are ill dressed in comparison with those of France, and there are more spots of uncultivated ground. The plough here is made with a single handle, which is a beam twelve feet long, six inches in diameter below, and tapered to about two inches at the upper end. They use goads for the oxen, not whips. The first swallows I have seen are to-day. There is a wine called Gatina, made in the neighborhood of Vercelli, both red and white. The latter resembles Calcavallo. There is also a red wine of Salusola, which is esteemed. It is very light. In the neighborhood of Vercelli begin the rice-fields. The water with which they are watered is very dear. They do not permit rice to be sown within two miles of the cities, on account of the insalubrity. Notwithstanding this, when the water is drawn off the fields, in August, the whole country is subject to agues and fevers. They estimate, that the same measure of ground yields three times as much rice as wheat, and with half the labor. They are now sowing. As soon as sowed, they let on the water two or three inches deep. After six weeks, or two months, they draw it off to weed; then let it on again, and it remains till August, when it is drawn off, about three or four weeks before the grain is ripe. In September they cut it. It is first threshed; then beaten in the mortar to separate the husk; then, by different siftings, it is separated into three qualities. Twelve rupes, equal to three hundred pounds of twelve ounces each, sell for sixteen livres, money of Piedmont, where the livre is exactly the shilling of England. Twelve rupes of maize sell for nine livres. The machine for separating the husk is thus made. In the axis of a water-wheel are a number of arms inserted, which, as they revolve, catches each the cog of a pestle, lifts it to a certain height, and lets it fall again. These pestles are five and a quarter inches square, ten feet long, and at their lower end formed into a truncated cone of three inches diameter, where cut off. The conical part is covered with iron. The pestles are ten and a half inches apart in the clear. They pass through two horizontal beams, which string them, as it were, together, and while the mortises in the beams are so loose, as to let the pestles work vertically, it restrains them to that motion. There is a mortar of wood, twelve or fifteen inches deep, under each pestle, covered with a board, the hole of which is only large enough to let the pestle pass freely. There are two arms in the axis for every pestle, so that the pestle gives two strokes for every revolution of the wheel. Poggio, a muleteer, who passes every week between Vercelli and Genoa, will smuggle a sack of rough rice for me to, Genoa; it being death to export it in that form. They have good cattle, and in good number, mostly cream-colored; and some middle-sized sheep. The streams furnish speckled trout.

April 20. *Novara. Buffalora. Sedriano. Milan.* From Vercelli to Novara the fields are all in rice, and now mostly under water. The dams separating the several water-plats or ponds, are set in willow. At Novara there are some figs in the gardens in situations well protected. From Novara to the Ticino it is mostly stony and waste, grown up in broom. From Ticino to Milan it is all in corn. Among the corn are willows, principally, a good many mulberries, some walnuts, and here and there an almond. The country still a plain, the soil black and rich, except between Novara and the Ticino, as before mentioned. There is very fine pasture round Vercelli and Novara to the distance of two miles, within which rice is not permitted. We cross the Sisto on the same kind of vibrating or pendulum boat as on the Po. The river is eighty or ninety yards wide; the rope fastened to an island two hundred yards above, and supported by five intermediate canoes. It is about one and a half inches in diameter. On these rivers they use a short oar of twelve feet long, the flat end of which is hooped with iron, shooting out a prong at each corner, so that it may be used occasionally as a setting-pole. There is snow on the Apennines, near Genoa. They have still another method here of planting the vine. Along rows of trees, they lash poles from tree to tree. Between the trees, are set vines, which, passing over the pole, are carried on to the pole of the, next tree, whose vines are in like manner brought to this, and twined together; thus forming the intervals between the rows of trees, alternately, into arbors and open space. They have another method also of making quick-set hedges. Willows are planted from one to two feet apart, and interlaced, so that every one is crossed by three or four others.

April 21, 22. *Milan.* Figs and pomegranates grow here, unsheltered, as I am told. I saw none, and therefore suppose them rare. They had formerly olives; but a great cold, in 1709, killed them, and they have not been replanted. Among a great many houses painted *al fresco*, the Casa Roma and Casa Candiani, by Appiani, and Casa Belgioiosa, by Martin, are superior. In the second, is a small cabinet, the ceiling of which is in small hexagons, within which are cameos and heads painted alternately, no two the same. The *salon* of the Casa-Belgioiosa is superior to any thing 1 have ever seen. The mixture called *scagliuola*, of which they make their walls and floors, is so like the finest marble, as to be scarcely distinguishable from it. The nights of the 20th and 21st instant, the rice ponds froze half an inch thick. Droughts of two or three months are not uncommon here, in summer. About five years ago, there was such a hail as to kill cats. The Count del Verme tells me of a pendulum odometer for the wheel of a carriage. Leases here are mostly for nine years. Wheat costs a louis d'or the one hundred and forty pounds. A laboring man receives sixty livres, and is fed and lodged. The trade of this country is principally rice, raw silk, and cheese.

April 23. *Casino*, five miles from Milan. I examined another rice-beater of six pestles. They are eight feet nine inches long. Their ends, instead of being a truncated cone, have nine teeth of iron, bound closely together. Each tooth is a double pyramid, joined at the base. When put together, they stand with the upper ends placed in contact, so as to form them into one great cone, and the lower ends diverging. The upper are socketed into the end of the pestle, and the lower, when a little blunted by use, are not unlike the jaw-teeth of the mammoth, with their studs. They say here, that pestles armed with these teeth, clean the rice faster, and break it less. The mortar, too, is of stone, which is supposed as good as wood, and more durable. One half of these pestles are always up. They rise about twenty-one inches; and each makes thirty-eight strokes in a minute; one hundred pounds of rough rice is put into the six mortars, and beaten somewhat less than a quarter of an hour. It is then taken out, put into a sifter of four feet diameter, suspended horizontally; sifted there; shifted into another of the same size; sifted there; returned to the mortars; beaten a little more than a quarter of an hour; sifted again; and it is finished. The six pestles will clear four thousand pounds in twenty-four hours. The pound here is twenty-eight ounces: the ounce equal to that of Paris. The best rice requires half an hour's boiling; a more indifferent kind, somewhat less. To sow the rice, they first plough the ground, then level it with a drag-harrow, and let on the water; when the earth has become soft, they smooth it with a shovel under the water, and then sow the rice in the water.

Rozzano. Parmesan cheese. It is supposed this was formerly made at Parma, and took its name thence; but none is made there now. It is made through all the country extending from Milan, for one hundred and fifty miles. The most is made about Lodi. The making of butter being connected with that of making cheese, both must be described together. There are, in the stables I saw, eighty-five cows, fed on hay and grass, not on grain. They are milked twice in twenty-four hours, ten cows yielding at the two milkings a *brenta* of milk, which is twenty-four of our gallons. The night's milk is scummed in the morning at daybreak, when the cows are milked again, and the new milk mixed with the old. In three hours, the whole mass is scummed a second time, the milk remaining in a kettle for cheese, and the cream being put into a cylindrical churn, shaped like a grind-stone, eighteen inches radius, and fourteen inches thick. In this churn, there are three staves pointing inwardly, endwise, to break the current of the milk. Through its centre passes an iron axis, with a handle at each end. It is turned, about an hour and an half, by two men, till the butter is produced. Then they pour off the butter-milk, and put in some water which they agitate backwards and forwards about a minute, and pour it off. They take out the butter, press it with their hands into loaves, and stamp it. It has no other washing. Sixteen American gallons of milk yield fifteen pounds of butter, which sell at twenty-four sous the pound.

The milk, which, after being scummed as before, had been put into a copper kettle, receives its due quantity of rennet, and is gently warmed, if the season requires it. In about four hours, it becomes a slip. Then the whey begins to separate. A little, of it is taken out. The curd is then thoroughly broken by a machine like a chocolate-mill. A quarter of an ounce of saffron is put to seven brentas of milk, to give color to the cheese. The kettle is then moved over the hearth, and heated by a quick fire till the curd is hard enough, being broken into small lumps by continued stirring. It is moved off the fire, most of the whey taken out, the curd compressed into a globe by the hand, a linen cloth slipped under it, and it is drawn out in that. A loose hoop is then laid on a bench, and the curd, as wrapped in the linen, is put into the hoop: it is a little pressed by the hand, the hoop drawn tight, and made fast. A board, two inches thick, is laid on it, and a stone on that, of about twenty pounds weight. In an hour, the whey is run off, and the cheese finished. They sprinkle a little salt on it every other day in summer, and every day in winter, for six weeks. Seven *brentas* of milk make a cheese of fifty pounds, which requires six months to ripen, and is then dried to forty-five pounds. It sells on the spot for eighty-eight livres, the one hundred pounds. There are now one hundred and fifty cheeses in this dairy. They are nineteen inches diameter, and six inches thick. They make a cheese a day, in summer, and two in three days, or one in two days, in winter.

The whey is put back into the kettle, the butter-milk poured into it, and of this, they make a poor cheese for the country people. The whey of this is given to the hogs. Eight men suffice to keep the cows, and to do all the business of this dairy. *Mascarponi*, a kind of curd, is made by pouring some butter-milk into cream, which is thereby curdled, and is then pressed in a linen cloth.

The ice-houses at Rozzano are dug about fifteen feet deep, and twenty feet diameter, and poles are driven down all round. A conical thatched roof is then put over them, fifteen feet high, and pieces of wood are laid at bottom, to keep the ice out of the water which drips from it, and goes off by a sink. Straw is laid on this wood, and then the house filled with ice, always putting straw between the ice and the walls, and covering ultimately with straw. About a third is lost by melting. Snow gives the most delicate flavor to creams; but ice is the most powerful congealer, and lasts longest. A tuft of trees surrounds these ice-houses.

Round Milan, to the distance of five miles, are corn, pasture, gardens, mulberries, willows, and vines. For, in this state, rice ponds are not permitted within five miles of the cities.

Binasco. Pavia. Near Casino the rice-ponds begin, and continue to within five miles of Pavia, the whole ground being in rice, pasture, and willows. The pasture is in the rice grounds which are resting. In the neighborhood of Pavia, again, are corn, pasture, &c. as round Milan. They gave me green pease at Pavia.

April 24. *Voghera. Tortona. Novi.* From Pavia to Novi corn, pasture, vines, mulberries, willows; but no rice. The country continues plain, except that the Apennines are approaching on the left. The soil, always good, is dark till we approach Novi, and then red. We cross the Po where it is three hundred yards wide, in a pendulum boat. The rope is fastened on one side of the river, three hundred yards above, and supported by eight intermediate canoes, with little masts in them to give a greater elevation to the rope. We pass in eleven minutes. Women, girls, and boys are working with the hoe, and breaking the clods with mauls.

April 25. *Voltaggio. Campo-Marone. Genoa.* At Novi, the Apennines begin to rise. Their growth of timber is oak, tall, small, and knotty, and chestnut. We soon lose the walnut, ascending, and find it again, about one fourth of the way down, on the south side. About halfway down, we find figs and vines, which continue fine and in great abundance. The Apennines are mostly covered with soil, and are in corn, pasture, mulberries and figs, in the parts before indicated. About half way from their foot to Genoa, at Campo-Marone, we find again the olive tree. Hence the produce becomes mixed, of all the kinds before mentioned. The method of sowing the Indian corn at Campo-Marone, is as follows. With a hoe shaped like the blade of a trowel, two feet long, and six inches broad at its upper end, pointed below, and a little curved, they make a trench. In that, they drop the grains six inches apart. Then two feet from that, they make another trench, throwing the earth they take out of that on the grain of the last one, with a singular slight and quickness; and so through the whole piece. The last trench is filled with the earth adjoining.

April 26. *Genoa.* Strawberries at Genoa. Scaffold poles for the upper parts of a wall, as for the third story, rest on the window sills of the story below. Slate is used here for paving, for steps, for stairs (the rise as well as tread), and for fixed Venetian blinds. At the Palazzo Marcello Durazzo, benches with straight legs, and bottoms of cane. At the Palazzo del Prencipe Lomellino, at Sestri, a phaeton with a canopy. At the former, tables folding into one plane. At Nervi they have pease, strawberries, &c. all the year round. The gardens of the Count Durazzo at Nervi, exhibit as rich a mixture of the *utile dulci*, as I ever saw. All the environs in Genoa are in olives, figs, oranges, mulberries, corn, and garden-stuff. Aloes in many places, but they never flower.

April 28. *Noli.* The Apennine and Alps appear to me to be one and the same continued ridge of mountains, separating every where the waters of the Adriatic Gulf from those of the Mediterranean. Where it forms an elbow, touching the Mediterranean, as a smaller circle touches a larger, within which it is inscribed, in the manner of a tangent, the name changes from Alps to Apennine. It is the beginning of the Apennine which constitutes the state of Genoa, the mountains there generally falling down in barren, naked precipices into the sea. Wherever there is soil on the lower parts, it is principally in olives and figs, in vines also, mulberries, and corn. Where there are hollows well protected, there are oranges. This is the case at Golfo della Spezia, Sestri, Bugiasco, Nervi, Genoa, Pegli, Savona, Finale, Oneglia (where there are abundance), St. Rerno, Ventimiglia, Mentone, and Monaco. Noli, into which I was obliged to put, by a change of wind, is forty miles from Genoa. There are twelve hundred inhabitants in the village, and many separate houses round about. One of the precipices hanging over the sea, is covered with aloes. But neither here, nor any where else I have been, could I procure satisfactory information that they ever flower. The current of testimony is to the contrary. Noli furnishes many fishermen. Paths penetrate up into the mountains in several directions, about three fourths of a mile; but these are practicable only for asses and mules. I saw no cattle nor sheep in the settlement. The wine they make, is white and indifferent. A curious cruet for oil and vinegar in one piece, I saw here. A bishop resides here, whose revenue is two thousand livres, equal to sixty-six guineas. I heard a nightingale here.

April 29. *Albenga.* In walking along the shore from Louano to this place, I saw no appearance of shells. The tops of the mountains are covered with snow, while there are olive trees, &c. on the lower parts. I do not remember to have seen assigned any where, the cause of the apparent color of the sea. Its water is generally clear and colorless, if taken up and viewed in a glass. That of the Mediterranean is remarkably so. Yet in the mass, it assumes, *by reflection*, the color of the sky or atmosphere, black, green, blue, according to the state of the weather. If any person wished to retire from his acquaintance, to live absolutely unknown, and yet in the midst of physical enjoyments, it should be in some of the little villages of this coast, where air, water, and earth concur to offer what each has, most precious. Here are nightingales, beccaficas, ortolans, pheasants, partridges, quails, a superb climate, and the power of changing it from summer to winter at any moment, by ascending the mountains. The earth furnishes wine, oil, figs, oranges, and every production of the garden, in every season. The sea yields lobsters, crabs, oysters, tunny, sardines, anchovies, &c. Ortolans sell, at this time, at thirty sous, equal to one shilling sterling, the dozen. At this season, they must be fattened. Through the whole of my route from Marseilles, I observe they plant a great deal of cane or reed, which is convenient while growing, as a cover from the cold and boisterous winds, and when cut, it serves for espaliers to vines, pease, &c. Through Piedmont, Lombardy, the Milanese, and Genoese, the garden bean is a great article of culture; almost as much so as corn. At Albenga, is a rich plain opening from between two ridges of mountains, triangularly, to the sea, and of several miles extent. Its growth is olives, figs, mulberries, vines, corn, and beans. There is some pasture. A bishop resides here, whose revenue is forty thousand livres. This place is said to be rendered unhealthy in summer, by the river which passes through the valley.

April 30. *Oneglia.* The wind continuing contrary, I took mules at Albenga for Oneglia. Along this tract are many of the tree called *caroubier*, being a species of locust. It is the *ceratonia siliqua* of Linnaeus. Its pods furnish food for horses, and also for the poor, in time of scarcity. It abounds in Naples and Spain. Oneglia and Port Maurice, which are within a mile of each other, are considerable places, and in a rich country. At St. Remo, are abundance of oranges and lemons, and some palm trees.

May 1. *Ventimiglia. Mentone. Monaco. Nice.* At Bordighera, between Ventimiglia and Mentone, are extensive plantations of palms, on the hill as well as in the plain. They bring fruit, but it does not ripen. Something is made of the midrib which is in great demand at Rome, on the Palm Sunday, and which renders this tree profitable here. From Mentone to Monaco, there is more good land, and extensive groves of oranges and lemons. Orange water sells here at forty sous, equal to sixteen pence sterling, the American quart. The distances on this coast are, from La Spezia, at the eastern end of the territories of Genoa, to Genoa, fifty-five miles, geometrical; to Savona, thirty; Albenga, thirty; Oneglia, twenty; Ventimiglia, twenty-five; Monaco, ten; Nice, ten; in the whole, one hundred and eighty miles. A superb road might be made along the margin of the sea from La Spezai, where the champaign country of Italy opens, to Nice, where the Alps go off northwardly, and the post roads of France begin; and it might even follow the margin of the sea quite to Cette. By this road, travellers would enter Italy without crossing the Alps, and all the little insulated villages of the Genoese would communicate together, and in time, form one continued village along that road.

May 3. *Luc, Brignoles. Tourves. Pourcieux. La Galiniere.* Long, small mountains, very rocky, the soil reddish, from bad to middling; in olives, grapes, mulberries, vines, and corn. Brignolles is an extensive plain, between two ridges of mountains, and along a water-course which continues to Tourves. Thence to Pourcieux we cross a mountain, low and easy. The country is rocky and poor. To La Galiniere are waving grounds, bounded by mountains of rock at a little distance. There are some enclosures of dry wall from Luc to La Galiniere; also, sheep and hogs. There is snow on the high mountains. I see no plums in the vicinities of Brignoles; which makes me conjecture that the celebrated plum of that name is not derived from this place.

May 8. *Orgon. Avignon. Vaucluse.* Orgon is on the Durance. From thence, its plain opens till it becomes common with that of the Rhone; so that from Orgon to Avignon is entirely a plain of rich dark loam, which is in willows, mulberries, vines, corn, and pasture. A very few figs. I see no olives in this plain. Probably the cold winds have too much power here. From the Bac de Nova (where we cross the Durance) to Avignon, is about nine American miles; and from the same Bac to Vaucluse, eleven miles. In the valley of Vaucluse, and on the hills impending over it, are olive trees. The stream issuing from the fountain of Vaucluse is about twenty yards wide, four or five feet deep, and of such rapidity that it could not be stemmed by a canoe. They are now mowing hay, and gathering mulberry leaves. The high mountains just back of Vaucluse, are covered with snow. Fine trout in the stream of Vaucluse, and the valley abounds peculiarly with nightingales. The *vin blanc* de M. de Rochequde of Avignon, resembles dry Lisbon. He sells it, at six years old, for twenty-two sous the bottle, the price of the bottle, &c. included.

Avignon. Remoulins. Some good plains, but generally hills, stony and poor. In olives, mulberries, vines, and corn. Where it is waste the growth is *chéne-vert*, box, furze, thyme, and rosemary.

May 10. *Lismes. Lunel.* Hills on the right, plains on the left. The soil reddish, a little stony, and of middling quality. The produce, olives, mulberries, vines, corn, saintfoin. No wood and few enclosures. Lunel is famous for its *vin de muscat blanc*, thence called Lunel, or *vin muscat de Lunel.* It is made from the raisin muscat, without fermenting the grain in the hopper. When fermented, it makes a red muscat, taking the tinge from the dissolution of the skin of the grape, which injures the quality. When a red muscat is required, they prefer coloring it with a little Alicant wine. But the white is best. The *pièce* of two hundred and forty bottles, after being properly drawn off from its lees, and ready for bottling, costs from one hundred and twenty to two hundred livres, the first, quality and last vintage. It cannot be bought old, the demand being sufficient to take it all the first year. There are not more than from fifty to one hundred *pièces* a year, made of this first quality. A *setterie* yields about one *pièce*, and my informer supposes there are about two *setteries* in an arpent. Portage to Paris, by land, is fifteen livres the quintal. The best *récoltes* are those of M. Bouquet and M. Tremoulet. The vines are in rows four feet apart, every way.

May 11. *Montpelier.* Snow on the Cevennes, still visible from here. With respect to the muscat grape, of which the wine is made, there are two kinds, the red and the white. The first has a red skin, but a white juice. If it be fermented in the *cuve*, the coloring matter which resides in the skin, is imparted to the wine. If not fermented in the *cuve*, the wine is white. Of the white grape, only a white wine can be made. The species of saintfoin cultivated here by the name of *sparsette*, is the *hedysarum onobrychis*. They cultivate a great deal of madder (*garance*) *rubia tinctorum* here, which is said to be immensely profitable. Monsieur de Gouan tells me, that the pine, of which they use the burs for fuel, is the *pinus sativus*, being two-leaved. They use-for an edging to the borders of their gardens, the santolina, which they call *garderobe*. I find the yellow clover here, in a garden, and the large pigeon succeeding well, confined in a house.

May 12. *Frontignan*. Some tolerably good plains in olives, vines, corn, saintfoin, and lucerne. A great proportion of the hills are waste. There are some enclosures of stone, and some sheep. The first four years of madder are unproductive; the fifth and sixth yield the whole value of the land. Then it must be renewed. The *sparsette* is the common or true saintfoin. It lasts about five years: in the best land it is cut twice, in May and September, and yields three thousand pounds of dry hay to the setterie, the first cutting, and five hundred pounds, the second. The *setterie* is of seventy-five *dextres en tout sens*, supposed about two arpents. Lucerne is the best of all forage; it is sowed herein the broad-cast, and lasts about twelve or fourteen years. It is cut four times a year, and yields six thousand pounds of dry hay, at the four cuttings, to the setterie. The territory in which the *vin muscat de Frontignan* is made, is about a league of three thousand *toises* long, and one fourth of a league broad. The soil is reddish and stony, often as much stone as soil. On the left, it is a plain, on the right hills. There are made about one thousand *pièces* (of two hundred and fifty bottles each) annually, of which six hundred are of the first quality, made on the *coteaux*. Of these, Madame Soubeinan makes two hundred, Monsieur Reboulle ninety, Monsieur Lambert, *medecin de la faculte de Montpelier*, sixty, Monsieur Thomas, *notaire*, fifty, Monsieur Argilliers fifty, Monsieur Audibert forty; equal to four hundred and ninety; and there are some small proprietors who make small quantities. The first quality is sold, *brut*, for one hundred and twenty livres the *pièce*; but it is then thick, and must have a winter and the *fouet*, to render it potable and brilliant. The *fouet* is like a chocolate-mill, the handle of iron, the brush of stiff hair. In bottles, this wine costs twenty-four sous, the bottle, &c. included. It is potable the April after it is made, is best that year, and after ten years begins to have a pitchy taste, resembling it to Malaga. It is not permitted to ferment more than half a day, because it would not be so liquorish. The best color, and its natural one, is the amber. By force of whipping, it is made white, but loses flavor. There are but two or three *pièces* a year of red Muscat made; there being but one vineyard of the red grape, which belongs to a baker called Pascal. This sells in bottles at thirty sous, the bottle included. Rondelle, *négociant en vin, Porte St. Bernard, fauxbourg St. Germain, Paris*, buys three hundred pieces of the first quality every year. The *coteaux* yield about half a piece to the *setterie*, the plains a whole piece. The inferior quality is not at all esteemed. It is bought by the merchants of Cette, as is also the wine of Beziers, and sold by them for Frontignan of the first quality. They sell thirty thousand *pièces* a year under that name. The town of Frontignan marks its casks with a hot iron: an individual of that place, having two casks emptied, was offered forty livres for the empty cask by a merchant of Cette. The town of Frontignan contains about two thousand inhabitants; it is almost on the level of the ocean. Transportation to Paris is fifteen livres the quintal, and takes fifteen days. The price of packages is about eight livres eight sous the one hundred bottles. A *setterie* of good vineyard sells for from three hundred and fifty to five hundred livres, and rents for fifty livres. A laboring man hires at one hundred and fifty livres the year, and is fed and lodged; a woman at half as much. Wheat sells at ten livres the *settier*, which weighs one hundred pounds, *poids de table*. They make some Indian corn here, which is eaten by the poor. The olives do not extend northward of this into the country above twelve or fifteen leagues. In general, the olive country in Languedoc is about fifteen leagues broad. More of the waste lands between Frontignan and Mirval are capable of culture; but it is a marshy country, very subject to fever and ague, and generally unhealthy. Thence arises, as is said, a want of hands.

Cette. There are in this town about ten thousand inhabitants. Its principal commerce is wine; it furnishes great quantities of grape-pumice for making *verdigrise.* They have a very growing commerce; but it is kept under by the privileges of Marseilles.

May 13. *Agde.* On the right of the Etang de Thau are plains of some width, then hills, in olives, vines, mulberry, corn, and pasture. On the left a narrow sand-bar, separating the Etang from the sea, along which it is proposed to make a road from Cette to Agde. In this case, the post would lead from Montpelier by Cette and Agde to Beziers, being leveller, and an hour or an hour and a half nearer. Agde contains six or eight thousand inhabitants.

May 14. *Beziers.* Rich plains in corn, saintfoin, and pasture; hills at a little distance to the right in olives; the soil both of hill and plain is red going from Agde to Beziers. But at Beziers the country becomes hilly, and is in olives, corn, saintfoin, pasture, some vines, and mulberries.

May 15. *Beziers. Argilies. Le Saumal.* From Argilies to Saumal are considerable plantations of vines. Those on the red hills, to the right, are said to produce good wine. No wood, no enclosures. There are sheep and good cattle. The Pyrenees are covered with snow. I am told they are so in certain parts all the year. The canal of Languedoc, along which I now travel, is six *toises* wide at bottom, and ten *toises* at the surface of the water, which is one *toise* deep. The barks which navigate it are seventy and eighty feet long, and seventeen or eighteen feet wide. They are drawn by one horse, and worked by two hands, one of which is generally a woman. The locks are mostly kept by women, but the necessary operations are much too laborious for them. The encroachments by the men, on the offices proper for the women, is a great derangement in the order of things. Men are shoemakers, tailors, upholsterers, staymakers, mantua-makers, cooks, housekeepers, house-cleaners, bed-makers, they *coiffe* the ladies, and bring them to bed: the women, therefore, to live, are obliged to undertake the offices which they abandon. They become porters, carters, reapers, sailors, lock-keepers, smiters on the anvil, cultivators of the earth, &c. Can we wonder, if such of them as have a little beauty, prefer easier courses to get their livelihood, as long as that beauty lasts? Ladies who employ men in the offices which should be reserved for their sex, are they not bawds in effect? For every man whom they thus emply, some girl, whose place he has thus taken, is driven to whoredom. The passage of the eight locks at Beziers, that is, from the opening of the first to the last gate took one hour and thirty-three minutes. The bark in which I go is about thirty-five feet long, drawn by one horse, and goes from two to three geographical miles an hour. The canal yields abundance of carp and eel. I see also small fish, resembling our perch and chub. Some plants of white clover, and some of yellow, on the banks of the canal near Capestan; santolina also, and a great deal of yellow iris. Met a raft of about three hundred and fifty beams, forty feet long, and twelve or thirteen inches in diameter, formed into fourteen rafts, tacked together. The extensive and numerous fields of saintfoin, in general bloom, are beautiful.

May 16. *Le Saumal. Marseillette.* May 17. *Marseilleite. Carcassonne.* From Saumal to Carcassonne we have always the river Aube close on our left. This river runs in the valley between the Cevennes and Pyrenees, serving as the common receptacle for both their waters. It is from fifty to one hundred and fifty yards wide, always rapid, rocky, and insusceptible of navigation. The canal passes in the side of hills made by that river, overlooks the river itself, and its plains, and has its prospect ultimately terminated on one side by mountains of rock, overtopped by the Pyrenees, on the other by small mountains, sometimes of rock, sometimes of soil, overtopped by the Cevennes. Marseillette is on a ridge, which separates the river Aube from the Etang de Marseillette. The canal, in its approach to this village, passes the ridge, and rides along the front, overlooking the Etang, and the plains on its border; and having passed the village, re-crosses the ridge, and resumes its general ground in front of the Aube. The land is in corn, saintfoin, pasture, vines, mulberries, willows, and olives.

May 18. *Carcassonne. Castelnaudari.* Opposite to Carcassonne the canal receives the river Fresquel, about thirty yards wide, which is its substantial supply of water from hence to Beziers. From Beziers to Agde the river Orb furnishes it, and the Eraut, from Agde to the Etang de Thau. By means of the *écluse ronde* at Agde, the waters of the Eraut can be thrown towards Beziers, to aid those of the Orb, as far as the *écluse de Porcaraigne*, nine geometrical miles.

Where the Fresquel enters the canal, there is, on the opposite side, a waste, to let off the superfluous waters. The horse-way is continued over this waste, by a bridge of stone of eighteen arches. I observe them fishing in the canal, with a skimming net of about fifteen feet diameter, with which they tell me they catch carp. Flax in blossom. Neither strawberries nor peas yet at Carcassonne. The Windsor-bean just come to table. From the *écluse de la Lande* we see the last olive trees near a *metairée*, or farm-house-, called *La Lande*. On a review of what I have seen and heard of this tree, the following seem to be its northern limits. Beginning on the Atlantic, at the Pyrenees, and along them to the meridian of La Lande, or of Carcassonne; up that meridian to the Cevennes, as they begin just there to raise themselves high enough to afford it shelter. Along the Cevennes, to the parallel of forty-five degrees of latitude, and along that parallel (crossing the Rhone near the mouth of the Isere) to the Alps; thence along the Alps and Apennines, to what parallel of latitude I know not. Yet here the tracing of the line becomes the most interesting. For from the Atlantic, so far we see this production the effect of shelter and latitude combined. But where does it venture to launch forth unprotected by shelter, and by the mere force of latitude alone? Where, for instance, does its northern limit cross the Adriatic? I learn, that the olive tree resists cold to eight degrees of Reaumur below the freezing-point, which corresponds to fourteen above zero of Fahrenheit: and that the orange resists to four degrees below freezing of Reaumur, which is twenty-three degrees above zero of Fahrenheit.

May 19. *Castelnaudari. St. Feriol. Escamaze. Lampy.* Some sheep and cattle; no enclosures. St. Feriol, Escamaze, and Lampy are in the montagnes noires. The country almost entirely waste. Some of it in shrubbery. The *voute d'Escamaze* is of one hundred and thirty-five yards. Round about Castelnaudari the country is hilly, as it has been constantly from Beziers; it is very rich. Where it is plain, or nearly plain, the soil is black: in general, however, it is hilly and reddish, and in corn. They cultivate a great deal of Indian corn here, which they call millet; it is planted, but not yet up.

May 20. *Castelnaudari. Naurouze. Villefranche. Baziege.* At Naurouze is the highest ground which the canal had to pass between the two seas. It became necessary, then, to find water still higher to bring it here. The river Fresquel heading by its two principal branches in the *montagnes noires*, a considerable distance off to the eastward, the springs of the most western one were brought together, and conducted to Naurouze, where its waters are divided, part furnishing the canal towards the ocean, the rest towards the Mediterranean, as far as the *écluse de Fresquel*, where, as has been before noted, the Lampy branch and the Alzau, under the name of the Fresquel, enter.

May 20. They have found that a lock of six *pieds* is best; however, eight *pieds* is well enough. Beyond this, it is bad. Monsieur Pin tells me of a lock of thirty *pieds* made in Sweden, of which it is impossible to open the gates. They therefore divided it into four locks. The small gates of the locks of this canal have six square *pieds* of surface. They tried the machinery of the jack for opening them. They were more easily opened, but very subject to be deranged, however strongly made. They returned, therefore, to the original wooden screw, which is excessively slow and laborious. I calculate that five minutes are lost at every basin by this screw, which, on the whole number of basins, is one eighth of the time necessary to navigate the canal: and of course, if a method of lifting the gate at one stroke could be found, it would reduce the passage from eight to seven days, and the freight equally. I suggested to Monsieur Pin and others a quadrantal gate, turning on a pivot, and lifted by a lever like a pump-handle, aided by a windlass and cord, if necessary. He will try it, and inform me of the success. The price of transportation from Cette to Bordeaux, through the canal and Garonne is ——— the quintal: round by the straits of Gibraltar is ———. Two hundred and forty barks, the largest of twenty-two hundred quintals (or say, in general, of one hundred tons), suffice to perform the business of this canal, which is stationary, having neither increased nor diminished for many years. When pressed, they can pass and repass between Toulouse and Beziers in fourteen days; but sixteen is the common period. The canal is navigated ten and a half months of the year: the other month and a half being necessary to lay it dry, cleanse it, and repair the works. This is done in July and August, when there would perhaps be a want of water.

May 21. *Baziège. Toulouse.* The country continues hilly, but very rich. It is in mulberries, willows, some vines, corn, maize, pasture, beans, flax. A great number of chateaux and good houses in the neighborhood of the canal. The people partly in farm-houses, partly in villages. I suspect that the farm-houses are occupied by the farmers, while the laborers (who are mostly by the day) reside in the villages. Neither strawberries nor pease yet at Baziege or Toulouse. Near the latter are some fields of yellow clover.

At Toulouse the canal ends. It has four communications with the Mediterranean. 1. Through the ponds of Thau, Frontignan, Palavas, Maguelone, and Manjo, the *canal de la Radela Aigues-mortes, le canal des Salines de Pecair,* and the arm of the Rhone called *Bras de Fer,* which ends at Fourgues, opposite to Arles, and thence down the Rhone. 2. At Cette, by a canal of a few hundred *toises,* leading out of the Etang de Thau into the sea. The vessels pass the Etang, though a length of nine thousand *toises,* with sails. 3. At Agde, by the river Eraut, twenty-five hundred *toises.* It has but five or six *pieds* of water at its mouth. It is joined to the canal at the upper part of this communication, by a branch of a canal two hundred and seventy *toises* long. 4. At Narbonne, by a canal they are now opening, which leads from the great canal near the aqueduct of the river Cesse, twenty-six hundred *toises,* into the

Aude. This new canal will have five lock-basins, of about twelve *pieds* fall each. Then you are to cross the Aude very obliquely, and descend a branch of it six thousand *toises*, through four lock-basins to Narbonne, and from Narbonne down the same branch, twelve hundred *toises* into the *Etang de Sigen*, across that Etang four thousand *toises*, issuing at an inlet, called *Grau de la Nouvelle*, into the Gulf of Lyons. But only vessels of thirty or forty tons can enter this inlet. Of these four communications, that of Cette only leads to a deep sea-port, because the exit is there by a canal, and not a river. Those by the Rhone, Eraut, and Aude, are blocked up by bars at the mouths of those rivers. It is remarkable, that all the rivers running into the Mediterranean are obstructed at their entrance by bars and shallows, which often change their position. This is the case with the Nile, Tiber, the Po, the Lez, le Lyoron, the Orbe, the Gly, the Tech, the Tet, he. Indeed, the formation of these bars seems not confined to the mouths of the rivers, though it takes place at them more certainly. Along almost the whole of the coast, from Marseilles towards the Pyrenees, banks of sand are thrown up parallel with the coast, which have insulated portions of the sea, that is, formed them into etangs, ponds, or sounds, through which here and there narrow and shallow inlets only are preserved by the currents of the rivers. These sounds fill up in time, with the mud and sand deposited in them by the rivers. Thus the Etang de Vendres, navigated formerly by vessels of sixty tons, is now nearly filled up by the mud and sand of the Aude. The Vistre and Vidourle, which formerly emptied themselves into the Gulf of Lyons, are now received by the *Etangs de Manjo* and Aiguesmortes, that is to say, the part of the Gulf of Lyons, which formerly received, and still receives those rivers, is now cut off from the sea by a bar of sand, which has been thrown up in it, and has formed it into sounds. Other proofs that the land gains there on the sea, are, that the towns of St. Giles and Notre Dame d'Asposts, formerly seaports, are no far from the sea, and that Aiguesmortes, where are still to be seen the iron rings to which vessels were formerly moored, and where St. Louis embarked for Palestine, has now in its vicinities only ponds, which cannot be navigated, and communicates with the sea by an inlet, called *Grau du Roy*, through which only fishing-barks can pass. It is pretty well established, that all the Delta of Egypt has been formed by the depositions of the Nile, and the alluvions of the sea, and it is probable that that operation is still going on. Has this peculiarity of the Mediterranean any connection with the scantiness of its tides, which, even at the equinoxes, are of two or three feet only? The communication from the western end of the canal to the ocean, is by the river Garonne. This is navigated by flat boats of eight hundred quintals, when the water is well; but when it is scanty, these boats carry only two hundred quintals, till they get to the mouth of the Tarn. It has been proposed to open a canal that far from Toulouse, along the right side of the river.

May 22. *Toulouse.* 23. *Agen.* 24. *Castres. Bordeaux.* The Garonne, and rivers emptying into it, make extensive and rich plains, which are in mulberries, willows, corn, maize, pasture, beans, and flax. The hills are in corn, maize, beans, and a considerable proportion of vines. There seems to be as much maize as corn in this country. Of the latter, there is more rye than wheat. The maize is now up, and about three inches high. It is sowed in rows two feet or two and a half feet apart, and is pretty thick in the row. Doubtless they mean to thin it. There is a great deal of a forage they call *farouche.* It is a species of red trefoil, with few leaves, a very coarse stalk, and a cylindrical blossom of two inches in length, and three quarters of an inch in diameter, consisting of floscules, exactly as does that of the red clover. It seems to be a coarse food, but very plentiful. They say it is for their oxen. These are very fine, large, and cream-colored. The services of the farm and of transportation are performed chiefly by them. There are a few horses and asses, but no mules. Even in the city of Bordeaux we see scarcely any beasts of draught but oxen. When we cross the Garonne at Langon, we find the plains entirely of sand and gravel, and they continue so to Bordeaux. Where they are capable of any thing, they are in vines, which are in rows, four, five, or six feet apart, and sometimes more. Near Langon is Sauterne, where the best white wines of Bordeaux are made. The waste lands are in fern, furze, shrubbery, and dwarf trees. The farmers live on their farms. At Agen, Castres, Bordeaux, strawberries and pease are now brought to table; so that the country on the canal of Languedoc seems to have later seasons than that east and west of it. What can be the cause? To the eastward, the protection of the Cevennes makes the warm season advance sooner. Does the neighborhood of the Mediterranean co-operate? And does that of the ocean mollify and advance the season to the westward? There are ortolans at Agen, but none at Bordeaux. The buildings on the canal and the Garonne are mostly of brick, the size of the bricks the same with that of the ancient Roman brick, as seen in the remains of their buildings in this country. In those of a circus at Bordeaux, considerable portions of which are standing, I measured the bricks, and found them nineteen or twenty inches long, eleven or twelve inches wide, and from one and a half to two inches thick; their texture as fine, compact, and solid as that of porcelain. The bricks now made, though of the same dimensions, are not so fine. They are burnt in a kind of furnace, and make excellent work. The elm tree shows itself at Bordeaux peculiarly proper for being spread flat for arbors. Many are done in this way on the Quay des Charterons. Strawberries, pease, and cherries at Bordeaux.

May 24, 25, 26, 27, 28. Bordeaux. The cantons in which the most celebrated wines of Bordeaux are made, are Medoc down the river, Grave adjoining the city, and the parishes next above; all on the same side of the river. In the first, is made red wine principally, in the two last, white. In Medoc they plant the vines in cross-rows of three and a half *pieds*. They keep them so low, that poles extended along the rows one way, horizontally, about fifteen or eighteen inches above the ground, serve to tie the vines to, and leave the cross row open to the plough. In Grave they set the plants in quincunx, i.e. in equilateral triangles of three and a half pieds every side; and they stick a pole of six or eight feet high to every vine, separately. The vine-stock is sometimes three or four feet high. They find these two methods equal in culture, duration, quantity, and quality. The former, however, admits the alternative of tending by hand or with the plough. The grafting of the vine, though a critical operation, is practised with success. When the graft has taken, they bend it into the earth, and let it take root above the scar. They begin to yield an indifferent wine at three years old, but not a good one till twenty-five years, nor after eighty, when they begin to yield less, and worse, and must be renewed. They give three or four workings in the year, each worth seventy or seventy-five livres the journal, which is of eight hundred and forty square ioises, and contains about three thousand plants. They dung a little in Medoc and Grave, because of the poverty of the soil; but very little; as more would affect the wine. The *journal* yields, *communions annis*, about three *pièces* (of two hundred and forty, or two hundred and fifty bottles each). The vineyards of first quality are all worked by their proprietors. Those of the second, rent for three hundred livres the journal: those of third, at two hundred livres. They employ a kind of overseer at four or five hundred livres the year, finding him lodging and drink: but he feeds himself. He superintends and directs, though he is expected to work but little. If the proprietor has a garden, the overseer tends that. They never hire laborers by the year. The day wages for a man are thirty sous, a woman's fifteen sous, feeding themselves. The women make the bundles of sarment, weed, pull off the snails, tie the vines, and gather the grapes. During the vintage they are paid high, and fed well.

Of Red wines, there are four vineyards of the first quality; viz. 1. *Chateau Margau*, belonging to the Marquis d'Agincourt, who makes about one hundred and fifty tons, of one thousand bottles each. He has engaged to Jernon, a merchant. 2. *La Tour de Segur, en Saint Lambert*, belonging to Monsieur Miresmenil, who makes one hundred and twenty-five tons. 3. *Hautbrion*, belonging two-thirds to M. le Comte de Femelle, who has engaged to Barton, a merchant: the other third to the Comte de Toulouse, at Toulouse. The whole is seventy-five tons. 4. *Chateau de la Fite*, belonging to the President Pichard, at Bordeaux, who makes one hundred and seventy-five tons. The wines of the three first, are not in perfection till four years old: those of *de la Fite*, being somewhat lighter, are good at three years; that is, the crop of 1786 is good in the spring of 1789. These growths, of the year 1783, sell now at two thousand livres the ton; those of 1784, on account of the superior quality of that vintage, sell at twenty-four hundred livres; those of 1785, at eighteen hundred livres; those of 1786, at eighteen hundred livres, though they had sold at first for only fifteen hundred livres. Red wines of the second quality, are Rozan, Dabbadie or Lionville, la Rose, Qui-rouen, Durfort; in all eight hundred tons, which sell at one thousand livres, new. The third class, are Galons, Mouton, Gassie, Arboete, Pontette, de Ferme, Candale; in all two thousand tons, at eight or nine hundred livres. After these, they are reckoned common wines, and sell from five hundred livres, down to one hundred and twenty livres, the ton. All red wines decline after a certain age, losing color, flavor, and body. Those of Bordeaux begin to decline at about seven years old.

Of White wines, those made in the canton of Grave, are most esteemed at Bordeaux. The best crops are, 1. *Pontac*, which formerly belonged to M. de Pontac, but now to M. de Lamont. He makes forty tons, which sell at four hundred livres, new. 2. *St. Brise*, belonging to M. de Pontac; thirty tons, at three hundred and fifty livres. 3. *De Carbonius*, belonging to the Benedictine monks, who make fifty tons, and never selling till three or four years old, get eight hundred livres the ton. Those made in the three parishes next above Grave, and more esteemed at Paris, are, 1. *Sauterne*. The best crop belongs to M. Diquem at Bordeaux, or to M. de Salus, his son-in-law; one hundred and fifty tons, at three hundred livres, new, and six hundred livres, old. The next best crop is M. de Fillotte's, one hundred tons, sold at the same price. 2. *Prignac*. The best is the President du Roy's, at Bordeaux. He makes one hundred and seventy-five tons, which sell at three hundred livres, new, and six hundred livres, old. Those of 1784, for their extraordinary quality, sell at eight hundred livres. 3. *Barsac*. The best belongs to the President Pichard, who makes one hundred and fifty tons, at two hundred and eighteen livres, new, and six hundred livres, old. Sauterne is the pleasantest; next Prignac, and lastly Barsac: but Barsac is the strongest; next Prignac, and lastly Sauterne; and all stronger than Grave. There are other good crops made in the same parishes of Sauterne, Prignac, and Barsac; but none as good as these. There is a virgin wine, which, though made of a red grape, is of a light rose color, because, being made without pressure, the coloring matter of the skin does not mix with the juice. There are other white wines, from the preceding prices down to seventy-five livres. In general, the white wines keep longest. They will be in perfection till fifteen or twenty years of age. The best vintage now to be bought, is of 1784; both of red and white. There has been no other good year since 1779. The celebrated vineyards before mentioned, are plains, as is generally the canton of Medoc, and that of the Grave. The soil of Hautbrion, particularly, which I examined, is a sand, in which is near as much round gravel or small stone, and very little loam: and this is the general soil of Medoc. That of Pontac, which I examined also, is a little different. It is clayey, with a fourth or fifth of fine rotten stone; and at two feet depth, it becomes all a rotten stone. M. de Lamont tells me, he has a kind of grape without seeds, which I did not formerly suppose to exist; but I saw at Marseilles dried raisins from Smyrna without seeds. I see in his farm at Pontac, some plants of white clover, and a good deal of yellow: also some small peach trees in the open ground. The principal English wine merchants at Bordeaux, are Jernon, Barton, Johnston, Foster, Skinner, Copinger, and M'Cartey: the chief French wine merchants, are Feger, Nerac, Bruneaux Jauge, and Du Verget. Desgrands, a wine-broker, tells me they never mix the wines of first quality: but that they mix the inferior ones to improve them. The smallest wines make the best brandy. They yield about a fifth or sixth.

May 28, 29. From Bordeaux to Blaye, the country near the river is hilly, chiefly in vines, some corn, some pasture: further out, are plains, boggy and waste. The soil, in both cases, clay and grit. Some sheep on the waste. To Etauliers, we have sometimes boggy plains, sometimes waving grounds and sandy, always poor, generally waste, in fern and furze, with some corn however, interspersed. To Mirambeau and St. Genis, it is hilly, poor, and mostly waste. There are some corn and maize however, and better trees than usual. Towards Pons, it becomes a little red, mostly rotten stone. There are vines, corn, and maize, which is up. At Pons we approach the Charente; the country becomes better, a blackish mould mixed with a rotten chalky stone: a great many vines, corn, maize, and farouche. From Lajart to Saintes and Rochefort, the soil is reddish, its foundation a chalky rock, at about a foot depth; in vines, corn, maize, clover, lucerne, and pasture. There are more and better trees than I have seen in all my journey; a great many apple and cherry trees: fine cattle and many sheep.

May 30. From Rochefort to La Rochelle, it is sometimes hilly and red, with a chalky foundation, middling good; in corn, pasture, and some waste: sometimes it is reclaimed marsh, in clover and corn, except the parts accessible to the tide, which are in wild grass. About Rochelle, it is a low plain. Towards Usseau, and halfway to Marans, level highlands, red, mixed with an equal quantity of broken chalk; mostly in vines, some corn, and pasture: then to Marans and halfway to St. Hermine, it is reclaimed marsh, dark, tolerably good, and all in pasture: there we rise to plains a little higher, red, with a chalky foundation, boundless to the eye, and altogether in corn and maize.

May 31. At St. Hermine, the country becomes very hilly, a red clay mixed with chalky stone, generally waste, in furze and broom, with some patches of corn and maize; and so it continues to Chantonay, and St. Fulgent. Through the whole of this road from Bordeaux, are frequent hedge rows, and small patches of forest wood, not good, yet better than I had seen in the preceding part of my journey. Towards Montaigu, the soil mends a little; the cultivated parts in corn and pasture, the uncultivated in broom. It is in very small enclosures of ditch and quickset. On approaching the Loire to Nantes, the country is leveller: the soil from Rochelle to this place may be said to have been sometimes red, but oftener gray, and always on a chalky foundation. The last census, of about 1770, made one hundred and twenty thousand inhabitants at Nantes. They conjecture there are now one hundred and fifty thousand, which equals it to Bordeaux.

June 1,2. The country from Nantes to L'Orient is very hilly and poor, the soil gray; nearly half is waste, in furze and broom, among which is some poor grass. The cultivated parts are in corn, some maize, a good many apple trees; no vines. All is in small enclosures of quick hedge and ditch. There are patches and hedge-rows of forest-wood, not quite deserving the name of timber. The people are mostly in villages; they eat rye-bread, and are ragged. The villages announce a general poverty, as does every other appearance. Women smite on the anvil, and work with the hoe, and cows are yoked to labor. There are great numbers of cattle, insomuch that butter is their staple. Neither asses nor mules: yet it is said that the fine mules I have met with on my journey, are raised in Poictou. There are but few *chateaux* here. I observe mill-ponds, and hoes with long handles. Have they not, in common with us, derived these from England, of which Bretagne is probably a colony? L'Orient is supposed to contain twenty-five thousand inhabitants. They tell me here, that to make a reasonable profit on potash and pearlash, as bought in America, the former should sell at thirty livres, the latter thirty-six livres, the quintal. Of turpentine they make no use in their vessels. Bayonne furnishes pitch enough; but tar is in demand, and ours sells well. The tower of L'Orient is sixty-five *pieds* above the level of the sea, one hundred and twenty *pieds* high, twenty-five *pieds* in diameter; the stairs four feet radius, and cost thirty thousand livres, besides the materials of the old tower.

June 3, 4, 5. The country and productions from L'Orient to Rennes, and from Rennes to Nantes, are precisely similar to those from Nantes to L'Orient. About Rennes, it is somewhat leveller, perhaps less poor, and almost entirely in pasture. The soil always gray. Some small, separate houses, which seem to be the residence of laborers, or very small farmers; the walls frequently of mud, and the roofs generally covered with slate. Great plantations of walnut, and frequently of pine. Some apple trees and sweet-briar still in bloom, and broom generally so. I have heard no nightingale since the last day of May. There are gates in this country made in such a manner, that the top rail of the gate overshoots backwards the hind post, so as to counterpoise the gate, and prevent its swagging.

Nantes. Vessels of eight feet draught only can come to Nantes. Those which are larger, lie at Painboeuf, ten leagues below Nantes, and five leagues above the mouth of the river. There is a continued navigation from Nantes to Paris, through the Loire, the canal de Briare and the Seine. Carolina rice is preferred to that of Lombardy for the Guinea trade, because it requires less water to boil it.

June 6, 7, 8. *Nantes. Ancenis. Angers. Tours.* Ascending the Loire from Nantes, the road, as far as Angers, leads over the hills, which are gray, oftener below than above mediocrity, and in corn, pasture, vines, some maize, flax, and hemp. There are no waste lands. About the limits of Bretagne and Anjou, which are between Loriottiere and St. George, the lands change for the better. Here and there, we get views of the plains on the Loire, of some extent, and good appearance, in corn and pasture. After passing Angers, the road is raised out of the reach of inundations, so as at the same time to ward them off from the interior plains. It passes generally along the river side; but sometimes leads through the plains, which, after we pass Angers, become extensive and good, in corn, pasture, some maize, hemp, flax, pease, and beans; many willows, also poplars and walnuts. The flax is near ripe. Sweet-briar in general bloom. Some broom here still, on which the cattle and sheep browse in winter and spring, when they have no other green food; and the hogs eat the blossoms and pods, in spring and summer. This blossom, though disagreeable when smelt in a small quantity, is of delicious fragrance when there is a whole field of it. There are some considerable vineyards in the river plains, just before we reach Les Trois Volets (which is at the one hundred and thirty-sixth milestone), and after that, where the hills on the left come into view, they are mostly in vines. Their soil is clayey and stony, a little reddish, and of southern aspect. The hills on the other side of the river, looking to the north, are not in vines. There is very good wine made on these hills; not equal indeed to the Bordeaux of best quality, but to that of good quality, and like it. It is a great article of exportation from Anjou and Touraine, and probably is sold abroad, under the name of Bordeaux. They are now mowing the first crop of hay. All along both hills of the Loire, is a mass of white stone, not durable, growing black with time, and so soft, that the people cut their houses out of the solid, with all the partitions, chimnies, doors, &c. The hill sides resemble cony burrows, full of inhabitants. The borders of the Loire are almost a continued village. There are many chateaux: many cattle, sheep, and horses; some asses.

Tours is at the one hundred and nineteenth mile-stone. Being desirous of inquiring here into a fact stated by Voltaire, in his *Questions Encylopédiques*, article *Coquilles*, relative to the growth of shells unconnected with animal bodies at the *Chateau* of Monsieur de la Sauvagiere, near Tours, I called on Monsieur Gentil, *premier sécrétaire de l'ntendance*, to whom the Intendant had written on my behalf, at the request of the Marquis de Chastellux.

I stated to him the fact as advanced by Voltaire, and found he was, of all men, the best to whom I could have addressed myself. He told me he had been in correspondence with Voltaire on that very subject, and was perfectly acquainted with Monsieur de la Sauvagiere, and the Faluniere where the fact is said to have taken place. It is at the Chateau de Grillemont, six leagues from Tours, on the road to Bordeaux, belonging now to Monsieur d'Orcai. He says, that De la Sauvagiere was a man of truth, and might be relied on for whatever facts he stated as of his own observation; but that he was overcharged with imagination, which, in matters of opinion and theory, often led him beyond his facts; that this feature in his character had appeared principally in what he wrote on the antiquities of Touraine; but that as to the fact in question, he believed him. That he himself, indeed, had not watched the same identical shells, as Sauvagiere had done, growing from small to great; but that he had often seen such masses of those shells of all sizes, from a point to a full size, as to carry conviction to his mind that they were in the act of growing; that he had once made a collection of shells for the Emperor's cabinet, reserving duplicates of them for himself; and that these afforded proofs of the same fact; that he afterwards gave those duplicates to a Monsieur du Verget, a physician of Tours, of great science and candor, who was collecting on a larger scale, and who was perfectly in sentiment with Monsieur de la Sauvagiere, and not only the Faluniere, but many other places about Tours, would convince any unbiassed observer, that shells are a fruit of the earth, spontaneously produced; and he gave me a copy of De la Sauvagiere's *Recueil de Dissertations*, presented him by the author, wherein is one *Sur la vegetation spontanée des coquilles du Chateau des Places*. So far, I repeat from him. What are we to conclude? That we have not materials enough yet, to form any conclusion. The fact stated by Sauvagiere is not against any law of nature, and is therefore possible; but it is so little analogous to her habitual processes, that, if true, it would be extraordinary: that to command our belief, therefore, there should be such a suite of observations, as that their untruth would be more extraordinary than the existence of the fact they affirm. The bark of trees, the skin of fruits and animals, the feathers of birds, receive their growth and nutriment from the internal circulation of a juice through the vessels of the individual they cover. We conclude from analogy, then, that the shells of the testaceous tribe receive also their growth from a like internal circulation. If it be urged, that this does not exclude the possibility of a like shell being produced by the passage of a fluid through the pores of the circumjacent body, whether of earth, stone, or water; I answer, that it is not within the usual economy of nature, to use two processes for one species of production. While I withhold my assent, however, from this hypothesis, I must deny it to every other I have ever seen, by which their authors pretend to account for the origin of shells in high places. Some of these are against the laws of nature, and therefore impossible; and others are built on positions more difficult to assent to, than that of De la Sauvagiere. They all suppose these shells to have covered submarine animals, and have then to answer the question, How came they fifteen thousand feet above the level of the sea? And they answer it, by demanding what cannot be conceded. One, therefore, who had rather have no opinion than a false one, will suppose this question one of those beyond the investigation of human sagacity; or wait till further and fuller observations enable him to decide it.

Chanteloup. I heard a nightingale to-day at Chanteloup. The gardener says it is the male, who alone sings, while the female sits; and that when the young are hatched, he also ceases. In the boudoir at Chanteloup, is an ingenious contrivance to hide the projecting steps of a staircase. Three steps were of necessity to project into the boudoir: they are therefore made triangular steps; and instead of being rested on the floor, as usual, they are made fast at their broad end to the stair door, swinging out and in, with that. When it shuts, it runs them under the other steps; when open it brings them out to their proper place. In the kitchen garden, are three pumps, worked by one horse. The pumps are placed in an equilateral triangle, each side of which is of about thirty-five feet. In the centre is a post, ten or twelve feet high, and one foot in diameter. In the top of this, enters the bent end of a lever, of about twelve or fifteen feet long, with a swingle-tree at the other end. About three feet from the bent end, it receives, on a pin, three horizontal bars of iron, which at their other end lay hold of one corner of a quadrantal crank (like a bell crank) moving in a vertical plane, to the other corner of which is hooked the vertical handle of the pump. The crank turns on its point as a centre, by a pin or pivot passing through it. The horse moving the lever horizontally in a circle, every point of the lever describes a horizontal circle. That which receives the three bars, describes a circle of six feet in diameter. It gives a stroke then of six feet to the handle of each pump, at each revolution.

Blois. Orleans. June 9, 10. At Blois, the road leaves the river, and traverses the hills, which are mostly reddish, sometimes gray, good enough, in vines, corn, saintfoin. From Orleans to the river Juines, at Etampes, it is a continued plain of corn, and saintfoin, tolerably good, sometimes gray, sometimes red. From Etampes to Etrechy, the country is mountainous and rocky, resembling that of Fontainebleau. *Quere*. If it may not be the same vein?

LETTER LVIII.—TO WILLIAM CARMICHAEL, June 14, 1787

TO WILLIAM CARMICHAEL.

Paris, June 14, 1787.

Dear Sir,

Having got back to Paris three days ago, I resume immediately the correspondence with which you have been pleased to honor me. I wish I could have begun it with more agreeable information than that furnished me by Mr. Grand, that the funds of the United States here are exhausted, and himself considerably in advance; and by the board of treasury at New York, that they have no immediate prospect of furnishing us supplies. We are thus left to shift for ourselves, without previous warning. As soon as they shall replenish Mr. Grand's hands, I will give you notice, that you may recommence your usual drafts on him; unless the board should provide a separate fund for you, dependant on yourself alone, which I have strongly and repeatedly pressed on them, in order to remove the indecency of suffering your drafts to pass through any intermediate hand for payment.

My letters from America came down to the 24th of April. The disturbances in the Eastern States were entirely settled. I do not learn that the government had made any examples. Mr. Hancock's health being re-established, the want of which had occasioned him to resign the government of Massachusetts, he has been re-elected to the exclusion of Governor Bowdoin. New York still refuses to pass the impost in any form, and were she to pass it, Pennsylvania will not uncouple it from the supplementary funds. These two States and Virginia, are the only ones, my letters say, which have paid any thing into the Continental treasury, for a twelvemonth past. I send you a copy of a circular letter from Congress to the several States, insisting on their removing all obstructions to the recovery of British debts. This was hurried, that it might be delivered to the Assembly of New York before they rose. It was delivered, but they did nothing in consequence of it. The convention to be assembled at Philadelphia will be an able one. Ten States were known to have appointed delegates. Maryland was about to appoint; Connecticut was doubtful; and Rhode Island had refused. We are sure, however, of eleven States. South Carolina has prohibited the importation of slaves for three years; which is a step towards a perpetual prohibition. Between six and seven hundred thousand acres of land are actually surveyed into townships, and the sales are to begin immediately. They are not to be sold for less than a dollar the acre, in public certificates. I wrote you from Bordeaux on the subject of Colonel Smith. I was sorry I missed him there, for other reasons as well as from a curiosity to know his errand. The Notables have laid the foundation of much good here: you have seen it detailed in the public papers. The Prince of Wales is likely to recover from his illness, which was very threatening. It is feared, that three powers have combined to lift the Prince of Orange out of his difficulties. Have you yet the cipher of which I formerly wrote to you, or any copy of it?

I am, with sincere esteem, Dear Sir, your most obedient and most humble servant,

Th: Jefferson.

LETTER LIX.—TO J. BANNISTER, JUNIOR, June 19, 1787

TO J. BANNISTER, JUNIOR.

Paris, June 19, 1787.

Dear Sir,

I have received your favor of April the 23d, from New York, and am sorry to find you have had a relapse. Time and temperance, however, will cure you; to which add exercise. I hope you have long ago had a happy meeting with your friends, with whom a few hours would be to me an ineffable feast. The face of Europe appears a little turbid, but all will subside. The Empress has endeavored to bully the Turk, who laughed at her, and she is going back. The Emperor's reformations have occasioned the appearance of insurrection in Flanders, and he, according to character, will probably tread back his steps. A change of system here with respect to the Dutch, is suspected; because the Kings of Prussia and England openly espouse the cause of the Stadtholder, and that of the Patriots is likely to fall. The American acquaintances whom you left here, not being stationary, you will hardly expect news of them. Mrs. Barrett, lately dead, was, I think, known to you. I had a letter from Ledyard lately, dated at St. Petersburg. He had but two shirts, and yet more shirts than shillings. Still he was determined to obtain the palm of being the first circumambulator of the earth. He says, that having no money, they kick him from place to place, and thus he expects to be kicked round the globe. Are you become a great walker? You know I preach up that kind of exercise. Shall I send you a *conte-pas*? It will cost you a dozen louis, but be a great stimulus to walking, as it will record your steps. I finished my tour a week or ten days ago. I went as far as Turin, Milan, Genoa; and never passed three months and a half more delightfully. I returned through the canal of Languedoc, by Bordeaux, Nantes, L'Orient, and Rennes; then returned to Nantes, and came up the Loire to Orleans. I was alone through the whole, and think one travels more usefully when alone, because he reflects more.

Present me in the most friendly terms to Mrs. Bannister and to your father, and be assured of the sincere esteem of, Dear Sir, your friend and servant,

Th: Jefferson.

LETTER LX.—TO JAMES MADISON, June 20, 1787*

TO JAMES MADISON.

Paris, June 20, 1787.

[Much of this letter is in cipher: but the notes annexed*

to it, have enabled the Editor to decipher and publish it.]

Dear Sir,

I wrote you last on the 30th of January, with a Postscript of February the 5th. Having set out the last day of that month to try the waters of Aix, and been journeying since, till the 10th instant, I have been unable to continue my correspondence with you. In the mean time, I have received your several favors of February the 15th, March the 18th and 19th, and April the 23d. The last arrived here about the 25th of May, while those of March the 18th and 19th, though written, five weeks earlier, arrived three weeks later. I mention this, to show you how uncertain is the conveyance through England.

The idea of separating the executive business of the confederacy from Congress, as the judiciary is already, in some degree, is just and necessary. I had frequently pressed on the members individually, while in Congress, the doing this by a resolution of Congress for appointing an executive committee, to act during the sessions of Congress, as the committee of the States was to act during their vacations. But the referring to this committee all executive business, as it should present itself, would require a more persevering self-denial than I suppose Congress to possess. It will be much better to make that separation by a federal act. The negative proposed to be given them on all the acts of the several legislatures, is now, for the first time, suggested to my mind. *Prima facie*, I do not like it. It fails in an essential character; that the hole and the patch should be commensurate. But this proposes to mend a small hole, by covering the whole garment. Not more than one out of one hundred State acts, concern the confederacy. This proposition, then, in order to give them one degree of power, which they ought to have, gives them ninety-nine more, which they ought not to have, upon a presumption that they will not exercise the ninety-nine. But upon every act there will be a preliminary question, Does this act concern the confederacy? And was there ever a proposition so plain, as to pass Congress without a debate? Their decisions are almost always wise; they are like pure metal. But you know of how much dross this is the result. Would not an appeal from the State judicature to a federal court, in all cases where the act of Confederation controlled the question, be as effectual a remedy, and exactly commensurate to the defect. A British creditor, for example, sues for his debt in Virginia; the defendant pleads an act of the State, excluding him from their courts; the plaintiff urges the confederation, and the treaty made under that, as controlling the State law; the judges are weak enough to decide according to the views of their legislature. An appeal to a federal court gets all to rights. It will be said, that this court may encroach on the jurisdiction of the State courts. It may. But there will be a power, to wit, Congress, to watch and restrain them. But place the same authority in Congress itself, and there will be no power above them to perform the same office. They will restrain within due bounds a jurisdiction exercised by others, much more rigorously than if exercised by themselves.

I am uneasy at seeing that the sale of our western lands is not yet commenced. That valuable fund for the immediate extinction of our debt will, I fear, be suffered to slip through our fingers. Every day exposes it to events, which no human foresight can guard against. When we consider the temper of the people of that country, derived from the circumstances which surround them, we must suppose their separation possible, at every moment. If they can be retained till their governments become settled and wise, they will remain with us always, and be a precious part of our strength and our virtue. But this affair of the Mississippi, by showing that Congress is capable of hesitating on a question, which proposes a clear sacrifice of the western to the maritime States, will with difficulty be obliterated. The proposition of my going to Madrid, to try to recover there the ground which has been lost at New York, by the concession of the vote of seven States, I should think desperate. With respect to myself, weighing the pleasure of the journey and bare possibility of success in one scale, and the strong probability of failure and the public disappointment directed on me, in the other, the latter preponderates. Add to this, that jealousy might be excited in the breast of a person, who could find occasions of making me uneasy.

The late changes in the ministry here, excite considerable hopes. I think we gain in them all. I am particularly happy at the reentry of Malesherbes into the Council. His knowledge and integrity render his value inappreciable, and the greater to me, because, while he had no views of office, we had established together the most unreserved intimacy. So far, too, I am pleased with Montmorin. His honesty proceeds from the heart as well as the head, and therefore may be more surely counted on. The King loves business, economy, order, and justice, and wishes sincerely the good of his people; but he is irascible, rude, very limited in his understanding, and religious bordering on bigotry. He has no mistress, loves his queen, and is too much governed by her. She is capricious, like her brother, and governed by him; devoted to pleasure and expense; and not remarkable for any other vices or virtues. Unhappily the King shows a propensity for the pleasures of the table. That for drink has increased lately, or at least it has become more known.

For European news in general, I will refer you to my letter to Mr. Jay. Is it not possible, that the occurrences in Holland may excite a desire in many of leaving that country, and transferring their effects out of it, and thus make an opening for shifting into their hands the debts due to this country, to its officers, and Farmers? It would be surely eligible. I believe Dumas, if put on the watch, might alone suffice; but he surely might, if Mr. Adams should go when the moment offers. Dumas has been in the habit of sending his letters open to me, to be forwarded to Mr. Jay. During my absence, they passed through Mr. Short's hands, who made extracts from them, by which I see he has been recommending himself and me for the money-negotiations in Holland. It might be thought, perhaps, that I have encouraged him in this. Be assured, my Dear Sir, that no such idea ever entered my head. On the contrary, it is a business which would be the most disagreeable to me of all others, and for which I am the most unfit person living. I do not understand bargaining, nor possess the dexterity requisite for the purpose. On the other hand, Mr. Adams, whom I expressly and sincerely recommend, stands already on ground for that business, which I could not gain in years. Pray set me to rights in the minds of those, who may have supposed me privy to this proposition. *En passant*, I will observe with respect to Mr. Dumas, that the death of the Count de Vergennes places Congress more at their ease, how to dispose of him. Our credit has been ill treated here in public debate, and our debt here deemed apocryphal. We should try to transfer this debt elsewhere, and leave nothing capable of exciting ill thoughts between us. I shall mention in my letter to Mr. Jay, a disagreeable affair which Mr. Barclay has been thrown into, at Bordeaux. An honester man cannot be found, nor a slower, nor more decisive one. His affairs, too, are so embarrassed and desperate, that the public reputation is, every moment, in danger of being compromitted with him. He is perfectly amiable and honest, with all his embarrassments.

By the next packet, I shall be able to send you some books, as also your watch and pedometer. The two last are not yet done. To search for books, and forward them to Havre, will require more time than I had between my return and the departure of this packet. Having been a witness, heretofore, to the divisions in Congress on the subject of their foreign ministers, it would be a weakness in me to suppose none with respect to myself, or to count with any confidence on the renewal of my commission, which expires on the 10th day of March next; and the more so, as instead of requiring the disapprobation of seven States, as formerly, that of one suffices for a recall, when Congress consists of only seven States, two, when of eight, &c. which I suppose to be habitually their numbers at present. Whenever I leave this place, it will be necessary to begin my arrangements six months before my departure; and these, once fairly begun and under way, and my mind set homewards, a change of purpose could hardly take place. If it should be the desire of Congress that I should continue still longer, I could wish to know it, at farthest, by the packet which will sail from New York in September. Because, were I to put off longer the quitting my house, selling my furniture, he, I should not have time left to wind up my affairs; and having once quitted, and sold off my furniture, I could not think of establishing myself here again. I take the liberty of mentioning this matter to you, not with a desire to change the purpose of Congress, but to know it in time. I have never fixed in my mind, the epoch of my return, so far as shall depend on myself, but I never supposed it very distant. Probably I shall not risk a second vote on this subject. Such trifling things may draw on me the displeasure of one or two States, and thus submit me to the disgrace of a recall.

I thank you for the paccan nuts, which accompanied your letter of March. Could you procure me a copy of the bill for proportioning crimes and punishments, in the form in which it was ultimately rejected by the House of Delegates? Young Mr. Bannister desired me to send him regularly the *Mercure de France*. I will ask leave to do this through you, and that you will adopt such method of forwarding them to him, as will save him from being submitted to postage, which they would not be worth. As a compensation for your trouble, you will be free to keep them till you shall have read them. I am, with sentiments of the most sincere esteem, Dear Sir, your friend and servant,

Th: Jefferson.

LETTER LXI.—TO JOHN JAY, June 21,1787

TO JOHN JAY.

Paris, June 21,1787.

Sir,

I had the honor of addressing you in a letter of May the 4th, from Marseilles, which was to have gone by the last packet. Bat it arrived a few hours too late for that conveyance, and has been committed to a private one, passing through England, with a promise that it should go through no post-office.

I was desirous, while at the sea-ports, to obtain a list of the American vessels which have come to them since the peace, in order to estimate their comparative importance to us, as well as the general amount of our commerce with this country, so far as carried on in our own bottoms. At Marseilles, I found there had been thirty-two, since that period; at Cette, not a single one; at Bayonne, one of our free ports, only one. This last fact I learned from other information, not having visited that place; as it would have been a deviation from my route, too considerable for the importance of the object. At Bordeaux, Nantes, and L'Orient, I could not obtain lists in the moment; but am in hopes I shall be able to get them ere long. Though more important to us, they will probably be more imperfect than that of Marseilles. At Nantes, I began with Monsieur Dobrée an arrangement of his claims. I visited the military stores, which have been detained there so long, opened some boxes of each kind, and found the state of their contents much better than had been represented. An exact list of the articles is to be sent me.

The importations into L'Orient of other fish-oils, besides those of the whale, brought to my notice there a defect in the letter of Monsieur de Calonne, of October the 22nd, which letter was formerly communicated to you. In that, whale oil only was named. The other fish-oils, therefore, have continued to pay the old duties. In a conference with Monsieur de Villedeuil, the present Comptroller General, since my return, I proposed the extending the exemption to all fish-oils, according to the letter of the Hanseatic treaty, which had formed the basis of the regulations respecting us. I think this will be agreed to. The delays of office first, then the illness of Monsieur de Colonne, and lastly, his removal and the throng of business occasioned by the *Assemblée des Notables*, have prevented the reducing the substance of the letter into the form of an *Arrêt*, as yet though I have continued soliciting it as much as circumstances would bear. I am now promised that it shall be done immediately, and it shall be so far retrospective to the date of the letter, as that all duties paid since that, shall be refunded.

The new accessions of the ministry are valued here. Good is hoped from the Archbishop of Toulouse, who succeeds the Count de Vergennes as *Chef du Conseil de finance*. Monsieur de Villedeuil, the Comptroller General, has been approved by the public, in the offices he has heretofore exercised. The Duke de Nivernois, called to the Council, is reckoned a good and able man; and Monsieur de Malesherbes, called also to the Council, is unquestionably the first character in the kingdom, for integrity, patriotism, knowledge, and experience in business. There is a fear that the Marechal de Castries is disposed to retire.

The face of things in Europe is a little turbid, at present; but probably all will subside. The Empress of Russia, it is supposed, will not push her pretensions against the Turks to actual war. Weighing the fondness of the Emperor for innovation, against his want of perseverance, it is difficult to calculate what he will do with his discontented subjects in Brabant and Flanders. If those provinces alone were concerned, he would probably give back; but this would induce an opposition to his plan, in all his other dominions. Perhaps he may be able to find a compromise. The cause of the Patriots in Holland is a little clouded at present.

England and Prussia seem disposed to interpose effectually. The former has actually ordered a fleet of six sail of the line, northwardly, under Gore; and the latter threatens to put her troops into motion. The danger of losing such a weight in their scale, as that of Prussia, would occasion this court to prefer conciliation to war. Add to this, the distress of their finances, and perhaps not so warm a zeal in the new ministry for the innovations in Holland. I hardly believe they will think it worth while to purchase the change of constitution proposed there, at the expense of a war. But of these things, you will receive more particular and more certain details from Mr. Dumas, to whom they belong.

Mr. Eden is appointed ambassador from England to Madrid. To the hatred borne us by his court and country, is added a recollection of the circumstances of the unsuccessful embassy to America, of which he made a part. So that I think he will carry to Madrid, dispositions to do us all the ill he can.

The late change in the ministry is very favorable to the prospects of the Chevalier de la Luzerne. The Count de Montmorin, Monsieur de Malesherbes, and Monsieur de Lamoignon, the *Garde des Sceaux*, are his near relations. Probably something will be done for him, and without delay. The promise of the former administration to the Count de Moutier, to succeed to this vacancy, should it take place, will perhaps be performed by the present one.

Mr. Barclay has probably informed you of his having been arrested in Bordeaux, for a debt contracted in the way of his commerce. He immediately applied to the parliament of that place, who ordered his discharge. This took place after five days' actual imprisonment. I arrived at Bordeaux a few days after his liberation. As the Procureur General of the King had interested himself to obtain it, with uncommon zeal, and that too on public principles, I thought it my duty to wait on him and return him my thanks. I did the same to the President of the parliament, for the body over which he presided; what would have been an insult in America, being an indispensable duty here. You will see by the enclosed printed paper, on what grounds the Procureur insisted on Mr. Barclay's liberation. Those on which the parliament ordered it, are not expressed. On my arrival here, I spoke with the minister on the subject. He observed, that the character of Consul is no protection in this country, against process for debt: that as to the character with which Mr. Barclay had been invested at the court of Morocco, it was questionable whether it would be placed on the diplomatic line, as it had not been derived immediately from Congress; that if it were, it would have covered him to Paris only, where he had received his commission, had he proceeded directly thither, but that his long stay at Bordeaux, must be considered as terminating it there. I observed to him, that Mr. Barclay had been arrested almost immediately on his arrival at Bordeaux. But, says he, the arrest was made void by the parliament, and still he has continued there several weeks. True, I replied, but his adversaries declared they would arrest him again, the moment he should be out of the jurisdiction of the parliament of Bordeaux, and have actually engaged the *Maréchausée* on the road, to do it. This seemed to impress him. He said he could obtain a letter of safe conduct which would protect him to Paris, but that immediately on his arrival here, he would be liable to arrest. I asked him, if such a letter could not be obtained to protect him to Paris, and back to Bordeaux, and even to America? He said, that for that, the consent of the greater part of his creditors would be necessary; and even with this, it was very doubtful whether it could be obtained: still, if I would furnish him with that consent, he would do what should depend on him. I am persuaded he will, and have written to Mr. Barclay to obtain the consent of his creditors. This is the footing on which this matter stands at present. I have stated it thus particularly, that you may know the truth, which will probably be misrepresented in the English papers, to the prejudice of Mr. Barclay. This matter has been a great affliction to him, but no dishonor where its true state is known. Indeed he is incapable of doing any thing not strictly honorable.

In a letter of August the 30th, 1785, I had the honor of mentioning to you what had passed here, on the subject of a convention for the regulation of the two post offices. I now inclose you a letter from the Baron D'Ogny, who is at the head of that department, which shows that he still expects some arrangement. I have heard it said, that M. de Creve-coeur is authorized to treat on this subject. You doubtless know if this be true. The articles may certainly be better adjusted there, than here. This letter from the Baron D'Ogny was in consequence of an application from a servant of mine, during my absence, which would not have been made had I been here. Nor will it be repeated; it being my opinion and practice to pay small sums of money, rather than to ask favors.

I have the honor to inclose you also, copies of a letter and papers from the Marechal de Castries, on the claim of an individual against the State of South Carolina, for services performed on board the Indian; and the petition of another, on a like claim: also copies of letters received from O'Bryan at Algiers, and from Mr. Lambe. A letter of the 26th of May, from Mr. Montgomery, at Alicant, informs me, that by a vessel arrived at Carthagena from Algiers, they learn the death of the Dey of that republic. Yet, as we hear nothing of it through any other channel, it may be doubted. It escaped me at the time of my departure to Aix, to make arrangements for sending you the gazettes regularly, by the packets. The whole are now sent, though a great part of them are so old as to be not worth perusal. Your favor of April the 24th, has been duly received.

I have the honor,to be, with sentiments of the most perfect esteem and respect. Sir, your most obedient and most humble servant,

Th: Jefferson.

LETTER LXII.—TO MADAME DE CORNY, June 30,1787

TO MADAME DE CORNY.

Paris, June 30,1787.

On my return to Paris, it was among my first attentions to go to the rue Chaussée d'Antin, No. 17, and inquire after my friends whom I had left there. I was told they were in England. And how do you like England, Madam? I know your taste for the works of art gives you little disposition to Anglomania. Their mechanics certainly exceed all others in some lines. But be just to your own nation. They have not patience, it is true, to set rubbing a piece of steel from morning to night, as a lethargic Englishman will do, full charged with porter. But do not their benevolence, their cheerfulness, their amiability, when compared with the growling temper and manners of the people among whom you are, compensate their want of patience? I am in hopes that when the splendor of their shops, which is all that is worth seeing in London, shall have lost the charm of novelty, you will turn a wishful eye to the good people of Paris, and find that you cannot be so happy with any others. The Bois de Boulogne invites you earnestly to come and survey its beautiful verdure, to retire to its umbrage from the heats of the season. I was through it to-day, as I am every day. Every tree charged me with this invitation to you. Passing by la Muette, it wished for you as a mistress. You want a country-house. This is for sale; and in the Bois de Boulogne, which I have always insisted to be most worthy of your preference. Come then, and buy it. If I had had confidence in your speedy return, I should have embarrassed you in earnest with my little daughter. But an impatience to have her with me, after her separation from her friends, added to a respect for your ease, has induced me to send a servant for her.

I tell you no news, because you have correspondents infinitely more *au fait* of the details at Paris than I am. And I offer you no services, because I hope you will come as soon as the letter could, which should command them. Be assured, however, that nobody is more disposed to render them, nor entertains for you a more sincere and respectful attachment, than him, who, after charging you with his compliments to Monsieur de Corny, has the honor of offering you the homage of those sentiments of distinguished esteem and regard, with which he is, Dear Madam, your most obedient and most humble servant,

Th: Jefferson.

LETTER LXIII.—TO JOHN ADAMS, July 1, 1787

TO JOHN ADAMS.

Paris, July 1, 1787.

Dear Sir,

I returned about three weeks ago from a very useless voyage; useless, I mean, as to the object which first suggested it, that of trying the effect of the mineral waters of Aix, in Provence, on my hand. I tried these, because recommended among six or eight others as equally beneficial, and because they would place me at the beginning of a tour to the seaports of Marseilles, Bordeaux, Nantes, and L'Orient, which I had long meditated, in hopes that a knowledge of the places and persons concerned in our commerce, and the information to be got from them, might enable me sometimes to be useful. I had expected to satisfy myself at Marseilles, of the causes of the difference of quality between the rice of Carolina, and that of Piedmont, which is brought in quantities to Marseilles. Not being able to do it, I made an excursion of three weeks into the rice country beyond the Alps, going through it from Vercelli to Pavia, about sixty miles. I found the difference to be, not in the management, as had been supposed both here and in Carolina, but in the species of rice; and I hope to enable them in Carolina, to begin the cultivation of the Piedmont rice, and carry it on, hand in hand, with their own, that they may supply both qualities which is absolutely necessary at this market. I had before endeavored to lead the depot of rice from Cowes to Honfleur, and hope to get it received there on such terms, as may draw that branch of commerce from England to this country. It is an object of two hundred and fifty thousand guineas a year. While passing through the towns of Turin, Milan, and Genoa, I satisfied myself of the practicability of introducing our whale-oil for their consumption, and suppose it would be equally so in the other great cities of that country. I was sorry that I was not authorized to set the matter on foot. The merchants with whom I chose to ask conferences met me freely, and communicated fully, knowing I was in a public character. I could, however, only prepare a disposition to meet our oil-merchants. On the article of tobacco, I was more in possession of my ground; and put matters into a train for inducing their government to draw their tobaccos directly from the United States, and not, as heretofore, from Great Britain. I am now occupied with the new ministry here, to put the concluding hand to the new regulations for our commerce with this country, announced in the letter of Monsieur de Calonne, which I sent you last fall. I am in hopes, in addition to those, to obtain a suppression of the duties on tar, pitch, and turpentine, and, an extension of the privileges of American *whale oil*, to their *fish oils* in general. I find that the quantity of cod-fish oil brought to L'Orient is considerable. This being got off hand (which will be in a few days), the chicaneries and vexations of the Farmers on the article of tobacco, and their elusions of the order of Bernis, call for the next attention. I have reasons to hope good dispositions in the new ministry towards our commerce with this country. Besides endeavoring, on all occasions, to multiply the points of contact and connection with this country, which I consider as our surest mainstay under every event, I have had it much at heart to remove from between us every subject of misunderstanding or irritation. Our debts to the King, to the Officers, and the Farmers, are of this description. The having complied with no part of our engagements in these, draws on us a great deal of censure, and occasioned a language in the *Assemblée des Notables*, very likely to produce dissatisfaction between us. Dumas being on the spot in Holland, I had asked of him some time ago, in confidence, his opinion of the practicability of transferring these debts from France to Holland, and communicated his answer to Congress, pressing them to get you to go over to Holland, and try to effect this business. Your knowledge of the ground, and former successes, occasioned me to take this liberty without consulting you, because I was sure you would not weigh your personal trouble against public good. I have had no answer from Congress; but hearing of your journey to Holland, have hoped that some money operation had led you there. If it related to the debts of this country, I would ask a communication of what you think yourself at liberty to communicate, as it might change the form of my answers to the eternal applications I receive. The debt to the officers of France, carries an interest of about two thousand guineas, so we may suppose its principal is between thirty and forty thousand. This makes more noise against us, than all our other debts put together.

I send you the *Arrêts* which begin the reformation here, and some other publications respecting America; together with copies of letters received from O'Bryan and Lambe. It is believed, that a naval armament has been ordered at Brest, in correspondence with that of England. We know, certainly, that orders are given to form a camp in the neighborhood of Brabant, and that Count Rochambeau has the command of it. Its amount I cannot assert. Report says fifteen thousand men. This will derange the plans of economy. I take the liberty of putting under your cover a letter for Mrs. Kinloch, of South Carolina, with a packet, and will trouble you to inquire for her, and have them delivered. The packet is of great consequence, and therefore referred to her care, as she will know the safe opportunities of conveying it. Should you not be able to find her, and can forward the packet to its address, by any very safe conveyance, I will beg you to do it.

I have the honor to be, with sentiments of the most perfect friendship and esteem, Dear Sir, your most obedient and most humble servant,

Th: Jefferson.

LETTER LXIV.—TO DAVID HARTLEY, July 2,1787

TO DAVID HARTLEY.

Paris, July 2,1787.

Dear Sir,

I received lately your favor of April the 23d, on my return from a journey of three or four months; and am always happy in an occasion of recalling myself to your memory. The most interesting intelligence from America, is that respecting the late insurrection in Massachusetts. The cause of this has not been developed to me to my perfect satisfaction. The most probable is, that those individuals were of the imprudent number of those who have involved themselves in debt beyond their abilities to pay, and that a vigorous effort in that government to compel the payment of private debts, and raise money for public ones, produced the resistance. I believe you may be assured, than an idea or desire of returning to any thing like their ancient government, never entered into their heads. I am not discouraged by this. For thus I calculate. An insurrection in one of thirteen States, in the course of eleven years that they have subsisted, amounts to one in any particular state, in one hundred and forty-three years, say a century and a half. This would not be near as many as have happened in every other government that has ever existed. So that we shall have the difference between a light and a heavy government as clear gain. I have no fear, but that the result of our experiment will be, that men may be trusted to govern themselves without a master. Could the contrary of this be proved, I should conclude, either that there is no God, or that he is a malevolent being. You have heard of the federal convention, now sitting at Philadelphia, for the amendment of the Confederation. Eleven States appointed delegates certainly; it was expected that Connecticut would also appoint, the moment its Assembly met. Rhode Island had refused. I expect they will propose several amendments; that that relative to our commerce will probably be adopted immediately, but that the others must wait to be adopted, one after another, in proportion as the minds of the States ripen for them. Dr. Franklin enjoys good health. I shall always be happy to hear from you, being, with sentiments of very sincere esteem and respect, Dear Sir, your most obedient and most humble servant,

Th: Jefferson.

LETTER LXV.—TO B. VAUGHAN, July 2, 1787

TO B. VAUGHAN.

Paris, July 2, 1787.

Dear Sir,

Your favor of February the 16th came to my hands in the moment I was setting out on a tour through the southern parts of France and northern of Italy, from which I am but just now returned. I avail myself of the earliest moment to acknowledge its receipt, and to thank you for the box of magnets which I found here. Though I do not know certainly by or from whom they come, I presume they came by Colonel Smith, who was here in my absence, and from Messrs. Nairne and Blunt, through your good offices. I think your letter of February the 16th flatters me with the expectation of another, with observations on the hygrometers I had proposed. I value what comes from you too much, not to remind you of it. Your favor by Mr. Garnett also came during my absence. I presume he has left Paris, as I can hear nothing of him. I have lost the opportunity, therefore, of seeing his method of resisting friction, as well as of showing, by attentions to him, respect for yourself and your recommendations. Mr. Paine (Common Sense) is here on his way to England. He has brought the model of an iron bridge, with which he supposes a single arch of four hundred feet may be made. It has not yet arrived in Paris. Among other projects, with which we begin to abound in America, is one for finding the longitude by the variation of the magnetic needle. The author supposes two points, one near each pole, through the northern of which pass all the magnetic meridians of the northern hemisphere, and through the southern those of the southern hemisphere. He determines their present position and periodical revolution. It is said his publication is plausible. I have not seen it.

What are you going to do with your naval armament on your side the channel. Perhaps you will ask me, what they are about to do here. A British navy and Prussian army hanging over Holland on one side, a French navy and army hanging over it on the other, looks as if they thought of fighting. Yet I think both parties too wise for that, too laudably intent on economizing, rather than on further embarrassing their finances. May they not propose to have a force on the spot to establish some neutral form of a constitution, which these powers will cook up among themselves, without consulting the parties for whom it is intended? The affair of Geneva shows such combinations possible. Wretched, indeed, is the nation, in whose affairs foreign powers are once permitted to intermeddle. Lord Wycombe is with us at present. His good sense, information, and discretion are much beyond his years, and promise good things for your country.

I beg you to accept assurances of the esteem/and respect, with which I have the honor to be, Dear Sir, your most obedient and most humble servant,

Th: Jefferson.

LETTER LXVI.—TO M. L'ABBE MORELLET, July 2, 1787

TO M. L'ABBE MORELLET.

Paris, July 2, 1787.

I am sorry, my Dear Sir, that your interest should be affected by the ill behavior of Barrois. But when you consider the facts, you will be sensible that I could not have indulged his indolence further, without increasing the injury to a more punctual workman. Stockdale, of London, had asked leave to print my Notes. I agreed to it; and promised he should have the plate of the map as soon as it should be corrected, and the copies struck off for you and myself. He thereupon printed his edition completely in three weeks. The printer, who was to strike off two hundred and fifty maps for me, kept the plate but five days. It was then delivered to Barrois, with notice that it could not be left longer with him, than should suffice to strike off his number. Repeated applications for it, by Mr. Short and my servant, were only answered by repeated promises, and times of delivery fixed, no one of which was performed. When I returned, he had been possessed of the plate upwards of two months. I was astonished and confounded, to be told it had not been sent to Stockdale, and that his edition had been lying dead on his hands three months. I sent to Barrois the very day of my return, to let him know, that justice to Stockdale did not permit me to defer sending him the plate any longer: yet I would wait five days, at the end of which he must deliver me the plate, whether his maps were done or not. I received no answer, but waited ten days. I then sent for the plate. The answer was, he was not at home. I sent again the next day. Answer, he was not at home. I sent the third day. Not at home. I then ordered the messenger to go back, and wait till he should come home. This produced an answer of two lines, *qu'il alloit soigner son ouvrier?* I wrote him word in return, to deliver the plate instantly. This I think was on a Saturday or Sunday. He told the messenger he would let me have it the Thursday following. I took patience, and sent on the Friday, but telling the messenger, if he refused to deliver it, to inform him I would be plagued no more with sending messages, but apply to the police. He then delivered it, and I sent it off immediately to London. He had kept it three months, of which three weeks were after my return. I think, Sir, you will be satisfied that justice to Stockdale, justice to myself, who had passed my word for sending on the plate, and sensibility to the shuffling conduct of Barrois, permitted me to act no otherwise. But no matter. Let his ill behavior make no odds between you and me. It will affect your interest, and that suffices to determine me to order back the plate, as soon as Stockdale has done with it. He will not require more days, than Barrois months. So that it will be here before you can want it. But it must never go into Barrois' hands again, nor of any person depending on him, or under his orders. The workman who struck off the two hundred and fifty for me, seems to have been diligent enough. Either he, or any other workman you please of that description, shall have it, to strike what number you wish. I forgot to observe, in its proper place, that when I was in the midst of my difficulties, I did myself the honor of calling on you, as well to have that of asking after your health on my return, as of asking your assistance to obtain the plate. Unluckily you were gone to Versailles; so I was obliged to proceed as well as I could. It is no excuse for Barrois, to say, he could not get his *imprimeur* to proceed. He should have applied to another. But as to you, it shall be set to rights in the manner I have before stated. Accept my regret that you were in the hands of so underserving a workman, and one who placed me under the necessity of interrupting a work which interested you. Be assured, at the same time, of the sincerity of those sentiments of esteem and respect with which I have the honor to be, Dear Sir, your most obedient and most humble servant,

Th: Jefferson.

OBSERVATIONS ON THE LETTER OF MONSIEUR DE CALONNE

[The following observations appear to have been addressed to the Count de Montmorin, about the 6th of July, 1787.]

Observations on the Letter of Monsieur de Calonne to Monsieur Jefferson, dated, Fontainbleau, October 22, 1786.

A committee was appointed, in the course of the last year, to take a view of the subjects of commerce which might be brought from the United States of America, in exchange for those of France, and to consider what advantages and facilities might be offered to encourage that commerce. The letter of Monsieur de Calonne was founded on their report. It was conclusive as to the articles on which satisfactory information had been then obtained, and reserved, for future consideration, certain others, needing further inquiry. It is proposed now to review those unfinished articles, that they may also be comprehended in the *Arrêt*, and the regulations on this branch of commerce be rendered complete.

1. The letter promised to diminish the *Droits du Roi et d'amirautè*, payable by an American vessel entering into a port at France, and to reduce what should remain into a single duty, which shall be regulated by the draught of the vessel, or her number of masts. It is doubted whether it will be expedient to regulate the duty, in either of these ways. If by the draught,of water, it will fall unequally on us as a nation; because we build our vessels sharp-bottomed, for swift sailing, so that they draw more water than those of other nations, of the same burthen. If by the number of masts, it will fall unequally on individuals; because we often see ships of one hundred and eighty tons, and brigs of three hundred and sixty. This, then, would produce an inequality among individuals, of six to one. The present principle is the most just, to regulate by the burthen. It is certainly desirable, that these duties should be reduced to a single one. Their names and numbers perplex and harass the merchant, more than their amount; subject him to imposition, and to the suspicion of it when there is none. An intention of general reformation in this article has been accordingly announced, with augmentation as to foreigners. We are in hopes, that this augmentation is not to respect us; because it is proposed as a measure of reciprocity, whereas, in some of our States, no such duties exist, and in others they are extremely light; because we have been made to hope a diminution, instead of augmentation; and because this distinction cannot draw on France any just claims from other nations; the *jura gentis amicissima*, conferred by her late treaties, having reference expressly to the nations of Europe only; and those conferred by the more ancient ones not being susceptible of any other interpretation, nor

admitting a pretension of reference to a nation which did not then exist, and which has come into existence under circumstances distinguishing its commerce from that of all other nations. Merchandise received from them, takes employment from the poor of France; ours gives it: theirs is brought in, the last stage of manufacture; ours in the first: we bring our tobaccos to be manufactured into snuff, our flax and hemp into linen and cordage, our furs into hats, skins into saddlery, shoes, and clothing; we take nothing till it has received the last hand.

2. Fish-oils. The Hanseatic treaty was the basis, on which the diminution of duty on this article was asked and granted. It is expressly referred to as such, in the letter of Monsieur de Calonne. Instead, however, of the expression, *huile et graisse de baleine et d'autres poisons*, used in that treaty, the letter uses the terms, '*huiles de baleine, spermaceti, et tout ce qui est compris sous ces denominations.*' And the Farmers have availed themselves of this variation, to refuse the diminution of duty on the oils of the *vache marine, chien de mer, esturgeon*, and other fish. It is proposed, therefore, to re-establish in the *Arrêt*, the expression of the Hanseatic treaty, and to add, from the same treaty, the articles '*baleine coupée et fanon de baleine.*'

The letter states these regulations as finally made by the King. The merchants, on this supposition, entered into speculations. But they found themselves called on for the old duties, not only on other fish-oils, but on the whale-oil. Monsieur de Calonne always promised, that the *Arrêt* should be retrospective to the date of the letter, so as to refund to them the duties they had thus been obliged to pay. To this, attention is prayed in forming the *Arrêt*. His majesty having been pleased, as an encouragement to the importation of our fish-oils, to abolish the *Droits de fabrication*, it is presumed that the purpose announced, of continuing those duties on foreign oils, will not be extended to us.

3. Rice. The duty on this, is only seven and a half deniers the quintal, or about one quarter per cent, on its first cost. While this serves to inform a government of the quantities imported, it cannot discourage that importation. Nothing further, therefore, is necessary on this article.

4. *Potasse*. This article is of principal utility to France, in her bleacheries of linen, glass-works, and soap-works; and the potash of America, being made of green wood, is known to be the best in the world. All duty on it was, therefore, abolished by the King. But the city of Rouen levies on it a duty of twenty sols the quintal, which is very sensible in its price, brings it dearer to the bleacheries near Paris, to those of Beauvais, Laval, &c. and to the glass-works, and encourages them to give a preference to the potash or soude of other nations. This is a counteraction of the views of the King, expressed in the letter, which it is hoped will be prevented.

5. Turpentine, tar, and pitch were not decided on, on the former occasion. Turpentine (*térébenthine*) pays ten sols the quintal, and ten sols the livre, making fifteen sols the quintal; which is ten per cent, on its prime cost. Tar (*goudron, braigras*) pays eight livres the *leth* of twelve barrels, and ten sols the livre, amounting to twenty sols the barrel; which is twelve and a half per cent, on its prime cost. Pitch (*brai sec*) pays ten sols the quintal, and ten sols the livre, making fifteen sols the quintal; which is twenty per cent, on its prime cost. Duties of from ten to twenty per cent., on articles of heavy carriage, prevent their importation. They eat up all the profits of the merchant, and often subject him to loss. This has been much the case with respect to turpentine, tar, and pitch, which are principal articles of remittance for the State of North Carolina. It is hoped, that it will coincide with the views of government, in making the present regulations, to suppress the duties on these articles, which, of all others, can bear them least.

LETTER LXVII.—TO T. M. RANDOLPH, JUNIOR, July 6, 1787

TO T. M. RANDOLPH, JUNIOR.

Paris, July 6, 1787.

Dear Sir,

Your favor of April the 14th came here during my absence on a journey through the southern parts of France and northern of Italy, from which I am but lately returned. This cause alone, has prevented your receiving a more early answer to it. I am glad to find, that among the various branches of science presenting themselves to your mind, you have fixed on that of politics as your principal pursuit. Your country will derive from this a more immediate and sensible benefit. She has much for you to do. For though we may say with confidence, that the worst of the American constitutions, is better than the best which ever existed before, in any other country, and that they are wonderfully perfect for a first essay, yet every human essay must have defects. It will remain, therefore, to those now coming on the stage of public affairs, to perfect what has been so well begun by those, going off it. Mathematics, Natural Philosophy, Natural History, Anatomy, Chemistry, Botany, will become amusements for your hours of relaxation, and auxiliaries to your principal studies. Precious and delightful ones they will be. As soon as such a foundation is laid in them, as you may build on as you please, hereafter, I suppose you will proceed to your main objects, Politics, Law, Rhetoric, and History. As to these, the place where you study them is absolutely indifferent. I should except Rhetoric, a very essential member of them, and which I suppose must be taught to advantage where you are. You would do well, therefore, to attend the public exercises in this branch also, and to do it with very particular diligence. This being done, the question arises, where you shall fix yourself for studying Politics, Law, and History. I should not hesitate to decide in favor of France, because you will, at the same time, be learning to speak the language of that country, become absolutely essential under our present circumstances. The best method of doing this, would be to fix yourself in some family where there are women and children, in Passy, Auteuil, or some other of the little towns in reach of Paris. The principal hours of the day you will attend to your studies, and in those of relaxation associate with the family. You will learn to speak better from women and children in three months, than from men in a year. Such a situation, too, will render more easy a due attention to economy of time and money. Having pursued your main studies here about two years, and acquired a facility in speaking French, take a tour of four or five months through this country and Italy, return then to Virginia, and pass a year in Williamsburg, under the care of Mr. Wythe; and you will be ready to enter on the public stage, with superior advantages. I have proposed to you to carry on the study of the law, with that of politics and history. Every political measure will, for ever, have an intimate connection with the laws of the land; and he who knows nothing of these, will always be perplexed, and often foiled by adversaries having the advantage of that knowledge over him. Besides, it is a source of infinite comfort to reflect, that under every change of fortune, we have a resource in ourselves, from which we may be able to derive an honorable subsistence. I would, therefore, propose not only the study, but the practice of the law for some time, to possess yourself of the habit of public speaking. With respect to modern languages, French, as I have before observed, is indispensable. Next to this, the Spanish is most important to an American. Our connection with Spain is already important, and will become daily more so. Besides this, the ancient part of American history is written chiefly in Spanish. To a person who would make a point of reading and speaking French and Spanish, I should doubt the utility of learning Italian. These three languages, being all degeneracies from the Latin, resemble one another so much, that I doubt the probability of keeping in the head a distinct knowledge of them all. I suppose that he who learns them all, will speak a compound of the three, and neither perfectly. The journey which I propose to you, need not be expensive, and would be very useful. With your talents and industry, with science, and that steadfast honesty which eternally pursues right, regardless of consequences, you may promise yourself every thing—but health, without which there is no happiness. An attention to health, then, should take place of every other object. The time necessary to secure this by active exercises, should be devoted to it, in preference to every other pursuit. I know the difficulty with which a studious man tears himself from his studies, at any given moment of the day. But his happiness, and that of his family, depend on it. The most uninformed mind with a healthy body, is happier than the wisest valetudinarian. I need not tell you, that if I can be useful to you in any part of this, or any other plan you shall adopt, you will make me happy by commanding my services.

Will you be so good, Sir, as to return my most respectful thanks for the diploma with which I am honored by the society instituted with you, for the encouragement of the study of Natural History. I am afraid it will never be in my power to contribute any thing to the object of the institution. Circumstances have thrown me into a very different line of life; and not choice, as I am happy to find in your case. In the year 1781, while confined to my room by a fall from my horse, I wrote some Notes, in answer to the inquiries of M. de Marbois, as to the natural and political state of Virginia. They were hasty and undigested: yet as some of these touch slightly on some objects of its natural history, I will take the liberty of asking the society to accept a copy of them. For the same reason, and because too, they touch on the political condition of our country, I will beg leave to present you with a copy, and ask the favor of you to find a conveyance for them, from London to Edinburgh. They are printed by Stockdale, bookseller, Piccadilly, and will be ready in three or four weeks from this time. I will direct him to deliver two copies to your order. Repeating, constantly, the proffer of my services, I shall only add assurances of the esteem and attachment, with which I am, Dear Sir, your friend and servant,

Th: Jefferson.

LETTER LXVIII.—TO STEPHEN CATHALAN, JUNIOR, July 21,1787

TO STEPHEN CATHALAN, JUNIOR.

Paris, July 21,1787.

Sir,

I received your favor of May the 9th, just as I was stepping into the barge on my departure from Cette; which prevented my answering it from that place. On my arrival here, I thought I would avail myself of the opportunity of paying your balance, to make a little acquaintance with Sir John Lambert. One or two unsuccessful attempts to find him at home, with the intermediate procrastinations well known to men of business, prevented my seeing him till yesterday, and have led me on to this moment, through a perpetual remorse of conscience for not writing to you, and in the constant belief that it would be to morrow and to morrow. At length, I have seen him, paid him the eighty-five livres which you have been so kind as to advance for me, and am actually at my writing table, returning you thanks for this kindness, and to yourself and the family for the thousand others I received at their hands, at Marseilles. My journey, after leaving you, wanted nothing but the company of Madame Cathalan and yourself, to render it perfectly agreeable. I felt the want of it peculiarly on the *canal de Languedoc*, where, with society, the mode of travelling would have been charming. I was much indebted to M. Minaudier, for a good equipment from Agde, and unceasing attentions to that place; for which I was indebted to your recommendations as well as to his goodness.

I am honored with your father's letters of June the 30th; and as he does not read English, and I cannot write French, I must beg leave to answer him through you. I thank him for his hints on the subject of tobacco. I am now pressing for arrangements as to that article, to take place on the expiration of Mr. Morris's contract, and the order of Bernis. What form this business will take, or what will be the nature of the arrangements, or whether there will be any, I am as yet unable to say. I will take care to inform you the moment there is a decision.

The public business with which Mr. Barclay has been charged rendering it necessary for him to repair to Congress, and the interest of his creditors, his family, and himself requiring his return to America, he has departed for that country. I know nothing of Mr. Barclay's affairs in this country. He has good possessions in America, which, he assured me, were much more than sufficient to satisfy all the demands against him. He went, determined to convert those immediately into money, and to collect the debts due to him there, that he might be enabled to pay his debts. My opinion of his integrity is such, as to leave no doubt in my mind, that he will do every thing in his power to render justice to his creditors; and I know so well his attachment to M. Cathalan, as to be satisfied, that if he makes any difference among his creditors, he will be among the most favored. Mr. Barclay is an honest and honorable man, and is more goaded towards the payment of his debts by his own feelings, than by all the processes of law, which could be set on foot against him.

No arrangements having ever been made as yet, for cases like that of the carpenter of the American ship Sally, I am unable to answer on that subject. I am in hopes, his money will last till he recovers his senses, or till we can receive instructions what to do in that and similar cases.

M. Cathalan wishes a copy of my Notes on Virginia. If you will be so good as to advise me by what channel they will go safely, I will do myself the honor of sending a copy, either of the original or of the translation. Present me affectionately to Mrs. Cathalan, the mother and daughter; tell the latter I feed on the hopes of seeing her one day at Paris. My friendly respects wait also on your father; and on yourself, assurances of the esteem and consideration with which I have the honor to be, Dear Sir, your most obedient and most humble servant,

Th: Jefferson.

LETTER LXIX.—TO THE DELEGATES OF RHODE ISLAND, July 22,1787

TO THE DELEGATES OF RHODE ISLAND.
Paris, July 22,1787.
Gentlemen,
I was honored, in the month of January last, with a letter from the honorable the Delegates of Rhode Island in Congress, enclosing a letter from the corporation of Rhode Island College to his Most Christian Majesty, and some other papers. I was then in the hurry of a preparation for a journey into the south of France, and therefore unable, at that moment, to make the inquiries which the object of the letter rendered necessary. As soon as I returned, which was in the last month, I turned my attention to that object, which was the establishment of a professorship of the French language in the College, and the obtaining a collection of the best French authors, with the aid of the King. That neither the College nor myself might be compromitted uselessly, I thought it necessary to sound, previously, those who were able to inform me what would be the success of the application. I was assured, so as to leave no doubt, that it would not be complied with; that there had never been an instance of the King's granting such a demand in a foreign country, and that they would be cautious of setting the precedent: that in this moment, too, they were embarrassed with the difficult operation of putting down all establishments of their own, which could possibly be dispensed with, in order to bring their expenditures down to the level of their receipts. Upon such information I was satisfied, that it was most prudent not to deliver the letter, and spare to both parties the disagreeableness of giving and receiving a denial. The King did give to two colleges in America copies of the works printing in the public press. But were this to be obtained for the College of Rhode Island, it would extend only to a volume or two of Buffon's works, still to be printed, Manilius's Astronomicon, and one or two other works in the press, which are of no consequence. I did not think this an object for the College worth being pressed. I beg the favor of you, gentlemen, to assure the corporation, that no endeavors of mine should have been spared, could they have effected their wish: and that they have been faithfully used in making the preliminary inquiries which are necessary, and which ended in an assurance, that nothing could be done. These papers having been transmitted to me through your delegation, will, I hope, be an apology for my availing myself of the same channel for communicating the result.
I have the honor to be, with sentiments of the most perfect esteem and respect, Gentlemen, your most obedient and most humble servant,
Th: Jefferson.

LETTER LXX.—TO THE COUNT DE MONTMORIN, July 23, 1787

TO THE COUNT DE MONTMORIN.

Paris, July 23, 1787.

Sir,

I had the honor, a few days ago, of putting into the hands of your Excellency, some observations on the other articles of American produce, brought into the ports of this country. That of our tobaccos, from the particular form of their administration here, and their importance to the King's revenues, has been placed on a separate line, and considered separately. I will now ask permission to bring that subject under your consideration.

The mutual extension of their commerce was among the fairest advantages to be derived to France and the United States, from the independence of the latter. An exportation of eighty millions, chiefly in raw materials, is supposed to constitute the present limits of the commerce of the United States with the nations of Europe; limits, however, which extend as their population increases. To draw the best proportion of this into the ports of France, rather than of any other nation, is believed to be the wish and interest of both. Of these eighty millions, thirty are constituted by the single article of tobacco. Could the whole of this be brought into the ports of France, to satisfy its own demands, and the residue to be re-vended to other nations, it would be a powerful link of commercial connection. But we are far from this. Even her own consumption, supposed to be nine millions, under the administration of the monopoly to which it is farmed, enters little, as an article of exchange, into the commerce of the two nations. When this article was first put into Farm, perhaps it did not injure the commercial interests of the kingdom; because nothing but British manufactures were then allowed to be given in return for American tobaccos. The laying the trade open, then, to all the subjects of France, could not have relieved her from a payment in money. Circumstances are changed; yet the old institution remains. The body to which this monopoly was given, was not mercantile. Their object is to simplify, as much as possible, the administration of their affairs. They sell for cash; they purchase, therefore, with cash. Their interest, their principles, and their practice seem opposed to the general interest of the kingdom, which would require, that this capital article should be laid open to a free exchange for the productions of this country. So far does the spirit of simplifying their operations govern this body, that, relinquishing the advantages to be derived from a competition of sellers, they contracted some time ago with a single person (Mr. Morris) for three years' supplies of American tobacco, to be paid for in cash. They obliged themselves, too, expressly, to employ no other person to purchase in America, during that term. In consequence of this, the mercantile houses of France, concerned in sending her productions to be exchanged for tobacco, cut off for three years from the hope of selling these tobaccos in France, were of necessity to abandon that commerce. In consequence of this, too, a single individual, constituted sole purchaser of so great a proportion of the tobaccos made, had the price in his own power. A great reduction in it took place, and that not only on the quantity he bought, but on the whole quantity made. The loss to the States producing the article, did not go to cheapen it for their friends here. Their price was fixed. What was gained on their consumption, was to enrich the person purchasing it; the rest, the monopolists and merchants of other countries. The effect of this operation was vitally felt by every farmer in America, concerned in the culture of this plant. At the end of the year, he found he had lost a fourth or a third of his revenue; the State, the same proportion of its subjects of exchange with other nations: the manufactures of this country, too, were either not to go there at all, or go through the channel of a new monopoly, which, freed from the control of competition in prices and qualities, was not likely to extend their consumption. It became necessary to relieve the two countries from the fatal effects of this double monopoly. I had the honor of addressing a letter, on the 15th day of August, 1785, to his late Excellency, the Count de Vergennes, upon this subject, a copy of which I do myself the honor herein to enclose. The effectual mode of relief was to lay the commerce open. But the King's interest was also to be guarded. A committee was appointed to take this matter into consideration; and the result was, an order to the Farmers General, that no such contract should be made again. And to furnish such aliment as might keep that branch of commerce alive, till the expiration of the present contract, they were required to put the merchants in general on a level with Mr. Morris, for the quantity of twelve or fifteen thousand hogsheads a year. That this relief, too, might not be intercepted from the merchants of the two suffering nations, by those of a neighboring one, and that the transportation of so bulky an article might go to nourish their own shipping, no tobaccos were to be counted of this purchase, but those brought in French or American vessels. Of this order, made at Bernis, his Excellency, Count de Vergennes, was pleased to honor me with a communication, by a letter of the 30th of May, 1786; desiring that I would publish it as well in America as to the American merchants in France. I did so; communicating it to Congress at the same time. This order, thus viewed, with the transactions which produced it, will be seen to have been necessary; and its punctual and candid execution has been rendered still more so, by the speculations of the merchants, entered into on the faith of it. Otherwise it would become the instrument of their ruin instead of their relief. A twelvemonth has elapsed some time since; and it is questioned, whether the Farmers General have purchased, within that time, the quantity prescribed, and on the conditions

prescribed. It would be impossible for the merchants to prove the negative; it will be easy for the Farmers General to show the affirmative, if it exists. I hope that a branch of commerce of this extent, will be thought interesting enough to both nations to render it the desire of your Excellency to require, as I deem it my duty to ask, a report of the purchases they have made, according to the conditions of the order of Bernis, specifying in that report, 1. The quantities purchased; 2. the prices paid; 3. the dates of the purchase and payment; 4. the flag of the vessel in which imported; 5. her name; 6. her port of delivery; and 7. the name of the seller. The four first articles make part of the conditions required by the order of Bernis; the three last may be necessary for the correction of any errors, which should happen to arise in the report.

But the order of Bernis was never considered but as a temporary relief. The radical evil will still remain. There will be but one purchaser in the kingdom, and the hazard of his refusal will damp every mercantile speculation. It is very much to be desired, that before the expiration of this order, some measure may be devised, which may bring this great article into free commerce between the two nations. Had this been practicable at the time it was put into Farm, that mode of collecting the revenue would probably never have been adopted: now that it has become practicable, it seems reasonable to discontinue this mode, and to substitute some of those practised on other imported articles, on which a revenue is levied, without absolutely suppressing them in commerce. If the revenue can be secured, the interests of a few individuals will hardly be permitted to weigh against those of as many millions, equally subjects of his Majesty, and against those, too, of a nation allied to him by all the ties of treaty, of interest, and of affection. The privileges of the most favored nation have been mutually exchanged by treaty. But the productions of other nations, which do not rival those of France, are suffered to be bought and sold freely within the kingdom. By prohibiting all his Majesty's subjects from dealing in tobacco, except with a single company, one third of the exports of the United States are rendered uncommerciable here. This production is so peculiarly theirs, that its shackles affect no other nation. A relief from these shackles will form a memorable epoch in the commerce of the two nations. It will establish at once a great basis of exchange serving, like a point of union, to draw to it other members of our commerce. Nature, too, has conveniently assorted our wants and our superfluities to each other. Each nation has exactly to spare the articles which the other wants. We have a surplus of rice, tobacco, furs, peltry, potash, lamp-oils, timber, which France wants; she has a surplus of wines, brandies, esculent oils, fruits, and manufactures of all kinds, which we want. The governments have nothing to do, but not to hinder their merchants from making the exchange. The difference of language, laws, and customs, will be some obstacle for a time; but the interest of the merchants will surmount them. A more serious obstacle is our debt to Great Britain. Yet, since the treaty between this country and that, I should not despair of seeing that debt paid, in part, with the productions of France, if our produce can obtain here a free course of exchange for them. The distant prospect is still more promising. A century's experience has shown, that we double our numbers every twenty or twenty-five years. No circumstance can be foreseen, at this moment, which will lessen our rate of multiplication for centuries to come. For every article of the productions and manufactures of this country, then, which can be introduced into habit there, the demand will double every twenty or twenty-five years. And to introduce the habit, we have only to let the merchants alone. Whether we may descend, by a single step, from the present state to that of perfect freedom of commerce in this article; whether any, and what, intermediate operation may be necessary to prepare the way to this; what cautions must be observed for the security of his Majesty's revenue, which we do not wish to impair, will rest with the wisdom of his ministers, whose knowledge of the subject will enable them to devise the best plans, and whose patriotism and justice will dispose them to pursue them. To the friendly dispositions of your Excellency, of which we have had such early and multiplied proofs, I take the liberty of committing this subject, particularly, trusting that some method may be devised of reconciling the collection of his Majesty's revenues with the interests of the two nations; and have the honor of assuring you of those sincere sentiments of esteem and respect, with which I am your Excellency's most obedient and most humble servant,

Th: Jefferson.

LETTER LXXI.—TO MR. SKIPWITH, July 28, 1787

TO MR. SKIPWITH.

Paris, July 28, 1787.

Dear Sir,

A long journey has prevented me from writing to any of my friends for some time past. This was undertaken with a view to benefit a dislocated and ill-set wrist, by the mineral waters of Aix, in Provence. Finding this hope vain, I was led from other views to cross the Alps as far as Turin, Milan, Genoa; to follow the Mediterranean as far as Cette, the canal of Languedoc, the Garonne, &c, to Paris. A most pleasing journey it proved; arts and agriculture offering something new at every step, and often things worth our imitation. But the accounts from our country give me to believe, that we are not in a condition to hope for the imitation of any thing good. All my letters are filled with details of our extravagance. From these accounts, I look back to the time of the war, as a time of happiness and enjoyment, when amidst the privation of many things not essential to happiness, we could not run in debt, because nobody would trust us; when we practised, of necessity, the maxim of buying nothing but what we had money in our pockets to pay for; a maxim, which, of all others, lays the broadest foundation for happiness. I see no remedy to our evils, but an open course of law. Harsh as it may seem, it would relieve the very patients who dread it, by stopping the course of their extravagance, before it renders their affairs entirely desperate. The eternal and bitter strictures on our conduct, which teem in every London paper, and are copied from them into others, fill me with anxiety on this subject. The state of things in Europe is rather threatening at this moment. The innovations of the Emperor in his dominions, have excited a spirit of resistance. His subjects in Brabant and Flanders are arming, and he has put forty-five thousand troops in motion towards that country. I believe they will come to blows. The parties in Holland have already spilt too much blood to be easily stopped. If left to themselves, I apprehend the Stadtholderians will be too strong; and if foreign powers interfere, the weight is still on their side. England and Prussia will be too much for France. As it is certain that neither of these powers wish for war, and that England and France are particularly averse to it, perhaps the matter may end in an armed mediation. If the mediators should not agree, they will draw their negotiations into length, and trust to the chapter of accidents for their final solution. With respect to our country, it stands well with the present ministry here. The non-payment of our debt is against us. We are occupied in procuring favorable terms of reception for our produce.

Adieu, my Dear Sir, and be assured of the sentiments of sincere esteem of your affectionate friend and servant,

Th: Jefferson.

LETTER LXXII.—TO J. W. EPPES, July 28,1787

TO J. W. EPPES.

Paris, July 28,1787.

Dear Jack,

The letter which you were so kind as to write to me the 22nd of May, 1786, was not delivered to me till the 3rd of May, 1787, when it found me in the neighborhood of Marseilles. Before that time you must have taken your degree, as mentioned in your letter. Those public testimonies which are earned by merit, and not by solicitation, may always be accepted without the imputation of vanity. Of this nature is the degree which your masters proposed to confer on you. I congratulate you sincerely on it. It will be a pleasing event to yourself; it will be the same to your parents and friends, and to none more than myself. Go on deserving applause, and you will be sure to meet with it: and the way to deserve it, is to be good, and to be industrious. I am sure you will be good, and hope you will be industrious. As to your future plan, I am too distant from you, to advise you on sure grounds. In general, I am of opinion that till the age of about sixteen, we are best employed on languages; Latin, Greek, French, and Spanish, or such of them as we can. After this, I think the College of William and Mary the best place to go through courses of Mathematics, Natural Philosophy in its different branches, and Law. Of the languages I have mentioned, I think Greek the least useful. Write me word, from time to time, how you go on. I shall always be glad to assist you with any books you may have occasion for, and you may count with certainty on every service I can ever render you, as well as on the sincere esteem of, Dear Jack, yours affectionately,

Th: Jefferson.

LETTER LXXIII.—TO A. DONALD, July 28, 1787

TO A. DONALD.

Paris, July 28, 1787.

Dear Sir,

I received with infinite satisfaction your letter of the 1st of March: it was the first information I had of your being in America. There is no person whom I shall see again with more cordial joy, whenever it shall be my lot to return to my native country; nor any one whose prosperity, in the mean time, will be more interesting to me. I find as I grow older, that I set a higher value on the intimacies of my youth, and am more afflicted by whatever loses one of them to me. Should it be in my power to render any service, in your shipment of tobacco to Havre de Grace, I shall do it with great pleasure. The order of Bernis has, I believe, been evaded by the Farmers General as much as possible. At this moment, I receive information from most of the seaports, that they refuse taking any tobacco, under the pretext, that they have purchased their whole quantity. From Havre I have heard nothing, and believe you will stand a better chance there than any where else. Being one of the ports of manufacture, too, it is entitled to a higher price. I have now desired that the Farmers may make a distinct return of their purchases, which are conformable to the order of Bernis. If they have really bought their quantity, on those terms, we must be satisfied: if they have not, I shall propose their being obliged to make it up instantly. There is a considerable accumulation of tobacco in the ports.

Among many good qualities which my countrymen possess, some of a different character unhappily mix themselves. The most remarkable are indolence, extravagance, and infidelity to their engagements. Cure the two first, and the last would disappear, because it is a consequence of them, and not proceeding from a want of morals. I know of no remedy against indolence and extravagance, but a free course of justice. Every thing else is merely palliative: but unhappily, the evil has gained too generally the mass of the nation, to leave the course of justice unobstructed. The maxim of buying nothing without the money in our pockets to pay for it, would make of our country one of the happiest upon earth. Experience during the war proved this; as I think every man will remember, that under all the privations it obliged him to submit to, during that period, he slept sounder, and awaked happier than he can do now. Desperate of finding relief from a free course of justice, I look forward to the abolition of all credit, as the only other remedy which can take place. I have seen, therefore, with pleasure, the exaggerations of our want of faith, with which the London papers teem. It is, indeed, a strong medicine for sensible minds, but it is a medicine. It will prevent their crediting us abroad, in which case, we cannot be credited at home. I have been much concerned at the losses produced by the fire of Richmond. I hope you have escaped them. It will give me much pleasure to hear from you, as often as you can spare a moment to write. Be assured that nobody entertains for you sentiments of more perfect and sincere esteem than, Dear Sir, your friend and servant,

Th: Jefferson.

LETTER LXXIV.—TO WILLIAM DRAYTON, July 30, 1787

TO WILLIAM DRAYTON.

Paris, July 30, 1787.

Sir,

Having observed that the consumption of rice in this country, and particularly in this capital, was very great, I thought it my duty to inform myself from what markets they draw their supplies, in what proportion from ours, and whether it might not be practicable to increase that proportion. This city being little concerned in foreign commerce, it is difficult to obtain information on particular branches of it in the detail. I addressed myself to the retailers of rice, and from them received a mixture of truth and error, which I was unable to sift apart in the first moment. Continuing, however, my inquiries, they produced at length this result; that the dealers here, were in the habit of selling two qualities of rice, that of Carolina, with which they were supplied chiefly from England, and that of Piedmont: that the Carolina rice was long, slender, white, and transparent, answers well when prepared with milk, sugar, &ic. but not so well when prepared *au gras*; that that of Piedmont was shorter, thicker, and less white, but that it presented its form better when dressed *au gras*, was better tasted, and therefore preferred by good judges for those purposes: that the consumption of rice, in this form, was much the most considerable, but that the superior beauty of the Carolina rice, seducing the eye of those purchasers who are attached to appearances, the demand for it was upon the whole as great as for that of Piedmont. They supposed this difference of quality to proceed from a difference of management; that the Carolina rice was husked with an instrument which broke it more, and that less pains were taken to separate the broken from the unbroken grains; imagining that it was the broken grains which dissolved in oily preparations: that the Carolina rice costs somewhat less than that of Piedmont; but that being obliged to sort the whole grains from the broken, in order to satisfy the taste of their customers, they ask and receive as much for the first quality of Carolina, when sorted, as for the rice of Piedmont; but the second and third qualities, obtained by sorting, are sold much cheaper. The objection to the Carolina rice then, being, that it crumbles in certain forms of preparation, and this supposed to be the effect of a less perfect machine for husking, I flattered myself I should be able to learn what might be the machine of Piedmont, when I should arrive at Marseilles, to which place I was to go in the course of a tour through the seaport towns of this country. At Marseilles, however, they differed as much in the account of the machine, as at Paris they had differed about other circumstances. Some said it was husked between mill-stones, others between rubbers of wood in the form of mill-stones, others of cork. They concurred in one fact, however, that the machine might be seen by me, immediately on crossing the Alps. This would be an affair of three weeks. I crossed them, and went through the rice country from Vercelli to Pavia, about sixty miles. I found the machine to be absolutely the same with that used in Carolina, as well as I could recollect a description which Mr. E. Rutledge had given me of it. It is on the plan of a powder-mill. In some of them, indeed, they arm each pestle with an iron tooth, consisting of nine spikes hooped together, which I do not remember in the description of Mr. Rutledge. I therefore had a tooth made, which I have the honor of forwarding you with this letter; observing, at the same time, that as many of their machines are without teeth as with them, and of course, that the advantage is not very palpable. It seems to follow, then, that the rice of Lombardy (for though called Piedmont rice, it does not grow in that country, but in Lombardy) is of a different species from that of Carolina; different in form, in color, and in quality. We know that in Asia they have several distinct species of this grain. Monsieur Poivre, a former Governor of the Isle of France, in travelling through several countries of Asia, observed with particular attention the objects of their agriculture, and he tells us, that in Cochin-China they cultivate six several kinds of rice, which he describes, three of them requiring water, and three growing on highlands. The rice of Carolina is said to have come from Madagascar, and De Poivre tells us, it is the white rice which is cultivated there. This favors the probability of its being of a different species originally, from that of Piedmont; and time, culture, and climate may have made it still more different. Under this idea, I thought it would be well to furnish you with some of the Piedmont rice, unhusked, but was told it was contrary to the laws to export it in that form. I took such measures as I could, however, to have a quantity brought out, and lest these should fail, I brought, myself, a few pounds. A part of this I have addressed to you by the way of London; a part comes with this letter; and I shall send another parcel by some other conveyance, to prevent the danger of miscarriage. Any one of them arriving safe, may serve to put in seed, should the society think it an object. This seed, too, coming from Vercelli, where the best rice is supposed to grow, is more to be depended on, than what may be sent me hereafter. There is a rice from the Levant, which is considered as of a quality still different, and some think it superior to that of Piedmont. The troubles which have existed in that country for several years back, have intercepted it from the European market, so that it is become almost unknown. I procured a bag of it, however, at Marseilles, and another of the best rice of Lombardy, which are on their way to this place, and when arrived, I will forward you a quantity of each, sufficient to enable you to judge of their qualities when prepared for the table. I have also taken measures to have a quantity of it brought from the Levant, unhusked. If I succeed, it shall be forwarded in like manner. I should think it certainly advantageous to cultivate, in Carolina and Georgia, the two qualities demanded at market; because the progress of culture, with us, may soon get beyond the demand for the white rice; and because, too, there is often a brisk demand for the one quality, when the market is glutted with the other. I should hope there would be no danger of losing the species of white rice, by a confusion with the other. This would be a real misfortune, as I should not hesitate to pronounce the white, upon the whole, the most precious of the two, for us.

The dry rice of Cochin-China has the reputation of being the whitest to the eye, best flavored to the taste, and most productive. It seems then to unite the good qualities of both the others known to us. Could it supplant them, it would be a great happiness, as it would enable us to get rid of those ponds of stagnant water, so fatal to human health and life. But such is the force of habit, and caprice of taste, that we could not be sure beforehand, it would produce this effect. The experiment, however, is worth trying, should it only end in producing a third quality, and increasing the demand. I will endeavor to procure some to be brought from Cochin-China. The event, however, will be uncertain and distant.

I was induced, in the course of my journey through the south of France, to pay very particular attention to the objects of their culture, because the resemblance of their climate to that of the southern parts of the United States authorizes us to presume we may adopt any of their articles of culture, which we would wish for. We should not wish for their wines, though they are good and abundant. The culture of the vine is not desirable in lands capable of producing any thing else. It is a species of gambling, and of desperate gambling too, wherein, whether you make much or nothing, you are equally ruined. The middling crop alone is the saving point, and that the seasons seldom hit. Accordingly, we see much wretchedness among this class of cultivators. Wine, too, is so cheap in these countries, that a laborer with us, employed in the culture of any other article, may exchange it for wine, more and better than he could raise himself. It is a resource for a country, the whole of whose good soil is otherwise employed, and which still has some barren spots, and a surplus of population to employ on them. There the vine is good, because it is something in the place of nothing. It may become a resource to us at a still earlier period: when the increase of population shall increase our productions beyond the demand for them, both at home and abroad. Instead of going on to make an useless surplus of them, we may employ our supernumerary hands on the vine. But that period is not yet arrived.

The almond tree is also so precarious, that none can depend for subsistence on its produce, but persons of capital.

The caper, though a more tender plant, is more certain in its produce, because a mound of earth of the size of a cucumber hill, thrown over the plant in the fall, protects it effectually against the cold of winter. When the danger of frost is over in the spring, they uncover it, and begin its culture. There is a great deal of this in the neighborhood of Toulon. The plants are set about eight feet apart, and yield, one year with another, about two pounds of caper each, worth on the spot six pence sterling the pound. They require little culture, and this may be performed either with the plough or hoe. The principal work is the gathering of the fruit as it forms. Every plant must be picked every other day, from the last of June till the middle of October. But this is the work of women and children. This plant does well in any kind of soil which is dry, or even in walls where there is no soil, and it lasts the life of a man. Toulon would be the proper port to apply for them. I must observe, that the preceding details cannot be relied on with the fullest certainty, because, in the canton where this plant is cultivated, the inhabitants speak no written language, but a medley, which I could understand but very imperfectly.

The fig and mulberry are so well known in America, that nothing need be said of them. Their culture, too, is by women and children, and therefore earnestly to be desired in countries where there are slaves. In these, the women and children are often employed in labors disproportioned to their sex and age. By presenting to the master objects of culture, easier and equally beneficial, all temptation to misemploy them would be removed, and the lot of this tender part of our species be much softened. By varying too the articles of culture, we multiply the chances for making something, and disarm the seasons, in a proportionable degree, of their calamitous effects.

The olive is a tree the least known in America, and yet the most worthy of being known. Of all the gifts of heaven to man, it is next to the most precious, if it be not the most precious. Perhaps it may claim a preference even to bread; because there is such an infinitude of vegetables, which it renders a proper and comfortable nourishment. In passing the Alps at the Col de Tende, where they are mere masses of rock, wherever there happens to be a little soil, there are a number of olive trees, and a village supported by them. Take away these trees, and the same ground, in corn, would not support a single family. A pound of oil, which can be bought for three or four pence sterling, is equivalent to many pounds of flesh, by the quantity of vegetables it will prepare, and render fit and comfortable food. Without this tree, the country of Provence and territory of Genoa, would not support one half, perhaps not one third, their present inhabitants. The nature of the soil is of little consequence, if it be dry. The trees are planted from fifteen to twenty feet apart, and when tolerably good, will yield fifteen or twenty pounds of oil yearly, one with another. There are trees which yield much more. They begin to render good crops at twenty years old, and last till killed by cold, which happens at some time or other, even in their best positions in France. But they put out again from their roots. In Italy, I am told, they have trees of two hundred years old. They afford an easy but constant employment through the year, and require so little nourishment, that if the soil be fit for any other production, it may be cultivated among the olive trees, without injuring them. The northern limits of this tree, are the mountains of the Cevennes, from about the meridian of Carcassonne to the Rhone, and from thence, the Alps and Apennines as far as Genoa, I know, and how much farther I am not informed. The shelter of these mountains may be considered as equivalent to a degree and a half of latitude, at least; because westward of the commencement of the Cevennes, there are no olive trees in 43 1/2° or even 43° of latitude, whereas, we find them now on the Rhone at Pierrelatte, in 44 1/2°, and formerly they were at Tains, above the mouth of the Isere, in 45°, sheltered by the near approach of the Cevennes and Alps, which only leave there a passage for the Rhone. Whether such a shelter exists or not, in the States of South Carolina and Georgia, I know not. But this we may say, either that it exists, or that it is not necessary there; because we know that they produce the orange in open air; and wherever the orange will stand at all, experience shows that the olive will stand well; being a hardier tree. Notwithstanding the great quantities of oil made in France, they have not enough for their own consumption, and therefore import from other countries. This is an article, the consumption of which will always keep pace with its production. Raise it; and it begets its own demand. Little is carried to America, because Europe has it not to spare. We therefore have not learned the use of it. But cover the southern States with it, and every man will become a consumer of oil, within whose reach it can be brought, in point of price. If the memory of those persons is held in great respect in South Carolina, who introduced there the culture of rice, a plant which sows life and death with almost equal hand, what obligations would be due to him who should introduce the olive tree, and set the example of its culture! Were the owner of slaves to view it only as the means of bettering their condition, how much would he better that, by planting one of those trees for every slave he possessed! Having been myself an eye-witness to the blessings which this tree sheds on the poor, I never had my wishes so kindled for the introduction of any article of new culture into our own country. South Carolina and Georgia appear to me to be the States, wherein its success, in favorable positions at least, could not be doubted, and I flattered myself, it would come within the views of the society for agriculture, to begin the experiments which are to prove its practicability. Carcassonne is the place from which the plants may be most certainly and cheaply obtained. They can be sent from thence by water to Bordeaux, where they may be embarked on vessels bound to Charleston. There is too little intercourse between Charleston and Marseilles, to propose this as the port of exportation. I offer my services to the society, for the obtaining and forwarding any number of plants which may be desired.

Before I quit the subject of climates, and the plants adapted to them, I will add, as a matter of curiosity, and of some utility too, that my journey through the southern parts of France, and the territory of Genoa, but still more the crossing of the Alps, enabled me to form a scale of the tenderer plants, and to arrange them according to their different powers of resisting cold. In passing the Alps at the Col de Tende, we cross three very high mountains, successively. In ascending, we lose these plants, one after another, as we rise, and find them again in the contrary order, as we descend on the other side; and this is repeated three times. Their order, proceeding from the tenderest to the hardiest, is as follows. Caper, orange, palm, aloe, olive, pomegranate, walnut, fig, almond. But this must be understood of the plant only; for as to the fruit, the order is somewhat different. The caper, for example, is the tenderest plant; yet, being so easily protected, it is among the most certain in its fruit. The almond, the hardiest plant, loses its fruit the oftenest, on account of its forwardness. The palm, hardier than the caper and orange, never produces perfect fruit here.

I had the honor of sending you, the last year, some seeds of the sulla of Malta, or Spanish saintfoin. Lest they should have miscarried, I now pack with the rice a canister of the same kind of seed, raised by myself. By Colonel Franks, in the month of February last, I sent a parcel of acorns of the cork-oak, which I desired him to ask the favor of the Delegates of South Carolina in Congress, to forward to you.

I have the honor to be, with sentiments of the most perfect esteem and respect, Sir, your most obedient and most humble servant,

Th: Jefferson.

LETTER LXXV.—TO JAMES MADISON, August 2, 1787

TO JAMES MADISON.

Paris, August 2, 1787.

Dear Sir,

My last was of June the 20th. Yours, received since that date, are of May the 15th, and June the 6th. In mine, I acknowledged the receipt of the paccan nuts which came sealed up. I have reason to believe those in the box have arrived at L'Orient. By the Mary, Captain Howland, lately sailed from Havre to New York, I shipped three boxes of books, one marked J. M. for yourself, one marked B. F. for Dr. Franklin, and one marked W. H. for William Hay in Richmond. I have taken the liberty of addressing them all to you, as you will see by the enclosed bill of lading, in hopes you will be so good as to forward the other two. You will have opportunities of calling on the gentlemen for the freight, &c. In yours, you will find the books, noted in the account enclosed herewith. You have now Mably's works complete, except that on Poland, which I have never been able to get, but shall not cease to search for. Some other volumes are wanting too, to complete your collection of Chronologies. The fourth volume of D'Albon was lost by the bookbinder, and I have not yet been able to get one to replace it. I shall continue to try. The *Memoires sur les Droits et Impositions en Europe* (cited by Smith) was a scarce and excessively dear book. They are now reprinting it. I think it will be in three or four quartos, of from nine to twelve livres a volume. When it is finished, I shall take a copy for you. Amelot's Travels into China, I can learn nothing of. I put among the books sent you, two somewhat voluminous, and the object of which will need explanation; these are the *Tableau de Paris* and *L'Espion Anglois.* The former is truly a picture of private manners in Paris, but presented on the dark side, and a little darkened moreover. But there is so much truth in its groundwork, that it will be well worth your reading. You will then know Paris (and probably the other large cities of Europe) as well as if you had been there for years. *L'Espion Anglois* is no caricature. It will give you a just idea of the wheels by which the machine of government is worked here. There are in it, also, many interesting details of the last war, which, in general, may be relied on. It may be considered as the small history of great events. I am in hopes, when you shall have read them, you will not think I have misspent your money for them. My method for making out this assortment was, to revise the list of my own purchases since the invoice of 1785, and to select such as I had found worth your having. Besides this, I have casually met with, and purchased, some few curious and cheap things.

I must trouble you on behalf of a Mr. Thomas Burke, at Loughburke near Loughrea in Ireland, whose brother, James Burke, is supposed to have died, in 1785, on his passage from Jamaica, or St. Eustatius, to New York. His property on board the vessel is understood to have come to the hands of Alderman Groom at New York. The enclosed copy of a letter to him will more fully explain it. A particular friend of mine here, applies to me for information, which I must ask the favor of you to procure, and forward to me.

Writing news to others, much pressed in time, and making this letter one of private business, I did not intend to have said any thing to you on political subjects. But I must press one subject. Mr. Adams informs me he has borrowed money in Holland, which, if confirmed by Congress, will enable them to pay, not only the interest due here to the foreign officers, but the principal. Let me beseech you to reflect on the expediency of transferring this debt to Holland. All our other debts in Europe do not injure our reputation so much as this. These gentlemen have connections both in and out of office, and these again their connections, so that our default on this article is further known, more blamed, and excites worse dispositions against us, than you can conceive. If you think as I do, pray try to procure an order for paying off their capital. Mr. Adams adds, that if any certain tax is provided for the payment of interest, Congress may borrow enough in Holland to pay off their whole debts in France, both public and private, to the crown, to the Farmers, and to Beaumarchais. Surely it will be better to transfer these debts to Holland. So critical is the state of that country, that I imagine the monied men of it, would be glad to place their money in foreign countries, and that Mr. Adams could borrow there for us, without a certain tax for the interest, and saving our faith too, by previous explanations on that subject. This country is really supposed on the eve of a * * * *. Such a spirit has risen within a few weeks, as could not have been believed. They see the great deficit in their revenues, and the hopes of economy lessen daily. The parliament refuse to register any act for a new tax, and require an Assembly of the States. The object of this Assembly is evidently to give law to the King, to fix a constitution, to limit expenses. These views are said to gain upon the nation.*

---

*[* The parts of this letter marked by asterisks, are in cipher, and unintelligible.]*

A final decision of some sort, should be made on Beaumarchais' affairs.

I am, with sentiments of the most perfect esteem, Dear Sir, your friend and servant,

Th: Jefferson.

LETTER LXXVI.—TO THOMAS BARCLAY, August 3, 1787

TO THOMAS BARCLAY.
Paris, August 3, 1787,
Dear Sir,
I am now to acknowledge the receipt of your several favors of June the 29th, and July the 6th and 8th.
I am of opinion that the affair of Geraud and Roland in Holland, had better be committed to Mr. Dumas in Holland, as lawsuits must always be attended to by some person on the spot. For the same reason, I think that of La Vayse and Puchilberg should be managed by the agent at L'Orient, and Gruel's by the agent at Nantes. I shall always be ready to assist the agents of L'Orient and Nantes, in any way in my power; but were the details to be left to me, they would languish, necessarily, on account, of my distance from the place, and perhaps suffer too, for want of verbal consultations with the lawyers entrusted with them. You are now with Congress, and can take their orders on the subject. I shall therefore, do nothing in these matters, in reliance that you will put them into such channel as they direct, furnishing the necessary documents and explanations.

With respect to French's affair, being perfectly satisfied myself, I have not ceased, nor shall I 'cease, endeavoring to satisfy others, that your conduct has been that of an honest and honorable debtor, and theirs the counterpart of Shylock in the play. I enclose you a letter containing my testimony on your general conduct, which I have written to relieve a debt of justice pressing on my mind, well knowing at the same time, you will not stand in need of it in America. Your conduct is too well known to Congress, your character to all the world, to need any testimonials.
The moment I close my despatches for the packet, which will be the 9th instant, I shall with great pleasure go to pay my respects to Mrs. Barclay at St. Germain, to satisfy her on the subject of your transactions, and to assure her that my resources shall be hers, as long as I have any. A multitude of letters to write, prevents my entering into the field of public news, further than to observe, that it is extremely doubtful whether the affairs of Holland will, or will not produce a war between France, on one side, and England and Prussia, on. the other.
I beg you to accept assurances of the sincere esteem and respect, with which I have the honor to be, Dear Sir, your friend
and servant,

Th: Jefferson.

LETTER LXXVII.—TO E. CARRINGTON, August 4,1787

TO E. CARRINGTON.

Paris, August 4,1787.

Dear Sir,

Since mine of the 16th of January, I have been honored by your favors of April the 24th and June the 9th. I am happy to find that the States have come so generally into the scheme of the federal convention, from which, I am sure, we shall see wise propositions. I confess, I do not go as far in the reforms thought necessary, as some of my correspondents in America; but if the convention should adopt such propositions, I shall suppose them necessary. My general plan would be, to make the States one as to every thing connected with foreign nations, and several as to every thing purely domestic. But with all the imperfections of our present government, it is, without comparison, the best existing, or that ever did exist. Its greatest defect is the imperfect manner in which matters of commerce have been provided for. It has been so often said, as to be generally believed, that Congress have no power by the Confederation to enforce any thing; for example, contributions of money. It was not necessary to give them that power expressly; they have it by the law of nature. When two parties make a compact, there results to each a power of compelling the other to execute it. Compulsion was never so easy as in our case, where a single frigate would soon levy on the commerce of any State the deficiency of its contributions; nor more safe than in the hands of Congress, which has always shown that it would wait, as it ought to do, to the last extremities, before it would execute any of its powers which are disagreeable. I think it very material, to separate, in the hands of Congress, the executive and legislative powers, as the judiciary already are, in some degree. This, I hope, will be done. The want of it has been the source of more evil, than we have experienced from any other cause. Nothing is so embarrassing nor so mischievous, in a great assembly, as the details of execution. The smallest trifle of that kind, occupies as long as the most important act of legislation, and takes place of every thing else. Let any man recollect, or look over, the files of Congress: he will observe the most important propositions hanging over, from week to week, and month to month, till the occasions have passed them, and the things never done. I have ever viewed the executive details as the greatest cause of evil to us, because they in fact place us as if we had no federal head, by diverting the attention of that head from great to small objects; and should this division of power not be recommended by the convention, it is my opinion, Congress should make it, itself, by establishing an executive committee.

I have the honor to be, with sincere esteem and respect, Dear Sir, your most obedient, humble servant,

Th: Jefferson,

LETTER LXXVIII.—TO DR. CURRIE, August 4, 1787

TO DR. CURRIE.

Paris, August 4, 1787.

Dear Sir,

I am favored with your letter of May the 2nd, and most cordially sympathize in your late immense losses. It is a situation in which a man needs the aid of all his wisdom and philosophy. But as it is better to turn from the contemplation of our misfortunes, to the resources we possess for extricating ourselves, you will, of course, have found solace in your vigor of mind, health of body, talents, habits of business, in the consideration that you have time yet to retrieve every thing, and a knowledge that the very activity necessary for this, is a state of greater happiness than the unoccupied one, to which you had a thought of retiring. I wish the bulk of my extravagant countrymen had as good prospects and resources as you. But with many of them, a feebleness of mind makes them afraid to probe the true state of their affairs, and procrastinate the reformation which alone can save something, to those who may yet be saved. How happy a people were we during the war, from the single circumstance that we could not run in debt! This counteracted all the inconveniences we felt, as the present facility of ruining ourselves overweighs all the blessings of peace. I know no condition happier than that of a Virginia farmer might be, conducting himself as he did during the war. His estate supplies a good table, clothes itself and his family with their ordinary apparel, furnishes a small surplus to buy salt, sugar, coffee, and a little finery for his wife and daughters, enables him to receive and to visit his friends, and furnishes him pleasing and healthy occupation. To secure all this, he needs but one act of self-denial, to put off buying any thing till he has the money to pay for it. Mr. Ammonett did not come. He wrote to me, however, and I am making inquiry for the town and family he indicated. As yet, neither can be heard of, and were they to be found, the length of time would probably bar all claims against them. I have seen no object present so many desperate faces. However, if inquiry can lighten our way, that shall not be wanting, and I will write to him as soon as we discover any thing, or despair of discovering. Littlepage has succeeded well in Poland. He has some office, it is said, worth five hundred guineas a year. The box of seeds you were so kind as to forward me, came safe to hand. The arrival of my daughter, in good health, has been a source of immense comfort to me. The injury of which you had heard, was a dislocated wrist, and though it happened eleven months ago, was a simple dislocation, and immediately aided by the best surgeon in Paris, it is neither well, nor ever will be, so as to render me much service. The fingers remain swelled and crooked, the hand withered, and the joint having a very confined motion. You ask me when I shall return. My commission expires next spring, and if not renewed, I shall return then. If renewed, I shall stay somewhat longer: how much, will not depend on me altogether. So far as it does, I cannot fix the epoch of my return, though I always flatter myself it is not very distant. My habits are formed to those of my own country. I am past the time of changing them, and am, therefore, less happy any where else than there.

I shall always be happy to hear from you, being with very sincere esteem, Dear Sir, your friend and servant,

Th: Jefferson.

LETTER LXXIX.—TO MR. HAWKINS, August 4, 1787

TO MR. HAWKINS.

Paris, August 4, 1787.

Dear Sir,

I have to acknowledge the receipt of your favors of March the 8th and June the 9th, and to give you many thanks for the trouble you have taken with the *dionæa muscipula*. I have not yet heard any thing of them, which makes me fear they have perished by the way. I believe the most effectual means of conveying them hither will be by the seed. I must add my thanks too for the vocabularies. This is an object I mean to pursue, as I am persuaded that the only method of investigating the filiation of the Indian nations, is by that of their languages.

I look up with you to the federal convention, for an amendment of our federal affairs; yet I do not view them in so disadvantageous a light at present, as some do. And above all things, I am astonished at some people's considering a kingly government as a refuge. Advise such to read the fable of the frogs, who solicited Jupiter for a king. If that does not put them to rights, send them to Europe, to see something of the trappings of monarchy, and I will undertake, that every man shall go back thoroughly cured. If all the evils which can arise among us, from the republican form of our government, from this day to the day of judgment, could be put into a scale against what this country suffers from its monarchical form, in a week, or England, in a month, the latter would preponderate. Consider the contents of the Red Book in England, or the Almanac Royale of France, and say what a people gain by monarchy. No race of kings has ever presented above one man of common, sense, in twenty generations. The best they can do is, to leave things to their ministers; and what are their ministers, but a committee, badly chosen? If the king ever meddles, it is to do harm. Adieu, my Dear Sir, and be assured of the esteem of your friend and servant,

Th: Jefferson.

LETTER LXXX.—TO COLONEL MONROE, August 5, 1787

TO COLONEL MONROE.

Paris, August 5, 1787.

Dear Sir,

A journey of between three and four months, into the southern parts of France and northern of Italy, has prevented my writing to you. In the mean time, you have changed your ground, and engaged in different occupations, so that I know not whether the news of this side the water will even amuse you. However, it is all I have for you. The storm which seemed to be raised suddenly in Brabant, will probably blow over. The Emperor, on his return to Vienna, pretended to revoke all the concessions which had been made by his Governors General, to his Brabantine subjects; but he, at the same time, called for deputies from among them to consult with. He will use their agency to draw himself out of the scrape, and all there I think will be quieted. Hostilities go on occasionally in Holland. France espouses the cause of the Patriots, as you know, and England and Prussia that of the Stadtholder. France and England are both unwilling to bring on a war, but a hasty move of the King of Prussia will perplex them. He has thought the stopping his sister sufficient cause for sacrificing a hundred or two thousand of his subjects, and as many Hollanders and French. He has therefore ordered twenty thousand men to march, without consulting England, or even his own ministers. He may thus drag England into a war, and of course this country, against their will. But it is certain they will do every thing they can, to prevent it; and that in this, at least, they agree.

Though such a war might be gainful to us, yet it is much to be deprecated by us at this time. In all probability, France would be unequal to such a war by sea and by land, and it is not our interest or even safe for us, that she should be weakened. The great improvements in their constitution, effected by the *Assemblée des Notables*, you are apprized of. That of partitioning the country into a number of subordinate governments, under the administration of Provincial Assemblies, chosen by the people, is a capital one. But to the delirium of joy which these improvements gave the nation, a strange reverse of temper has suddenly succeeded. The deficiencies of their revenue were exposed, and they were frightful. Yet there was an appearance of intention to economize and reduce the expenses of government. But expenses are still very, inconsiderately incurred, and all reformation in that point despaired of. The public credit is affected; and such a spirit of discontent has arisen, as has never been seen. The parliament refused to register the edict for a stamp tax, or any other tax, and call for the States General, who alone, they say, can impose a new tax. They speak with a boldness unexampled. The King has called them to Versailles to-morrow, where he will hold a *lit de justice* and compel them to register the tax. How the chapter will finish, we must wait to see. By a vessel lately sailed from Havre to New York, I have sent you some more *livraisons* of the *Encyclopédie*, down to the 22nd inclusive. They were in a box with Dr. Currie's, and addressed to Mr. Madison, who will forward them to Richmond. I have heard you are in the Assembly. I will beg the favor of you, therefore, to give me, at the close of the session, a history of the most remarkable acts passed, the parties and views of the House, &c. This, with the small news of my country, crops and prices, furnish you abundant matter to treat me, while I have nothing to give you in return, but the history of the follies of nations in their dotage. Present me in respectful and friendly terms to Mrs. Monroe, and be assured of the sincere sentiments of esteem and attachment, with which I am Dear Sir, your friend and servant,

Th: Jefferson.

LETTER LXXXI.—TO JOHN JAY, August 6,1787

TO JOHN JAY.

Paris, August 6,1787.

The last letter I had the honor of addressing you was dated June the 21st. I have now that of enclosing you a letter from the Swedish ambassador, praying that inquiry may be made for a vessel of his nation, piratically carried off, and measures taken relative to the vessel, cargo, and crew. Also a letter from William Russell and others, citizens of America, concerned in trade to the island of Guadaloupe, addressed to the Marechal de Castries, and complaining of the shutting to them the port of Point a Pitre, and receiving them only at Basse-terre. This was enclosed to me by the subscribers, to be delivered to the Marechal de Castries. But the present is not the moment to move in that business: and moreover, I suppose, that whenever parties are within the reach of Congress, they should apply to them, and my instructions come through that channel. Matters, arising within the kingdom of France, to which my commission is limited, and not admitting time to take the orders of Congress, I suppose I may move in originally. I also enclose you the copy of a letter from Mr. Barclay, closing his proceedings in our affairs with Morocco. Before this reaches you, he will have had the honor of presenting himself to you in person. After his departure, the parliament of Bordeaux decided that he was liable to arrest. This was done on a letter from the minister, informing them that Mr. Barclay was invested with no character which privileged him from arrest. His constant character of consul was no protection, and they did not explain whether his character to Morocco was not originally diplomatic, or was expired. Mr. Barclay's proceedings under this commission being now closed, it would be incumbent on me to declare with respect to them, as well as his consular transactions, my opinion of the judgment, zeal, and disinterestedness with which he has conducted himself; were it not that Congress has been so possessed of those transactions from time to time, as to judge for themselves. I cannot but be uneasy, lest my delay of entering on the subject of the consular convention, may be disapproved. My hope was and is, that more practicable terms might be obtained: in this hope, I do nothing till further orders, observing by an extract from the journals you were pleased to send me, that Congress have referred the matter to your consideration, and conscious that we are not suffering in the mean time, as we have not a single consul in France, since the departure of Mr. Barclay. I mentioned to you in my last, the revival of the hopes of the Chevalier de la Luzerne. I thought it my duty to remind the Count de Montmorin, the other day, of the long absence of their minister from Congress. He told me, the Chevalier de la Luzerne would not be sent back, but that we might rely, that in the month of October a person would be sent, with whom we should be content. He did not name the person, though there is no doubt that it is the Count de Mourtier. It is an appointment, which, according to the opinion I have formed of him, bids as fair to give content, as any one which could be made.

I also mentioned in my last letter, that I had proposed the reducing the substance of Monsieur de Calonne's letter into the form of an *Arrêt*, with some alterations, which, on consultation with the merchants at the different ports I visited, I had found to be necessary. I received soon after a letter from the Comptroller General, informing me, that the letter of Monsieur de Calonne was in a course of execution. Of this, I enclose you a copy. I was, in that moment, enclosing to him my general observations on that letter, a copy of which is also enclosed. In these I stated all the alterations I wished to have made. It became expedient soon after, to bring on the article of tobacco; first, to know whether the Farmers had executed the order of Bernis, and also to prepare some arrangements to succeed the expiration of this order. So that I am now pursuing the whole subject of our commerce, 1. to have necessary amendments made in Monsieur de Calonne's letter; 2. to put it into a more stable form; 3. to have full execution of the order of Bernis; 4. to provide arrangements for the article of tobacco, after that order shall be expired. By the copy of my letter on the two last points, you will perceive that I again press the abolition of the Farm of this article. The conferences on that subject give no hope of effecting that. Some poor palliative is probably all we shall obtain. The Marquis de la Fayette goes hand in hand with me in all these transactions, and is an invaluable auxiliary to me. I hope it will not be imputed either to partiality or affectation, my naming this gentleman so often in my despatches. Were I not to do it, it would be a suppression of truth, and the taking to myself the whole merit where he has the greatest share.

The Emperor, on his return to Vienna, disavowed the concessions of his Governors General to his subjects of Brabant. He at the same time proposed their sending deputies to him, to consult on their affairs. They refused in the first moment; but afterwards nominated deputies; without giving them any power, however, to concede any thing. In the mean time, they are arming and training themselves. Probably the Emperor will avail himself of the aid of these deputies, to tread back his steps. He will be the more prompt to do this, that he may be in readiness to act freely, if he finds occasion, in the new scenes preparing in Holland. What these will be, cannot be foreseen. You well know, that the original party-divisions of that country were into Stadtholderians, Aristocrats, and Democrats. There was a subdivision of the Aristocrats, into violent and moderate, which was important. The violent Aristocrats would have wished to preserve all the powers of government in the hands of the Regents, and that these should remain self-elective: but choosing to receive a modification of these powers from the Stadtholder, rather than from the people, they threw themselves into his scale. The moderate Aristocrats would have consented to a temperate mixture of democracy, and particularly, that the Regents should be elected by the people. They were the declared enemies of the Stadtholder, and acted in concert with the Democrats, forming with them what was called the Patriots. It is the opinion of dispassionate people on the spot, that their views might have been effected. But the democratic party aimed at more. They talked of establishing tribunes of the people, of annual accounts, of depriving the magistrates at the will of the people, &c.; of enforcing all this with the arms in the hands of the *corps francs*; and in some places, as at Heusden, Sprang, &c. began the execution of these projects. The moderate Aristocrats found it difficult to strain their principles to this pitch. A schism took place between them and the Democrats, and the former have for some time been dropping off from the latter into the scale of the Stadtholder. This is the fatal coalition which governs without obstacle in Zealand, Friesland, and Guelderland, which constitutes the States of Utrecht, at Amersfort, and, with their aid, the plurality in the States General. The States of Holland, Groningen, and Overyssel, vote as yet in the opposition. But the coalition gains ground in the States of Holland, and has been prevalent in the Council of Amsterdam. If its progress be not stopped by a little moderation in the Democrats, it will turn the scale decidedly in favor of the Stadtholder, in the event of their being left to themselves without foreign interference. If foreign powers interfere, their prospect does not brighten. I see no sure friends to the Patriots but France, while Prussia and England are their assured enemies. Nor is it probable, that characters so greedy, so enterprising, as the Emperor and Empress, will be idle during such a struggle. Their views have long shown which side they would take. That France has engaged to interfere, and to support the Patriots, is beyond doubt. This engagement was entered into during the life of the late King of Prussia, whose eye was principally directed on the Emperor, and whose dispositions towards the Prince of Orange would have permitted him to be clipped a little close. But the present King comes in with warmer dispositions towards the Princess his sister. He has shown decidedly, that he will support her, even to the destruction of the balance of Europe, and the disturbance of its peace. The King of England has equally decided to support that house, at the risk of plunging his nation into another war. He supplies the Prince with money at this moment. A particular remittance of one hundred and twenty thousand guineas is known of. But his ministry is divided. Pitt is against the King's opinion, the Duke of Richmond and the rest of the ministers for it. Or, at least, such is the belief here. Mr. Adams will have informed you more certainly. This division in the English ministry, with the ill condition of their finances for war, produces a disposition even in the King, to try first every pacific measure: and that country and this were laboring jointly to stop the course of hostilities in

Holland, to endeavor to effect an accommodation, and were scarcely executing at all the armaments ordered in their ports; when all of a sudden an inflammatory letter, written by the Princess of Orange to the King of Prussia, induces him, without consulting England, without consulting even his own Council, to issue orders by himself to his generals, to march twenty thousand men to revenge the insult supposed to be offered to his sister. With a pride and egotism planted in the heart of every King, he considers her being stopped in the road, as a sufficient cause to sacrifice a hundred or two thousand of his own subjects, and as many of his enemies, and to spread fire, sword, and desolation over the half of Europe. This hasty measure has embarrassed England, undesirous of war, if it can be avoided, yet unwilling to separate from the power who is to render its success probable. Still you may be assured, that that court is going on in concurrence with this, to prevent extremities, if possible; always understood, that if the war cannot be prevented, they will enter into it as parties, and in opposition to one another. This event is, in my opinion, to be deprecated by the friends of France. She never was equal to such a war by land, and such a one by sea; and less so now, than in any moment of the present reign. You remember that the nation was in a delirium of joy on the convocation of the *Notables*, and on the various reformations agreed on between them and the government. The picture of the distress of their finances was indeed frightful, but the intentions to reduce them to order seemed serious. The constitutional reformations have gone on well, but those of expenses make little progress. Some of the most obviously useless have indeed been lopped off, but the remainder is a heavy mass, difficult to be reduced. Despair has seized every mind, and they have passed from an extreme of joy to one of discontent. The parliament, therefore, oppose the registering any new tax, and insist on an Assembly of the States General. The object of this is to limit expenses, and dictate a constitution. The edict for the stamp tax has been the subject of reiterated orders and refusals to register. At length, the King has summoned the parliament to Versailles to hold a bed of justice, in which he will order them, in person, to register the edict. At the moment of my writing, they are gone to Versailles for this purpose. There will yet remain to them, to protest against the register, as forced, and to issue orders against its execution on pain of death. But as the King would have no peaceable mode of opposition left, it remains to be seen, whether they will push the matter to this extremity. It is evident, I think, that the spirit of this country is advancing towards a revolution in their constitution. There are not wanting persons at the helm, friends to the progress of this spirit. The Provincial Assemblies will be the most probable instrument of effecting it.

Since writing thus far, I have received an intimation, that it will be agreeable not to press our commercial regulations at this moment, the ministry being too much occupied with the difficulties surrounding them, to spare a moment on any subject which will admit of delay. Our business must, therefore, be suspended for a while. To press it out of season, would be to defeat, it. It would be felt as a vital benefit here, could we relieve their finances, by paying what we owe. Congress will judge by Mr. Adams's letters, how far the transferring all our debts in this country to Holland is practicable. On the replenishing their treasury with our principal and interest, I should not be afraid to ask concessions in favor of our West India trade. It would produce a great change of opinion as to us and our affairs. In the *Assemblée des Notables*, hard things were said of us. They were induced, however, in committing us to writing, to smother their ideas a little. In their votes, now gone to be printed, our debt is described in these words. The twenty-first article of the account, formed of the interest of the claims of his Majesty on the United States of America, cannot be drawn out for the present, except as a document. The recovery of these claims, as well principal as perhaps even interest, although they appear to rest on the most solid security, may, nevertheless, be long delayed, and should not, consequently, be taken into account in estimating the annual revenue. This article amounts to one million and six hundred thousand livres.' Above all things, it is desirable to hush the foreign officers by payment. Their wants, the nature of their services, their access to high characters, and connections with them, bespeak the reasons for this. I hear also that Mr. Beaumarchais means to make himself heard, if a memorial which he sends by an agent in the present packet is not attended to, as he thinks it ought to be. He called on me with it, and desired me to recommend his case to a decision, and to note in my despatch, that it was the first time he had spoken to me on the subject. This is true, it being the first time I ever saw him; but my recommendations would be as displaced as unnecessary. I assured him Congress would do in that business what justice should require, and their means enable them. The information sent me by Mr. Montgomery from Alicant, of the death of the Dey of Algiers, was not true. I had expressed my doubt of it in my last, when I communicated it. I send herewith the newspapers to this date, and a remonstrance of the parliament, to show you in what language the King can be addressed at this day. I have received no journal of Congress since the beginning of November last, and will thank you for them, if printed.

I have the honor to be, with sentiments of the most perfect esteem and respect, Sir, your most obedient and most humble servant,

Th: Jefferson.

P. S. August 7. The parliament were received yesterday very harshly by the King. He obliged them to register the two edicts for the *impôt territorial* and stamp tax. When speaking in my letter of the reiterated orders and refusals to register, which passed between the King and parliament, I omitted to insert the King's answer to a deputation of parliament, which attended him at Versailles. It may serve to show the spirit which exists between them. It was in these words, and these only:—'*Je vous ferai savoir mes intentions. Allez-vous-en. Qu'on ferme la porte.*'

LETTER LXXXII.—TO JOHN CHURCHMAN, August 8, 1787

TO JOHN CHURCHMAN.

Paris, August 8, 1787.

Sir,

I have duly received your favor of June the 6th, and immediately communicated its contents to a member of the Academy. He told me that they had received the other copy of your memorial, which you mention to have sent through another channel; that your ideas were not conveyed so explicitly, as to enable them to decide finally on their merit, but that they had made an entry in their journals, to preserve to you the claim of the original idea. As far as we can conjecture it here, we imagine you make a table of variations of the needle, for all the different meridians whatever. To apply this table to use in the voyage between America and Europe, suppose the variation to increase a degree in every one hundred and sixty miles. Two difficulties occur; 1. a ready and accurate method of finding the variation of the place; 2. an instrument so perfect, as that (though the degree on it shall represent one hundred and sixty miles) it shall give the parts of the degree so minutely, as to answer the purpose of the navigator. The variation of the needle at Paris, actually, is 21° west. I make no question you have provided against the doubts entertained here, and I shall be happy that our country may have the honor of furnishing the old world, what it has so long sought in vain.

I am with much respect, Sir, your most obedient, humble servant,

Th: Jefferson.

LETTER LXXXIII.—TO MONSIEUR L HOMMANDE, August 9, 1787

TO MONSIEUR L HOMMANDE.

Paris, August 9, 1787.

Sir,

At the time you honored me with your letter of May the 31st, I was not returned from a journey I had taken into Italy. This circumstance, with the mass of business which had accumulated during my absence, must apologize for the delay of my answer. Every discovery, which multiplies the subsistence of man, must be a matter of joy to every friend to humanity. As such, I learn with great satisfaction, that you have found the means of preserving flour more perfectly than has been done hitherto. But I am not authorized to avail my country of it, by making any offer for its communication. Their policy is to leave their citizens free, neither restraining nor aiding them in their pursuits. Though the interposition of government in matters of invention has its use, yet it is in practice so inseparable from abuse, that they think it better not to meddle with it. We are only to hope, therefore, that those governments, who are in the habit of directing all the actions of their subjects by particular law, may be so far sensible of the duty they are under of cultivating useful discoveries, as to reward you amply for yours, which is among the most interesting to humanity.

I have the honor to be, with great consideration and respect, Sir, your most obedient and most humble servant,

Th: Jefferson.

LETTER LXXXIV.—TO PETER CARR, August 10, 1787

TO PETER CARR.

Paris, August 10, 1787.

Dear Peter,

I have received your two letters of December the 30th and April the 18th, and am very happy to find by them, as well as by letters from Mr. Wythe, that you have been so fortunate as to attract his notice and good will: I am sure you will find this to have been one of the most fortunate events of your life, as I have ever been sensible it was of mine. I enclose you a sketch of the sciences to which I would wish you to apply, in such order as Mr. Wythe shall advise: I mention also the books in them worth your reading, which submit to his correction. Many of these are among your father's books, which you should have brought to you. As I do not recollect those of them not in his library, you must write to me for them, making out a catalogue of such as you think you shall have occasion for in eighteen months from the date of your letter, and consulting Mr. Wythe on the subject. To this sketch I will add a few particular observations.

1. Italian. I fear the learning this language will confound your French and Spanish. Being all of them degenerated dialects of the Latin, they are apt to mix in conversation. I have never seen a person speaking the three languages, who did not mix them. It is a delightful language, but late events having rendered the Spanish more useful, lay it aside to prosecute that.

2. Spanish. Bestow great attention on this, and endeavor to acquire an accurate knowledge of it. Our future connections with Spain and Spanish America, will render that language a valuable acquisition. The ancient history of a great part of America, too, is written in that language. I send you a dictionary.

3. Moral Philosophy. I think it lost time to attend lectures on this branch. He who made us would have been a pitiful bungler, if he had made the rules of our moral conduct a matter of science. For one man of science, there are thousands who are not. What would have become of them? Man was destined for society. His morality, therefore, was to be formed to this object. He was endowed with a sense of right and wrong, merely relative to this. This sense is as much a part of his nature, as the sense of hearing, seeing, feeling; it is the true foundation of morality, and not the τὸ καλὸν truth, &c, as fanciful writers have imagined. The moral sense, or conscience, is as much a part of man, as his leg or arm. It is given to all human beings, in a stronger

or weaker degree, as force of members is given them in a greater or less degree. It may be strengthened by exercise, as may any particular limb of the body. This sense is submitted, indeed, in some degree, to the guidance of reason; but it is a small stock which is required for this: even a less one than what we call common sense. State a moral case to a ploughman and a professor. The former will decide it as well, and often better than the latter, because he has not been led astray by artificial rules. In this branch, therefore, read good books, because they will encourage, as well as direct your feelings. The writings of Sterne, particularly, form the best course of morality that ever was written. Besides these, read the books mentioned in the enclosed paper: and, above all things, lose no occasion of exercising your dispositions to be grateful, to be generous, to be charitable, to be humane, to be true, just, firm, orderly, courageous, &c. Consider every act of this kind, as an exercise which will strengthen your moral faculties, and increase your worth.

4. Religion, Your reason is now mature enough to examine this object. In the first place, divest yourself of all bias in favor of novelty and singularity of opinion. Indulge them in any other subject rather than that of religion. It is too important, and the consequences of error may be too serious. On the other hand, shake off all the fears and servile prejudices, under which weak minds are servilely crouched. Fix reason firmly in her seat, and call to her tribunal every fact, every opinion. Question with boldness even the existence of a God; because, if there be one, he must more approve the homage of reason, than that of blindfolded fear. You will naturally examine, first, the religion of your own country. Read the Bible, then, as you would read Livy or Tacitus. The facts which are within the ordinary course of nature, you will believe on the authority of the writer, as you do those of the same kind in Livy and Tacitus. The testimony of the writer weighs in their favor, in one scale, and their not being against the laws of nature, does not weigh against them. But those facts in the Bible, which contradict the laws of nature, must be examined with more care, and under a variety of faces. Here you must recur to the pretensions of the writer to inspiration from God. Examine upon what evidence his pretensions are founded, and whether that evidence is so strong, as that its falsehood would be more improbable than a change of the laws of nature, in the case he relates. For example, in the book of Joshua we are told the sun stood still several hours. Were we to read that fact in Livy or Tacitus, we should class it with their showers of blood, speaking of statues, beasts, &c. But it is said, that the writer of that book was inspired. Examine, therefore, candidly, what evidence there is of his having been inspired. The pretension is entitled to your inquiry, because millions believe it. On the other hand, you are astronomer enough to know, how contrary it is to the law of nature, that a body revolving on its axis, as the earth does, should have stopped, should not, by that sudden stoppage, have prostrated animals, trees, buildings, and should after a certain time have resumed its revolution, and

that without a second general prostration. Is this arrest of the earth's motion, or the evidence which affirms it, most within the law of probabilities? You will next read the New Testament. It is the history of a personage called Jesus. Keep in your eye the opposite pretensions, 1. of those who say he was begotten by God, born of a virgin, suspended, and reversed the laws of nature at will, and ascended bodily into heaven: and, 2. of those who say he was a man, of illegitimate birth, of a benevolent heart, enthusiastic mind, who set out without pretensions to divinity, ended in believing them, and was punished capitally for sedition, by being gibbeted, according to the Roman law, which punished the first commission of that offence by whipping, and the second by exile or death *in furca.* See this law in the Digest, Lib. 48, tit. 19, § 28. 3. and Lipsius, Lib. 2. *De Cruce*, cap. 2. These questions are examined in the books I have mentioned, under the head of Religion, and several others. They will assist you in your inquiries; but keep your reason firmly on the watch in reading them all. Do not be frightened from this inquiry by any fear of its consequences. If it ends in a belief that there is no God, you will find incitements to virtue in the comfort and pleasantness you feel in its exercise, and the love of others which it will procure you. If you find reason to believe there is a God, a consciousness that you are acting under his eye, and that he approves you, will be a vast additional incitement: if that there be a future state, the hope of a happy existence in that, increases the appetite to deserve it: if that Jesus was also a God, you will be comforted by a belief of his aid and love. In fine, I repeat, you must lay aside all prejudice on both sides, and neither believe nor reject any thing, because any other person, or description of persons, have rejected or believed it. Your own reason is the only oracle given you by Heaven, and you are answerable not for the rightness, but uprightness of the decision. I forgot to observe, when speaking of the New Testament, that you should read all the histories of Christ, as well of those whom a council of ecclesiastics have decided for us to be Pseudo-evangelists, as those they named Evangelists. Because these Pseudo-evangelists pretended to inspiration as much as the others, and you are to judge their pretensions by your own reason, and not by the reason of those ecclesiastics. Most of these are lost. There are some, however, still extant, collected by Fabricius, which I will endeavor to get and send you.

5. Travelling. This makes men wiser, but less happy. When men of sober age travel, they gather knowledge, which they may apply usefully for their country; but they are subject ever after to recollections mixed with regret; their affections are weakened by being extended over more objects; and they learn new habits, which cannot be gratified when they return home. Young men who travel are exposed to all these inconveniences in a higher degree, to others still more serious, and do not acquire that wisdom for which a previous foundation is requisite, by repeated and just observations at home. The glare of pomp and pleasure is analogous to the motion of the blood; it

absorbs all their affection and attention; they are torn from it as from the only good in this world, and return to their home as to a place of exile and condemnation. Their eyes are for ever turned back to the object they have lost, and its recollection poisons the residue of their lives. Their first and most delicate passions are hackneyed on unworthy objects here, and they carry home the dregs, insufficient to make themselves or any body else happy. Add to this, that a habit of idleness, an inability to apply themselves to business is acquired, and renders them useless to themselves and their country. These observations are founded in experience. There is no place where your pursuit of knowledge will be so little obstructed by foreign objects, as in your own country, nor any wherein the virtues of the heart will be less exposed to be weakened. Be good, be learned, and be industrious, and you will not want the aid of travelling, to render you precious to your country, dear to your friends, happy within yourself. I repeat my advice, to take a great deal of exercise, and on foot. Health is the first requisite after morality. Write to me often, and be assured of the interest I take in your success, as well as the warmth of those sentiments of attachment with which I am, Dear Peter, your affectionate friend,

Th: Jefferson.

LETTER LXXXV.—TO DR. GILMER, August 11, 1787

TO DR. GILMER.

Paris, August 11, 1787.

Dear Doctor,

Your letter of January the 9th, 1787, came safely to hand in the month of June last. Unluckily you forgot to sign it, and your hand-writing is so Protean, that one cannot be sure it is yours. To increase the causes of incertitude, it was dated Pen-Park, a name which I only know, as the seat of John Harmer. The hand-writing, too, being somewhat in his style, made me ascribe it hastily to him, indorse it with his name, and let it lie in my bundle to be answered at leisure. That moment of leisure arriving, I sat down to answer it to John Harmer, and now, for the first time, discover marks of its being yours, and particularly those expressions of friendship to myself and family, which you have ever been so good as to entertain, and which are to me among the most precious possessions. I wish my sense of this, and my desires of seeing you rich and happy, may not prevent my seeing any difficulty in the case you state of George Harmer's wills; which, as you state them, are thus.

1. A will, dated December the 26th, 1779, written in his own hand, and devising to his brother the estates he had received from him.

2. Another will, dated June the 25th, 1782, written also in his own hand, devising his estate to trustees, to be conveyed to such of his relations, I. H., I. L., or H. L., as should become capable of acquiring property, or, on failure of that, to be sold, and the money remitted them.

3. A third will, dated September the 12th, 1786, devising all his estate at Marrowbone, and his tracts at Horse-pasture and Poison-field to you; which will is admitted to record, and of course has been duly executed.

You say the learned are divided on these wills. Yet I see no cause of division, as it requires little learning to decide, that 'the first deed and last will must always prevail.' I am afraid, therefore, the difficulty may arise on the want of words of inheritance in the devise to you: for you state it as a devise to 'George Gilmer' (without adding 'and to his heirs') of 'all the *estate* called Marrowbone,' 'the *tract* called Horse-pasture,' and 'the tract called Poison-field.' If the question is on this point, and you have copied the words of the will exactly, I suppose you take an estate in fee simple in Marrowbone, and for life only in Horse-pasture and Poison-field; the want of words of inheritance in the two last cases, being supplied as to the first, by the word 'estate,' which has been repeatedly decided to be descriptive of the quantum of interest devised, as well as of its locality. I am in hopes, however, you have not copied the words exactly, that there are words of inheritance to all the devises, as the testator certainly knew their necessity, and that the conflict only will be between the different wills, in which case, I see nothing which can be opposed to the last. I shall be very happy to eat at Pen-park some of the good mutton and beef of Marrowbone, Horse-pasture, and Poison-field, with yourself and Mrs. Gilmer, and my good old neighbors. I am as happy no where else, and in no other society, and all my wishes end, where I hope my days will end, at Monticello. Too many scenes of happiness mingle themselves with all the recollections of my native woods and fields, to suffer them to be supplanted in my affection by any other. I consider myself here as a traveller only, and not a resident. My commission expires next spring, and if not renewed, I shall of course return then. If renewed, I shall remain here some time longer. How much, I cannot say; yet my wishes shorten the period. Among the strongest inducements, will be that of your society and Mrs. Gilmer's, which I am glad to find brought more within reach, by your return to Pen-park. My daughters are importunate to return also. Patsy enjoys good health, and is growing to my stature. Maria arrived here about a month ago, after a favorable voyage, and in perfect health. My own health has been as good as ever, after the first year's probation. If you knew how agreeable to me are the details of the small news of my neighborhood, your charity would induce you to write frequently. Your letters lodged in the post-office at Richmond (to be forwarded to New York) come with certainty. We are doubtful yet, whether there will be war or not. Present me with warm affection to Mrs. Gilmer, and be assured yourself of the unvarying sentiments of esteem and attachment, with which I am, Dear Doctor, your sincere friend and servant,

Th: Jefferson.

LETTER LXXXVI.—TO JOSEPH JONES, August 14, 1787

TO JOSEPH JONES.

Paris, August 14, 1787.

Dear Sir,

I have never yet thanked you, but with the heart, for the act of Assembly confirming the agreement with Maryland, the pamphlet, and papers, I received from you a twelvemonth ago. Very soon after their receipt, I got my right wrist dislocated, which prevented me long from writing, and as soon as that was able to bear it, I took a long journey, from which I am but lately returned. I am anxious to hear what our federal convention recommends, and what the States will do in consequence of their recommendation. * * * * With all the defects of our constitution, whether general or particular, the comparison of our governments with those of Europe, is like a comparison of heaven and hell. England, like the earth, may be allowed to take the intermediate station. And yet I hear there are people among you, who think the experience of our governments has already proved, that republican governments will not answer. Send those gentry here, to count the blessings of monarchy. A king's sister, for instance, stopped in the road, and on a hostile journey, is sufficient cause for him to march immediately twenty thousand men to revenge this insult, when he had shown himself little moved by the matter of right then in question.

From all these broils we are happily free, and that God may keep us long so, and yourself in health and happiness, is the prayer of,

Dear Sir, your most obedient

and most humble servant,

Th: Jefferson.

LETTER LXXXVII.—TO GENERAL WASHINGTON, August 14, 1787

TO GENERAL WASHINGTON.

Paris, August 14, 1787.

Dear Sir,

I was happy to find, by the letter of August the 1st, 1786, which you did me the honor to write to me, that the modern dress for your statue, would meet your approbation. I found it strongly the sentiment of West, Copely, Trumbull, and Brown, in London; after which it would be ridiculous to add, that it was my own. I think a modern in an antique dress, as just an object of ridicule, as a Hercules or Marius with a periwig and chapeau bras.

I remember having written to you, while Congress sat at Annapolis, on the water communication between ours and the western country, and to have mentioned, particularly, the information I had received of the plain face of the country between the sources of Big-beaver and Cayohoga, which made me hope that a canal, of no great expense, might unite the navigation of Lake Erie and the Ohio. You must since have had occasion of getting better information on this subject, and if you have, you would oblige me by a communication of it. I consider this canal, if practicable, as a very important work.

I remain in hopes of great and good effects from the decision of the Assembly over which you are presiding. To make our States one as to all foreign concerns, preserve them several as to all merely domestic, to give to the federal head some peaceable mode of enforcing its just authority, to organize that head into legislative, executive, and judiciary departments, are great desiderata in our federal constitution. Yet with all its defects, and with all those of our particular governments, the inconveniences resulting from them are so light, in comparison with those existing in every other government on earth, that our citizens may certainly be considered as in the happiest political situation which exists.

The *Assemblée des Notables* has been productive of much good in this country. The reformation of some of the most oppressive laws has taken place, and is taking place. The allotment of the State into subordinate governments, the administration of which is committed to persons chosen by the people, will work in time a very beneficial change in their constitution. The expense of the trappings of monarchy, too, is lightening. Many of the useless officers, high and low, of the King, Queen, and Princes, are struck off. Notwithstanding all this, the discovery of the abominable abuses of public money by the late Comptroller General, some new expenses of the court, not of a piece with the projects of reformation, and the imposition of new taxes, have, in the course of a few weeks, raised a spirit of discontent in this nation, so great and so general, as to threaten serious consequences. The parliaments in general, and particularly that of Paris, put themselves at the head of this effervescence, and direct its object to the calling the States General, who have not been assembled since 1614. The object is to fix a constitution, and to limit expenses. The King has been obliged to hold a bed of justice, to enforce the registering the new taxes: the parliament, on their side, propose to issue a prohibition against their execution. Very possibly this may bring on their exile. The mild and patriotic character of the new ministry is the principal dependence against this extremity.

The turn which the affairs of Europe will take, is not yet decided.

A war, wherein France, Holland, and England should be parties, seems, *primâ facie*, to promise much advantage to us. But, in the first place, no war can be safe for us, which threatens France with an unfavorable issue. And, in the next, it will probably embark us again into the ocean of speculation, engage us to overtrade ourselves, convert us into sea-rovers, under French and Dutch colors, divert us from agriculture, which is our wisest pursuit, because it will in the end contribute most to real wealth, good morals, and happiness. The wealth acquired by speculation and plunder, is fugacious in its nature, and fills society with the spirit of gambling. The moderate and sure income of husbandry begets permanent improvement, quiet life, and orderly conduct, both public and private. We have no occasion for more commerce than to take off our superfluous produce, and the people complain that some restrictions prevent this; yet the price of articles with us, in general, shows the contrary. Tobacco, indeed, is low, not because we cannot carry it where we please, but because we make more than the consumption requires. Upon the whole, I think peace advantageous to us, necessary for Europe, and desirable for humanity. A few days will decide, probably, whether all these considerations are to give way to the bad passions of Kings, and those who would be Kings.

I have the honor to be, with very sincere esteem and respect, Dear Sir, your most obedient and most humble servant,

Th: Jefferson.

P. S. August 15. The parliament is exiled to Troyes this morning. T. J.

LETTER LXXXVIII.—TO COLONEL HUMPHREYS, August 14, 1787

TO COLONEL HUMPHREYS.

Paris, August 14, 1787.

Dear Sir,

I remember when you left us, it was with a promise to supply all the defects of correspondence in our friends, of which we complained, and which you had felt in common with us. Yet I have received but one letter from you, which was dated June the 5th, 1786, and I answered it August the 14th, 1786. Dropping that, however, and beginning a new account, I will observe to you, that wonderful improvements are making here in various lines. In architecture, the wall of circumvallation round Paris, and the palaces by which we are to be let out and in, are nearly completed; four hospitals are to be built instead of the old *hôtel-dieu*; one of the old bridges has all its houses demolished, and a second nearly so; a new bridge is begun at the Place Louis XV.; the Palais Royal is gutted, a considerable part in the centre of the garden being dug out, and a subterranean circus begun, wherein will be equestrian exhibitions, &c. In society, the *habit habille* is almost banished, and they begin to go even to great suppers in frock: the court and diplomatic corps, however, must always be excepted. They are too high to be reached by any improvement. They are the last refuge from which etiquette, formality, and folly will be driven. Take away these, and they would be on a level with other people.

[After describing the unsettled state of Europe, as in some

of the preceding letters, the writer proceeds.]

So much for the blessings of having Kings, and magistrates who would be Kings. From these events our young republics may learn useful lessons, never to call on foreign powers to settle their differences, to guard against hereditary magistrates, to prevent their citizens from becoming so established in wealth and power, as to be thought worthy of alliance by marriage with the nieces, sisters, &c. of Kings, and, in short, to besiege the throne of Heaven with eternal prayers, to extirpate from creation this class of human lions, tigers, and mammoths, called Kings; from whom, let him perish who does not say, 'Good Lord, deliver us;' and that so we may say, one and all, or perish, is the fervent prayer of him who has the honor to mix with it sincere wishes for your health and happiness, and to be, with real attachment and respect, Dear Sir, your affectionate friend and humble servant,

Th: Jefferson.

LETTER LXXXIX.—TO JOHN JAY, August 15, 1787

TO JOHN JAY.

Sir,

Paris, August 15, 1787.

An American gentleman leaving Paris this afternoon, to go by the way of L'Orient to Boston, furnishes me the rare occasion of a conveyance, other than the packet, sure and quick. My letter by the packet informed you of the bed of justice, for enregistering the stamp tax and land tax. The parliament, on their return came to an *Arrêtée* (a resolution) which, besides protesting against the enregistering, as done by force, laid the foundation for an *Arrêt de defence* (an act) against the execution of the two new laws. The question on the final *Arrêt* was adjourned to the day before yesterday. It is believed they did not conclude on this *Arrêt*, as it has not appeared. However, there was a concourse of about ten thousand people at the parliament house, who, on their adjournment, received them with acclamations of joy, loosened the horses of the most eminent speakers against the tax from their carriages, and drew them home. This morning, the parliament is exiled to Troyes. It is believed to proceed, principally, from the fear of a popular commotion here.

The officer charged by this court, to watch the English squadron, which was under sailing orders, returned about a week ago with information that it had sailed, having shaped its course west-wardly. This is another step towards war. It is the more suspicious, as their minister here denies the fact. Count Adhemar is here from London, by leave from his court. The Duke of Dorset, the British ambassador here, has lately gone to London on leave. Neither of these ambassadors has the confidence of his court, on the point of abilities. The latter merits it for his honesty. The minister of the British court, resident here, remains; but Mr. Eden, their ambassador to Spain, under pretence of taking this in his route, is in truth their *fac-totum* in the present emergency. Nothing worth noting has occurred since my last, either in the Dutch or Austrian Netherlands.

I have the honor to be, with the most perfect esteem and respect, Sir, your most obedient and most humble servant,

Th: Jefferson.

LETTER XC.—TO JOHN ADAMS, August 30, 1787

TO JOHN ADAMS.

Paris, August 30, 1787.

Dear Sir,

Since your favor of July the 10th, mine have been of July the 17th, 23rd, and 28th. The last enclosed a bill of exchange from Mr. Grand, on Tessier, for £46. 17s. 10d. sterling, to answer General Sullivan's bill for that sum. I hope it got safe to hand, though I have been anxious about it, as it went by post, and my letters through that channel sometimes miscarry.

From the separation of the *Notables* to the present moment, has been perhaps the most interesting interval ever known in this country. The propositions of the government, approved by the *Notables*, were precious to the nation, and have been in an honest course of execution, some of them being carried into effect, and others preparing. Above all, the establishment of the Provincial Assemblies, some of which have begun their sessions, bid fair to be the instrument for circumscribing the power of the crown, and raising the people into consideration. The election given to them, is what will do this. Though the minister, who proposed these improvements, seems to have meant them as the price of the new supplies, the game has been so played, as to secure the improvements to the nation, without securing the price. The *Notables* spoke softly on the subject of the additional supplies. But the parliament took them up roundly, refused to register the edicts for the new taxes, till compelled in a bed of justice, and suffered themselves to be transferred to Troyes, rather than withdraw their opposition. It is urged principally against the King, that his revenue is one hundred and thirty millions more than that of his predecessor was, and yet he demands one hundred and twenty millions further. You will see this well explained in the '*Conference entre un Ministre d'etat et un Conseiller au parliament,*' which I send you with some small pamphlets. In the mean time, all tongues in Paris (and in France as it is said) have been let loose, and never was a license of speaking against the government, exercised in London more freely or more universally. Caricatures, placards, *bons-mots*, have been indulged in by all ranks of people, and I know of no well attested instance of a single punishment. For some time, mobs of ten, twenty, and thirty thousand people collected daily, surrounded the Parliament house, huzzaed the members, even entered the doors and examined into their conduct, took the horses out of the carriages of those who did well, and drew them home. The government thought it prudent to prevent these, drew some regiments into the neighborhood, multiplied the guards, had the streets constantly patrolled by strong parties, suspended privileged places, forbade all clubs, &c. The mobs have ceased: perhaps this may be partly owing to the absence of Parliament. The Count d'Artois, sent to hold a bed of justice in the *Cour des Aides*, was hissed and hooted without reserve, by the populace; the carriage of Madame de (I forget the name), in the Queen's livery, was stopped by the populace, under a belief that it was Madame de Polignac, whom they would have insulted; the Queen, going to the theatre at Versailles with Madame de Polignac, was received with a general hiss. The King, long in the habit of drowning his cares in wine, plunges deeper and deeper. The Queen cries, but sins on. The Count d'Artois is detested, and Monsieur, the general favorite. The Archbishop of Toulouse is made minister principal, a virtuous, patriotic, and able character. The Marechal de Castries retired yesterday, notwithstanding strong solicitations to remain in office. The Marechal de Segur retired at the same time, prompted to it by the court. Their successors are not yet known. Monsieur de St. Priest goes ambassador to Holland, in the room of Verac, transferred to Switzerland, and the Count de Moustier goes to America, in the room of the Chevalier de la Luzerne, who has a promise of the first vacancy. These nominations are not yet made formally, but they are decided on, and the parties are ordered to prepare for their destination.

As it has been long since I have had a confidential conveyance to you, I have brought together the principal facts from the adjournment of the Notables, to the present moment, which, as you will perceive from their nature, required a confidential conveyance. I have done it the rather, because, though you will have heard many of them, and seen them in the public papers, yet, floating in the mass of lies which constitute the atmosphere of London and Paris, you may not have been sure of their truth; and I have mentioned every truth of any consequence, to enable you to stamp as false, the facts pretermitted. I think that in the course of three months, the royal authority has lost, and the rights of the nation gained, as much ground by a revolution of public opinion only, as England gained in all her civil wars under the Stuarts. I rather believe, too, they will retain the ground gained, because it is defended by the young and the middle-aged, in opposition to the old only. The first party increases, and the latter diminishes daily, from the course of nature. You may suppose, that in this situation, war would be unwelcome to France. She will surely avoid it, if not forced into it by the courts of London and Berlin. If forced, it is probable she will change the system of Europe totally, by an alliance with the two empires, to whom nothing would be more desirable. In the event of such a coalition, not only Prussia, but the whole European world must receive from them their laws. But France will probably endeavor to preserve the present system, if it can be done, by sacrificing, to a certain degree, the pretensions of the patriotic party in Holland. But of all these matters, you can judge, in your position, where less secrecy is observed, better than I can.

I have news from America as late as July the 19th. Nothing had transpired from the federal convention. I am sorry they began their deliberations by so abominable a precedent, as that of tying up the tongues of their members. Nothing can justify this example, but the innocence of their intentions, and ignorance of the value of public discussions. I have no doubt that all their other measures will be good and wise. It is really an assembly of demigods. General Washington was of opinion, that they should not separate till October.

I have the honor to be, with every sentiment of friendship and respect, Dear Sir, your most obedient and most humble servant,

Th: Jefferson.

LETTER XCI.—TO MR. WYTHE, September 16,1787

TO MR. WYTHE.

Paris, September 16,1787.

Dear Sir,

I am now to acknowledge the receipt of your favors of December the 13th and 22nd, 1786, and of January, 1787. These should not have been so long unanswered, but that they arrived during my absence on a journey of between three and four months, through the southern parts of France and northern of Italy. In the latter country, my time allowed me to go no further than Turin, Milan, and Genoa: consequently, I scarcely got into classical ground. I took with me some of the writings, in which endeavors have been made to investigate the passage of Annibal over the Alps, and was just able to satisfy myself, from a view of the country, that the descriptions given of his march are not sufficiently particular, to enable us, at this day, even to guess at his track across the Alps. In architecture, painting, sculpture, I found much amusement: but more than all, in their agriculture, many objects of which might be adopted with us to great advantage. I am persuaded, there are many parts of our lower country where the olive tree might be raised, which is assuredly the richest gift of Heaven. I can scarcely except bread. I see this tree supporting thousands among the Alps, where there is not soil enough to make bread for a single family. The caper, too, might be cultivated with us. The fig we do raise. I do not speak of the vine, because it is the parent of misery. Those who cultivate it are always poor, and he who would employ himself with us in the culture of corn, cotton, &c. can procure, in exchange for them, much more wine, and better, than he could raise by its direct culture.

I sent you formerly copies of the documents on the Tagliaferro family, which I had received from Mr. Febroni. I now send the originals. I have procured for you a copy of Polybius, the best edition; but the best edition of Vitruvius which is with the commentaries of Ficinus, is not to be got here. I have sent to Holland for it. In the mean time, the Polybius comes in a box containing books for Peter Carr, and for some of my friends in Williamsburg and its vicinities. I have taken the liberty of addressing the box to you. It goes to New York in the packet-boat which carries this letter, and will be forwarded to you by water, by Mr. Madison. Its freight to New York is paid here. The transportation from thence to Williamsburg, will be demanded of you, and shall stand as the equivalent to the cost of Polybius and Vitruvius, if you please. The difference either way, will not be worth the trouble of raising and transmitting accounts. I send you herewith a state of the contents of the box, and for whom each article is. Among these are some, as you will perceive, of which I ask your acceptance. It is a great comfort to me, that while here, I am able to furnish some amusement to my friends, by sending them such productions of genius, ancient and modern, as might otherwise escape them; and I hope they will permit me to avail myself of the occasion, while it lasts.

This world is going all to war. I hope ours will remain clear of it. It is already declared between the Turks and Russians, and considering the present situation of Holland, it cannot fail to spread itself all over Europe. Perhaps it may not be till next spring, that the other powers will be engaged in it: nor is it as yet clear, how they will arrange themselves. I think it not impossible, that France and the two empires may join against all the rest. The Patriotic party in Holland will be saved by this, and the Turks sacrificed. The only thing which can prevent the union of France and the two empires, is the difficulty of agreeing about the partition of the spoils. Constantinople is the key of Asia. Who shall have it, is the question. I cannot help looking forward to the re-establishment of the Greeks as a people, and the language of Homer becoming again a living language, as among possible events. You have now with you Mr. Paradise, who can tell you how easily the modern may be improved into the ancient Greek.

You ask me in your letter, what ameliorations I think necessary in our federal constitution. It is now too late to answer the question, and it would always have been presumption in me to have done it. Your own ideas, and those of the great characters who were to be concerned with you in these discussions, will give the law, as they ought to do, to us all. My own general idea was, that the States should severally preserve their sovereignty in whatever concerns themselves alone, and that whatever may concern another State, or any foreign nation, should be made a part of the federal sovereignty: that the exercise of the federal sovereignty should be divided among three several bodies, legislative, executive, and judiciary, as the State sovereignties are: and that some peaceable means should be contrived, for the federal head to force compliance on the part of the States. I have reflected on your idea of wooden or ivory diagrams, for the geometrical demonstrations. I should think wood as good as ivory; and that in this case, it might add to the improvement of the young gentlemen, that they should make the figures themselves. Being furnished by a workman with a piece of vineer, no other tool than a penknife and a wooden rule would be necessary. Perhaps pasteboards, or common cards, might be still more convenient. The difficulty is, how to reconcile figures which must have a very sensible breadth, to our ideas of a mathematical line, which, as it has neither breadth nor thickness, will revolt more at these, than at simple lines drawn on paper or slate. If, after reflecting on this proposition, you would prefer having them made here, lay your commands on me, and they shall be executed.

I return you a thousand thanks for your goodness to my nephew. After my debt to you for whatever I am myself, it is increasing it too much, to interest yourself for his future fortune. But I know that to you, a consciousness of doing good is a luxury ineffable. You have enjoyed it already, beyond all human measure, and that you may long live to enjoy it, and to bless your country and friends, is the sincere prayer of him, who is, with every possible sentiment of esteem and respect, Dear Sir, your most obedient and most humble servant,

Th: Jefferson.

LETTER XCII.—TO JOHN JAY, September 19, 1787

TO JOHN JAY.

Sir,

Paris, September 19, 1787.

My last letters to you were of the 6th and 15th of August; since which, I have been honored with yours of July the 24th, acknowledging the receipt of mine of the 14th and 23d of February. I am anxious to hear you have received that also of May the 4th, written from Marseilles. According to the desires of Congress, expressed in their vote confirming the appointments of Francisco Giuseppa and Girolamo Chiappi, their agents in Morocco, I have written letters to these gentlemen, to begin a correspondence with them. To the first, I have enclosed the ratification of the treaty with the Emperor of Morocco, and shall send it either by our agent at Marseilles, who is now here, or by the Count Daranda, who sets out for Madrid in a few days, having relinquished his embassy here. I shall proceed on the redemption of our captives at Algiers, as soon as the commissioners of the treasury shall enable me, by placing the money necessary under my orders. The prisoners redeemed by the religious order of Mathurins, cost about four hundred dollars each, and the General of the order told me, that they had never been able to redeem foreigners on so good terms as their own countrymen. Supposing that their redemption, clothing, feeding, and transportation should amount to five hundred dollars each, there must be, at least, a sum of ten thousand dollars set apart for this purpose. Till this is done, I shall take no other step than the preparatory one, of destroying at Algiers all idea of our intending to redeem the prisoners. This, the General of the Mathurins told me, was indispensably necessary, and that it must not, on any account, transpire, that the public would interest themselves for their redemption. This was rendered the more necessary, by the declaration of the Dey to the Spanish consul, that he should hold him responsible, at the Spanish price, for our prisoners, even for such as should die. Three of them have died of the plague. By authorizing me to redeem at the prices usually paid by the European nations, Congress, I suppose, could not mean the Spanish price, which is not only unusual but unprecedented, and would make our vessels the first object with those pirates. I shall pay no attention, therefore, to the Spanish price, unless further instructed. Hard as it may seem, I should think it necessary, not to let it be known even to the relations of the captives, that we mean to redeem them.

I have the honor to inclose you a paper from the admiralty of Guadaloupe, sent to me as a matter of form, and to be lodged, I suppose, with our marine records. I enclose, also, a copy of a letter from the Count de Florida Blanca to Mr. Carmichael, by which you will perceive, they have referred the settlement of the claim of South Carolina for the use of their frigate, to Mr. Gardoqui, and to the Delegates of South Carolina in Congress.

I had the honor to inform you in my last letter, of the parliament's being transferred to Troyes. To put an end to the tumults in Paris, some regiments were brought nearer, the patroles were strengthened and multiplied, some mutineers punished by imprisonment: it produced the desired effect. It is confidently believed, however, that the parliament will be immediately recalled, the stamp tax and land tax repealed, and other means devised of accommodating their receipts and expenditures. Those supposed to be in contemplation, are, a rigorous levy of the old tax of the *deux vingtiemes*, on the rich, who had, in a great measure, withdrawn their property from it, as well as on the poor, on whom it had principally fallen. This will greatly increase the receipts: while they are proceeding on the other hand, to reform their expenses far beyond what they had promised. It is said these reformations will amount to eighty millions. Circumstances render these measures more and more pressing. I mentioned to you in my last letter, that the officer charged by the ministry to watch the motion of the British squadron, had returned with information that it had sailed westwardly. The fact was not true. He had formed his conclusion too hastily, and thus led the ministry into error. The King of Prussia, urged on by England, has pressed more and more the affairs of Holland and lately has given to the States General of Holland four days only to comply with his demand. This measure would, of itself, have rendered it impossible for France to proceed longer in the line of accommodation with Prussia. In the same moment, an event takes place, which seems to render all attempt at accommodation idle. The Turks have declared war against the Russians, and that under circumstances which exclude all prospect of preventing its taking place. The King of Prussia having deserted his ancient friends, there remain only France and Turkey, perhaps Spain also, to oppose the two empires, Prussia and England. By such a piece of Quixotism, France might plunge herself into ruin with the Turks and Dutch, but would save neither. But there is certainly a confederacy secretly in contemplation, of which the public have not yet the smallest suspicion; that is between France and the two empires. I think it sure that Russia has desired this, and that the Emperor, after some hesitation, has acceded. It rests on this country to close. Her indignation against the King of Prussia will be some spur. She will thereby save her party in Holland, and only abandon the Turks to that fate she cannot ward off, and which their precipitation has brought on themselves, by the instigation of the English ambassador at the Porte, and against the remonstrances of the French ambassador. Perhaps this formidable combination, should it take place, may prevent the war of the western powers, as it would seem that neither England nor Prussia would carry their false calculations so far, as, with the aid of the Turks only, to oppose themselves to such a force. In that case, the Patriots of Holland would be peaceably established in the powers of their government, and the war go on against the Turks only, who would probably be driven from Europe. This new arrangement would be a total change of the European system, and a favorable one for our friends. The probability of a general war, in which this country would be engaged on one side, and England on the other, has appeared to me sufficient to justify my writing to our agents in the different ports of France, to put our merchants on their guard, against risking their property in French or English bottoms. The Emperor, instead of treading back his steps in Brabant, as was expected, has pursued the less honorable plan of decoying his subjects thence by false pretences, to let themselves be invested by his troops, and this done, he dictates to them his own terms. Yet it is not certain the matter will end with that.

The Count De Moustier is nominated Minister Plenipotentiary to America; and a frigate is ordered to Cherbourg, to carry him over. He will endeavor to sail by the middle of the next month, but if any delay should make him pass over the whole of October, he will defer his voyage to the spring, being unwilling to undertake a winter passage. Monsieur de St. Priest is sent ambassador to Holland, in the room of Monsieur de Verac, appointed to Switzerland. The Chevalier de Luzerne might, I believe,have gone to Holland, but he preferred a general promise of promotion, and the possibility that it might be to the court of London. His prospects are very fair. His brother, the Count de la Luzerne, (now Governor in the West Indies) is appointed minister of the marine, in the place of Monsieur de Castries, who has resigned. The Archbishop of Toulouse is appointed ministre principal, and his brother Monsieur de Brienne, minister of war, in the place of Monsieur de Segur. The department of the Comptroller has had a very rapid succession of tenants. From Monsieur de Calonne it passed to Monsieur de Forqueux, from him to Villedeuil, and from him to Lambert, who holds it at present, but divided with a Monsieur Cabarrus (whom I believe you knew in Spain), who is named *Directeur du tresor royal,* the office into which M. Necker came at first. I had the honor to inform you, that before the departure of the Count de Luzerne to his government in the West Indies, I had pressed on him the patronage of our trade with the French islands; that he appeared well disposed, and assured me he would favor us as much as his instructions, and the laws of the colonies, would permit. I am in hopes, these dispositions will be strengthened by his residence in the islands, and that his acquaintance among the people there will be an additional motive to favor them. Probably they will take advantage of his appointment, to press indulgences in commerce with us. The ministry is of a liberal complexion, and well disposed to us. The war may add to the motives for opening their islands to other resources for their subsistence, and for doing what may be agreeable to us. It seems to me at present, then, that the moment of the arrival of the Count de la Luzerne will be the moment for trying to obtain a freer access to their islands. It would be very material to do this, if possible, in a permanent way, that is to say, by treaty. But I know of nothing we have to offer in equivalent. Perhaps the payment of our debt to them might be made use of as some inducement, while they are so distressed for money. Yet the borrowing the money in Holland will be rendered more difficult by the same event, in proportion as it will increase the demand for money by other powers.

The gazettes of Ley den and France, to this date, are enclosed, together with some pamphlets on the internal affairs of this country.

I have the honor to be, with sentiments of the most perfect esteem and respect, Sir, your most obedient and most humble servant,

Th: Jefferson.

LETTER XCIII.—TO CHARLES THOMSON, September 20, 1787

TO CHARLES THOMSON.

Paris, September 20, 1787.

Dear Sir,

Your favor of April the 28th did not come to my hands till the 1st instant. Unfortunately, the boxes of plants, which were a day too late to come by the April packet, missed the packet of June the 10th also, and only came by that of July the 25th. They are not yet arrived at Paris, but I expect them daily. I am sensible of your kind attention to them, and that as you were leaving New York, you took the course which bade fair to be the best. That they were forgotten in the hands in which you placed them, was probably owing to much business, and more important. I have desired Mr. Madison to refund to you the money, you were so kind as to advance for me. The delay of your letter will apologize for this delay of the repayment. I thank you also, for the extract of the letter you were so kind as to communicate to me, on the antiquities found in the western country. I wish that the persons who go thither, would make very exact descriptions of what they see of that kind, without forming any theories. The moment a person forms a theory, his imagination sees in every object, only the traits which favor that theory. But it is too early to form theories on those antiquities. We must wait with patience till more facts are collected. I wish your Philosophical Society would collect exact descriptions of the several monuments as yet known, and insert them naked in their Transactions, and continue their attention to those hereafter to be discovered. Patience and observation may enable us, in time, to solve the problem, whether those who formed the scattering monuments in our western country, were colonies sent off from Mexico or the founders of Mexico itself; whether both were the descendants or the progenitors of the Asiatic red men. The Mexican tradition, mentioned by Dr. Robertson, is an evidence, but a feeble one, in favor of the one opinion. The number of languages radically different, is a strong evidence in favor of the contrary one. There is an American by the name of Ledyard, he who was with Captain Cook on his last voyage, and wrote an account of that voyage, who has gone to St. Petersburg; from thence he was to go to Kamtschatka; to cross over thence to the northwest coast of America, and to penetrate through the main continent, to our side of it. He is a person of ingenuity and information. Unfortunately, he has too much imagination. However, if he escapes safely, he will give us new, curious, and useful information. I had a letter from him, dated last March, when he was about to leave St. Petersburg on his way to Kamtschatka.

With respect to the inclination of the strata of rocks, I had observed them between the Blue Ridge and North Mountains in Virginia, to be parallel with the pole of the earth. I observed the same thing in most instances in the Alps, between Cette and Turin: but in returning along the precipices of the Apennines, where they hang over the Mediterranean, their direction was totally different and various: and you mention, that in our western country, they are horizontal. This variety proves they have not been formed by subsidence, as some writers of theories of the earth have pretended; for then they should always have been in circular strata, and concentric. It proves, too, that they have not been formed by the rotation of the earth on its axis, as might have been suspected, had all these strata been parallel with that axis. They may, indeed, have been thrown up by explosions, as Whitehurst supposes, or have been the effect of convulsions. But there can be no proof of the explosion, nor is it probable that convulsions have deformed every spot of the earth. It is now generally agreed that rock grows, and it seems that it grows in layers in every direction, as the branches of trees grow in all directions. Why seek further the solution of this phenomenon? Every thing in nature decays. If it were not reproduced then by growth, there would be a chasm.

I remember you asked me in a former letter, whether the steam-mill in London was turned by the steam immediately, or by the intermediate agency of water raised by the steam. When I was in London, Boulton made a secret of his mill. Therefore, I was permitted to see it only superficially. I saw no water-wheels, and therefore supposed none. I answered you, accordingly, that there were none. But when I was at Nismes, I went to see the steam-mill there, and they showed it to me in all its parts. I saw that their steam raised water, and that this water turned a wheel. I expressed my doubts of the necessity of the inter-agency of water, and that the London mill was without it. But they supposed me mistaken; perhaps I was so: I have had no opportunity since of clearing up the doubt.

I had a letter from Mr. Churchman, but not developing his plan of knowing the longitude, fully. I wrote him what was doubted about it, so far as we could conjecture what it was.

I am with very great and sincere esteem, Dear Sir, your friend and servant,

Th: Jefferson.

LETTER XCIV.—TO JOHN JAY, September 22,1787

TO JOHN JAY.

Paris, September 22,1787.

Sir,

The letters of which the inclosed are copies, are this moment received, and as there is a possibility that they may reach Havre before the packet sails, I have the honor of enclosing them to you. They contain a promise of reducing the duties on tar, pitch, and turpentine, and that the government will interest itself with the city of Rouen, to reduce the local duty on potash. By this you will perceive, that we are getting on a little in this business, though under their present embarrassments, it is difficult to procure the attention of the ministers to it. The parliament has enregistered the edict for a rigorous levy of the *deux vingtièmes*. As this was proposed by the King in lieu of the *impôt territorial*, there is no doubt now, that the latter, with the stamp tax, will be immediately repealed. There can be no better proof of the revolution in the public opinion, as to the powers of the monarch, and of the force, too, of that opinion. Six weeks ago, we saw the King displaying the plenitude of his omnipotence, as hitherto conceived, to enforce these two acts. At this day, he is forced to retract them by the public voice; for as to the opposition of the parliamemt, that body is too little esteemed to produce this effect in any case, where the public do not throw themselves into the same scale.

I have the honor to be, with the most perfect esteem and respect, Sir, your most obedient and most humble servant,

Th: Jefferson.

LETTER XCV.—TO JOHN JAY, September 22, 1787

TO JOHN JAY.

Paris, September 22, 1787.

Sir,

When I had the honor of addressing you this morning, intelligence was handing about, which I did not think well enough authenticated to communicate to you. As it is now ascertained, I avail myself of the chance that another post may yet reach Havre, before the departure of the packet. This will depend on the wind, which has for some days been unfavorable. I must premise that this court, about ten days ago, declared, by their *Chargé des Affaires* in Holland, that if the Prussian troops continued to menace Holland with an invasion, his Majesty was determined, in quality of ally, to succor that province. An official letter from the Hague, of the 18th instant, assures that the Prussian army entered the territory of Holland on the 15th, that most of the principal towns had submitted, some after firing a gun or two, others without resistance: that the Rhingrave de Salm had evacuated Utrecht, with part of the troops under his command, leaving behind him one hundred and forty-four pieces of cannon, with great warlike stores: that the standard of Orange was hoisted every where: that no other cockade could be worn at the Hague: that the States General were to assemble that night for reinstating the Stadtholder in all his rights. The letter concludes, 'We have this moment intelligence that Woerden has capitulated; so that Amsterdam remains without defence.' So far the letter. We know, otherwise, that Monsieur de St. Priest, who had set out on his embassy to the Hague, has stopped at Antwerp, not choosing to proceed further till new orders. This Court has been completely deceived, first by its own great desire to avoid a war, and secondly by calculating that the King of Prussia would have acted on principles of common sense, which would surely have dictated, that a power, lying between the jaws of Russia and Austria, should not separate itself from France, unless, indeed, he had assurances of dispositions in those two powers, which are not supposed to exist. On the contrary, I am persuaded that they ask the alliance of France, whom we suppose to be under hesitations between her reluctance to abandon the Turks, her jealousy of increasing by their spoils the power of the two empires, and her inability to oppose them. If they cannot obtain her alliance, they will surely join themselves to England and Prussia.

Official advices are received, that the first division of the Russian army has passed the Borysthenes into the Polish Ukraine, and is marching towards the frontiers of Turkey. Thus, we may consider the flames of war as completely kindled in two distinct parts of this quarter of the globe, and that though

France and England have not yet engaged themselves in it, the probabilities are that they will do it.

I have the honor to be, with the most perfect esteem and respect, Sir, your most obedient and most humble servant,

Th: Jefferson.

LETTER XCVI.—TO MR. CARNES, September 22, 1787

TO MR. CARNES.

Paris, September 22, 1787.

Sir,

I am honored by your favor of the 17th instant. A war between France and England does not necessarily engage America in it; and I think she will be disposed rather to avail herself of the advantages of a neutral power. By the former usage of nations, the goods of a friend were safe, though taken in an enemy bottom, and those of an enemy were lawful prize, though found in a free bottom. But in our treaties with France, &c. we have established the simpler rule, that a free bottom makes free goods, and an enemy bottom, enemy goods. The same rule has been adopted by the treaty of armed neutrality between Russia, Sweden, Denmark, Holland, and Portugal, and assented to by France and Spain. Contraband goods, however, are always excepted, so that they may still be seized; but the same powers have established that naval stores are not contraband: and this may be considered now as the law of nations. Though England acquiesced under this during the late war, rather than draw on herself the neutral powers, yet she never acceded to the new principle, and her obstinacy on this point is what has prevented the late renewal of her treaty with Russia. On the commencement of a new war, this principle will probably be insisted on by the neutral powers, whom we may suppose to be Sweden, Denmark, Portugal, America, and perhaps Spain. *Quere*; if England will again acquiesce. Supposing these details might be useful to you, I have taken the liberty of giving them, and of assuring you of the esteem with which I am, Sir, your very humble servant,

Th: Jefferson.

LETTER XCVII.—TO JOHN JAY, September 24, 1787

TO JOHN JAY.

Paris, September 24, 1787.

Sir,

The times are now so critical, that every day brings something new and important, not known the day before. Observing the wind still unfavorable, I am in hopes the packet may not sail to-morrow, and that this letter may be at Havre in time for that conveyance. Mr. Eden has waited on Count Montmorin to inform him, officially, that England must consider its convention with France, relative to the giving notice of its naval armaments, as at an end, and that they are arming generally. This is considered here as a declaration of war. The Dutch ambassador told me yesterday, that he supposed the Prussian troops probably in possession of the Hague. I asked him if it would interrupt the course of business, commercial or banking, in Amsterdam; and particularly, whether our depot of money there was safe. He said, the people of Amsterdam would be surely so wise as to submit, when they should see that they could not oppose the Stadtholder: therefore he supposed our depot safe, and that there would be no interruption of business. It is the hour of the departure of the post: so I have only time to add assurances of the respect and esteem, with which I have the honor to be, Sir, your most obedient, humble servant,

Th: Jefferson.

LETTER XCVIII,—TO JOHN ADAMS, September 28, 1787

TO JOHN ADAMS.

Paris, September 28, 1787.

Dear Sir,

I received your favor by Mr. Cutting, and thank you sincerely for the copy of your book. The departure of a packet-boat, which always gives me full employment for some time before, has only permitted me to look into it a little. I judge of it from the first volume, which I thought formed to do a great deal of good. The first principle of a good government, is certainly a distribution of its powers into executive, judiciary, and legislative, and a subdivision of the latter into two or three branches. It is a good step gained, when it is proved that the English constitution, acknowledged to be better than all which have preceded it, is only better, in proportion as it has approached nearer to this distribution of powers. From this, the last step is easy, to show by a comparison of our constitutions with that of England, how much more perfect they are. The article of Confederations is certainly worthy of your pen. It would form a most interesting addition, to show, what has been the nature of the Confederations which have existed hitherto, what were their excellencies, and what their defects.

A comparison of ours with them would be to the advantage of ours, and would increase the veneration of our countrymen for it. It is a misfortune, that they do not sufficiently know the value of their constitutions, and how much happier they are rendered by them, than any other people on earth, by the governments under which they live.

You know all that has happened in the United Netherlands. You know also that our friends, Van Staphorsts, will be among the most likely to become objects of severity, if any severities should be exercised. Is the money in their hands entirely safe? If it is not, I am sure you have already thought of it. Are we to suppose the game already up, and that the Stadtholder is to be reestablished, perhaps erected into a monarch, without the country lifting a finger in opposition to it? If so, it is a lesson the more for us. In fact, what a crowd of lessons do the present miseries of Holland teach us? Never to have an hereditary officer of any sort: never to let a citizen ally himself with kings: never to call in foreign nations to settle domestic differences: never to suppose that any nation will expose itself to war for us, &c. Still I am not without hopes, that a good rod is in soak for Prussia, and that England will feel the end of it. It is known to some, that Russia made propositions to the Emperor and France, for acting in concert; that the Emperor consents, and has disposed four camps of one hundred and eighty thousand men, from the limits of Turkey to those of Prussia. This court hesitates, or rather its Premier hesitates; for the Queen, Montmorin, and Breteuil are for the measure. Should it take place, all may yet come to rights, except for the Turks, who must retire from Europe, and this they must do, were France Quixotic enough to undertake to support them. We, I hope, shall be left free to avail ourselves of the advantages of neutrality: and yet, much I fear, the English, or rather their stupid King, will force us out of it. For thus I reason. By forcing us into the war against them, they will be engaged in an expensive land war, as well as a sea war. Common sense dictates, therefore, that they should let us remain neuter: ergo, they will not let us remain neuter. I never yet found any other general rule for foretelling what they will do, but that of examining what they ought not to do.

I have the honor to be, with my best respects to Mrs. Adams, and sentiments of perfect esteem and regard to yourself, Sir, your most obedient and most humble servant,

Th: Jefferson

LETTER XCIX.—TO COLONEL SMITH, September 28,1787

TO COLONEL SMITH.

Paris, September 28,1787.

Dear Sir,

I have duly received your favor by Mr. Cutting. I had before had a transient acquaintance with him, and knew him to be sensible. Your recommendation is always a new merit. I really think, and had taken the liberty some time ago of hinting to Congress, that they would do well to have a diplomatic character at Lisbon. There is no country whose commerce is more interesting to us. I wish Congress would correspond to the wishes of that court, in sending a person there, and to mine, in sending yourself. For I confess, I had rather see you there than at London, because I doubt whether it be honorable for us to keep any body at London, unless they keep some person at New York. Of all nations on earth, they require to be treated with the most hauteur. They require to be kicked into common good manners. You ask, if you shall say any thing to Sullivan about the bill. No. Only that it is paid. I have, within these two or three days, received letters from him explaining the matter. It was really for the skin and bones of the moose, as I had conjectured. It was my fault, that I had not given him a rough idea of the expense I would be willing to incur for them. He had made the acquisition an object of a regular campaign, and that too of a winter one. The troops he employed sallied forth, as he writes me, in the month of March—much snow—a herd attacked—one killed—in the wilderness—a road to cut twenty miles—to be drawn by hand from the frontiers to his house—bones to be cleaned, &c. &c. &c. In fine, he put himself to an infinitude of trouble, more than I meant: he did it cheerfully, and I feel myself really under obligations to him. That the tragedy might not want a proper catastrophe, the box, bones, and all are lost: so that this chapter of Natural History will still remain a blank. But I have written to him not to send me another. I will leave it for my successor to fill up, whenever I shall make my bow here. The purchase for Mrs. Adams shall be made, and sent by Mr. Cutting. I shall always be happy to receive her commands. Petit shall be made happy by her praises of his last purchase for her. I must refer you to Mr. Adams for the news. Those respecting the Dutch you know as well as I. Nor should they be written but with the pen of Jeremiah. Adieu, mon ami! Yours affectionately,

Th: Jefferson.

LETTER C.—TO MONSIEUR LE COMTE DE BUFFON, October 3, 1787

TO MONSIEUR LE COMTE DE BUFFON.

Paris, October 3, 1787.

Sir,

I had the honor of informing you, some time ago, that I had written to some of my friends in America, desiring they would send me such of the spoils of the moose, caribou, elk, and deer, as might throw light on that class of animals; but more particularly, to send me the complete skeleton, skin, and horns of the moose, in such condition as that the skin might be sewed up and stuffed, on its arrival here. I am happy to be able to present to you at this moment, the bones and skin of a moose, the horns of another individual of the same species, the horns of the caribou, the elk, the deer, the spiked-horned buck, and the roebuck of America. They all come from New Hampshire and Massachusetts, and were received by me yesterday. I give you their popular names, as it rests with yourself to decide their real names. The skin of the moose was dressed with the hair on, but a great deal of it has come off, and the rest is ready to drop off. The horns of the elk are remarkably small. I have certainly seen some of them, which would have weighed five or six times as much. This is the animal which we call elk in the southern parts of America, and of which I have given some description in the Notes on Virginia, of which I had the honor of presenting you a copy. I really doubt, whether the flat-horned elk exists in America: and I think this may be properly classed with the elk, the principal difference being in the horns. I have seen the *daim*, the *cerf*, the *chevreuil*, of Europe. But the animal we call elk, and which may be distinguished as the round-horned elk, is very different from them. I have never seen the *brand-hirtz* or *cerf d'Ardennes*, nor the European elk. Could I get a sight of them, I think I should be able to say which of them the American elk resembles most, as I am tolerably well acquainted with that animal. I must observe, also, that the horns of the deer, which accompany these spoils, are not of the fifth or sixth part of the weight of some that I have seen. This individual has been of three years of age, according to our method of judging. I have taken measures, particularly, to be furnished with large horns of our elk and our deer, and therefore beg of you not to consider those now sent, as furnishing a specimen of their ordinary size. I really suspect you will find that the moose, the round-horned elk, and the American deer are species not existing in Europe. The moose is, perhaps, of a new class. I wish these spoils, Sir, may have the merit of adding any thing new to the treasures of nature, which have so fortunately come under your observation, and of which she seems to have given you the key:

they will in that case be some gratification to you, which it will always be pleasing to me to have procured; having the honor to be, with sentiments of the most perfect esteem and respect, Sir, your most obedient and most humble servant,

Th: Jefferson.

LETTER CI.—TO MR. DUMAS, October 4,1787

TO MR. DUMAS.

Paris, October 4,1787.

Sir,

I received your favor of the 23rd of September two days ago. That of the 28th and 29th was put in my hands this morning. I immediately waited on the ambassadors, ordinary and extraordinary, of the United Netherlands, and also on the envoy of Prussia, and asked their good offices to have an efficacious protection extended to your person, your family, and your effects, observing, that the United States know no party, but are the friends and allies of the United Netherlands as a nation, and would expect from their friendship, that the person who is charged with their affairs, until the arrival of a minister, should be covered from all insult and injury, which might be offered him by a lawless mob; well assured that their minister, residing with Congress, would on all occasions receive the same. They have been so good as to promise me, each, that he will in his first despatches press this matter on the proper power, and give me reason to hope that it will be efficacious for your safety. I will transmit your letter to Mr. Jay by the Count de Moustier, who sets out within a week for New York, as Minister Plenipotentiary for France, in that country. I sincerely sympathize in your sufferings, and wish that what I have done may effect an end to them; being with much respect and esteem, Sir, your most obedient and most humble servant,

Th: Jefferson.

LETTER CII.—TO JOHN JAY, October 8, 1787

TO JOHN JAY.

Paris, October 8, 1787.

Sir,

I had the honor of writing you on the 19th of September, twice on the 22nd, and again on the 24th. The two first went by the packet, the third by a vessel bound to Philadelphia. I have not yet learned by what occasion the last went. In these several letters, I communicated to you the occurrences of Europe, as far as they were then known. Notwithstanding the advantage which the Emperor seemed to have gained over his subjects of Brabant, by the military arrangements he had been permitted to make under false pretexts, he has not obtained his ends. He certainly wished to enforce his new regulations; but he wished more to be cleared of all domestic difficulties, that he might be free to act in the great scenes which are preparing for the theatre of Europe. He seems, therefore, to have instructed his Governor General of the Netherlands to insist on compliance as far as could be insisted, without producing resistance by arms; but at the same time, to have furnished him with a sufficiently complete recantation, to prevent the effects of insurrection. The Governor pressed; the people were firm; a small act of force was then attempted, which produced a decided resistance, in which the people killed several of the military: the last resource was then used, which was the act of recantation; this produced immediate tranquillity, and every thing there is now finally settled, by the Emperor's relinquishment of his plans.

My letter of the evening of September the 22nd informed you that the Prussian troops had entered Holland, and that of the 24th, that England had announced to this court that she was arming generally. These two events being simultaneous, proved that the two sovereigns acted in concert. Immediately after, the court of London announced to the other courts of Europe, that if France entered Holland with armed force, she would consider it as an act of hostility, and declare war against her; sending Mr. Grenville here, at the same time, to make what she called a conciliatory proposition. This proposition was received as a new insult, Mr. Grenville very coolly treated, and he has now gone back. It is said, he has carried the ultimatum of France. What it is, particularly, has not transpired; it is only supposed, in general, to be very firm. You will see, in one of the Leyden gazettes, one of the letters written by the ministers of England to the courts of their respective residence, communicating the declaration before mentioned. In the mean time, Holland has been sooner reduced by the Prussian troops, than could have been expected. The abandonment of Utrecht by the Rhingrave of Salm, seems to have thrown the people under a general panic, during which every place submitted, except Amsterdam. That had opened conferences with the Duke of Brunswick; but as late as the 2nd instant, no capitulation was yet concluded. The King of Prussia, on his first move, demanded categorically of the King of Poland, what part he intended to act in the event of war. The latter answered, he should act as events should dictate; and is, in consequence of this species of menace from Prussia, arming himself. He can bring into the field about seventy thousand good cavalry. In the mean time, though nothing transpires publicly of the confederation between France and the two empires, mentioned in my letter of September the 19th, it is not the less sure that it is on the carpet, and will take place. To the circumstances before mentioned, may be added, as further indications of war, the naming as Generalissimo of their marine on the Atlantic, Monsieur de Suffrein, on the Mediterranean, Monsieur Albert de Rioms, the recalling Monsieur de St. Priest, their ambassador, from Antwerp, before he had reached the Hague, and the activity of their armies by sea. On the other hand, the little movement by land would make one suppose they expected to put the King of Prussia into other hands. They too, like the Emperor, are arranging matters at home. The rigorous levy of the *deux vingtiemes* is enregistered, the stamp act and *impot territorial* are revoked, the parliament recalled, the nation soothed by these acts, and inspired by the insults of the British court. The part of the Council still leaning towards peace are become unpopular, and perhaps may feel the effects of it. No change in the administration has taken place since my last, unless we may consider as such, Monsieur Cabarrus's refusal to stand in the lines. Thinking he should be forced to follow, too seriously, plans formed by others, he has declined serving.

Should this war take place, as is quite probable, and should it be as general as it threatens to be, our neutrality must be attended with great advantages. Whether of a nature to improve our morals or our happiness, is another question. But is it sure that Great Britain, by her searches, her seizures, and other measures for harassing us, will permit us to preserve our neutrality? I know it may be argued, that the land-war, which she would superadd to her sea-war, by provoking us to join her enemies, should rationally hold her to her good behavior with us. But since the accession of the present monarch, has it not been passion, and not reason, which, nine times out of ten, has dictated her measures? Has there been a better rule of prognosticating what he would do, than to examine what he ought not to do? When I review his dispositions and review his conduct, I have little hope of his permitting our neutrality. He will find subjects of provocation in various articles of our treaty with France, which will now come into view, in all their consequences, and in consequences very advantageous to the one, and injurious to the other country. I suggest these doubts, on a supposition that our magazines are not prepared for war, and in the opinion that provisions for that event should be thought of.

The enclosed letter from Mr. Dumas came to me open, though directed to you. I immediately waited on the ambassadors, ordinary and extraordinary, of Holland, and the envoy of Prussia, and prayed them to interest themselves to have his person, his family, and his goods protected. They promised me readily to do it, and have written accordingly; I trust it will be with effect. I could not avoid enclosing you the letter from Monsieur Bouebe, though I have satisfied him he is to expect nothing from Congress for his inventions. These are better certified than most of those things are; but if time stamps their worth, time will give them to us. He expects no further answer. The gazettes of Leyden and France to this date accompany this, which will be delivered you by the Count de Moustier, Minister Plenipotentiary from this country.

I have the honor to be, with sentiments of the most perfect esteem and respect, Sir, your most obedient and most humble servant,

Th: Jefferson.

LETTER CIII.—TO JAMES MADISON, October 8, 1787

TO JAMES MADISON.

Paris, October 8, 1787.

Dear Sir,

The bearer hereof, the Count de Moustier, successor to Monsieur de la Luzerne, would, from his office, need no letter of introduction to you or to any body. Yet I take the liberty of recommending him to you, to shorten those formal approaches, which the same office would otherwise expose him to, in making your acquaintance. He is a great enemy to formality, etiquette, ostentation, and luxury. He goes with the best dispositions to cultivate society, without poisoning it by ill example. He is sensible, disposed to view things favorably, and being well acquainted with the constitution of England, her manners, and language, is the better prepared for his station with us. But I should have performed only the lesser, and least pleasing half of my task, were I not to add my recommendations of Madame de Brehan. She is goodness itself. You must be well acquainted with her. You will find her well disposed to meet your acquaintance, and well worthy of it. The way to please her, is to receive her as an acquaintance of a thousand years' standing. She speaks little English. You must teach her more, and learn French from her. She hopes, by accompanying Monsieur de Moustier, to improve her health, which is very feeble, and still more, to improve her son in his education, and to remove him to a distance from the seductions of this country. You will wonder to be told, that there are no schools in this country to be compared to ours in the sciences. The husband of Madame de Brehan is an officer, and obliged by the times to remain with the army. Monsieur de Moustier brings your watch. I have worn it two months, and really find it a most incomparable one. It will not want the little re-dressing, which new watches generally do, after going about a year. It costs six hundred livres. To open it in all its parts, press the little pin on the edge with the point of your nail; that opens the crystal; then open the dial-plate in the usual way; then press the stem, at the end within the loop, and it opens the back for winding up or regulating.

De Moustier is remarkably communicative. With adroitness he may be pumped of any thing. His openness is from character, not from affectation. An intimacy with him may, on this account, be politically valuable.

I am, Dear Sir, your affectionate friend and servant,

Th: Jefferson.

LETTER CIV.—TO JOHN JAY, October 8, 1787

TO JOHN JAY.

(Private.) Paris, October 8, 1787.

Dear Sir,

The Count de Moustier, Minister Plenipotentiary from the court of Versailles to the United States, will have the honor of delivering you this. The connection of your offices will necessarily connect you in acquaintance; but I beg leave to present him to you, on account of his personal as well as his public character. You will find him open, communicative, candid, simple in his manners, and a declared enemy to ostentation and luxury. He goes with a resolution to add no aliment to it by his example, unless he finds that the dispositions of our countrymen require it indispensably. Permit me, at the same time, to solicit your friendly notice, and through you, that also of Mrs. Jay, to Madame la Marquise de Brehan, sister-in-law to Monsieur de Moustier. She accompanies him, in hopes that a change of climate may assist her feeble health, and also, that she may procure a more valuable education for her son, and safer from seduction, in America than in France. I think it impossible to find a better woman, more amiable, more modest, more simple in her manners, dress, and way of thinking. She will deserve the friendship of Mrs. Jay, and the way to obtain hers, is to receive her and treat her without the shadow of etiquette.

The Count d'Aranda leaves us in a day or two. He desired me to recall him to your recollection, and to assure you of his friendship. In a letter which I mean as a private one, I may venture details too minute for a public one, yet not unamusing, or unsatisfactory. I may venture names too, without the danger of their getting into a newspaper. There has long been a division in the Council here, on the question of war and peace. Monsieur de Montmorin and Monsieur de Breteuil have been constantly for war. They are supported in this by the Queen. The King goes for nothing. He hunts one half the day, is drunk the other, and signs whatever he is bid. The Archbishop of Toulouse desires peace. Though brought in by the Queen, he is opposed to her in this capital object, which would produce an alliance with her brother. Whether the Archbishop will yield or not, I know not. But an intrigue is already begun for ousting him from his place, and it is rather probable it will succeed. He is a good and patriotic minister for peace, and very capable in the department of finance. At least he is so in theory. I have heard his talents for execution censured.

Can I be useful here to Mrs. Jay or yourself, in executing any commissions, great or small? I offer you my services with great cordiality. You know whether any of the wines of this country may attract your wishes. In my tour, last spring, I visited the best vineyards of Burgundy, Cote-rotie, Hermitage, Lunelle, Frontignan, and white and red Bordeaux, got acquainted with the proprietors, and can procure for you the best crops from the vigneron himself. Mrs. Jay knows if there is any thing else here, in which I could be useful to her. Command me without ceremony, as it will give me real pleasure to serve you; and be assured of the sincere attachment and friendship, with which I am, Dear Sir, your most obedient and most humble servant,

Th: Jefferson.

LETTER CV.—TO MONSIEUR LE COMTE DE MOUSTIER, October 9,1787

TO MONSIEUR LE COMTE DE MOUSTIER.

Paris, October 9,1787.

Mr. Jefferson has the honor of presenting his respects to Monsieur le Comte de Moustier, and of taking leave of him by letter, which he is prevented doing in person, by an unexpected visit to Versailles to-day. He will hope to have the pleasure of sometimes hearing from him, and will take the liberty occasionally, of troubling him with a letter. He considers the Count de Moustier as forming with himself the two end links of that chain which holds the two nations together, and is happy to have observed in him dispositions to strengthen rather than to weaken it. It is a station of importance, as on the cherishing good dispositions and quieting bad ones, will depend in some degree the happiness and prosperity of the two countries. The Count de Moustier will find the affections of the Americans with France, but their habits with England. Chained to that country by circumstances, embracing what they loathe, they realize the fable of the living and the dead bound together. Mr. Jefferson troubles the Count de Moustier with two letters, to gentlemen whom he wishes to recommend to his particular acquaintance, and to that of Madame de Brehan. He bids Monsieur de Moustier a most friendly adieu, and wishes him every thing which may render agreeable his passage across the water, and his residence beyond it.

LETTER CVI.—TO MADAME DE BREHAN, October 9, 1787

TO MADAME DE BREHAN.

Paris, October 9, 1787.

Persuaded, Madam, that visits at this moment must be troublesome I beg you to accept my adieus, in this form. Be assured, that no one mingles with them more regret at separating from you. I will ask your permission to inquire of you by letter sometimes, how our country agrees with your health and your expectations, and will hope to hear it from yourself. The imitation of European manners, which you will find in our towns, will, I fear, be little pleasing. I beseech you to practise still your own, which will furnish them a model of what is perfect. Should you be singular, it will be by excellence, and after a while you will see the effect of your example.

Heaven bless you, Madam, and guard you under all circumstances; give you smooth waters, gentle breezes, and clear skies, hushing all its elements into peace, and leading with its own hand the favored bark, till it shall have safely landed its precious charge on the shores of our new world.

Th: Jefferson.

LETTER CVII.—TO MR. DUMAS, October 14, 1787

TO MR. DUMAS.

Paris, October 14, 1787.

Sir,

I have duly received your favors of October the 23rd and 26th. With respect to the mission you suggest, in the former, no powers are lodged in the hands of Mr. Adams and myself. Congress commissioned Mr. Adams, Doctor Franklin, and myself, to treat with the Emperor on the subjects of amity and commerce: at the same time, they gave us the commission to Prussia, with which you are acquainted. We proposed treating through the Imperial ambassador here. It was declined on their part, and our powers expired, having been given but for two years. Afterwards, the same ambassador here was instructed to offer to treat with us. I informed him our powers were expired, but that I would write to Congress on the subject. I did so, but have never yet received an answer. Whether this proceeds from a change of opinion in them, or from the multiplicity of their occupations, I am unable to say: but this state of facts will enable you to see that we have no powers, in this instance, to take the measures you had thought of. I sincerely sympathize with you in your sufferings. Though forbidden by my character to meddle in the internal affairs of an allied State, it is the wish of my heart that their troubles may have such an issue, as will secure the greatest degree of happiness to the body of the people: for it is with the mass of the nation we are allied, and not merely with their governors. To inform the minds of the people, and to follow their will, is the chief duty of those placed at their head. What party in your late struggles was most likely to do this, you are more competent to judge than I am. Under every event, that you maybe safe and happy, is the sincere wish of him, who has the honor to be, with sentiments of great esteem, Sir, your most obedient and most humble servant,

Th: Jefferson.

LETTER CVIII.—TO MADAME DE CORNY, October 18, 1787

TO MADAME DE CORNY.

Paris, October 18, 1787.

I now have the honor, Madam, to send you the Memoire of M. de Calonne. Do not injure yourself by hurrying its perusal. Only, when you shall have read it at your ease, be so good as to send it back, that it may be returned to the Duke of Dorset. You will read it with pleasure. It has carried comfort to my heart, because it must do the same to the King and the nation. Though it does not prove M. de Calonne to be more innocent than his predecessors, it shows him not to have been that exaggerated scoundrel, which the calculations and the clamors of the public have supposed. It shows that the public treasures have not been so inconceivably squandered, as the parliaments of Grenoble, Toulouse, &c. had affirmed. In fine, it shows him less wicked, and France less badly governed, than I had feared. In examining my little collection of books, to see what it could furnish you on the subject of Poland, I find a small piece which may serve as a supplement to the history I had sent you. It contains a mixture of history and politics, which I think you will like—How do you do this morning? I have feared you exerted and exposed yourself too much yesterday. I ask you the question, though I shall not await its answer. The sky is clearing, and I shall away to my hermitage. God bless you, my Dear Madam, now and always. Adieu.

Th: Jefferson.

LETTER CIX.—TO THE COUNT DE MONTMORIN, October 23, 1787

TO THE COUNT DE MONTMORIN.

Paris, October 23, 1787.

Sir,

I take the liberty of troubling your Excellency on the subject of the *Arrêt*, which has lately appeared, for prohibiting the importation of whale-oils and spermaceti, the produce of foreign fisheries. This prohibition, being expressed in general terms, seems to exclude the whale-oils of the United States of America, as well as of the nations of Europe. The uniform disposition, however, which his Majesty and his ministers have shown to promote the commerce between France and the United States, by encouraging our productions to come hither, and particularly those of our fisheries, induces me to hope, that these were not within their view, at the passing of this *Arrêt*. I am led the more into this opinion, when I recollect the assiduity exercised for several months, in the year 1785, by the committee appointed by government to investigate the objects of commerce of the two countries, and to report the encouragements of which it was susceptible; the result of that investigation, which his Majesty's Comptroller General did me the honor to communicate, in a letter of the 22nd of October, 1786, stating therein the principles which should be established for the future regulation of that commerce, and particularly distinguishing the article of whale-oils by an abatement of the duties on them for the present, and a promise of farther abatement after the year 1790; the thorough re-investigation with which Monsieur de Lambert honored this subject when the letter of 1786 was to be put into the form of an *Arrêt*; that *Arrêt* itself, bearing date the 29th of December last, which ultimately confirmed the abatements of duty present and future, and declared that his Majesty reserved to himself to grant other favors to that production, if, on further information, he should find it for the interest of the two nations; and finally, the letter in which Monsieur de Lambert did me the honor to enclose the *Arrêt*, and to assure me, that the duties which had been levied on our whale-oils, contrary to the intention of the letter of 1786, should be restored. On a review, then, of all these circumstances, I cannot but presume, that it has not been intended to reverse, in a moment, views so maturely digested, and uniformly pursued; and that the general expressions of the *Arrêt* of September the 28th had within their contemplation the nations of Europe only. This presumption is further strengthened by having observed, that in the treaties of commerce, made since the epoch of our independence, the *jura gentis amicissimæ* conceded to other nations, are expressly restrained to those of the 'most favored

European nation': his Majesty wisely foreseeing that it would be expedient to regulate the commerce of a nation, which brings nothing but raw materials to employ the industry of his subjects, very differently from that of the European nations, who bring mostly what has already passed through all the stages of manufacture.

On these circumstances, I take the liberty of asking information from your Excellency, as to the extent of the late *Arrêt*: and if I have not been mistaken in supposing it did not mean to abridge that of December the 29th, I would solicit an explanatory *Arrêt*, to prevent the misconstruction of it, which will otherwise take place. It is much to be desired too, that this explanation could be given as soon as possible, in order that it may be handed out with the *Arrêt* of September the 28th. Great alarm may otherwise be spread among the merchants, and adventurers in the fisheries, who, confiding in the stability of regulations, which his Majesty's wisdom had so long and well matured, have embarked their fortunes in speculations in this branch of business.

The importance of the subject to one of the principal members of our Union, induces me to attend with great anxiety the re-assurance from your Excellency, that no change has taken place in his Majesty's views on this subject; and that his dispositions to multiply, rather than diminish, the combinations of interest between the two people, continue unaltered.

Commerce is slow in changing its channel. That between this country and the United States is as yet but beginning; and this beginning has received some checks. The *Arrêt* in question would be a considerable one, without the explanation I have the honor to ask. I am persuaded, that a continuation of the dispositions which have been hitherto manifested towards us, will insure effects, political and commercial, of value to both nations.

I have had too many proofs of the friendly interest your Excellency is pleased to take in whatever may strengthen the bands and connect the views of the two countries, to doubt your patronage of the present application; or to pretermit any occasion of repeating assurances of those sentiments of high respect and esteem, with which I have the honor to be

your Excellency's most obedient

and most humble servant,

Th: Jefferson.

LETTER CX.—TO JOHN JAY, November 3, 1787

TO JOHN JAY.

Paris, November 3, 1787.

Sir,

My last letters to you were of the 8th and 27th of October. In the former? I mentioned to you the declaration of this country, that they would interpose with force, if the Prussian troops entered Holland; the entry of those troops into Holland; the declaration of England, that if France did oppose force, they would consider it as an act of war; the naval armaments on both sides; the nomination of the Bailli de Suffrein as Generalissimo on the ocean; and the cold reception of Mr. Grenville here, with his conciliatory propositions, as so many symptoms which seemed to indicate a certain and immediate rupture. It was indeed universally and hourly expected. But the king of Prussia, a little before these last events, got wind of the alliance on the carpet between France and the two empires: he awaked to the situation in which that would place him: he made some application to the court of St. Petersburg, to divert the Empress from the proposed alliance, and supplicated the court of London not to abandon him. That court had also received a hint of the same project; both seemed to suspect, for the first time, that it would be possible for France to abandon the Turks, and that they were likely to get more than they had played for at Constantinople: for they had meant nothing more there, than to divert the Empress and Emperor from the affairs of the west, by employing them in the east, and, at the same time, to embroil them with France as the patroness of the Turks. The court of London engaged not to abandon Prussia: but both of them relaxed a little the tone of their proceedings. The King of Prussia sent a Mr. Alvensleben here, expressly to explain and soothe: the King of England, notwithstanding the cold reception of his propositions by Grenville, renewed conferences here through Eden and the Duke of Dorset. The minister, in the affection of his heart for peace, readily joined in conference, and a declaration and counter-declaration were cooked up at Versailles, and sent to London for approbation. They were approved, arrived here at one o'clock the 27th, were signed that night at Versailles, and on the next day, I had the honor of enclosing them to you, under cover to the Count de Moustier, whom I supposed still at Brest, dating my letter as of the 27th, by mistake for the 28th. Lest, however, these papers should not have got to Brest before the departure of the Count de Moustier, I now enclose you other copies. The English declaration states a notification of this court, in September, by Barthelemy, their minister at London, 'that they would send succors into Holland,' as the first cause of England's arming; desires an explanation of the intentions of this court, as to the affairs of Holland, and proposes to disarm; on condition, however, that the King of France shall not retain any hostile views in any quarter, for what has been done in Holland. This last phrase was to secure Prussia, according to promise. The King of France acknowledges the notification by his minister at London, promises he will do nothing in consequence of it, declares he has no intention to intermeddle with force in the affairs of Holland, and that he will entertain hostile views in no quarter, for what has been done there. He disavows having ever had any intention to interpose with force in the affairs of that republic. This disavowal begins the sentence, which acknowledges he had notified the contrary to the court of London, and it includes no apology to soothe the feelings which may be excited in the breasts of the Patriots of Holland, at hearing the King declare he never did intend to aid them with force, when promises to do this were the basis of those very attempts to better their constitution, which have ended in its ruin, as well as their own.

I have analyzed these declarations, because, being somewhat wrapped up in their expressions, their full import might escape, on a transient reading; and it is necessary it should not escape. It conveys to us the important lesson, that no circumstances of morality, honor, interest, or engagement, are sufficient to authorize a secure reliance on any nation, at all times, and in all positions. A moment of difficulty, or a moment of error, may render for ever useless the most friendly dispositions in the King, in the major part of his ministers, and the whole of his nation. The present pacification is considered by most, as only a short truce. They calculate on the spirit of the nation, and not on the aged hand which guides its movements. It is certain, that from this moment the whole system of Europe changes. Instead of counting together England, Austria, and Russia, as heretofore, against France, Spain, Holland, Prussia, and Turkey, the division will probably be, England, Holland, and Prussia, against France, Austria, Russia, and perhaps Spain. This last power is not sure, because the dispositions of its heir apparent are not sure. But whether the present be truce or peace, it will allow time to mature the conditions of the alliance between France and the two empires, always supposed to be on the carpet. It is thought to be obstructed by the avidity of the Emperor, who would swallow a good part of Turkey, Silesia, Bavaria, and the rights of the Germanic body. To the two or three first articles, France might consent, receiving in gratification a well rounded portion of the Austrian Netherlands, with the islands of Candia, Cyprus, Rhodes, and perhaps Lower Egypt. But all this is in embryo, uncertainly known, and counterworked by the machinations of the courts of London and Berlin. The following solution of the British armaments is supposed in a letter of the 25th ultimo, from Colonel Blachden of Connecticut, now at Dunkirk, to the Marquis de la Fayette. I will cite it in his own words. "A gentleman who left London two days ago, and came to this place to-day, informs me that it is now generally supposed that Mr. Pitt's great secret, which has puzzled the whole nation so long, and to accomplish which design, the whole force of the nation is armed, is to make a vigorous effort for the recovery of America. When I recollect the delay they have made in delivering the forts in America, and that little more than a year ago, one of the British ministry wrote to the King a letter, in which were these remarkable words, 'If your Majesty pleases, America may yet be yours;' add to this, if it were possible for the present ministry in England to effect such a matter, they would secure their places and their power for a long time, and should they fail in the end, they would be certain of holding them during the attempt, which it is in their power to prolong as much as they please, and at all events, they would boast of having endeavored the recovery of what a former ministry had abandoned, it is possible." A similar surmise has come in a letter from a person in Rotterdam to one at this place. I am satisfied that the King of England believes the mass of our people to be tired of their independence, and desirous of returning under his government; and that the same opinion prevails in the ministry and nation. They have hired their news-writers to repeat this lie in their gazettes so long, that they have become the dupes of it themselves. But there is no occasion to recur to this, in order to account for their arming. A more rational purpose avowed, that purpose executed, and when executed, a solemn agreement to disarm, seem to leave no doubt, that the re-establishment of the Stadtholder was their object. Yet it is possible, that having found that this court will not make war in this moment for any ally, new views may arise, and they may think the moment favorable for executing any purposes they may have, in our quarter. Add to this, that reason is of no aid in calculating their movements. We are, therefore, never safe till our magazines are filled with arms. The present season of truce, or peace, should, in my opinion, be improved without a moment's respite, to effect this essential object, and no means be omitted, by which money may be obtained for the purpose. I say this, however, with due deference to the opinion of Congress, who are better judges of the necessity and practicability of the measure.

I mentioned to you, in a former letter, the application I had made to the Dutch ambassadors and Prussian envoy, for the protection of Mr. Dumas. The latter soon after received an assurance, that he was put under the protection of the States of Holland; and the Dutch ambassador called on me a few days ago, to inform me, by instruction from his constituents, 'that the States General had received a written application from Mr. Adams, praying their protection of Dumas: that they had instructed their greffier, Fagel, to assure Mr. Adams, by letter, that he was under the protection of the States of Holland; but to inform him, at the same time, that Mr. Dumas's conduct, out of the line of his office, had been so extraordinary, that they would expect *de l'honnêteté de Mr. Adams*, that he would charge some other person with the affairs of the United States, during his absence.'

Your letter, of September the 8th, has been duly received. I shall pay due attention to the instructions relative to the medals, and give any aid I can, in the case of Boss's vessel. As yet, however, my endeavors to find *Monsieur Pauly, avocat au conseil d'état, rue Coquilliere*, have been ineffectual. There is no such person living in that street. I found a *Monsieur Pauly, avocat au parlement*, in another part of the town; he opened the letter, but said it could not mean him. I shall advertise in the public papers. If that fails, there will be no other chance of finding him. Mr. Warnum will do well, therefore, to send some other description by which the person may be found. Indeed some friend of the party interested should be engaged to follow up this business, as it will require constant attention, and probably a much larger sum of money than that named in the bill inclosed in Mr. Warnum's letter.

I have the honor to enclose you a letter from O'Bryan to me, containing information from Algiers, and one from Mr. Montgomery at Alicant. The purpose of sending you this last, is to show you how much the difficulties of ransom are increased since the Spanish negotiations. The Russian captives have cost about eight thousand livres apiece, on an average. I certainly have no idea that we should give any such sum; and, therefore, if it should be the sense of Congress to give such a price, I would be glad to know it by instruction. My idea is, that we should not ransom but on the footing of the nation which pays least, that it may be as little worth their while to go in pursuit of us, as any nation. This is cruelty to the individuals now in captivity, but kindness to the hundreds that would soon be so, were we to make it worth the while of those pirates to go out of the Streights, in quest of us. As soon as money is provided, I shall put this business into train. I have taken measures to damp, at Algiers, all expectations of our proposing to ransom, at any price. I feel the distress which this must occasion to our countrymen there, and their connections; but the object of it is their ultimate good, by bringing down their holders to such a price as we ought to pay, instead of letting them remain in such expectations as cannot be gratified. The gazettes of France and Leyden accompany this.

I have the honor to be, with sentiments of the most perfect esteem and respect, Sir, your most obedient humble servant,

Th: Jefferson.

[The annexed are translations of the declaration and counter-declaration, referred to in the preceding letter.]

DECLARATION.

The events which have taken place in the republic of the United Provinces appearing no longer to leave any subject of discussion, and still less of dispute, between the two courts, the undersigned are authorized to ask, if it be the intention of his Most Christian Majesty to act in pursuance of the notification given, on the 16th of last month, by the Minister Plenipotentiary of his Most Christian Majesty, which, announcing his purpose of aiding Holland, has occasioned maritime armaments on the part of his Majesty, which armaments have become reciprocal.

If the court of Versailles is disposed to explain itself on this subject, and on the conduct adopted towards the republic, in a manner conformably to the desire, evinced by each party, to preserve a good understanding between the two courts, it being also understood, at the same time, that no hostile view is entertained, in any quarter, in consequence of the past; his Majesty, always eager to manifest his concurrence in the friendly sentiments of his Most Christian Majesty, agrees forthwith that the armaments, and, in general, all preparations for war, shall be mutually discontinued, and that the marines of the two nations shall be placed on the footing of a peace establishment, such as existed on the first of January of the present year.

Signed. Dorset Wm. Eden.

At Versailles, the 27th of October, 1787.

COUNTER-DECLARATION.

It neither being, nor ever having been, the intention of his Majesty to interpose by force in the affairs of the republic of the United Provinces, the communication made to the court of London by M. Barthelemy having had no other object than to announce to that court an intention, the motives of which no longer-exist, especially since the King of Prussia has made known his resolution, his Majesty makes no difficulty in declaring, that he has no wish to act in pursuance of the communication aforesaid, and that he entertains no hostile view in any quarter, relative to what has passed in Holland.

Consequently, his Majesty, desiring to concur in the sentiments of his Britannic Majesty, for the preservation of a good understanding between the two courts, consents with pleasure to the proposition of his Britannic Majesty, that the armaments, and, in general, all preparations for war, shall be mutually discontinued, and that the marines of the two nations shall be replaced upon the footing of the peace establishment, as it existed on the first day of January of the present year.

Signed. Montmorin.

At Versailles, the 27th of October, 1787.

LETTER CXI.—TO JOHN JAY, November 3, 1787

TO JOHN JAY.

(Private.) Paris, November 3, 1787.

Dear Sir,

I shall take the liberty of confiding sometimes to a private letter, such details of the small history of the court or cabinet, as may be worthy of being known, and yet not proper to be publicly communicated. I doubt whether the administration is yet in a permanent form. The Count de Montmorin and Baron de Breteuil are, I believe, firm enough in their places. It was doubted whether they would wait for the Count de la Luzerne, if the war had taken place: but at present I suppose they will. I wish it also, because M. de Hector, his only competitor, has on some occasions shown little value for the connection with us. Lambert, the Comptroller General, is thought to be very insecure. I should be sorry also to lose him. I have worked several days with him, the Marquis de la Fayette, and Monsieur du Pont (father of the young gentleman gone to America with the Count de Moustier), to reduce into one *Arrêt* whatever concerned our commerce. I have found him a man of great judgment and application, possessing good general principles on subjects of commerce, and friendly dispositions towards us. He passed the *Arrêt* in a very favorable form, but it has been opposed in the Council, and will, I fear, suffer some alteration in the article of whale-oil. That of tobacco, which was put into a separate instrument, experiences difficulties also, which do not come from him. M. du Pont has rendered us essential services on these occasions. I wish his son could be so well noticed, as to make a favorable report to his father; he would, I think, be gratified by it, and his good dispositions be strengthened, and rendered further useful to us. Whether I shall be able to send you these regulations by the present packet, will depend on their getting through the Council in time. The Archbishop continues well with his patroness. Her object is, a close connection with her brother. I suppose he convinces her, that peace will furnish the best occasion of cementing that connection.

It may not be uninstructive to give you the origin and nature of his influence with the Queen. When the Duke de Choiseul proposed the marriage of the Dauphin with this lady, he thought it proper to send a person to Vienna, to perfect her in the language. He asked his friend, the Archbishop of Toulouse, to recommend to him a proper person. He recommended a certain Abbe. The Abbe, from his first arrival at Vienna, either tutored by his patron, or prompted by gratitude, impressed on the Queen's mind the exalted talents and merit of the Archbishop, and continually represented him as the only man fit to be placed at the helm of affairs. On his return to Paris, being retained near the person of the Queen, he kept him constantly in her view. The Archbishop was named of the *Assembly des Notables*, had occasion enough there to prove his talents, and Count de Vergennes, his great enemy, dying opportunely, the Queen got him into place. He uses the Abbe even yet, for instilling all his notions into her mind. That he has imposing talents and patriotic dispositions, I think is certain. Good judges think him a theorist only, little acquainted with the details of business, and spoiling all his plans by a bungled execution. He may perhaps undergo a severe trial. His best actions are exciting against him a host of enemies, particularly the reduction of the pensions, and reforms in other branches of economy. Some think the other ministers are willing he should stay in, till he has effected this odious, yet necessary work, and that they will then make him the scape-goat of the transaction. The declarations too, which I send you in my public letter, if they should become public, will probably raise an universal cry. It will all fall on him, because Montmorin and Breteuil say, without reserve, that the sacrifice of the Dutch has been against their advice. He will, perhaps, not permit these declarations to appear in this country. They are absolutely unknown: they were communicated to me by the Duke of Dorset, and I believe no other copy has been given here. They will be published doubtless in England, as a proof of their triumph, and may from thence make their way into this country. If the Premier can stem a few months, he may remain long in office, and will never make war if he can help it. If he should be removed, the peace will probably be short. He is solely chargeable with the loss of Holland. True, they could not have raised money by taxes to supply the necessities of war; but could they do it were their finances ever so well arranged? No nation makes war now-a-days, but by the aid of loans: and it is probable, that in a war for the liberties of Holland, all the treasures of that country would have been at their service. They have now lost the cow which furnishes the milk of war. She will be on the side of their enemies, whenever a rupture shall take place: and no arrangement of their finances can countervail this circumstance.

I have no doubt, you permit access to the letters of your foreign ministers, by persons only of the most perfect trust. It is in the European system to bribe the clerks high, in order to obtain copies of interesting papers. I am sure you are equally attentive to the conveyance of your letters to us, as you know that all are opened that pass through any post-office of Europe. Your letters which come by the packet, if put into the mail at New York, or into the post-office at Havre, wear proofs that they have been opened. The passenger to whom they are confided, should be cautioned always to keep them in his own hands, till he can deliver them personally in Paris.

I have the honor to be, with very sincere esteem and respect, Dear Sir, your most obedient and most humble servant,

Th: Jefferson.

LETTER CXII.—TO THE COUNT DE MONTMORIN, November 6, 1787

TO THE COUNT DE MONTMORIN.

Sir,

Paris, November 6, 1787.

I take the liberty of asking your Excellency's perusal of the enclosed case of an American hostage, confined in the prisons of Dunkirk. His continuance there seems to be useless, and yet endless. Not knowing how far the government can interfere for his relief, as it is a case wherein private property is concerned, I do not presume to ask his liberation absolutely: but I will solicit from your Excellency such measures in his behalf, as the laws and usages of the country may permit.

The Comptroller General having been so good as to explain to me in a conversation, that he wished to know what duties were levied in England on American whale-oil, I have had the honor of informing him by letter, that the ancient duties on that article are seventeen pounds, six shillings, and six pence, sterling, the ton, and that some late additional duties make them amount to about eighteen pounds sterling. That the common whale-oil sells there but for about twenty pounds sterling, the ton, and of course the duty amounts to a prohibition. This duty was originally laid on all foreign fish-oil, with a view to favor the British and American fisheries. When we became independent, and of course foreign to Great Britain, we became subject to the foreign duty. No duty, therefore, which France may think proper to lay on this article, can drive it to the English market. It could only oblige the inhabitants of Nantucket to abandon their fishery. But the poverty of their soil offering them no other resource, they must quit their country, and either establish themselves in Nova Scotia, where, as British fishermen, they may participate of the British premium, in addition to the ordinary price of their whale-oil, or they must accept the conditions which this government offers, for the establishment they have proposed at Dunkirk. Your Excellency will judge, what conditions may counterbalance, in their minds, the circumstances of the vicinity of Nova Scotia, sameness of langague,[sp.] laws, religion, customs, and kindred. Remaining in their native country, to which they are most singularly attached, excluded from commerce with England, taught to look to France as the only country from which they can derive sustenance, they will, in case of war, become useful rovers against its enemies. Their position, their poverty, their courage, their address, and their hatred, will render them formidable scourges on the British commerce. It is to be considered then, on the one hand, that the duty which M. de Calonne had proposed to retain on their oil, may endanger the shifting this useful body of seamen out of our joint scale into that of the British; and also may suppress a considerable subject of exchange for the productions of France: on the other hand, that it may produce an addition to his Majesty's revenue. What I have thus far said, is on the supposition, that the duty may operate a diminution of the price received by the fishermen. If it act in the contrary direction, and produce an augmentation of price to the consumer, it immediately brings into competition a variety of other oils, vegetable and animal, a good part of which France receives from abroad, and the fisherman, thus losing his market, is compelled equally to change either his calling or country. When M. de Calonne first agreed to reduce the duties to what he has declared, I had great hopes the commodity could bear them, and that it would become a medium of commerce between France and the United States. I must confess, however, that my expectations have not been fulfilled, and that but little has come here as yet. This induces me to fear, that it is so poor an article, that any duty whatever will suppress it. Should this take place, and the spirit of emigration once seize those people, perhaps an abolition of all duty might then come too late to stop, what it would now easily prevent. I fear there is danger in the experiment; and it remains for the wisdom of his Majesty and his ministers to decide, whether the prospect of gain to the revenue, or establishing a national fishery, may compensate this danger. If the government should decide to retain the duty, I shall acquiesce in it cheerfully, and do every thing in my power to encourage my countrymen still to continue their occupation.

The actual session of our several legislatures would render it interesting to forward immediately the regulations proposed on our commerce; and the expiration of the order of Bernis, at the close of this month, endangers a suspension and derangement in the commerce of tobacco, very embarrassing to the merchants of the two countries. Pardon me therefore, Sir, if I appear solicitous to obtain the ultimate decision of his Majesty's Council on these subjects, and to ask as early a communication of that decision, as shall be convenient.

I have the honor to be, with sentiments of the most profound esteem and respect, your Excellency's most obedient and most humble servant,

Th: Jefferson.

LETTER CXIII.—TO JOHN ADAMS, November 13, 1787

TO JOHN ADAMS.

Paris, November 13, 1787.

Dear Sir,

This will be delivered you by young Mr. Rutledge. Your knowledge of his father will introduce him to your notice. He merits it, moreover, on his own account.

I am now to acknowledge your favors of October the 8th and 26th. That of August the 25th was duly received, nor can I recollect by what accident I was prevented from acknowledging it in mine of September the 28th. It has been the source of my subsistence hitherto, and must continue to be so, till I receive letters on the affairs of money from America. Van Staphorsts and Willinks have answered my drafts. Your books for Marquis de la Fayette are received here. I will notify it to him, who is at present with his Provincial Assembly in Auvergne.

Little is said lately of the progress of the negotiations between the courts of Petersburg, Vienna, and Versailles. The distance of the former, and the cautious, unassuming character of its minister here, is one cause of delays: a greater one is, the greediness and instable character of the Emperor. Nor do I think that the Principal here, will be easily induced to lend himself to any connection, which shall threaten a war within a considerable number of years. His own reign will be that of peace only, in all probability; and were any accident to tumble him down, this country would immediately gird on its sword and buckler, and trust to occurrences for supplies of money. The wound their honor has sustained, festers in their hearts; and it may be said with truth, that the Archbishop and a few priests, determined to support his measures, because proud to see their order come again into power, are the only advocates for the line of conduct which has been pursued. It is said, and believed through Paris literally, that the Count de Montmorin '*pleuroit comme un enfant*,' when obliged to sign the counter-declaration. Considering the phrase as figurative, I believe it expresses the distress of his heart. Indeed, he has made no secret of his individual opinion. In the mean time, the Principal goes on with a firm and patriotic spirit in reforming the cruel abuses of the government, and preparing a new constitution, which will give to this people as much liberty as they are capable of managing. This, I think, will be the glory of his administration, because, though a good theorist in finance, he is thought to execute badly. They are about to open a loan of one hundred millions to supply present wants, and it is said, the preface of the *Arrêt* will contain a promise of the convocation of the States General during the ensuing year. Twelve or fifteen Provincial Assemblies are already in action, and are going on well: and I think, that, though the nation suffers in reputation, it will gain infinitely in happiness under the present administration. I enclose to Mr. Jay a pamphlet, which I will beg of you to forward. I leave it open for your perusal. When you shall have read it, be so good as to stick a wafer in it. It is not yet published, nor will be for some days. This copy has been ceded to me as a favor.

How do you like our new constitution? I confess there are things in it, which stagger all my dispositions to subscribe to what such an Assembly has proposed. The House of federal representatives will not be adequate to the management of affairs, either foreign or federal. Their President seems a bad edition of a Polish King. He may be elected from four years to four years, for life. Reason and experience prove to us, that a chief magistrate, so continuable, is an office for life. When one or two generations shall have proved, that this is an office for life, it becomes, on every succession, worthy of intrigue, of bribery, of force, and even of foreign interference. It will be of great consequence to France and England, to have America governed by a Galloman or Angloman. Once in office, and possessing the military force of the Union, without the aid or check of a council, he would not be easily dethroned, even if the people could be induced to withdraw their votes from him. I wish that at the end of the four years, they had made him for ever ineligible a second time. Indeed, I think all the good of this new constitution might have been couched in three or four new articles to be added to the good, old, and venerable fabric, which should have been preserved even as a religious relique. Present me and my daughters affectionately to Mrs. Adams. The younger one continues to speak of her warmly. Accept yourself assurances of the sincere esteem and respect, with which I have the honor to be, Dear Sir, your friend and servant,

Th: Jefferson.

LETTER CXIV.—TO COLONEL SMITH, November 13, 1787

TO COLONEL SMITH.

Paris, November 13, 1787.

Sir,

I am now to acknowledge the receipt of your favors of October the 4th, 8th, and 26th. In the last, you apologize for your letters of introduction to Americans coming here. It is so far from needing apology on your part, that it calls for thanks on mine. I endeavor to show civilities to all the Americans who come here, and who will give me opportunities of doing it: and it is a matter of comfort to know, from a good quarter, what they are, and how far I may go in my attentions to them.

Can you send me Woodmason's bills for the two copying presses, for the Marquis de la Fayette and the Marquis de Chastellux? The latter makes one article in a considerable account, of old standing, and which I cannot present for want of this article. I do not know whether it is to yourself or Mr. Adams I am to give my thanks for the copy of the new constitution. I beg leave, through you, to place them where due. It will yet be three weeks before I shall receive them from America. There are very good articles in it; and very bad. I do not know which preponderate. What we have lately read in the history of Holland, in the chapter on the Stadtholder, would have sufficed to set me against a chief magistrate eligible for a long duration, if I had ever been disposed towards one: and what we have always read of the elections of Polish Kings, should have for ever excluded the idea of one continuable for life. Wonderful is the effect of impudent and persevering lying. The British ministry have so long hired their gazetteers to repeat, and model into every form, lies about our being in anarchy, that the world has at length believed them, the English nation has believed them, the ministers themselves have come to believe them, and what is more wonderful, we have believed them ourselves. Yet where does this anarchy exist? Where did it ever exist, except in the single instance of Massachusetts? And can history produce an instance of rebellion so honorably conducted? I say nothing of its motives. They were founded in ignorance, not wickedness. God forbid, we should ever be twenty years without such a rebellion. The people cannot be all, and always, well informed. The part which is wrong will be discontented, in proportion to the importance of the facts they misconceive. If they remain quiet under such misconceptions, it is a lethargy, the forerunner of death to the public liberty. We have had thirteen States independent for eleven years. There has been one rebellion. That comes to one rebellion in a century and a half for each State. What country before ever existed a century and a half without a rebellion? And what country can preserve its liberties, if its rulers are not warned from time to time, that this people preserve the spirit of resistance? Let them take arms. The remedy is to set them right as to facts, pardon, and pacify them. What signify a few lives lost in a century or two? The tree of liberty must be refreshed from time to time with the blood of patriots and tyrants. It is its natural manure. Our convention has been too much impressed by the insurrection of Massachusetts: and on the spur of the moment, they are setting up a kite to keep the hen-yard in order. I hope in God, this article will be rectified before the new constitution is accepted. You ask me, if any thing transpires here on the subject of South America? Not a word. I know that there are combustible materials there, and that they wait the torch only. But this country probably will join the extinguishers. The want of facts worth communicating to you, has occasioned me to give a little loose to dissertation. We must be contented to amuse, when we cannot inform.

Present my respects to Mrs. Smith, and be assured of the sincere esteem of, Dear Sir, your friend and servant,

Th: Jefferson.

LETTER CXV.—TO WILLIAM CARMICHAEL, December 11, 1787

TO WILLIAM CARMICHAEL.

Paris, December 11, 1787.

Dear Sir,

I am later in acknowledging the receipt of your favors of October the 15th, and November the 5th and 15th, because we have been long expecting a packet, which I hoped would bring communications worth detailing to you; and she arrived only a few days ago, after a very long passage indeed. I am very sorry you have not been able to make out the cipher of my letter of September the 25th, because it contained things which I wished you to know at that time. They have lost now a part of their merit; * but still I wish you could decipher them, as there remains a part, which it might yet be agreeable to you to understand. I have examined the cipher, from which it was written. It as precisely a copy of those given to Messrs. Barclay and Lambe. In order that you may examine whether yours corresponds, I will now translate into cipher, the three first lines of my letter of June the 14th.

This will serve to show, whether your cipher corresponds with mine, as well as my manner of using it. But I shall not use it in future, till I know from you the result of your re-examination of it. I have the honor now, to return you the letter you had been so good as to enclose to me. About the same time of Liston's conversation with you, similar ones were held with me by Mr. Eden. He particularly questioned me on the effect of our treaty with France, in the case of a war, and what might be our dispositions. I told him without hesitation, that our treaty obliged us to receive the armed vessels of France, with their prizes, into our ports, and to refuse the admission of prizes made on her by her enemies; that there was a clause by which we guarantied to France her American possessions, and which might, perhaps, force us into the war, if these were attacked. 'Then it will be war,' said he, 'for they will assuredly be attacked.' I added, that our dispositions would be to be neutral, and that I thought it the interest of both those powers that we should be so, because it would relieve both from all anxiety as to the feeding their West India islands, and England would, moreover, avoid a heavy land war on our continent, which would cripple all her proceedings elsewhere. He expected these sentiments from me personally, and he knew them to be analogous to those of our country. We had often before had occasions of knowing each other: his peculiar bitterness towards us had sufficiently appeared, and I had never concealed from him, that I considered the British as our natural enemies, and as the only nation on earth, who wished us ill from the bottom of their souls. And I am satisfied, that were our continent to be swallowed up by the ocean, Great Britain would be in a bonfire from one end to the other. Mr. Adams, as you know, has asked his recall. This has been granted, and Colonel Smith is to return too; Congress having determined to put an end to their commission at that court. I suspect and hope they will make no new appointment.

Our new constitution is powerfully attacked in the American newspapers. The objections are, that its effect would be to form the thirteen States into one; that, proposing to melt all down into one general government, they have fenced the people by no declaration of rights; they have not renounced the power of keeping a standing army; they have not secured the liberty of the press; they have reserved the power of abolishing trials by jury in civil cases; they have proposed that the laws of the federal legislatures shall be paramount the laws and constitutions of the States; they have abandoned rotation in office; and particularly their President may be re-elected from four years to four years, for life, so as to render him a King for life, like a King of Poland; and they have not given him either the check or aid of a council. To these, they add calculations of expense, &c. &.c. to frighten the people. You will perceive that those objections are serious and some of them not without foundation. The constitution, however, has been received with a very general enthusiasm, and as far as can be judged from external demonstrations, the bulk of the people are eager to adopt it. In the eastern States, the printers will print nothing against it, unless the writer subscribes his name. Massachusetts and Connecticut have called conventions in January, to consider of it. In New York, there is a division. The Governor (Clinton) is known to be hostile to it. Jersey, it is thought, will certainly accept it. Pennsylvania is divided; and all the bitterness of her factions has been kindled anew on it. But the party in favor of it is strongest, both in and out of the legislature. This is the party anciently of Morris, Wilson, &c., Delaware will do what Pennsylvania shall do. Maryland is thought favorable to it; yet it is supposed Chase and Paca will oppose it. As to Virginia, two of her Delegates, in the first place, refused to sign it. These were Randolph, the Governor, and George Mason. Besides these, Henry, Harrison, Nelson, and the Lees are against it. General Washington will be for it, but it is not in his character to exert himself much in the case. Madison will be its main pillar; but though an immensely powerful one, it is questionable whether he can bear the weight of such a host. So that the presumption is, that Virginia will reject it. We know nothing of the dispositions of the States south of this. Should it fall through, as is possible, notwithstanding the enthusiasm with which it was received in the first moment, it is probable that Congress will propose, that, the objections which the people shall make to it being once known, another convention shall be assembled, to adopt the improvements generally acceptable, and omit those found disagreeable. In this way, union may be produced under a happy constitution, and one which shall not be too energetic, as are the constitutions of Europe. I give you these details, because, possibly, you may not have received them all. The sale of our western lands is immensely successful. Five millions of acres have been sold at private sale, for a dollar an acre, in certificates; and at the public sales, some of them had sold as high as two dollars and forty cents the acre. The sales had not been begun two months. By these means, taxes, &c. our domestic debt, originally twenty-eight millions of dollars, was reduced, by the 1st day of last October, to twelve millions, and they were then in treaty-for two millions of acres more, at a dollar, private sale. Our domestic debt will thus be soon paid off, and that done, the sales will go on for money, at a cheaper rate, no doubt, for the payment of our foreign debt. The *petite guerre*, always waged by the Indians, seems not to abate the ardor of purchase or emigration. Kentucky is now counted at sixty thousand. Frankland is also growing fast.

I have been told, that the cutting through the Isthmus of Panama, which the world has so often wished, and supposed practicable, has at times been thought of by the government of Spain, and that they once proceeded so far, as to have a survey and examination made of the ground; but that the result was, either impracticability or too great difficulty. Probably the Count de Campomanes, or Don Ulloa, can give you information on this head. I should be exceedingly pleased to get as minute details as possible on it, and even copies of the survey, report, &c. if they could be obtained at a moderate expense. I take the liberty of asking your assistance in this.

I have the honor to be, with great respect and esteem, Sir, your most obedient and most humble servant,

Th: Jefferson.

LETTER CXVI.—TO JOHN ADAMS

TO JOHN ADAMS.
Paris, December 12, 1787.
Dear Sir,
In the month of July, I received from Fiseaux & Co. of Amsterdam, a letter notifying me that the principal of their loan to the United States would become due the first day of January. I answered them that I had neither powers nor information on the subject, but would transmit their letter to the board of treasury. I did so, by the packet which sailed from Havre, August the 10th. The earliest answer possible would have been by the packet which arrived at Havre three or four days ago. But by her I do not receive the scrip of a pen from any body. This makes me suppose, that my letters are committed to Paul Jones, who was to sail a week after the departure of the packet; and that possibly, he may be the bearer of orders from the treasury, to repay Fiseaux' loan, with the money you borrowed. But it is also possible, he may bring no order on the subject. The slowness with which measures are adopted on our side the water, does not permit us to count on punctual answers; but, on the contrary, renders it necessary for us to suppose, in the present case, that no orders will arrive in time, and to consider whether any thing, and what, should be done. As it may be found expedient to transfer all our foreign debts to Holland, by borrowing there, and as it may always be prudent to preserve a good credit in that country, because we may be forced into wars, whether we will or not, I should suppose it very imprudent to suffer our credit to be annihilated, for so small a sum as fifty-one thousand guelders. The injury will be greater too, in proportion to the smallness of the sum; for they will ask, 'How can a people be trusted for large sums, who break their faith for such small ones?' You know best what effect it will have on the minds of the money-lenders of that country, should we fail in this payment. You know best also, whether it is practicable and prudent for us, to have this debt paid without orders. I refer the matter, therefore, wholly to your consideration, willing to participate with you in any risk and any responsibility, which may arise. I think it one of those cases, where it is a duty to risk one's self. You will perceive, by the enclosed, the necessity of an immediate answer, and that, if you think any thing can and should be done, all the necessary authorities from you should accompany your letter. In the mean time, should I receive any orders from the treasury by Paul Jones, I will pursue them, and consider whatever you shall have proposed or done, as *non avenue.*
I am, with much affection, Dear Sir, your most obedient and most humble servant,
Th: Jefferson.

LETTER CXVII.—TO JAMES MADISON, December 20, 1787

TO JAMES MADISON.

Paris, December 20, 1787.

Dear Sir,

My last to you was of October the 8th, by the Count de Moustier. Yours of July the 18th, September the 6th, and October the 24th, were successively received, yesterday, the day before, and three or four days before that. I have only had time to read the letters; the printed papers communicated with them, however interesting, being obliged to lie over till I finish my despatches for the packet, which despatches must go from hence the day after to-morrow. I have much to thank you for; first and most for the ciphered paragraph respecting myself. These little informations are very material towards forming my own decisions. I would be glad even to know, when any individual member thinks I have gone wrong in any instance. If I know myself, it would not excite ill blood in me, while it would assist to guide my conduct, perhaps to justify it, and to keep me to my duty, alert. I must thank you too, for the information in Thomas Burke's case; though you will have found by a subsequent letter, that I have asked of you a further investigation of that matter. It is to gratify the lady who is at the head of the convent wherein my daughters are, and who, by her attachment and attention to them, lays me under great obligations, I shall hope, therefore, still to receive from you the result of all the further inquiries my second letter had asked. The parcel of rice which you informed me had miscarried, accompanied my letter to the Delegates of South Carolina. Mr. Bourgoin was to be the bearer of both, and both were delivered together into the hands of his relation here, who introduced him to me, and who, at a subsequent moment, undertook to convey them to Mr. Bourgoin. This person was an engraver, particularly recommended to Dr. Franklin and Mr. Hopkinson. Perhaps he may have mislaid the little parcel of rice among his baggage. I am much pleased, that the sale of western lands is so successful. I hope they will absorb all the certificates of our domestic debt speedily, in the first place, and that then, offered for cash, they will do the same by our foreign ones.

The season admitting only of operations in the cabinet, and these being in a great measure secret, I have little to fill a letter, I will therefore make up the deficiency, by adding a few words on the constitution proposed by our convention.

I like much the general idea of framing a government, which should go on of itself, peaceably, without needing continual recurrence to the State legislatures. I like the organization of the government into legislative, judiciary, and executive. I like the power given the legislature to levy taxes, and for that reason solely, I approve of the greater House being chosen by the people directly. For though I think a House, so chosen, will be very far inferior to the present Congress, will be very illy qualified to legislate for the Union, for foreign nations, &c.; yet this evil does not weigh against the good of preserving inviolate the fundamental principle, that the people are not to be taxed but by representitives[sp.] chosen immediately by themselves. I am captivated by the compromise of the opposite claims of the great and little States, of the latter to equal, and the former to proportional influence. I am much pleased, too, with the substitution of the method of voting by persons, instead of that of voting by States: and I like the negative given to the Executive, conjointly with a third of either House; though I should have liked it better, had the judiciary been associated for that purpose, or invested separately with a similar power. There are other good things of less moment.

I will now tell you what I do not like. First, the omission of a bill of rights, providing clearly, and without the aid of sophism, for freedom of religion, freedom of the press, protection against standing armies, restriction of monopolies, the eternal and unremitting force of the *habeas corpus* laws, and trials by jury in all matters of fact triable by the laws of the land, and not by the laws of nations. To say, as Mr. Wilson does, that a bill of rights was not necessary, because all is reserved in the case of the general government which is not given, while in the particular ones, all is given which is not reserved, might do for the audience to which it was addressed: but it is surely a *gratis dictum*, the reverse of which might just as well be said; and it is opposed by strong inferences from the body of the instrument, as well as from the omission of the clause of our present Confederation, which had made the reservation in express terms. It was hard to conclude, because there has been a want of uniformity among the States as to the cases triable by jury, because some have been so incautious as to dispense with this mode of trial in certain cases, therefore the more prudent States shall be reduced to the same level of calamity. It would have been much more just and wise to have concluded the other way, that as most of the States had preserved with jealousy this sacred palladium of liberty, those who had wandered, should be brought back to it: and to have established general right rather than general wrong. For I consider all the ill as established, which maybe established. I have a right to nothing, which another has a right to take away; and Congress will have a right to take away trials by jury in all civil cases. Let me add, that a bill of rights is what the people are entitled to against every government on earth, general or particular; and what no just government should refuse, or rest on inference.

The second feature I dislike, and strongly dislike, is the abandonment, in every instance, of the principle of rotation in office, and most particularly in the case of the President. Reason and experience tell us, that the first magistrate will always be re-elected if he may be re-elected. He is then an officer for life.

This once observed, it becomes of so much consequence to certain nations, to have a friend or a foe at the head of our affairs, that they will interfere with money and with arms. A Galloman, or an Angloman, will be supported by the nation he befriends. If once elected, and at a second or third election outvoted by one or two votes, he will pretend false votes, foul play, hold possession of the reins of government, be supported by the States voting for him, especially if they be the central ones, lying in a compact body themselves, and separating their opponents; and they will be aided by one nation in Europe, while the majority are aided by another. The election of a President of America, some years hence, will be much more interesting to certain nations of Europe, than ever the election of a King of Poland was. Reflect on all the instances in history, ancient and modern, of elective monarchies, and say, if they do not give foundation for my fears; the Roman Emperors, the Popes while they were of any importance, the German Emperors till they became hereditary in practice, the Kings of Poland, the Deys of the Ottoman dependencies. It may be said, that if elections are to be attended with these disorders, the less frequently they are repeated the better. But experience says, that to free them from disorder, they must be rendered less interesting by a necessity of change. No foreign power, nor domestic party, will waste their blood and money to elect a person, who must go out at the end of a short period. The power of removing every fourth year by the vote of the people, is a power which they will not exercise, and if they were disposed to exercise it, they would not be permitted. The King of Poland is removable every day by the diet. But they never remove him. Nor would Russia, the Emperor, &c. permit them to do it. Smaller objections are, the appeals on matters of fact as well as law; and the binding all persons, legislative, executive, and judiciary, by oath, to maintain that constitution. I do not pretend to decide, what would be the best method of procuring the establishment of the manifold good things in this constitution, and of getting rid of the bad. Whether by adopting it, in hopes of future amendment; or, after it shall have been duly weighed and canvassed by the people, after seeing the parts they generally dislike, and those they generally approve, to say to them, 'We see now what you wish. You are willing to give to your federal government such and such powers: but you wish, at the same time, to have such and such fundamental rights secured to you, and certain sources of convulsion taken away. Be it so. Send together your deputies again. Let them establish your fundamental rights by a sacrosanct declaration, and let them pass the parts of the constitution you have approved. These will give powers to your federal government sufficient for your happiness.' This is what might be said, and would probably produce a speedy, more perfect, and more permanent form of government. At all events, I hope you will not be discouraged from making other trials, if the present one should fail. We are never permitted to despair of the commonwealth. I have thus told you freely what I like, and what I dislike, merely as a matter of curiosity; for I know it is not in my power to offer matter of information to your judgment, which has been formed after hearing and weighing every thing which the wisdom of man could offer on these subjects. I own, I am not a friend to a very energetic government. It is always oppressive. It places the governors indeed more at their ease, at the expense of the people. The late rebellion in Massachusetts has given more alarm, than I think it should have done. Calculate that one rebellion in thirteen States in the course of eleven years, is but one for each State in a century and a half. No country should be so long without one. Nor will any degree of power in the hands of government prevent insurrections. In England, where the hand of power is heavier than with us, there are seldom half a dozen years without an insurrection. In France, Where it is still heavier, but less despotic, as Montesquieu supposes, than in some other countries, and where there are always two or three hundred thousand men ready to crush insurrections, there have been three in the course of the three years I have been here, in every one of which greater numbers were engaged than in Massachusetts, and a great deal more blood was spilt. In Turkey, where the sole nod of the despot is death, insurrections are the events of every day. Compare again the ferocious depredations of their insurgents, with the order, the moderation, and the almost self-extinguishment of ours. And say, finally, whether peace is best preserved by giving energy to the government, or information to the people. This last is the most certain and the most legitimate engine of government. Educate and inform the whole mass of the people. Enable them to see that it is their interest to preserve peace and order, and they will preserve them. And it requires no very high degree of education to convince them of this. They are the only sure reliance for the preservation of our liberty. After all, it is my principle that the will of the majority should prevail. If they approve the proposed constitution in all its parts, I shall concur in it cheerfully, in hopes they will amend it, whenever they shall find it works wrong. This reliance cannot deceive us, as long as we remain virtuous; and I think we shall be so, as long as agriculture is our principal object, which will be the case, while there remain vacant lands in any part of America. When we get piled upon one another in large cities, as in Europe, we shall become corrupt as in Europe, and go to eating one another as they do there. I have tired you by this time with disquisitions which you have already heard repeated by others, a thousand and a thousand times; and, therefore, shall only add assurances of the esteem and attachment, with which I have the honor to be, Dear Sir, your affectionate friend and servant,

Th: Jefferson.

P. S. The instability of our laws is really an immense evil. I think it would be well to provide in our constitutions, that there shall always be a twelvemonth between the engrossing a bill and passing it: that it should then be offered to its passage without changing a word: and that if circumstances should be thought to require a speedier passage, it should take two thirds of both Houses, instead of a bare majority.

LETTER CXVIII.—TO E. CARRINGTON, December 21, 1787

TO E. CARRINGTON

Paris, December 21, 1787.

Dear Sir,

I have just received your two favors of October the 23rd and November the 10th. I am much obliged to you for your hints in the Danish business. They are the only information I have on that subject, except the resolution of Congress, and warn me of a rock on which I should most certainly have split. The vote plainly points out an agent, only leaving it to my discretion to substitute another. My judgment concurs with that of Congress as to his fitness. But I shall inquire for the surest banker at Copenhagen to receive the money, not because I should have had any doubts, but because I am informed others have them. Against the failure of a banker, were such an accident, or any similar one to happen, I cannot be held accountable in a case, where I act without particular interest. My principal idea in proposing the transfer of the French debt, was, to obtain on the new loans a much longer day for the reimbursement of the principal, hoping that the resources of the United States could have been equal to the article of interest alone. But I shall endeavor to quiet, as well as I can, those interested. A part of them will probably sell out at any rate: and one great claimant may be expected to make a bitter attack on our honor. I am very much pleased to hear, that our western lands sell so successfully. I turn to this precious resource, as that which will, in every event, liberate us from our domestic debt, and perhaps too from our foreign one: and this, much sooner than I had expected. I do not think any thing could have been done with them in Europe. Individual speculators and sharpers had duped so many with their unlocated land-warrants, that every offer would have been suspected.

As to the new constitution, I find myself nearly a neutral. There is a great mass of good in it, in a very desirable form; but there is also, to me, a bitter pill or two. I have written somewhat lengthily to Mr. Madison on this subject, and will take the liberty to refer you to that part of my letter to him. I will add one question to what I have said there. Would it not have been better to assign to Congress exclusively, the article of imposts for federal purposes, and to have left direct taxation exclusively to the States? I should suppose the former fund sufficient for all probable events, aided by the land office.

The form which the affairs of Europe may assume, is not yet decipherable by those out of the cabinet. The Emperor gives himself, at present, the airs of a mediator. This is necessary to justify a breach with the Porte. He has his eye at the same time on Germany, and particularly on Bavaria, the Elector of which has, for a long time, been hanging over the grave. Probably, France would now consent to the exchange of the Austrian Netherlands, to be created into a kingdom for the Duke de Deux-ponts, against the electorate of Bavaria. This will require a war. The Empress longs for Turkey, and viewing France as her principal obstacle, would gladly negotiate her acquiescence. To spur on this, she is coquetting it with England. The King of Prussia, too, is playing a double game between France and England. But I suppose the former incapable of forgiving him, or of ever reposing confidence in him. Perhaps the spring may unfold to us the final arrangement, which will take place among the powers of this continent.

I often doubt whether I should trouble Congress or my friends with these details of European politics. I know they do not excite that interest in America, of which it is impossible for one to divest himself here. I know too, that it is a maxim with us, and I think it is a wise one, not to entangle ourselves with the affairs of Europe. Still, I think, we should know them. The Turks have practised the same maxim of not meddling in the complicated wrangles of this continent. But they have unwisely chosen to be ignorant of them also, and it is this total ignorance of Europe, its combinations, and its movements, which exposes them to that annihilation possibly about taking place. While there are powers in Europe which fear our views, or have views on us, we should keep an eye on them, their connections, and oppositions, that in a moment of need, we may avail ourselves of their weakness with respect to others as well as ourselves, and calculate their designs and movements, on all the circumstances under which they exist. Though I am persuaded, therefore, that these details are read by many with great indifference, yet I think it my duty to enter into them, and to run the risk of giving too much, rather than too little information.

I have the honor to be, with perfect esteem and respect, Dear Sir, your most obedient and most humble servant,

Th: Jefferson.

P. S. The resolution of Congress, relative to the prize money received here, speaks of that money as paid to me. I hope this matter is properly understood. The treasury board desired me to receive it, and apply it to such and such federal purposes; and they would pay the dividends of the claimants in America. This would save the expense of remittance. I declined, however, receiving the money, and ordered it into the hands of their banker, who paid it away for the purposes to which they had destined it. I should be sorry an idea should get abroad, that I had received the money of those poor fellows, and applied it to other purposes. I shall, in like manner, order the Danish and Barbary money into the hands of bankers, carefully avoiding ever to touch a sou of it, or having any other account to make out than what the banker will furnish. T. J.

LETTER CXIX.—TO MONSIEUR LIMOZIN, December 22, 1787

TO MONSIEUR LIMOZIN.

Paris, December 22, 1787.

Sir,

I have the honor now to acknowledge the receipt of your favors of the 18th and 19th of November, and two of the 18th of the present month. I did not write to you immediately on the receipt of the two first, because the observation they contained were to be acted on here. I was much obliged to you for them, as I have been frequently before for others, and you will find that I have profited by them in the *Arrêt* which is to come out for the regulation of our commerce, wherein most of the things are provided for, which you have from time to time recommended. With respect to the article of yellow wax, I think there is a general clause in the *Arrêt*, which will take it in; but I am not sure of it. If there be not, it is now too late to get any alteration made. You shall receive the *Arrêt* the moment it is communicated to me.

I have examined the case of Captain Thomas, with all the dispositions possible, to interpose for him. But on mature reflection, I find it is one of those cases wherein my solicitation would be ill received. The government of France, to secure to its subjects the carrying trade between her colonies and the mother country, have made a law, forbidding any foreign vessels to undertake to carry between them. Notwithstanding this, an American vessel has undertaken, and has brought a cargo. For me to ask that this vessel shall be received, would be to ask a repeal of the law, because there is no more reason for receiving her, than there will be for receiving the second, third, &c, which shall act against the same law, nor for receiving an American vessel, more than the vessels of other nations. Captain Thomas has probably engaged in this business, not knowing the law; but ignorance of the law is no excuse, in any country. If it were, the laws would lose their effect, because it can be always pretended. Were I to make this application to the Comptroller General, he might possibly ask me, whether, in a like case, of a French vessel in America acting through ignorance, against law, we would suspend the law as to her? I should be obliged honestly to answer, that with us there is no power which can suspend the law for a moment; and Captain Thomas knows that this answer would be the truth. The Senegal company seems to be as much engaged in it as he is. I should suppose his most probable means of extrication, would be with their assistance, and availing himself of their privileges, and the apparent authority he has received from the officers of government there. I am sorry his case is such a one, as I cannot present to the minister. A jealousy of our taking away their carrying trade, is the principal reason which obstructs our admission into their West India islands. It would not be right for me to strengthen that jealousy.

I have the honor to be, with much esteem, Sir, your most obedient, humble servant,

Th: Jefferson.

LETTER CXX.—TO JOHN JAY, December 31, 1787

TO JOHN JAY.

Paris, December 31, 1787.

Sir,

Since the receipt of the letter of Monsieur de Calonne, of October the 22nd, 1786, I have several times had the honor of mentioning to you, that I was endeavoring to get the substance of that letter reduced into an *Arrêt*, which, instead of being revocable by a single letter of a Comptroller General, would require an *Arrêt* to repeal or alter it, and of course must be discussed in full Council, and so give time to prevent it. This has been pressed as much as it could be with prudence. One cause of delay has been the frequent changes of the Comptroller General; as we had always our whole work to begin again, with every new one. Monsieur Lambert's continuance in office for some months has enabled us, at length, to get through the business; and I have just received from him a letter, and the *Arrêt* duly authenticated; of which I have the honor to send you a number of printed copies. You will find, that the several alterations and additions are made, which, on my visit, to the seaports, I had found to be necessary, and which my letters of June the 21st and August the 6th particularly mentioned to you. Besides these, we have obtained some new articles of value, for which openings arose in the course of the negotiation. I say we have done it, because the Marquis de la Fayette has gone hand in hand with me through this business, and has been a most invaluable aid. I take the liberty of making some observations on the articles of the *Arrêt*, severally, for their explanation, as well as for the information of Congress.

Article 1. In the course of our conferences with the Comptroller General, we had prevailed on him to pass this article with a suppression of all duty. When he reported the *Arrêt*, however, to the Council, this suppression was objected to, and it was insisted to re-establish the duties of seven livres and ten sous, and of ten sous the livre, reserved in the letter of M. de Calonne. The passage of the *Arrêt* was stopped, and the difficulty communicated to me. I urged every thing I could, in letters and in conferences, to convince them that whale-oil was an article which could bear no duty at all. That if the duty fell on the consumer, he would choose to buy vegetable oils; if on the fisherman, he could no longer live by his calling, remaining in his own country; and that if he quitted his own country, the circumstances of vicinity, sameness of language, laws, religion, and manners, and perhaps the ties of kindred, would draw him to Nova Scotia, in spite of every encouragement which could be given at Dunkirk; and that thus those fishermen would be shifted out of a scale friendly to France, into one always hostile. Nothing, however, could prevail. It hung on this article alone, for two months, during which we risked the total loss of the *Arrêt* on the stability in office of Monsieur Lambert; for if he had gone out, his successor might be less favorable; and if Monsieur Necker were the successor, we might lose the whole, as he never set any store by us, or the connection with us. About ten days ago, it became universally believed that Monsieur Lambert was to go out immediately. I therefore declined further insisting on the total suppression, and desired the *Arrêt* might pass, leaving the duties on whale-oil, as Monsieur de Calonne had promised them; but with a reservation, which may countenance our bringing on this matter again, at a more favorable moment.

Article 2. The other fish-oils are placed in a separate article; because, whatever encouragements we may hereafter obtain for whale-oils, they will not be extended to those which their own fisheries produce.

Article 3. A company had silently, and by unfair means, obtained a monopoly for the making and selling spermaceti candles: as soon as we discovered it, we solicited its suppression, which is effected by this clause.

Article 4. The duty of an eighth per cent, is merely to oblige the masters of vessels to enter their cargoes, for the information of government; without inducing them to attempt to smuggle.

Article 6. Tar, pitch, and turpentine of America, coming in competition with the same articles produced in the southwestern parts of France, we could obtain no greater reduction, than two and a half per cent. The duties before were from four to six times that amount.

Article 10. The right of *entrepôt*, given by this article, is almost the same thing, as the making all their ports, free ports for us. The ships are indeed subject to be visited, and the cargoes must be reported in ports of *entrepôt*, which need not be done in the free ports. But the communication between the *entrepôt* and the country is not interrupted by continual search of all persons passing into the country, which has proved so troublesome to the inhabitants of our free ports, as that a considerable proportion of them have wished to give back the privilege of their freedom.

Article 13. This article gives us the privileges and advantages of native subjects, in all their possessions in Asia, and in the scales leading thereto. This expression means, at present, the isles of France and Bourbon, and will include the Cape of Good Hope, should any future event put it into the hands of France. It was with a view to this, that I proposed the expression, because we were then in hourly expectation of a war, and it was suspected that France would take possession of that place. It will, in no case, be considered as including any thing westward of the Cape of Good Hope. I must observe further, on this article, that it will only become valuable, on the suppression of their East India Company; because, as long as their monopoly continues, even native subjects cannot enter their Asiatic ports, for the purposes of commerce. It is considered, however, as certain, that this Company will be immediately suppressed.

The article of tobacco could not be introduced into the *Arrêt*; because it was necessary to consider the Farmers General as parties to that arrangement. It rests, therefore, of necessity, on the basis of a letter only. You will perceive that this is nothing more than a continuation of the order of Bernis, only leaving the prices unfixed; and like that, it will require a constant and vexatious attention, to have its execution enforced.

The States who have much to carry, and few carriers, will observe, perhaps, that the benefits of these regulations are somewhat narrowed, by confining them to articles brought hither in French or American bottoms. But they will consider, that nothing in these instruments moves from us. The advantages they hold out are all given by this country to us, and the givers will modify their gifts as they please. I suppose it to be a determined principle of this court not to suffer our carrying business, so far as their consumption of our commodities extends, to become a nursery for British seamen. Nor would this, perhaps, be advantageous to us, considering the dispositions of the two nations towards us. The preference which our shipping will obtain on this account, may counterpoise the discouragements it experiences from the aggravated dangers of the Barbary States. Nor is the idea unpleasing, which shows itself in various parts of these papers, of naturalizing American bottoms, and American citizens in France and in its foreign possessions. Once established here, and in their eastern settlements, they may revolt less at the proposition to extend it to those westward. They are not yet, however, at that point; we must be contented to go towards it a step at a time, and trust to future events for hastening our progress.

With respect to the alliance between this and the two imperial courts, nothing certain transpires. We are enabled to conjecture its progress, only from facts which now and then show themselves. The following may be considered as indications of it. 1. The Emperor has made an attempt to surprise Belgrade. The attempt failed, but will serve to plunge him into the war, and to show that he had assumed the character of mediator, only to enable himself to gain some advantage by surprise. 2. The mediation of France is probably at an end, and their abandonment of the Turks agreed on; because they have secretly ordered their officers to quit the Turkish service. This fact is known to but few, and not intended to be known: but I think it certain. 3. To the offer of mediation lately made by England and Prussia, the court of Petersburg answered, that having declined the mediation of a friendly power (France), she could not accept that of two courts, with whose dispositions she had reason to be dissatisfied. 4. The States General are said to have instructed their ambassador here, lately, to ask of M. de Montmorin, whether the inquiry had been made, which they had formerly desired; 'By what authority the French engineers had been placed in the service of Holland?' And that he answered, that the inquiry had not been made, nor should be made. Though I do not consider the channel through which I get this fact, as absolutely sure, yet it is so respectable, that I give credit to it myself. 5. The King of Prussia is withdrawing his troops from Holland. Should this alliance show itself it would seem that France, thus strengthened, might dictate the re-establishment of the affairs of Holland, in her own form. For it is not conceivable, that Prussia would dare to move, nor that England would alone undertake such a war, and for such a purpose. She appears, indeed, triumphant at present; but the question is, Who will triumph last?

I enclose you a letter from Mr. Dumas. I received one from him myself, wherein he assures me, that no difficulties shall be produced, by what he had suggested relative to his mission to Brussels. The gazettes of France and Leyden to this date accompany this letter, which, with the several papers put under your cover, I shall send to M. Limozin, our agent at Havre, to be forwarded by the Juno, Captain Jenkins, which sails from that port for New York, on the 3d of January.

I have the honor to be, with sentiments of the most perfect esteem and respect, Sir, your most obedient and most humble servant,

Th: Jefferson.

LETTER CXXI.—TO MONSIEUR LAMBERT, January 3, 1788

TO MONSIEUR LAMBERT.

Paris, January 3, 1788.

Sir,

I am honored with your Excellency's letter of the 29th of December, enclosing the *Arrêt* on the commerce between France and the United States. I availed myself of the occasion of a vessel sailing this day from Havre for New York, to forward it to Congress. They will receive with singular satisfaction, this new testimony of his Majesty's friendship for the United States, of his dispositions to promote their interest, and to strengthen the bands which connect the two nations.

Permit me, Sir, to return you, personally, my sincere thanks for the great attention you have paid to this subject, for the sacrifices you have kindly made of a time so precious as yours, every moment of which is demanded and is occupied by objects interesting to the happiness of millions; and to proffer you the homage of those sincere sentiments of attachment and respect, with which I have the honor to be, your Excellency's most obedient and most humble servant,

Th: Jefferson.

LETTER CXXII.—TO LE COMTE BERNSTORFF, January 21, 1788

TO LE COMTE BERNSTORFF, *Minister of Foreign Affairs, Copenhagen.*

Paris, January 21, 1788.

Sir,

I am instructed by the United States of America, in Congress assembled, to bring again under the consideration of his Majesty, the King of Denmark, and of his ministers, the case of the three prizes taken from the English during the late war, by an American squadron under the command of Commodore Paul Jones, put into Bergen in distress, there rescued from our possession by orders from the court of Denmark, and delivered back to the English. Dr. Franklin, then Minister Plenipotentiary from the United States at the court of Versailles, had the honor of making applications to the court of Denmark, for a just indemnification to the persons interested, and particularly by a letter of the 22nd of December, 1779, a copy of which I have now the honor of enclosing to your Excellency. In consequence of this, the sum of ten thousand pounds was proposed to him, as an indemnification, through the Baron de Waltersdorff, then at Paris. The departure of both those gentlemen from this place, soon after, occasioned an intermission in the correspondence on this subject. But the United States continue to be very sensibly affected by this delivery of their prizes to Great Britain, and the more so, as no part of their conduct had forfeited their claim to those rights of hospitality, which civilized nations extend to each other. Not only a sense of justice due to the individuals interested in those prizes, but also an earnest desire that no subject of discontent may check the cultivation and progress of that friendship, which they wish may subsist and increase between the two countries, prompt them to remind his Majesty of the transaction in question; and they flatter themselves, that his Majesty will concur with them in thinking, that as restitution of the prizes is not practicable, it is reasonable and just that he should render, and that they should accept, a compensation equivalent to the value of them. And the same principles of justice towards the parties, and of amity to the United States, which influenced the breast of his Majesty to make, through the Baron de Waltersdorff, the proposition of a particular sum, will surely lead him to restore their full value, if that were greater, as is believed, than the sum proposed. In order to obtain, therefore, a final arrangement of this demand, Congress have authorized me to depute a special agent to Copenhagen, to attend the pleasure of his Majesty. No agent could be so adequate to this business, as the Commodore Paul Jones, who commanded the squadron which took the prizes. He will therefore have the honor of delivering this letter to your Excellency, in person; of giving such information as may be material, relative to the whole transaction; of entering into conferences for its final adjustment; and being himself principally interested, not only in his own right, but as the natural patron of those who fought under him, whatever shall be satisfactory to him, will have a great right to that ultimate approbation, which Congress have been pleased to confide to me.

I beg your Excellency to accept the homage of that respect, which your exalted station, talents, and merit impress, as well as those sentiments of esteem and regard, with which I have the honor to be

Your Excellency's most obedient

and most humble servant,

Th: Jefferson.

LETTER CXXIII.—TO WILLIAM RUTLEDGE, February 2, 1788

TO WILLIAM RUTLEDGE.

Paris, February 2, 1788.

Dear Sir,

I should have sooner answered your favor of January the 2nd, but that we have expected for some time, to see you here. I beg you not to think of the trifle I furnished you with, nor to propose to return it, till you shall have that sum more than you know what to do with. And on every other occasion of difficulty, I hope you will make use of me freely. I presume you will now remain at London, to see the trial of Hastings. Without suffering yourself to be imposed on by the pomp in which it will be enveloped, I would recommend to you to consider and decide for yourself these questions. If his offence is to be decided by the law of the land, why is he not tried in that court in which his fellow citizens are tried, that is, the King's Bench? If he is cited before another court, that he may be judged, not according to the law of the land, but by the discretion of his judges, is he not disfranchised of his most precious right, the benefit of the laws of his country, in common with his fellow citizens? I think you will find, in investigating this subject, that every solid argument is against the extraordinary court, and that every one in its favor is specious only. It is a transfer from a judicature of learning and integrity, to one, the greatness of which is both illiterate and unprincipled. Yet such is the force of prejudice with some, and of the want of reflection in others, that many of our constitutions have copied this absurdity, without suspecting it to be one. I am glad to hear that our new constitution is pretty sure of being accepted by States enough to secure the good it contains, and to meet with such opposition in some others, as to give us hopes it will be accommodated to them, by the amendment of its most glaring faults, particularly the want of a declaration of rights.

The long expected edict for the Protestants at length appears here. Its analysis is this. It is an acknowledgment (hitherto withheld by the laws) that Protestants can beget children, and that they can die, and be offensive unless buried. It does not give them permission to think, to speak, or to worship. It enumerates the humiliations to which they shall remain subject, and the burthens to which they shall continue to be unjustly exposed. What are we to think of the condition of the human mind in a country, where such a wretched thing as this has thrown the State into convulsions, and how must we bless our own situation in a country, the most illiterate peasant of which is a Solon, compared with the authors of this law. There is modesty often, which does itself injury; our countrymen possess this. They do not know their own superiority. You see it; you are young, you have time and talents to correct them. Study the subject while in Europe, in all the instances which will present themselves to you, and profit your countrymen of them, by making them to know and value themselves.

Adieu, my dear Sir, and be assured of the esteem with which I am your friend and servant,

Th: Jefferson.

LETTER CXXIV.—TO THE COMMISSIONERS OF THE TREASURY, Feb. 7, 1788

TO THE COMMISSIONERS OF THE TREASURY.

Paris, February 7, 1788.

Gentlemen,

Your favors of November the 10th and 13th, and December the 5th, have been duly received. Commodore Jones left this place for Copenhagen, the 5th instant, to carry into execution the resolution of Congress, of October the 25th. Whatever monies that court shall be willing to allow, shall be remitted to your bankers, either in Amsterdam or Paris, as shall be found most beneficial, allowing previously to be withdrawn Commodore Jones's proportion, which will be necessary for his subsistence. I desired him to endeavor to prevail on the Danish minister, to have the money paid in Amsterdam or Paris, by their banker in either of those cities, if they have one.

M. Ast (secretary to the consulate) is at L'Orient. Whether he comes up with the papers, or sends them, they shall be received, sealed up, and taken care of. I will only ask the favor of you, that I may never be desired to break the seals, unless very important cause for it should arise.

I have just received from Messrs. Willincks and Van Staphorsts, a letter of January the 31st, in which are these words: 'The official communication we have of the actual situation and prospect of the finances of the United States, would render such a partial payment as that to Fiseaux's house of no avail towards the support of the public credit, unless effectual measures shall be adopted, to provide funds for the two hundred and seventy thousand florins, interest, that will be due the first of June next; a single day's retard in which would ground a prejudice of long duration.' They informed me, at the same time, that they have made to you the following communication; that Mr. Stanitski, our principal broker, and holder of thirteen hundred and forty thousand dollars, of certificates of our domestic debt, offers to have our loan of a million of guilders (of which six hundred and twenty-two thousand eight hundred and forty are still unfilled) immediately made up, on condition that he may retain thereout one hundred and eighty thousand guilders, being one year's interest on his certificates, allowing a deduction of ten per cent, from his said interest, as a compensation for his receiving it in Amsterdam instead of America, and not pretending that this shall give him any title to ask any payment of future interest in Europe. They observe, that this will enable them to face the demands of Dutch interest, till the 1st of June, 1789, pay the principal of Fiseaux' debt, and supply the current expenses of your legation in Europe. On these points, it is for you to decide. I will only take the liberty to observe, that if they shall receive your acceptance of the proposition, some days credit will still be to be given for producing the cash, and that this must be produced fifteen days before it is wanting, because that much previous notice is always given to the creditors, that their money is ready. It is, therefore, but three months from this day, before your answer should be in Amsterdam. It might answer a useful purpose also, could I receive a communication of that answer ten days earlier than they. The same stagnation attending our passage from the old to the new form of government, which stops the feeble channel of money hitherto flowing towards our treasury, has suspended also what foreign credit we had. So that, at this moment, we may consider the progress of our loan as stopped. Though much an enemy to the system of borrowing, yet I feel strongly the necessity of preserving the power to borrow. Without this, we might be overwhelmed by another nation, merely by the force of its credit. However, you can best judge whether the payment of a single year's interest on Stanitski's certificates, in Europe, instead of America, may be more injurious to us than the shock of our credit in Amsterdam, which may be produced by a failure to pay our interest.

I have only to offer any services which I can render in this business, either here or by going to Holland, at a moment's warning, if that should be necessary.

I have the honor to be, with sentiments of the most perfect esteem and respect, Gentlemen, your most obedient and most humble servant,

Th: Jefferson.

LETTER CXXV.—TO DOCTOR PRICE, February 7, 1788

TO DOCTOR PRICE.

Paris, February 7, 1788.

Dear Sir,

It is rendering mutual service to men of virtue and understanding, to make them acquainted with one another. I need no other apology for presenting to your notice the bearer hereof, Mr. Barlow. I know you were among the first who read the "Vision of Columbus," while yet in manuscript: and think the sentiments I heard you express of that poem, will induce you to be pleased with the acquaintance of their author. He comes to pass a few days only at London, merely to know something of it. As I have little acquaintance there, I cannot do better for him than to ask you to be so good as to make him known to such persons, as his turn and his time might render desirable to him.

I thank you for the volume you were so kind as to send me some time ago. Every thing you write is precious, and this volume is on the most precious of all our concerns. We may well admit morality to be the child of the understanding rather than of the senses, when we observe that it becomes dearer to us as the latter weaken, and as the former grows stronger by time and experience, till the hour arrives in which all other objects lose all their value. That that hour may be distant with you, my friend, and that the intermediate space may be filled with health and happiness, is the sincere prayer of him who is, with sentiments of great respect and friendship, Dear Sir, your most obedient, humble servant,

Th: Jefferson.

LETTER CXXVI.—TO A. DONALD, February.7, 1788

TO A. DONALD.

Paris, February.7, 1788.

Dear Sir,

I received duly your friendly letter of November the 12th. By this time, you will have seen published by Congress, the new regulations obtained from this court, in favor of our commerce. You will observe, that the arrangement relative to tobacco is a continuation of the order of Berni for five years, only leaving the price to be settled between the buyer and seller. You will see too, that all contracts for tobacco are forbidden, till it arrives in France. Of course, your proposition for a contract is precluded.

I fear the prices here will be low, especially if the market be crowded. You should be particularly attentive to the article, which requires that the tobacco should come in French or American bottoms, as this article will, in no instance, be departed from.

I wish with all my soul, that the nine first conventions may accept the new constitution, because this will secure to us the good it contains, which I think great and important. But I equally wish, that the four latest conventions, which ever they be, may refuse to accede to it, till a declaration of rights be annexed. This would probably command the offer of such a declaration, and thus give to the whole fabric, perhaps, as much perfection as any one of that kind ever had. By a declaration of rights, I mean one which shall stipulate freedom of religion, freedom of the press, freedom of commerce against monopolies, trial by juries in all cases, no suspensions of the *habeas corpus*, no standing armies. These are fetters against doing evil, which no honest government should decline. There is another strong feature in the new constitution, which I as strongly dislike. That is, the perpetual re-eligibility of the President. Of this I expect no amendment at present, because I do not see that any body has objected to it on your side the water. But it will be productive of cruel distress to our country, even in your day and mine. The importance to France and England, to have our government in the hands of a friend or foe, will occasion their interference by money, and even by arms. Our President will be of much more consequence to them than a King of Poland. We must take care, however, that neither this, nor any other objection to the new form, produces a schism in our Union. That would be an incurable evil, because near friends falling out, never re-unite cordially; whereas, all of us going together, we shall be sure to cure the evils of our new constitution, before they do great harm. The box of books I had taken the liberty to address to you, is but just gone from Havre for New York. I do not see, at present, any symptoms strongly indicating war. It is true, that the distrust existing between the two courts of Versailles and London, is so great, that they can scarcely do business together. However, the difficulty and doubt of obtaining money make both afraid to enter into war. The little preparations for war, which we see, are the effect of distrust, rather than of a design to commence hostilities. And in such a state of mind, you know, small things may produce a rupture: so that though peace is rather probable, war is very possible.

Your letter has kindled all the fond recollections of ancient times; recollections much dearer to me than any thing I have known since. There are minds which can be pleased by honors and preferments; but I see nothing in them but envy and enmity. It is only necessary to possess them, to know how little they contribute to happiness, or rather how hostile they are to it. No attachments soothe the mind so much as those contracted in early life; nor do I recollect any societies which have given me more pleasure, than those of which you have partaken with me. 1 had rather be shut up in a very modest cottage, with my books, my family, and a few old friends, dining on simple bacon, and letting the world roll on as it liked, than to occupy the most splendid post, which any human power can give. I shall be glad to hear from you often. Give me the small news as well as the great. Tell Dr. Currie, that I believe I am indebted to him a letter, but that like the mass of our countrymen, I am not, at this moment, able to pay all my debts; the post being to depart in an hour, and the last stroke of a pen I am able to send by it, being that which assures you of the sentiments of esteem and attachment, with which I am, Dear Sir, your affectionate friend and servant,

Th: Jefferson.

LETTER CXXVII.—TO M. WARVILLE, February 12, 1888

TO M. WARVILLE.

Paris, February 12, 1888.

Sir,

I am very sensible of the honor you propose to me, of becoming a member of the society for the abolition of the slave-trade. You know that nobody wishes more ardently, to see an abolition, not only of the trade, but of the condition of slavery: and certainly nobody will be more willing to encounter every sacrifice for that object. But the influence and information of the friends to this proposition in France will be far above the need of my association. I am here as a public servant, and those whom I serve, having never yet been able to give their voice against the practice, it is decent for me to avoid too public a demonstration of my wishes to see it abolished. Without serving the cause here, it might render me less able to serve it beyond the water. I trust you will be sensible of the prudence of those motives, therefore, which govern my conduct on this occasion, and be assured of my wishes for the success of your undertaking, and the sentiments of esteem and respect, with which I have the honor to be, Sir, your most obedient, humble servant,

Th: Jefferson.

LETTER CXXVIII.—TO JOHN ADAMS, March 2, 1788

TO JOHN ADAMS.

Paris, March 2, 1788.—Sunday.

Dear Sir,

I received this day, a letter from Mrs. Adams, of the 26th ultimo, informing me you would set out on the 29th for the Hague. Our affairs at Amsterdam press on my mind like a mountain. I have no information to go on, but that of Willincks and Van Staphorsts, and according to that, something seems necessary to be done. I am so anxious to confer with you on this subject, and to see you and them together, and get some effectual arrangement made in time, that I determine to meet you at the Hague. I will set out the moment some repairs are made to my carriage: it is promised me at three o'clock to-morrow; but probably they will make it night, and that I may not set out till Tuesday morning. In that case, I shall be at the Hague on Friday night: in the mean time, you will perhaps have made all your bows there. I am sensible how irksome this must be to you, in the moment of your departure. But it is a great interest of the United States, which is at stake, and I am sure you will sacrifice to that your feelings and your interest. I hope to shake you by the hand within twenty-four hours after you receive this; and in the mean time, I am, with much esteem and respect, Dear Sir, your affectionate friend and humble servant,

Th: Jefferson.

LETTER CXXIX.—TO JOHN JAY, March 16, 1788

TO JOHN JAY.

Amsterdam, March 16, 1788.

Sir,

In a letter of the 13th instant, which I had the honor of addressing you from this place, I mentioned in general terms, the object of my journey hither, and that I should enter into more particular details, by the confidential conveyance which would occur through Mr. Adams and Colonel Smith.

The board of treasury had, in the month of December, informed me and our bankers here, that it would be impossible for them to make any remittances to Europe for the then ensuing year, and that they must, therefore, rely altogether on the progress of the late loan. But this, in the mean time, after being about one third filled, had ceased to get forward. The bankers who had been referred to me for advice, by Mr. Adams, stated these circumstances, and pressed their apprehension for the ensuing month of June, when two hundred and seventy thousand florins would be wanting for interest. In fine, they urged an offer of the holders of the former bonds, to take all those remaining on hand, provided they might receive out of them the interest on a part of our domestic debt, of which they had also become the holders. This would have been one hundred and eighty thousand florins. To this proposition, I could not presume any authority to listen. Thus pressed between the danger of failure on one hand, and this proposition on the other, I heard of Mr. Adams being gone to the Hague to take leave. His knowledge of the subject was too valuable to be neglected under the present difficulty, and it was the last moment in which we could be availed of it. I set out immediately, therefore, for the Hague, and we came on to this place together, in order to see what could be done. It was easier to discover, than to remove, the causes which obstructed the progress of the loan. Our affairs here, like those of other nations, are in the hands of particular bankers. These employ particular, and they have their particular circle of money-lenders. These moneylenders, as I have before mentioned, while placing a part of their money in our foreign loans, had at the same time employed another part in a joint speculation, to the amount of eight hundred and forty thousand dollars, in our domestic debt. A year's interest was becoming due on this, and they wished to avail themselves of our want of money for the foreign interest, to obtain payment of the domestic. Our first object was to convince our bankers, that there was no power on this side the Atlantic which could accede to this proposition, or give it any countenance. They at length, therefore, but with difficulty, receded from this ground, and agreed to enter into conferences with the brokers and lenders, and to use every exertion to clear the loan from the embarrassment in which this speculation had engaged it. What will be the result of these conferences, is not yet known. We have hopes, however, that it is not desperate, because the bankers consented yesterday, to pay off the capital of fifty-one thousand florins, which had become due on the first day of January, and which had not yet been paid. We have gone still further. The treasury board gives no hope of remittances, till the new government can procure them. For that government to be adopted, its legislature assembled, its system of taxation and collection arranged, the money gathered from the people into the treasury, and then remitted to Europe, must extend considerably into the year 1790. To secure our credit then, for the present year only, is but to put off the evil day to the next. What remains of the last loan, when it shall be filled up, will little more than clear us of present demands, as may be seen by the estimate enclosed. We thought it better, therefore, to provide at once for the years 1789 and 1790 also; and thus to place the government at its ease, and her credit in security, during that trying interval. The same estimate will show, that another million of florins will be necessary to effect this. We stated this to our bankers, who concurred in our views, and that to ask the whole sum at once would be better than to make demands from time to time, so small, as that they betray to the money-holders the extreme feebleness of our resources. Mr. Adams, therefore, has executed bonds for another million of florins; which, however, are to remain unissued till Congress shall have ratified the measure that this transaction is something or nothing, at their pleasure. We suppose its expediency so apparent, as to leave little doubt of its ratification. In this case, much time will have been saved by the execution of the bonds at this moment, and the proposition will be presented here under a more favorable appearance, according to the opinion of the bankers. Mr. Adams is under a necessity of setting out to-morrow morning, but I shall stay two or three days longer, to attend to and encourage the efforts of the bankers; though it is yet doubtful whether they will ensure us a safe passage over the month of June. Not having my letters here to turn to, I am unable to say whether the last I wrote, mentioned the declaration of the Emperor that he should take part in the war against the Turks. This declaration appeared a little before, or a little after that letter, I do not recollect which. Some little hostilities have taken place between them. The court of Versailles seems to pursue immoveably its pacific system, and from every appearance in the country from which I write, we must conclude that its tragedy is wound up. The triumph appears complete, and tranquillity perfectly established. The numbers who have emigrated are differently estimated, from twenty to forty thousand. A little before I left Paris, I received a piece of intelligence, which should be communicated, leaving you to lay what stress on it, it may seem to deserve. Its authenticity may be surely relied on. At the time of the late pacification, Spain had about fifteen ships of the line nearly ready for sea. The convention for disarming did not extend to her, nor did she disarm. This gave inquietude to the court of London, and they demanded an explanation. One was given, they say, which is perfectly satisfactory. The Russian minister at Versailles, getting knowledge of this, became suspicious on his part. He recollected that Spain, during the late war, had been opposed to the entrance of a Russian fleet into the Mediterranean, and concluded, if England was not the object of this armament, Russia might be. It is known that that power means to send a fleet of about twenty-four ships into the Mediterranean this summer. He sent to the Count de Montmorin, and expressed his apprehensions. The Count de Montmorin declared, that the object of Spain in that armament was totally different; that he was not sure she would succeed; but that France and Spain were to be considered as one, and that the former would become guarantee for the latter, that she would make no opposition to the Russian fleet. If neither England nor Russia be the object, the question recurs, Who is it for? You know best, if our affairs with Spain are in a situation to give jealousy to either of us. I think it very possible, that the satisfaction of the court of London may have been pretended or premature. It is possible also, that the affairs of Spain in South America may require them to assume a threatening appearance. I give you the facts, however, and you will judge whether they are objects of attention or of mere curiosity.

I have the honor to be, with sentiments of sincere esteem and respect, Sir, your most obedient and most humble servant,

Th: Jefferson.

P. S. I enclose herewith an extract of a letter from the Count de Vergennes to the French ambassador at the Hague, which will make a remarkable chapter in the history of the late revolution here. It is not public, nor should be made so by us. Probably those who have been the victims of it, will some day publish it.

LETTER CXXX.—TO MR. DUMAS, March 29, 1788

TO MR. DUMAS.

Amsterdam, March 29, 1788.

Sir,

I have now to acknowledge the receipt of your favors of the 14th, 18th, and 23rd instant. I would have preferred doing it in person, but the season, and the desire of seeing what I have not yet seen, invite me to take the route of the Rhine. I shall leave this place to-morrow morning, and probably not reach Paris till the latter end of April. In the moment we were to have conferred on the subject of paying the arrears due to you, a letter of the 20th of February, from the board of treasury, was received, forbidding the application of money to any purpose, (except our current claims,) till the June interest should be actually in hand. Being by the letter, tied up from giving an order in your favor, I return you the letter you had written to Mr. Jay, on the supposition that the order for your arrears was given. It has been suggested, however, that if you could receive bonds of the loan, you could make them answer your purpose, and the commissioners say, this would in no wise interfere with the views of the treasury board, nor the provision for the June interest. I have, therefore, recommended to them in writing, to give you bonds to the amount of your balance, if you choose to take them, rather than to wait. I wish this may answer your purpose. I remember that in the conversation which I had the honor of having with you, on the evening I was at the Hague, you said that your enemies had endeavored to have it believed, that Congress would abandon you, and withdraw your appointments. An enemy generally says and believes what he wishes, and your enemies, particularly, are not those who are most in the counsels of Congress, nor the best qualified to tell what Congress will do. From the evidences you have received of their approbation, and from their well known steadiness and justice, you must be assured of a continuance of their favor, were they to continue under the present form. Nor do I see any thing in the new government which threatens us with less firmness. The Senate, who will make and remove their foreign officers, must, from its constitution, be a wise and steady body. Nor would a new government begin its administration by discarding old servants; servants who have put all to the risk, and when the risk was great, to obtain that freedom and security under which themselves will be what they shall be. Upon the whole, my Dear Sir, tranquillize yourself and your family upon this subject. All the evidence, which exists as yet, authorizes you to do this, nor can I foresee any cause of disquiet in future. That none may arise, that yourself and family may enjoy health, happiness, and the continued approbation of those by whom you wish most to be approved, is the sincere wish of him, who has the honor to be, with sentiments of sincere esteem and attachment, your most obedient and most humble servant,

Th: Jefferson.

LETTER CXXXI.—TO THE COMMISSIONERS OF THE TREASURY, March 29, 1788

TO THE COMMISSIONERS OF THE TREASURY.

Gentlemen,

Amsterdam, March 29, 1788.

I cannot close my letter, without some observations on the transfer of our domestic debt to foreigners. This circumstance, and the failure to pay off Fiseaux' loan, were the sole causes of the stagnation of our late loan. For otherwise our credit would have stood on more hopeful grounds than heretofore. There was a condition in the last loan, that, the lenders furnishing one third of the money, the remaining two thirds of the bonds should remain eighteen months unsold, and at their option to take or not, and that in the mean time, the same bankers should open no other loan for us. These same lenders became purchasers of our domestic debt, and they were disposed to avail themselves of the power they had thus acquired over us as to our foreign demands, to make us pay the domestic one. Should the present necessities have obliged you to comply with their proposition for the present year, I should be of opinion it ought to be the last instance. If the transfer of these debts to Europe meet with any encouragement from us, we can no more borrow money here, let our necessities be what they will. For who will give ninety-six per cent, for the foreign obligations of the same nation, whose domestic ones can be bought at the same market for fifty-five per cent.; the former, too, bearing an interest of only five per cent., while the latter yields six. If any discouragements can be honestly thrown on this transfer, it would seem advisable, in order to keep the domestic debt at home. It would be a very effectual one, if, instead of the title existing in our treasury books alone, it was made to exist in loose papers, as our loan office debts do. The European holder would then be obliged to risk the title paper of his capital, as well as his interest, in the hands of his agent in America, whenever the interest was to be demanded; whereas, at present, he trusts him with the interest only. This single circumstance would put a total stop to all future sales of domestic debt at this market. Whether this, or any other obstruction, can or should be thrown in the way of these operations, is not for me to decide; but I have thought the subject worthy your consideration.

I have the honor to be, with sentiments of the most perfect esteem and respect, Gentlemen, your most obedient and most humble servant,

Th: Jefferson.

LETTER CXXXII.—TO GENERAL WASHINGTON, May 2, 1788

TO GENERAL WASHINGTON.

Paris, May 2, 1788.

Dear Sir,

I am honored with your Excellency's letter by the last packet, and thank you for the information it contains on the communication between the Cayahoga and Big Beaver. I have ever considered the opening a canal between those two water courses, as the most important work in that line, which the state of Virginia could undertake. If will infallibly turn through the Potomac all the commerce of Lake Erie, and the country west of that, except what may pass down the Mississippi; and it is important that it be soon done, lest that commerce should, in the mean time, get established in another channel. Having, in the spring of the last year, taken a journey through the southern parts of France, and particularly examined the canal of Languedoc, through its whole course, I take the liberty of sending you the notes I made on the spot, as you may find in them something perhaps, which may be turned to account, some time or other, in the prosecution of the Potomac canal. Being merely a copy from my travelling notes, they are undigested and imperfect, but may still, perhaps, give hints capable of improvement in your mind.

The affairs of Europe are in such a state still, that it is impossible to say what form they will take ultimately. France and Prussia, viewing the Emperor as their most dangerous and common enemy, had heretofore seen their common safety as depending on a strict connection with one another. This had naturally inclined the Emperor to the scale of England, and the Empress also, as having views in common with the Emperor, against the Turks. But these two powers would, at any time, have gladly quitted England, to coalesce with France, as being the power which they met every where, opposed as a barrier to all their schemes of aggrandizement. When, therefore, the present King of Prussia took the eccentric measure of bidding defiance to France, by placing his brother-in-law on the throne of Holland, the two empires immediately seized the occasion of soliciting an alliance with France. The motives for this appeared so plausible, that it was believed the latter would have entered into this alliance, and that thus the whole political system of Europe would have taken a new form. What has prevented this court from coming into it, we know not. The unmeasurable ambition of the Emperor, and his total want of moral principle and honor, are suspected. A great share of Turkey, the recovery of Silesia, the consolidation of his dominions by the Bavarian exchange, the liberties of the Germanic body, all occupy his mind together; and his head is not well enough organized, to pursue so much only of all this, as is practicable. Still it was thought that France might safely have coalesced with these powers, because Russia and herself holding close together, as their interests would naturally dictate, the Emperor could never stir, but with their permission. France seems, however, to have taken the worst of all parties, that is, none at all. She folds her arms, lets the two empires go to work to cut up Turkey as they can, and holds Prussia aloof, neither as a friend nor foe. This is withdrawing her opposition from the two empires, without the benefit of any condition whatever. In the mean time, England has clearly overreached herself. She excited the war between the Russians and Turks, in hopes that France, still supporting the Turks, would be embarrassed with the two empires. She did not foresee the event which has taken place, of France abandoning the Turks, and that which may take place, of her union with the two empires. She allied herself with Holland, but cannot obtain the alliance of Prussia. This latter power would be very glad to close again the breach with France, and therefore, while there remains an opening for this, holds off from England, whose fleets could not enter into Silesia, to protect that from the Emperor. Thus you see, that the old system is unhinged, and no new one hung in its place. Probabilities are rather in favor of a connection between the two empires, France, and Spain. Several symptoms show themselves, of friendly dispositions between Russia and France, unfriendly ones between Russia and England, and such as are barely short of hostility between England and France. But into real hostilities, this country would with difficulty be drawn. Her finances are too deranged, her internal union too much dissolved, to hazard a war. The nation is pressing on fast, to a fixed constitution. Such a revolution in the public opinion has taken place, that the crown already feels its powers bounded, and is obliged, by its measures, to acknowledge limits.

A States-General will be called at some epoch not distant; they will probably establish a civil list, and leave the government to temporary provisions of money, so as to render frequent assemblies of the national representative necessary. How that representative will be organized, is yet uncertain. Among a thousand projects, the best seems to me, that of dividing them into two Houses, of Commons and Nobles; the Commons to be chosen by the Provincial Assemblies, who are chosen themselves by the people, and the Nobles by the body of *Noblesse*, as in Scotland. But there is no reason to conjecture, that this is the particular scheme which will be preferred.

The war between the Russians and Turks has made an opening for our Commodore Paul Jones. The Empress has invited him into her service. She insures to him the rank of rear-admiral; will give him a separate command, and it is understood, that he is never to be commanded. I think she means to oppose him to the Captain Pacha, on the Black Sea. He is by this time, probably, at St. Petersburg. The circumstances did not permit his awaiting the permission of Congress, because the season was close at hand for opening the campaign. But he has made it a condition, that he shall be free at all times to return to the orders of Congress, whenever they shall please to call for him; and also, that he shall not, in any case be expected to bear arms against France. I believe Congress had it in contemplation to give him the grade of admiral, from the date of his taking the Serapis. Such a measure now, would greatly gratify him, second the efforts of fortune in his favor, and better the opportunities of improving him for our service, whenever the moment shall come in which we may want him.

The danger of our incurring something like a bankruptcy in Holland, which might have been long, and even fatally felt in a moment of crisis, induced me to take advantage of Mr. Adams's journey to take leave at the Hague, to meet him there, get him to go on to Amsterdam, and try to avert the impending danger. The moment of paying a great sum of annual interest was approaching. There was no money on hand; the board of treasury had notified that they could not remit any; and the progress of the loan, which had been opened there, had absolutely stopped. Our bankers there gave me notice of all this; and that a single day's failure in the payment of interest, would have the most fatal effect on our credit. I am happy to inform you, we were able to set the loan a going again, and that the evil is at least postponed. Indeed, I am tolerably satisfied, that if the measures we proposed, are ratified by Congress, all European calls for money (except the French debt) are secure enough, till the end of the year 1790; by which time, we calculated that the new government might be able to get money into the treasury. Much conversation with the bankers, brokers, and money-holders, gave me insight into the state of national credit there, which I had never before been able satisfactorily to get. The English credit is the first, because they never open a loan, without laying and appropriating taxes for the payment of the interest, and there has never been an instance of their failing one day, in that payment. The Emperor and Empress have good credit, because they use it little, and have hitherto been very punctual. This country is among the lowest, in point of credit. Ours stands in hope only. They consider us as the surest nation on earth for the repayment of the capital; but as the punctual payment of interest is of absolute necessity in their arrangements, we cannot borrow but with difficulty and disadvantage. The monied men, however, look towards our new government with a great degree of partiality, and even anxiety. If they see that set out on the English plan, the first degree of credit will be transferred to us. A favorable occasion will arise to our new government of asserting this ground to themselves. The transfer of the French debt, public and private, to Amsterdam, is certainly desirable. An act of the new government, therefore, for opening a loan in Holland for the purpose, laying taxes at the same time for paying annually the interest and a part of the principal, will answer the two valuable purposes, of ascertaining the degree of our credit, and of removing those causes of bickering and irritation, which should never be permitted to subsist with a nation, with which it is so much our interest to be on cordial terms as with France. A very small portion of this debt, I mean that part due to the French officers, has done us an injury, of which those in office in America cannot have an idea. The interest is unpaid for the last three years; and these creditors, highly connected, and at the same time needy, have felt and communicated hard thoughts of us. Borrowing, as we have done, three hundred thousand florins a year, to pay our interest in Holland, it would have been worth while to have added twenty thousand more, to suppress those clamors. I am anxious about every thing which may affect our credit. My wish would be, to possess it in the highest degree, but to use it little. Were we without credit, we might be crushed by a nation of much inferior resources, but possessing higher credit. The present system of war renders it necessary to make exertions far beyond the annual resources of the State, and consume in one year the efforts of many. And this system we cannot change. It remains, then, that we cultivate our credit with the utmost attention.

I had intended to have written a word to your Excellency on the subject of the new constitution, but I have already spun out my letter to an immoderate length. I will just observe, therefore, that according to my ideas, there is a great deal of good in it. There are two things, however, which I dislike strongly, 1. The want of a declaration of rights. I am in hopes the opposition in Virginia will remedy this, and produce such a declaration. 2. The perpetual re-eligibility of the President. This, I fear, will make that an office for life, first, and then hereditary. I was much an enemy to monarchies before I came to Europe. I am ten thousand times more so, since I have seen what they are. There is scarcely an evil known in these countries, which may not be traced to their king, as its source, nor a good, which is not derived from the small fibres of republicanism existing among them. I can further say, with safety, there is not a crowned head in Europe, whose talents or merits would entitle him to be elected a vestryman by the people of any parish in America. However, I shall hope, that before there is danger of this change taking place in the office of President, the good sense and free spirit of our countrymen will make the changes necessary to prevent it. Under this hope, I look forward to the general adoption of the new constitution with anxiety, as necessary for us under our present circumstances. I have so much trespassed on your patience already, by the length of this letter, that I will add nothing further, than those assurances of sincere esteem and attachment, with which I have the honor to be, your Excellency's most obedient and most humble servant,

Th: Jefferson.

LETTER CXXXIII.—TO JAMES MADISON, May 3,1788

TO JAMES MADISON.

Paris, May 3,1788.

Dear Sir,

Mine of February the 6th acknowledged the receipt of yours of December the 9th and 20th; since that, those of February the 19th and 20th have come to hand. The present will be delivered you by Mr. Warville, whom you will find truly estimable, and a great enthusiast for liberty. His writings will have shown you this.

For public news, I must refer you to my letters to Mr. Jay. Those I wrote to him from Amsterdam will have informed you of my journey thither. While there, I endeavored to get, as well as I could, into the state of national credit there; for though I am an enemy to the using our credit but under absolute necessity, yet the possessing a good credit I consider as indispensable, in the present system of carrying on war. The existence of a nation having no credit, is always precarious. The credit of England is the best. Their paper sells at par on the exchange of Amsterdam, the moment any of it is offered, and they can command there any sum they please. The reason is, that they never borrow, without establishing taxes for the payment of the interest, and they never yet failed one day in that payment. The Emperor and Empress have good credit enough. They use it little and have been ever punctual. This country cannot borrow at all there; for though they always pay their interest within the year, yet it is often some months behind. It is difficult to assign to our credit its exact station in this scale. They consider us as the most certain nation on earth for the principal; but they see that we borrow of themselves to pay the interest, so that this is only a conversion of their interest into principal. Our paper, for this reason, sells for from four to eight per cent, below par, on the exchange, and our loans are negotiated with the Patriots only. But the whole body of money-dealers, Patriot and Stadtholderian, look forward to our new government with a great degree of partiality and interest. They are disposed to have much confidence in it, and it was the prospect of its establishment, which enabled us to set the loan of last year into motion again. They will attend steadfastly to its first money operations. If these are injudiciously begun, correction, whenever they shall be corrected, will come too late. Our borrowings will always be difficult and disadvantageous. If they begin well, our credit will immediately take the first station. Equal provision for the interest, adding to it a certain prospect for the principal, will give us a preference to all nations, the English not excepted. The first act of the new government should be some operation, whereby they may assume to themselves this station. Their European debts form a proper subject for this. Digest the whole, public and private, Dutch, French, and Spanish, into a table, showing the sum of interest due every year, and the portions of principal payable the same year. Take the most certain branch of revenue, and one which shall suffice to pay the interest, and leave such a surplus as may accomplish all the payments of the capital, as terms somewhat short of those, at which they will become due. Let the surpluses of those years, in which no reimbursement of principal falls, be applied to buy up our paper on the exchange of Amsterdam, and thus anticipate the demands of principal. In this way our paper will be kept up at par; and this alone will enable us to command in four and twenty hours, at any time, on the exchange of Amsterdam, as many millions as that capital can produce. The same act which makes this provision for the existing debts, should go on to open a loan to their whole amount; the produce of that loan to be applied, as fast as received, to the payment of such parts of the existing debts as admit of payment. The rate of interest to be as the government should privately instruct their agent, because it must depend on the effect these measures would have on the exchange. Probably it could be lowered from time to time. Honest and annual publications of the payments made, will inspire confidence, while silence would conceal nothing from those interested to know.

You will perceive by the *comte rendu* which I send you, that this country now calls seriously for its interest at least. The nonpayment of this, hitherto, has done our credit little injury, because the government here, saying nothing about it, the public have supposed they wished to leave us at our ease as to the payment. It is now seen that they call for it, and they will publish annually the effect of that call. A failure here, therefore, will have the same effect on our credit hereafter, as a failure at Amsterdam. I consider it, then, as of a necessity not to be dispensed with, that these calls be effectually provided for. If it shall be seen, that the general provision before hinted at cannot be in time, then it is the present government which should take on itself to borrow in Amsterdam what may be necessary. The new government should by no means be left by the old to the necessity of borrowing a stiver, before it can tax for its interest. This will be to destroy the credit of the new government in its birth. And I am of opinion, that if the present Congress will add to the loan of a million (which Mr. Adams and myself have proposed this year) what may be necessary for the French calls to the year 1790, the money can be obtained at the usual disadvantage. Though I have not at this moment received such authentic information from our bankers as I may communicate to Congress, yet I know privately from one of them (Mr. Jacob Van Staphorst, who is here), that they had on Hand a fortnight ago four hundred thousand florins, and the sale going on well. So that the June interest, which had been in so critical a predicament, was already secured. If

the loan of a million on Mr. Adams's bonds of this year be ratified by Congress, the applications of the money on hand may go on immediately, according to the statement I sent to Mr. Jay. One article in this I must beg you to press on the treasury board; that is, an immediate order for the payment of the three years' arrearages to the French officers. They were about holding a meeting to take desperate measures on this subject, when I was called to Holland. I desired them to be quiet till my return, and since my return I have pressed a further tranquillity till July, by which time I have given them reason to hope I may have an answer from the treasury board to my letters of March. Their ill humor can be contained no longer; and as I know no reason why they may not be paid at that time, I shall have nothing to urge in our defence after that.

You remember the report, drawn by Governor Randolph, on the navigation of the Mississippi. When I came to Europe, Mr. Thomson was so kind as to have me a copy of it made out. I lent it to Dr. Franklin, and he mislaid it, so that it could never be found. Could you make interest with him to have me another copy made, and send it to me? By Mr. Warville I send your pedometer. To the loop at the bottom of it you must sew a tape, and at the other end of the tape a small hook (such as we use under the name of hooks and eyes), cut a little hole in the bottom of your left watch-pocket, pass the hook and tape through it, and down between the breeches and drawers, and fix the hook on the edge of your knee-band, an inch from the knee-buckle; then hook the instrument itself by its swivel-hook on the upper edge of the watch-pocket. Your tape being well adjusted in length, your double steps will be exactly counted by the instrument, the shortest hand pointing out the thousands, the flat hand the hundreds, and the long hand the tens and units. Never turn the hands backward; indeed, it is best not to set them to any given place, but to note the number they stand at when you begin to walk. The adjusting the tape to its exact length is a critical business, and will cost you many trials. But once done, it is done for ever. The best way is to have a small buckle fixed on the middle of the tape, by which you can take it up, and let it out at pleasure. When you choose it should cease to count, unhook it from the top of the watch-pocket, and let it fall down to the bottom of the pocket.

I am, with sentiments of the most sincere esteem and attachment, Dear Sir, your affectionate friend and servant,

Th: Jefferson.

LETTER CXXXIV.—TO JOHN JAY, May 4, 1788

TO JOHN JAY.

Paris, May 4, 1788.

Sir,

I had the honor of addressing you in two letters of the 13th and 16th of March from Amsterdam, and have since received Mr. Ramson's of February the 20th. I staid at Amsterdam about ten or twelve days after the departure of Mr. Adams, in hopes of seeing the million of the last year filled up. This, however, could not be accomplished on the spot. But the prospect was so good as to have dissipated all fears; and since my return here, I learn (not officially from our bankers, but) through a good channel, that they have received near four hundred thousand florins since the date of the statement I sent you in my letter of March the 16th; and I presume we need not fear the completion of that loan, which will provide for all our purposes of the year 1788, as stated in that paper. I hope, therefore, to receive from the treasury orders in conformity thereto, that I may be able to proceed to the redemption of our captives. A provision for the purposes of the years 1789 and 1790, as stated in the same paper, will depend on the ratification by Congress of Mr. Adams's bonds of this year for another million of florins. But there arises a new call from this government, for its interest at least. Their silence hitherto has made it be believed in general, that they consented to the nonpayment of our interest to them, in order to accommodate us. You will perceive in the seventy-fifth and seventy-sixth pages of the *compte rendu*, which I have the honor to send you, that they call for this interest, and will publish whether it be paid or not; and by No. 25, page eighty-one, that they count on its regular receipt for the purposes of the year. These calls, for the first days of January, 1789 and 1790, will amount to about a million and a half of florins more; and if to be raised by loan, it must be for two millions, as well to cover the expenses of the loan, as that loans are not opened for fractions of millions. This publication seems to render a provision for this interest as necessary as for that of Amsterdam.

I had taken measures to have it believed at Algiers, that our government withdrew its attention from our captives there. This was to prepare their captors for the ransoming them at a reasonable price. I find, however, that Captain O'Bryan is apprized that I have received some authority on this subject. He writes me a cruel letter, supposing me the obstacle to their redemption. Their own interest requires that I should leave them to think thus hardly of me. Were the views of government communicated to them, they could not keep their own secret, and such a price would be demanded for them, as Congress, probably, would think ought not to be given, lest it should be the cause of involving thousands of others of their citizens in the same condition. The moment I have money, the business shall be set in motion.

By a letter from Joseph Chiappe, our agent at Mogadore, I am notified of a declaration of the Emperor of Morocco, that if the States General of the United Netherlands do not, before the month of May, send him an ambassador, to let him know whether it is war or peace between them, he will send one to them with five frigates; and that if their dispositions be unfavorable, their frigates shall proceed to America to make prizes on the Dutch, and to sell them there. It seems to depend on the Dutch, therefore, whether the Barbary powers shall learn the way to our coasts, and whether we shall have to decide the question of the legality of selling in our ports vessels taken from them. I informed you, in a former letter, of the declaration made by the court of Spain to that of London, relative to its naval armament, and also of the declaration of the Count de Montmorin to the Russian minister here on the same subject. I have good information, that the court of Spain has itself made a similar and formal declaration to the minister of Russia at Madrid. So that Russia is satisfied she is not the object. I doubt whether the English are equally satisfied as to themselves. The season has hitherto prevented any remarkable operation between the Turks and the two empires. The war, however, will probably go on, and the season now admits of more important events. The Empress has engaged Commodore Paul Jones in her service. He is to have the rank of rear-admiral, with a separate command, and it is understood that he is in no case to be commanded. He will probably be opposed to the Captain Pacha on the Black Sea. He received this invitation at Copenhagen, and as the season for commencing the campaign, was too near to admit time for him to ask and await the permission of Congress, he accepted the offer, only stipulating, that he should be always free to return to the orders of Congress whenever called for, and that he should not be expected to bear arms against France. He conceived, that the experience he should gain would enable him to be more useful to the United States, should they ever have occasion for him. It has been understood, that Congress had had it in contemplation to give him the grade of rear-admiral, from the date of the action of the Serapis, and it is supposed, that such a mark of their approbation would have a favorable influence on his fortune in the north. Copies of the letters which passed between him and the Danish minister are herewith transmitted. I shall immediately represent to Count Bernstorff, that the demand for our prizes can have no connection with a treaty of commerce; that there is no reason why the claims of our seamen should await so distant and uncertain an event; and press the settlement of this claim.

This country still pursues its line of peace. The ministry seem now all united in it; some from a belief of their inability to carry on a war; others from a desire to arrange their internal affairs, and improve their constitution. The differences between the King and parliaments threaten a serious issue. Many symptoms indicate that the government has in contemplation some act of highhanded authority. An extra number of printers have for several days been employed, the apartment wherein they are at work being surrounded by a body of guards, who permit no body either to come out or go in. The commanders of the provinces, civil and military, have been ordered to be at their stations on a certain day of the ensuing week. They are accordingly gone: so that the will of the King is probably to be announced through the whole kingdom on the same day. The parliament of Paris, apprehending that some innovation is to be attempted, which may take from them the opportunity of deciding on it after it shall be made known, came last night to the resolution of which I have the honor to enclose you a manuscript copy. This you will perceive to be, in effect, a declaration of rights. I am obliged to close here the present letter, lest I should miss the opportunity of conveying it by a passenger who is to call for it. Should the delay of the packet admit any continuation of these details, they shall be the subject of another letter, to be forwarded by post. The gazettes of Leyden and France accompany this.

I have the honor to be, with sentiments of the most perfect esteem and respect, Sir, your most obedient and most humble servant,

Th: Jefferson.

LETTER CXXXV.—TO THE COUNT DE MOUSTIER, May 17, 1788

TO THE COUNT DE MOUSTIER.

Paris, May 17, 1788.

Dear Sir,

I have at length an opportunity of acknowledging the receipt of your favors of February, and March the 14th, and congratulating you on your resurrection from the dead, among whom you had been confidently entombed by the news-dealers of Paris. I am sorry that your first impressions have been disturbed by matters of etiquette, where surely they should least have been expected to occur. These disputes are the most insusceptible of determination, because they have no foundation in reason. Arbitrary and senseless in their nature, they are arbitrarily decided by every nation for itself. These decisions are meant to prevent disputes, but they produce ten, where they prevent one. It would have been better, therefore, in a new country, to have excluded etiquette altogether; or if it must be admitted in some form or other, to have made it depend on some circumstance founded in nature, such as the age or station of the parties. However, you have got over all this, and I am in hopes have been able to make up a society suited to your own dispositions. Your situation will doubtless be improved by the adoption of the new constitution, which I hope will have taken place before you receive this. I see in this instrument a great deal of good. The consolidation of our government, a just representation, an administration of some permanence, and other features of great value, will be gained by it. There are, indeed, some faults, which revolted me a good deal in the first moment; but we must be contented to travel on towards perfection, step by step. We must be contented with the ground which this constitution will gain for us, and hope that a favorable moment will come for correcting what is amiss in it. I view in the same light the innovations making here. The new organization of the judiciary department is undoubtedly for the better. The reformation of the criminal code is an immense step taken towards good. The composition of the Plenary court is indeed vicious in the extreme; but the basis of that court may be retained, and its composition changed. Make of it a representative of the people, by composing it of members sent from the Provincial Assemblies, and it becomes a valuable member of the constitution. But it is said, the court will not consent to do this: the court, however, has consented to call the States General, who will consider the Plenary court but as a canvass for them to work on. The public mind is manifestly advancing on the abusive prerogatives of their governors, and bearing them down. No force in the government can withstand this, in the long run. Courtiers had rather give up power than pleasures; they will barter, therefore, the usurped prerogatives of the King for the money of the people. This is the agent by which modern nations will recover their rights. I sincerely wish that, in this country, they may be contented with a peaceable and passive opposition. At this moment we are not sure of this; though as yet it is difficult to say what form the opposition will take. It is a comfortable circumstance, that their neighboring enemy is under the administration of a minister disposed to keep the peace. Engage in war who will, may my country long continue your peaceful residence, and merit your good offices with that nation, whose affections it is their duty and interest to cultivate.

Accept these and all other the good wishes of him, who has the honor to be, with sincere esteem and respect, Dear Sir, your most obedient and most humble servant,

Th: Jefferson.

LETTER CXXXVI.—TO JOHN JAY, May 23,1788

TO JOHN JAY.

Paris, May 23,1788.

Sir,

When I wrote my letter of the 4th instant, I had no reason to doubt that a packet would have sailed on the 10th, according to the established order. The passengers had all, except one, gone down to Havre in this expectation. However, none has sailed, and perhaps none will sail, as I think the suppression of the packets is one of the economies in contemplation. An American merchant, concerned in the commerce of the whale-oil, proposed to government to despatch his ships from Havre and Boston at stated periods, and to take on board the French courier and mail, and the proposition has been well enough received. I avail myself of a merchant vessel going from Havre, to write the present.

In my letter of the 4th, I stated to you the symptoms which indicated that government had some great stroke of authority in contemplation. That night they sent guards to seize Monsieur d'Epremenil and Monsieur Goiskind, two members of parliament, in their houses. They escaped, and took sanctuary in the Palais (or parliament house). The parliament assembled itself extraordinarily, summoned the Dukes and Peers specially, and came to the resolution of the 5th, which they sent to Versailles by deputies, determined not to leave the palace till they received an answer. In the course of that night a battalion of guards surrounded the house. The two members were taken by the officers from among their fellows, and sent off to prison, the one to Lyons, the other (d'Epremenil), the most obnoxious, to an island in the Mediterranean. The parliament then separated. On the 8th, a bed of justice was held at Versailles, wherein were enregistered the six ordinances which had been passed in Council on the 1st of May, and which I now send you. They were in like manner enregistered in beds of justice, on the same day, in nearly all the parliaments of the kingdom. By these ordinances, 1. The criminal law is reformed, by abolishing examination on the *sellette*, which, like our holding up the hand at the bar, remained a stigma on the party, though innocent; by substituting an oath, instead of torture, on the *question préalable*, which is used after condemnation, to make the prisoner discover his accomplices; (the torture, abolished in 1780, was on the *question préparatoire*, previous to judgment, in order to make the prisoner accuse himself;) by allowing counsel to the prisoner for his defence; obliging the judges to specify in their judgments the offence for which he is condemned; and respiting execution a month, except in the case of sedition. This reformation is unquestionably good, and within the ordinary legislative powers of the crown. That it should remain to be made at this day, proves that the monarch is the last person in his kingdom who yields to the progress of philanthropy and civilization. 2. The organization of the whole judiciary department is changed, by the institution of subordinate jurisdictions, the taking from the parliaments the cognizance of all causes of less value than twenty thousand livres, reducing their numbers to about a fourth, and suppressing a number of special courts. Even this would be a great improvement, if it did not imply that the King is the only person in this nation, who has any rights or any power. 3. The right of registering the laws is taken from the parliaments, and transferred to a Plenary court, created by the King. This last is the measure most obnoxious to all persons. Though the members are to be for life, yet a great proportion of them are from descriptions of men always candidates for the royal favor in other lines. As yet, the general consternation has not sufficiently passed over, to say whether the matter will end here. I send you some papers, which indicate symptoms of resistance. These are the resolution of the *Noblesse* of Brittany, the declaration of the Advocate General of Provence, which is said to express the spirit of that province; and the *Arrêté of the Châtelet*, which is the hustings-court of the city of Paris. Their refusal to act under the new character assigned them, and the suspension of their principal functions, are very embarrassing. The clamors this will excite, and the disorders it may admit, will be loud, and near to the royal ear and person. The parliamentary fragments permitted to remain, have already some of them refused, and probably all will refuse, to act under that form. The assembly of the clergy which happens to be sitting, have addressed the King to call the States General immediately. Of the Dukes and Peers (thirty-eight in number), nearly half are either minors or superannuated; two thirds of the acting half seem disposed to avoid taking a part; the rest, about eight or nine, have refused, by letters to the King, to act in the new courts. A proposition excited among the Dukes and Peers, to assemble and address the King for a modification of the Plenary court, seems to show that the government would be willing to compromise on that head. It has been prevented by the Dukes and Peers in opposition, because they suppose that no modification to be made by the government will give to that body the form they desire, which is that of a representative of the nation. They foresee that if the government is forced to this, they will call them, as nearly as they can, in the ancient forms; in which case, less good will be to be expected from them. But they hope they may be got to concur in a declaration of rights, at least, so that the nation may be acknowledged to have some fundamental rights, not alterable by their ordinary legislature, and that this may form a ground-work for future improvements. These seem to be the views of the most enlightened and disinterested characters of the opposition. But they may be frustrated by the nation's making no cry at all, or by a hasty and premature appeal to arms. There is neither head nor body in the nation, to promise a successful opposition to two hundred thousand regular troops. Some think the army could not be depended on by the government; but the breaking men to military discipline, is breaking their spirits to principles of passive obedience. A firm, but quiet opposition, will be the most likely to succeed. Whatever turn this crisis takes, a revolution in their constitution seems inevitable, unless foreign war supervene, to suspend the present contest. And a foreign war they will avoid, if possible, from an inability to get money. The loan of one hundred and twenty millions, of the present year, is filled up by such subscriptions as may be relied on. But that of eighty millions, proposed for the next year, cannot be filled up, in the actual situation of things.

The Austrians have been successful in an attack upon Schabatz, intended as a preliminary to that of Belgrade. In that on Dubitza, another town in the neighborhood of Belgrade, they have been repulsed, and as is suspected, with considerable loss. It is still supposed the Russian fleet will go into the Mediterranean, though it will be much retarded by the refusal of the English government to permit its sailors to engage in the voyage. Sweden and Denmark are arming from eight to twelve ships of the line each. The English and Dutch treaty you will find in the Leyden gazettes of May the 9th and 13th. That between England and Prussia is supposed to be stationary. Monsieur de St. Priest, the ambassador from this court to the Hague, has either gone, or is on the point of going. The Emperor of Morocco has declared war against England. I enclose you his orders in our favor, on that occasion. England sends a squadron to the Mediterranean for the protection of her commerce, and she is reinforcing her possessions in the two Indies. France is expecting the arrival of an embassy from Tippoo Saib, is sending some regiments to the East Indies, and a fleet of evolution into the Atlantic. Seven ships of the line and several frigates, sailed from Cadiz on the 22nd of April, destined to perform evolutions off the Western Islands, as the Spaniards say, but really to their American possessions, as is suspected. Thus the several powers are by little and little, taking the position of war, without an immediate intention of waging it. But that the present ill humor will finally end in war, is doubted by nobody.

In my letter of February the 5th, I had the honor of informing you of the discontent produced by our *Arrêt* of December the 29th, among the merchants of this country, and of the deputations from the chambers of commerce to the minister, on that subject. The articles attacked, were the privileges on the sale of our ships, and the *entrepôt* for codfish. The former I knew to be valuable: the latter I supposed not so; because during the whole of the time we have had four free ports in this kingdom, we have never used them for the smuggling of fish. I concluded, therefore, the ports of *entrepôt* would not be used for that purpose. I saw that the ministers would sacrifice something to quiet the merchants, and was glad to save the valuable article relative to our ships, by abandoning the useless one for our codfish. It was settled, therefore, in our conferences, that an *Arrêt* should be passed, abridging the former one only as to the entrepot of codfish. I was in Holland when the *Arrêt* came out; and did not get a copy of it till yesterday. Surprised to find that fish-oil was thereby also excluded from the entrepot, I have been to-day to make some inquiry into the cause; and from what I can learn, I conclude it must have been a mere error in the clerk who formed the *Arrêt*, and that it escaped attention on its passage. The *entrepôt* of whale-oil was not objected to by a single deputy at the conferences, and the excluding it is contrary to the spirit of encouragement the ministers have shown a disposition to give. I trust, therefore, I may get it altered on the first occasion which occurs, and I believe one will soon occur. In the mean time, we do not store a single drop for re-exportation, as all which comes here is needed for the consumption of this country; which will alone, according to appearances, become so considerable as to require all we can produce.

By a letter of the 8th instant, from our bankers, I learn that they had disposed of bonds enough to pay our June interest, and to replace the temporary advances made by Mr. Grand, and from a fund placed here by the State of Virginia. I have desired them, accordingly, to replace these monies, which had been lent for the moment only, and in confidence of immediate repayment. They add, that the payment of the June interest and the news from America, will, as they trust, enable them to place the remaining bonds of the last year's million. I suppose, indeed, that there is no doubt of it, and that none would have been expressed, if those two houses could draw better together than they do. In the mean time, I hope the treasury board will send an order for so much as may be necessary for executing the purposes of Congress, as to our captives at Algiers.

I send you herewith, a *Mémoire* of Monsieur Caseaux, whose name is familiar on the journals of Congress. He prepared it to be delivered to the King, but I believe he will think better, and not deliver it. The gazettes of France and Leyden accompany this.

I have the honor to be, Sir, your most obedient and most humble servant,

Th: Jefferson.

P. S. May 27, 1788. I have kept my letter open to the moment of Mr. Warville's departure (he being the bearer of it), that I might add any new incidents that should occur. The refusal of the *Châtelet* and *Grande Chambre* of Paris to act in the new character assigned them, continues. Many of the *grandes bailliages* accept, some conditionally, some fully. This will facilitate greatly the measures of government, and may possibly give them a favorable issue. The parliament of Toulouse, considering the edicts as nullities, went on with their business. They have been exiled in consequence. Monsieur de St. Priest left

Paris for the Hague, on the 23rd. I mention this fact, because it denotes the acquiescence of this government in the late revolution there. A second division of a Spanish fleet will put to sea soon. Its destination not declared. Sweden is arming to a greater extent than was at first supposed. From twelve so sixteen sail of the line are spoken of, on good grounds, Denmark, for her own security, must arm in proportion to this. T. J.

LETTER CXXXVII.—TO JOHN BROWN, May 26,1788

TO JOHN BROWN.

Paris, May 26,1788.

Dear Sir,

It was with great pleasure I saw your name on the roll of Delegates, but I did not know you had actually come onto New-York, till Mr. Paradise informed me of it. Your removal from Carolina to Kentucky was not an indifferent event to me. I wish to see that country in the hands of people well disposed, who know the value of the connection between that and the maritime States, and who wish to cultivate it. I consider their happiness as bound up together, and that every measure should be taken, which may draw the bands of union tighter. It will be an efficacious one to receive them into Congress, as I perceive they are about to desire to this be added an honest and disinterested conduct in Congress, as to every thing relating to them, we may hope for a perfect harmony. The navigation of the Mississippi was, perhaps, the strongest trial to which the justice of the federal government could be put. If ever they thought wrong about it, I trust they have got to rights. I should think it proper for the western country to defer pushing their right to that navigation to extremity, as long as they can do without it, tolerably; but that the moment it becomes absolutely necessary for them, it will become the duty of the maritime states to push it to every extremity, to which they would their own right of navigating the Chesapeake, the Delaware, the Hudson, or any other water. A time of peace will not be the surest for obtaining this object. Those, therefore, who have influence in the new country, would act wisely, to endeavor to keep things quiet till the western parts of Europe shall be engaged in war. Notwithstanding the aversion of the courts of London and Versailles to war, it is not certain that some incident may not engage them in it. England, France, Spain, Russia, Sweden, and Denmark will all have fleets at sea, or ready to put to sea immediately. Who can answer for the prudence of all their officers? War is their interest. Even their courts are pacific from impotence only, not from disposition. I wish to Heaven that our new government may see the importance of putting themselves immediately into a respectable position. To make provision for the speedy payment of their foreign debts, will be the first operation necessary. This will give them credit. A concomitant one should be, magazines and manufactures of arms. This country is at present in a crisis of very uncertain issue. I am in hopes it will be a favorable one to the rights and happiness of the people; and that this will take place quietly. Small changes in the late regulations will render them wholly good. The campaign opens between the Turks and the two empires, with an aspect rather favorable to the former. The Russians seem not yet thawed from the winter's torpitude. They have no army yet in motion: and the Emperor has been worsted in two thirds of the small actions, which they have had as yet. He is said to be rather retiring. I do not think, however, that the success of the Turks in the partisan affairs which have taken place, can authorize us to presume, that they will be superior also in great decisions. Their want of discipline and skill in military manoeuvres is of little consequence in small engagements, and of great in larger ones. Their grand army was at Adrianople by the last accounts, and to get from thence to Belgrade will require a month. It will be that time at least then, before we can have any very interesting news from them. In the mean time, the plague rages at Constantinople to a terrible degree. I cannot think but that it would be desirable to all commercial nations, to have that nation and all its dependencies driven from the sea-coast, into the interior parts of Asia and Africa. What a field would, thus be restored to commerce! The finest parts of the old world are now dead, in a great degree, to commerce, to arts, to science, and to society. Greece, Syria, Egypt, and the northern coast of Africa, constituted the whole world almost for the Romans, and to us they are scarcely known, scarcely accessible at all. The present summer will enable us to judge, what turn this contest will take. I am greatly anxious to hear that nine States accept our new constitution. We must be contented to accept of its good, and to cure what is evil in it hereafter. It seems necessary for our happiness at home; I am sure it is so for our respectability abroad. I shall, at all times, be glad to hear from you, from New York, from Kentucky, or whatever region of the earth you inhabit; being with sentiments of very sincere esteem and attachment, Dear Sir, your friend and servant,

Th: Jefferson.

LETTER CXXXVIII.—TO WILLIAM CARMICHAEL, May 27, 1788

TO WILLIAM CARMICHAEL.

Paris, May 27, 1788.

Dear Sir,

Your favors of April the 14th and 29th, and May the 8th, have lately come to hand. That of January the 29th, by M. de Moinedo, had been left here during my absence on a journey to Amsterdam. That gentleman had gone, as I presume, before my return, from my being unable to learn any thing of him.

With respect to the Isthmus of Panama, I am assured by Burgoine (who would not chose to be named, however), that a survey was made, that a canal appeared very practicable, and that the idea was suppressed for political reasons altogether. He has seen and minutely examined the report. This report is to me a vast *desideratum*, for reasons political and philosophical. I cannot help suspecting the Spanish squadrons to be gone to South America, and that some disturbances have been excited there by the British. The court of Madrid may suppose we would not see this with an unwilling eye. This may be true as to the uninformed part of our people: but those who look into futurity farther than the present moment or age, and who combine well what is, with what is to be, must see that our interests, well understood, and our wishes are, that Spain shall (not for ever, but) very long retain her possessions in that quarter; and that her views and ours must, in a good degree, and for a long time, concur. It is said in our gazettes, that the Spaniards have sunk one of our boats on the Mississippi, and that our people retaliated on one of theirs. But my letters, not mentioning this fact, have made me hope it is not true, in which hope your letter confirms me. There are now one hundred thousand inhabitants in Kentucky. They have accepted the offer of independence, on the terms proposed by Virginia, and they have decided that their independent government shall begin on the first day of the next year. In the mean time, they claim admittance into Congress. Georgia has ceded her western territory to the United States, to take place with the commencement of the new federal government. I do not know the boundaries. There has been some dispute of etiquette with the new French minister, which has disgusted him.

The following is a state of the progress and prospects of the new plan of government.

The conduct of Massachusetts has been noble. She accepted the constitution, but voted that it should stand as a perpetual instruction to her Delegates, to endeavor to obtain such and such reformations; and the minority, though very strong both in numbers and abilities, declared *viritim* and *seriatim*, that acknowledging the principle that the majority must give the law, they would now support the new constitution with their tongues, and with their blood, if necessary. I was much pleased with many and essential parts of this instrument, from the beginning. But I thought I saw in it many faults, great and small. What I have read and reflected, has brought me over from several of my objections, of the first moment, and to acquiesce under some others. Two only remain, of essential consideration, to wit, the want of a bill of rights, and the expunging the principle of necessary rotation in the offices of President and Senator. At first, I wished that when nine States should have accepted the constitution, so as to insure us what is good in it, the other four might hold off till the want of the bill of rights at least, might be supplied. But I am now convinced that the plan of Massachusetts is the best, that is, to accept and to amend afterwards. If the States which were to decide after her, should all do the same, it is impossible but they must obtain the essential amendments. It will be more difficult, if we lose this instrument, to recover what is good in it, than to correct what is bad, after we shall have adopted it. It has, therefore, my hearty prayers, and I wait with anxiety for news of the votes of Maryland, South Carolina, and Virginia. There is no doubt that General Washington will accept the presidentship; though he is silent on the subject. He would not be chosen to the Virginia convention. A riot has taken place in New York, which I will state to you from an eye-witness. It has long been a practice with the surgeons of that city, to steal from the grave bodies recently buried. A citizen had lost his wife: he went, the first or second evening after her burial, to pay a visit to her grave.. He found that it had been disturbed, and suspected from what quarter. He found means to be admitted to the anatomical lecture of that day, and on his entering the room, saw the body of his wife, naked and under dissection. He raised the people immediately. The body, in the mean time, was secreted. They entered into and searched the houses of the physicians whom they most suspected, but found nothing. One of them however more guilty or more timid than the rest, took asylum in the prison. The mob considered this an acknowledgment of guilt. They attacked the prison. The Governor ordered militia to protect the culprit, and suppress the mob. The militia, thinking the mob had just provocation, refused to turn out. Hereupon the people of more reflection, thinking it more dangerous that even a guilty person should be punished without the forms of law, than that he should escape, armed themselves, and went to protect the physician. They were received by the mob with a volley of stones, which wounded several of them. They hereupon fired on the mob and killed four. By this time, they received a reinforcement of other citizens of the militia horse, the appearance of which, in the critical moment, dispersed the mob. So ended this chapter of history, which I have detailed to you, because it may be represented as a political riot, when politics had nothing to do with it. Mr. Jay and Baron Steuben were both grievously wounded in the head by stones. The former still kept his bed, and the latter his room, when the packet sailed, which was the 24th of April. I am, with sentiments of great esteem and respect, Dear Sir, your most obedient and most humble servant,

Th: Jefferson.

LETTER CXXXIX.—TO JOHN JAY, May 27, 1788

TO JOHN JAY.

(Private.) Paris, May 27, 1788.

Dear Sir,

The change which is likely to take place in the form of our government, seems to render it proper, that, during the existence of the present government, an article should be mentioned which concerns me personally. Uncertain, however, how far Congress may have decided to do business when so near the close of their administration; less capable than those on the spot of foreseeing the character of the new government; and not fully confiding in my own judgment, where it is so liable to be seduced by feeling, I take the liberty of asking your friendly counsel, and that of my friend Mr. Madison, and of referring the matter to your judgments and discretion.

Mr. Barclay when in Europe was authorized to settle all the European accounts of the United States: he settled those of Dr. Franklin and Mr. Adams, and it was intended between us, that he should settle mine. But as what may be done at any time is often put off to the last, this settlement had been made to give way to others, and that of Beaumarchais being pressed on Mr. Barclay before his departure for Morocco, and having long retarded his departure, it was agreed that my affair should await his return from that mission: you know the circumstances which prevented his return to Paris after that mission was finished. My account is therefore unsettled, but I have no anxiety on any article of it, except one, that is, the outfit. This consists of, 1. clothes; 2. carriage and horses; 3. household furniture. When Congress made their first appointments of ministers to be resident in Europe, I have understood (for I was not then in Congress) that they allowed them all their expenses, and a fixed sum over and above for their time. Among their expenses, was necessarily understood their outfit. Afterwards they thought proper to give them fixed salaries of eleven thousand one hundred and eleven dollars and one ninth a year; and again, by a resolution of May the 6th and 8th, 1784, the 'salaries' of their ministers at foreign courts were reduced to nine thousand dollars, to take place on the 1st of August ensuing. On the 7th of May I was appointed, in addition to Mr. Adams and Dr. Franklin, for the negotiation of treaties of commerce; but this appointment being temporary, for two years only, and not as of a resident minister, the article of outfit did not come into question. I asked an advance of six months' salary, that I might be in cash to meet the first expenses; which was ordered. The year following, I was appointed to succeed Dr. Franklin at this court. This was the first appointment of a minister resident, since the original ones, under which all expenses were to be paid. So much of the ancient regulation, as respected annual expenses, had been altered to a sum certain; so much of it as respected first expenses, or outfit, remained unaltered; and I might therefore expect, that the actual expenses for outfit were to be paid. When I prepared my account for settlement with Mr. Barclay, I began a detail of the articles of clothes, carriage, horses, and household furniture. I found that they were numerous, minute, and incapable, from their nature, of being vouched; and often entered in my memorandum-book under a general head only, so that I could not specify them. I found they would exceed a year's salary. Supposing, therefore, that, mine being the first case, Congress would make a precedent of it, and prefer a sum fixed for the outfit, as well as the salary, I have charged it in my account at a year's salary; presuming there can be no question that an outfit is a reasonable charge. It is the usage here (and I suppose at all courts), that a minister resident, shall establish his house in the first instant. If this is to be done out of his salary, he will be a twelvemonth at least without a copper to live on. It is the universal practice, therefore, of all nations, to allow the outfit as a separate article from the salary. I have inquired here into the usual amount of it. I find that, sometimes, the sovereign pays the actual cost. This is particularly the case of the Sardinian ambassador now coming here, who is to provide a service of plate, and every article of furniture, and other matters of first expense, to be paid for by his court. In other instances, they give a service of plate, and a fixed sum for all other articles, which fixed sum is in no case lower than a year's salary.

I desire no service of plate, having no ambition for splendor. My furniture, carriage, and apparel are all plain, yet they have cost me more than a year's salary. I suppose that in every country, and in every condition of life, a year's expense would be found a moderate measure for the furniture of a man's house. It is not more certain to me, that the sun will rise to-morrow, than that our government must allow the outfit, on their future appointment of foreign ministers; and it would be hard on me, so to stand between the discontinuance of a former rule, and institution of a future one, as to have the benefit of neither. I know, I have so long known the character of our federal head, in its present form, that I have the most unlimited confidence in the justice of its decisions. I think I am so far known to many of the present Congress, as that I may be cleared of all views of making money out of any public employment, or of desiring any thing beyond actual and decent expenses, proportioned to the station in which they have been pleased to place me, and to the respect they would wish to see attached to it. It would seem right, that they should decide the claims of those who have acted under their administration, and their pretermission of any article, might amount to a disallowance of it in the opinion of the new government. It would be painful to me to meet that government with a claim under this kind of cloud, and to pass it in review before their several Houses of legislation, and boards of administration, to whom I shall be unknown; and being for money actually expended, it would be too inconvenient to me to relinquish it in silence. I anxiously ask it, therefore, to be decided on by Congress before they go out of office, if it be not out of the line of proceeding they may have chalked out for themselves. If it be against their inclination to determine it, would it be agreeable to them to refer it to the new government, by some resolution, which should show they have not meant to disallow it, by passing it over? Not knowing the circumstances under which Congress may exist and act at the moment you shall receive this, I am unable to judge what should be done on this subject. It is therefore that I ask the aid of your friendship and that of Mr. Madison, that you will do for me in this regard, what you think it is right should be done, and what it would be right for me to do, were I on the spot, or were I apprized of all existing circumstances. Indeed, were you two to think my claim an improper one, I would wish it to be suppressed, as I have so much confidence in your judgment, that I should suspect my own in any case where it varied from yours, and more especially, in one where it is liable to be warped by feeling. Give me leave, then, to ask your consultation with Mr. Madison on this subject; and to assure you that whatever you are so good as to do herein, will be perfectly approved, and considered as a great obligation conferred on him, who has the honor to be, with sentiments of the most perfect esteem and attachment, Dear Sir, your friend and servant,

Th: Jefferson.

LETTER CXL.*—TO JAMES MADISON, May 28, 1788

TO JAMES MADISON.

Paris, May 28, 1788.

Dear Sir,

The enclosed letter for Mr. Jay, being of a private nature. I have thought it better to put it under your cover, lest it might be opened by some of his clerks, in the case of his absence. But I enclose a press copy of it for yourself, as you will perceive the subject of it referred to you, as well as to him. I ask your aid in it so far as you think right, and to have done what you think right. If you will now be so good as to cast your eye over the copy enclosed, what follows the present sentence, will be some details, supplementary to that only, necessary for your information, but not proper for me to state to Mr. Jay.

[It will be seen that a few words of this letter are in cipher. It is published, however, as written, because enough of it is literal to interest the reader, to whom also a specimen of the cipher, used by the Author, may not be unacceptable.]*

378.227.1247. though appointed a minister resident at the court of 514. he never was 663. in that character. He was continually passing from 1042. to 514. and 514. to 1042., so that he had no occasion to establish a household at either. Accordingly, he staid principally in furnished lodgings. Of all our ministers, he had the least occasion for an outfit, and I suppose spent almost nothing on that article. He was of a disposition, too, to restrain himself within any limits of expense whatever, and it suited his recluse turn, which is, to avoid society. Should he judge of what others should do, by what he did, it would be an improper criterion. He was in Europe as a voyageur only, and it was while the salary was five hundred guineas more than at present.

145.1267.1046.7. he came over, when, instead of outfit and salary, all expenses were paid. Of rigorous honesty, and careless of appearances, he lived for a considerable time as an economical private individual. After he was fixed at 812.141. and the salary at a sum certain, he continued his economical style, till, out of the difference between his expenses and his salary, he could purchase furniture for his house. This was the easier, as the salary was at two thousand five hundred guineas then. He was obliged, too, to be passing between 1042. and 812.141. so as to avoid any regular current of expenses. When he established himself, his pecuniary affairs were under the direction of 964.814.7.101.994., one of the most estimable characters on earth, and the most attentive and honorable economists. Neither had a wish to lay up a copper, but both wished to make both ends meet. I suspected, however, from an expression dropped in conversation, that they were not able to do this, and that a deficit in their accounts appeared in their winding up. If this conjecture be true, it is a proof that the salary, so far from admitting savings, is unequal to a very plain style of life; for such was theirs. I presume Congress will be asked to allow it, and it is evident to me, from what I saw while in 1093. that it ought to be done, as they did not expend a shilling which should have been avoided. Would it be more eligible to set the example of making good a deficit, or to give him an outfit, which will cover it? The impossibility of living on the sum allowed, respectably, was the true cause of his insisting on his recall. 821.267.1292. He came over while all expenses were paid. He rented a house with standing furniture, such as tables, chairs, presses, &c., and bought all other necessaries. The latter were charged in his account; the former was included in the article of house-rent, and paid during the whole time of his stay here; and as the established rate of hire for furniture is from thirty to forty per cent, per annum, the standing furniture must have been paid for three times over, during the eight years he staid here. His salary was two thousand five hundred guineas. When Congress reduced it to less than two thousand, he refused to accede to it, asked his recall, and insisted that whenever they chose to alter the conditions on which he came out, if he did not approve of it, they ought to replace him in America on the old conditions. He lived plain, but as decently as his salary would allow. He saved nothing, but avoided debt. He knew he could not do this on the reduced salary, and therefore asked his recall with decision.

To 935.145. succeeded. He had established a certain style of living. The same was expected from 1214. and there were five hundred guineas a year less to do it on. It has been aimed at, however, as far as was practicable. This rendered it constantly necessary to step neither to the right nor to the left, to incur any expense which could possibly be avoided, and it called for an almost womanly attention to the details of the household, equally perplexing, disgusting, and inconsistent with business. You will be sensible, that, in this situation, no savings could be made for reimbursing the half year's salary, ordered to be advanced under the former commission, and more than as much again, which was unavoidably so applied, without order, for the purchase of the outfit. The reason of the thing, the usage of all nations, the usage of our own, by paying all expenses of preceding ministers, which gave them the outfit, as far as their circumstances appeared to them to render it necessary, have made me take for granted all along, that it would not be refused to me: nor should I have mentioned it now, but that the administration is passing into other hands, and more complicated forms. It would be disagreeable to me to be presented to them, in the first instance, as a suitor. Men come into business at first with visionary principles. It is practice alone, which can correct and conform them to the actual current of affairs. In the mean time, those to whom their errors were first applied, have been their victims. The government may take up the project of appointing foreign ministers without outfits, and they may ruin two or three individuals, before they find that that article is just as indispensable as the salary. They must then fall into the current of general usage, which has become general, only because experience has established its necessity. Upon the whole, be so good as to reflect on it, and to do, not what your friendship to me, but your opinion of what is right, shall dictate.

Accept, in all cases, assurances of the sincere esteem and respect with which I am, Dear Sir, your friend and servant,

Th: Jefferson.

LETTER CXLI.—TO PETER CARU, May 23, 1788

TO PETER CARU.

Paris, May 23, 1788.

Dear Peter,

The preceding letter [* For the letter referred to, see ante, LXXIV.] was written at its date, and I supposed you in possession of it, when your letters of December the 10th, 1787, and March the 18th, 1788, told me otherwise. Still I supposed it on its way to you, when a few days ago, having occasion to look among some papers in the drawer, where my letters are usually put away, till an opportunity of sending them occurs, I found that this letter had slipped among them, so that it had never been forwarded. I am sorry for it, on account of the remarks relative to the Spanish language only. Apply to that with all the assiduity you can. That language and the English covering nearly the whole face of America, they should be well known to every inhabitant, who means to look beyond the limits of his farm. I like well the distribution of your time, mentioned in your letter of March the 18th; and the counsels of Mr. Wythe, so kindly extended to you, leave it necessary for me to add nothing of that kind. Be assiduous in learning, take much exercise for your health, and practise much virtue. Health, learning, and virtue, will insure your happiness; they will give you a quiet conscience, private esteem, and public honor. Beyond these, we want nothing but physical necessaries, and they are easily obtained. My daughters are well, and join me in love to yourself, your mother, brothers, and sisters.

I am, with very sincere esteem, Dear Peter, your affectionate

friend,

Th: Jefferson.

LETTER CXLII.—TO THE COMTE DE BERNSTORFF, June 19, 1788

TO THE COMTE DE BERNSTORFF.

Paris, June 19, 1788.

I had the honor of addressing your Excellency, by Admiral Paul Jones, on the 21st of January, on the subject of the prizes taken under his command during the late war, and sent into Bergen. I communicated at the same time a copy of the powers which the Congress of the United States of America had been pleased to confide to me therein, having previously shown the original to the Baron de Blome, Envoy Extraordinary of his Majesty, the King of Denmark, at this court; and I furnished, at the same time, to Admiral Paul Jones, such authority as I was empowered to delegate, for the arrangement of this affair. That officer has transmitted me a copy of your Excellency's letter to him of the 4th of April, wherein you are pleased to observe, that the want of full powers on his part was an invincible obstacle to the definitive discussion of this claim with him, and to express your dispositions to institute a settlement at this place. Always assured of the justice and honor of the court of Denmark, and encouraged by the particular readiness of your Excellency to settle and remove this difficulty from between the two nations, I take the liberty of recalling your attention to it. The place of negotiation proposed by your Excellency, meets no objection from us, and it removes, at the same time, that which the want of full powers in Admiral Paul Jones had produced in your mind. These full powers Congress have been pleased to honor me with. The arrangement taken between the person to be charged with your full powers and myself, will be final and conclusive. You are pleased to express a willingness to treat at the same time on the subjects of amity and commerce. The powers formerly communicated on our part, were given to Mr. Adams, Doctor Franklin, and myself, for a limited term only. That term has expired, and the other two gentlemen returned to America; so that no person is commissioned at this moment to renew those conferences. I may safely, however, assure your Excellency, that the same friendly dispositions still continue, and the same desire of facilitating and encouraging a commerce between the two nations, which produced the former appointment. But our nation is, at this time, proposing a change in the organization of its government. For this change to be agreed to by all the members of the Union, the new administration chosen and brought into activity, their domestic matters arranged, which will require their first attention, their foreign system afterwards decided on and carried into full execution, will require very considerable length of time. To place under the same delay the private claims which I have the honor to present to your Excellency, would be hard on the persons interested: because these claims have no connection with the system of commercial connection, which may be established between the two nations, nor with the particular form of our administration. The justice due to them is complete, and the present administration as competent to final settlement as any future one will be, should a future change take place. These individuals have already lingered nine years in expectation of their hard and perilous earnings. Time lessens their numbers continually, disperses their representatives, weakens the evidence of their right, and renders more and more impracticable his Majesty's dispositions to repair the private injury, to which public circumstances constrained him. These considerations, the just and honorable intentions of your Excellency, and the assurances you give us in your letter, that no delay is wished on your part, give me strong hopes that we may speedily obtain that final arrangement, which express instructions render it my duty to urge. I have the honor, therefore, of agreeing with your Excellency, that the settlement of this matter, formerly begun at Paris, shall be continued there; and to ask that you will be pleased to give powers and instructions for this purpose to such persons as you shall think proper, and in such full form as may prevent those delays, to which the distance between Copenhagen and Paris might otherwise expose us.

I have the honor to be, with sentiments of the most profound respect, your Excellency's most obedient and most humble servant,

Th: Jefferson.

LETTER CXLIII.—TO THE COUNT DE MONTMORIN, June 20, 1788

TO THE COUNT DE MONTMORIN.

Paris, June 20, 1788.

Sir,

Having had the honor of mentioning to your Excellency the wish of Congress, that certain changes should be made in the articles for a consular convention, which had been sent to them, I have now that, conformably to the desire you expressed, of giving a general idea of the alterations to be proposed.

The fourth article gives to the consuls the immunities of the law of nations. It has been understood, however, that the laws of France do not admit of this; and that it might be desirable to expunge this article. In this we are ready to concur, as in every other case, where an article might call for changes in the established laws, either inconvenient or disagreeable.

After establishing in favor of consuls, the general immunities of the law of nations, one consequence of which would have been, that they could not have been called upon to give testimony in courts of justice, the fifth article requires, that after the observance of certain formalities, which imply very high respect, they shall make a declaration; but *in their own houses* [*chez eux*] as may be pretended, if not justly inferred, from the expressions in the article. But our laws require, indispensably, a personal examination of witnesses in the presence of the parties, of their counsel, the jury, and judges, each of whom has a right to ask of them all questions pertinent to the fact. The first and highest officers of our government are obliged to appear personally to the order of a court, to give evidence. The court takes care that they are treated with respect. It is proposed, therefore, to omit this article for these particular reasons, as well as for the general one, that the fourth being expunged, this, which was but an exception to that, falls of course.

The seventh, eighth, tenth, and fourteenth articles extend their pre-eminences far beyond those, which the laws of nations would have given. These articles require that the declarations made in the presence of consuls, and certified by them, shall be received in evidence in all courts whatever: and, in some instances, give to their certificates a credibility which excludes all other testimony. The cases are rare, in which our laws admit written evidence of facts; and such evidence, when admitted, must have been given in the presence of both parties, and must contain the answers to all the pertinent questions, which they may have desired to ask of the witness: and to no evidence, of whatever nature, written or oral, do our laws give so high credit, as to exclude all counter-proof. These principles are of such ancient foundation in our system of jurisprudence, and are so much valued and venerated by our citizens, that perhaps it would be impossible to execute articles, which should contravene them, nor is it imagined that these stipulations can be so interesting to this country, as to balance the inconvenience and hazard of such an innovation with us. Perhaps it might be found, that the laws of both countries require a modification of this article; as it is inconceivable that the certificate of an American consul in France could be permitted by one of its courts to establish a fact, the falsehood of which should be notorious to the court itself.

The eighth article gives to the consuls of either nation a jurisdiction, in certain cases, over foreigners of any other. On a dispute arising in France, between an American and a Spaniard or an Englishman, it would not be fair to abandon the Spaniard or Englishman to an American consul. On the contrary, the territorial judge, as neutral, would seem to be the most impartial. Probably, therefore, it will be thought convenient for both parties, to correct this stipulation.

A dispute arising between two subjects of France, the one being in France and the other in the United States, the regular tribunals of France would seem entitled to a preference of jurisdiction. Yet the twelfth article gives it to their consul in America; and to the consul of the United States in France, in a like case between their citizens.

The power given by the tenth article, of arresting and sending back a vessel, its captain, and crew, is a very great one indeed, and, in our opinion, more safely lodged with the territorial judge. We would ourselves trust the tribunals of France to decide, when there is just cause for so high-handed an act of authority over the persons and property of so many of our citizens, to all of whom these tribunals will stand in a neutral and impartial relation, rather than any single person whom we may appoint as consul, who will seldom be learned in the laws, and often susceptible of influence from private interest and personal pique. With us, applications for the arrest of vessels, and of their masters, are made to the admiralty courts. These are composed of the most learned and virtuous characters in the several States, and the maritime law, common to all nations, is the rule of their proceedings. The exercise of foreign jurisdiction, within the pale of their own laws, in a very high case, and wherein those laws have made honorable provisions, would be a phenomenon never yet seen in our country, and which would be seen with great jealousy and uneasiness. On the contrary, to leave this power with the territorial judge will inspire confidence and friendship, and be really, at the same time, more secure against abuse. The power of arresting deserted seamen seems necessary for the purposes of navigation and commerce, and will be more attentively and effectually exercised by the consul, than by the territorial judge. To this part of the tenth article, therefore, as well as to that which requires the territorial judge to assist the consul in the exercise of this function, we can accede. But the extension of the like power to passengers, seems not necessary for the purposes either of navigation or commerce. It does not come, therefore, within the functions of the consul, whose institution is for those two objects only, nor within the powers of a commissioner, authorized to treat and conclude a convention, solely for regulating the powers, privileges, and duties of consuls. The arrest and detention of passengers, moreover, would often be in contradiction to our bills of rights, which, being fundamental, cannot be obstructed in their operation by any law or convention whatever.

Consular institutions being entirely new with us, Congress think it wise to make their first convention probationary, and not perpetual. They propose, therefore, a clause for limiting its duration to a certain term of years. If after the experience of a few years, it should be found to answer the purposes intended by it, both parties will have sufficient inducements to renew it, either in its present form, or with such alterations and amendments, as time, experience, and other circumstances may indicate.

The convention, as expressed in the French language, will fully answer our purposes in France, because it will there be understood. But it will not equally answer the purposes of France in America, because it will not there be understood. In very few of the courts, wherein it may be presented, will there be found a single judge or advocate, capable of translating it at all, much less of giving to all its terms, legal and technical, their exact equivalent in the laws and language of that country. Should any translation which Congress would undertake to publish, for the use of our courts, be conceived on any occasion not to render fully the idea of the French original, it might be imputed as an indirect attempt to abridge or extend the terms of a contract, at the will of one party only. At no place are there better helps than here, for establishing an English text equivalent to the French, in all its phrases; no persons can be supposed to know what is meant by these phrases, better than those who form them; and no time more proper to ascertain their meaning in both languages than that at which they are formed. I have, therefore, the honor to propose, that the convention shall be faithfully expressed in English as well as in French, in two columns, side by side, that these columns be declared each of them to be text, and to be equally original and authentic in all courts of justice.

This, Sir, is a general sketch of the alterations, which our laws and our manner of thinking render necessary in this convention, before the faith of our country is engaged for its execution. Some of its articles, in their present form, could not be executed at all, and others would produce embarrassments and ill humor, to which it would not be prudent for our government to commit itself. Inexact execution on the one part, would naturally beget dissatisfaction and complaints on the other; and an instrument intended to strengthen our connection, might thus become the means of loosening it. Fewer articles, better observed, will better promote our common interests. As to ourselves, we do not find the institution of consuls very necessary. Its history commences in times of barbarism, and might well have ended with them. During these, they were, perhaps, useful, and may still be so in countries not yet emerged from that condition. But all civilized nations at this day understand so well the advantages of commerce, that they provide protection and encouragement for merchant strangers and vessels coming among them. So extensive, too, have commercial connections now become, that every mercantile house has correspondents in almost every port. They address their vessels to these correspondents, who are found to take better care of their interests, and to obtain more effectually the protection of the laws of the country for them, than the consul of their nation can. He is generally a foreigner, unpossessed of the little details of knowledge of greatest use to them. He makes national questions of all the difficulties which arise; the correspondent prevents them. We carry on commerce with good success in all parts of the world; yet we have not a consul in a single port, nor a complaint for the want of one, except from the persons who wish to be consuls themselves. Though these considerations may not be strong enough to establish the absolute inutility of consuls, they may make us less anxious to extend their privileges and jurisdictions, so as to render them objects of jealousy and irritation, in the places of their residence. That this government thinks them useful, is sufficient reason for us to give them all the functions and facilities which our circumstances will admit. Instead, therefore, of declining every article which will be useless to us, we accede to every one which will not be inconvenient. Had this nation been alone concerned, our desire to gratify them might have tempted us to press still harder on the laws and opinions of our country. But your Excellency knows, that we stand engaged in treaties with some nations, which will give them occasion to claim whatever privileges we yield to any other. This renders circumspection more necessary. Permit me to add one other observation. The English allow to foreign consuls scarcely any functions within their ports. This proceeds, in a great measure, from the character of their laws, which eye, with peculiar jealousy, every exemption from their control. Ours are the same in their general character, and rendered still more unpliant, by our having thirteen parliaments to relax, instead of one. Upon the whole, I hope your Excellency will see the causes of the delay which this convention has met with, in the difficulties it presents, and our desire to surmount them: and will be sensible that the alterations proposed, are dictated to us by the necessity of our circumstances, and by a caution, which cannot be disapproved, to commit ourselves to no engagements which we foresee we might not be able o fulfil.

These alterations, with some other smaller ones, which may be offered on the sole principle of joint convenience, shall be the subject of more particular explanation, whenever your Excellency shall honor me with a conference thereon. I shall then, also, point out the verbal changes which appear to me necessary, to accommodate the instrument to the views before expressed. In the mean time, I have the honor to be, with sentiments of the most perfect respect and esteem, your Excellency's most obedient and most humble servant,

Th: Jefferson.

LETTER CXLIV.—TO DOCTOR GORDON, July 16, 1788

TO DOCTOR GORDON.

Paris, July 16, 1788.

Sir,

In your favor of the 8th instant, you mentioned that you had written to me in February last. This letter never came to hand. That of April the 24th came here during my absence on a journey through Holland and Germany; and my having been obliged to devote the first moments after my return to some very pressing matters, must be my apology for not having been able to write to you till now. As soon as I knew that it would be agreeable to you to have such a disposal of your work for translation, as I had made for Dr. Ramsay, I applied to the same bookseller with propositions on your behalf. He told me, that he had lost so much by that work, that he could hardly think of undertaking another, and, at any rate, not without first seeing and examining it. As he was the only bookseller I could induce to give any thing on the former occasion, I went to no other with my proposal, meaning to ask you to send me immediately as much of the work as is printed. This you can do by the Diligence, which comes three times a week from London to Paris. Furnished with this, I will renew my proposition, and do the best for you I can; though I fear that the ill success of the translation of Dr. Ramsay's work, and of another work on the subject of America, will permit less to be done for you than I had hoped. I think Dr. Ramsay failed from the inelegance of the translation, and the translator's having departed entirely from the Doctor's instructions. I will be obliged to you, to set me down as subscriber for half a dozen copies, and to ask Mr. Trumbull (No. 2, North street, Rathbone Place) to pay you the whole subscription price for me, which he will do on showing him this letter. These copies can be sent by the Diligence. I have not yet received the pictures Mr. Trumbull was to send me, nor consequently that of M. de la Fayette. I will take care of it when it arrives. His title is simply, Le Marquis de la Fayette.

You ask, in your letter of April the 24th, details of my sufferings by Colonel Tarleton. I did not suffer by him. On the contrary, he behaved very genteelly with me. On his approach to Charlottesville, which is within three miles of my house at Monticello, he despatched a troop of his horse, under Captain McLeod, with the double object of taking me prisoner, with the two Speakers of the Senate and Delegates, who then lodged with me, and of remaining there in *vidette*, my house commanding a view often or twelve miles round about. He gave strict orders to Captain McLeod to suffer nothing to be injured. The troop failed in one of their objects, as we had notice of their coming, so that the two Speakers had gone off about two hours before their arrival at Monticello, and myself, with my family, about five minutes. But Captain McLeod preserved every thing with sacred care, during about eighteen hours that he remained there. Colonel Tarleton was just so long at Charlottesville, being hurried from thence by the news of the rising of the militia, and by a sudden fall of rain which threatened to swell the river and intercept his return. In general he did little injury to the inhabitants on that short and hasty excursion, which was of about sixty miles from their main army, then in Spotsylvania, and ours in Orange. It was early in June, 1781. Lord Cornwallis then proceeded to the Point of Fork, and encamped his army from thence all along the main James River, to a seat of mine called Elk-hill, opposite to Elk Island, and a little below the mouth of the Byrd Creek. (You will see all these places exactly laid down in the map annexed to my Notes on Virginia, printed by Stockdale.) He remained in this position ten days, his own head-quarters being in my house, at that place. I had time to remove most of the effects out of the house. He destroyed all my growing crops of corn and tobacco; he burned all my barns, containing the same articles of the last year, having first taken what corn he wanted; he used, as was to be expected, all my stock of cattle, sheep, and hogs, for the sustenance of his army, and carried off all the horses capable of service; of those too young for service he cut the throats; and he burned all the fences on the plantation so as to leave it an absolute waste. He carried off also about thirty slaves. Had this been to give them freedom, he would have done right: but it was to consign them to inevitable death from the small-pox and putrid fever, then raging in his camp. This I knew afterwards to be the fate of twenty-seven of them. I never had news of the remaining three, but presume they shared the same fate. When I say that Lord Cornwallis did all this, I do not mean that he carried about the torch in his own hands, but that it was all done under his eye; the situation of the house in which he was, commanding a view of every part of the plantation, so that he must have seen every fire. I relate these things on my own knowledge, in a great degree, as I was on the ground soon after he left it. He treated the rest of the neighborhood somewhat in the same style, but not with that spirit of total extermination with which he seemed to rage over my possessions. Wherever he went, the dwelling-houses were plundered of every thing which could be carried off. Lord Cornwallis's character in England would forbid the belief that he shared in the plunder; but that his table was served with the plate thus pillaged from private houses, can be proved by many hundred eye-witnesses. From an estimate I made at that time, on the best information I could collect, I supposed the State of Virginia lost under Lord Cornwallis's hands, that year, about thirty thousand slaves; and that of these, about twenty-seven thousand died of the small-pox and camp-fever, and the rest were partly sent to the West Indies, and exchanged for rum, sugar, coffee, and fruit, and partly sent to New York, from whence they went, at the peace, either to Nova Scotia or England. From this last place, I believe they have been lately sent to Africa. History will never relate the horrors committed by the British army, in the southern States of America. They raged in Virginia six months only, from the middle of April to the middle of October, 1781, when they were all taken prisoners; and I give you a faithful specimen of their transactions for ten days of that time, and on one spot only. *Ex pede Herculem.* I suppose their whole devastations during those six months, amounted to about three millions sterling. The copiousness of this subject has only left me space to assure you of the sentiments of esteem and respect, with which I am, Sir, your most obedient, humble servant,

Th: Jefferson.

LETTER CXLV.—TO JAMES MADISON, July 19, 1788

TO JAMES MADISON, *of William and Mary College.*

Paris, July 19, 1788.

Dear Sir,

My last letter to you was of the 13th of August last. As you seem willing to accept of the crumbs of science on which we are subsisting here, it is with pleasure I continue to hand them on to you, in proportion as they are dealt out. Herschel's volcano in the moon you have doubtless heard of, and placed among the other vagaries of a head, which seems not organized for sound induction. The wildness of the theories hitherto proposed by him, on his own discoveries, seems to authorize us to consider his merit as that of a good optician only. You know also, that Doctor Ingenhouse had discovered, as he supposed from experiment, that vegetation might be promoted by occasioning streams of the electrical fluid to pass through a plant, and that other physicians had received and confirmed this theory. He now, however, retracts it, and finds by more decisive experiments, that the electrical fluid can neither forward nor retard vegetation. Uncorrected still of the rage of drawing general conclusions from partial and equivocal observations, he hazards the opinion that light promotes vegetation. I have heretofore supposed from observation, that light affects the color of living bodies, whether vegetable or animal; but that either the one or the other receives nutriment from that fluid, must be permitted to be doubted of, till better confirmed by observation. It is always better to have no ideas, than false ones; to believe nothing, than to believe what is wrong. In my mind, theories are more easily demolished than rebuilt.

An Abbe here, has shaken, if not destroyed, the theory of De Dominis, Descartes and Newton, for explaining the phenomenon of the rainbow. According to that theory, you know, a cone of rays issuing from the sun, and falling on a cloud in the opposite part of the heavens, is reflected back in the form of a smaller cone, the apex of which is the eye of the observer: so that the eye of the observer must be in the axis of both cones, and equally distant from every part of the bow. But he observes, that he has repeatedly seen bows, the one end of which has been very near to him, and the other at a very great distance. I have often seen the same thing myself. I recollect well to have seen the end of a rainbow between myself and a house, or between myself and a bank, not twenty yards distant; and this repeatedly. But I never saw, what he says he has seen, different rainbows at the same time, intersecting each other. I never saw coexistent bows, which were not concentric also. Again, according to the theory, if the sun is in the horizon, the horizon intercepts the lower half of the bow, if above the horizon, that intercepts more than the half, in proportion. So that generally the bow is less than a semicircle, and never more. He says he has seen it more than a semicircle. I have often seen the leg of the bow below my level. My situation at Monticello admits this, because there is a mountain there in the opposite direction of the afternoon's sun, the valley between which and Monticello is five hundred feet deep. I have seen a leg of a rainbow plunge down on the river running through the valley. But I do not recollect to have remarked at any time, that the bow was more than half a circle. It appears to me, that these facts demolish the Newtonian hypothesis, but they do not support that erected in its stead by the Abbe. He supposes a cloud between the sun and observer, and that through some opening in that cloud, the rays pass, and form an iris on the opposite part of the heavens, just as a ray passing through a hole in the shutter of a darkened room, and falling on a prism there, forms the prismatic colors on the opposite wall. According to this, we might see bows of more than the half circle, as often as of less. A thousand other objections occur to this hypothesis, which need not be suggested to you. The result is, that we are wiser than we were, by having an error the less in our catalogue; but the blank occasioned by it, must remain for some happier hypothesist to fill up.

The dispute about the conversion and reconversion of water and air, is still stoutly kept up. The contradictory experiments of chemists, leave us at liberty to conclude what we please. My conclusion is, that art has not yet invented sufficient aids, to enable such subtle bodies to make a well defined impression on organs as blunt as ours: that it is laudable to encourage investigation, but to hold back conclusion. Speaking one day with Monsieur de Buffon on the present ardor of chemical inquiry, he affected to consider chemistry but as cookery, and to place the toils of the laboratory on a footing with those of the kitchen. I think it, on the contrary, among the most useful of sciences, and big with future discoveries for the utility and safety of the human race. It is yet, indeed, a mere embryon. Its principles are contested; experiments seem contradictory; their subjects are so minute as to escape our senses; and their result too fallacious to satisfy the mind. It is probably an age too soon, to propose the establishment of a system. The attempt, therefore, of Lavoisier to reform the chemical nomenclature, is premature. One single experiment may destroy the whole filiation of his terms, and his string of sulfates, sulfiles, and sulfures may have served no other end, than to have retarded the progress of the science, by a jargon, from the confusion of which, time will be requisite to extricate us. Accordingly, it is not likely to be admitted generally.

You are acquainted with the properties of the composition of nitre, salt of tartar, and sulphur, called *pulvis fulminans*. Of this, the explosion is produced by heat alone. Monsieur Bertholet, by dissolving silver in the nitrous acid, precipitating it with lime-water, and drying the precipitate on ammoniac, has discovered a powder, which fulminates most powerfully, on coming into contact with any substance whatever. Once made, it cannot be touched. It cannot be put into a bottle, but must remain in the capsula, where dried. The property of the spathic acid, to corrode flinty substances, has been lately applied by a Mr. Puymaurin, to engrave on glass, as artists engrave on copper, with aquafortis.

M. de la Place has discovered, that the secular acceleration and retardation of the moon's motion, is occasioned by the action of the sun, in proportion as his excentricity changes, or, in other words, as the orbit of the earth increases or diminishes. So that this irregularity is now perfectly calculable.

Having seen announced in a gazette, that some person had found, in a library of Sicily, an Arabic translation of Livy, which was thought to be complete, I got the *chargé des affaires* of Naples here, to write to Naples to inquire into the fact. He obtained in answer, that an Arabic translation was found, and that it would restore to us seventeen of the books lost, to wit, from the sixtieth to the seventy-seventh, inclusive: that it was in possession of an Abbe Vella, who, as soon as he shall have finished a work he has on hand, will give us an Italian, and perhaps a Latin translation of this Livy. There are persons, however, who doubt the truth of this discovery, founding their doubts on some personal circumstances relating to the person who says he has this translation. I find, nevertheless, that the *chargé des affaires* believes in the discovery, which makes me hope it may be true.

A countryman of ours, a Mr. Ledyard of Connecticut, set out from hence some time ago for St. Petersburg, to go thence to Kamtschatka, thence to cross over to the western coast of America, and penetrate through the continent, to the other side of it. He had got within a few days' journey of Kamtschatka, when he was arrested by order of the Empress of Russia, sent back, and turned adrift in Poland. He went to London; engaged under the auspices of a private society, formed there for pushing discoveries into Africa; passed by this place, which he left a few days ago for Marseilles, where he will embark for Alexandria and Grand Cairo; thence explore the Nile to its source; cross the head of the Niger, and descend that to its mouth. He promises me, if he escapes through his journey, he will go to Kentucky, and endeavor to penetrate westwardly to the South Sea.

The death of M. de Buffon you have heard long ago. I do not know whether we shall have anything posthumous of his. As to political news, this country is making its way to a good constitution. The only danger is, they may press so fast as to produce an appeal to arms, which might have an unfavorable issue for them. As yet the appeal is not made. Perhaps the war, which seems to be spreading from nation to nation, may reach them this would insure the calling of the States General, and this, as is supposed, the establishment of a constitution.

I have the honor to be, with sentiments of sincere esteem and respect, Dear Sir, your friend and servant,

Th: Jefferson.

LETTER CXLVI.—TO E. RUTLEDGE, July 18, 1788

TO E. RUTLEDGE.

Paris, July 18, 1788.

Dear Sir,

Messrs. Berard were to have given me particular accounts of the proceeds of the shipments of rice made to them. But they have failed. I fear, from what they mention, that the price has been less advantageous than usual; which is unlucky, as it falls the first essay. If on the whole, however, you get as much as you would have done by a sale on the spot, it should encourage other adventures, because the price at Havre or Rouen is commonly higher, and because I think you may, by trials, find out the way to avail yourselves of the Paris retail price. The Carolina rice, sold at Paris, is separated into three kinds; 1. the whole grains; 2. the broken grains; 3. the small stuff; and sell at ten, eight, and six livres the French pound, retail. The whole grains, which constitute the first quality, are picked out by hand. I would not recommend this operation to be done with you, because labor is dearer there than here. But I mention these prices, to show, that after making a reasonable deduction for sorting, and leaving a reasonable profit to the retailer, there should still remain a great wholesale price. I shall wish to know from you, how much your cargo of rice shipped to Berard netts you, and how much it would have *netted* in hard money, if you had sold it at home.

You promise, in your letter of October the 23rd, 1787, to give me in your next, at large, the conjectures of your philosopher on the descent of the Creek Indians from the Carthaginians, supposed to have been separated from Hanno's fleet, during his periplus. I shall be very glad to receive them, and see nothing impossible in his conjecture. I am glad he means to appeal to similarity of language, which I consider as the strongest kind of proof it is possible to adduce. I have somewhere read, that the language of the ancient Carthaginians is still spoken by their descendants, inhabiting the mountainous interior parts of Barbary, to which they were obliged to retire by the conquering Arabs. If so, a vocabulary of their tongue can still be got, and if your friend will get one of the Creek languages, the comparison will decide. He probably may have made progress in this business: but if he wishes any inquiries to be made on this side the Atlantic, I offer him my services cheerfully; my wish being, like his to ascertain the history of the American aborigines.

I congratulate you on the accesion of your State to the new federal constitution. This is the last I have yet heard of, but I expect daily to hear that my own has followed the good example, and suppose it to be already established. Our government wanted bracing. Still we must take care not to run from one extreme to another; not to brace too high. I own, I join those in opinion, who think a bill of rights necessary. I apprehend too, that the total abandonment of the principle of rotation in the offices of President and Senator, will end in abuse. But my confidence is, that there will, for a long time, be virtue and good sense enough in our countrymen, to correct abuses. We can surely boast of having set the world a beautiful example of a government reformed by reason alone, without bloodshed. But the world is too far oppressed to profit by the example. On this side of the Atlantic, the blood of the people has become an inheritance, and those who fatten on it, will not relinquish it easily. The struggle in this country is, as yet, of doubtful issue. It is, in fact, between the monarchy and the parliaments. The nation is no otherwise concerned, but as both parties may be induced to let go some of its abuses, to court the public favor. The danger is, that the people, deceived by a false cry of liberty, may be led to take side with one party, and thus give the other a pretext for crushing them still more. If they can avoid the appeal to arms, the nation will be sure to gain much by this controversy. But if that appeal is made, it will depend entirely on the disposition of the army, whether it issue in liberty or despotism. Those dispositions are not as yet known. In the mean time, there is great probability that the war kindled in the east, will spread from nation to nation, and, in the long run, become general.

I am, with the most sincere esteem and attachment, my dear; Sir, your friend and servant,

Th: Jefferson.

LETTER CXLVII.—TO MR. BELLINI, July 25,1788

TO MR. BELLINI.

Paris, July 25,1788.

Dear Sir,

Though I have written to you seldom, you are often the object of my thoughts, and always of my affection. The truth is, that the circumstances with which I am surrounded, offer little worth detailing to you. You are too wise to feel an interest in the squabbles, in which the pride, the dissipations, and the tyranny of kings, keep this hemisphere constantly embroiled. Science, indeed, finds some aliment here, and you are one of her sons. But this I have pretty regularly communicated to Mr. Madison, with whom, I am sure, you participate of it. It is with sincere pleasure I congratulate you on the good fortune of our friend Mazzei, who is appointed here, to correspond with the King of Poland. The particular character given him is not well defined, but the salary is, which is more important. It is eight thousand livres a year, which will enable him to live comfortably, while his duties will find him that occupation, without which he cannot exist. Whilst this appointment places him at his ease, it affords a hope of permanence also. It suspends, if not entirely prevents, the visit he had intended to his native country, and the return to his adoptive one, which the death of his wife had rendered possible. This last event has given him three quarters of the globe elbow-room, which he had ceded to her, on condition she would leave him quiet in the fourth. Their partition of the next world will be more difficult, if it be divided only into two parts, according to the protestant faith. Having seen by a letter you wrote him, that you were in want of a pair of spectacles, I undertook to procure you some, which I packed in a box of books addressed to Mr. Wythe, and of which I beg your acceptance. This box lay forgotten at Havre the whole of the last winter, but was at length shipped, and I trust has come to hand. I packed with the spectacles three or four pair of glasses, adapted to the different periods of life, distinguished from each other by numbers, and easily changed. You see I am looking forward in hope of a long life for you; and that it may be long enough to carry you through the whole succession of glasses, is my sincere prayer. Present me respectfully to Mrs. Bellini, assure her of my affectionate remembrance of her, and my wishes for her health and happiness; and accept yourself very sincere professions of the esteem and attachment with which I am, Dear Sir, your affectionate friend and servant,

Th: Jefferson.

LETTER CXLVIII.—TO JAMES MADISON, July 31, 1788

TO JAMES MADISON.

Paris, July 31, 1788.

Dear Sir,

My last letters to you were of the 3rd and the 25th of May. Yours from Orange, of April the 22nd, came to hand on the 10th instant.

My letter to Mr. Jay containing all the public news that is well authenticated, I will not repeat it here, but add some details in the smaller way, which you may be glad to know. The disgrace of the Marquis de la Fayette, which, at any other period of their history, would have had the worst consequences for him, will, on the contrary, mark him favorably to the nation, at present. During the present administration, he can expect nothing; but perhaps it may serve him with their successors, whenever a change shall take place. No change of the Principal will probably take place, before the meeting of the States General; though a change is to be wished, for his operations do not answer the expectations formed of him. These had been calculated, on his brilliancy in society. He is very feebly aided too. Montmorin is weak, though a most worthy character. He is indolent and inattentive too, in the extreme. Luzerne is considerably inferior in abilities to his brother, whom you know. He is a good man too, but so much out of his element, that he has the air of one *huskanoyed.* The *Garde des Sceaux* is considered as the Principal's bull-dog, braving danger like the animal. His talents do not pass mediocrity. The Archbishop's brother, and the new minister Villedeuil, and Lambert, have no will of their own. They cannot raise money for the peace establishment the next year, without the States General; much less if there be war; and their administration will probably end with the States General.

Littlepage, who was here as a secret agent for the King of Poland, rather overreached himself. He wanted more money. The King furnished it, more than once. Still he wanted more, and thought to obtain a high bid, by saying he was called for in America, and asking leave to go there. Contrary to his expectation, he received leave; but he went to Warsaw instead of America, and from thence, to join the * * * * I do not know

[Several paragraphs of this letter are in cipher, A few words here could not be deciphered.]*

these facts certainly, but collect them, by putting several things together. The King then sent an ancient secretary here, in whom he had much confidence, to look out for a correspondent, a mere letter-writer for him. A happy hazard threw Mazzei in his way. He recommended him, and he is appointed. He has no diplomatic character whatever, but is to receive eight thousand livres a year, as an intelligencer. I hope this employment may have some permanence. The danger is, that he will over-act his part.

The Marquis de la Luzerne had been for many years married to his brother's wife's sister, secretly. She was ugly and deformed, but sensible, amiable, and rather rich. When he was ambassador to London, with ten thousand guineas a year, the marriage was avowed, and he relinquished his cross of Malta, from which he derived a handsome revenue for life, and which was very open to advancement. Not long ago, she died. His real affection for her, which was great and unfeigned, and perhaps the loss of his order, for so short-lived a satisfaction, has thrown him almost into a state of despondency. He is now here.

I send you a book of Dupont's, on the subject of the commercial treaty with England. Though its general matter may not be interesting, yet you will pick up, in various parts of it, such excellent principles and observations, as will richly repay the trouble of reading it. I send you, also, two little pamphlets of the Marquis de Condorcet, wherein is the most judicious statement I have seen, of the great questions which agitate this nation at present. The new regulations present a preponderance of good over their evil; but they suppose that the King can model the constitution at will, or, in other words, that his government is a pure despotism. The question then arising is, whether a pure despotism in a single head, or one which is divided among a king, nobles, priesthood, and numerous magistracy, is the least bad. I should be puzzled to decide: but I hope they will have neither, and that they are advancing to a limited, moderate government, in which the people will have a good share.

I sincerely rejoice at the acceptance of our new constitution by nine States. It is a good canvass, on which some strokes only want retouching. What these are, I think are sufficiently manifested by the general voice from north to south, which calls for a bill of rights. It seems pretty generally understood, that this should go to juries, *habeas corpus*, standing armies, printing, religion, and monopolies. I conceive there may be difficulty in finding general modifications of these, suited to the habits of all the States. But if such cannot be found, then it is better to establish trials by jury, the right of *habeas corpus*, freedom of the press, and freedom of religion, in all cases, and to abolish standing armies in time of peace, and monopolies in all cases, than not to do it in any. The few cases wherein these things may do evil, cannot be weighed against the multitude, wherein the want of them will do evil. In disputes between a foreigner and a native, a trial by jury may be improper. But if this exception cannot be agreed to, the remedy will be to model the jury, by giving the *medietas linguæ*, in civil as well as criminal cases. Why suspend the *habeas corpus* in insurrections and rebellions? The parties who may be arrested, may be charged instantly with a well-defined crime: of course, the judge will remand them. If the public safety requires, that the government should have a man imprisoned on less probable testimony in those than in other emergencies, let him be taken and tried, retaken and retried, while the necessity continues, only giving him redress against the government, for damages. Examine the history of England. See how few of the cases of the suspension of the *habeas corpus* law have been worthy of that suspension. They have been either real treason, wherein the parties might as well have been charged at once, or sham plots, where it was shameful they should ever have been suspected. Yet for the few cases, wherein the suspension of the *habeas corpus* has done real good, that operation is now become habitual, and the minds of the nation almost prepared to live under its constant suspension. A declaration, that the federal government will never restrain the presses from printing any thing they please, will not take away the liability of the printers for false facts printed. The declaration, that religious faith shall be unpunished, does not give impunity to criminal acts, dictated by religious error. The saying—there shall be no monopolies, lessens the incitements to ingenuity, which is spurred on by the hope of a monopoly for a limited time, as of fourteen years; but the benefit of even limited monopolies is too doubtful, to be opposed to that of their general suppression. If no check can be found to keep the number of standing troops within safe bounds, while they are tolerated as far as necessary, abandon them altogether, discipline well the militia, and guard the magazines with them. More than magazine guards will be useless, if few, and dangerous, if many. No European nation can ever send against us such a regular army as we need fear, and it is hard, if our militia are not equal to those of Canada or Florida. My idea then, is, that though proper exceptions to these general rules are desirable, and probably practicable, yet if the exceptions cannot be agreed on, the establishment of the rules, in all cases, will do ill in very few. I hope, therefore, a bill of rights will be formed, to guard the people against the federal government, as they are already guarded against their State governments, in most instances. The abandoning the principle of necessary rotation in the Senate, has, I see, been disapproved by many: in the case of the President, by none. I readily, therefore, suppose my opinion wrong, when opposed by the majority, as in the former instance, and the totality, as in the latter. In this, however, I should have done it with more complete satisfaction, had we all judged from the same position.

Solicitations, which cannot be directly refused, oblige me to trouble you often with letters, recommending and introducing to you persons who go from hence to America. I will beg the favor of you to distinguish the letters wherein I appeal to recommendations from other persons, from those which I write on my own knowledge. In the former, it is never my intention to compromit myself or you. In both instances, I must beg you to ascribe the trouble I give you, to circumstances which do not leave me at liberty to decline it.

I am, with very sincere esteem, Dear Sir, your affectionate friend and servant,

Th: Jefferson.

LETTER CXLIX.—TO JOHN JAY, August 3, 1788

TO JOHN JAY.

Paris, August 3, 1788.

Sir,

My last letters to you were of the 4th and 23d of May, with a Postscript of the 27th. Since that, I have been honored with yours of April the 24th, May the 16th, and June the 9th.

The most remarkable internal occurrences since my last are these. The *Noblesse* of Bretagne, who had received with so much warmth the late innovations in the government, assembled, and drew up a memorial to the King, and chose twelve members of their body to come and present it. Among these was the Marquis de la Rouerie (Colonel Armand). The King, considering the *Noblesse* as having no legal right to assemble, declined receiving the memorial. The deputies, to give greater weight to it, called a meeting of the landed proprietors of Bretagne, resident at Paris, and proposed to them to add their signatures—They did so, to the number of about sixty, of whom the Marquis de la Fayette was one. The twelve deputies, for having called this meeting, were immediately sent to the Bastile where they now are, and the Parisian signers were deprived of such favors as they held of the court. There were only four of them, however, who held any thing of that kind. The Marquis de la Fayette was one of these. They had given him a military command, to be exercised in the south of France, during the months of August and September of the present year. This they took from him; so that he is disgraced, in the ancient language of the court, but in truth, honorably marked in the eyes of the nation. The ministers are so sensible of this, that they have had, separately, private conferences with him, to endeavor, through him, to keep things quiet. From the character of the province of Bretagne, it was much apprehended, for some days, that the imprisonment of their deputies would have produced an insurrection. But it took another turn. The *Cours intermédiaire* of the province, acknowledged to be a legal body, deputed eighteen members of their body to the King. To these he gave an audience, and the answer, of which I send you a copy. This is hard enough. Yet I am in hopes the appeal to the sword will be avoided, and great modifications in the government be obtained without bloodshed. As yet none has been spilt, according to the best evidence I have been able to obtain, notwithstanding what the foreign newspapers have said to the contrary. The convocation of the States General has now become inevitable. Whenever the time shall be announced certainly, it will keep the nation quiet till they meet. According to present probabilities, this must be in the course of the next summer; but to what movements their meeting and measures may give occasion, cannot be foreseen. Should a foreign war take place, still they must assemble the States General, because they cannot, but by their aid, obtain money to carry it on. Monsieur de Malesherbes will, I believe, retire from the King's Council. He has been much opposed to the late acts of authority. The Baron de Breteuil has resigned his secretaryship of the domestic department; certainly not for the same reasons, as he is known to have been of opinion, that the King had compromitted too much of his authority. The real reason has probably been, an impatience of acting under a principal minister. His successor is M. de Villedeuil, lately Comptroller General.

The ambassadors of Tippoo Saib have arrived here. If their mission has any other object than that of pomp and ceremony, it is not yet made known. Though this court has not avowed that they are in possession of Trincomale, yet the report is believed, and that possession was taken by General Conway, in consequence of orders given in the moment that they thought a war certain. The dispute with the States General of the United Netherlands, on account of the insult to M. de St. Priest, does not tend as yet towards a settlement. He has obtained leave to go to the waters, and perhaps from thence he may come to Paris, to await events. Sweden has commenced hostilities against Russia, by the taking a little fortress by land. This having been their intention, it is wonderful, that when their fleet lately met three Russian ships of one hundred guns each, they saluted instead of taking them. The Empress has declared war against them in her turn. It is well understood, that Sweden is set on by England, and paid by the Turks. The prospect of Russia has much brightened by some late successes. Their fleet of galleys and gun-boats, twenty-seven in number, having been attacked by fifty-seven Turkish vessels of the same kind, commanded by the Captain Pacha, these were repulsed, with the loss of three vessels. In the action, which was on the 18th of June, Admiral Paul Jones commanded the right wing of the Russians, and the Prince of Nassau the left. On the 26th of the same month, the Turkish principal fleet, that is to say, their ships of the line, frigates, &c, having got themselves near the swash, at the mouth of the Borysthenes, the Prince of Nassau took advantage of their position, attacked them while so engaged in the mud that they could not manoeuvre, burnt six, among which were the admiral's and vice-admiral's, took two, and made between three and four thousand prisoners. The first reports gave this success to Admiral Paul Jones; but it is now rendered rather probable that he was not there, as he commands the vessels of war which are said not to have been there. It is supposed, that his presence in the affair of the 18th was accidental. But if this success has been so complete as it is represented, the Black Sea must be tolerably open to the Russians: in which case, we may expect, from what we know of that officer, that he will improve to the greatest advantage the situation of things on that sea. The Captain Pacha's standard was taken in the last action, and himself obliged to make his escape in a small vessel. Prince Potemkin immediately got under march for Oczakow, to take advantage of the consternation into which that place was thrown.

The Spanish squadron, after cruising off the Western Isles and Cape St. Vincent, has returned into port.

A dispute has arisen between the Papal See and the King of Naples, which may, in its progress, enable us to estimate what degree of influence that See retains at the present day. The kingdom of Naples, at an early period of its history, became feudatory to the See of Rome, and in acknowledgment thereof, has annually paid a hackney to the Pope in Rome, to which place it has always been sent by a splendid embassy. The hackney has been refused by the King this year, and the Pope, giving him three months to return to obedience, threatens, if he does not, to proceed seriously against him.

About three weeks ago a person called on me, and informed me, that Silas Deane had taken him in for a sum of one hundred and twenty guineas, and that being unable to obtain any other satisfaction, he had laid hands on his account book and letter book, and had brought them off to Paris, to offer them first to the United States, if they would repay him his money, and if not, that he should return to London, and offer them to the British minister. I desired him to leave them with me four and twenty hours, that I might judge whether they were worth our notice. He did so. They were two volumes. One contained all his accounts with the United States, from his first coming to Europe to January the 10th, 1781. Presuming that the treasury board was in possession of this account till his arrival in Philadelphia, August, 1778, and that he had never given in the subsequent part, I had that subsequent part copied from the book, and now enclose it, as it may on some occasion or other, perhaps, be useful in the treasury office. The other volume contained all his correspondences from March the 30th to August the 23d, 1777. I had a list of the letters taken by their dates and addresses, which will enable you to form a general idea of the collection. On perusal of many of them, I thought it desirable that they should not come to the hands of the British minister, and from an expression dropped by the possessor of them, I believe he would have fallen to fifty or sixty guineas. I did not think them important enough, however, to justify my purchasing them without authority; though, with authority, I should have done it. Indeed, I would have given that sum to cut out a single sentence, which contained evidence of a fact, not proper to be committed to the hands of enemies. I told him I would state his proposition to you, and await orders. I gave him back the books, and he returned to London without making any promise, that he would await the event of the orders you might think proper to give.

News of the accession of nine States to the new form of federal government has been received here about a week. I have the honor to congratulate you sincerely on this event. Of its effect at home, you are in the best situation to judge. On this side the Atlantic, it is considered as a very wise reformation. In consequence of this, speculations are already begun here, to purchase up our domestic liquidated debt. Indeed, I suspect that orders may have been previously lodged in America to do this, as soon as the new constitution was accepted effectually. If it is thought that this debt should be retained at home, there is not a moment to lose; and I know of no means of retaining it, but those I suggested to the treasury board, in my letter to them of March the 29th. The transfer of these debts to Europe will excessively embarrass, and perhaps totally prevent the borrowing any money in Europe, till these shall be paid off. This is a momentous object, and, in my opinion, should receive instantaneous attention.

The gazettes of France, to the departure of my letter, will accompany it, and those of Leyden to the 22nd of July, at which time their distribution in this country was prohibited. How long the prohibition may continue, I cannot tell. As far as I can judge, it is the only paper in Europe worth reading. Since the suppression of the packet-boats, I have never been able to find a safe conveyance for a letter to you, till the present by Mrs. Barclay. Whenever a confidential person shall be going from hence to London, I shall send my letters for you to the care of Mr. Trumbull, who will look out for safe conveyances. This will render the epochs of my writing very irregular. There is a proposition under consideration, for establishing packet-boats on a more economical plan, from Havre to Boston; but its success is uncertain, and still more, its duration.

I have the honor to be, with sentiments of the most perfect esteem and respect, Sir, your most obedient and most humble servant,

Th: Jefferson.

LETTER CL.—TO COLONEL MONROE, August 9, 1788

TO COLONEL MONROE.

Paris, August 9, 1788.

Dear Sir,

Since my last to you, I have to thank your for your favors of July the 27th, 1787, and April the 10th, 1788, and the details they contained; and in return, will give you now the leading circumstances of this continent.

This nation is at present under great internal agitation. The authority of the crown on one part, and that of the parliaments on the other, are fairly at issue. Good men take part with neither, but have raised an opposition, the object of which is to obtain a fixed and temperate constitution. There was a moment when this opposition ran so high, as to endanger an appeal to arms, in which case, perhaps, it would have been crushed. The moderation of government has avoided this, and they are yielding daily one right after another to the nation. They have given them Provincial Assemblies, which will be very perfect representations of the nation, and stand somewhat in the place of our State Assemblies; they have reformed the criminal law; acknowledged the King cannot lay a new tax, without the consent of the States General; and they will call the States General the next year. The object of this body, when met, will be a bill of rights, a civil list, a national assembly meeting at certain epochs, and some other matters of that kind. So that I think it probable this country will, within two or three years, be in the enjoyment of a tolerably free constitution, and that without its having cost them a drop of blood; for none has yet been spilt, though the English papers have set the whole nation to cutting throats.

Be assured of those sentiments of esteem and attachment, with which I am, Dear Sir, your friend and servant,

Th: Jefferson.

LETTER CLI.—TO MONSIEUR DE CREVE-COEUR, August 9, 1788

TO MONSIEUR DE CREVE-COEUR.

Paris, August 9, 1788.

Dear Sir,

While our second revolution is just brought to a happy end with you, yours here is but cleverly under way. For some days I was really melancholy with the apprehension, that arms would be appealed to, and the opposition crushed in its first efforts. But things seem now to wear a better aspect. While the opposition keeps at its highest wholesome point, government, unwilling to draw the sword, is not forced to do it. The contest here is exactly what it was in Holland: a contest between the monarchical and aristocratical parts of the government for a monopoly of despotism over the people. The aristocracy in Holland, seeing that their common prey was likely to escape out of their clutches, chose rather to retain its former portion, and therefore coalesced with the single head. The people remained victims. Here, I think, it will take a happier turn. The parliamentary part of the aristocracy is alone firmly united. The *Noblesse* and Clergy, but especially the former, are divided partly between the parliamentary and the despotic party, and partly united with the real patriots, who are endeavoring to gain for the nation what they can, both from the parliamentary and the single despotism. I think I am not mistaken in believing, that the King and some of his ministers are well affected to this band; and surely, that they will make great cessions to the people, rather than small ones to the parliament. They are, accordingly, yielding daily to the national reclamations, and will probably end in according a well-tempered constitution. They promise the States General for the next year, and I have good information that an Arrêt will appear the day after to-morrow, announcing them for May, 1789. How they will be composed, and what they will do, cannot be foreseen. Their convocation, however, will tranquillize the public mind, in a great degree, till their meeting. There are, however, two intervening difficulties. 1. Justice cannot till then continue completely suspended, as it now is. The parliament will not resume their functions, but in their entire body. The *bailliages* are afraid to accept of them. What will be done? 2. There are well-founded fears of a bankruptcy before the month of May. In the mean time, the war is spreading from nation to nation. Sweden has commenced hostilities against Russia; Denmark is showing its teeth against Sweden; Prussia against Denmark; and England too deeply engaged in playing the back game, to avoid coming forward, and dragging this country and Spain in with her. But even war will not prevent the assembly of the States General, because it cannot be carried on without them. War, however, is not the most favorable moment for divesting the monarchy of power. On the contrary, it is the moment when the energy of a single hand shows itself in the most seducing form.

A very considerable portion of this country has been desolated by a hail. I considered the newspaper accounts of hailstones of ten pounds weight as exaggerations. But in a conversation with the Duke de la Rochefoucault the other day, he assured me, that though he could not say he had seen such himself, yet he considered the fact as perfectly established. Great contributions, public and private, are making for the sufferers. But they will be like the drop of water from the finger of Lazarus. There is no remedy for the present evil, nor way to prevent future ones, but to bring the people to such a state of ease, as not to be ruined by the loss of a single crop. This hail may be considered as the *coup de grace* to an expiring victim. In the arts there is nothing new discovered since you left us, which is worth communicating. Mr. Paine's iron bridge was exhibited here with great approbation. An idea has been encouraged of executing it in three arches at the King's garden. But it will probably not be done.

I am, with sentiments of perfect esteem and attachment, Dear Sir, your most obedient and most humble servant,

Th: Jefferson.

LETTER CLII.—TO JOHN JAY, August 10, 1788

TO JOHN JAY.

Paris, August 10, 1788.

Sir,

I have waited till the last moment of Mrs. Barclay's departure, to write you the occurrences since my letter of the 3rd instant. We have received the Swedish account of an engagement between their fleet and the Russian, on the Baltic, wherein they say they took one, and burned another Russian vessel, with the loss of one on their side, and that the victory remained with them. They say, at the same time, that their fleet returned into port, and the Russians kept the sea; we must, therefore, suspend our opinion till we get the Russian version of this engagement. The Swedish manifesto was handed about to-day at Versailles, by the Swedish ambassador, in manuscript. The King complains that Russia has been ever endeavoring to sow divisions in his kingdom, in order to re-establish the ancient constitution; that he has long borne it, through a love of peace, but finds it no longer bearable: that still, however, he will make peace on these conditions; 1. That the Empress punishes her minister for the note he gave in to the court of Stockholm; 2. that she restore Crimea to the Turks; and 3. that she repay to him all the expenses of his armament. The Russian force, in vessels of war on the Black Sea, are five frigates, and three ships of the line; but those of the line are shut up in port, and cannot come out till Oczakow shall be taken. This fleet is commanded by Paul Jones, with the rank of rear-admiral. The Prince of Nassau commands the galleys and gun-boats. It is now ascertained, that the States General will assemble the next year, and probably in the month of May. Tippoo Saib's ambassadors had their reception to-day at Versailles with unusual pomp. The presence was so numerous, that little could be caught of what they said to the king, and he answered to them: from what little I could hear, nothing more passed than mutual assurances of good will. The name of the Marechal de Richelieu is sufficiently remarkable in history, to justify my mentioning his death, which happened two days ago; he was aged ninety-two years.

I have the honor to be, with sentiments of the most perfect esteem and respect, Sir, your most obedient and most humble servant,

Th: Jefferson.

LETTER CLIII.—TO JOHN JAY, August 11, 1788

TO JOHN JAY.

Paris, August 11, 1788.

Sir,

In my letter of the last night, written in the moment of Mrs. Barclay's departure, I had the honor of mentioning to you, that it was now pretty certain that the States General would be assembled in the next year, and probably in the month of May. This morning an *Arrêt* is published, announcing that their meeting is fixed on the first day of May next, of which I enclose you a copy by post, in hopes it will get to Bordeaux in time for Mrs. Barclay. This *Arrêt* ought to have a great effect towards tranquillizing the nation. There are still, however, two circumstances which must continue to perplex the administration. The first is, the want of money, occasioned not only by the difficulty of filling up the loan of the next year, but by the withholding the ordinary supplies of taxes, which is said to have taken place in some instances: this gives apprehension of a bankruptcy under some form or other, and has occasioned the stocks to fall, in the most alarming manner. The second circumstance is, that justice, both civil and criminal, continues suspended. The parliament will not resume their functions, but with their whole body, and the greater part of the *bailliages* declined acting; the present *Arrêt* announces a perseverance in this plan. I have information from Algiers, of the 5th of June, that the plague is raging there, with great violence; that one of our captives was dead of it, and another ill, so that we have there, in all, now, only fifteen or sixteen; that the captives are more exposed to its ravages, than others; that the great redemptions by the Spaniards, Portuguese, and Neapolitans, and the havoc made by the plague, had now left not more than four hundred slaves in Algiers; so that their redemption was become not only exorbitant, but almost inadmissible; that common sailors were held at four hundred pounds sterling, and that our fifteen or sixteen could probably not be redeemed for less than from twenty-five to thirty thousand dollars. An Algerine cruiser, having twenty-eight captives of Genoa aboard, was lately chased ashore, by two Neapolitan vessels: the crew and captives got safe ashore, and the latter, of course, recovered their freedom. The Algerine crew was well treated, and would be sent back by the French. But the government of Algiers demands of France, sixty thousand sequins, or twenty-seven thousand pounds sterling, for the captives escaped; that is, nearly one thousand pounds each. The greater part of the regency were for an immediate declaration of war against France; but the Dey urged the heavy war the Turks were at present engaged in; that it would be better not to draw another power on them, at present; that they would decline renewing the treaty of one hundred years, which expired two years ago, so as to be free to act hereafter; but, for the present, they ought to accept payment for the captives, as a satisfaction. They accordingly declared to the French consul, that they would put him, and all his countrymen there, into irons, unless the sixty thousand sequins were paid: the consul told them, his instructions were, positively, that they should not be paid. In this situation stood matters between that pettifogging nest of robbers and this great kingdom, which will finish, probably, by crouching under them, and paying the sixty thousand sequins. From the personal characters of the present administration, I should have hoped, under any other situation than the present, they might have ventured to quit the beaten track of politics hitherto pursued, in which the honor of their nation has been calculated at nought, and to join in a league for keeping up a perpetual cruise against these pirates, which, though a slow operation, would be a sure one for destroying all their vessels and seamen, and turning the rest of them to agriculture. But a desire of not bringing upon themselves another difficulty, will probably induce the ministers to do as their predecessors have done.

August 12. The enclosed paper of this morning gives some particulars of the action between the Russians and Swedes, the manifesto of the Empress, and the declaration of the court of Versailles, as to the affair of Trincomale.

I have the honor to be, with sentiments of perfect esteem and respect, Sir, your most obedient and most humble servant,

Th: Jefferson.

LETTER CLIV.—TO WILLIAM CARMICHAEL, August 12, 1788

TO WILLIAM CARMICHAEL.

Paris, August 12, 1788.

Dear Sir,

Since my last to you, I have been honored with yours of the 18th and 29th of May, and 5th of June. My latest American intelligence is of the 24th of June, when nine certainly, and probably ten States, had accepted the new constitution, and there was no doubt of the eleventh (North Carolina), because there was no opposition there. In New York, two thirds of the State were against it, and certainly if they had been called to the decision, in any other stage of the business, they would have rejected it; but before they put it to the vote, they would certainly have heard that eleven States had joined in it, and they would find it safer to go with those eleven, than put themselves into opposition, with Rhode Island only. Though I am much pleased with this successful issue of the new constitution, yet I am more so, to find that one of its principal defects (the want of a declaration of rights) will pretty certainly be remedied. I suppose this, because I see that both people and conventions, in almost every State, have concurred in demanding it. Another defect, the perpetual re-eligibility of the same President, will probably not be cured, during the life of General Washington. His merit has blinded our countrymen to the danger of making so important an officer re-eligible. I presume there will not be a vote against him, in the United States. It is more doubtful, who will be Vice-President. The age of Dr. Franklin, and the doubt whether he would accept it, are the only circumstances that admit a question, but that he would be the man. After these two characters of first magnitude, there are so many which present themselves equally, on the second line, that we cannot see which of them will be singled out. John Adams, Hancock, Jay, Madison, Rutledge, will be all voted for. Congress has acceded to the prayer of Kentucky to become an independent member of the Union. A committee was occupied in settling the plan of receiving them, and their government is to commence on the 1st day of January next.

You are, I dare say, pleased, as I am, with the promotion of our countryman, Paul Jones. He commanded the right wing, in the first engagement between the Russian and Turkish galleys; his absence from the second, proves his superiority over the Captain Pacha, as he did not choose to bring his ships into the shoals in which the Pacha ventured, and lost those entrusted to him. I consider this officer as the principal hope of our future efforts on the ocean. You will have heard of the action between the Swedes and Russians, on the

Baltic; as yet, we have only the Swedish version of it. I apprehend this war must catch from nation to nation, till it becomes general.

With respect to the internal affairs of this country, I hope they will be finally well arranged, and without having cost a drop of blood. Looking on as a by-stander, no otherwise interested, than as entertaining a sincere love for the nation in general, and a wish to see their happiness promoted, keeping myself clear of the particular views and passions of individuals, I applaud extremely the patriotic proceedings of the present ministry. Provincial Assemblies established, the States General called, the right of taxing the nation without their consent abandoned, *corvées* abolished, torture abolished, the criminal code reformed, are facts which will do eternal honor to their administration, in history. But were I their historian, I should not equally applaud their total abandonment of their foreign affairs. A bolder front in the beginning, would have prevented the first loss, and consequently, all the others. Holland, Prussia, Turkey, and Sweden, lost without the acquisition of a single new ally, are painful reflections for the friends of France. They may, indeed, have in their places the two empires, and perhaps Denmark; in which case, physically speaking, they will stand on as good ground as before, but not on as good moral ground. Perhaps, seeing more of the internal working of the machine, they saw, more than we do, the physical impossibility of having money to carry on a war. Their justification must depend on this, and their atonement, on the internal good they are doing to their country; this makes me completely their friend.

I am, with great esteem and attachment, Dear Sir, you friend and servant,

Th: Jefferson.

LETTER CLV.—TO M. CATHALAN, August 13,1788

TO M. CATHALAN.

Paris, August 13,1788.

Sir,

I have to acknowledge the receipt of your two favors, of June, and July the 11th, and to thank you for the political intelligence they contained, which is always interesting to me. I will ask a continuance of them, and especially that you inform me, from time to time, of the movements in the ports of Marseilles and Toulon, which may seem to indicate peace or war. These are the most certain presages possible; and being conveyed to me from all the ports, they will always enable me to judge of the intentions or expectations of the ministry, and to notify you of the result of the intelligence from all the ports, that you may communicate it to the American commerce.

I have the pleasure to inform you, that the new constitution proposed to the United States, has been established by the votes of nine States. It is happy for us to get this operation over before the war kindled in Europe could affect us, as by rendering us more respectable, we shall be more probably permitted, by all parties, to remain neutral.

I take the liberty of putting under your cover a letter for Mr. Bernard, containing some seeds, and another to Giuseppe Chiappe, our consul at Mogadore. I thank you for your settlement of the price of the *Observations Météorologiques*, and I have repaid the sixty livres to Sir John Lambert, in your name. When the nursery man, whom you have been so good as to employ to prepare the olives and olive plants, to be sent to Charleston, shall be executing that commission, I shall be glad if he will, at the same time, prepare a few plants only, of the following kinds. Figs, the best kind for drying, and the best kind for eating fresh, raisins, the best kind for drying, prugnolles, cork trees, pistaches, capers. I desire only a few plants of each of these, that they may not take too much of the place of the olives, which is our great object, and the sole one we have at heart. If you will be so good as to give the nursery man this order immediately, it will save you the necessity of recurring to my letter, when the season comes.

I have the honor to be, with great and sincere esteem, Sir, your most obedient and most humble servant,

Th: Jefferson.

LETTER CLVI.—TO JOHN JAY, August 20,1788

TO JOHN JAY.

Paris, August 20,1788.

Sir,

I had the honor to write to you on the 3rd, 10th, and 11th instant, with a postscript of the 12th; all of which went by Mrs. Barclay. Since that date, we have received an account of a third victory obtained by the Russians over the Turks, on the Black Sea, in which the Prince of Nassau, with his galleys, destroyed two frigates, three smaller vessels, and six galleys. The Turkish power on that sea is represented, by their enemies, as now annihilated. There is reason to believe, however, that this is not literally true, and that aided by the supplies furnished by the English, they are making extraordinary efforts to re-establish their marine. The Russian minister here has shown the official report of Admiral Greigh, on the combat of July the 17th, in which he claims the victory, and urges in proof of it, that he kept the field of battle. This report is said to have been written on it. As this paper, together with the report of the Swedish admiral, is printed in the Leyden gazette of the 15th instant, I enclose it to you. The court of Denmark has declared, it will furnish Russia the aid stipulated in their treaty: and it is not doubted they will go beyond this, and become principals in the war. The next probable moves are, that the King of Prussia will succor Sweden; and Poland, Russia, by land: and a possible consequence is, that England may send a squadron into the Baltic, to restore equilibrium in that sea. In my letter of the 11th, I observed to you, that this country would have two difficulties to struggle with, till the meeting of their States General, and that one of these was the want of money: this has, in fact, overborne all their resources, and the day before yesterday, they published an *Arrêt*, suspending all reimbursements of capital, and reducing the payments of the principal mass of demands for interest, to twelve sous in the livre; the remaining eight sous to be paid with certificates. I enclose you a newspaper with the *Arrêt*. In this paper you will see the exchange of yesterday, and I have inserted that of the day before, to show you the fall. The consternation is, as yet, too great to let us judge of the issue. It will probably ripen the public mind to the necessity of a change in their constitution, and to the substituting the collected wisdom of the whole, in place of a single will, by which they have been hitherto governed. It is a remarkable proof of the total incompetency of a single head to govern a nation well, when, with a revenue of six hundred millions, they are led to a declared bankruptcy, and to stop the wheels of government, even in its most essential movements, for want of money.

I send the present letter by a private conveyance to a sea-port, in hopes a conveyance may be found by some merchant vessel.

I have the honor to be, with sentiments of the most perfect esteem and respect, Sir, your most obedient and most humble servant,

Th: Jefferson.

LETTER CLVII.—TO MR. CUTTING, August 23, 1788

TO MR. CUTTING.

Paris, August 23, 1788.

Dear Sir,

I have duly received your favors of the 3rd, 8th, 14th, and 15th instant, and have now the honor of enclosing you a letter of introduction to Doctor Ramsay.

I think a certainty that England and France must enter into the war, was a great inducement to the ministry here to suspend the portion of public payments, which they have lately suspended. By this operation, they secure two hundred and three millions of livres, or eight millions and a half of guineas, in the course of this and the ensuing year, which will be sufficient for the campaign of the first year: for what is to, follow, the States General must provide. The interesting question now is, how the States General shall be composed? There are three opinions. 1. To place the three estates, Clergy, *Noblesse*, and Commons, in three different Houses. The Clergy would, probably, like this, and some of the Nobility; but it has no partisans out of those orders. 2. To put the Clergy and *Noblesse* into one House, and the Commons into another. The *Noblesse* will be generally for this. 3. To put the three orders into one House, and make the Commons the majority of that House. This re-unites the greatest number of partisans, and I suspect it is well patronized in the ministry, who, I am persuaded, are proceeding *bona fide*, to improve the constitution of their country. As to the opposition which the English expect from the personal character of the King, it proves they do not know what his personal character is. He is the honestest man in his kingdom, and the most regular and economical. He has no foible which will enlist him against the good of his people; and whatever constitution will promote this, he will befriend. But he will not befriend it obstinately: he has given repeated proofs of a readiness to sacrifice his opinion to the wish of the nation. I believe he will consider the opinion of the States General, as the best evidence of what will please and profit the nation, and will conform to it. All the characters at court may not be of this disposition, and from thence may, possibly, arise representations, capable of leading the King astray; but upon a full view of all circumstances, I have sanguine hopes, that such a constitution will be established here, as will regenerate the energy of the nation, cover its friends, and make its enemies tremble. I am, with very great esteem, Dear Sir, your friend and servant,

Th: Jefferson.

LETTER CLVIII.—TO JOHN JAY, September 3, 1788

TO JOHN JAY.

Paris, September 3, 1788.

Sir,

By Mrs. Barclay I had the honor of sending you letters of the 3rd, 10th, and 11th of August; since which, I wrote you of the 20th of the same month, by a casual conveyance, as is the present.

In my letter of the 20th, I informed you of the act of public bankruptcy which had taken place here. The effect of this would have been a forced loan of about one hundred and eighty millions of livres, in the course of the present and ensuing year. But it did not yield a sufficient immediate relief. The treasury became literally moneyless, and all purposes depending on this mover came to a stand. The Archbishop was hereupon removed, with Monsieur Lambert, the Comptroller General; and Mr. Necker was called in, as Director General of the finance. To soften the Archbishop's dismission, a cardinal's hat is asked for him from Rome, and his nephew promised the succession to the Archbishopric of Sens. The public joy, on this change of administration, was very great indeed. The people of Paris were amusing themselves with trying and burning the Archbishop in effigy, and rejoicing on the appointment of Mr. Necker. The commanding officer of the city-guards undertook to forbid this, and not being obeyed, he charged the mob with fixed bayonets, killed two or three, and wounded many: this stopped their rejoicings for that day; but enraged at being thus obstructed in amusements wherein they had committed no disorder whatever, they collected in great numbers the next day, attacked the guards in various places, burnt ten or twelve guard-houses, killed two or three of the guards, and had about six or eight of their own number killed. The city was hereupon put under martial law, and after a while, the tumult subsided, and peace was restored. The public stocks rose ten per cent, on the day of Mr. Necker's appointment: he was immediately offered considerable sums of money, and has been able so far to wave the benefit of the act of bankruptcy, as to pay in cash all demands, except the *remboursements des capitaux*. For these, and for a sure supply of other wants, he will depend on the States General, and will hasten their meetings, as is thought. No other change has yet taken place in the administration. The minister of war, however, must certainly follow his brother, and some think, and all wish, that Monsieur de Lamoignon, the *Garde des Sceaux*, may go out also. The administration of justice is still suspended. The whole kingdom seems tranquil at this moment.

Abroad, no event worth noting has taken place since my last. The court of Denmark has not declared it will do any thing more, than furnish the stipulated aid to Russia. The King of Prussia has as yet made no move, which may decide whether he will engage in the war, nor has England sent any squadron into the Baltic. As the season for action is considerably passed over, it is become more doubtful, whether any other power will enter the lists till the next campaign; this will give time for stopping the further progress of the war, if they really wish to stop it. Two camps of twenty-five thousand men each are forming in this country on its northern limits. The Prince of Conde has the command of one, and the Duke de Broglio of the other.

I trouble you with the enclosed letter from a Henry Watson, claiming prize monies, as having served under Admiral Paul Jones, which I suppose should go to the treasury, or war-office.

I have the honor to be, with sentiments of the most perfect esteem and respect, Sir, your most obedient and most humble; servant,

Th: Jefferson,

LETTER CLIX.—TO THE COMMISSIONERS OF THE TREASURY, Sep. 6, 1788

TO THE COMMISSIONERS OF THE TREASURY.

Paris, September 6, 1788.

Gentlemen,

Your favor of July the 3rd came to hand some days ago, and that of July the 22nd in the afternoon of yesterday. Knowing that a Mr. Vannet was to leave Paris this morning to go to Virginia in a vessel bound from Havre to Potomac, I have engaged him to receive the papers which are the subject of those letters, to take care of them from thence to Havre, and on the voyage; and when he shall have arrived in Potomac, instead of going directly to Richmond, as he intended, he will proceed with them himself to New York. I shall pay here all expenses to their delivery at the ship's side in America, freight included: unless, perhaps, he may find it necessary to put another covering over them, if he should not be able to get them into the cabin; in this case, you will have to reimburse him for that. I engage to him that you shall pay him their transportation from the ship's side to New York, and his own reasonable expenses from the place of his landing to New York, and back to the place of landing. As he takes that journey for this object only, it would be reasonable that you give him some gratuity for his time and trouble, and I suppose it would be accepted by him; but I have made no agreement for this. The papers are contained in a large box and a trunk. They were sent here by Mr. Ast, during my absence in Holland. When they arrived at the gates of Paris, the officers of the customs opened the trunk, to see whether it contained dutiable articles; but finding only books and papers, they concluded the contents of the box to be of the same nature, and did not open that. You receive it, therefore, as it came from the hands of Mr. Ast. A small trunk, which came as a third package from Mr. Ast, and which has never been opened, I have put into the great trunk, without displacing, or ever having touched a single paper, except as far as was necessary to make room for that. I shall have the whole corded and plumbed by the Custom-house here, not only to prevent their being opened at the Custom-houses on the road, and at the port of exportation, but to prove to you, whether they shall have been opened by any body else after going out of my hands. If the stamped leads are entire, and the cords uncut, when you receive them, you will be sure they have not been opened; they will be wrapt in oil-cloth here to guard them against the damps of the sea; and, as I mentioned before, Mr. Vannet will put them under another covering, if he finds it necessary, at Havre.

At the same time with your last letter, I received from the office of Foreign Affairs the ratification by Congress of the loan of 1788, for another million of guilders. As the necessity of this loan resulted from the estimate made by Mr. Adams and myself, which estimate was laid before Congress, I suppose their ratification of the loan implies that of the estimate. One article of this was for the redemption of our captives at Algiers. Though your letter says nothing on this subject, I am in hopes you have sent orders to the commissioners of the loans at Amsterdam to furnish, as soon as they shall have it, what may be necessary for this pressing call. So also for the foreign officers. If the ratification of the loan has been made by Congress, with a view to fulfil the objects of the estimate, a general order from you to the commissioners of the loans at Amsterdam, to pay the monies from time to time, according to that estimate, or to such other as you shall furnish them with, might save the trouble of particular orders on every single occasion, and the disappointments arising from the delay or miscarriage of such orders: but it is for you to decide on this.

I have the honor to be, with sentiments of the most perfect respect, Gentlemen, your most obedient and most humble servant,

Th: Jefferson.

LETTER CLX.—TO THE COUNT DE MONTMORIN,

TO THE COUNT DE MONTMORIN.

Paris, September 11, 1788.

Sir,

In the course of the last war, the house of Schweighaeuser and Dobree of Nantes, and Puchilberg of L'Orient, presented to Dr. Franklin a demand against the United States of America. He, being acquainted with the circumstances of the demand, and knowing it to be unfounded, refused to pay it. They thereupon procured seizure, by judiciary authority, of certain arms and other military stores which we had purchased in this country, and had deposited for embarkation at Nantes: and these stores have remained in that position ever since. Congress have lately instructed me to put an end to this matter. Unwilling to trouble your Excellency, whenever it can be avoided, I proposed to the parties to have the question decided by arbitrators, to be chosen by us jointly. They have refused it, as you will see by their answers to my letters, copies of both which I have the honor to enclose you. I presume it to be well settled in practice, that the property of one sovereign is not permitted to be seized within the dominions of another; and that this practice is founded not only in mutual respect, but in mutual utility. To what the contrary practice would lead, is evident in the present case, wherein military stores have been stopped, in the course of a war, in which our greatest difficulties proceeded from the want of military stores. In their letter, too, they make a merit of not having seized one of our ships of war, and certainly the principle which admits the seizure of arms, would admit that of a whole fleet, and would often furnish an enemy the easiest means of defeating an expedition. The parties obliging me, then, to have recourse to your Excellency on this occasion, I am under the necessity of asking an order from you for the immediate delivery of the stores and other property of the United States at Nantes, detained by the house of Schweighaeuser and Dobree, and that of Puchilberg, or by either of them, under a pretence of a judicial seizure.

I have the honor to be, with sentiments of the most perfect respect and esteem, your Excellency's most obedient and most humble servant,

Th: Jefferson.

LETTER CLXI.—TO M. DE REYNEVAL, September 16, 1788

TO M. DE REYNEVAL.

Sir,

Paris, September 16, 1788.

I have the honor now to enclose you my observations on the alteration proposed in the consular convention. There remain only three articles of those heretofore in question between us, to which I am unable to agree; that is to say, the second, proposing still to retain personal immunities for the consuls, and others attached to their office; the eighth, proposing that the navigation code of each nation shall be established in the territories of the other; and the ninth, insisting that the ship's roll shall be conclusive evidence that a person belongs to the ship.

There are several new matters introduced into the draught: some of these are agreed to; others cannot be admitted, as being contrary to the same principles which had obliged me to disagree to some of the former articles. The greatest part of the eleventh, and the whole of the twelfth new articles, are in this predicament. They propose, that no person shall be arrested on board a merchant vessel, for any cause, but in presence of the consul; that no such vessel shall be visited, but in his presence; and that when the officers of justice have reason to believe that a criminal has taken refuge on board a vessel of war, the captain's word shall be conclusive evidence that he is not there.

To the objections which I had the honor of stating in my letter to his Excellency, the Count de Montmorin, I have now that of adding some other observations, of which I request your perusal. I enclose with them a draught, on the basis of the one you were pleased to give me, altered so as to reconcile it to the spirit of our laws.

I have the honor to be, with sentiments of the most perfect esteem and respect, Sir, your most obedient and most humble servant,

Th: Jefferson.

LETTER CLXII.—TO THE MARQUIS DE LA ROUERIE, September 16,1788

TO THE MARQUIS DE LA ROUERIE.

Paris, September 16,1788.

Sir,

On receiving the first letters which you did me the honor to write to me on the arrears due to you from the United States, I informed you that I had nothing to do in the money department; that the subject of your letters belonged altogether to the treasury board, and to Mr. Grand, their banker here, to the former of whom I forwarded your letters. As I felt an anxiety, however, that the foreign officers should be paid, I took the liberty of pressing the treasury board, from time to time, to exert themselves for that effect; and I availed myself of an opportunity which occurred last spring, of setting on foot measures, which, with their approbation, might furnish the means of effecting this payment. So far my information to you went, and I added a supposition, that the treasury board would probably give orders on the subject, in the course of the month of July. But I made you no promise; it would have been strange if I had; nor does my office, nor any thing I have ever said or done, subject me to the demand of immediate payment, which you are pleased to make on me, nor call on me for any declaration or answer, positive or negative.

Finding that my interference, which was friendly only, and avowed to be inofficial, has given occasion to your letter of yesterday, in a style which I did not expect, and to which I can have no motive for further exposing myself, I must take the liberty of desiring that the correspondence between us on this subject may cease. I presume that the certificate given you points out the person, here or elsewhere, to whom your applications are to be made, and that he will inform you when he receives orders on your subject.

I am, Sir, your humble servant,

Th: Jefferson.

LETTER CLXIII.—TO WILLIAM SHORT, September 20, 1788

TO WILLIAM SHORT.

Paris, September 20, 1788.

Dear Sir,

The evening of your departure, a letter came by the way of London and New York, addressed to you, and probably from Virginia. I think you wished your American letters to remain here; I shall therefore keep it. The passport now enclosed came the day after your departure; so also did a mass of American letters for me, as low down as August the 10th. I shall give you their substance. The convention of Virginia annexed to their ratification of the new constitution a copy of the State declaration of rights, not by way of condition, but to announce their attachment to them. They added also propositions for specific alterations of the constitution. Among these was one for rendering the President incapable of serving more than eight years, in any term of sixteen. New York has followed the example of Virginia, expressing the substance of her bill of rights (that is, Virginia's), and proposing amendments: these last differ much from those of Virginia; but they concur as to the President, only proposing that he shall be incapable of being elected more than twice. But I own I should like better than either of these, what Luther Martin tells us was repeatedly voted and adhered to by the federal convention, and only altered about twelve days before their rising, when some members had gone off; to wit, that he should be elected for seven years, and incapable for ever after. But New York has taken another step, which gives uneasiness; she has written a circular letter to all the legislatures, asking their concurrence in an immediate convention for making amendments. No news yet from North Carolina. Electors are to be chosen the first Wednesday in January; the President to be elected the first Wednesday in February; the new legislature to meet the third week in March:—the place is not yet decided on. Philadelphia was first proposed, and had six and a half votes; the half vote was Delaware, one of whose members wanted to take a vote on Wilmington; then Baltimore was proposed and carried, and afterwards rescinded: so that the matter stood open as ever on the 10th of August; but it was allowed the dispute lay only between New York and Philadelphia, and rather thought in favor of the last. The Rhode Island Delegates had retired from Congress. Dr. Franklin was dangerously ill of the gout and stone on the 21st of July. My letters of August the 10th not mentioning him, I hope he was recovered. Warville, &c. were arrived. Congress had referred the decision, as to the independence of Kentucky, to the new government. Brown ascribes this to the jealousy of the northern

States, who want Vermont to be received at the same time, in order to preserve a balance of interests in Congress. He was just setting out for Kentucky, disgusted, yet disposed to persuade to an acquiescence, though doubting they would immediately separate from the Union. The principal obstacle to this, he thought, would be the Indian war.

The following is a quotation from a letter from Virginia, dated July the 12th. 'P———n, though much impaired in health, and in every respect in the decline of life, showed as much zeal to carry the new constitution, as if he had been a young man; perhaps more than he discovered in the commencement of the late revolution,in his opposition to Great Britain. W———e acted as chairman to the committee of the whole, and of course took but little part in the debate; but was for the adoption, relying on subsequent amendments. B———r said nothing, but was for it. The G——
—r exhibited a curious spectacle to view. Having refused to sign the paper, every body supposed him against it; but he afterwards had written a letter, and having taken a part, which might be called rather vehement than active, he was constantly laboring to show, that his present conduct was consistent with that letter, and that letter with his refusal to sign. M—d—n took the principal share in the debate for it; in which, together with the aid I have already mentioned, he was somewhat assisted by I—nn—s, Lee, M———l, C———n, and G. N———s. M—s—n, H———y, and Gr———n were the principal supporters of the opposition. The discussion, as might be expected, where the parties were so nearly on a balance, was conducted generally with great order, propriety, and respect of either party to the other.'

The assembly of Virginia, hurried to their harvests, would not enter into a discussion of the district bill, but suspended it to the next session. E. Winston is appointed a judge, vice Gabriel Jones, resigned. R. Goode and Andrew Moore, Counsellors, vice B. Starke, dead, and Joseph Egglestone, resigned. It is said Wilson, of Philadelphia, is talked of to succeed Mr. A. in London. *Quære?*

The dispute about Virgil's tomb and the laurel, seems to be at length settled, by the testimony of two travellers, given separately, and without a communication with each other. These both say, that attempting to pluck off a branch of the laurel, it followed their hand, being, in fact, nothing more than a plant or bough recently cut, and stuck in the ground for the occasion. The Cicerone acknowledged the roguery, and said they practised it with almost every traveller, to get money. You will, of course, tug well at the laurel which shall be shown you, to see if this be the true solution.

The President Dupaty is dead. Monsieur de Barentin, *prémier president de la cour des aides*, is appointed *Garde des Sceaux*. The stocks are rather lower than when you left this. Present me in the most friendly terms to Messrs. Shippen and

Rutledge. I rely on your communicating to them the news, and, therefore, on their pardoning me for not repeating it in separate letters to them. You can satisfy them how necessary this economy of my time and labor is. This goes to Geneva *poste restante.* I shall not write again till you tell me where to write to.

Accept very sincere assurances of the affection, with which I am, Dear Sir, your friend and servant,

Th; Jefferson.

LETTER CLXIV.—TO JOHN JAY, September 24,1788

TO JOHN JAY.

Paris, September 24,1788.

Sir,

Understanding that the vessel is not yet sailed from Havre, which is to carry my letters of the 3rd and 5th instant, I am in hopes you will receive the present with them. The Russian accounts of their victories on the Black Sea must have been greatly exaggerated. According to these, the Captain Pacha's fleet was annihilated; yet themselves have lately brought him on the stage again, with fifteen ships of the line, in order to obtain another victory over him. I believe the truth to be, that he has suffered some checks, of what magnitude it is impossible to say, where one side alone is heard, and that he is still master of that sea. He has relieved Oczakow, which still holds out; Choczim also is still untaken, and the Emperor's situation is apprehended to be bad. He spun his army into a long cord, to cover several hundred miles of frontier, which put it in the power of the Turks to attack with their whole force wherever they pleased. Laudon, now called to head the imperial army, is endeavoring to collect it; but in the mean time the campaign is drawing to a close, and has been worse than fruitless. The resistance of Russia to Sweden has been successful in every point by sea and land, This, with the interference of Denmark, and the discontent of the Swedish nation; at the breach of their constitution, by the King's undertaking an offensive war without the consent of the Senate, has obliged him to withdraw his attacks by land, and to express a willingness for peace; one third of his officers have refused to serve. England and Prussia have offered their mediation between Sweden and Russia, in such equivocal terms, as to leave themselves at liberty to say it was an offer, or was not, just as it shall suit them. Denmark is asking the counter-offer of mediation from this court. If England and Prussia make a peace effectually in the north (which it is absolutely in their power to do), it will be a proof they do not intend to enter into the war; if they do not impose a peace, I should suspect they mean to engage themselves; as one can hardly suppose they would let the war go on in its present form, wherein Sweden must be crushed between Russia and Denmark.

The *Garde des Sceaux*, M. de Lamoignon, was dismissed the 14th instant, and M. de Barentin is appointed in his room. The deputies of Bretagne are released from the Bastile, and M. d'Epermesnil and M. Sabatier recalled from their confinement. The parliament is not yet reinstated; but it is confidently said it will be this week. The stocks continue low, and the treasury under a hard struggle to keep the government in motion. It is believed the meeting of the States General will be as early as January, perhaps December. I have received a duplicate of the ratification of the loan of 1788, by Congress, and a duplicate of a letter of July the 22nd, from the treasury board, on another subject, but none on that of the captives, or foreign officers. I suppose some cause of delay must have intervened between the ratification of Congress, and the consequent orders of the treasury board.

I have the honor to be, with sentiments of the most perfect esteem and respect, Sir, your most obedient and most humble servant;

Th: Jefferson,

LETTER CLXV.—TO M. DE REYNEVAL, October 1, 1788

TO M. DE REYNEVAL.

Paris, October 1, 1788

Sir,

I have now the honor of enclosing to you a copy of the letter of September the 16th, which I had that of writing to his Excellency the Count de Montmorin, with the papers therein referred to, and of soliciting the order I have asked for. The originals were sent at the date before mentioned. Notwithstanding the refusal of the houses of Schweighaeuser and Dobree, and of Puchilberg, to settle their claim against the United States by arbitration, as I proposed to them, the United States will still be ready to do them justice. But those houses must first retire from the only two propositions they have ever made; to wit, either a payment of their demand without discussion, or a discussion before the tribunals of the country. In the mean time, I shall hope an acknowledgment with respect to us, of the principle which holds as to other nations; that our public property here cannot be seized by the territorial judge. It is the more interesting to us, as we shall be more and longer exposed than other nations, to draw arms and military stores from Europe. Our preference of this country has occasioned us to draw them from hence alone, since the peace: and the friendship we have constantly experienced from the government, will, we doubt not, on this and every other occasion, insure to us the protection of what we purchase. I have the honor to be, Sir, your friend and servant,

Th: Jefferson.

LETTER CLXVI.—TO MR. CUTTING, October 2, 1788

TO MR. CUTTING.

Paris, October 2, 1788.

Dear Sir,

I am now to acknowledge the receipt of your favors of the 16th and 23rd ultimo and to thank you for the intelligence they conveyed. That respecting the case of the interrogatories in Pennsylvania, ought to make noise. So evident a heresy in the common law ought not to be tolerated on the authority of two or three civilians, who happened, unfortunately, to make authority in the courts of England. I hold it essential, in America, to forbid that any English decision which has happened since the accession of Lord Mansfield to the bench, should ever be cited in a court: because, though there have come many good ones from him, yet there is so much sly poison instilled into a great part of them, that it is better to proscribe the whole. Can you inform me what has been done by England on the subject of our wheat and flour? The papers say it is prohibited, even in Hanover. How do their whale-fisheries turn out, this year? I hope a deep wound will be given them in that article soon, and such as will leave us in no danger from their competition.

I am, with very great esteem, Dear Sir, your most obedient, humble servant,

Th: Jefferson.

LETTER CLXVII.—TO JOHN JAY, November 14, 1788

TO JOHN JAY.

Paris, November 14, 1788.

Sir,

In my letter of December the 21st, 1787, I had the honor of acknowledging the receipts of your two favors of July the 27th, 1787, which had come to my hands December the 19th, and brought with them my full powers for treating on the subject of the consular convention. Being then much engaged in getting forward the *Arrêt* which came out the 29th of December, and willing to leave some interval between that act, and the solicitation of a reconsideration of our consular convention, I had declined mentioning it, for some time, and was just about to bring it on the carpet, when it became necessary for me to go to Amsterdam. Immediately after my return, which was about the last of April, I introduced the subject to the Count de Montmorin, and have followed it unremittingly, from that time. The office of Marine, as well as that of Foreign Affairs, being to be consulted in all the stages of the negotiation, has protracted its conclusions till this time: it is at length signed this day, and I have now the honor to enclose the original, for the ratification of Congress. The principal changes effected are the following:

The clauses of the Convention of 1784, clothing consuls with privileges of the law of nations, are struck out, and they are expressly subjected, in their persons and property, to the laws of the land.

That giving the right of sanctuary to their houses, is reduced to a protection of their chancery room and its papers.

Their coercive powers over passengers are taken away; and over those, whom they might have termed deserters of their nation, are restrained to deserted seamen only.

The clause, allowing them to arrest and send back vessels, is struck out, and instead of it, they are allowed to exercise a police over the ships of their nation generally.

So is that, which declared the indelibility of the character of subject, and the explanation and extension of the eleventh article of the treaty of amity.

The innovations in the laws of evidence are done away: and the convention is limited to twelve years' duration. Convinced that the fewer examples, the better, of either persons or causes unamenable to the laws of the land, I could have wished, still more had been done; but more could not be done, with good humor. The extensions of authority given by the convention of 1784, were so homogeneous with the spirit of this government, that they were prized here. Monsieur de Reyneval has had the principal charge of arranging this instrument with me; and, in justice to him, I must say, I could not have desired more reasonable and friendly dispositions, than he demonstrated through the whole of it.

I enclose herewith the several schemes successively proposed between us, together with the copies of the written observations given in with them, and which served as texts of discussion, in our personal conferences. They may serve as a commentary on any passage which may need it, either now or hereafter, and as a history how any particular passage comes to stand as it does. No. 1. is the convention of 1784. No. 2. is my first scheme. No. 3. theirs in answer to it. No. 4. my next, which brought us so near together, that, in a conference on that, we arranged it in the form in which it has been signed. I add No. 5. the copy of a translation which I have put into their hands, with a request, that if they find any passages in which the sense of the original is not faithfully rendered, they will point them out to me; otherwise, we may consider it as having their approbation. This, and the convention of 1784, (marked No. 1.) are placed side by side, so as to present to the eye, with less trouble, the changes made; and I enclose a number of printed copies of them, for the use of the members, who will have to decide on the ratification. It is desirable that the ratification should be sent here for exchange, as soon as possible.

With respect to the consular appointments, it is a duty on me to add some observations, which my situation here has enabled me to make. I think it was in the spring of 1784, that Congress (harassed by multiplied applications from foreigners, of whom nothing was known but on their own information, or on that of others as unknown as themselves) came to a resolution, that the interest of America would not permit the naming any person not a citizen, to the office of consul, vice-consul, agent, or commissary. This was intended as a general answer to that swarm of foreign pretenders. It appears to me, that it will be best, still to preserve a part of this regulation. Native citizens, on several valuable accounts, are preferable to aliens, and to citizens alien-born. They possess our language, know our laws, customs, and commerce; have, generally, acquaintance in the United States; give better satisfaction; and are more to be relied on, in point of fidelity. Their disadvantages are, an imperfect acquaintance with the language of this country, and an ignorance of the organization of its judicial and executive powers, and consequent awkwardness, whenever application to either of these is necessary, as it frequently is. But it happens, that in some of the principal ports of France, there is not a single American (as in Marseilles, L'Orient, and Havre), in others but one (as in Nantes and Rouen), and in Bordeaux only, are there two or three. Fortunately for the present moment, most of these are worthy of appointments. But we should look forward to future times, when there may happen to be no native citizens in a port, but such as, being bankrupt, have taken asylum in France from their creditors, or young ephemeral adventurers in commerce, without substance or conduct, or other descriptions, which might disgrace the consular office, without protecting our commerce. To avail ourselves of our good native citizens, when we have one in a port, and when there are none, to have yet some person to attend to our affairs, it appears to me advisable to declare, by a standing law, that no person but a native citizen shall be capable of the office of consul, and that the consul's presence in his port should suspend, for the time, the functions of the vice-consul. This is the rule of 1784, restrained to the office of consul, and to native citizens. The establishing this, by a standing law, will guard against the effect of particular applications, and will shut the door against such applications, which will otherwise be numerous. This done, the office of vice-consul may be given to the best subject in the port, whether citizen or alien, and that of consul, be kept open for any native citizen of superior qualifications, who might come afterwards to establish himself in the port.

The functions of the vice-consul would become dormant during the presence of his principal, come into activity again on his departure, and thus spare us and them the painful operation of revoking and reviving their commissions perpetually. Add to this, that during the presence of the consul, the vice-consul would not be merely useless, but would be a valuable counsellor to his principal, new in the office, the language, laws, and customs of the country. Every consul and vice-consul should be restrained in his jurisdiction, to the port for which he is named, and the territory nearer to that than to any other consular or vice-consular port, and no idea be permitted to arise, that the grade of consul gives a right to any authority whatever over a vice-consul, or draws on any dependence.

It is now proper I should give some account of the state of our dispute with Schweighaeuser and Dobree. In the conversation I had with Dobree, at Nantes, he appeared to think so rationally on this subject, that I thought there would be no difficulty in accommodating it with him, and I wished rather to settle it by accommodation, than to apply to the minister. I afterwards had it intimated to him, through the medium of Mr. Carnes, that I had it in idea, to propose a reference to arbitrators. He expressed a cheerful concurrence in it. I thereupon made the proposition to him formally, by letter, mentioning particularly, that we would choose our arbitrators of some neutral nation, and, of preference, from among the Dutch refugees here. I was surprised to receive an answer from him, wherein, after expressing his own readiness to accede to this proposition, he added, that on consulting Mr. Puchilberg, he had declined it; nevertheless, he wished a fuller explanation from me, as to the subjects to be submitted to arbitration. I gave him that explanation, and he answered finally, that Mr. Puchilberg refused all accommodation, and insisted that the matter should be decided by the tribunals of the country. Accommodation being at an end, I wrote to Monsieur de Montmorin, and insisted on the usage of nations, which does not permit the effects of one sovereign, to be seized in the territories of another, and subjected to judiciary decision there. I am promised that the stores shall be delivered; but the necessary formalities will occasion some delay. The King being authorized to call all causes before himself, ours will be evoked from the tribunal where it is, and will be ended by an order to deliver up the stores arrested, leaving it to the justice of Congress, to do afterwards what is right, as to the demand of Schweighaeuser and Dobree. I wish I could receive instructions what to do with the stores, when delivered. The arms had certainly better be sent to America, as they are good, and yet will sell here for little or nothing. The gun-stocks and old iron had better be sold here; but what should be done with the anchors? Being thoroughly persuaded that Congress wish that substantial justice should be done to Schweighaeuser and Dobree, I shall, after the stores are secured, repeat my proposition of arbitration to them. If they then refuse it, I shall return all the papers to America, and consider my powers for settling this matter as at an end.

I have received no answer yet from Denmark on the subject of the prizes; nor do I know whether to ascribe this silence to an intention to evade the demand, or to the multitude of affairs they have had on their hands lately. Patience seems to be prudence, in this case; to indispose them, would do no good, and might do harm. I shall write again soon, if no answer be received in the mean time.

I have the honor to be, with sentiments of the most perfect esteem and respect, Sir, your most obedient and most humble

servant,

Th: Jefferson.

[The following is the translation of the convention referred

to as No. 5. in the preceding letter.]

Convention between his Most Christian Majesty and the United States of America, for the purpose of defining and establishing the Functions and Privileges of their respective Consuls and Vice-Consuls.

His Majesty the Most Christian King, and the United States of America, having, by the twenty-ninth article of the treaty of amity and commerce concluded between them, mutually granted the liberty of having, in their respective States and ports, Consuls, Vice-Consuls, Agents, and Commissaries, and being willing, in consequence thereof, to define and establish, in a reciprocal and permanent manner, the functions and privileges of Consuls and Vice-Consuls, which they have judged it convenient to establish of preference, his M. C. Majesty has nominated the Sieur Count of Montmorin of St. Herent, Marechal of his Camps and Armies, Knight of his Orders and of the Golden Fleece, his Counsellor in all his Councils, Minister and Secretary of State, and of his Commandments and Finances, having the department of foreign affairs, and the United States have nominated Thomas Jefferson, citizen of the United States of America and their Minister Plenipotentiary near the King, who after having communicated to each other their respective full powers, have agreed on what follows:

Article I. The Consuls and Vice-Consuls named by the M. C. K. and the United States, shall be bound to present their commissions according to the forms which shall be established respectively by the M. C. K. within his dominions, and by the Congress within the United States; there shall be delivered to them, without any charges, the *Exequatur* necessary for the exercise of their functions; and on exhibiting the said *Exequatur*, the governors, commanders, heads of justice, bodies corporate, tribunals, and other officers having authority in the ports and places of their consulates, shall cause them to enjoy immediately, and without difficulty, the pre-eminences, authority, and privileges, reciprocally granted, without exacting from the said Consuls and Vice-Consuls any fee, under any pretext whatever.

Article II. The Consuls and Vice-Consuls, and persons attached to their functions, that is to say, their chancellors and secretaries, shall enjoy a full and entire immunity for their chancery and the papers which shall be therein contained: they shall be exempt from aU, personal service, from soldiers' billets, militia, watch, guard, guardianship, trusteeship, as well as from all duties, taxes, impositions, and charges whatsoever, except on the estate real and personal of which they may be the proprietors or possessors, which shall be subject to the taxes imposed on the estates of all other individuals: and in all other instances they shall be subject to the laws of the land, as the natives are.

Those of the said Consuls and Vice-Consuls who shall exercise commerce, shall be respectively subject to all taxes, charges, and impositions established on other merchants.

They shall place over the outward door of their house the arms of their sovereign: but this mark of indication shall not give to the said house any privilege of asylum for any person or property whatsoever.

Article III. The respective Consuls and Vice-Consuls may establish agents in the different ports and places of their departments, where necessity shall require. These agents maybe chosen among the merchants, either national or foreign, and furnished with a commission from one of the said Consuls; they shall confine themselves respectively to the rendering to their respective merchants, navigators, and vessels, all possible service, and to inform the nearest Consul of the wants of the said merchants, navigators, and vessels, without the said agents otherwise participating in the immunities, rights, and privileges attributed to Consuls and Vice-Consuls, and without power, under any pretext whatever, to exact from the said merchants any duty or emolument whatsoever.

Article IV. The Consuls and Vice-Consuls respectively, may establish a chancery, where shall be deposited the consular determinations, acts, and proceedings, as also testaments, obligations, contracts, and other acts done by or between persons of their nation, and effects left by decedents, or saved from shipwreck.

They may, consequently, appoint fit persons to act in the said chancery, qualify and swear them in, commit to them the custody of the seal, and authority to seal commissions, sentences, and other consular acts, and also to discharge the functions of notaries and registers of the consulate.

Article V. The Consuls and Vice-Consuls respectively, shall have the exclusive right of receiving in their chancery, or on board their vessels, the declarations and all other the acts which the captains, masters, crews, passengers, and merchants of their nation may choose to make there, even their testaments and other disposals by last will: and the copies of the said acts, duly authenticated by the said Consuls or Vice-Consuls, under the seal of their consulate, shall receive faith in law, equally as their originals would, in all the tribunals of the dominions of the M. C. King and of the United States.

They shall also have, and exclusively, in case of the absence of the testamentary executor, guardian, or lawful representative, the right to inventory, liquidate, and proceed to the sale of the personal estate left by subjects or citizens of their nation, who shall die within the extent of their consulate; they shall proceed therein with the assistance of two merchants of their said nation, or, for want of them, of any other at their choice, and shall cause to be deposited in their chancery, the effects and papers of the said estates; and no officer, military, judiciary, or of the police of the country, shall disturb them or interfere therein, in any manner whatsoever: but the said Consuls and Vice-Consuls shall not deliver up the said effects, nor the proceeds thereof, to the lawful representatives or to their order, till they shall have caused to be paid all debts which the deceased shall have contracted in the country; for which purpose the creditor shall have a right to attach the said effects in their hands, as they might in those of any other individual whatever, and proceed to obtain sale of them, till payment of what shall be lawfully due to them. When the debts shall not have been contracted by judgment, deed, or note, the signature whereof shall be known, payment shall not be ordered, but on the creditor's giving sufficient surety resident in the country, to refund the sums he shall have unduly received, principal, interest, and costs; which surety, nevertheless, shall stand duly discharged after the term of one year, in time of peace, and of two, in time of war, if the discharge cannot be formed before the end of this term, against the* representatives who shall present themselves.

And in order that the representatives may not be unjustly kept out of the effects of the deceased, the Consuls and Vice-Consuls shall notify his death in some one of the gazettes published within their consulate, and that they shall retain the said effects in their hands four months, to answer all just demands which shall be presented; and they shall be bound, after this delay, to deliver to the persons succeeding thereto, what shall be more than sufficient for the demands which shall have been formed.

Article VI. The Consuls and Vice-Consuls, respectively, shall receive the declarations, protests, and reports of all captains and masters of their respective nations, on account of average losses sustained at sea; and these captains and masters shall lodge in the chancery of the said Consuls and Vice-Consuls, the acts which they may have made in other ports, on account of the accidents which may have happened to them on their voyage. If a subject of the M. C. K. and a citizen of the United States, or a foreigner, are interested in the said cargo, the average shall be settled by the tribunals of the country, and not by the Consuls or Vice-Consuls; but when only the subjects or citizens of their own nation shall be interested, the respective Consuls or Vice-Consuls shall appoint skilful persons to settle the damages and average.

Article VII. In cases where by tempest, or other accident, French ships or vessels shall be stranded on the coasts of the United States, and ships or vessels of the United States shall be stranded on the coasts of the dominions of the M. C. K.,the Consul or Vice-Consul nearest to the place of shipwreck shall do whatever he may judge proper, as well for the purpose of saving the said ship or vessel, its cargo and appurtenances, as for the storing and the security of the effects and merchandise saved. He may take an inventory of them, without the intermeddling of any officers of the military, of the customs, of justice, or of the police of the country, otherwise than to give to the Consuls, Vice-Consuls, captain, and crew of the vessels shipwrecked or stranded, all the succor and favor which they shall ask of them, either for the expedition and security of the saving and of the effects saved, as to prevent all disturbance.

And in order to prevent all kind of dispute and discussion in the said cases of shipwreck, it is agreed that when there shall be no Consul or Vice-Consul to attend to the saving of the wreck, or that the residence of the said Consul or Vice-Consul (he not being at the place of the wreck) shall be more distant from the said place than that of the competent judge of the country, the latter shall immediately proceed therein, with all the despatch, certainty, and precautions, prescribed by the respective laws; but the said territorial judge shall retire, on the arrival of the Consul or Vice-Consul, and shall deliver over to him the report of his proceedings, the expenses of which the Consul and Vice-Consul shall cause to be reimbursed to him, as well as those of saving the wreck.

The merchandise and effects saved, shall be deposited in the nearest Custom-house, or other place of safety, with the inventory thereof, which shall have been made by the Consul or Vice-Consul, or by the judge who shall have proceeded in their absence, that the said effects and merchandise may be afterwards delivered (after levying therefrom the costs), and without form of process, to the owners, who, being furnished with an order for their delivery, from the nearest Consul or Vice-Consul, shall reclaim them by themselves, or by their order, either for the purpose of re-exporting such merchandise, in which case, they shall-pay no kind of duty of exportation, or for that of selling them in the country, if they be not prohibited there; and in this last case, the said merchandise, if they be damaged, shall be allowed an abatement of entrance duties, proportioned to the damage they have sustained, which shall be ascertained by the affidavits taken at the time the vessel was wrecked or struck.

Article VIII. The Consuls and Vice-Consuls shall exercise police over all the vessels of their respective nations, and shall have on board the said vessels, all power and jurisdiction in civil matters, in all the disputes which may there arise; they shall have an entire inspection over the said vessels, their crew, and the changes and substitutions there to be made. For which purpose they may go on board the said vessels whenever they may judge it necessary: well understood, that the functions hereby allowed shall be confined to the interior of the vessels, and that they shall not take place in any case, which shall have any interference with the police of the ports where the said vessels shall be.

Article IX. The Consuls and Vice-Consuls may cause to be arrested the captains, officers, mariners, sailors, and all other persons, being part of the crews of the vessels of their respective nations, who shall have deserted from the said vessels, in order to send them back, and transport them out of the country. For which purpose, the said Consuls and Vice-Consuls shall address themselves to the courts, judges, and officers competent, and shall demand the said deserters in writing, proving by an exhibition of the registers of the vessel or ship's roll, that those men were part of the said crews: and on this demand, so proved (saving, however, where the contrary is proved), the delivery shall not be refused; and there shall be given all aid and assistance to the said Consuls and Vice-Consuls, for the search, seizure, and arrest of the said deserters, who shall even be detained and kept in the prisons of the country, at their request and expense, until they shall have found an opportunity of sending them back. But if they be not sent back within three months, to be counted from the day of their arrest, they shall be set at liberty, and shall be no more arrested for the same cause.

Article X. In cases where the respective subjects, or citizens, shall have committed any crime, or breach of the peace, they shall be amenable to the judges of the country.

Article XI. When the said offenders shall be a part of the crew of a vessel of their nation, and shall have withdrawn themselves on board the said vessel, they may be there seized and arrested by order of the judges of the country: these shall give notice thereof to the Consul or Vice-Consul, who may repair on board, if he thinks proper: but this notification shall not, in any case, delay execution of the order in question. The persons arrested shall not afterwards be set at liberty, until the Consul or Vice-Consul shall have been notified thereof; and they shall be delivered to him, if he requires it, to be put again onboard of the vessel on which they were arrested, or of others of their nation, and to be sent out of the country.

Article XII. All differences and suits between the subjects of the M. C. K. in the U. S., or between the citizens of the United States within the dominions of the M. C. K. and particularly all disputes relative to the wages and terms of engagement of the crews of the respective vessels, and all differences of whatever nature they be, which may arise between the privates of the said crews, or between any of them and their captains, or between the captains of different vessels of their nation, shall be determined by the respective Consuls and Vice-Consuls, either by a reference to arbitrators, or by a summary judgment, and without costs.

No officer of the country, civil or military, shall interfere therein, or take any part whatever in the matter: and the appeals from the said consular sentences shall be carried before the tribunals of France or of the United States, to whom it may appertain to take cognizance thereof.

Article XIII. The general utility of commerce, having caused to be established within the dominions of the M. C. K. particular tribunals and forms, for expediting the decision of commercial affairs, the merchants of the U. S. shall enjoy the benefit of these establishments; and the Congress of the U. S. will provide in the manner the most conformable to its laws, equivalent advantages in favor of the French merchants, for the prompt despatch and decision of affairs of the same nature.

Article XIV. The subjects of the M. C. K. and citizens of the U. S. who shall prove by legal evidence, that they are of the said nations respectively, shall, in consequence, enjoy an exemption from all personal service in the place of their settlement.

Article XV. If any other nation acquires, by virtue of any convention whatever, a treatment more favorable with respect to the consular pre-eminences, powers, authority, and privileges, the Consuls and Vice-Consuls of the M. C. K. or of the U. S., reciprocally, shall participate therein, agreeably to the terms stipulated by the second, third, and fourth articles of the treaty of amity and commerce, concluded between the M. C. K. and the U. S.

Article XVI. The present convention shall be in full force during the term of twelve years, to be counted from the day of the exchange of ratifications, which shall be given in proper form, and exchanged on both sides, within the space of one year, or sooner, if possible.

In faith whereof, we, Ministers Plenipotentiary, have signed the present convention, and have thereto set the seal of our arms.

Done at Versailles, the 14th of November, one thousand seven hundred and eighty eight.

L. C. De MONTMORIN. L. S.

Signed.

Th: Jefferson. L. S.

LETTER CLXVIII.—TO JAMES MADISON, November 18, 1788

TO JAMES MADISON.

Paris, November 18, 1788.

Dear Sir,

My last to you was of the 31st of July; since which, I have received yours of July the 24th, August the 10th, and 23rd. The first part of this long silence in me was occasioned by a knowledge that you were absent from New York; the latter part, by a want of opportunity, which has been longer than usual. Mr. Shippen being just arrived here, and to set out to-morrow for London, I avail myself of that channel of conveyance. Mr. Carrington was so kind as to send me the second volume of the American Philosophical Transactions, the Federalist, and some other interesting pamphlets; and I am to thank you for another copy of the Federalist, and the report of the instructions to the ministers for negotiating peace. The latter unluckily omitted exactly the passage I wanted, which was what related to the navigation of the Mississippi. With respect to the Federalist, the three authors had been named to me. I read it with care, pleasure, and improvement, and was satisfied there was nothing in it by one of those hands, and not a great deal by a second. It does the highest honor to the third, as being, in my opinion, the best commentary on the principles of government, which ever was written. In some parts, it is discoverable that the author means only to say what may be best said in defence of opinions, in which he did not concur. But in general, it establishes firmly the plan of government. I confess, it has rectified me on several points. As to the bill of rights, however, I still think it should be added; and I am glad to see, that three States have at length considered the perpetual re-eligibility of the President, as an article which should be amended. I should deprecate with you, indeed, the meeting of a new convention. I hope they will adopt the mode of amendment by Congress and the Assemblies, in which case, I should not fear any dangerous innovation in the plan. But the minorities are too respectable, not to be entitled to some sacrifice of opinion in the majority; especially, when a great proportion of them would be contented with a bill of rights. Here, things internally, are going on well. The *Notables* now in session, have, indeed, passed one vote, which augurs ill to the rights of the people; but if they do not obtain now so much as they have a right to, they will in the long run. The misfortune is, that they are not yet ripe for receiving the blessings to which they are entitled. I doubt, for instance, whether the body of the nation, if they could be consulted, would accept of a *habeas corpus* law, if offered them by the King. If the *Etats Generaux*, when they assemble, do not aim at too much, they may begin a good constitution. There are three articles which they may easily obtain; 1. their own meeting, periodically; 2. the exclusive right of taxation; 3. the right of registering laws and proposing amendments to them, as exercised now by the parliaments. This last would be readily approved by the court, on account of their hostility against the parliaments, and would lead immediately to the origination of laws: the second has been already solemnly avowed by the King; and it is well understood, there would be no opposition to the first. If they push at much more, all may fail. I shall not enter further into public details, because my letter to Mr. Jay will give them. That contains a request of permission to return to America the next spring, for the summer only. The reasons therein urged, drawn from my private affairs, are very cogent. But there is another, more cogent on my mind, though of a nature not to be explained in a public letter. It is the necessity of attending my daughters, myself, to their own country, and depositing them safely in the hands of those, with whom I can safely leave them. I have deferred this request as long as circumstances would permit, and am in hopes it will meet with no difficulty. I have had too many proofs of your friendship, not to rely on your patronage of it, as, in all probability, nothing can suffer by a short absence. But the immediate permission is what I am anxious about; as by going in April and returning in October, I shall be sure of pleasant and short passages, out and in. I must intreat your attention, my friend, to this matter, and that the answers may be sent me through several channels.

Mr. Liniozin, at Havre, sent you, by mistake, a package belonging to somebody else. I do not know what it contained, but he has written to you on the subject, and prayed me to do the same, he is likely to suffer if it be not returned.

Supposing that the funding their foreign debt will be among the first operations of the new government, I send you two estimates; the one by myself, the other by a gentleman infinitely better acquainted with the subject, showing what fund will suffice to discharge the principal and interest, as it shall become due, aided by occasional loans, which the same fund will repay. I enclose them to you, because collating them together, and with your own ideas, you will be able to advise something better than either; but something must be done. This government will expect, I fancy, a very satisfactory provision for the payment of their debt, from the first session of the new Congress. Perhaps, in this matter, as well as the arrangement of your foreign affairs, I may be able, when on the spot with you, to give some information and suggest some hints, which may render my visit to my native country not altogether useless. I consider as no small advantage, the resuming the tone of mind of my constituents, which is lost by long absence, and can only be recovered by mixing with them; and shall, particularly, hope for much profit and pleasure, by contriving to pass as much time as possible with you. Should you have a trip to Virginia in contemplation, for that year, I hope you will time it so as that we may be there together. I will camp you at Monticello, where, if illy entertained otherwise, you shall not want books. In firm hope of a happy meeting with you in the spring, or early in summer, I conclude, with assurances of the sincere esteem and attachment, with which I am, Dear Sir, your affectionate friend and servant,

Th: Jefferson.

LETTER CLXIX.—TO A. DONALD, November 18,1788

TO A. DONALD.

Paris, November 18,1788.

Dear Sir,

Often solicited by persons on this side the water, to inquire for their friends in America, about whose fate they are uncertain, I can only hand on their requests to my friends in America. The enclosed letter from, the Chevalier de Sigougne desires some inquiry after his brother, whom he supposes to have settled at Todd's Bridge. As this is within your reach, I must refer the request to your humanity, and beg of you, if you can hear of him, you will be so good as to give me an account of him, returning me the enclosed letter at the same time.

The campaign between the Turks and Russians has been tolerably equal. The Austrians have suffered through the whole of it. By the interposition of Prussia and England, peace is likely to be made between Russia, Denmark, and Sweden. This is a proof that England does not mean to engage in the war herself. This country will certainly engage herself in no manner, externally, before the meeting of her States General. This assembly has been so long disused, that the forms of its convocation occasion difficulty. The *Notables* have been convened to prescribe them, and they are now in session. I am in hopes this will end in giving a good degree of liberty to this country. They enjoy, at present, the most perfect tranquillity within; their stocks, however, continue low, and money difficult to be got for current expenses. It is hoped, that Mr. Necker's talents and popularity, with the aid of a National Assembly, will extricate them from their difficulties. We have been daily expecting to hear of the death of the King of England: our last news is of the 11th, when he was thought in the utmost danger. This event might produce a great change in the situation of things: it is supposed Mr. Fox would come into place, and he has been generally understood to be disposed for war. Should the King survive, I think the continuance of peace more probable at present, than it has been for some time past. Be so good as to contrive the enclosed letter, by a very safe conveyance. Remember me in the most friendly terms to Dr. Currie, and be assured yourself of the esteem and attachment, with which I am. Dear Sir, your affectionate friend and servant,

Th: Jefferson.

LETTER CLXX.—TO JOHN JAY, November 19, 1788

TO JOHN JAY.

Sir,

Paris, November 19, 1788.

Since my letter of September the 5th, wherein I acknowledged Mr. Remsen's favor of July the 25th, I have written those of September the 24th, and of the 14th instant. This last will accompany the present, both going by the way of London, for want of a direct opportunity; but they go by a private hand.

No late event worth notice has taken place between the Turks and Austrians. The former continue in the territories of the latter, with all the appearances of superiority. On the side of Russia, the war wears an equal face, except that the Turks are still masters of the Black sea. Oczakow is not yet taken. Denmark furnished to Russia its stipulated quota of troops with so much alacrity, and was making such other warlike preparations, that it was believed they meant to become principals in the war against Sweden. Russia and England hereupon interposed efficaciously. Their ministers appointed to meditate, gave notice to the court of Copenhagen, that they would declare war against them in the name of their two sovereigns, if they did not immediately withdraw their troops from the Swedish territories. The court of London has since said, that their minister (Elliott) went further in this than he was authorized. However, the Danish troops are retiring. Poland is augmenting its army from twenty to an hundred thousand men. Nevertheless, it seems as if England and Prussia meant in earnest to stop the war in that quarter, contented to leave the two empires in the hands of the Turks. France, desired by Sweden to join the courts of London and Berlin in their mediation between Sweden and Russia, has declined it. We may be assured, she will meddle in nothing external before the meeting of the States General. Her temporary annihilation in the political scale of Europe, leaves to England and Prussia the splendid roll, of giving the law without meeting the shadow of opposition. The internal tranquillity of this country is perfect: their stocks, however, continue low, and the difficulty of getting money to face current expenses very great. In the contest between the King and parliament, the latter, fearing the power of the former, passed the convoking the States General. The government found itself obliged by other difficulties, also, to recur to the same expedient. The parliament, after its recall, showed that it was now become apprehensive of the States General, and discovered a determination to cavil at their form, so as to have a right to deny their legality, if that body should undertake to abridge their powers. The court, hereupon, very adroitly determined to call the same *Notables*, who had been approved by the nation the last year, to decide on the form of convoking the *Etats Generaux*: thus withdrawing itself from the disputes which the parliament might excite, and committing them with the nation. The *Notables* are now in session. The government had manifestly discovered a disposition that the *Tiers-Etat*, or Commons, should have as many representatives in the States General, as the Nobility and Clergy together: but five Bureaux of the *Notables* have voted by very great majorities, that they should have only an equal number with each of the other orders singly. One bureau, by a majority of a single voice, had agreed to give the Commons the double number of representatives. This is the first symptom of a decided combination between the Nobility and Clergy, and will necessarily throw the people into the scale of the King. It is doubted, whether the States can be called so early as January, though the government, urged by the want of money, is for pressing the convocation. It is still more uncertain what the States will do when they meet: there are three objects which they may attain, probably without opposition from the court; 1. A periodical meeting of the States; 2. their exclusive right of taxation; 3. the right of en-registering laws and proposing amendments to them, as now exercised by the parliaments. This would lead, as it did in England, to the right of originating laws. The parliament would, by the last measure, be reduced to a mere judiciary body, and would probably oppose it. But against the King and nation their opposition could not succeed. If the States stop here, for the present moment, all will probably end well, and they may, in future sessions, obtain a suppression of *lettres de cachet*, a free press, a civil list, and other valuable mollifications of their government. But it is to be feared, that an impatience to rectify every thing at once, which prevails in some minds, may terrify the court, and lead them to appeal to force, and to depend on that alone.

Before this can reach you, you will probably have heard of an *Arrêt*, passed the 28th of September, for prohibiting the introduction of foreign whale-oils, without exception. The English had glutted the markets of this country with their oils: it was proposed to exclude them, and an *Arrêt* was drawn, with an exception for us: in the last stage of the *Arrêt*, the exception was struck out, without my having any warning, or even suspicion of this. I suspect this stroke came from the Count de la Luzerne, minister of marine; but I cannot affirm it positively. As soon as I was apprized of this, which was several days after it passed (because it was kept secret till published in their seaports), I wrote to the Count de Montmorin a letter, of which the enclosed is a copy, and had conferences on the subject, from time to time, with him and the other ministers. I found them prepossessed by the partial information of their Dunkirk fishermen; and therefore thought it necessary to give them a view of the whole subject in writing, which I did, in the piece, of which I enclose you a printed copy. I therein entered into more details, than the question between us seemed rigorously to require. I was led to them by other objects.

The most important was to disgust Mr. Necker, as an economist, against their new fishery, by letting him foresee its expense. The particular manufactures suggested to them, were in consequence of repeated applications from the shippers of rice and tobacco: other details, which do not appear immediately pertinent, were occasioned by circumstances which had arisen in conversation, or an apparent necessity of giving information on the whole matter. At a conference, in the presence of M. Lambert, on the 16th (where I was ably aided by the Marquis de la Fayette, as I have been through the whole business), it was agreed to except us from the prohibition. But they will require rigorous assurance, that the oils coming under our name are really of our fishery. They fear we shall cover the introduction of the English oils from Halifax. The *Arrêt* for excepting us was communicated to me, but the formalities of proving the oils to be American were not yet inserted. I suppose they will require every vessel to bring a certificate from their Consul or Vice-Consul residing in the State from which it comes. More difficult proofs were sometimes talked of. I supposed I might surely affirm to them, that our government would do whatever it could to prevent this fraud, because it is as much our interest as theirs to keep the market for the French and American oils only. I am told Massachusetts has prohibited the introduction of foreign fish-oils into her ports. This law, if well executed, will be an effectual guard against fraud; and a similar one in the other States, interested in the fishery, would much encourage this government to continue her indulgence to us. Though the *Arrêt*, then, for the re-admission of our oils is not yet passed, I think I may assure you it will be so in a few days, and of course that this branch of commerce, after so threatening an appearance, will be on a better footing than ever, as enjoying, jointly with the French oil, a monopoly of their markets. The continuance of this will depend on the growth of their fishery. Whenever they become able to supply their own wants, it is very possible they may refuse to take our oils; but I do not believe it possible for them to raise their fishery to that, unless they can continue to draw off our fishermen from us. Their seventeen ships, this year, had one hundred and fifty of our sailors on board. I do not know what number the English have got into their service. You will readily perceive, that there are particulars in these printed observations, which it would not be proper to suffer to become public. They were printed, merely that a copy might be given to each minister, and care has been taken to let them go into no other hands.

I must now trouble Congress with a petition on my own behalf. When I left my own house in October, 1783, it was to attend Congress as a member, and in expectation of returning in five or six months. In the month of May following, however, I was desired to come to Europe, as member of a commission, which was to continue two years only. I came off immediately, without going home to make any other arrangements in my affairs, thinking they would not suffer greatly before I should return to them. Before the close of the two years, Doctor Franklin retiring from his charge here, Congress were pleased to name me to it; so that I have been led on by events to an absence of five years, instead of five months. In the mean time, matters of great moment to others as well as myself, and which can be arranged by nobody but myself, will await no longer. Another motive, of still more powerful co-agency on my mind, is the necessity of carrying my family back to their friends and country. I must, therefore, ask of Congress a leave of short absence. Allowing three months on the sea, going and coming, and two months at my own house, which will suffice for my affairs, I need not be from Paris but between five and six months. I do not foresee any thing which can suffer during my absence. The consular convention is finished, except as to the exchange of ratification, which will be the affair of a day only. The difference with Schweighaeuser and Dobree, relative to our arms, will be finished. That of Denmark, if ever finished, will probably be long spun out. The ransom of the Algerine captives is the only matter likely to be on hand. That cannot be set on foot till the money is raised in Holland, and an order received for its application: probably these will take place, so that I may set it into motion, before my departure; if not, I can still leave it on such a footing, as to be put into motion the moment the money can be paid. And even when the leave of Congress shall be received, I will not make use of it, if there is any thing of consequence which may suffer; but would, postpone my departure till circumstances will admit it. But should these be as I expect they will, it will be vastly desirable to me to receive the permission immediately, so that I may go out as soon as the vernal equinox is over, and be sure of my return in good time and season in the fall. Mr. Short, who had had thoughts of returning to America, will postpone that return till I come back. His talents and character allow me to say, with confidence, that nothing will suffer in his hands. The friendly dispositions of Monsieur de Montmorin would induce him readily to communicate with Mr. Short in his present character; but should any of his applications be necessary to be laid before the Council, they might suffer difficulty: nor could he attend the diplomatic societies, which are the most certain sources of good intelligence. Would Congress think it expedient to remove the difficulties, by naming him secretary of legation, so that he would act of course as *chargé des affaires* during my absence? It would be just, that the difference between the salary of a secretary and a secretary of legation should cease, as soon as he should cease to be charged with the affairs of the United States; that is to say, on my return: and he would expect that. So that this difference for five or six months would be an affair of about one hundred and seventy guineas only, which would be not more than equal to the additional expense that would be brought on him necessarily by the change of character. I mention these particulars, that Congress may see the end as well as beginning of the proposition, and have only to add, 'their will be done.' Leave for me being obtained, I will ask it, Sir, of your friendship, to avail yourself of various occasions to the ports of France and England to convey me immediate notice of it, and relieve me as soon as possible from the anxiety of expectation, and the uncertainty in which I shall be. We have been in daily expectation of hearing of the death of the King of England. Our latest news are of the 11th. He had then been despaired of for three or four days; but as my letter is to pass through England, you will have later accounts of him than that can give you. I send you the newspapers to this date, and have the honor to be, with the greatest esteem and respect, Sir, your most obedient, humble servant,

Th: Jefferson.

P. S. The last crop of corn in France has been so short, that they apprehend want. Mr. Necker desires me to make known this scarcity to our merchants, in hopes they would send supplies. I promised him I would. If it could be done without naming him, it would be agreeable to him, and probably advantageous to the adventurers. T. J.

[The annexed are the observations on the subject of admitting our whale-oil in the markets of France, referred to in the preceding letter.]

Whale-oil enters, as a raw material, into several branches of manufacture, as of wool, leather, soap: it is used also in painting, architecture, and navigation. But its great consumption is in lighting houses and cities. For this last purpose, however, it has a powerful competitor in the vegetable oils. These do well in warm, still weather, but they fix with cold, they extinguish easily with the wind, their crop is precarious, depending on the seasons, and to yield the same light, a larger wick must be used, and greater quantity of oil consumed. Estimating all these articles of difference together, those employed in lighting cities find their account in giving about twenty-five per cent, more for whale than for vegetable oils. But higher than this the whale-oil, in its present form, cannot rise; because it then becomes more advantageous to the city lighters to use others. This competition, then, limits its price, higher than which no encouragement can raise it; and it becomes, as it were, a law of its nature. But, at this low price, the whale-fishery is the poorest business into which a merchant or sailor can enter. If the sailor, instead of wages, has a part of what is taken, he finds that this, one year with another, yields him less than he could have got as wages in any other business. It is attended, too, with great risk, singular hardships, and long absence from his family, if the voyage is made solely at the expense of the merchant, he finds that, one year with another, it does not reimburse him his expense. As for example; an English ship of three hundred tons and forty-two hands brings home, *communibus annis*, after four months' voyage, twenty-five tons of oil, worth four hundred and thirty-seven pounds ten shillings sterling. But the wages of the officers and seamen will be four hundred pounds; the outfit, then, and the merchants' profit, must be paid by the government: and it is accordingly on this idea, that the British bounty is calculated. From the poverty of this business, then, it has happened, that the nations who have taken it up have successively abandoned it. The Basques began it: but though the most economical and enterprising of the inhabitants of France, they could not continue it; and it is said, they never employed more than thirty ships a year. The Dutch and Hanse towns succeeded them. The latter gave it up long ago. The English carried it on, in competition with the Dutch, during the last and beginning of the present century: but it was too little profitable for them, in comparison with other branches of commerce open to them.

In the mean time, the inhabitants of the barren island of Nantucket had taken up this fishery, invited to it by the whales presenting themselves on their own shore. To them, therefore, the English relinquished it, continuing to them, as British subjects, the importation of their oils into England, duty free, while foreigners were subject to a duty of eighteen pounds five shillings sterling a ton. The Dutch were enabled to continue it long, because, 1. They are so near the northern fishing grounds, that a vessel begins her fishing very soon after she is out of port. 2. They navigate with more economy than the other nations of Europe. 3. Their seamen are content with lower wages: and, 4. Their merchants, with a lower profit on their capital. Under all these favorable circumstances, however, this branch of business, after long languishing, is at length nearly extinct with them. It is said, they did not send above half a dozen ships in pursuit of the whale this present year. The *Nantuckois*, then, were the only people who exercised this fishery to any extent at the commencement of the late war. Their country, from its barrenness yielding no subsistence, they were obliged to seek it in the sea which surrounded them. Their economy was more rigorous than that of the Dutch. Their seamen, instead of wages, had a share in what was taken: this induced them to fish with fewer hands, so that each had a greater dividend in the profit; it made them more vigilant in seeking game, bolder in pursuing it, and parsimonious in all their expenses. London was their only market. When, therefore, by the late revolution, they became aliens in Great Britain, they became subject to the alien duty of eighteen pounds five shillings the ton of oil, which being more than equal to the price of the common whale-oil, they are obliged to abandon that fishery. So that this people, who, before the war, had employed upwards of three hundred vessels a year in the whale-fishery (while Great Britain had herself never employed one hundred), have now almost ceased to exercise it. But they still had the seamen, the most important material for this fishery; and they still retained the spirit for fishing: so that, at the re-establishment of peace, they were capable, in a very short time, of reviving their fishery in all its splendor. The British government saw that the moment was critical. They knew that their own share in that fishery was as nothing: that the great mass of fishermen was left with a nation now separated from them: that these fishermen, however, had lost their ancient market; had no other resource within their country to which they could turn and they hoped, therefore, they might, in the present moment of distress, be decoyed over to their establishments, and be added to the mass of their seamen. To effect this, they offered extravagant advantages to all persons who should exercise the whale-fishery from British establishments. But not counting with much confidence on a long connection with their remaining possessions on the continent of America, foreseeing that the *Nantuckois* would settle in them, preferably, if put on an equal footing with those of Great Britain, and that thus they might have to purchase them a second time, they confined their high offers to settlers in Great Britain. The *Nantuckois*, left without resource by the loss of their market, began to think of removing to the British dominions; some to Nova Scotia, preferring smaller advantages in the neighborhood of their ancient country and friends; others to Great Britain, postponing country and friends to high premiums. A vessel was already arrived from Halifax to Nantucket, to take off some of those who proposed to remove; two families had gone on board, and others were going, when a letter was received there, which had been written by Monsieur le Marquis de la Fayette, to a gentleman in Boston, and transmitted by him to Nantucket. The purport of the letter was to dissuade their accepting the British proposals, and to assure them that their friends in France would endeavor to do something for them. This instantly suspended their design: not another went on board, and the vessel returned to Halifax with only the two families.

In fact the French government had not been inattentive to the views of the British, nor insensible to the crisis. They saw the danger of permitting five or six thousand of the best seamen existing, to be transferred by a single stroke to the marine strength of their enemy, and to carry over with them an art which they possessed almost exclusively. The counterplan which they set on foot was to tempt the *Nantuckois*, by high offers, to come and settle in France. This was in the year 1785. The British, however, had in their favor, a sameness of language, religion, laws, habits, and kindred. Nine families only, of thirty-three persons in the whole, came to Dunkirk; so that this project was not likely to prevent their emigration to the English establishments, if nothing else had happened.

France had effectually aided in detaching the United States of America from the force of Great Britain: but as yet they seemed to have indulged only a silent wish to detach them from her commerce. They had done nothing to induce that event. In the same year, 1785, while M. de Calonne was in treaty with the *Nantuckois*, an estimate of the commerce of the United States was submitted to the Count de Vergennes, and it was shown, that, of three millions of pounds sterling, to which their exports amounted, one third might be brought to France, and exchanged against her productions and manufactures, advantageously for both nations; provided the obstacles of prohibition, monopoly, and duty, were either done away, or moderated as far as circumstances would admit. A committee, which had been appointed to investigate a particular one of these objects, was thereupon instructed to extend its researches to the whole, and see what advantages and facilities the government could offer, for the encouragement of a general commerce with the United States. The committee was composed of persons well skilled in commerce; and after laboring assiduously for several months, they made their report: the result of which was given in the letter of his Majesty's Comptroller General, of the 22nd of October, 1786, wherein he stated the principles which should be established, for the future regulation of the commerce between France and the United States. It was become tolerably evident, at the date of this letter, that the terms offered to the *Nantuckois* would not produce their emigration to Dunkirk; and that it would be safest, in every event, to offer some other alternative, which might prevent their acceptance of the British offers. The obvious one was, to open the ports of France to their oils, so that they might still exercise their fishery, remaining in their native country, and find a new market for its produce, instead of that which they had lost. The article of whale-oil was, accordingly, distinguished in the letter of M. de Calonne, by an immediate abatement of duty, and promise of further abatement, after the year 1790. This letter was instantly sent to America, and bid fair to produce there the effect intended, by determining the fishermen to carry on their trade from their own homes, with the advantage only of a free market in France, rather than remove to Great Britain, where a free market and great bounty were offered them. An *Arrêt* was still to be prepared, to give legal sanction to the letter of M. de Calonne. Monsieur Lambert, with a patience and assiduity almost unexampled, went through all the investigations necessary to assure himself, that the conclusion of the committee had been just. Frequent conferences on this subject were held in his presence; the deputies of the chambers of commerce were heard, and the result was, the *Arrêt* of December the 29th, 1787, confirming the abatements of duty, present and future, which the letter of October, 1786, had promised, and reserving to his Majesty, to grant still further favors to that production, if, on further information, he should find it for the interest of the two nations.

The English had now begun to deluge the markets of France with their whale-oils; and they were enabled by the great premiums given by their government, to undersell the French fisherman, aided by feebler premiums, and the American, aided by his poverty alone. Nor is it certain, that these speculations were not made at the risk of the British government, to suppress the French and American fishermen in their only market. Some remedy seemed necessary. Perhaps it would not have been a bad one, to subject, by a general law, the merchandise of every nation and of every nature, to pay additional duties in the ports of France, exactly equal to the premiums and drawbacks given on the same merchandise by their own government. This might not only counteract the effect of premiums in the instance of whale-oils, but attack the whole British system of bounties and drawbacks, by the aid of which they make London the centre of commerce for the whole earth. A less general remedy, but an effectual one, was, to prohibit the oils of all European nations: the treaty with England requiring only, that she should be treated as well as the most favored European nation. But the remedy adopted was, to prohibit all oils, without exception.

To know how this remedy will operate, we must consider the quantity of whale-oil which France consumes annually, the quantity she obtains from her own fishery; and, if she obtains less than she consumes, we are to consider what will follow the prohibition.

The annual consumption of France, as stated by a person who has good opportunities of knowing it, is as follows.

	lbs. pesant.	*quinteaux.*	*tons.*
Paris, according to the registers of 1786,................................	2,800,000	28,000	1750
Twenty-seven other cities, lighted by M. Sangrain,.......................	800,000	8,000	500
Rouen,.................................	*500,000*	*5,000*	*312*
Bordeaux,..............................	*600,000*	*6,000*	*375*
Lyons,.................................	*300,000*	*3,000*	*187*
Other cities, leather and light,......	*3,000,000*	*30,000*	*1875*
	8,000,000	*80,000*	*5,000*

Other calculations, or say rather, conjectures, reduce the consumption to about half this. It is treating these conjectures with great respect, to place them on an equal footing with the estimate of the person before alluded to, and to suppose the truth half way between them. But we will do it, and call the present consumption of France only sixty thousand quintals, or three thousand seven hundred and fifty tons a year. This consumption is increasing fast, as the practice of lighting cities is becoming more general, and the superior advantages of lighting them with whale-oil are but now beginning to be known.

What do the fisheries of France furnish? She has employed, this year, fifteen vessels in the southern, and two in the northern fishery, carrying forty-five hundred tons in the whole, or two hundred and sixty-five each, on an average. The English ships, led by Nantuckois as well as the French, have never averaged in the southern fishery, more than one fifth of their burthen, in the best year. The fifteen ships of France, according to this ground of calculation, and supposing the present to have been one of the best years, should have brought, one with another, one fifth of two hundred and sixty-five tons, or fifty-three tons each. But we are told, they have brought near the double of that, to wit, one hundred tons each, and fifteen hundred tons in the whole. Supposing the two northern vessels to have brought home the cargo which is common from the northern fishery, to wit, twenty-five tons each, the whole produce this year will then be fifteen hundred and fifty tons. This is five and a half months'provision, or two fifths of the annual consumption. To furnish for the whole year, would require forty ships of the same size, in years as fortunate as the present, and eighty-five, *communibus annis*; forty-four tons, or one sixth of the burthen, being as high an average as should be counted on, one year with another: and the number must be increased, with the increasing consumption. France, then, is evidently not yet in a condition to supply her own wants. It is said, indeed, she has a large stock on hand, unsold, occasioned by the English competition. Thirty-three thousand quintals, including this year's produce, are spoken of: this is between six and seven months'provision; and supposing by the time this is exhausted that the next year's supply comes in, that will enable her to go on five or six months longer; say a twelvemonth in the whole. But, at the end of the twelvemonth, what is to be done? The manufacturers depending on this article, cannot maintain their competition against those of other countries, if deprived of their equal means. When the alternative, then, shall be presented, of letting them drop, or opening the ports to foreign whale-oil, it is presumable the latter will be adopted, as the lesser evil. But it will be too late for America. Her fishery, annihilated during the late war, only began to raise its head, on the prospect of a market held out by this country. Crushed by the *Arrêt* of September the 28th, in its first feeble effort to revive, it will rise no more. Expeditions, which require the expense of the outfit of vessels, and from nine to twelve months' navigation, as the southern fishery does, most frequented by the Americans, cannot be undertaken in sole reliance on a market, which is opened and shut from one day to another, with little or no warning. The English alone, then, will remain to furnish these supplies, and they must be received, even from them. We must accept bread from our enemies, if our friends cannot furnish it. This comes exactly to the point, to which that government has been looking. She fears no rival in the whale-fishery, but America: or rather, it is the whale-fishery of America, of which she is endeavoring to possess herself. It is for this object, she is making the present extraordinary efforts, by bounties and other encouragements: and her success, so far, is very flattering. Before the war, she had not one hundred vessels in the whale-trade, while America employed three hundred and nine. In 1786, Great Britain employed one hundred and fifty-one vessels; in 1787, two hundred and eighty-six; in 1788, three hundred and fourteen, nearly the ancient American number: while the latter has fallen to about eighty. They have just changed places then; England having gained, exactly what America has lost. France, by her ports and markets, holds the balance between the two contending parties, and gives the victory, by opening and shutting them, to which she pleases. We have still precious remains of seamen, educated in this fishery, and capable by their poverty, their boldness, and address, of recovering it from the English, in spite of their bounties. But this Arret endangers the transferring to Great Britain every man of them, who is not invincibly attached to his native soil. There is no other nation in present condition to maintain a competition with Great Britain in the whale-fishery. The expense, at which it is supported on her part, seems enormous. Two hundred and fifty-five vessels, of seventy-five thousand four hundred and thirty-six tons, employed by her, this year, in the northern fishery, at forty-two men each; and fifty-nine in the southern, at eighteen men each, make eleven thousand seven hundred and seventy-two men. These are known to have cost the government fifteen pounds each, or one hundred and seventy-six thousand five hundred and eighty pounds, in the whole, and that, to employ the principal part of them from three to four months only. The northern ships have brought home twenty, and the southern sixty tons of oil, on an average; making eighty-six hundred and forty tons. Every ton of oil, then, has cost the government twenty pounds in bounty. Still, if they can beat, us out of the field, and have it to themselves, they will think their money well employed. If France undertakes, solely, the competition against them, she must do it at equal expense. The trade is too poor to support itself. The eighty-five ships, necessary to supply even her present consumption, bountied, as the English are, will require a sacrifice of twelve hundred and eighty-five thousand two hundred livres a year, to maintain three thousand five hundred and seventy seamen, and that, a part of the year only; and if she will put it to twelve thousand men, in competition with England, she must sacrifice, as they do, four or five millions a year. The same number of men might, with the same bounty, be kept in as constant employ, carrying stone from Bayonne to Cherburg, or coal from Newcastle to Havre, in which navigations they would be always at hand, and become as good seamen. The English consider among their best sailors, those employed to carry coal from Newcastle to London. France cannot expect to raise her fishery, even to the supply of her own consumption, in one year, or in several years. Is it not better, then, by keeping her ports open to the United States, to enable them to aid in maintaining the field against the common adversary, till she shall be in condition to take it herself, and to supply her own wants? Otherwise her supplies must aliment that very force, which is keeping her under. On our part, we can never be dangerous competitors to France. The extent to which we can exercise this fishery, is limited to that of the barren island of Nantucket, and a few similar barren spots; its duration, to the pleasure of this government, as we have no other market. A material observation must be added here: sudden vicissitudes of opening and shutting ports, do little injury to merchants settled on the opposite coast, watching for the opening, like the return of a tide, and ready to enter with it. But they ruin the adventurer, whose distance requires six months' notice. Those who are now arriving from America, in consequence of the Arret of December the 29th, will consider it as the false light which has led them to their ruin. They will be apt to say, that they come to the ports of France by invitation of that *Arrêt*, that the subsequent one of September the 28th, which drives them from those ports, founds itself on a single principle, viz. 'that the prohibition of foreign oils is the most useful encouragement which can be given to that branch of industry.' They will say, that, if this be a true principle, it was as true on the 29th of December 1787, as on the 20th of September, 1788: it was then weighed against other motives, judged weaker and overruled, and it is hard it should be now revived, to ruin them.

The refinery for whale-oil, lately established at Rouen, seems to be an object worthy of national attention. In order to judge of its importance, the different qualities of whale-oil must be noted. Three qualities are known in the American and English markets. 1st. That of the spermaceti whale. 2nd. Of the Greenland whale. 3rd. Of the Brazil whale. 1. The spermaceti whale found by the *Nantuckois*, in the neighborhood of the Western Islands, to which they had gone in pursuit of other whales, retired thence to the coast of Guinea, afterwards to that of Brazil, and begins now to be best found in the latitude of the Cape of Good Hope, and even of Cape Horn. He is an active, fierce animal, and requires vast address and boldness in the fisherman. The inhabitants of Brazil make little expeditions from their coast, and take some of these fish. But the Americans are the only distant people, who have been in the habit of seeking and attacking him, in numbers. The British, however, led by the *Nantuckois*, whom they have decoyed into their service, have begun this fishery. In 1785, they had eighteen ships in it; in 1787, thirty-eight; in 1788, fifty-four, or, as some say, sixty-four. I have calculated on the middle number, fifty-nine. Still they take but a very small proportion of their own demand; we furnish the rest. Theirs is the only market to which we carry that oil, because it is the only one where its properties are known. It is luminous, resists coagulation by cold, to the forty-first degree of Fahrenheit's thermometer, and fourth of Reaumur's, and yields no smell at all: it is used, therefore, within doors, to lighten shops, and even in the richest houses, for antichambers, stairs, galleries, &c. It sells at the London market for treble the price of common whale-oil. This enables the adventurer to pay the duty of eighteen pounds five shillings sterling the ton, and still to have a living profit. Besides the mass of oil produced from the whole body of the whale, his head yields three or four barrels of what is called head-matter, from which is made the solid spermaceti, used for medicine and candles. This sells by the pound at double the price of the oil. The disadvantage of this fishery is, that the sailors are from nine to twelve months absent on the voyage; of course, they are not at hand on any sudden emergency, and are even liable to be taken, before they know that war is begun. It must be added, on the subject of this whale, that he is rare and shy, soon abandoning the grounds where he is hunted. This fishery, less losing than the other, and often profitable, will occasion it to be so thronged, soon, as to bring it on a level with the other. It will then require the same expensive support, or to be abandoned.

2. The Greenland whale-oil is next in quality. It resists coagulation by cold, to thirty-six degrees of Fahrenheit, and two of Reaumur, but it has a smell insupportable within doors, and is not luminous. It sells, therefore, in London, at about sixteen pounds the ton. This whale is clumsy and timid; he dives when struck, and comes up to breathe by the first cake of ice, where the fishermen need little address or courage to find and take him. This is the fishery mostly frequented by European nations; it is this fish which yields the fin in quantity, and the voyages last about three or four months.

The third quality is that of the small Brazil whale. He was originally found on the coast of Nantucket, and first led that people to this pursuit: he retired, first to the Banks of Newfoundland, then to the Western Islands, and is now found within soundings on the coast of Brazil, during the months of December, January, February, and March. His oil chills at fifty-two degrees of Fahrenheit, and eight of Reaumur, is black and offensive; worth, therefore, but thirteen pounds the ton, in London. In warm summer nights, however, it burns better than the Greenland oil.

To the qualities of the oils thus described, it is to be added, that an individual has discovered methods, 1. of converting a great part of the oils of the spermaceti-whale, into the solid substance called spermaceti, heretofore produced from his head alone; 2. of refining the Greenland whale-oil, so as to take from it all smell, and render it limpid and luminous as that of the spermaceti-whale; 3. of curdling the oil of the Brazil whale into tallow, resembling that of beef, and answering all its purposes. This person is engaged by the company, which has established the refinery at Rouen: their works will cost them half a million of livres; will be able to refine all the oil which can be used in the kingdom, and even to supply foreign markets. The effects of the refinery, then, would be, 1. to supplant the solid spermaceti of all other nations, by theirs, of equal quality and lower price; 2. to substitute, instead of spermaceti-oil, their black whale-oil refined, of equal quality and lower price; 3. to render the worthless oil of the Brazil, equal in value to tallow; and 4. by accommodating these oils to uses, to which they could never otherwise have been applied, they will extend the demand beyond its present narrow limits, to any supply which can be furnished, and thus give the most effectual encouragement and extension to the whale-fishery. But these works were calculated on the *Arrêt* of December the 29th, which admitted here, freely and fully, the produce of the American fishery. If confined to that of the French fishery alone, the enterprise may fail, for want of matter to work on.

After this review of the whale-fishery as a political institution, a few considerations shall be added on its produce, as a basis of commercial exchange between France and the United States. The discussions it has undergone, on former occasions, in this point of view, leaves little new to be now urged.

The United States, not possessing mines of the precious metals, can purchase necessaries from other nations, so far only as their produce is received in exchange. Without enumerating our smaller articles, we have three of principal importance, proper for the French market; to wit, tobacco, whale-oil, and rice. The first and most important, is tobacco. This might furnish an exchange for eight millions of the productions of this country; but it is under a monopoly, and that not of a mercantile, but of a financiering company, whose interest is, to pay in money and not in merchandise, and who are so much governed by the spirit of simplifying their purchases and proceedings, that they find means to elude every endeavor on the part of government, to make them diffuse their purchases among the merchants in general. Little profit is derived from this, then, as an article of exchange for the produce and manufactures of France. Whale-oil might be next in importance; but that is now prohibited. American rice is not yet of great, but it is of growing consumption in France, and being the only article of the three which is free, it may become a principal basis of exchange. Time and trial may add a fourth, that is, timber. But some essays, rendered unsuccessful by unfortunate circumstances, place that, at present, under a discredit, which it will be found hereafter not to have merited. The English know its value, and were supplied with it, before the war. A spirit of hostility, since that event, led them to seek Russian rather than American supplies; a new spirit of hostility has driven them back from Russia, and they are now making contracts for American timber. But of the three articles before mentioned, proved by experience to be suitable for the French market, one is prohibited, one under monopoly, and one alone free, and that the smallest and of very limited consumption. The way to encourage purchasers, is, to multiply their means of payment. Whale-oil might be an important one. In one scale, are the interests of the millions who are lighted, shod, or clothed with the help of it, and the thousands of laborers and manufacturers, who would be employed in producing the articles which might be given in exchange for it, if received from America: in the other scale, are the interests of the adventurers in the whale-fishery each of whom, indeed, politically considered, may be of more importance to the State, than a simple laborer or manufacturer; but to make the estimate with the accuracy it merits, we should multiply the numbers in each scale into their individual importance, and see which preponderates.

Both governments have seen with concern, that their commercial intercourse does not grow as rapidly as they would wish. The system of the United States is, to use neither prohibitions nor premiums. Commerce, there, regulates itself freely, and asks nothing better. Where a government finds itself under the necessity of undertaking that regulation, it would seem, that it should conduct it as an intelligent merchant would; that is to say, invite customers to purchase, by facilitating their means of payment, and by adapting goods to their taste. If this idea be just, government here has two operations to attend to, with respect to the commerce of the United States; 1. to do away, or to moderate, as much as possible, the prohibitions and monopolies of their materials for payment; 2. to encourage the institution of the principal manufactures, which the necessities, or the habits of their new customers call for. Under this latter head, a hint shall be suggested, which must find its apology in the motive from which it flows; that is, a desire of promoting mutual interests and close friendship. Six hundred thousand of the laboring poor of America, comprehending slaves under that denomination, are clothed in three of the simplest manufactures possible; to wit, oznaburgs, plains, and duffel blankets. The first is a linen; the two last, woollens. It happens, too, that they are used exactly by those who cultivate the tobacco and rice, and in a good degree by those employed in the whale-fishery. To these manufactures they are so habituated, that no substitute will be received. If the vessels which bring tobacco, rice, and whale-oil, do not find them in the ports of delivery, they must be sought where they can be found; that is, in England, at present. If they were made in France, they would be gladly taken in exchange there. The quantities annually used by this description of people, and their value, are as follows:

Oznaburgs 2,700,000 aunes, at sixteen sous the aune, worth

2,160,000

Plains 1,350,000 aunes, at two livres the aune,

2,700,000

Duffel Blankets 300,000 aunes, at seven and 4/5ths livres each

2,160,000

7,020,000

It would be difficult to say, how much should be added, for the consumption of inhabitants of other descriptions; a great deal surely. But the present view shall be confined to the one description named. Seven millions of livres, are nine millions of days' work, of those who raise, spin, and weave the wool and flax; and, at three hundred working days to the year, would maintain thirty thousand people. To introduce these simple manufactures, suppose government to give five per cent, on the value of what should be exported of them, for ten years to come: if none should be exported, nothing would be to be paid: but on the other hand, if the manufactures, with this encouragement, should rise to the full demand, it will be a sacrifice of three hundred and fifty-one thousand livres a year, for ten years only, to produce a perpetual subsistence for more than thirty thousand people (for the demand will grow with our population); while she must expend perpetually one million two hundred and eighty-five thousand livres a year, to maintain the three thousand five hundred and seventy seamen, who would supply her with whale-oil. That is to say, for each seaman, as much as for thirty laborers and manufacturers.

But to return to our subject, and to conclude.

Whether, then, we consider the *Arrêt* of September the 28th, in a political or a commercial light, it would seem, that the United States should be excepted from its operation. Still more so, when they invoke against it the amity subsisting between the two nations, the desire of binding them together by every possible interest and connection, the several acts in favor of this exception, the dignity of legislation, which admits not of changes backwards and forwards, the interests of commerce, which requires steady regulations, the assurances of the friendly motives which have led the King to pass these acts, and the hope, that no cause will arise, to change either his motives or his measures towards us.

LETTER CLXXI.—TO JOHN JAY, November 29, 1788

TO JOHN JAY.

Paris, November 29, 1788.

Sir,

In the hurry of making up my letter of the 19th instant, I omitted the enclosed printed paper, on the subject of whale-oil. That omission is now supplied by another conveyance, by the way of London. The explanatory *Arrêt* is not yet come out. I still take for granted, it will pass, though there be an opposition to it in the Council. In the mean time, orders are given to receive our oils which may arrive. The apprehension of a want of corn has induced them to turn their eyes to foreign supplies; and to show their preference of receiving them from us, they have passed the enclosed *Arrêt*, giving a premium on wheat and flour from the United States, for a limited time. This, you will doubtless think proper to have translated and published. The *Notables* are still in session: the votes of the separate bureaux have not yet been reduced to a joint act, in an assembly of the whole. I see no reason to suppose they will change the separate votes relative to the representation of the *Tiers Etat* in the States General. In the mean time, the stream of public indignation, heretofore directed against the court, sets strongly against the *Notables*. It is not yet decided when the States will meet: but certainly they cannot, till February or March. The Turks have retired across the Danube. This movement indicates their going into winter-quarters, and the severity of the weather must hasten it. The thermometer was yesterday at eight degrees of Fahrenheit, that is, twenty-four degrees below freezing; a degree of cold equal to that of the year 1740, which they count here among their coldest winters. This having continued many days, and being still likely to continue, and the wind from northeast, render it probable, that all enterprise must be suspended between the three great belligerent powers. Poland is likely to be thrown into great convulsions. The Empress of Russia has peremptorily demanded such aids from Poland, as might engage it in the war. The King of Prussia, on the other hand, threatens to march an army on their borders. The vote of the Polish confederacy for one hundred thousand men, was a coalition of the two parties, in that single act only. The party opposed to the King, have obtained a majority, and have voted that this army shall be independent of him. They are supported by Prussia, while the King depends on Russia. Authentic information from England leaves not a doubt, that the King is lunatic; and that, instead of the effect, is the cause of the illness, under which he has been so near dying. I mention this, because the English newspapers, speaking by guess on that as they do on all other subjects, might mislead you as to his true situation; or rather, might mislead others, who know less than you do, that a thing is not rendered the more probable, by being mentioned in those papers.

I enclose those of Leyden to the present date, with the gazettes of France, and have the honor to be, with sentiments of the most perfect esteem and respect, Sir, your most obedient, humble servant,

Th: Jefferson

LETTER, CLXXII.—TO GENERAL WASHINGTON, December 4, 1788

TO GENERAL WASHINGTON.

Paris, December 4, 1788.

Sir,

Your favor of August the 31st came to hand yesterday; and a confidential conveyance offering, by the way of London, I avail myself of it, to acknowledge the receipt.

I have seen, with infinite pleasure, our new constitution accepted by eleven States, not rejected by the twelfth; and that the thirteenth happens to be a state of the least importance. It is true, that the minorities in most of the accepting States have been very respectable; so much so, as to render it prudent, were it not otherwise reasonable, to make some sacrifice to them. I am in hopes, that the annexation of a bill of rights to the constitution will alone draw over so great a proportion of the minorities, as to leave little danger in the opposition of the residue; and that this annexation may be made by Congress and the Assemblies, without calling a convention, which might endanger the most valuable parts of the system. Calculation has convinced me, that circumstances may arise, and probably will arise, wherein all the resources of taxation will be necessary for the safety of the State. For though I am decidedly of opinion, we should take no part in European quarrels, but cultivate peace and commerce with all, yet who can avoid seeing the source of war in the tyranny of those nations, who deprive us of the natural right of trading with our neighbors? The produce of the United States will soon exceed the European demand: what is to be done with the surplus, when there shall be one? It will be employed, without question, to open, by force, a market for itself, with those placed on the same continent with us, and who wish nothing better. Other causes, too, are obvious, which may involve us in war; and war requires every resource of taxation and credit. The power of making war often prevents it, and in our case, would give efficacy to our desire of peace. If the new government wears the front which I hope it will, I see no impossibility in the availing ourselves of the wars of others, to open the other parts of America to our commerce, as the price of our neutrality.

The campaign between the Turks and two Empires has been clearly in favor of the former. The Emperor is secretly trying to bring about a peace. The alliance between England, Prussia, and Holland, (and some suspect Sweden also) renders their mediation decisive, wherever it is proposed. They seemed to interpose it so magisterially between Denmark and Sweden, that the former submitted to its dictates, and there was all reason to believe, that the war in the northwestern parts of Europe would be, quieted. All of a sudden, a new flame bursts out in Poland. The King and his party are devoted to Russia. The opposition rely on the protection of Prussia. They have lately become the majority in the confederated diet, and have passed a vote for subjecting their army to a commission independent of the King, and propose a perpetual diet, in which case he will be a perpetual cipher. Russia declares against such a change in their constitution, and Prussia has put an army into readiness, for marching, at a moment's warning, on the frontier of Poland. These events are too recent, to see, as yet, what turn they will take, or what effect they will have on the peace of Europe. So is that also, of the lunacy of the King of England, which is a decided fact, notwithstanding all the stuff the English papers publish, about his fevers, his deliriums, &c. The truth is, that the lunacy declared itself almost at once, and with as few concomitant complaints, as usually attend the first developement of that disorder. I suppose a regency will be established, and if it consists of a plurality of members, it will, probably, be peaceable. In this event, it will much favor the present wishes of this country, which are so decidedly for peace, that they refused to enter into the mediation between Sweden and Russia, lest it should commit them. As soon as the convocation of the States General was announced, a tranquillity took place through the whole kingdom: happily, no open rupture had taken place, in any part of it. The parliament were re-instated in their functions, at the same time. This was all they desired; and they had called for the States General, only through fear that the crown could not otherwise be forced to re-instate them. Their end obtained, they began to foresee danger to themselves, in the States General. They began to lay the foundation for caviling at the legality of that body, if its measures should be hostile to them. The court, to clear itself of the dispute, convened the *Notables*, who had acted with general approbation on the former occasion, and referred to them the forms of calling and organizing the States General. These *Notables* consist principally of Nobility and Clergy; the few of the *Tiers Etat* among them, being either parliament men, or other privileged persons. The court wished, that, in the future States General, the members of the *Tiers Etat* should equal those of both the other orders, and that they should form but one House, all together, and vote by persons, not by orders. But the *Notables*, in the true spirit of Priests and Nobles, combining together against the people, have voted, by five bureaux out of six, that the people, or *Tiers Etat*, shall have no greater number of deputies, than each of the other orders separately, and that they shall vote by orders: so that two orders concurring in a vote, the third will be overruled; for it is not here as in England, where each of the three branches has a negative on the other two. If this project of theirs succeeds, a combination between the two Houses of Clergy and Nobles will render the representation of the *Tiers Etat* merely nugatory. The bureaux are to assemble together, to consolidate their separate votes: but I see no reasonable hope of their changing this. Perhaps the King, knowing that he may count on the support of the nation, and attach it more closely to him, may take on himself to disregard the opinion of the *Notables* in this instance, and may call an equal representation of the people, in which precedents will support him. In every event, I think the present disquiet will end well. The nation has been awaked by our Revolution; they feel their strength, they are enlightened, their lights are spreading, and they will not retrograde. The first States General may establish three important points, without opposition from the court; 1. their own periodical convocation; 2. their exclusive right of taxation (which has been confessed by the King); 3. the right of registering laws, and of previously proposing amendments to them, as the parliaments have, by usurpation, been in the habit of doing. The court will consent to this, from its hatred to the parliaments, and from the desire of having to do with one, rather than many legislatures. If the States are prudent, they will not aim at more than this at first, lest they should shock the dispositions of the court, and even alarm the public mind, which must be left to open itself, by degrees, to successive improvements. These will follow, from the nature of things: how far they can proceed, in the end, towards a thorough reformation of abuse, cannot be foreseen. In my opinion, a kind of influence, which none of their plans of reform take into account, will elude them all; I mean the influence of women in the government. The manners of the nation allow them to visit, alone, all persons in office, to solicit the affairs of the husband, family, or friends, and their solicitations bid defiance to laws and regulations. This obstacle may seem less to those, who, like our countrymen, are in the precious habit of considering right, as a barrier against all solicitation. Nor can such an one, without the evidence of his own eyes, believe in the desperate state to which things are reduced in this country, from the omnipotence of an influence, which, fortunately for the happiness of the sex itself, does not endeavor to extend itself, in our country, beyond the domestic line.

Your communications to the Count de Moustier, whatever they may have been, cannot have done injury to my endeavors here, to open the West Indies to us. On this head, the ministers are invincibly mute, though I have often tried to draw them into the subject. I have therefore found it necessary to let it lie, till war, or other circumstances, may force it on. Whenever they are in war with England, they must open the islands to us, and perhaps, during that war, they may see some price which might make them agree to keep them always open. In the mean time, I have laid my shoulder to the opening the markets of this country to our produce, and rendering its transportation a nursery for our seamen. A maritime force is the only one, by which we can act on Europe. Our navigation law (if it be wise to have any) should be the reverse of that of England. Instead of confining importations to home-bottoms, or those of the producing nation, I think we should confine exportations to home-bottoms, or to those of nations having treaties with us. Our exportations are heavy, and would nourish a great force of our own, or be a tempting price to the nation to whom we should offer a participation of it, in exchange for free access to all their possessions. This is an object to which our government alone is adequate, in the gross; but I have ventured to pursue it here, so far as the consumption of our productions by this country extends. Thus, in our arrangements relative to tobacco, none can be received here, but in French or American bottoms. This is employment for near two thousand seamen, and puts nearly that number of British out of employ. By the *Arrêt* of December, 1787, it was provided, that our whale-oils should not be received here, but in French or American bottoms; and by later regulations, all oils, but those of France and America, are excluded. This will put one hundred English whale vessels immediately out of employ, and one hundred and fifty ere long; and call so many of French and American into service. We have had six thousand seamen formerly in this business, the whole of whom we have been likely to lose. The consumption of rice is growing fast in this country, and that of Carolina gaining ground on every other kind. I am of opinion, the whole of the Carolina rice can be consumed here. Its transportation employs two thousand five hundred sailors, almost all of them English at present; the rice being deposited at Cowes, and brought from thence here. It would be dangerous to confine this transportation to French and American bottoms, the ensuing year, because they will be much engrossed by the transportation of wheat and flour hither, and the crop of rice might lie on hand for want of vessels; but I see no objections to the extension of our principle to this article also, beginning with the year 1790. However, before there is a necessity of deciding on this, I hope to be able to consult our new government in person, as I have asked of Congress a leave of absence for six months, that is to say, from April to November next. It is necessary for me to pay a short visit to my native country, first, to reconduct my family thither, and place them in the hands of their friends, and secondly, to place my private affairs under certain arrangements. When I left my own house, I expected to be absent but five months, and I have been led by events to an absence of five years. I shall hope, therefore, for the pleasure of personal conferences with your Excellency, on the subject of this letter, and others interesting to our country; of getting my own ideas set to rights by a communication of yours, and of taking again the tone of sentiment of my own country, which we lose in some degree, after a certain absence. You know, doubtless, of the death of the Marquis de Chastellux. The Marquis de la Fayette is out of favor with the court, but high in favor with the nation. I once feared for his personal liberty, but I hope he is on safe ground at present.

On the subject of the whale-fishery, I enclose you some observations I drew up for the ministry here, in order to obtain a correction of their *Arrêt* of

September last, whereby they had involved our oils with the English, in a general exclusion from their ports. They will accordingly correct this, so that our oils will participate with theirs, in the monopoly of their markets. There are several things incidentally introduced, which do not seem pertinent to the general question: they were rendered necessary by particular circumstances, the explanation of which would add to a letter already too long. I will trespass no further, than to assure you of the sentiments of sincere attachment and respect, with which I have the honor to be your Excellency's most obedient, humble servant,

Th: Jefferson.

P. S. The observations enclosed, though printed, have been put into confidential hands only. T. J.

LETTER CLXXIII.—TO JOHN ADAMS, December 5, 1788

TO JOHN ADAMS.

Paris, December 5, 1788.

Dear Sir,

I had the pleasure of writing to you on the 2nd of August, and of adding a Postscript of August the 6th.

You recollect well the *Arrêt* of December the 29th, 1787, in favor of our commerce, and which, among other things, gave free admission to our whale-oil, under a duty of about two louis a ton. In consequence of the English treaty, their oils flowed in, and over-stocked the market. The light duty they were liable to under the treaty, still lessened by false estimates and aided by the high premiums of the British government, enabled them to undersell the French and American oils. This produced an outcry of the Dunkirk fishery. It was proposed to exclude all European oils, which would not infringe the British treaty. I could not but encourage this idea, because it would give to the French and American fisheries a monopoly of the French market. The *Arrêt* was so drawn up; but, in the very moment of passing it, they struck out the word European, so that our oils became involved. This, I believe, was the effect of a single person in the ministry. As soon as it was known to me, I wrote to Monsieur de Montmorin, and had conferences with him and the other ministers. I found it necessary to give them information on the subject of the whale-fishery, of which they knew little but from the partial information of their Dunkirk adventurers. I therefore wrote the observations (of which I enclose you a printed copy), had them printed to entice them to read them, and particularly developed the expense at which they are carrying on that fishery, and at which they must continue it, if they do continue it. This part was more particularly intended for Mr. Necker, who was quite a stranger to the subject, who has principles of economy, and will enter into calculations. Other subjects are incidentally introduced; though little connected with the main question, they had been called for by other circumstances. An immediate order was given for the present admission of our oils, till they could form an *Arrêt*; and, at a conference, the draught of an *Arrêt* was communicated to me, which re-established that of December the 29th. They expressed fears, that, under cover of our name, the Nova Scotia oils would be introduced; and a blank was left in the draught for the means of preventing that. They have since proposed, that the certificate of their consul shall accompany the oils, to authorize their admission, and this is what they will probably adopt. It was observed, that if our States would prohibit all foreign oils from being imported into them, it would be a great safeguard, and an encouragement to them to continue the admission. Still there remains an expression in the *Arrêt*, that it is provisory only. However, we must be contented with it as it is; my hope being, that the legislature will be transferred to the National Assembly, in whose hands it will be more stable, and with whom it will be more difficult to obtain a repeal, should the ministry hereafter desire it. If they could succeed in drawing over as many of our Nantucket men as would supply their demands of oil, we might then fear an exclusion; but the present *Arrêt*, as soon as it shall be passed, will, I hope, place us in safety till that event, and that event may never happen. I have entered into all these details, that you may be enabled to quiet the alarm which must have been raised by the *Arrêt* of September the 28th, and assure the adventurers that they may pursue their enterprises as safely as if that had never been passed, and more profitably, because we participate now of a monopolized, instead of an open market. The enclosed observations, though printed, have only been given to the ministers, and one or two other confidential persons. You will see that they contain matter which should be kept from the English, and will therefore trust them to the perusal only of such persons as you can confide in. We are greatly indebted to the Marquis de la Fayette for his aid on this, as on every other occasion. He has paid the closest attention to it, and combated for us with the zeal of a native.

The necessity of reconducting my family to America, and of placing my affairs there under permanent arrangements, has obliged me to ask of Congress a six months' absence, to wit, from April to November next. I hope, therefore, to have the pleasure of seeing you there, and particularly, that it will be at New York that I shall find you. Be so good as to present my sincere esteem to Mrs. Adams, and believe me to be, with very affectionate attachment, Dear Sir, your friend and servant,

Th: Jefferson.

LETTER CLXXIV.—TO MR. SHORT, December 8, 1788

TO MR. SHORT.

Paris, December 8, 1788.

Dear Sir,

My last to you was of the 21st of November, addressed to Milan, *poste restante*, according to the desire expressed through Mrs. Paradise. I have lately received yours of the 19th of November, and sincerely felicitate you on your recovery. I wish you may have suffered this to be sufficiently established before you set out on your journey. The present letter will probably reach you amidst the classical enjoyments of Rome. I feel myself kindle at the reflection, to make that journey; but circumstances will oblige me to postpone it at least. We are here under a most extraordinary degree of cold. The thermometer has been ten degrees of Reaumur below freezing: this is eight degrees of Fahrenheit above zero, and was the degree of cold here in the year 1740. The long continuance of this severity, and the snow now on the ground, give physical prognostications of a hard winter. You will be in a privileged climate, and will have had an enviable escape from this. The *Notables* are not yet separated, nor is their treasonable vote against the people yet consolidated; but it will be. The parliament have taken up the subject, and passed a very laudable vote in opposition. They have made it the occasion of giving sketches of what should be a bill of rights. Perhaps this opposition of authority may give the court an option between the two. Stocks are rising slowly, but steadily. The loan of 1784 is at thirteen loss; the *caisse d'escompte*, four thousand and seventy-five. The Count de Bryenne has retired, and M. de Puysegur succeeded to his place. Madame de Chambonois (sister of M. de Langear) is dead of the small-pox. Pio is likely to receive a good appointment in his own country, which will take him from us. Corn is likely to become extremely scarce in France, Spain, and England. This country has offered a premium of forty sous the quintal on flour of the United States, and thirty sous the quintal on our wheat, to be brought here between February and June.

General Washington writes me, that industry and economy begin to take place of that idleness and extravagance which had succeeded the close of the war. The Potomac canal is in great forwardness. J. M. writes me word, that Mr. Jay and General Knox are talked of in the Middle States for Vice-Presidents, but he queries whether both will not prefer their present births. It seems agreed, that some emendations will be made to the new constitution. All are willing to add a bill of rights; but they fear the power of internal taxation will be abridged. The friends of the new government will oppose the method of amendment by a federal convention, which would subject the whole instrument to change, and they will support the other method, which admits Congress, by a vote of two thirds, to submit specific changes to the Assemblies, three fourths of whom must concur to establish them.

The enclosed letter is from Pallegrino, one of the Italian laborers established in our neighborhood. I fancy it contains one for his father. I have supposed it would not be unpleasant to you to have the delivery of it, as it may give you a good opportunity of conferring with one of that class as much as you please. I obey at the same time my own wishes to oblige the writer. Mazzei is at this time ill, but not in danger. I am impatient to receive further letters from you, which may assure me of the solidity of your recovery, being, with great anxiety for your health and happiness, Dear Sir, your affectionate friend and servant,

Th: Jefferson.

[The annexed is here inserted in the Author's MS. To whom addressed, does not appear.]

The Minister Plenipotentiary for the United States of America finds himself under the necessity of declining to authenticate writings destined to be sent to the United States, for this main reason, that such authentication is not legal evidence there. After a reason so sufficient, it seems superfluous to add, that, were his authentication admissible in the courts of the United States, he could never give it to any seal or signature, which had not been put in his presence; that he could never certify a copy, unless both that and the original were in a hand-writing legible to him, and had been compared together by him, word by word: that so numerous are the writings presented, that their authentication alone would occupy the greater part of his time, and, withdrawing him from his proper duties, would change the nature of his office to that of a notary. He observes to those who do him the honor of addressing themselves to him on this subject, that the laws for the authentication of foreign writings are not the same through all the United States, some requiring an authentication under the seal of the *Prevoté* of a city, and others admitting that of a Notary: but that writings authenticated in both these manners, will, under the one or the other, be admitted in most, if not all of the United States. It would seem advisable, then, to furnish them with this double authentication.

LETTER CLXXV.—TO DOCTOR GILMER, December 16, 1788

TO DOCTOR GILMER.

Paife, December 16, 1788.

Dear Doctor,

Your last letter of December the 23rd was unlucky, like the former one, in arriving while I was absent on a call of public business in Holland. I was discouraged from answering the law part of it on my return, because I foresaw such a length of time between the date of that and receipt of the answer, as would give it the air of a prescription after the death of the patient. I hope the whole affair is settled, and that you are established in good titles to all the lands. Still, however, being on the subject, I cannot help adding a word, in answer to the objection which you say is raised on the words 'the estate,' instead of 'my estate.' It has long been confessed in the courts, that the first decision, that a devise of lands to a person without words of inheritance, should carry an estate for life only, was an absurd decision, founded on feudal principles, after feudal ideas had long been lost by the unlettered writers of their own wills: and it has often been said, that were the matter to begin again, it should be decided that such a devise should carry a fee simple, as every body is sensible testators intend, by these expressions. The courts, therefore, circumscribe the authority of this chain of decisions, all hanging on the first link, as much as possible; and they avail themselves of every possible circumstance which may render any new case unlike the old one, and authorize them to conform their judgments to common sense, and the will of the testator. Hence they decide, that in a devise of 'my estate at M.' to such a one, without words of inheritance, the word estate is descriptive of the duration of the interest bequeathed, as well as its locality. From the same desire of getting back into the paths of common sense, they would not suffer the particle 'the' instead of 'my', to make a difference. 'My estate at M.' means not only my lands at M., but my fee simple in them. 'The estate at M.' means not only 'the lands the testator holds at M., but the fee simple he has in them.' Another objection will be made, perhaps, viz. that the testator devises in the same clause his estate called Marrow-bone, his tract called Horse-pasture, and his tract called Poison-field; that it is probable he intended to give the same interest in all; and as it is confessed that the word tract conveys but an estate for life, we must conclude that the word estate was meant to convey the same. I should reverse the argument, and say, as it confessed the word estate, conveys an estate in fee simple, we must conclude the word tract was meant to convey the same; that this conclusion coincides with the wishes of the courts, as bringing them back to what is right and consentaneous to the intention of the testator, as furnishing them a circumstance to distinguish the case from the original one, and withdraw it from its authority; whereas, the contrary conclusion tends to lead them further from the meaning of testators, and to fix them in error.

But I perceive that my wishes to see the weight of no objection where you are interested, are leading me to write an argument, where I had promised I would say only a word. I will, therefore, talk the subject over with you at Monticello, or Pen-park. I have asked of Congress a leave of five or six months' absence next year, that I may carry my daughters home, and assist in the arrangement of my affairs. I shall pass two of the months at Monticello, that is to say, either June and July, or July and August, according to the time I may sail, which I hope will be in April: and then go on to New York and Boston, from whence I shall embark again for Europe, so as to get here before the winter sets in. I look forward with great fondness to the moment, when I can again see my own country and my own neighbors, and endeavor to anticipate as little as possible the pain of another separation from them. I hope I shall find you all under the peaceable establishment of the new constitution, which, as far as I can judge from public papers, seems to have become necessary for the happiness of our country. I thank you for your kind inquiries about my wrist. I followed advice with it, till I saw, visibly, that the joint had never been replaced, and that it was absurd to expect that cataplasms and waters would reduce dislocated bones. From that moment I have done nothing. I have for ever lost the use of my hand, except that I can write: and a withered hand and swelled and crooked fingers, still remaining twenty-seven months after the accident, make me fear I do not yet know the worst of it. But this, too, we will talk over at Monticello, and endeavor that it be the only pain to which our attention may be recalled. Adieu, my dear friend. Kiss and bless every body for me, Mrs. Gilmer especially. Assure her and yourself of the sincere and constant attachment of, Dear Doctor, your affectionate friend and servant,

Th: Jefferson.

LETTER CLXXVI.—TO THOMAS PAINE, December 23,1788

TO THOMAS PAINE.

Paris, December 23,1788.

Dear Sir,

It is true that I received very long ago your favors of September the 9th and 15th, and that I have been in daily intention of answering them, fully and confidentially; but you know such a correspondence between you and me cannot pass through the post, nor even by the couriers of ambassadors. The French packet-boats being discontinued, I am now obliged to watch opportunities by Americans going to London, to write my letters to America. Hence it has happened, that these, the sole opportunities by which I can write to you without fear, have been lost, by the multitude of American letters I had to write. I now determine, without foreseeing any such conveyance, to begin my letter to you, so that when a conveyance occurs, I shall only have to add recent occurrences. Notwithstanding the interval of my answer which has taken place, I must beg a continuance of your correspondence; because I have great confidence in your communications, and since Mr. Adams's departure, I am in need of authentic information from that country.

I will begin with the subject of your bridge, in which I feel myself interested; and it is with great pleasure that I learn, by your favor of the 16th, that the execution of the arch of experiment exceeds your expectations. In your former letter you mention, that, instead of arranging your tubes and bolts as ordinates to the cord of the arch, you had reverted to your first idea, of arranging them in the direction of radii. I am sure it will gain both in beauty and strength. It is true that the divergence of these radii recurs as a difficulty, in getting the rails on upon the bolts; but I thought this fully removed by the answer you first gave me, when I suggested that difficulty, to wit, that you should place the rails first, and drive the bolts through them, and not, as I had imagined, place the bolts first, and put the rails on them. I must doubt whether what you now suggest will be as good as your first idea; to wit, to have every rail split into two pieces longitudinally, so that there shall be but the halves of the holes in each, and then to clamp the two halves together. The solidity of this method cannot be equal to that of the solid rail, and it increases the suspicious parts of the whole machine, which, in a first experiment, ought to be rendered as few as possible. But of all this the practical iron men are much better judges than we theorists. You hesitate between the catenary and portion of a circle. I have lately received from Italy a treatise on the equilibrium of arches, by the Abbe Mascheroni. It appears to be a very scientifical work. I have not yet had time to engage in it; but I find that the conclusions of his demonstrations are, that every part of the catenary is in perfect equilibrium. It is a great point, then, in a new experiment, to adopt the sole arch, where the pressure will be equally borne by every point of it. If any one point is pushed with accumulated pressure, it will introduce a danger, foreign to the essential part of the plan. The difficulty you suggest, is, that the rails being all in catenaries, the tubes must be of different lengths, as these approach nearer or recede farther from each other, and therefore you recur to the portions of concentric circles, which are equidistant in all their parts. But I would rather propose, that you make your middle rail an exact catenary, and the interior and exterior rails parallels to that. It is true, they will not be exact catenaries, but they will depart very little from it; much less than portions of circles will. Nothing has been done here on the subject since you went away. There is an Abbe D'Arnal at Nismes, who had obtained an exclusive privilege for navigating the rivers of this country by the aid of the steam-engine. This interests Mr. Rumsey, who had hoped the same thing. D'Arnal's privilege was published in a paper of the 10th of November. Probably, therefore, his application for it was previous to the delivery of Mr. Rumsey's papers to the secretary of the Academy of Sciences, which was in the latter part of the month of August. However, D'Arnal is not a formidable competitor. He is not in circumstances to make any use himself of his privilege, and he has so illy succeeded with a steam-mill he erected at Nismes, that he is not likely to engage others to venture in his projects. To say another word of the catenarian arch, without caring about mathematical demonstrations, its nature proves it to be in equilibrio in every point. It is the arch formed by a string fixed at both ends, and swaying loose in all the intermediate points. Thus at liberty, they must finally take that position, wherein every one will be equally pressed; for if any one was more pressed than the neighboring point, it would give way, from the flexibility of the matter of the string.

I am, with sentiments of sincere esteem and attachment, Dear Sir, your friend and servant,

Th: Jefferson.

LETTER CLXXVII.—TO JOHN JAY, January 11, 1789

TO JOHN JAY.

Paris, January 11, 1789.

Sir,

My last letters were of the 14th, 19th, and 29th of November, by the way of London. The present will go the same way, through a private channel.

All military operations in Europe seem to have been stopped, by the excessive severity of the weather. In this country, it is unparalleled in so early a part of the winter, and in duration, having continued since the middle of November, during which time it has been as low as nine degrees below nought, that is to say, forty degrees below freezing, by Fahrenheit's thermometer; and it has increased the difficulties of the administration here. They had, before, to struggle with the want of money, and want of bread for the people, and now, the want of fuel for them, and want of employment. The siege of Oczakow is still continued, the soldiers sheltering themselves in the Russian manner, in subterraneous barracks; and the Captain Pacha has retired with his fleet. The death of the King of Spain has contributed, with the insanity of the English King, to render problematical the form which the affairs of Europe will ultimately take. Some think a peace possible between the Turks and two Empires, with the cession of Crimea to the former, as less important to Russia than Poland, which she is in danger of losing. In this case, the two Empires might attack the King of Prussia, and the scene of war be only changed. He is certainly uneasy at the accident happened to his principal ally. There seems no doubt, but that the Prince of Wales will be sole regent; but it is also supposed, they will not give him the whole executive power, and particularly, that of declaring war without the consent of the parliament. Should his personal dispositions, therefore, and that of a new ministry, be the same which the King had, of co-operating with Prussia, yet the latter cannot count on their effect. Probably, the parliament will not consent to war, so that I think we may consider the two great powers of France and England as absolutely at rest for some time.

As the character of the Prince of Wales is becoming interesting, I have endeavored to learn what it truly is. This is less difficult in his case, than in that of other persons of his rank, because he has taken no pains to hide himself from the world. The information I most rely on, is from a person here, with whom I am intimate, who divides his time between Paris and London, an Englishman by birth, of truth, sagacity, and science. He is of a circle, when in London, which has had good opportunities of knowing the

Prince; but he has also, himself, had special occasions of verifying their information, by his own personal observation. He happened, when last in London, to be invited to a dinner of three persons. The Prince came by chance, and made the fourth. He ate half a leg of mutton; did not taste of small dishes, because small; drank Champagne and Burgundy as small beer during dinner, and Bordeaux after dinner, as the rest of the company. Upon the whole, he ate as much as the other three, and drank about two bottles of wine without seeming to feel it. My informant sat next him, and being till then unknown to the Prince, personally, (though not by character), and lately from France, the Prince confined his conversation almost entirely to him. Observing to the Prince that he spoke French without the least foreign accent, the Prince told him, that when very young, his father had put only French servants about him, and that it was to that circumstance he owed his pronunciation. He led him from this to give an account of his education, the total of which was the learning a little Latin. He has not a single element of Mathematics, of Natural or Moral Philosophy, or of any other science on earth, nor has the society he has kept been such as to supply the void of education. It has been that of the lowest, the most illiterate and profligate persons of the kingdom, without choice of rank or mind, and with whom the subjects of conversation are only horses, drinking-matches, bawdy houses, and in terms the most vulgar. The young nobility, who begin by associating with him, soon leave him, disgusted with the insupportable profligacy of his society; and Mr. Fox, who has been supposed his favorite, and not over nice in the choice of company, would never keep his company habitually. In fact, he never associated with a man of sense. He has not a single idea of justice, morality, religion, or of the rights of men, or any anxiety for the opinion of the world. He carries that indifference for fame so far, that he would probably not be hurt were he to lose his throne, provided he could be assured of having always meat, drink, horses, and women. In the article of women, nevertheless, he is become more correct, since his connection with Mrs. Fitzherbert, who is an honest and worthy woman: he is even less crapulous than he was. He had a fine person, but it is becoming coarse. He possesses good native common sense; is affable, polite, and very good humored. Saying to my informant on another occasion, 'your friend, such a one, dined with me yesterday, and I made him damned drunk;' he replied, 'I am sorry for it; I had heard that your royal highness had left off drinking;' the Prince laughed, tapped him on the shoulder very good-naturedly, without saying a word, or ever after showing any displeasure. The Duke of York, who was for some time cried up as the prodigy of the family, is as profligate, and of less understanding. To these particular traits, from a man of sense and truth, it would be superfluous to add the general terms of praise or blame, in which he is spoken of by other persons, in whose impartiality and penetration, I have less confidence. A sample is better than a description. For the peace of

Europe, it is best that the King should give such gleamings of recovery, as would prevent the regent or his ministry from thinking themselves firm, and yet, that he should not recover. This country advances with a steady pace towards the establishment of a constitution, whereby the people will resume the great mass of those powers, so fatally lodged in the hands of the King. During the session of the *Notables*, and after their votes against the rights of the people, the Parliament of Paris took up the subject, and passed a vote in opposition to theirs, (which I send you.) This was not their genuine sentiment: it was a manoeuvre of the young members, who are truly well disposed, taking advantage of the accidental absence of many old members, and bringing others over by the clause, which, while it admits the negative of the States General in legislation, reserves still to the parliament the right of enregistering, that is to say, another negative. The *Notables* persevered in their opinion. The Princes of the blood (Monsieur and the Duke d'Orleans excepted) presented and published a memoire, threatening a scission. The parliament were proposing to approve of that memoire (by way of rescinding their former vote), and were prevented from it by the threat of a young member, to impeach (*denoncer*) the memoire and the Princes who signed it. The vote of the *Notables*, therefore, remaining balanced by that of the parliament, the voice of the nation becoming loud and general for the rights of the *Tiers-Etat*, a strong probability that if they were not allowed one half the representation, they would send up their members with express instructions to agree to no tax and to no adoption of the public debts, and the court really wishing to give them a moiety of the representation, this was decided on ultimately. You are not to suppose that these dispositions of the court proceed from any love of the people, or justice towards their rights. Courts love the people always, as wolves do the sheep. The fact is this. The court wants money. From the *Tiers-Etat* they cannot get it, because they are already squeezed to the last drop. The clergy and the nobles, by their privileges and their influence, have hitherto screened their property, in a great degree, from public contribution. That half of the orange, then, remains yet to be squeezed, and for this operation there is no agent powerful enough, but the people. They are, therefore, brought forward as the favorites of the court, and will be supported by them. The moment of crisis will be the meeting of the States; because their first act will be, to decide whether they shall vote by persons or by orders. The clergy will leave nothing unattempted to obtain the latter; for they see that the spirit of reformation will not confine itself to the political, but will extend to the ecclesiastical establishment also. With respect to the nobles, the younger members are generally for the people, and the middle aged are daily coming over to the same side: so that by the time the States meet, we may hope there will be a majority of that body, also, in favor of the people, and consequently for voting by persons, and not by orders.

You will perceive, by the report of Mr. Necker (in the gazette of France), 1. a renewal of the renunciation of the power of imposing a new tax by the King, and a like renunciation of the power of continuing any old one; 2. an acknowledgment that the States are to appropriate the public monies, which will go to the binding the court to a civil list; 3. a consent to the periodical meeting of the States; 4. to consider of the restrictions of which *lettres de cachet* are susceptible; 5. the degree of liberty to be given to the press; 6. a bill of rights; and 7. there is a passage which looks towards the responsibility of ministers. Nothing is said of communicating to them a share in the legislation. The ministry, perhaps, may be unwilling to part with this, but it will be insisted on in the States. The letters of convocation will not appear till towards the latter end of the month: neither time nor place are yet declared, but Versailles is talked of, and we may well presume that some time in April will be fixed on. In the mean time, Mr. Necker gets money to keep the machine in motion. Their funds rose slowly, but steadily, till within these few days, when there was a small check. However, they stand very well, and will rise. The *caisse d'escompte* lent the government twenty-five millions, two days ago. The navy of this country sustained a heavy loss lately, by the death of the Bailli de Suffrein. He was appointed Generalissimo of the Atlantic, when war was hourly expected with England, and is certainly the officer on whom the nation would have reposed its principal hopes, in such a case. We just now hear of the death of the Speaker of the House of Commons, before the nomination of a regent, which adds a new embarrassment to the re-establishment of government in England. Since writing mine of November the 29th, yours of the 23rd of September has come to hand. As the General of the Mathurins was to be employed in the final redemption of our captives, I thought that their previous support had better be put into his hands, and conducted by himself in such a way as not to counterwork his plan of redemption, whenever we can enable him to begin on it. I gave him full powers as to the amount and manner of subsisting them. He has undertaken it, informing me, at the same time, that it will be on a very low scale, to avoid suspicion of its coming from the public. He spoke of but three sous a day per man, as being sufficient for their physical necessaries, more than which, he thinks it not advisable to give. I have no definitive answer yet from our bankers, whether we may count on the whole million last agreed to be borrowed, but I have no doubt of it, from other information, though I have not their formal affirmative. The gazettes of Leyden and France to this date, accompany this. I have the honor to be, with sentiments of the most perfect esteem and respect, Sir, your most obedient and most humble servant,

Th: Jefferson.

LETTER CLXXVIII.—TO JAMES MADISON, January 12, 1789

TO JAMES MADISON.

Paris, January 12, 1789.

Dear Sir,

My last to you was of the 18th of November; since which, I have received yours of the 21st of September, and October the 8th, with the pamphlet on the Mohicon language, for which, receive my thanks. I endeavor to collect all the vocabularies I can of the American Indians, as of those of Asia, persuaded, that if they ever had a common parentage, it will appear in their languages.

I was pleased to see the vote of Congress, of September the 16th, on the subject of the Mississippi, as I had before seen, with great uneasiness, the pursuit of other principles, which I could never reconcile to my own ideas of probity or wisdom, and from which, and my knowledge of the character of our western settlers, I saw that the loss of that country was a necessary consequence. I wish this return to true policy may be in time to prevent evil. There has been a little foundation for the reports and fears relative to the Marquis de la Fayette. He has, from the beginning, taken openly part with those who demand a constitution; and there was a moment that we apprehended the Bastile: but they ventured on nothing more, than to take from him a temporary service, on which he had been ordered; and this, more to save appearances for their own authority, than any thing else; for at the very time they pretended that they had put him into disgrace, they were constantly conferring and communicating with him. Since this, he has stood on safe ground, and is viewed as among the foremost of the patriots. Every body here is trying their hand at forming declarations of rights. As something of that kind is going on with you also, I send you two specimens from hence. The one is by our friend of whom I have just spoken. You will see that it contains the essential principles of ours, accommodated as much as could be, to the actual state of things here. The other is from a very sensible man, a pure theorist, of the sect called the *Economists*, of which Turgot was considered as the head. The former is adapted to the existing abuses, the latter goes to those possible, as well as to those existing.

With respect to Doctor Spence, supposed to have been taken by the Algerines, I think the report extremely improbable. O'Bryan, one of our captives there, has constantly written to me, and given me information on every subject he thought interesting. He could not have failed to know if such a capture had been made, though before his time, nor to inform me of it. I am under perpetual anxiety for our captives there. The money, indeed, is not yet ready at Amsterdam; but when it shall be, there are no orders from the board of treasury to the bankers, to furnish what may be necessary for the redemption of the captives: and it is so long since Congress approved the loan, that the orders of the treasury for the application of the money would have come, if they had intended to send any. I wrote to them early on the subject, and pointedly. I mentioned it to Mr. Jay also, merely that he might suggest it to them. The payments to the foreign officers will await the same formality.

I thank you for your attention to the case of Mrs. Burke. We have no news of Doctor Franklin since July last, when he was very ill. Though the silence of our letters on that subject is a proof that he is well, yet there is an anxiety here among his friends. We have lately had three books published, which are of great merit, in different lines. The one is in seven volumes, octavo, by an Abbe Barthelemy, wherein he has collected every subject of Grecian Literature, after a labor of thirty years. It is called 'Les Voyages d'Anacharsis.' I have taken a copy for you, because the whole impression was likely to be run off at once. The second is a work on government, by the Marquis de Condorcet, two volumes, octavo. I shall secure you a copy. The third are the works of the King of Prussia, in sixteen volumes, octavo. These were a little garbled at Berlin, before printed. The government lays its hands on all which come here, and change some leaves. There is a genuine edition published at Basle, where even the garblings of Berlin are re-established. I doubt the possibility of getting a copy, so vigilant is the government as to this work. I shall obtain you one, if it be possible. As I write all the public news to Mr. Jay, I will not repeat it to you. I have just received the Flora Caroliniana of Walter, a very learned and good work. I am, with very sincere esteem and respect, Dear Sir, your friend and servant,

Th: Jefferson.

LETTER CLXXIX.—TO JOHN JAY, January 14, 1789

TO JOHN JAY.

Sir,

Paris, January 14, 1789.

In my letter of the 11th, I have said nothing of the *Arrêt* explanatory of that of September the 28th, on the subject of whale-oils, which my letter of November the 19th gave you reason to expect. Though this explanatory *Arrêt* has been passed so long ago as the 7th of December, it has not been possible for me to obtain an authentic copy of it, till last night. I now enclose that to you, with a copy of a letter to me from Mr. Necker, on the subject. The reception of our oils in the mean time, is provided for by an intermediate order. You will observe, that in the *Arrêt* it is said to be passed '*provisoirement*,' and that Mr. Necker expressly holds up to us in his letter, a repeal, whenever the national fishery supplies their wants. The *Arrêt*, however, is not limited in its duration, and we have several chances against its repeal. It may be questioned, whether Mr. Necker thinks the fishery worth the expense. It may be well questioned, whether, either with or without encouragement, the nation, whose navigation is the least economical of all in Europe, can ever succeed in the whale-fishery, which calls for the most rigorous economy. It is hoped that a share in the legislation will pass immediately into the hands of the States General, so as to be no longer in the power of the *commis* of a bureau, or even of his minister, to smuggle a law through, unquestioned; and we may even hope that the national demand for this oil will increase faster than both their and our fisheries together will supply. But in spite of all these hopes, if the English should find means to cover their oils under our name, there will be great danger of a repeal. It is essential, then, that our government take effectual measures to prevent the English from obtaining genuine sea-papers, that they enable their consuls in the ports of France (as soon as they shall be named) to detect counterfeit papers, and that we convince this government that we use our best endeavors, with good faith, as it is clearly our interest to do; for the rivalship of the English is the only one we have to fear. It had already begun to render our oils invendible in the ports of France. You will observe that Mr. Necker renews the promise of taking off the ten sous pour livre, at the end of the next year.

Oczakow is at length taken by assault. The assailants were fourteen thousand, and the garrison twelve thousand, of whom seven thousand were cut to pieces before they surrendered. The Russians lost three thousand men. This is the Russian version, of which it is safe to believe no part, but that Oczakow is taken. The Speaker of the English House of Commons, having died suddenly, they have chosen Mr. Grenville, a young man of twenty-seven years of age. This proves that. Mr. Pitt is firm with the present parliament.

I have the honor to be, with sentiments of the most perfect esteem and respect, Sir, your most obedient and most humble servant,

Th: Jefferson.

LETTER CLXXX.—TO MADAME NECKER, January 24, 1789

TO MADAME NECKER.

Paris, January 24, 1789.

I have received, Madam, with a great deal of sensibility, the letter of the 22nd instant, with which you were pleased to honor me on the claims of Monsieur Klein against the United States; and immediately endeavored to inform myself of their foundation, by an examination of the journals of Congress. Congress consisting of many persons, can only speak by the organ of their records. If they have any engagements, they are to be found there. If not found there, they can never have existed. I proceeded to this examination, with all the partialities which were naturally inspired by the interest you are so good as to take in his behalf, the desire of doing what will be agreeable to you, and a disposition to obtain for him the justice which might be his due. I have extracted, literally, from those journals, every thing I find in them on his subject, and I take the liberty of enclosing you those extracts. From them, as well as from what I recollect of the ordinary train of business about the years 1778 and 1779, I presume the following to be very nearly the history of Monsieur Klein's case.

Congress were generally desirous of adding to their army during the war. Among other methods attempted, it was usual for foreigners (multitudes of whom went to ask command), when they found there was no vacancy, to propose to raise troops themselves, on condition they should have commissions to command them. I suppose that Messrs. Klein, Fearer, and Kleinsmit (named in the resolution of Congress of 1778, and whom, from their names, I conjecture to be Germans) offered to enlist a body of men from among the German prisoners taken with General Burgoyne at Saratoga, on condition that Fearer and Kleinsmit should be captains over them, and Klein, lieutenant colonel. Three months seem to have been allowed them for raising their corps. However, at the end of ten months it seems they had engaged but twenty-four men, and that all of these, except five, had deserted. Congress, therefore, put an end to the project, June the 21st, 1779, (and not in July, 1780, as Monsieur Klein says) by informing him they had no further use for his services, and giving him a year's pay and subsistence to bring him to Europe. He chose to stay there three and a half longer, as he says, to solicit what was due to him. Nothing could ever have been due to him, but pay and subsistence for the ten months he was trying to enlist men, and the donation of a year's pay and subsistence; and it is not probable he would wait three years and a half to receive these. I suppose he has staid, in hopes of finding some other opening for employment. If these articles of pay and subsistence have not been paid to him, he has the certificates of the paymaster and commissary to prove it; because it was an invariable rule, when demands could not be paid, to give the party a certificate, to establish the sum due to him. If he has not such a certificate, it is a proof he has been paid. If he has it, he can produce it, and in that case, I will undertake to represent his claim to our government, and will answer for their justice.

It would be easy to correct several inaccuracies in the letter of Monsieur Klein, such as that Congress engaged to give him a regiment; that he paid the recruiting money out of his own pocket; that his soldiers had nothing but bread and water; that Congress had promised him they would pay his soldiers in specie, &c.; some of which are impossible, and others very improbable; but these would be details too lengthy, Madam, for you to be troubled with. Klein's object is to be received at the hospital of invalids. I presume he is not of the description of persons entitled to be received there, and that his American commission and American grievances are the only ground he has, whereon to raise a claim to reception. He has therefore tried to make the most of them. Few think there is any immorality in scandalizing governments or ministers; and M. Klein's distresses render this resource more innocent in him, than it is in most others.

Your commands, Madam, to give what information I could, have drawn thus much from me. I would not wish to weaken the hopes he so justly rests on your, known goodness and benevolence. On the contrary, the weaker his claims elsewhere, the stronger they will plead in your bosom to procure him relief; and whatever may be done for him here, I repeat it, that if he has any just demand against the United States, and will furnish me with proofs of it, I will solicit it with zeal, and, I trust, with effect. To procure him justice will be one gratification, and a great additional one will be, that he has procured me the occasion of offering you my portion of the general tribute so justly due, for all the good you have done, and all you are perpetually endeavoring to do. Accept then, Madam, I pray you, this homage from one, whose motives are pure truth and justice, when he assures you of the sincerity of those sentiments of esteem and respect, with which he has the honor to be, Madam, your most obedient and most

humble servant,

Th: Jefferson.

LETTER CLXXXI.—TO JOHN JAY, February 1, 1789

TO JOHN JAY.

Paris, February 1, 1789.

Sir,

My last letters have been of the 11th, 14th, and 21st of January. The present conveyance being through the post to Havre, from whence a vessel is to sail for New York, I avail myself of it, principally to send you the newspapers. That of Leyden of the 24th, contains a note of the *Chargé des Affaires* of France, at Warsaw, which is interesting. It shows a concert between France and Russia; it is a prognostication that Russia will interfere in the affairs of Poland, and if she does, it is most probable that the King of Prussia must be drawn into the war. The revolution which has taken place in Geneva, is a remarkable and late event. With the loss of only two or three lives, and in the course of one week, riots, begun at first on account of a rise in the price of bread, were improved and pointed to a reformation of their constitution; and their ancient constitution has been almost completely re-established. Nor do I see any reason to doubt of the permanence of the re-establishment. The King of England has shown such marks of returning reason, that the regency bill was postponed in the House of Lords, on the 19th instant. It seems now probable, there may be no change of the ministry, perhaps no regent. We may be sure, however, that the present ministry make the most of those favorable symptoms. There has been a riot in Brittany, begun on account of the price of bread, but converted into a quarrel between the *Noblesse* and *Tiers-Etat*. Some few lives were lost in it. All is quieted for the present moment. In Burgundy and Franche Compte, the opposition of the nobles to the views of government is very warm. Every where else, however, the revolution is going on quietly and steadily, and the public mind ripening so fast, that there is great reason to hope a good result from the States General. Their numbers (about twelve hundred) give room to fear, indeed, that they may be turbulent. Having never heard of Admiral Paul Jones since the action, in which he took a part before Oczakow, I began to be a little uneasy. But I have now received a letter from him, dated at St. Petersburg, the 31 st of January, where he had just arrived, at the desire of the Empress. He has hitherto commanded on the Black Sea. He does not know whether he shall be employed there, or where, the ensuing campaign. I have no other interesting intelligence, which would not lead me into details, improper for the present mode of conveyance. After observing, therefore, that the gazettes of France and Leyden, to the present date, accompany this, I shall only add assurance of the sincere esteem and respect, with which I have the honor to be, Dear Sir, your most obedient and most humble servant,

Th: Jefferson.

LETTER CLXXXII.—TO JOHN JAY, February 4, 1789

TO JOHN JAY.

Paris, February 4, 1789.

Sir,

Your favor of November the 25th, by Gouverneur Morris, is duly received. I must beg you to take the trouble of deciphering yourself what follows, and to communicate it to nobody but the President, at least for the present.

We had before understood, through different channels, that the conduct of the Count de Moustier was politically and morally offensive. It was delicate for me to speak on the subject to the Count de Montmorin. The invaluable mediation of our friend, the Marquis de la Fayette, was therefore resorted to, and the subject explained, though not pressed. Later intelligence showing the necessity of pressing it, it was yesterday resumed, and represented through the same medium to the Count de Montmorin, that recent information proved to us, that his minister's conduct had rendered him personally odious in America, and might even influence the dispositions of the two nations; that his recall was become a matter of mutual concern; that we had understood he was instructed to remind the new government of their debt to this country, and that he was in the purpose of doing it in very harsh terms; that this could not increase their desire of hastening payment, and might wound their affections: that, therefore, it was much to be desired that his discretion should not be trusted to, as to the form in which the demand should be made, but that the letter should be written here, and he instructed to add nothing but his signature: nor was his private conduct omitted. The Count de Montmorin was sensibly impressed. He very readily determined that the letter should be formed here, but said that the recall was a more difficult business: that as they had no particular fact to allege against the Count de Moustier, they could not recall him from that ministry, without giving him another, and there was no vacancy at present. However, he would hazard his first thoughts on the subject, saving the right of correcting them by further consideration. They were these: that there was a loose expression in one of de Moustier's letters, which might be construed into a petition for leave of absence; that he would give him permission to return to France; that it had been before decided, on the request of the Marquis de la Luzerne, that Otto should go to him to London; that they would send a person to America as *Chargé des Affaires* in place of Otto, and that if the President (General Washington) approved of him, he should be afterwards made minister. He had cast his eye on Colonel Ternant, and desired the Marquis to consult me, whether he would be agreeable. At first I hesitated, recollecting to have heard

Ternant represented in America, as an hypochondriac, discontented man, and paused for a moment between him and Barthelemy, at London, of whom I have heard a great deal of good. However, I concluded it safer to take one whom we knew and who knew us. The Marquis was decidedly of this opinion. Ternant will see that his predecessor is recalled for unconciliatory deportment, and that he will owe his own promotion to the approbation of the President. He established a solid reputation in Europe, by his conduct when Generalissimo of one of the United Provinces, during their late disturbances; and it is generally thought, that if he had been put at the head of the principal province, instead of the Rhingrave de Salm, he would have saved that cause. Upon the whole, I believe you may expect that the Count de Moustier will have an immediate leave of absence, which will soon after become a recall in effect. I will try also to have the consuls admonished as to the line of conduct they should observe. I shall have the honor of writing you a general letter, within a few days. I have now that of assuring you of the sentiments of sincere esteem and respect, with which I am, Dear Sir, your most obedient and most humble servant,

Th: Jefferson.

LETTER CLXXXIII.—TO WILLIAM SHORT, February 9,1789

TO WILLIAM SHORT.

Paris, February 9,1789.

Dear Sir,

I wrote you last on the 22nd of January, on which day I received yours of December the 31st, and since that, the other of January the 14th. We have now received news from America down to the middle of December. They had then had no cold weather. All things relative to our new constitution were going on well. Federal senators are; New Hampshire, President Langdon and Bartlett. Massachusetts, Strong and Dalton. Connecticut, Dr. Johnson and Ellsworth. New Jersey, Patterson and Ellmer. Pennsylvania, Robert Morris and M'Clay. Delaware, Reed and Bassett. Virginia, Richard Henry Lee and Grayson. Maryland, Charles Carroll, of Carrolton, and John Henry. All of these are federalists, except those of Virginia; so that a majority of federalists are secured in the Senate, and expected in the House of Representives. General Washington will be President, and probably Mr. Adams Vice-President. So that the constitution will be put under way by those who will give it a fair trial. It does not seem probable that the attempt of New York, to have another convention to make amendments, will succeed, though Virginia concurs in it. It is tolerably certain that Congress will propose amendments to the Assemblies, as even the friends of the constitution are willing to make amendments; some from a conviction they are necessary, others, from a spirit of conciliation. The addition of a bill of rights will, probably, be the most essential change. A vast majority of anti-federalists have got into the Assembly of Virginia, so that Mr. Henry is omnipotent there. Mr. Madison was left out as a senator by eight or nine votes; and Henry has so modeled the districts for representatives, as to tack Orange to counties where himself has great influence, that Madison may not be elected into the lower federal House, which was the place he had wished to serve in, and not the Senate. Henry pronounced a philippic against Madison in open Assembly, Madison being then at Philadelphia. Mifflin is President of Pennsylvania, and Peters, Speaker. Colonel Howard is Governor of Maryland. Beverly Randolph, Governor of Virginia; (this last is said by a passenger only, and he seems not very sure.) Colonel Humphreys is attacked in the papers for his French airs, for bad poetry, bad prose, vanity, &c. It is said his dress, in so gay a style, gives general disgust against him. I have received a letter from him. He seems fixed with General Washington. Mayo's bridge, at Richmond, was completed, and carried away in a few weeks. While up, it was so profitable that he had great offers for it. A turnpike is established at Alexandria, and succeeds. Rhode Island has again refused to call a convention. Spain has granted to Colonel Morgan, of New Jersey, a vast tract of land on the western side of the Mississippi, with the monopoly of the navigation of that river. He is inviting settlers, and they swarm to him. Even the settlement of Kentucky is likely to be much weakened by emigrations to Morgan's grant. Warville has returned, charmed with our country. He is going to carry his wife and children to settle there. Gouverneur Morris has just arrived here; deputed, as is supposed, to settle Robert Morris's affairs, which continue still deranged. Doctor Franklin was well when he left America, which was about the middle of December.

I send Mr. Rutledge two letters by this post. Be so good as to present him my esteem, and to be assured yourself, of the sincere esteem and attachment with which I am and shall ever be? Dear Sir, your affectionate friend and servant,

Th: Jefferson.

LETTER CLXXXIV.—TO M. DE VILLEDEUIL, February 10, 1789

TO M. DE VILLEDEUIL.

Paris, February 10, 1789.

Sir,

I take the liberty of troubling your Excellency with the following case, which I understand to be within your department. Mr. Jay, secretary for Foreign Affairs, to the United States of America, having occasion to send me despatches of great importance, and by a courier express, confided them to a Mr. Nesbitt, who offered himself in that character. He has delivered them safely: but, in the moment of delivering them, explained to me his situation, which is as follows. He was established in commerce at L'Orient, during the war. Losses by shipwreck, by capture, and by the conclusion of the peace at a moment when he did not expect it, reduced him to bankruptcy, and he returned to America, with the consent of his creditors, to make the most of his affairs there. He has been employed in this ever since, and now wishing to see his creditors, and to consult them on their mutual interests, he availed himself of Mr. Jay's demand for a courier, to come under the safe conduct of that character to Paris, where he flattered himself he might obtain that of your Excellency, for the purpose of seeing his creditors, settling, and arranging with them. He thinks a twelvemonth will be necessary for this. Understanding that it is not unusual to grant safe conducts in such cases, and persuaded it will be for the benefit of his creditors, I take the liberty of enclosing his memoir to your Excellency, and of soliciting your favorable attention to it, assured that it will not be denied him, if it be consistent with the established usage; and if inadmissible, praying that your Excellency will have the goodness to give me as early an answer as the other arduous occupations in which you are engaged, will admit, in order that he may know whether he may see his creditors, or must return without. I am encouraged to trouble your Excellency with this application, by the goodness with which you have been pleased to attend to our interests on former occasions, and by the desire of availing myself of every occasion of proffering to you the homage of those sentiments of attachment and respect, with which I have the honor to be your Excellency's most obedient and most humble servant,

Th: Jefferson.

LETTER CLXXXV.—TO MR. CARNES, February 15,1789

TO MR. CARNES.

Paris, February 15,1789.

Sir,

I am now to acknowledge the receipt of your favors of January the 23rd, and February the 9th and 10th. Your departure for America so soon, puzzles me as to the finishing the affair of Schweighaeuser and Dobree, in which I could have reposed myself on you. It remains, that I ask you to recommend some person who may be perfectly relied on, in that business. In fact, it is probably the only one I shall have occasion to trouble them with before my own departure for America, which I expect to take place in May; and I fix my return to Paris, in December. While I ask your recommendation of a person to finish Dobree's business with fidelity, I must ask your secrecy on the subject of that very business, so as not to name it at all, even to the person you shall recommend.

With respect to the distressed American who needs one hundred and forty livres to enable him to return to America, I have no authority to apply any public monies to that purpose, and the calls of that nature are so numerous, that I am obliged to refuse myself to them in my private capacity. As to Captain Newell's case, you are sensible, that being in the channel of the laws of the land, to ask a special order from government, would expose us, in reciprocity to like demands from them in America, to which our laws would never permit us to accede. Speaking conscientiously, we must say it is wrong in any government to interrupt the regular course of justice. A minister has no right to intermeddle in a private suit, but when the laws of the country have been palpably perverted to the prejudice of his countryman.

When you shall be so kind as to recommend to me a correspondent in your port during your absence, I will ask the favor of you also to give me some idea of the time you expect to return.

I have the honor, after wishing you pleasant and prosperous voyages, to assure you of the esteem and attachment, with which I am, Sir, your most obedient, humble servant,

Th: Jefferson.

LETTER CLXXXVI.—TO DR. BANCROFT, March 2, 1789

TO DR. BANCROFT.

Paris, March 2, 1789

Dear Sir,

I have just received a letter of January the 31st from Admiral Paul Jones, at Petersburg, which charging me with the execution of some commissions, and these requiring money, he tells me you will answer my drafts, to the amount of four or five thousand livres, on his account. Be so good as to inform me whether you will pay such drafts.

A Monsieur Foulloy, who has been connected with Deane, lately offered me for sale two volumes of Deane's letter books and account books, that he had taken instead of money, which Deane owed him. I have purchased them on public account. He tells me Deane has still six or eight volumes more, and being to return soon to London, he will try to get them also, in order to make us pay high for them. You are sensible of the impropriety of letting such books get into hands which might make an unfriendly use of them. You are sensible of the immorality of an ex-minister's selling his secrets for money and, consequently, that there can be no immorality in tempting him with money to part with them; so that they may be restored to that government to whom they properly belong. Your former acquaintance with Deane may, perhaps, put it in your power to render our country the service of recovering those books. It would not do to propose it to him as for Congress. What other way would best bring it about, you know best. I suppose his distresses and his crapulous habits will not render him difficult on this head. On the supposition that there are six or eight volumes, I think you might venture as far as fifty guineas, and proportionably for fewer. I will answer your draft to this amount and purpose, or you may retain it out of any monies you may propose to pay me for admiral Jones. There is no time to lose in this negotiation, as, should Foulloy arrive there before it is closed, he will spoil the bargain. If you should be able to recover these books, I would ask the favor of you to send them to me by the Diligence, that I may carry them back with me to America. I make no apology for giving you this trouble. It is for our common country, and common interest.

I am, with sincere and great esteem and attachment, Dear Sir, your most obedient, humble servant,

Th: Jefferson.

LETTER CLXXXVII.—TO M. DE MALESHERBES, March 11, 1789

TO M. DE MALESHERBES.

Sir,

Paris, March 11, 1789.

Your zeal to promote the general good of mankind, by an interchange of useful things, and particularly in the line of agriculture, and the weight which your rank and station would give to your interposition, induce me to ask it, for the purpose of obtaining one of the species of rice which grows in Cochin-China on high lands, and which needs no other watering than the ordinary rains. The sun and soil of Carolina are sufficiently powerful to insure the success of this plant, and Monsieur de Poivre gives such an account of its quality, as might induce the Carolinians to introduce it instead of the kind they now possess, which, requiring the whole country to be laid under water during a certain season of the year, sweeps off numbers of the inhabitants annually, with pestilential fevers. If you would be so good as to interest yourself in the procuring for me some seeds of the dry rice of Cochin-China, you would render the most precious service to my countrymen, on whose behalf I take the liberty of asking your interposition: very happy, at the same time, to have found such an occasion of repeating to you the homage of those sentiments of respect and esteem, with which I have the honor to be, Sir, your most obedient and most humble servant,

Th: Jefferson.

LETTER CLXXXVIII.—TO JOHN JAY, March 12, 1789

TO JOHN JAY.

Sir,

Paris, March 12, 1789.

I had the honor of addressing you, on the 1st instant, through the post. I write the present, uncertain whether Mr. Nesbitt, the bearer of your last, will be the bearer of this, or whether it may not have to wait some other private occasion. They have reestablished their packet-boats here, indeed; but they are to go from Bordeaux, which, being between four and five hundred miles from hence, is too far to send a courier with any letters but on the most extraordinary occasions and without a courier, they must pass through the post-office. I shall, therefore, not make use of this mode of conveyance, but prefer sending my letters by a private hand by the way of London. The uncertainty of finding private conveyances to London, is the principal objection to this.

On the receipt of your letter, advising me to purchase the two volumes of Deane's letters and accounts, I wrote to the person who had them, and after some offers and refusals, he let me have them for twenty-five louis, instead of twenty louis asked at first. He told me that Deane had still six or eight volumes more, and that when he should return to London he would try to get them, in order to make himself whole for the money he had lent Deane. As I knew he would endeavor to make us pay dear for them, and it appeared to be your opinion, and that of the members you had consulted, that it was an object worthy attention, I wrote immediately to a friend in London to endeavor to purchase them from Deane himself, whose distresses and crapulous habits will probably render him more easy to deal with. I authorized him to go as far as fifty guineas. I have as yet no answer from him. I enclose you a letter which I wrote last month to our bankers in Holland. As it will itself explain the cause of its being written, I shall not repeat its substance here. In answer to my proposition, to pay bills for the medals and the redemption of our captives, they quote a resolution of Congress (which, however, I do not find in the printed journals), appropriating the loans of 1787 and 1788 to the payment of interest on the Dutch loans till 1790, inclusive, and the residue to salaries and contingencies in Europe, and they argue, that, according to this, they are not to pay any thing in Europe till they shall first have enough to pay all the interest which will become due to the end of the year 1790; and that it is out of personal regard, that they relax from this so far as to pay diplomatic salaries. So that here is a clear declaration they will answer no other demands, till they have in hand money enough for all the interest to the end of the year 1790. It is but a twelvemonth since I have had occasion to pay attention to the proceedings of those gentlemen; but during that time I have observed, that as soon as a sum of interest is becoming due, they are able to borrow just that, and no more; or at least only so much more as may pay our salaries, and keep us quiet. Were they not to borrow for the interest, the failure to pay that would sink the value of the capital, of which they are considerable sharers. So far their interests and ours concur. But there, perhaps, they may separate. I think it possible they may choose to support our credit to a certain point, and let it go no further, but at their will; to keep it so poised, as that it may be at their mercy. By this, they will be sure to keep us in their own hands. They write word to the treasury, that in order to raise money for the February interest, they were obliged to agree with the subscribers, that Congress should open no other loan at Amsterdam this year, till this one be filled up, and that this shall not be filled but by the present subscribers, and they not obliged to fill it. This is delivering us, bound hand and foot, to the subscribers, that is, to themselves. Finding that they would not raise money for any other purposes, without being pushed, I wrote the letter I enclose you. They answer, as I have stated, by refusing to pay, alleging the appropriation of Congress. I have written again to press them further, and to propose to them the payment of thirty thousand florins only, for the case of our captives, as I am in hopes this may do. In the close of my letter to them, you will observe I refer them, as to the article of foreign officers, to the board of treasury. I had, in truth, received the printed journals a few days before, but had not yet had time to read them carefully, and, particularly, had not then noted the vote of Congress of August the 20th, directing me to attend to that article. I shall not fail to do what I can in it; but I am afraid they will consider this also as standing on the same ground with the other contingent articles.

This country, being generally engaged in its elections, affords nothing new and worthy of communication. The hopes of accommodation between Turkey and the two empires do not gain strength. The war between Russia and Denmark on the one hand, and Sweden on the other, is likely also to go on, the mediation of England being rendered of little force by the accident to its Executive. The progress of this war, and also of the broils in Poland, may possibly draw the King of Prussia into it during the ensuing campaign: and it must, before it be finished, take in this country, and perhaps England. The ill humor on account of the Dutch revolution continues to rankle here. They have recalled their ambassador from the Hague, manifestly to show their dissatisfaction with that court, and some very dry memorials have lately been exchanged on the subject of the money this country assumed to pay the Emperor for the Dutch. I send you very full extracts of these, which will show you the dispositions of the two courts towards each other. Whether, and when this country will be able to take an active part, will depend on the issue of their States General. If they fund their public debts judiciously, and will provide further funds for a war, on the English plan, 1 believe they will be able to borrow any sums they please. In the mean time, the situation of England will leave them at leisure to settle their internal affairs well. That ministry, indeed, pretend their King is perfectly re-established. No doubt they will make the most of his amendment, which is real, to a certain degree. But as, under pretence of this, they have got rid of the daily certificate of the physicians, and they are possessed of the King's person, the public must judge hereafter from such facts only as they can catch. There are several at present, which, put together, induce a presumption that the King is only better, not well. And should he be well, time will be necessary to give a confidence, that it is not merely a lucid interval. On the whole, I think we may conclude that that country will not take a part in the war this year, which was by no means certain before.

M. del Pinto, formerly minister of Portugal at London, and the same who negotiated the treaty with us, being now put at the head of the ministry of that country, I presume that negotiation may be renewed successfully, if it be the desire of our government. Perhaps an admission of our flour into their ports may be obtained now, as M. del Pinto seemed impressed with our reasoning on that subject, and promised to press it on his court, though he could not then venture to put it into the treaty. There is not the same reason to hope any relaxation as to our reception in Brazil, because he would scarcely let us mention that at all. I think, myself, it is their interest to take away all temptations to our cooperation in the emancipation of their colonies; and I know no means of doing this, but the making it our interest that they should continue dependant, nor any other way of making this our interest, but by allowing us a commerce with them. However, this is a mode of reasoning which their ministry, probably, could not bear to listen to. I send herewith the gazettes of France and Leyden, and have the honor to be, Sir, your most obedient and most humble servant,

Th: Jefferson.

LETTER CLXXXIX.—TO F. HOPKINSON, March 13, 1789

TO F. HOPKINSON.

Paris, March 13, 1789.

Dear Sir,

Since my last, which was of December the 21st, yours of December the 9th and 21st are received. Accept my thanks for the papers and pamphlets which accompanied them, and mine and my daughters for the book of songs. I will not tell you how much they have pleased us, nor how well the last of them merits praise for its pathos, but relate a fact only, which is, that while my elder daughter was playing it on the harpsichord, I happened to look towards the fire, and saw the younger one all in tears. I asked her if she was sick? She said, 'No; but the tune was so mournful.'

The Editor of the *Encyclopédie* has published something as to an advanced price on his future volumes, which, I understand, alarms the subscribers. It was in a paper which I do not take, and therefore I have not yet seen it, nor can I say what it is. I hope that by this time you have ceased to make wry faces about your vinegar, and that you have received it safe and good. You say that I have been dished up to you as an anti-federalist, and ask me if it be just. My opinion was never worthy enough of notice, to merit citing; but since you ask it, I will tell it to you. I am not a federalist, because I never submitted the whole system of my opinions to the creed of any party of men whatever, in religion, in philosophy, in politics, or in any thing else, where I was capable of thinking for myself. Such an addiction is the last degradation of a free and moral agent. If I could not go to heaven but with a party, I would not go there at all. Therefore, I protest to you, I am not of the party of federalists. But I am much farther from that of the anti-federalists. I approved, from the first moment, of the great mass of what is in the new constitution; the consolidation of the government; the organization into executive, legislative, and judiciary; the subdivision of the legislative; the happy compromise of interests between the great and little States, by the different manner of voting in the different Houses; the voting by persons instead of States; the qualified negative on laws given to the executive, which, however, I should have liked better if associated with the judiciary also, as in New York; and the power of taxation. I thought at first that the latter might have been limited. A little reflection soon convinced me it ought not to be. What I disapproved from the first moment, also, was the want of a bill of rights, to guard liberty against the legislative as well as executive branches of the government; that is to say, to secure freedom in religion, freedom of the press, freedom from monopolies, freedom from unlawful imprisonment, freedom from a permanent military, and a trial by jury, in all cases determinable by the laws of the land. I disapproved, also, the perpetual re-eligibility of the President. To these points of disapprobation I adhere. My first wish was, that the nine first conventions might accept the constitution, as the means of securing to us the great mass of good it contained, and that the four last might reject it, as the means of obtaining amendments. But I was corrected in this wish, the moment I saw the much better plan of Massachusetts, and which had never occurred to me. With respect to the declaration of rights, I suppose the majority of the United States are of my opinion: for I apprehend all the anti-federalists, and a very respectable proportion of the federalists, think that such a declaration should now be annexed. The enlightened part of Europe have given us the greatest credit for inventing this instrument of security for the rights of the people, and have been not a little surprised to see us so soon give it up. With respect to the re-eligibility of the President, I find myself differing from the majority of my countrymen; for I think there are but three States of the eleven which have desired an alteration of this. And, indeed, since the thing is established, I would wish it not to be altered during the life of our great leader, whose executive talents are superior to those, I believe, of any man in the world, and who, alone, by the authority of his name, and the confidence reposed in his perfect integrity, is fully qualified to put the new government so under way, as to secure it against the efforts of opposition. But having derived from our error all the good there was in it, I hope we shall correct it, the moment we can no longer have the same name at the helm.

These, my dear friend, are my sentiments, by which you will see I was right in saying, I am neither federalist nor anti-federalist; that I am of neither party, nor yet a trimmer between parties. These, my opinions, I wrote, within a few hours after I had read the constitution, to one or two friends in America. I had not then read one single word printed on the subject. I never had an opinion in politics or religion, which I was afraid to own. A costive reserve on these subjects might have procured me more esteem from some people, but less from myself. My great wish is, to go on in a strict but silent performance of my duty: to avoid attracting notice, and to keep my name out of newspapers, because I find the pain of a little censure, even when it is unfounded, is more acute than the pleasure of much praise. The attaching circumstance of my present office, is, that I can do its duties unseen by those for whom they are done. You did not think, by so short a phrase in your letter, to have drawn on yourself such an egotistical dissertation. I beg your pardon for it, and will endeavor to merit that pardon by the constant sentiments of esteem and attachment, with which I am, Dear Sir, your sincere friend and servant,

Th: Jefferson.

LETTER CXC.—TO MADAME DE BREHAN, March 14, 1789

TO MADAME DE BREHAN.

Paris, March 14, 1789.

Dear Madam,

I had the honor of writing to you on the 15th of February; soon after which, I had that of receiving your favor of December the 29th. I have a thousand questions to ask you about your journey to the Indian treaty, how you like their persons, their manners, their costumes, cuisine, &c. But this I must defer till I can do it personally in New York, where I hope to see you for a moment in the summer, and to take your commands for France. I have little to communicate to you from this place. It is deserted: every body being gone into the country to choose or be chosen deputies to the States General. I hope to see that great meeting before my departure. It is to be on the 27th of next month. A great political revolution will take place in your country, and that without bloodshed. A King with two hundred thousand men at his orders, is disarmed by the force of the public opinion and the want of money. Among the economies becoming necessary, perhaps one may be the opera. They say, it has cost the public treasury an hundred thousand crowns the last year. A new theatre is established since your departure; that of the *Opera Buffone*, where Italian operas are given, and good music. It is in the *Château des Tuileries*. Paris is every day enlarging and beautifying. I do not count among its beauties, however, the wall with which they have enclosed us. They have made some amends for this, by making fine boulevards within and without the walls. These are in considerable forwardness, and will afford beautiful rides round the city, of between fifteen and twenty miles in circuit. We have had such a winter, Madam, as makes me shiver yet, whenever I think of it. All communications, almost, were cut off. Dinners and suppers were suppressed, and the money laid out in feeding and warming the poor, whose labors were suspended by the rigor of the season. Loaded carriages passed the Seine on the ice, and it was covered with thousands of people from morning till night, skating and sliding. Such sights were never seen before, and they continued two months. We have nothing new and excellent in your charming art of painting. In fact, I do not feel an interest in any pencil but that of David. But I must not hazard details on a subject wherein I am so ignorant, and you such a connoisseur. Adieu, my dear Madam; permit me always the honor of esteeming and being esteemed by you, and of tendering you the homage of that respectful attachment with which I am, and shall ever be, Dear Madam, your most obedient, humble servant,

Th: Jefferson.

LETTER CXCI.—TO JAMES MADISON, March 15, 1789

TO JAMES MADISON.

Paris, March 15, 1789.

Dear Sir,

I wrote you last on the 12th of January; since which I have received yours of October the 17th, December the 8th and 12th. That of October the 17th came to hand only February the 23rd.

How it happened to be four months on the way, I cannot tell, as I never knew by what hand it came. Looking over my letter of January the 12th, I remark an error of the word 'probable' instead of' improbable,' which, doubtless, however, you had been able to correct.

Your thoughts on the subject of the declaration of rights, in the letter of October the 17th, I have weighed with great satisfaction. Some of them had not occurred to me before, but were acknowledged just, in the moment they were presented to my mind. In the arguments in favor of a declaration of rights, you omit one which has great weight with me; the legal check which it puts into the hands of the judiciary. This is a body, which, if rendered independent and kept strictly to their own department, merits great confidence for their learning and integrity. In fact, what degree of confidence would be too much, for a body composed of such men as Wythe, Blair, and Pendleton? On characters like these, the '*civium ardor prava jubentium*' would make no impression. I am happy to find that, on the whole, you are a friend to this amendment. The declaration of rights is, like all other human blessings, alloyed with some inconveniences, and not accomplishing fully its object. But the good, in this instance, vastly overweighs the evil. I cannot refrain from making short answers to the objections which your letter states to have been raised. 1. That the rights in question are reserved, by the manner in which the federal powers are granted. Answer. A constitutive act, may, certainly, be so formed, as to need no declaration of rights. The act itself has the force of a declaration, as far as it goes; and if it goes to all material points, nothing more is wanting. In the draught of a constitution which I had once a thought of proposing in Virginia, and printed afterwards, I endeavored to reach all the great objects of public liberty, and did not mean to add a declaration of rights. Probably the object was imperfectly executed; but the deficiencies would have been supplied by others, in the course of discussion. But in a constitutive act which leaves some precious articles unnoticed, and raises implications against others, a declaration of rights becomes necessary, by way of supplement. This is the case of our new federal constitution. This instrument forms us into one State, as to certain objects, and gives us a legislative and executive body for these objects. It should, therefore, guard us against their abuses of power, within the field submitted to them. 2. A positive declaration of some essential rights could not be obtained in the requisite latitude. Answer. Half a loaf is better than no bread. If we cannot secure all our rights, let us secure what we can. 3. The limited powers of the federal government, and jealousy of the subordinate governments, afford a security which exists in no other instance. Answer. The first member of this seems resolvable into the first objection before stated. The jealousy of the subordinate governments is a precious reliance. But observe that those governments are only agents. They must have principles furnished them, whereon to found their opposition. The declaration of rights will be the text, whereby they will try all the acts of the federal government. In this view, it is necessary to the federal government also; as by the same text, they may try the opposition of the subordinate governments. 4. Experience proves the inefficacy of a bill of rights. True. But though it is not absolutely efficacious under all circumstances, it is of great potency always, and rarely inefficacious. A brace the more will often keep up the building which would have fallen, with that brace the less. There is a remarkable difference between the characters of the inconveniences which attend a declaration of rights, and those which attend the want of it. The inconveniences of the declaration are, that it may cramp government in its useful exertions. But the evil of this is short-lived, moderate, and reparable. The inconveniences of the want of a declaration are permanent, afflicting, and irreparable. They are in constant progression from bad to worse. The executive, in our governments, is not the sole, it is scarcely the principal object of my jealousy. The tyranny of the legislatures is the most formidable dread at present, and will be for many years. That of the executive will come in its turn; but it will be at a remote period. I know there are some among us, who would now establish a monarchy. But they are inconsiderable in number and weight of character. The rising race are all republicans. We were educated in royalism; no wonder, if some of us retain that idolatry still. Our young people are educated in republicanism; an apostacy from that to royalism is unprecedented and impossible. I am much pleased with the prospect that a declaration of rights will be added; and I hope it will be done in that way, which will not endanger the whole frame of government, or any essential part of it.

I have hitherto avoided public news in my letters to you, because your situation insured you a communication of my letters to Mr. Jay. This circumstance being changed, I shall, in future, indulge myself in these details to you. There had been some slight hopes that an accommodation might be effected between the Turks and two empires; but these hopes do not strengthen, and the season is approaching which will put an end to them, for another campaign at least. The accident to the King of England has had great influence on the affairs of Europe. His mediation, joined with that of Prussia, would certainly have kept Denmark quiet, and so have left the two empires in the hands of the Turks and Swedes. But the inactivity to which England is reduced, leaves Denmark more free, and she will probably go on in opposition to Sweden. The King of Prussia, too, had advanced so far, that he can scarcely retire. This is rendered the more difficult by the troubles he has excited in Poland. He cannot, well abandon the party he had brought forward there; so that it is very possible he may be engaged in the ensuing campaign. France will be quiet this year, because this year, at least, is necessary for settling her future constitution. The States will meet the 27th of April: and the public mind will. I think, by that time, be ripe for a just decision of the question, whether they shall vote by orders or persons. I think there is a majority of the Nobles already for the latter. If so, their affairs cannot but go on well. Besides settling for themselves a tolerably free constitution, perhaps as free a one as the nation is as yet prepared to bear, they will fund their public debts. This will give them such a credit, as will enable them to borrow any money they may want, and of course, to take the field again, when they think proper. And I believe they mean to take the field as soon as they can. The pride of every individual in the nation suffers under the ignominies they have lately been exposed to, and I think the States General will give money for a war, to wipe off the reproach. There have arisen new bickerings between this court and that of the Hague; and the papers which have passed, show the most bitter acrimony rankling at the heart of this ministry. They have recalled their ambassador from the Hague, without appointing a successor. They have given a note to the Diet of Poland, which shows a disapprobation of their measures. The insanity of the King of England has been fortunate for them, as it gives them time to put their house in order. The English papers tell you the King is well; and even the English ministry say so. They will naturally set the best foot foremost; and they guard his person so well, that it is difficult for the public to contradict them. The King is probably better, but not well, by a great deal. 1. He has been bled, and judicious physicians say, that in his exhausted state, nothing could have induced a recurrence to bleeding, but symptoms of relapse. 2. The Prince of Wales tells the Irish deputation, he will give them a definitive answer in some days; but if the King had been well, he could have given it at once. 3. They talk of passing a standing law, for providing a regency in similar cases. They apprehend then, they are not yet clear of the danger of wanting a regency.

4. They have carried the King to church; but it was his private chapel. If he be well, why do not they show him publicly to the nation, and raise them from that consternation into which they have been thrown, by the prospect of being delivered over to the profligate hands of the Prince of Wales. In short, judging from little facts, which are known in spite of their teeth, the King is better, but not well. Possibly he is getting well, but still time will be

wanting to satisfy even the ministry, that it is not merely a lucid interval. Consequently, they cannot interrupt France this year in the settlement of her affairs, and after this year it will be too late.

As you will be in a situation to know when the leave of absence will be granted me, which I have asked, will you be so good as to communicate it, by a line, to Mr. Lewis and Mr. Eppes? I hope to see you in the summer, and that if you are not otherwise engaged, you will encamp with me at Monticello for a while.

I am, with great and sincere attachment, Dear Sir, your affectionate friend and servant,

Th: Jefferson.

LETTER, CXCII.—TO THOMAS PAINE, March 17,1789

TO THOMAS PAINE.

Paris, March 17,1789.
Dear Sir,
My last letter to you extended from December the 23rd to January the 11th. A confidential opportunity now arising, I can acknowledge the receipt of yours of January the 15th, at the date of which you could not have received mine.
You knew, long ago, that the meeting of the States is to be at Versailles, on the 27th of April. This country is entirely occupied in its elections, which go on quietly and well. The Duke d'Orleans is elected for Villers Cotterets. The Prince of Conde has lost the election he aimed at; nor is it certain he can be elected any where. We have no news from Auvergne, whither the Marquis de la Fayette is gone. In general, all the men of influence in the country are gone into the several provinces, to get their friends elected, or be elected themselves. Since my letter to you, a tumult arose in Bretagne, in which four or five lives were lost. They are now quieter, and this is the only instance of a life lost, as yet, in this revolution. The public mind is now so far ripened by time and discussion, that there seems to be but one opinion on the principal points. The question of voting by persons or orders is the most controverted; but even that seems to have gained already a majority among the Nobles. I fear more from the number of the Assembly, than from any other cause. Twelve hundred persons are difficult to keep to order, and will be so, especially, till they shall have had time to frame rules of order. Their funds continue stationary, and at the level they have stood at for some years past. We hear so little of the parliaments for some time past, that one is hardly sensible of their existence. This unimportance is probably the forerunner of their total re-modification by the nation. The article of legislation is the only interesting one on which the court has not explicitly declared itself to the nation. The Duke d'Orleans has given instructions to his proxies in the *bailliages*, which would be deemed bold in England, and are reasonable beyond the reach of an Englishman, who, slumbering under a kind of half reformation in politics and religion, is not excited by any thing he sees or feels, to question the remains of prejudice. The writers of this country, now taking the field freely, and unrestrained, or rather revolted by prejudice, will rouse us all from the errors in which we have been hitherto rocked.
We had, at one time, some hope, that an accommodation would have been effected between the Turks and two empires. Probably the taking Oczakow, while it has attached the Empress more to the Crimea, is not important enough to the Turks, to make them consent to peace. These hopes are

vanishing. Nor does there seem any prospect of peace between Russia and Sweden. The palsied condition of England leaves it probable, that Denmark will pursue its hostilities against Sweden. It does not seem certain whether the King of Prussia has advanced so far in that mediation, and in the troubles he has excited in Poland, as to be obliged to become a party. Nor will his becoming a party draw in this country, the present year, if England remains quiet. Papers which have lately passed between this court and the government of Holland, prove that this nourishes its discontent, and only waits to put its house in order, before it interposes. They have recalled their ambassador from the Hague, without naming a successor. The King of Sweden, not thinking that Russia and Denmark are enough for him, has arrested a number of his Nobles, of principal rank and influence. It is a bold measure, at least, and he is too boyish a character to authorize us to presume it a wise one, merely because he has adopted it. His army was before disgusted. He now puts the Nobles and all their dependants on the same side, and they are sure of armed support, by Russia on the north, and Denmark on the south. He can have no salvation but in the King of Prussia.

I have received two letters from Ledyard, the one dated Alexandria, August the 15th, the other Grand Cairo, September the 10th; and one lately from Admiral Paul Jones, dated St. Petersburg, January the 31st. He was just arrived there, on the call of the Empress, and was uncertain where he should be employed the next campaign. Mr. Littlepage has returned from the Black Sea to Warsaw, where he has been perfectly received by the King. I saw this from under the King's own hand, and was pleased with the parental expressions towards him.

We have no news from America later than the middle of January. My letters inform me, that even the friends of the new constitution have come over to the expediency of adding a declaration of rights. There is reason to hope that this will be proposed by Congress to the several legislatures, and that the plan of New York for calling a new convention, will be rejected. Hitherto, no State had acceded to it but Virginia, in which Henry and anti-federalism had got full possession of their legislature. But the people are better disposed. My departure for America is likely to be retarded, by the want of a Congress to give me permission. I must attend it from the new government. I am anxious to know how much we ought to believe of the recovery of the King of England. By putting little facts together, I see that he is not well. Mr. Rumsey (who came in while I was writing the preceding page) tells me you have a long letter ready for me. I shall be happy to receive it.

I am, with great and sincere attachment, Dear Sir, your affectionate friend and servant,

Th: Jefferson.

LETTER CXIII.—TO COLONEL HUMPHREYS, March 18, 1789

TO COLONEL HUMPHREYS.

Paris, March 18, 1789.

Dear Sir,

Your favor of November the 29th, 1788, came to hand the last month. How it happened that mine of August, 1787, was fourteen months on its way, is inconceivable. I do not recollect by what conveyance I sent it. I had concluded, however, either that it had miscarried, or that you had become indolent, as most of our countrymen are, in matters of correspondence.

The change in this country since you left it, is such as you can form no idea of. The frivolities of conversation have given way entirely to politics. Men, women, and children talk nothing else: and all, you know, talk a great deal. The press groans with daily productions, which, in point of boldness, make an Englishman stare, who hitherto has thought himself the boldest of men. A complete revolution in this government, has, within the space of two years (for it began with the *Notables* of 1787), been effected merely by the force of public opinion, aided, indeed, by the want of money, which the dissipations of the court had brought on. And this revolution has not cost a single life, unless we charge to it a little riot lately in Bretagne, which began about the price of bread, became afterwards political, and ended in the loss of four or five lives. The assembly of the States General begins the 27th of April. The representation of the people will be perfect. But they will be alloyed by an equal number of nobility and clergy. The first great question they will have to decide, will be, whether they shall vote by orders or persons. And I have hopes, that the majority of the Nobles are already disposed to join the *Tiers-Etat*, in deciding that the vote shall be by persons. This is the opinion *a la mode* at present, and mode has acted a wonderful part in the present instance. All the handsome young women, for example, are for the *Tiers-Etat* and this is an army more powerful in France, than the two hundred thousand men of the King. Add to this, that the court itself is for the *Tiers-Etat*, as the only agent which can relieve their wants: not by giving money themselves (they are squeezed to the last drop), but by pressing it from the non-contributing orders. The King stands engaged to pretend no more to the power of laying, continuing, or appropriating taxes; to call the States General periodically; to submit *lettres de cachet* to legal restrictions; to consent to freedom of the press; and that all this shall be fixed by a fundamental constitution, which shall bind his successors. He has not offered a participation in the legislature, but it will surely be insisted on. The public mind is so ripened on all these subjects, that there seems to be now but one opinion. The clergy, indeed, think separately, and the old men among the Nobles: but their voice is suppressed by the general one of the nation. The writings published on this occasion are, some of them, very valuable; because, unfettered by the prejudices under which the English labor, they give a full scope to reason, and strike out truths, as yet unperceived and unacknowledged on the other side the channel. An Englishman, dozing under a kind of half reformation, is not excited to think by such gross absurdities as stare a Frenchman in the face, wherever he looks, whether it be towards the throne or the altar. In fine, I believe this nation will, in the course of the present year, have as full a portion of liberty dealt out to them, as the nation can bear at present, considering how uninformed the mass of their people is. This circumstance will prevent the immediate establishment of the trial by jury. The palsied state of the executive in England is a fortunate circumstance for France, as it will give her time to arrange her affairs internally. The consolidation and funding their debts, will give government a credit which will enable them to do what they please. For the present year the war will be confined to the two empires and Denmark, against Turkey and Sweden. It is not yet evident, whether Prussia will be engaged. If the disturbances of Poland break out into overt acts, it will be a power divided in itself, and so of no weight. Perhaps by the next year England and France may be ready to take the field. It will depend on the former principally, for the latter, though she may be then able, must wish still a little time to see her new arrangements well under way. The English papers and English ministry say the King is well. He is better, but not well: no malady requires a longer time to insure against its return than insanity. Time alone can distinguish accidental insanity from habitual lunacy.

The operations which have taken place in America lately fill me with pleasure. In the first place, they realize the confidence I had, that, whenever our affairs go obviously wrong, the good sense of the people will interpose, and set them to rights. The example of changing a constitution, by assembling the wise men of the State, instead of assembling armies, will be worth as much to the world as the former examples we had given them. The constitution, too, which was the result of our deliberations, is unquestionably the wisest ever yet presented to men, and some of the accommodations of interest which it has adopted are greatly pleasing to me, who have before had occasions of seeing how difficult those interests were to accommodate. A general concurrence of opinion seems to authorize us to say it has some defects. I am one of those who think it a defect, that the important rights, not placed in security by the frame of the constitution itself, were not explicitly secured by a supplementary declaration. There are rights which it is useless to surrender to the government, and which governments have yet always been fond to invade. These are the rights of thinking, and publishing our thoughts by speaking or writing; the right of free commerce; the right of personal freedom. There are instruments for administering the government so peculiarly trust-worthy, that we should never leave the legislature at liberty to change them. The new constitution has secured these in the executive and legislative departments; but not in the judiciary. It should have established trials by the people themselves, that is to say, by jury. There are instruments so dangerous to the rights of the nation, and which place them so totally at the mercy of their governors, that those governors, whether legislative or executive, should be restrained from keeping such instruments on foot, but in well defined cases. Such an instrument is a standing army. We are now allowed to say, such a declaration of rights, as a supplement to the constitution, where that is silent, is wanting, to secure us in these points. The general voice has legitimated this objection. It has not, however, authorized me to consider as a real defect, what I thought, and still think one, the perpetual re-eligibility of the President. But three States out of eleven having declared against this, we must suppose we are wrong, according to the fundamental law of every society, the *lex majoris partis*, to which we are bound to submit. And should the majority change their opinion, and become sensible that this trait in their constitution is wrong, I would wish it to remain uncorrected, as long as we can avail ourselves of the services of our great leader, whose talents and whose weight of character, I consider as peculiarly necessary to get the government so under way, as that it may afterwards be carried on by subordinate characters.

I must give you sincere thanks for the details of small news contained in your letter. You know how previous that kind of information is to a person absent from his country, and how difficult it is to be procured. I hope to receive soon permission to visit America this summer, and to possess myself anew, by conversation with my countrymen, of their spirit and their ideas. I know only the Americans of the year 1784. They tell me this is to be much a stranger to those of 1789. This renewal of acquaintance is no indifferent matter to one, acting at such a distance, as that instructions cannot be received hot and hot. One of my pleasures, too, will be that of talking over the old and new with you.

In the mean time, and at all times, I have the honor to be, with great and sincere esteem. Dear Sir, your friend and servant,

Th: Jefferson,

LETTER CXCIV.—TO DOCTOR WILLARD, March 24, 1789

TO DOCTOR WILLARD.

Paris, March 24, 1789.

Sir,

I have been lately honored with your letter of September the 24th, 1788, accompanied by a diploma for a Doctorate of Laws, which the University of Harvard has been pleased to confer on me. Conscious how little I merit it, I am the more sensible of their goodness and indulgence to a stranger, who has had no means ef serving or making himself known to them. I beg you to return them my grateful thanks, and to assure them that this notice from so eminent a seat of science is very precious to me.

The most remarkable publications we have had in France, for a year or two past, are the following. *Les Voyages d'Anacharsis, par Abbe Barthelemi*, seven volumes, octavo. This is a very elegant digest of whatever is known of the Greeks; useless, indeed, to him who has read the original authors, but very proper for one who reads modern languages only. The works of the King of Prussia. The Berlin edition is in sixteen volumes, octavo. It is said to have been gutted at Berlin; and here it has been still more mangled. There are one or two other editions published abroad, which pretend to have rectified the maltreatment both of Berlin and Paris. Some time will be necessary to settle the public mind as to the best edition.

Montignot has given us the original Greek, and a French translation of the seventh book of Ptolemy's great work, under the title of *Etat des Etoiles fixes au second siecle*, in quarto. He has given the designation of the same stars by Flamsteed and Bayer, and their position in the year 1786. A very remarkable work is the *Mechanique Analytique of La Grange*, in quarto. He is allowed to be the greatest mathematician now living, and his personal worth is equal to his science. The object of his work is to reduce all the principles of mechanics to the single one of the equilibrium, and to give a simple formula applicable to them all. The subject is treated in the algebraic method, without diagrams to assist the conception. My present occupations not permitting me to read any thing which requires a long and undisturbed attention, I am not able to give you the character of this work from my own examination. It has been received with great approbation in Europe. In Italy, the works of Spallanzani on Digestion and Generation are valuable. Though, perhaps, too minute, and therefore tedious, he has developed some useful truths, and his book is well worth attention; it is in four volumes, octavo. Clavigero, an Italian also, who has resided thirty-six years in Mexico, has given us a History of that country, which certainly merits more respect than any other work on the same subject. He corrects many errors of Dr. Robertson; and though sound philosophy will disapprove many of his ideas, we must still consider it as an useful work, and assuredly the best we possess on the same subject. It is in four thin volumes, small quarto. De la Lande has not yet published a fifth volume.

The chemical dispute about the conversion and reconversion of air and water, continues still undecided. Arguments and authorities are so balanced, that we may still safely believe, as our fathers did before us, that these principles are distinct. A schism of another kind has taken place among the chemists. A particular set of them here have undertaken to remodel all the terms of the science, and to give to every substance a new name, the composition, and especially the termination of which, shall define the relation in which it stands to other substances of the same family. But the science seems too much in its infancy as yet, for this reformation; because, in fact, the reformation of this year must be reformed again the next year, and so on, changing the names of substances as often as new experiments develope properties in them undiscovered before. The new nomenclature has, accordingly, been already proved to need numerous and important reformations. Probably it will not prevail. It is espoused by the minority only here, and by very few, indeed, of the foreign chemists. It is particularly rejected in England.

In the arts, I think two of our countrymen have presented the most important inventions. Mr. Paine, the author of 'Common Sense,' has invented an iron bridge, which promises to be cheaper by a great deal than stone, and to admit of a much greater arch. He supposes it may be ventured for an arch of five hundred feet. He has obtained a patent for it in England, and is now executing the first experiment with an arch of between ninety and one hundred feet. Mr. Rumsey has also obtained a patent for his navigation by the force of steam in England, and is soliciting a similar one here. His principal merit is in the improvement of the boiler, and instead of the complicated machinery of oars and paddles, proposed by others, the substitution of so simple a thing as the reaction of a stream of water on his vessel. He is building a sea-vessel at this time in England, and she will be ready for an experiment in May. He has suggested a great number of mechanical improvements in a variety of branches, and, upon the whole, is the most original and the greatest mechanical genius I have ever seen. The return of La Peyrouse (whenever that shall happen) will probably add to our knowledge in Geography, Botany, and Natural History. What a field have we at our doors to signalize ourselves in! The Botany of America is far from being exhausted, its Mineralogy is untouched, and its Natural History or Zoology totally mistaken and misrepresented. As far as I have seen, there is not one single species of terrestrial birds common to Europe and America, and I question if there be a single species of quadrupeds. (Domestic animals are to be excepted.) It is for such institutions as that over which you preside so worthily, Sir, to do justice to our country, its productions, and its genius. It is the work to which the young men, whom you are forming, should lay their hands. We have spent the prime of our lives in procuring them the precious blessing of liberty. Let them spend theirs in showing that it is the great parent of science and of virtue; and that a nation will be great in both, always in proportion as it is free. Nobody wishes more warmly for the success of your good exhortations on this subject, than he who has the honor to be, with sentiments of great esteem and respect, Sir, your most obedient, humble servant,

Th: Jefferson.

LETTER CXCV.—TO J. SARSFIELD, April 3, 1789

TO J. SARSFIELD.

Paris, April 3, 1789.

Sir,

I could not name to you the day of my departure from Paris, because I do not know it. I have not yet received my *congé*, though I hope to receive it soon, and to leave this some time in May, so that I may be back before the winter.

Impost is a duty paid on any imported article, in the moment of its importation, and of course, it is collected in the sea-ports only. Excise is a duty on any article, whether imported or raised at home, and paid in the hands of the consumer or retailer; consequently, it is collected through the whole country. These are the true definitions of these words as used in England, and in the greater part of the United States. But in Massachusetts, they have perverted the word excise to mean a tax on all liquors, whether paid in the moment of importation or at a later moment, and on nothing else. So that in reading the debates of the Massachusetts convention, you must give this last meaning to the word excise.

Rotation is the change of officers required by the laws at certain epochs, and in a certain order: thus, in Virginia, our justices of the peace are made sheriffs one after the other, each remaining in office two years, and then yielding it to his next brother in order of seniority. This is the just and classical meaning of the word. But in America we have extended it (for want of a proper word) to all cases of officers who must be necessarily changed at a fixed epoch, though the successor be not pointed out in any particular order, but comes in by free election. By the term rotation in office, then, we mean an obligation on the holder of that office to go out at a certain period. In our first Confederation, the principle of rotation was established in the office of President of Congress, who could serve but one year in three, and in that of a member of Congress, who could serve but three years in six.

I believe all the countries in Europe determine their standard of money, in gold as well as silver. Thus, the laws of England direct that a pound Troy of gold, of twenty-two carats fine, shall be cut into forty-four and a half guineas, each of which shall be worth twenty-one and a half shillings, that is, into 956 3/4 shillings. This establishes the shilling at 5.518 grains of pure gold. They direct that a pound of silver, consisting of 11 1/10 ounces of pure silver, and 9/10 of an ounce alloy, shall be cut into sixty-two shillings. This establishes the shilling at 85.93 grains of pure silver, and, consequently, the proportion of gold to silver as 85.93 to 5.518, or as 15.57 to 1. If this be the true proportion between the value of gold and silver at the general market of Europe, then the value of the shilling, depending on two standards, is the same, whether a payment be made in gold or in silver. But if the proportion at the general market of Europe be as fifteen to one, then the Englishman who owes a pound weight of gold at Amsterdam, if he sends the pound of gold to pay it, sends 1043.72 shillings; if he sends fifteen pounds of silver, he sends only 1030.5 shillings; if he pays half in gold and half in silver, he pays only 1037.11 shillings. And this medium between the two standards of gold and silver, we must consider as furnishing the true medium value of the shilling. If the parliament should now order the pound of gold (of one-twelfth alloy as before) to be cut into a thousand shillings instead of nine hundred and fifty-six and three fourths, leaving the silver as it is, the medium or true value of the shilling would suffer a change of half the difference; and in the case before stated, to pay a debt of a pound weight of gold, at Amsterdam, if he sent the pound weight of gold, he would send 1090.9 shillings; if he sent fifteen pounds of silver, he would send 1030.5 shillings; if half in gold and half in silver, he would send 1060.7 shillings; which shows, that this parliamentary operation would reduce the value of the shilling in the proportion of 1060.7 to 1037.11.

Now this is exactly the effect of the late change in the quantity of gold contained in your louis. Your *marc d'argent fin* is cut into 53.45 livres (fifty-three livres and nine sous), the *marc de l'or fin* was cut, heretofore, by law, into 784.6 livres (seven hundred and eighty-four livres and twelve sous); gold was to silver, then, as 14.63 to 1. And if this was different from the proportion at the markets of Europe, the true value of your livre stood half way between the two standards. By the ordinance of October the 30th, 1785, the marc of pure gold has been cut into 828.6 livres. If your standard had been in gold alone, this would have reduced the value of the livre, in the proportion of 828.6 to 784.6. But as you had a standard of silver as well as gold, the true standard is the medium between the two; consequently, the value of the livre is reduced only one half the difference, that is, as 806.6 to 784.6, which is very nearly three per cent. Commerce, however, has made a difference of four per cent., the average value of the pound sterling, formerly twenty-four livres, being now twenty-five livres. Perhaps some other circumstance has occasioned an addition of one per cent, to the change of your standard.

I fear I have tired you by these details. I did not mean to be so lengthy when I began. I beg you to consider them as an appeal to your judgment, which I value, and from which I will expect a correction, if they are wrong.

I have the honor to be, with very great esteem and attachment, Dear Sir, your most obedient and most humble servant,

Th: Jefferson.

LETTER CXCVI.—TO THE MARQUIS DE LA FAYETTE, May 6,1789

TO THE MARQUIS DE LA FAYETTE.

Paris, May 6,1789.

My Dear Friend,

As it becomes more and more possible that the *Noblesse* will go wrong, I become uneasy for you. Your principles are decidedly with the *Tiers-Etat*, and your instructions against them. A complaisance to the latter on some occasions, and an adherence to the former on others, may give an appearance of trimming between the two parties, which may lose you both. You will, in the end, go over wholly to the *Tiers-Etat*, because it will be impossible for you to live in a constant sacrifice of your own sentiments to the prejudices of the *Noblesse*. But you would be received by the *Tiers-Etat*, at any future day, coldly, and without confidence. This appears to me the moment to take at once that honest and manly stand with them, which your own principles dictate. This will win their hearts for ever, be approved by the world, which marks and honors you as the man of the people, and will be an eternal consolation to yourself. The *Noblesse*, and especially the *Noblesse of Auvergne*, will always prefer men who will do their dirty work for them. You are not made for that. They will therefore soon drop you, and the people, in that case, will perhaps not take you up. Suppose a scission should take place. The Priests and Nobles will secede, the nation will remain in place, and, with the King, will do its own business. If violence should be attempted, where will you be? You cannot then take side with the people in opposition to your own vote, that very vote which will have helped to produce the scission. Still less can you array yourself against the people. That is impossible. Your instructions are indeed a difficulty. But to state this at its worst, it is only a single difficulty, which a single effort surmounts. Your instructions can never embarrass you a second time, whereas an acquiescence under them will re-produce greater difficulties every day, and without end. Besides, a thousand circumstances offer as many justifications of your departure from your instructions. Will it be impossible to persuade all parties, that (as for good legislation two Houses are necessary) the placing the privileged classes together in one House, and the unprivileged in another, would be better for both than a scission? I own I think it would. People can never agree without some sacrifices; and it appears but a moderate sacrifice in each party, to meet on this middle ground. The attempt to bring this about might satisfy your instructions, and a failure in it would justify your siding with the people, even to those who think instructions are laws of conduct. Forgive me, my dear friend, if my anxiety for you makes me talk of things I know nothing about. You must not consider this as advice. I know you and myself too well to presume to offer advice. Receive it merely as the expression of my uneasiness, and the effusion of that sincere friendship, with which I am, my dear Sir, yours affectionately,

Th: Jefferson.

LETTER CXCVII.—TO WILLIAM CARMICHAEL, May 8, 1789

TO WILLIAM CARMICHAEL.

Paris, May 8, 1789.

Dear Sir,

Your favor of January the 26th, to March the 27th, is duly received, and I thank you for the interesting papers it contained. The answer of Don Ulloa, however, on the subject of the canal through the American isthmus, was not among them, though mentioned to be so. If you have omitted it through accident, I shall thank you for it at some future occasion, as I wish much to understand that subject thoroughly. Our American information comes down to the 16th of March. There had not yet been members enough assembled of the new Congress, to open the tickets. They expected to do it in a day or two. In the mean time, it was said from all the States, that their vote had been unanimous for General Washington, and a good majority in favor of Mr. Adams, who is certainly, therefore, Vice-President. The new government would be supported by very cordial and very general dispositions in its favor from the people. I have not yet seen a list of the new Congress. This delay in the meeting of the new government has delayed the determination on my petition for leave of absence. However, I expect to receive it every day, and am in readiness to sail the instant I receive it, so that this is probably the last letter I shall write you hence, till my return. While there, I shall avail government of the useful information I have received from you, and shall not fail to profit of any good occasion which may occur, to show the difference between your real situation, and what it ought to be. I consider Paris and Madrid as the two only points, at which Europe and America should touch closely, and that a connection at these points should be fostered.

We have had in this city a very considerable riot, in which about one hundred people have been probably killed. It was the most unprovoked, and is therefore, justly, the most unpitied catastrophe of that kind I ever knew. Nor did the wretches know what they wanted, except to do mischief. It seems to have had no particular connection with the great national question now in agitation. The want of bread is very seriously dreaded through the whole kingdom. Between twenty and thirty ship-loads of wheat and flour has already arrived from the United States, and there will be about the same quantity of rice sent from Charleston to this country directly, of which about half has arrived. I presume that, between wheat and rice, one hundred ship-loads may be counted on in the whole from us. Paris consumes about a ship-load a day, (say two hundred and fifty tons.) The total supply of the West

Indies, for this year, rests with us, and there is almost a famine in Canada and Nova Scotia. The States General were opened the day before yesterday. Viewing it as an opera, it was imposing; as a scene of business, the King's speech was exactly what it should have been, and very well delivered; not a word of the Chancellor's was heard by any body, so that, as yet, I have never heard a single guess at what it was about. Mr. Necker's was as good as such a number of details would permit it to be. The picture of their resources was consoling, and generally plausible. I could have wished him to have dwelt more on those great constitutional reformations, which his *Rapport au Roy* had prepared us to expect. But they observe, that these points are proper for the speech of the Chancellor. We are in hopes, therefore, they were in that speech, which, like the Revelations of St. John, were no revelations at all. The *Noblesse*, on coming together, show that they are not as much reformed in their principles as we had hoped they would be. In fact, there is real danger of their totally refusing to vote by persons. Some found hopes on the lower clergy, which constitute four-fifths of the deputies of that order. If they do not turn the balance in favor of the *Tiers-Etat*, there is real danger of a scission. But I shall not consider even that event as rendering things desperate. If the King will do business with the *Tiers-Etat*, which constitutes the nation, it may be well done without Priests or Nobles. From the best information I can obtain, the King of England's madness has terminated in an imbecility, which may very possibly be of long continuance. He is going with his Queen to Germany. England chained to rest, the other parts of Europe may recover or retain tranquillity.

I have the honor to be, with great and sincere esteem, Dear Sir, your most obedient and most humble servant,

Th: Jefferson..

LETTER CXCVIII.—TO JOHN JAY, May 9, 1789

TO JOHN JAY.

Paris, May 9, 1789.

Sir,

Since my letter of March the 1st, by the way of Havre, and those of March the 12th and 15th, by the way of London, no opportunity of writing has occurred, till the present to London.

There are no symptoms of accommodation between the Turks and two empires, nor between Russia and Sweden. The Emperor was, on the 16th of the last month, expected to die, certainly; he was, however, a little better when the last news came away, so that hopes were entertained of him; but it is agreed that he cannot get the better of his complaints ultimately, so that his life is not at all counted on. The Danes profess, as yet, to do no more against Sweden than furnish their stipulated aid. The agitation of Poland is still violent, though somewhat moderated by the late change in the demeanor of the King of Prussia. He is much less thrasonic than he was. This is imputed to the turn which the English politics may be rationally expected to take. It is very difficult to get at the true state of the British King j but from the best information we can get, his madness has gone off, but he is left in a state of imbecility and melancholy. They are going to carry him to Hanover, to see whether such a journey may relieve him. The Queen accompanies him. If England. should, by this accident, be reduced to inactivity, the southern countries of Europe may escape the present war. Upon the whole, the prospect for the present year, if no unforeseen accident happens, is certain peace for the powers not already engaged, a probability that Denmark will not become a principal, and a mere possibility that Sweden and Russia may be accommodated. The interior disputes of Sweden are so exactly detailed in the Leyden gazette, that I have nothing to add on that subject.

The revolution of this country has advanced thus far without encountering any thing which deserves to be called a difficulty. There have been riots in a few instances, in three or four different places, in which there may have been a dozen or twenty lives lost. The exact truth is not be got at. A few days ago, a much more serious riot took place in this city, in which it became necessary for the troops to engage in regular action with the mob, and probably about one hundred of the latter were killed. Accounts vary from twenty to two hundred. They were the most abandoned banditti of Paris, and never was a riot more unprovoked and unpitied. They began, under a pretence that a paper manufacturer had proposed in an assembly, to reduce their wages to fifteen sous a day. They rifled his house, destroyed every thing in his magazines and shops, and were only stopped in their career of mischief, by the carnage above mentioned. Neither this nor any other of the riots, have had a professed connection with the great national reformation going on. They are such as have happened every year since I have been here, and as will continue to be produced by common incidents. The States General were opened on the 4th instant, by a speech from the throne, one by the *Garde des Sceaux*, and one from Mr. Necker. I hope they will be printed in time to send you herewith: lest they should not, I will observe, that that of Mr, Necker stated the real and ordinary deficit to be fifty-six millions, and that he showed that this could be made up without a new tax, by economies and bonifications which he specified. Several articles of the latter are liable to the objection, that they are proposed on branches of the revenue, of which the nation has demanded a suppression. He tripped too lightly over the great articles of constitutional reformation, these being not as clearly announced in this discourse as they were in his *Rapport au Roy*, which I sent you some time ago. On the whole, his discourse has not satisfied the patriotic party. It is now, for the first time, that their revolution is likely to receive a serious check, and begins to wear a fearful appearance. The progress of light and liberality in the order of the *Noblesse* has equalled expectation in Paris only, and its vicinities. The great mass of deputies of that order, which come from the country, show that the habits of tyranny over the people, are deeply rooted in them. They will consent, indeed, to equal taxation; but five-sixths of that chamber are thought to be, decidedly, for voting by orders; so that, had this great preliminary question rested on this body, which formed heretofore the sole hope, that hope would have been completely disappointed. Some aid, however, comes in from a quarter whence none was expected. It was imagined the ecclesiastical elections would have been generally in favor of the higher clergy; on the contrary, the lower clergy have obtained five-sixths of these deputations. These are the sons of peasants, who have done all the drudgery of the service, for ten, twenty, and thirty guineas a year, and whose oppressions and penury, contrasted with the pride and luxury of the higher clergy, have rendered them perfectly disposed to humble the latter. They have done it, in many instances, with a boldness they were thought insusceptible of. Great hopes have been formed, that these would concur with the *Tiers-Etat*, in voting by persons. In fact, about half of them seem as yet so disposed; but the bishops are intriguing, and drawing them over with the address which has ever marked ecclesiastical intrigue. The deputies of the *Tiers-Etat* seem, almost to a man, inflexibly determined against the vote by orders. This is the state of parties, as well as can be judged from conversation only, during the fortnight they have been now together. But as no business has been yet begun, no votes as yet taken, this calculation cannot be considered as sure. A middle proposition is talked of, to form the two privileged orders into one chamber. It is thought more possible to bring them into it, than the *Tiers-*

Etat. Another proposition is, to distinguish questions, referring those of certain descriptions to a vote by persons, others to a vote by orders. This seems to admit of endless altercation, and the *Tiers-Etat* manifest no respect for that, or any other modification whatever. Were this single question accommodated, I am of opinion, there would not occur the least difficulty in the great and essential points of constitutional reformation. But on this preliminary question the parties are so irreconcilable, that it is impossible to foresee what issue it will have. The *Tiers-Etat*, as constituting the nation, may propose to do the business of the nation, either with or without the minorities in the Houses of Clergy and Nobles, which side with them. In that case, if the King should agree to it, the majorities in those two Houses would secede, and might resist the tax-gatherers. This would bring on a civil war. On the other hand, the privileged orders, offering to submit to equal taxation, may propose to the King to continue the government in its former train, resuming to himself the power of taxation. Here, the tax-gatherers might be resisted by the people. In fine, it is but too possible, that between parties so animated, the King may incline the balance as he pleases. Happy that he is an honest, unambitious man, who desires neither money nor power for himself; and that his most operative minister, though he has appeared to trim a little, is still, in the main, a friend to public liberty.

I mentioned to you in a former letter, the construction which our bankers at Amsterdam had put on the resolution of Congress, appropriating the last Dutch loan, by which the money for our captives would not be furnished till the end of the year 1790. Orders from the board of treasury have now settled this question. The interest of the next month is to be first paid, and after that, the money for the captives and foreign officers is to be furnished, before any other payment of interest. This insures it when the next February interest becomes payable. My representations to them, on account of the contracts I had entered into for making the medals, have produced from them the money for that object, which is lodged in the hands of Mr. Grand.

Mr. Necker, in his discourse, proposes among his bonifications of revenue, the suppression of our two free ports of Bayonne and L'Orient, which, he says, occasion a loss of six hundred thousand livres annually, to the crown, by contraband. (The speech being not yet printed, I state this only as it struck my ear when he delivered it. If I have mistaken it, I beg you to receive this as my apology, and to consider what follows, as written on that idea only.) I have never been able to see that these free ports were worth one copper to us. To Bayonne our trade never went, and it is leaving L'Orient. Besides, the right of *entrepot* is a perfect substitute for the right of free port. The latter is a little less troublesome only, to the merchants and captains. I should think, therefore, that a thing so useless to us and prejudicial to them might be relinquished by us, on the common principles of friendship. I know the merchants of these ports will make a clamor, because the franchise covers their contraband with all the world. Has Monsieur de Moustier said any thing to you on this subject? It has never been mentioned to me. If not mentioned in either way, it is rather an indecent proceeding, considering that this right of free port is founded in treaty. I shall ask of M. de Montmorin, on the first occasion, whether he has communicated this to you through his minister; and if he has not, I will endeavor to notice the infraction to him in such manner, as neither to reclaim nor abandon the right of free port, but leave our government free to do either.

The gazettes of France and Leyden, as usual, will accompany this. I am in hourly expectation of receiving from you my leave of absence, and keep my affairs so arranged, that I can leave Paris within eight days after receiving the permission.

I have the honor to be, with sentiments of the most perfect esteem and respect, Sir, your most obedient and most humble

servant,

Th: Jefferson.

LETTER CXCIX.—TO GENERAL WASHINGTON, May 10, 1780

TO GENERAL WASHINGTON.

Paris, May 10, 1780,

Sir,

I am now to acknowledge, the honor of your two letters of November the 27th and February the 13th, both of which have come to hand since my last to you of December the 4th and 5th. The details you are so good as to give me on the subject of the navigation of the waters of the Potomac and Ohio, are very pleasing to me, as I consider the union of those two rivers, as among the strongest links of connection between the eastern and western sides of our confederacy. It will, moreover, add to the commerce of Virginia, in particular, all the upper parts of the Ohio and its waters. Another vast object, and of much less difficulty, is to add also, all the country on the lakes and their waters. This would enlarge our field immensely, and would certainly be effected by an union of the upper waters of the Ohio and lake Erie. The Big Beaver and Cayahoga offer the most direct line, and according to information I received from General Hand, and which I had the honor of writing you in the year 1783, the streams in that neighborhood head in lagoons, and the country is flat. With respect to the doubts which you say are entertained by some, whether the upper waters of Potomac can be rendered capable of navigation, on account of the falls and rugged banks, they are answered, by observing, that it is reduced to a maxim, that whenever there is water enough to float a batteau, there may be navigation for a batteau. Canals and locks may be necessary, and they are expensive; but I hardly know what expense would be too great for the object in question. Probably, negotiation with the Indians, perhaps even settlement, must precede the execution of the Cayahoga canal. The States of Maryland and Virginia should make a common object of it. The navigation, again, between Elizabeth River and the Sound is of vast importance, and in my opinion, it is much better that these should be done at public than private expense.

Though we have not heard of the actual opening of the new Congress, and consequently, have not official information of your election as President of the United States, yet, as there never could be a doubt entertained of it, permit me to express here my felicitations, not to yourself, but to my country. Nobody who has tried both public and private life, can doubt but that you were much happier on the banks of the Potomac than you will be at New York. But there was nobody so well qualified as yourself, to put our new machine into a regular course of action; nobody, the authority of whose name could have so effectually crushed opposition at home, and produced respect abroad. I am sensible of the immensity of the sacrifice on your part. Your measure of fame was full to the brim; and therefore, you have nothing to gain. But there are cases wherein it is a duty to risk all against nothing, and I believe this was exactly the case. We may presume, too, according to every rule of probability, that after doing a great deal of good, you will be found to have lost nothing but private repose.

In a letter to Mr. Jay, of the 19th of November, I asked a leave of absence to carry my children back to their own country, and to settle various matters of a private nature, which were left unsettled, because I had no idea of being absent so long. I expected that letter would have been received in time to be decided on by the government then existing. I know now that it would arrive when there was no Congress, and consequently, that if must have awaited your arrival at New York. I hope you found the request not an unreasonable one. I am excessively anxious to receive the permission without delay, that I may be able to get back before the winter sets in. Nothing can be so dreadful to me, as to be shivering at sea for two or three months, in a winter passage. Besides, there has never been a moment at which the presence of a minister here could be so well dispensed with, from certainty of no war this summer, and that the government will be so totally absorbed in domestic arrangements, as to attend to nothing exterior. Mr. Jay will, of course, communicate to you some ciphered letters lately written, and one of this date. My public letter to him contains all the interesting public details. I enclose with the present, some extracts of a letter from Mr. Paine, which he desired me to communicate: your knowledge of the writer will justify my giving you the trouble of these communications, which their interesting nature and his respectability will jointly recommend to notice. I am in great pain for the Marquis de la Fayette. His principles, you know, are clearly with the people; but having been elected for the *Noblesse* of Auvergne, they have laid him under express instructions to vote for the decision by orders and not persons. This would ruin him with the *Tiers-Etat*, and it is not possible he could continue long to give satisfaction to the *Noblesse.* I have not hesitated to press on him to burn his instructions, and follow his conscience as the only sure clue, which will eternally guide a man clear of all doubts and inconsistencies. If he cannot effect a conciliatory plan, he will surely take his stand manfully at once with the *Tiers-Etat.* He will in that case be what he pleases with them, and I am in hopes that base is now too solid to render it dangerous to be mounted on it. In hopes of being able, in the course of the summer, to pay my respects to you personally in New York, I have the honor to be, with sentiments of the most perfect respect and attachment, Sir, your most obedient and most humble servant,

Th: Jefferson.

[Extract of the letter from Thomas Paine, referred to in the

preceding, to General Washington.]

'London, March the 12th, 1789. I do not think it is worth while for Congress to appoint any minister at this court. The greater distance Congress observes on this point, the better. It will be all money thrown away to go to any expense about it, at least during the present reign. I know the nation well, and the line of acquaintance I am in enables me to judge better on this matter than any other American can judge, especially at a distance. I believe I am not so much in the good graces of the Marquis of Lansdowne as I used to be. I do not answer his purpose. He was always talking of a sort of re-connection of England and America, and my coldness and reserve on this subject checked communication. I believe he would be a good minister for England, with respect to a better agreement with France.'

(Same letter continued) 'April 10. The acts for regulating the trade with America are to be continued as last year. A paper from the Privy Council respecting the American fly is before parliament. I had some conversation with Sir Joseph Banks upon this subject, as he was the person whom the Privy Council referred to. I told him that the Hessian fly attacked only the green plant, and did not exist in the dry grain. He said, that with respect to the Hessian fly they had no apprehension, but it was the weevil they alluded to. I told him the weevil had always, more or less, been in the wheat countries of America, and that if the prohibition was on that account, it was as necessary fifty or sixty years ago as now; that I believed it was only a political manoeuvre of the ministry to please the landed interest, as a balance for prohibiting the exportation of wool, to please the manufacturing interest. He did not reply, and as we are on very sociable terms, I went farther, by saying, the English ought not to complain of the non-payment of debts from America, while they prohibit the means of payment. I suggest to you a thought on this subject.

The debts due before the war ought to be distinguished from the debts contracted since, and all and every mode of payment and remittance under which they might have been discharged at the time they were contracted, ought to accompany those debts so long as any of them shall continue unpaid, because the circumstances of payment became united with the debt, and cannot be separated by subsequent acts of one side only. If this was taken up in America, and insisted on as a right coeval with, and inseparable from those debts, it would force some of the restrictions here to give way. While writing this, I am informed that the minister has had a conference with some of the American creditors, and proposed to them to assume the debts, and give them ten shillings in the pound. The conjecture is, that he means, when the new Congress is established, to demand the payment. If you are writing to General Washington, it may not be amiss to mention this, and if I hear further on this matter, I will inform you. But as, being a money matter, it cannot come forward but through parliament; there will be notice given of the business. This would be a proper time to show that the British acts since the peace militate against the payment, by narrowing the means by which those debts might have been paid when they were contracted, and which ought to be considered as constituent parts of the contract.'

LETTER CC.—TO JAMES MADISON, May 11,1789

TO JAMES MADISON.

Paris, May 11,1789.

Dear Sir,

My last to you was of the 15th of March. I am now in hourly expectation of receiving my leave of absence. The delay of it a little longer will endanger the throwing my return into the winter, the very idea of which is horror itself to me. I am in hopes this is the last letter I shall have the pleasure of writing you before my departure.

The madness of the King of England has gone off, but left him in a state of imbecility and melancholy. They talk of carrying him to Hanover. If they do, it will be a proof he does not mend, and that they take that measure, to authorize them to establish a regency. But if he grows better, they will perhaps keep him at home, to avoid the question, Who shall be regent? As that country cannot be relied on in the present state of its executive, the King of Prussia has become more moderate; he throws cold water on the fermentation he had excited in Poland. The King of Sweden will act as nobody, not even himself, can foresee; because he acts from the caprice of the moment, and because the discontents of his army and nobles may throw him under internal difficulties, while struggling with external ones. Denmark will probably only furnish its stipulated aid to Russia. France is fully occupied with internal arrangements. So that, on the whole, the prospect of this summer is, that the war will continue between the powers actually engaged in the close of the last campaign, and extend to no others; certainly it will not extend, this year, to the southern States of Europe. The revolution of France has gone on with the most unexampled success, hitherto. There have been some mobs, occasioned by the want of bread, in different parts of the kingdom, in which there may have been some lives lost; perhaps a dozen or twenty. These had no professed connection, generally, with the constitutional revolution. A more serious riot happened lately in Paris, in which about one hundred of the mob were killed. This execution has been universally approved, as they seemed to have no view but mischief and plunder. But the meeting of the States General presents serious difficulties, which it had been hoped the progress of reason would have enabled them to get over. The nobility of and about Paris have come over, as was expected, to the side of the people, in the great question of voting by persons or orders. This had induced a presumption, that those of the country were making the same progress, and these form the great mass of the deputies of that order. But they are found to be where they were centuries ago, as to their disposition to keep distinct from the people, and even to tyrannize over them. They agree, indeed, to abandon their pecuniary privileges. The clergy seem at present much divided. Five-sixths of that representation consists of the lower clergy, who, being the sons of the peasantry, are very well with the *Tiers-Etat.* But the Bishops are intriguing, and drawing them over daily. The *Tiers-Etat* is so firm to vote by persons or to go home, that it is impossible to conjecture what will be the result. This is the state of parties, as well as we can conjecture from the conversation of the members; for as yet no vote has been given, which will enable us to calculate on certain ground.

Having formerly written to you on the subject of our finances, I enclose you now an abstract of a paper on that subject, which Gouverneur Morris communicated to me. You will be a better judge of its merit than I am. It seems to me worthy good attention.

I have a box of books packed for you, which I shall carry to Havre, and send by any ship bound to New York or Philadelphia. I have been so inexact, as to take no list of them before nailing up the box. Be so good as to do this, and I will take with me my bookseller's account, which will enable us to make a statement of them. They are chiefly *Encyclopédies*, from the 23rd to the 30th *livraison.* Paul Jones has desired me to send to yourself and Colonel Carrington each, his bust. They are packed together in the same box. There are three other boxes, with two in each, for other gentlemen. I shall send them all together, and take the liberty of addressing them to you. I rejoice extremely to hear you are elected, in spite of all cabals. I fear your post will not permit me to see you but in New York, and consequently for a short time only. I shall much regret this.

I am, with sentiments of sincere attachment and respect, Dear Sir, your friend and servant,

Th: Jefferson.

LETTER CCI.—TO MONSIEUR DE PONTIERE, May 17, 1789

TO MONSIEUR DE PONTIERE.

Paris, May 17, 1789.

Sir,

I am honored with your letter of the 6th instant, and am sincerely sorry that you should experience inconveniences for the want of the arrearages due to you from the United States. I have never ceased to take every measure, which could promise to procure to the foreign officers the payment of these arrears. At present the matter stands thus. Congress have agreed to borrow a sum of money in Holland, to enable them to pay the individual demands in Europe. They have given orders that these arrearages shall be paid out of this money, when borrowed, and certain bankers in Amsterdam are charged to borrow the money. I am myself of opinion, they will certainly procure the money in the course of the present year; but it is not for me to affirm this, nor to make any engagement. The moment the money is ready, it shall be made known to Colonel Gourion, who, at the desire of many of the officers, has undertaken to communicate with me on the subject, and to inform them, from time to time, of the progress of this business. He will readily answer your letters on this subject. I depart in a few days for America, but shall leave such instructions here, as that this matter will suffer no delay on that account.

I have the honor to be. Sir, your most obedient, humble servant,

Th: Jefferson.

LETTER CCII.—TO MR. VAUGHAN, May 17, 1789

TO MR. VAUGHAN.

Paris, May 17, 1789.

Dear Sir,

I am to acknowledge, all together, the receipt of your favors of March the 17th, 26th, and May the 7th, and to return you abundant thanks for your attention to the article of dry rice, and the parcel of seeds you sent me. This is interesting, because, even should it not take place of the wet rice, in South Carolina, it will enable us to cultivate this grain in Virginia, where we have not lands disposed for the wet rice. The collection of the works of Monsieur de Poivre has not, as I believe, been ever published. It could hardly have escaped my knowledge, if they had been ever announced. The French translation of the book on trade has not yet come to my hands. Whenever I receive the copies, they shall be distributed, and principally among the members of the *Etats Generaux*. I doubt whether, at this session, they will take up the subject of commerce. Whenever they do, they will find better principles no where than in that book. I spoke with Mr. Stewart yesterday on the subject of the distribution, and if I should be gone before the books come to hand, he will execute the commission. Your nation is very far from the liberality that treatise inculcates. The proposed regulation on the subject of our wheat is one proof. The prohibition of it in England would, of itself, be of no great moment, because I do not know that it is much sent there. But it is the publishing a libel on our wheat, sanctioned with the name of parliament, and which can have no object but to do us injury, by spreading a groundless alarm in those countries of Europe where our wheat is constantly and kindly received. It is a mere assassination. If the insect they pretend to fear, be the Hessian fly, it never existed in the grain. If it be the weevil, our grain always had that; and the experience of a century has proved, that either the climate of England is not warm enough to hatch the egg and continue the race, or that some other unknown cause prevents any evil from it. How different from this spirit, my dear Sir, has been your readiness to help us to the dry rice, to communicate to us the bread tree, &tc. Will any of our climates admit the cultivation of the latter? I am too little acquainted with it to judge. I learn that your newspapers speak of the death of Ledyard, at Grand Cairo. I am anxious to know whether there be foundation for this. I have not yet had time to try the execution of the wood hygrometer proposed by Dr. Franklin. Though I have most of the articles ready made, I doubt now whether I shall be able to do it before my departure for America, the permission for which I expect every hour; and I shall go off the instant I receive it. While there, I shall have the pleasure of seeing your father and friends. I expect to return in the fall.

In the mean time, I have the honor to be, with very great esteem and respect, Dear Sir, your most obedient, humble servant,

Th: Jefferson.

LETTER CCIII.—TO THOMAS PAINE, May 19,1789

TO THOMAS PAINE.

Paris, May 19,1789.

Dear Sir,

Your favors of February the 16th to April the 13th, and of May the 3rd and 10th, are received; and the two last are sent to Mr. Leroy, who will communicate them to the Academy.

You know that the States General have met, and probably have seen the speeches at the opening of them. The three orders sit in distinct chambers. The great question, whether they shall vote by orders or persons can never be surmounted amicably. It has not yet been proposed in form; but the votes which have been taken on the outworks of that question show, that the *Tiers-Etat* are unanimous, a good majority of the Clergy (consisting of the *Curés*) disposed to side with the *Tiers-Etat*, and in the chamber of the *Noblesse* there are only fifty-four in that sentiment, against one hundred and ninety, who are for voting by orders. Committees to find means of conciliation are appointed by each chamber; but conciliation is impossible. Some think the Nobles could be induced to unite themselves with the higher Clergy into one House, the lower Clergy and *Tiers-Etat* forming another. But the *Tiers-Etat* are immovable. They are not only firm, but a little disdainful. The question is, what will ensue? One idea is to separate, in order to consult again their constituents, and to take new instructions. This would be doing nothing, for the same instructions would be repeated; and what, in the mean time, is to become of a government absolutely without money, and which cannot be kept in motion with less than a million of livres a day? The more probable expectation is as follows. As soon as it shall become evident, that no amicable determination of the manner of voting can take place, the *Tiers-Etat* will send an invitation to the two other orders, to come and take their places in the common chamber. A majority of the Clergy will go, and the minority of the Noblesse. The chamber thus composed, will declare that the States General are constituted, will notify it to the King, and that they are ready to proceed to business. If the King refuses to do business with them, and adheres to the Nobles, the common chamber will declare all taxes at an end, will form a declaration of rights, and do such other acts as the circumstances will permit, and go home. The tax-gatherers will then be resisted, and it may well be doubted whether the soldiery and their officers will not divide, as the *Tiers-Etat* and Nobles. But it is more likely that the King will agree to do business with the States General, so constituted, professing that the necessities of the moment force this, and that he means to negotiate (as they go along) a reconciliation between the seceding members, and those which remain. If the matter takes this turn, there may be small troubles and ebullitions excited by the seceding *Noblesse* and higher Clergy; but no serious difficulty can arise. M. de Lamoignon, the *Garde des Sceaux* of the last year, has shot himself. The Emperor's complaint is pulmonary, and incurable. The Grand Seignior is dead; his successor, young and warlike. I congratulate you sincerely on the success of your bridge. I was sure of it before from theory: yet one likes to be assured from practice also. I am anxious to see how Mr. Rumsey's experiment succeeds.

May the 21st. I have this moment received a letter from Ledyard, dated Cairo, November the 15th. He therein says, 'I am doing up my baggage, and most curious baggage it is, and I leave Cairo in two or three days. I travel from hence southwest, about three hundred leagues, to a black King: there my present conductors leave me to my fate. Beyond, I suppose, I go alone. I expect to hit the continent across, between the parallels of twelve and twenty degrees north latitude. I shall, if possible, write you from the kingdom of this black gentleman.' This seems to contradict the story of his having died at Cairo, in January, as he was then, probably, in the interior parts of Africa. If Sir Joseph Banks has no news from him later than the letter of September, it may do him pleasure, if you will communicate the above. If he or any other person knows whether there is any foundation for the story of his death, I will thank you to inform me of it. My letter being to go off to-morrow, I shall only add assurances of the esteem and respect, with which I am, Dear Sir, your friend and servant,

Th: Jefferson.

LETTER CCIV.—TO MONSIEUR DE ST. ETIENNE, June 3, 1789

TO MONSIEUR DE ST. ETIENNE.

Paris, June 3, 1789.

Sir,

After you quitted us yesterday evening, we continued our conversation (Monsieur de la Fayette, Mr. Short, and myself) on the subject of the difficulties which environ you. The desirable object being to secure the good which the King has offered, and to avoid the ill which seems to threaten, an idea was suggested, which appearing to make an impression on Monsieur de la Fayette, I was encouraged to pursue it on my return to Paris, to put it into form, and now to send it to you and him. It is this; that the King, in a *seance royale*, should come forward with a Charter of Rights in his hand, to be signed by himself and by every member of the three orders. This charter to contain the five great points which the *Resultat* of December offered on the part of the King; the abolition of pecuniary privileges offered by the privileged orders, and the adoption of the national debt, and a grant of the sum of money asked from the nation. This last will be a cheap price for the preceding articles; and let the same act declare your immediate separation till the next anniversary meeting. You will carry back to your constituents more good than ever was effected before without violence, and you will stop exactly at the point where violence would otherwise begin. Time will be gained, the public mind will continue to ripen and to be informed, a basis of support may be prepared with the people themselves, and expedients occur for gaining still something further at your next meeting, and for stopping again at the point of force. I have ventured to send yourself and Monsieur de la Fayette a sketch of my ideas of what this act might contain, without endangering any dispute. But it is offered merely as a canvass for you to work on, if it be fit to work on at all. I know too little of the subject, and you know too much of it, to justify me in offering any thing but a hint. I have done it, too, in a hurry: insomuch, that since committing it to writing, it occurs to me that the fifth article may give alarm; that it is in a good degree included in the fourth, and is, therefore, useless. But after all, what excuse can I make, Sir, for this presumption. I have none but an unmeasurable love for your nation, and a painful anxiety lest despotism, after an unaccepted offer to bind its own hands, should seize you again with tenfold fury. Permit me to add to these, very sincere assurances of the sentiments of esteem and respect, with which I have the honor to be, Sir, your most obedient and most humble servant,

Th: Jefferson.

[The annexed is the Charter accompanying the preceding letter.]

A Charter of Rights, solemnly established by the King and Nation.

1. The States General shall assemble, uncalled, on the first day of November, annually, and shall remain together so long as they shall see cause. They shall regulate their own elections and proceedings, and until they shall ordain otherwise, their elections shall be in the forms observed in the present year, and shall be triennial.

2. The States General alone shall levy money on the nation, and shall appropriate it.

3. Laws shall be made by the States General only, with the consent of the King.

4. No person shall be restrained of his liberty, but by regular process from a court of justice, authorized by a general law. (Except that a Noble may be imprisoned by order of a court of justice, on the prayer of twelve of his nearest relations.) On complaint of an unlawful imprisonment, to any judge whatever, he shall have the prisoner immediately brought before him, and shall discharge him, if his imprisonment be unlawful. The officer, in whose custody the prisoner is, shall obey the orders of the judge; and both judge and officer shall be responsible, civilly and criminally, for a failure of duty herein.

5. The military shall be subordinate to the civil authority.

7. Printers shall be liable to legal prosecution for printing and publishing false facts, injurious to the party prosecuting; but they shall be under no other restraint.

7. All pecuniary privileges and exemptions, enjoyed by any description of persons, are abolished.

8. All debts already contracted by the King, are hereby made the debts of the nation; and the faith thereof is pledged for their payment in due time.

9. Eighty millions of livres are now granted to the King, to be raised by loan, and reimbursed by the nation: and the taxes heretofore paid, shall continue to be paid to the end of the present year, and no longer.

10. The States General shall now separate, and meet again on the 1st day of November next.

Done, on behalf of the whole nation, by the King and their representatives in the States General, at Versailles, this ——— day of June, 1789.

Signed by the King, and by every member individually, and in his presence.

LETTER CCV.—TO THE MARQUIS DE LA FAYETTE, June 12, 1789

TO THE MARQUIS DE LA FAYETTE.

Paris, June 12, 1789.

My Dear Sir,

As I may not be able to get at you at Versailles, I write this to deliver it myself at your door. With respect to the utility or inutility of your minority's joining the Commons, I am unable to form an opinion for myself. I know too little of the subject to see what may be its consequences.

I never knew an instance of the English parliament's undertaking to relieve the poor by a distribution of bread in time of scarcity. In fact, the English commerce is so extensive and so active, that though bread may be a little more or less plenty, there can never be an absolute failure. The island is so narrow, that corn can be readily carried from the sea-ports to its interior parts. But were an absolute want to happen, and were the parliament to undertake a distribution of corn, I think, that according to the principles of their government, they would only vote a sum of money, and address the King to employ it for the best. The business is, in its nature, executive, and would require too great a variety of detail to be managed by an act of parliament. However, I repeat it, that I never heard or read of an instance of the parliament's interfering to give bread. If I see you at Versailles to-day, I can be more particular.

I am with great sincerity, my dear Sir, your affectionate friend and servant,

Th: Jefferson,

LETTER CCVI.—TO JOHN JAY, June 17, 1789

TO JOHN JAY.

Sir

Paris, June 17, 1789.

I had the honor of addressing you on the 9th and 12th of May, by the way of London. This goes through the same channel to the care of Mr. Trumbull. Having received no letter from you of later date than the 25th of November, I am apprehensive that there may have been miscarriages, and the more so, as I learn, through another channel, that you have particularly answered mine of November the 19th.

The death of the Grand Seignior, which has happened, renders the continuance of the war more probable, as it has brought to the throne a successor of a more active and ardent temper, and who means to put himself at the head of his armies. He has declared the Captain Pacha his Generalissimo. The prospects for Russia, on the other hand, are less encouraging. Her principal ally, the Emperor, is at death's door, blazing up a little indeed, from time to time like an expiring taper, but certainly to extinguish soon. Denmark, too, is likely to be restrained by the threats of England and Prussia, from contributing even her stipulated naval succors. It is some time since I have been able to obtain any account of the King of England, on which I can rely with confidence. His melancholy continues, and to such a degree, as to render him absolutely indifferent to every thing that passes, so that he seems willing to let his ministers do every thing they please, provided they will let him alone. When forced to speak, his comprehension seems better than it was in the first moments after his phrensy went off. His health is bad: he does not go into public at all, and very few are admitted to see him. This is his present state, according to the best accounts I have been able to get lately. His ministers dictate boldly in the north, because they know it is impossible they should be engaged in the war, while this country is so completely palsied.

You will have seen by my former letters, that the question, whether the States General should vote by persons or by orders, had stopped their proceedings in the very first instance in which it could occur, that is, as to the verification of their powers, and that they had appointed committees to try if there were any means of accommodation. These could do nothing. The King then proposed that they should appoint others, to meet persons whom he should name, on the same subject. These conferences also proved ineffectual. He then proposed a specific mode of verifying. The clergy accepted it unconditionally; the *Noblesse*, with such conditions and modifications, as did away their acceptance altogether. The Commons, considering this as a refusal, came to the resolution of the 10th instant (which I have the honor to send you), inviting the two other orders to come and take their places in the common room, and notifying that they should proceed to the verification of powers, and to the affairs of the nation, either with or without them. The Clergy have, as yet, given no answer. A few of their members have accepted the invitation of the Commons, and have presented themselves in their room, to have their powers verified; but how many it will detach, in the whole, from that body, cannot be known till an answer be decided on. The *Noblesse* adhered to their former resolutions, and even the minority, well disposed to the Commons, thought they could do more good in their own chamber, by endeavoring to increase their numbers and fettering the measures of the majority, than by joining the Commons. An intrigue was set on foot, between the leaders of the majority in that House, the Queen, and Princes. They persuaded the King to go for some time to Marly: he went. On the same day, the leaders moved in the chamber of Nobles, that they should address the King, to declare his own sentiments on the great question between the orders. It was intended that this address should be delivered to him at Marly, where, separated from his ministers, and surrounded by the Queen and Princes, he might be surprised into a declaration for the Nobles. The motion was lost, however, by a very great majority, that chamber being not yet quite ripe for throwing themselves into the arms of despotism. Necker and Montmorin, who had discovered this intrigue, had warned some of the minority to defeat it, or they could not answer for what would happen. These two and St. Priest, are the only members of the Council in favor of the Commons. Luzerne, Puy-Segur, and the others, are high aristocrats. The Commons having verified their powers, a motion was made the day before yesterday, to declare themselves constituted, and to proceed to business. I left them at two o'clock yesterday; the debates not then finished. They differed only about forms of expression, but agreed in the substance, and probably decided yesterday, or will decide to-day. Their next move, I fancy, will be to suppress all taxes, and instantly re-establish them till the end of their session, in order to prevent a premature dissolution: and then they will go to work on a declaration of rights and a constitution. The *Noblesse*, I suppose, will be employed altogether in counter operations; the Clergy, that is to say, the higher Clergy, and such of the *Curés* as they can bring over to their side, will be waiting and watching, merely to keep themselves in their saddles. Their deportment, hitherto, is that of meekness and cunning. The fate of the nation depends on the conduct of the King and his ministers. Were they to side openly with the Commons, the revolution would be completed without a convulsion, by the establishment of a constitution, tolerably free, and in which the distinction of Noble and Commoner would be suppressed. But this is scarcely possible. The King is honest, and wishes the good of his people; but the expediency of an hereditary aristocracy is too difficult a question for him. On the contrary, his prejudices, his habits, and his connections decide him in his heart to support it. Should they decide openly for the *Noblesse*, the Commons, after suppressing taxes, and finishing their declaration of rights, would probably go home; a bankruptcy takes place in the instant, Mr. Necker must go out, a resistance to the tax-gatherers follows, and probably a civil war. These consequences are too evident and violent, to render this issue likely. Though the Queen and Princes are infatuated enough to hazard it, the party in the ministry would not. Something, therefore, like what I hinted in my letter of May the 12th, is still the most likely to take place. While the Commons, either with or without their friends of the other two Houses, shall be employed in framing a constitution, perhaps the government may set the other two Houses to work on the same subject: and when the three schemes shall be ready, joint committees may be negotiated, to compare them together, to see in what parts they agree; and probably they will agree in all, except the organization of the future States General. As to this, it may be endeavored, by the aid of wheedling and intimidation, to induce the two privileged chambers to melt themselves into one, and the Commons, instead of one, to agree to two Houses of legislation. I see no other middle ground to which they can be brought.

It is a tremendous cloud, indeed, which hovers over this nation, and he at the helm has neither the courage nor the skill necessary to weather it. Eloquence in a high degree, knowledge in matters of account, and order, are distinguishing traits in his character. Ambition is his first passion, virtue his second. He has not discovered that sublime truth, that a bold, unequivocal virtue is the best handmaid even to ambition, and would carry him further, in the end, than the temporizing, wavering policy he pursues. His judgment is not of the first order, scarcely even of the second; his resolution frail; and upon the whole, it is rare to meet an instance of a person so much below the reputation he has obtained. As this character, by the post and times in which Providence has placed it, is important to be known, I send it to you as drawn by a person of my acquaintance, who knows him well. He is not, indeed, his friend, and allowance must, therefore, be made for the high coloring. But this being abated, the facts and groundwork of the drawing are just. If the *Tiers* separate, he goes at the same time; if they stay together, and succeed in establishing a constitution to their mind, as soon as that is placed in safety, they will abandon him to the mercy of the court, unless he can recover the confidence which he has lost at present, and which, indeed, seems to be irrecoverable.

The inhabitants of St. Domingo, without the permission of the government, have chosen and sent deputies to the States General. The question of their admission is to be discussed by the States. In the mean time, the government had promised them an Assembly in their own Island, in the course of the present year. The death of the Dauphin, so long expected, has at length happened. Montmorin told Ternant the other day, that De Moustier had now asked a *congé*, which would be sent him immediately. So that unless a change of ministry should happen, he will, probably, be otherwise disposed of. The gazettes of France and Leyden accompany this. I have the honor to be, with the most perfect esteem and respect, Sir, your most obedient, humble servant,

Th: Jefferson.

P. S. June 18. The motion under debate with the Commons, for constituting their Assembly, passed yesterday by a majority of four hundred and odd, against eighty odd. The latter were for it in substance, but wished some particular amendment. They proceeded instantly to the subject of taxation. A member who called on me this moment, gave me a state of the proceedings of yesterday, from memory, which I enclose you. He left the House a little before the question was put, because he saw there was no doubt of its passing, and his brother, who remained till the decision, informed him of it. So that we may expect, perhaps, in the course of to-morrow, to see whether the government will interpose with a bold hand, or will begin a negotiation. But in the mean time, this letter must go off. I will find some other opportunity, however, of informing you of the issue. T. J.

^^^ [Character of Mr. Necker, accompanying the preceding letter.]

Nature bestowed on Mr. Necker an ardent passion for glory, without, at the same time, granting him those qualities required for its pursuit by direct means. The union of a fruitful imagination with a limited talent, with which she has endowed him, is always incompatible with those faculties of the mind which qualify their possessor to penetrate, to combine, and to comprehend all the relations of objects.

He had probably learned in Geneva, his native country, the influence which riches exercise on the success of ambition, without having recourse to the school of Paris, where he arrived about the twenty-eighth year of his age. A personal affair with his brother, in which the chiefs of the republic conducted themselves unjustly towards him, the circumstances of which, moreover, exposed him to ridicule, determined him to forsake his country. On taking his leave, he assured his mother that he would make a great fortune at Paris. On his arrival, he engaged himself as clerk, at a salary of six hundred livres, with the banker Thelusson, a man of extreme harshness in his intercourse with his dependants. The same cause which obliged other clerks to abandon the service of Thelusson, determined Necker to continue in it. By submitting to the brutality of his master with a servile resignation, whilst, at the same time, he devoted the most unremitting attention to his business, he recommended himself to his confidence, and was taken into partnership. Ordinary abilities only were requisite to avail him of the multitude of favorable circumstances, which, before he entered into the administration, built up a fortune of six millions of livres. He owed much of his good fortune to his connections with the Abbe Terrai, of whose ignorance he did not scruple to profit. His riches, his profession, his table, and a virtuous, reasonable, and well informed wife, procured him the acquaintance of many persons of distinction, among whom were many men of letters, who celebrated his knowledge and wisdom.

The wise and just principles by which Turgot aimed to correct the Abuses of the administration, not having been received with favor, he seized the occasion to flatter ignorance and malignity, by publishing his work against the freedom of the corn trade.

He had published, two years before, an eulogy on Colbert. Both these productions exhibited the limited capacity of a banker, and, in no degree, the enlarged views of a statesman. Not at all delicate in the choice of his means, he succeeded to his wish in his object, which was the establishing himself in public opinion. Elevated by a secret cabal to the direction of the finances, he began by refusing the salaries of his office. He affected a spirit of economy and austerity, which imposed even on foreign nations, and showed the possibility of making war without laying new taxes. Such at least was his boast; but, in reality, they have been increased under his administration, about twenty millions, partly by a secret augmentation of the bailies and of the poll-tax, partly by some verifications of the twentieths, and partly by the natural progression, which is tested by the amount of taxes on consumption, the necessary result of the successive increase of population, of riches, and of expensive tastes.

All these circumstances reared for him an astonishing reputation, which his fall has consecrated. People will not reflect, that, in the short period of his ministry, he had more than doubled his fortune. Not that he had peculated on the public treasury; his good sense and pride forbade a resort to this manoeuvre of weak minds; but by resorting to loans and the costly operations of the bank, to provide the funds of war, and being still connected with the house to which he addressed himself for much the greater part of his negotiations. They have not remarked that his great principles of economy have nothing more than a false show, and that the loans resorted to, in order to avoid the imposition of taxes, have been the source of the mischief which has reduced the finances to their present alarming condition.

As to his *compte rendu*; he has been forgiven the nauseous panegyric which he has passed upon himself, and the affectation of introducing his wife into it, for the purpose of praising her; and we are spared the trouble of examining his false calculations. M. de Calonne has undertaken this investigation. Without being able to vindicate himself, he has already begun to unmask his antagonist, and he promises to do it effectually.

Necessity has recalled this man to the ministry: and it must be confessed, that he is beyond comparison a less mischievous minister than his predecessors. I would compare him to a steward, who, by his management, does not entirely ruin his master, but who enriches himself at his expense. The desire of glory should inspire him as much as possible with the energy requisite for the public business. There is every likelihood that his ministry will not endure long enough, to cause it to feel the effects of his false principles of administration: and it is he alone who is able, if any one can, to preserve order in the finances, until the reform is effected which we hope from the assembling of the States General. In the mean time, the public estimation of his talents and virtue is not so high as it has been. There are persons who pretend that he is more firmly established in public opinion than he ever was. They deceive themselves. The ambitious desire he has always manifested of getting again into the administration, his work on the Importance of Religious Opinions, and the Memoires of M. de Calonne, have greatly impaired his reputation.

LETTER CCVII.—TO JAMES MADISON, June 18, 1789

TO JAMES MADISON.

Paris, June 18, 1789.

Sir,

My last to you was of May the 11th. Yours of March the 29th came to hand ten days ago; and about two days ago, I received a cover of your hand-writing, under which were a New York paper of May the 4th, and a letter from Mr. Page to Mazzei. There being no letter from you, makes me hope there is one on the way, which will inform me of my *congé*. I have never received Mr. Jay's answer to my public letter of November the 19th, which you mention him to have written, and which I fear has been intercepted. I know only from you, that my letter got safe to hand. My baggage has been made up more than a month, so that I shall leave Paris almost in the instant of receiving the permission.

The campaign begins under unfavorable auspices for Russia. The death of the Grand Seignior, who was personally disposed for peace, has brought a young and ardent successor to the throne, determined to push the war to extremity. Her only ally, the Emperor, is *in articulo mortis*, and the grand Duke of Tuscany, should he succeed, loves peace and money. Denmark is forbidden by England and Prussia to furnish even its stipulated maritime aid. There is no appearance of any other power's engaging in the war. As far as I can discover, the King of England is somewhat better in his head, but under such a complete depression of spirits, that he does not care how the world goes, and leaves his ministers to do as they please. It is impossible for you to conceive how difficult it is to know the truth relative to him, he is environed in such an atmosphere of lies. Men who would not speak a falsehood on any other subject, lie on this, from a principle of duty; so that even eye-witnesses cannot be believed without scanning their principles and connections; and few will stand this, of the very few permitted to see him.

Committees of conciliation having failed in their endeavors to bring together the three chambers of the States General, the King proposed a specific mode of verifying their powers; for that having been the first question which presented itself to them, was the one in which the question of voting by persons or orders was first brought on. The clergy accepted unconditionally. The *Noblesse* accepted on conditions which reduced the acceptance to nothing at all. The Commons considered this as a refusal on the part of the Nobles, and thereupon took their definitive resolution, to invite the other two orders to come and verify their powers in common, and to notify them they should proceed with or without them to verify, and to do the business of the nation. This was on the 10th. On the 15th, they moved to declare themselves the National Assembly. The debates on this were finished yesterday, when the proposition was agreed to, by four hundred and odd, against eighty odd. The minority agreed in substance, but wished some particular amendment. They then immediately made the proposition relative to taxes, which I enclose you, as this moment stated to me, by memory, by a member who left the Assembly a little before the question, because there was no opposition to the matter, but only to the form. He assures me, on the information of another member who was present, that Target's motion passed. We shall know, I think, within a day or two, whether the government will risk a bankruptcy and civil war, rather than see all distinction of orders done way, which is what the Commons will push for. If the fear of the former alternative prevails, they will spin the matter into negotiation. The Commons have in their chamber almost all the talents of the nation; they are firm and bold, yet moderate. There is indeed, among them, a number of very hot-headed members; but those of most influence are cool, temperate, and sagacious. Every step of this House has been marked with caution and wisdom. The *Noblesse*, on the contrary, are absolutely out of their senses. They are so furious, they can seldom debate at all. They have few men of moderate talents, and not one of great, in the majority. Their proceedings have been very injudicious. The Clergy are waiting to profit of every incident to secure themselves, and have no other object in view. Among the Commons, there is an entire unanimity on the great question of voting by persons. Among the *Noblesse*, there are about sixty for the Commons, and about three times that number against them. Among the Clergy, about twenty have already come over and joined the Commons, and in the course of a few days, they will be joined by many more, not indeed making the majority of that House, but very near it. The Bishops and Archbishops have been very successful by bribes and intrigues, in detaching the *Curés* from the Commons, to whom they were at first attached to a man. The Commons are about, five hundred and fifty-four in number, of whom three hundred and forty-four are of the Jaw. These do not possess an influence founded in property; but in their habits of business and acquaintance with the people, and in their means of exciting them as they please. The *Curés*, throughout the kingdom, form the mass of the Clergy; they are the only part favorably known to the people, because solely charged with the duties of baptism, burial, confession, visitation of the sick, instruction of the children, and aiding the poor; they are themselves of the people, and united with them. The carriages and equipage only of the higher Clergy, not their persons, are known to the people, and are in detestation with them. The soldiers will follow their officers, that is to say, their captains, lieutenants, and ensigns. These are of the lower nobility, and therefore much divided. The colonels and higher officers are of the higher nobility, are seldom with the soldiers, little known to them, not possessing their attachment. These circumstances give them little weight in the partition of the army.

I give you these miscellaneous observations, that knowing somewhat the dispositions of the parties, you may be able to judge of the future for yourself, as I shall not be here to continue its communication to you.

In hopes to see you soon, I conclude with assurances of the perfect esteem and respect, with which I am, Dear Sir, your friend and servant,

Th: Jefferson.

LETTER CCVIII.—TO JOHN JAY, June 24,1789

TO JOHN JAY.

Sir,

Paris, June 24,1789.

My letter of the 17th and 18th instant gave you the progress of the States General to the 17th, when the *Tiers* had declared the illegality of all the existing taxes, and their discontinuance from the end of their present session. The next day, being a *jour de fete*, could furnish no indication of the impression that vote was likely to make on the government. On the 19th, a Council was held at Marly, in the afternoon. It was there proposed, that the King should interpose by a declaration of his sentiments in a *seance royale.* The declaration prepared by M. Necker, while it censured, in general, the proceedings both of the Nobles and Commons, announced the King's views, such as substantially to coincide with the Commons. It was agreed to in Council, as also that the *seance royale* should be held on the 22nd, and the meetings till then be suspended. While the Council was engaged in this deliberation at Marly, the chamber of the Clergy was in debate, whether they should accept the invitation of the *Tiers* to unite with them in the common chamber. On the first question, to unite simply and unconditionally, it was decided in the negative by a very small majority. As it was known however, that some members who had voted in the negative, would be for the affirmative, with some modifications, the question was put with these modifications, and it was determined by a majority of eleven members, that their body should join the *Tiers.* These proceedings of the Clergy were unknown to the Council at Marly, and those of the Council were kept secret from every body. The next morning (the 20th), the members repaired to the House as usual, found the doors shut and guarded, and a proclamation posted up for holding a *seance royale* on the 22nd, and a suspension of their meetings till then. They presumed, in the first moment, that their dissolution was decided, and repaired to another place, where they proceeded to business. They there bound themselves to each other by an oath, never to separate of their own accord, till they had settled a constitution for the nation on a solid basis, and if separated by force, that they would re-assemble in some other place. It was intimated to them, however, that day, privately, that the proceedings of the *seance royale* would be favorable to them. The next day they met in a church, and were joined by a majority of the Clergy. The heads of the aristocracy saw that all was lost without some violent exertion. The King was still at Marly. Nobody was permitted to approach him but their friends. He was assailed by lies in all shapes. He was made to believe that the Commons were going to absolve the army from their oath of fidelity to him, and to raise their pay.

They procured a committee to be held, consisting of the King and his ministers, to which Monsieur and the Count d'Artois should be admitted. At this committee, the latter attacked Mr. Necker personally, arraigned his plans, and proposed one which some of his engines had put into his hands. Mr. Necker, whose characteristic is the want of firmness, was browbeaten and intimidated, and the King shaken. He determined that the two plans should be deliberated on the next day, and the *seance royale* put off a day longer. This encouraged a fiercer attack on Mr. Necker the next day; his plan was totally dislocated, and that of the Count d'Artois inserted into it. Himself and Monsieur de Montmorin offered their resignation, which was refused; the Count d'Artois saying to Mr. Necker, 'No, Sir, you must be kept as the hostage; we hold you responsible for all the ill which shall happen.' This change of plan was immediately whispered without doors. The nobility were in triumph, the people in consternation. When the King passed, the next day, through the lane they formed from the Chateau to the *Hotel des Etats* (about half a mile), there was a dead silence. He was about an hour in the House, delivering his speech and declaration, copies of which I enclose you. On his coming out, a feeble cry of 'Vive le Roy' was raised by some children, but the people remained silent and sullen. When the Duke d'Orleans followed, however, their applauses were excessive. This must have been sensible to the King. He had ordered, in the close of his speech, that the members should follow him, and resume their deliberations the next day. The *Noblesse* followed him, and so did the Clergy, except about thirty, who, with the *Tiers*, remained in the room and entered into deliberation. They protested against what the King had done, adhered to all their former proceedings, and resolved the inviolability of their own persons. An officer came twice to order them out of the room, in the King's name, but they refused to obey. In the afternoon, the people, uneasy, began to assemble in great numbers in the courts and vicinities of the palace. The Queen was alarmed, and sent for Mr. Necker. He was conducted amidst the shouts and acclamations of the multitude, who filled all the apartments of the palace. He was a few minutes only with the Queen, and about three quarters of an hour with the King. Not a word has transpired of what passed at these interviews. The King was just going to ride out. He passed through the crowd to his carriage, and into it, without being in the least noticed. As Mr. Necker followed him, universal acclamations were raised of '*Vive Monsieur Necker, vive le sauveur de la France opprimée.*' He was conducted back to his house with the same demonstrations of affection and anxiety. About two hundred deputies of the *Tiers*, catching the enthusiasm of the moment, went to his house, and extorted from him a promise that he would not resign. These circumstances must wound the heart of the King, desirous as he is, to possess the affections of his subjects. As soon as the proceedings at Versailles were known at Paris, a run began on the *caisse d'escompte*, which is the first symptom always of the public diffidence and alarm. It is the less in condition to meet the run, as Mr. Necker has been forced to make free with its funds, for the daily support of the government. This is the state of things as late as I am able to give them with certainty, at this moment. My letter not being to go off till to-morrow evening, I shall go to Versailles to-morrow, and be able to add the transactions of this day and to-morrow.

June 25. Just returned from Versailles, I am enabled to continue my narration. On the 24th, nothing remarkable passed, except an attack by the mob of Versailles on the Archbishop of Paris, who had been one of the instigators of the court, to the proceedings of the, *seance royale*. They threw mud and stones at his carriage, broke the windows of it, and he in a fright promised to join the *Tiers*.

This day (the 25th) forty-eight of the Nobles have joined the *Tiers*. Among these is the Duke d'Orleans. The Marquis de la Fayette could not be of the number, being restrained by his instructions. He is writing to his constituents, to change his instructions or to accept his resignation. There are with the *Tiers* now one hundred and sixty-four members of the Clergy, so that the common chamber consists of upwards of eight hundred members. The minority of the Clergy, however, call themselves the Chamber of the Clergy, and pretend to go on with business. I found the streets of Versailles much embarrassed with soldiers. There was a body of about one hundred horse drawn up in front of the Hotel of the States, and all the avenues and doors guarded by soldiers. Nobody was permitted to enter but the members, and this was by order of the King; for till now, the doors of the common room have been open, and at least two thousand spectators attending their debates constantly. They have named a deputation to wait on the King, and desire a removal of the soldiery from their doors, and seem determined, if this is not complied with, to remove themselves elsewhere.

Instead of being dismayed with what has passed, they seem to rise in their demands, and some of them to consider the erasing every vestige of a difference of order, as indispensable to the establishment and preservation of a good constitution. I apprehend there is more courage than calculation in this project. I did imagine, that seeing that Mr. Necker and themselves were involved as common enemies in the hatred of the aristocrats, they would have been willing to make common cause with him, and to wish his continuance in office; and that Mr. Necker, seeing that all the trimming he has used towards the court and Nobles has availed him nothing, would engage himself heartily and solely on the popular side, and view his own salvation in that alone. The confidence which the people place in him, seems to merit some attention. However, the mass of the common chamber are absolutely indifferent to his remaining in office. They consider his head as unequal to the planning a good constitution, and his fortitude to a co-operation in the effecting it. His dismission is more credited to-day than it was yesterday. If it takes place, he will retain his popularity with the nation, as the members of the States will not think it important to set themselves against it, but on the contrary, will be willing that he should continue on their side, on his retirement. The run on the *caisse d'escompte* continues. The members of the States admit, that Mr. Necker's departure out of office will occasion a stoppage of public payments. But they expect to prevent any very ill effect, by assuring the public against any loss, and by taking immediate measures for continuing payment. They may, perhaps, connect these measures with their own existence, so as to interest the public in whatever catastrophe may be aimed at them. The gazettes of France and Leyden accompany this. During the continuance of this crisis and my own stay, I shall avail myself of every private conveyance to keep you informed of what passes.

I have the honor to be, with the most perfect esteem and respect, Sir, your most obedient and most humble servant,

Th: Jefferson.

LETTER CCIX.—TO JOHN JAY, June 29, 1789

TO JOHN JAY.

Paris, June 29, 1789.

Sir,

My letter of the 25th gave you the transactions of the States General to the afternoon of that day. On the next, the Archbishop of Paris joined the *Tiers*, as did some others of the Clergy and *Noblesse*. On the 27th, the question of the St. Domingo deputation came on, and it was decided that it should be received. I have before mentioned to you the ferment into which the proceedings at the *seance royale* of the 23rd had thrown the people. The soldiery also were affected by it. It began in the French guards, extended to those of every other denomination (except the Swiss), and even to the body-guards of the King. They began to quit their barracks, to assemble in squads, to declare they would defend the life of the King, but would not cut the throats of their fellow-citizens. They were treated and caressed by the people, carried in triumph through the streets, called themselves the soldiers of the nation, and left no doubt on which side they would be, in case of a rupture. Similar accounts came in from the troops in other parts of the kingdom, as well those which had not heard of the *seance royale*, as those which had, and gave good reason to apprehend that the soldiery, in general, would side with their fathers and brothers, rather than with their officers. The operation of this medicine, at Versailles, was as sudden as it was powerful. The alarm there was so complete, that in the afternoon of the 27th, the King wrote a letter to the President of the Clergy, the Cardinal de la Rochefoucault, in these words: [* A translation is here given.]

** My Cousin, Wholly engaged in promoted the general good of my kingdom, and desirous, above all things, that the Assembly of the States General should apply themselves to objects of general interest, after the voluntary acceptance by your order of my declaration of the 23rd of the present month; I pass my word that my faithful Clergy will, without delay, unite themselves with the other two orders, to hasten the accomplishment of my paternal views. Those whose powers are too limited, may decline voting until new powers are procured. This will be a new mark of attachment which my*

Clergy will give me. I pray God, my Cousin, to have you in

his holy keeping. LOUIS.'

A like letter was written to the Duke de Luxemburgh, President of the *Noblesse.* The two chambers entered into debate on the question, whether they should obey the letter of the King. There was a considerable opposition; when notes written by the Count d'Artois to sundry members, and handed about among the rest, decided the matter, and they went in a body and took their seats with the *Tiers*, and thus rendered the union of the orders in one chamber complete. As soon as this was known to the people of Versailles, they assembled about the palace, demanded the King and Queen, who came and showed themselves in a balcony. They rent the skies with cries of 'Vive la Roy,' 'Vive la Reine.' They, called for the Dauphin, who was also produced, and was the subject of new acclamations. After feasting themselves and the royal family with this tumultuary reconciliation, they went to the house of Mr. Necker and M. de Montmorin, with shouts of thankfulness and affection. Similar emotions of joy took place in Paris, and at this moment, the triumph of the Tiers is considered as complete. Tomorrow they will recommence business, voting by persons on all questions: and whatever difficulties may be opposed in debate by the malcontents of the Clergy and Nobility, every thing must be finally settled at the will of the *Tiers.* It remains to see whether they will leave to the nobility any thing but their titulary appellations. I suppose they will not. Mr. Necker will probably remain in office. It would seem natural that he should endeavor to have the hostile part of the Council removed, but I question if he finds himself firm enough for that. A perfect co-operation with the *Tiers* will be his wisest game. This great crisis being now over, I shall not have matter interesting enough to trouble you with, as often as I have done lately. There has nothing remarkable taken place in any other part of Europe.

I have the honor to be, with the most perfect esteem and respect, Sir, your most; obedient and most humble servant,

Th: Jefferson.

LETTER CCX.—TO THE MARQUIS DE LA FAYETTE, July 6, 1789

TO THE MARQUIS DE LA FAYETTE.

Paris, July 6, 1789.

Dear Sir,

I never made an offer to any body to have corn or flour brought here from America: no such idea ever entered my head. Mr. Necker desired me to give information in America, that there would be a want of flour. I did so in a letter to Mr. Jay, which he published with my name to it, for the encouragement of the merchants. Those here, who have named me on this subject, must have mistaken me for Mr. Parker. I have heard him say, he offered to Mr. Necker to bring a large supply, yet I do not think I ever repeated this: or if I did, it must have been in a company I relied on. I will thank you to satisfy Mr. Necker of the truth. It would be disagreeable, and perhaps mischievous, were he to have an idea that I encouraged censures on him. I will bring you the paper you desire to-morrow; and shall dine at the Dutchess Danville's, where I shall be happy to meet you.

Adieu. Yours affectionately.

Th: Jefferson.

LETTER CCXI.—TO THE MARQUIS DE LA FAYETTE, July 7,1789

TO THE MARQUIS DE LA FAYETTE.

Paris, July 7,1789.

Dear Sir,

Your letter of yesterday gave me the first information that Monsieur de Mirabeau had suggested to the honorable the Assembly of the Nation, that I had made an offer to Mr. Necker to obtain from America a quantity of corn or flour, which had been refused. I know not how Monsieur de Mirabeau has been led into this error. I never in my life made any proposition to Mr. Necker on the subject: I never said I had made such a proposition. Some time last autumn, Mr. Necker did me the honor to desire I would have notified in the United States, that corn and flour would meet with a good sale in France. I conveyed this notice, in a letter to Mr. Jay, Secretary for Foreign Affairs, as you will see by the extract of my letter published by him in an American gazette, which I have the honor to send you. I must beg leave to avail myself of your friendship and of your position to have a communication of these facts made to the honorable Assembly of the Nation, of which you are a member, and to repeat to you those sentiments of respect and attachment, with which I have the honor to be, my dear Sir, your most obedient and most

humble servant,

Th: Jefferson.

LETTER CCXII.—TO MR. NECKER, July 8, 1789

TO MR. NECKER.

Paris, July 8, 1789

Sir,

I have the honor to enclose you a copy of my letter to Monsieur de la Fayette. When I called on him yesterday, he had already spoken to Monsieur de Mirabeau, who acknowledged he had been in an error in what he had advanced in the Assembly of the Nation, as to the proposition supposed to have been made by me to your Excellency, and undertook to declare his error, when the subject should be resumed by the Assembly, to whom my letter to the Marquis de la Fayette will be also read.

I have thought it a duty, Sir, thus to correct, in the first moment, an error, by which your name had been compromitted by an unfounded use of mine, and shall be happy in every occasion of proving to you those sentiments of profound respect and attachment, with which I have the honor to be, your Excellency's most obedient and most humble servant,

Th: Jefferson.

LETTER CCXIII.—TO THE COUNT DE MONTMORIN, July 8, 1789

TO THE COUNT DE MONTMORIN.

Paris, July 8, 1789.

Sir,

My hotel having been lately robbed for the third time, I take the liberty of uniting my wish with that of the inhabitants of this quarter, that it might coincide with the arrangements of police, to extend to us the protection of a guard. While the *Douane* remained here, no accident of that kind happened, but since their removal, other houses in the neighborhood have been robbed as well as mine. Perhaps it may lessen the difficulties of this request, that the house occupied by the people of the *Douane*, will lodge abundantly a *corps de garde*. On the one side of that house is Chaillot, on the other the Roule, on the third the Champs Elysees, where accidents are said to happen very frequently, all of which are very distant from any *corps de garde*.

I have the honor to be, with sentiments of the most perfect respect and esteem, your Excellency's most obedient and most humble servant,

Th: Jefferson.

LETTER CCXIV.—TO THE MARQUIS DE LA FAYETTE, July 9, 1789

TO THE MARQUIS DE LA FAYETTE.

Paris, July 9, 1789.

Dear Sir,

Having been curious to form some estimate of the quantity of corn and flour which have been supplied to France this year, I applied to a person in the Farms to know upon what quantities the premium had been paid. He could not give me information, but as to the Atlantic ports, into which there have been imported from the United States, from March to May inclusive, forty-four thousand one hundred and sixteen quintals of corn, twelve thousand two hundred and twenty-one quintals of flour, making fifty-six thousand three hundred and thirty-seven quintals in the whole. Add to this what has been imported since May, suppose nearly twenty thousand quintals a month, and what has been furnished to the French islands, which has prevented an equal quantity being exported from France, and you will have the proportion drawn from us. Observe, that we have regular and constant markets for our corn and flour in Spain, Portugal, and all the West India islands, except the French. These take nearly our whole quantity. This year, France, the French West Indies, and Canada were added. But a regular course of trade is not quitted in an instant, nor constant customers deserted for accidental ones. This is the reason that so small a proportion has come here.

I am, Dear Sir, with great sincerity, your affectionate friend and servant,

Th: Jefferson.

LETTER CCXV.—TO THE MARQUIS DE LA FAYETTE, July 10, 1789

TO THE MARQUIS DE LA FAYETTE.

Paris, July 10, 1789.

Dear Sir,

The acknowledgment by Monsieur de Mirabeau to the National Assembly, that he had been in an error as to the offer he supposed me to have made, and the reading to them my letter, seem to be all that was requisite for any just purpose. As I was unwilling my name should be used to injure the minister, I am also unwilling it should be used to injure Monsieur de Mirabeau. I learn that his enemies in Paris are framing scandalous versions of my letter. I think, therefore, with you, it may be better to print it, and I send you a copy of it. I gave copies of it to Monsieur de Montmorin and Monsieur Necker, as was my duty.

I am, with sincere affection, my Dear Sir, your friend and servant,

Th: Jefferson.

LETTER CCXVI.—TO THOMAS PAINE, July 11, 1789

TO THOMAS PAINE.

Paris, July 11, 1789.

Dear Sir,

Since my last, which was of May the 19th, I have received yours of June the 17th and 18th. I am struck with the idea of the geometrical wheel-barrow, and will beg of you a farther account, if it can be obtained. I have no news yet of my *congé*.

Though you have doubtless heard most of the proceedings of the States General since my last, I will take up the narration where that left it, that you may be able to separate the true from the false accounts you have heard. A good part of what was conjecture in that letter, is now become true history.

The National Assembly, then, (for that is the name they take,) having shown through every stage of these transactions a coolness, wisdom, and resolution to set fire to the four corners of the kingdom, and to perish with it themselves, rather than to relinquish an iota from their plan of a total change of government, are now in complete and undisputed possession of the sovereignty. The executive and aristocracy are at their feet; the mass of the nation, the mass of the clergy, and the army are with them: they have prostrated the old government, and are now beginning to build one from the foundation. A committee, charged with the arrangement of their business, gave in, two days ago, the following order of proceedings.

'1. Every government should have for its only end, the preservation of the rights of man: whence it follows, that to recall constantly the government to the end proposed, the constitution should begin by a declaration of the natural and imprescriptible rights of man.

'2. Monarchical government being proper to maintain those rights, it has been chosen by the French nation. It suits especially a great society; it is necessary for the happiness of France. The declaration of the principles of this government, then, should follow immediately the declaration of the rights of man.

'3. It results from the principles of monarchy, that the nation, to assure its own rights, has yielded particular rights to the monarch: the constitution, then, should declare, in a precise manner, the rights of both. It should begin by declaring the rights of the French nation, and then should declare the rights of the King.

'4. The rights of the King and nation not existing but for the happiness of the individuals who compose it, they lead to an examination of the rights of citizens.

'5. The French nation not being capable of assembling individually to exercise all its rights, it ought to be represented. It is necessary, then, to declare the form of its representation and the rights of its representatives.

'6. From the union of the powers of the nation and King, should result the enacting and execution of the laws: thus, then, it should first be determined how the laws shall be established; afterwards should be considered, how they shall be executed.

'7. Laws have for their object the general administration of the kingdom, the property, and the actions of the citizens. The execution of the laws which concern the general administration, requires Provincial and Municipal Assemblies. It is necessary to examine, therefore, what should be the organization of the Provincial Assemblies, and what of the Municipal.

'8. The execution of the laws, which concern the property and actions of the citizens, calls for a judiciary power. It should be determined how that should be confided, and then its duties and limits.

'9. For the execution of the laws and the defence of the kingdom, there exists a public force. It is necessary, then, to determine the principles which should direct it, and how it should be employed.

'Recapitulation.

'Declaration of the rights of man. Principles of the monarchy. Rights of the nation. Rights of the King. Rights of the citizens.

'Organization and rights of the National Assembly. Forms necessary for the enaction of laws. Organization and functions of the Provincial and Municipal Assemblies. Duties and limits of the judiciary power. Functions and duties of the military power.'

You see that these are the materials of a superb edifice, and the hands which have prepared them are perfectly capable of putting them together, and of filling up the work, of which these are only the outlines. While there are some men among them of very superior abilities, the mass possess such a degree of good sense, as enables them to decide well. I have always been afraid their numbers might lead to confusion. Twelve hundred men in one room are too many. I have still that fear. Another apprehension is, that a majority cannot be induced to adopt the trial by jury, and I consider that as the only anchor ever yet imagined by man, by which a government can be held to the principles of its constitution. Mr. Paradise is the bearer of this letter. He can supply those details which it would be so tedious to write.

I am, with great esteem, Dear Sir, your friend and servant,

Th: Jefferson.

CPSIA information can be obtained
at www.ICGtesting.com
Printed in the USA
LVHW040728040323
740706LV00028B/391

9 789356 894686